The History of Jesus Christ

THE HISTORY OF JESUS CHRIST

By R. L. BRUCKBERGER

PREFACE BY

✠EUGÈNE CARDINAL TISSERANT

TRANSLATED FROM THE FRENCH BY

DENVER LINDLEY

New York · The Viking Press

Nihil obstat

Myles M. Bourke, S.S.L., S.T.D.

Censor Librorum

Imprimatur

✠ Francis Cardinal Spellman

Archbishop of New York

L'Histoire de Jésus-Christ © 1965 by Editions Bernard Grasset
The History of Jesus Christ Copyright © 1965 by R. L. Bruckberger
All rights reserved

First published in 1965 by The Viking Press, Inc., 625 Madison Avenue, New York, N.Y. 10022

Published simultaneously in Canada by The Macmillan Company of Canada Limited

Library of Congress catalog card number: 64-20684. Printed in U.S.A.

Grateful acknowledgment is made to the Confraternity of Christian Doctrine, Washington, D.C., for permission to quote from the Confraternity translation of the Scriptures, and to the Cardinal Archbishop of Westminster and Burns & Oates Ltd. for permission to quote from the translation by Monsignor Ronald A. Knox (copyright 1944, 1948, and 1950 Sheed & Ward, Inc., New York). Lines from "Nineteen Hundred and Nineteen" (page 456) and "Among School Children" (page 458) from *Collected Poems of W. B. Yeats* are reprinted with permission of The Macmillan Company, New York, The Macmillan Co. of Canada Ltd., and Mrs. W. B. Yeats. Copyright 1928 by The Macmillan Company. Renewed 1956 by Georgie Yeats.

CONTENTS

PREFACE

Saint Thomas Aquinas, wishing to determine which religious orders are to be preferred, bestowed the palm on those that combine teaching with contemplation: *Maius est contemplata aliis tradere, quam solum contemplari.* Such is the purpose of the Preaching Brothers and such the purpose of the Reverend Father Bruckberger.

He has read and reread the Gospels; he has meditated on every chapter in them, yet without neglecting the other parts of the Bible. He has practiced the apostolic ministry and acquired a living knowledge of the mentality of our contemporaries. It is for them that he writes.

The History of Jesus Christ is not the commentary of a synoptist, in which the first concern would be to arrange each detail of the Gospels in chronological order according to some learned plan. The Reverend Father Bruckberger has selected what seemed to him most important, that which permits a better understanding of the significance of this unique and incredible fact: the life of a God made man. The Incarnation is a mystery; but the earthly life of Jesus, God incarnate, belongs to history. It has been recorded by four writers; two of them lived in intimacy with him of whom they speak, whereas the other two, Mark and Luke, report what they learned by hearsay, the former setting down quite spontaneously the details he had heard, the latter writing with a historian's care, which he announces in advance in the preamble of his Gospel.

Pope Pius XI proclaimed, with his usual vigor, that Christians are the spiritual heirs of the Hebrew people. The Reverend Father Bruckberger does not hesitate to write that Christianity is more Jewish than modern Judaism, for in Jesus it has preserved, "in a sacramental and real manner," the priesthood, the sacrifice, prophecy, personal messianism, the apocalypse, and the Promise.

Jesus was the victim of the Pharisees, whom he had often accused of legalism. But after the destruction of Jerusalem, in the year 70, the Pharisees insured the survival of the Jewish people by providing the Diaspora with an official doctrine. The temple at Jerusalem has not been raised again, and the weekly meetings in the synagogues are very different from the daily rites of earlier times.

The continuity of the religious thought of the Old Testament has been assured by the Christian Church. Before that was possible, however, Jesus had to destroy, in those around him, the myth of the liberating Messiah who would put an end to the Roman occupation. This idea was so firmly rooted in his compatriots that on the very morning of the Ascension the Apostles asked their divine Master whether he was not going to "restore the kingdom of Israel."

Thereafter the primitive Church had to free itself from those who wished to impose upon the neophytes, won from paganism, the ritual observances of the books of the Law. The Reverend Father Bruckberger has clearly demonstrated the rupture between the traditional Judaism of our Lord's contemporaries and the later Judaism, whose unitary doctrine and legal practices inspired the author of the Koran.

Frequently, in the course of his exposition, he refers to events that we ourselves have witnessed, for the purpose of making more comprehensible the episodes related by the Evangelists. For example, he recalls with emotion the mobilization in 1914—which caused Frenchmen to abandon from one moment to the next their families, their homes, and their fields, in response to the appeal of their fatherland—to justify the unprecedented decision by the sons of Zebedee to abandon their father and their nets in order to follow Jesus. Another example is the use made of the situation in France during the Second World War and the enforced collaboration of the government with the occupying authorities, in order to make clear the psychological attitude of the Jewish people and its elite in the last days of the earthly life of Jesus, and to show that his death was brought about by the inevitable conflict between the political realism of the Sanhedrin and the hope that animated the people.

Half of the Reverend Father Bruckberger's volume is devoted to the final days of Holy Week, which may also be called the "Terrible Week," for it saw a total reversal of the triumph of Palm Sunday in the tragedy of the Passion. The plan of these chapters is announced in words that it is well to quote: "I shall say that he really wished to die a cruel death, I shall say why he wished to die thus. I shall say that they wanted to kill him, that finally they did kill him, I shall say that they wanted him to die the death of rebellious slaves, the death of blasphemers. I shall say why they wanted to kill him thus. I shall say how all this came about and why, given the situation between his adversaries and him, it could hardly have turned out otherwise."

At the beginning of his chapter on Maundy Thursday, the Reverend Father Bruckberger recalls the words of Saint John, that Jesus had to die for his nation but also to bring unity to the children of God scattered abroad. The Last Supper is the basis of ecumenicalism. It was at the end of the ritual banquet of the Jewish Passover that Jesus gave to his disciples, with unique solemnity, the precept of mutual charity that was to characterize them throughout the centuries. Jesus, born under the Law, wished to the end to obey the Law. In the most painful moments of the trial to which he was brought by the leaders of his people, he never spoke against the legitimate authorities.

In reference to Herod, to whom Jesus did not deign to reply—Jesus, who was willing to talk to all, poor and rich, fishermen of the lake and women of the streets—a warning is issued to those of our contemporaries who have fallen prey to frivolity, "blindness of soul and deafness of heart," for whom there is only one scourge: boredom.

Men of our time are like the pagans at the time of Saint Paul, "devoid of hope in a world without God." To restore meaning to their lives they must be willing to reassume their proper places in a world where nothing is justified except through God, and learn once more to adore Him and give thanks to Him for all that exists.

The Reverend Father Bruckberger's intention is to announce, and at the same time explain to our contemporaries in their own language, the extraordinary good news of Jesus crucified. I hope there will be many who will take his book into their hands, for I am convinced that believers and unbelievers alike will profit from it, provided they are of good will.

✠ EUGÈNE CARDINAL TISSERANT

Paris, March 21, 1965

AUTHOR'S NOTE

Here is the book of my whole life; I have been engaged in its preparation always. I dedicate it to my masters, both the living and the dead, to them who gave me some understanding of the Kingdom of God and taught me to speak of it in a certain way. I name these good masters in the order in which I came to know them and in which they influenced me: Cardinal Salièges, Father Lacomme, Jacques Maritain, Father M. J. Lagrange, Father Louis-Bertrand Gillon, Georges Bernanos. May the homage of this book be a tribute to them all.

While preparing this book I have thought constantly about the young people of the world. It is among them above all that I hope for readers. I have also thought about Christians; they are most fortunate to have Jesus Christ as their Lord. But I have thought a great deal as well about nonbelievers; I could wish to make them doubtful of their doubt.

It is impossible to write the sort of book I am now presenting to the public without confronting, a hundred times and with embarrassment, the problem of Biblical translations, and without solving this problem for oneself in some fashion more or less in accord with the truth: no translation can be wholly satisfactory. To give a single example—whose importance will become clearer in the course of this book—Hebrew has only one word to designate the seed of plants, the sperm of male animals, race, posterity, offspring, etc. By choosing each time just one of these translations, which cannot be inclusive, one loses much in perspective. The Vulgate stays closer to the original by translating this word almost always as *semen*.

This book is not, properly speaking, a work of exegesis. Not that I fail to attach the greatest importance to exegesis, especially on questions of date and authenticity—quite the contrary. I am fully aware, for example, of the problems that arise in connection with the composition of the Gospel according to Matthew and of "The Epistle to the Hebrews." But when I say "The Gospel according to Matthew" and when I attribute "The Epistle to the Hebrews" purely and simply to Saint Paul, I am using a convenient language and one that is understood by everybody.

As for the heroine of the Gospel, Mary Magdalene, I am equally well aware that the exegetes have chosen to cut her into three pieces. On this point I am not in agreement with the great majority of modern exegetes, as I have explained elsewhere in this book. But I do not believe either that the exegetes, even taken as a body, are infallible: that they are not has been easy to see for the past hundred and fifty years. If only there are more discoveries like that of the Dead Sea Scrolls, it will become increasingly easy to see.

I have principally made use of *The Bible of Jerusalem, The Pleïade Bible,* and for the Gospels the admirable *Synoptics* of Lavergne. But I have constantly had recourse to the Latin of the Vulgate, and, with the assistance of experts, to the Greek or Hebrew of the original. I have sometimes felt free to paraphrase the Biblical text, always indicating the places where I have done so, in order to illustrate my interpretation and to throw light on it from a particular angle. It was often my wish that this venerable text might convey the impression of being read for the first time.

—R. L. BRUCKBERGER

New York City, November 14, 1964

TRANSLATOR'S NOTE

In attempting to follow the author's practice in the use of translations of the Bible, the translator has relied primarily on the Confraternity-Douay Edition and secondarily on the translation by Monsignor Ronald A. Knox. Where the author has gone back to the Vulgate or to the Greek, the translator has followed suit.

Part One

The Personality of Jesus Christ

CHAPTER I

The Son of Man

THE HISTORY of a man is the inscription of his personality on his time, and the deciphering of that inscription. Most men barely have a history; they leave on the sands of time the faint tracings of an insect. But some go deeper, reach the rock, rend it, hollow it out, shape it, and their course is indelible.

A history of Napoleon exists. We also have Napoleon's memoirs. No one interested in the subject could neglect Napoleon's own point of view about himself and his life. Jesus Christ left no memoirs, but an idea of his personal view of himself can be formed from what the Gospels tell us about his actions, gestures, and words.

One peculiarity strikes us at once. All through the Gospels a single question keeps returning to Jesus again and again like the flood tide recurrently seeking a cliff. "Who are you? Who do you say that you are? Are you he that is to come, or must we wait for another? Explain what you mean about yourself." Friends, enemies—everyone, at one time or another, puts this question to him; he himself sometimes puts it to others: "Who do you believe that I am?" Not Socrates, not Alexander, not Napoleon was asked who he was; men thought they knew, and, in effect, they did.

It seems that Jesus took pleasure in evoking and maintaining this atmosphere of interrogation about his origins and his true mission. His replies were not always clear, sometimes they sidestepped the question, sometimes he replied in riddles or in parables, but he made sure the question would be repeated.

3

John 8:58   One day he gave an astounding reply. "Before Abraham was," he said, "*I am.*" A speech with which no utterance of any other man can be compared, a speech impossible for an Evangelist to invent if it had not been said by him who had the right to say it. A speech in which without warning eternity erupts into time. A false evangelist, wishing to magnify his hero to the dimensions of eternity, would have made the tenses agree; he would have written: "Before Abraham was, *I was.*" The tranquil affirmation of that solemn present, prior to Abraham, *I am,* has an authority that takes one's breath.

Or perhaps one should believe that Jesus was mad and that he said these words simply by chance. Unsupportable hypothesis! All the actions, all the words of Jesus are those of a man completely master of himself and possessed of perfect clearness of mind. Even so, this testimony of Jesus concerning himself stands as an insurmountable barrier. Here, indeed, is Jesus' point of view about himself! Without explaining this affirmation, which opens out upon infinity, the Christian accepts it; he grasps its meaning; it gives him from the start the dimensions of the hero of the Gospels.

But for others, for those who are not Christians, this claim is an insuperable offense to reason. It is only by forgetting such a speech that the nonbeliever can, from his point of view, attempt to explain who this man Jesus was. He has, however, lost the key; every explanation breaks down in incoherence, and the Gospel begins to seethe with contradictions. Nevertheless, the naturalistic historian stubbornly persists, he compares documents and works of criticism, separating those documents he thinks authentic from those he considers apocryphal. Inevitably, through inclination and training, he enlarges the apocryphal section until he ends by asking himself whether Jesus ever really existed. "Before Abraham was, I am." It is better to act as if that tormenting assertion had never been uttered; the naturalistic historian is compelled to pass over it in silence, to omit it, for he cannot give it any meaning. It does in fact elude all naturalistic explanation, being in itself more incredible than all the miracles, even including the Resurrection.

"Before Abraham was, *I am.*" That present tense, which breaks the sentence, that present, all alone, agreeing with nothing but its subject, must have evoked in the minds of its hearers the famous sentence in
Ex. 3:14   which God defines Himself outside time: "I am He that am." Therefore, when Saint John in his old age returns in memory to what he has seen and heard, it is quite natural for him to choose a starting point
John 1:1, 14   outside time. "In the beginning," he says, "was the Word. And the Word dwelt with God. And the Word was God. . . . And the Word

was made flesh. And he pitched his tent among us. And we saw his glory."

"In the beginning . . ." Deliberately, John opens his history of Jesus Christ with the very phrase that opens the whole history of the world, the history of humanity and of the salvation of that humanity in this world, as it is described in the book of Genesis, first book of all in the Old Testament. Let us admire this correspondence: in the one case as in the other there is an absolute beginning in time, but this beginning is supported by the prior eternity of God:

"In the beginning God created the heavens and the earth . . ."   Gen. 1:1

"In the beginning was the Word, and the Word was with God,   John 1:1
and the Word was God. . . ."

In the beginning, God alone: it is He who creates the world, who makes it habitable, and who creates the human family to make its habitation there. It is God again who makes Himself flesh, and who comes to inhabit this world, among us, like one of us, Himself a member of this human family.

All the discoveries of science concerning the immensity of space and the origins of life and of man do not controvert the account in Genesis any more than archaeological and historical discoveries can shake the simple declaration of Saint John. The account in Genesis of the creation of the world and the declaration of John about the Incarnation move on a quite different plane: that of a revelation by God of facts that are unverifiable in the natural world but that bind God Himself in His relations with time and with humanity.

Many say there never was any such revelation. It is not my purpose here to convince them on this point. I am simply trying to define the tradition and the context in which this man named Jesus arose.

What can be verified by all is the stupendous coherence of this revelation, extending over millennia. John the Evangelist takes up the work of the writer of Genesis as naturally as a single author passes from one chapter in his book to the next. From the times of Abraham and Moses, and no doubt longer still, this revelation has advanced, has grown more precise, more and more urgent and complete, through tens upon tens of generations, through migrations, wars, exiles, in the slothfulness of prosperity and under the blows of misfortune. One can understand to some degree the continuity of the Catholic tradition, jealously guarded by a doctrinal authority and a most vigilant magistracy, but the chances God took with the Jewish people surpass all imagining. It will be forever the glory of that people to have borne this revelation faithfully through the millennia.

In the time of the Old Testament there was no juridical continuity to conserve and enrich revelation: the sacerdotal tradition did not identify itself with the transmission of prophecy. Each Prophet was directly invested by God; he obeyed a compulsion he had not sought or merited. Generally, he was filled with terror at having to be the bearer of so heavy a message. Nevertheless, he delivered his message, and generally, once more, the venture justified his fears and ended very badly for him. He was persecuted, imprisoned, tortured, exiled, or even killed. But the same people who persecuted him or who allowed him to be persecuted treasured his message and transmitted it. Each Prophet was a beginning. At his death, there was no human guarantee that revelation had not died with him. One can understand and appreciate the anguish of the people of Israel when a generation passed without a prophetic message: "Since then no prophet has arisen in Israel. . . ." And then, suddenly, it all begins again: "In this time a prophet arose from the midst of the people. . . ."

Deut. 34:10

All these Prophets, great and small, shepherds or princes, young or old, illiterate or learned, scattered at random over the centuries, take up the same message, enrich it, define it. Sometimes indeed they seem to be contradicting one another. But through sublime intuition the people of Israel preserve all of it with obscure fidelity, affectionate and fierce, putting their faith in a far-off event that will justify all, that will in some divine fashion resolve the apparent contradictions. The history of this revelation, from a simple human point of view, is a magnificent epic; how can the naturalistic historian possibly explain it? If prophetic continuity were the effect of rational calculation, why should it contain these apparent contradictions? If it were the result of individual religious emotion, it would lack coherence, it would no longer possess continuity.

Whatever unhappy destiny Israel often kept in store for her Prophets, the Prophets would not have been possible without the people of Israel. The Prophets were the elect of God, but they were of the people; it was to this people that they confided their message, it was this people that safeguarded it. Israel herself was a wholly prophetic nation, to such a degree that Saint Paul could say that everything that happened to her happened in parables. Until the death of Christ, her history is quite literally the history of the guardianship of man's salvation. Israel was the precious vessel that contained the hope of the entire human race. Clearly such a destiny, such a continuity, such steadfastness, enduring through thousands of years, transcends natural history and attains a level at which humanity issues out of itself into a vocation.

The fruit of this vocation, of this millennial fidelity, was to be an exceptional being, at once the elect of God and the elect of this people. The whole ancient history of Israel is no more than the awaiting of this exceptional being who would express in his own person the predilection God had vowed to His people as well as the attachment and the gratitude Israel had vowed to her God. Throughout the centuries, millions of Israelites have lived and died in this hope and this expectation. Through century after century, millions of Israelites have cherished in their hearts the violent desire to contemplate the face of him who was to come. Many have shed their blood in affirmation of this hope. The Prophets had defined in advance the lineaments of this glorious scion of Israel, and pious Jews repeated daily verses describing the face of him whom they called the Messiah, the Christ, that is to say, the Anointed of the Lord.

It is in itself a strange thing that a man should be led to speak of himself in the third person. It does not seem natural except in children or to characterize some exalted mission that surpasses even the individual charged with it. Louis XIV could very well say "the King" when speaking of himself, but in this case there is no identity between the person and the function. The relation of the one to the other is contingent and may be broken, at least by death. Caesar, speaking of himself in his memoirs, says simply "Caesar."

The case of Jesus is different, unique. Speaking of himself in the third person, he never uses his own name, he does not say "Jesus" as Caesar says "Caesar." No more does he use a social or political title; he had no official position in the society of his day. He makes use of a designation that surprises us by its air of universal significance and its poetic savor. This designation could be applied to any one of us; nevertheless it has a sacred radiance, not only because he chose it for his own, but also because it is bathed in an ambiance of legend. Jesus called himself "the Son of Man."

At first sight, the remarkable thing about this appellation is the solidarity it avows between the man who was Jesus and the whole human race, for the title is as universal as the species itself. It is a name which could belong to anyone at all among us, but Jesus made it his own to such a degree that no one since has even dreamed of appropriating it for himself. Moreover, it would not satisfy anyone's ambition, precisely because there is nothing distinctive about it, it does not add anything to the status of man. Nevertheless, what boldness in speaking of himself to emphasize just this quality! To be human, completely human, not to fall below that state or to inflate it—that is the duty of everyone in all circumstances, happy or unhappy. Who can flatter himself that he has always achieved it? The ambition of Jesus, if he had one and if it is revealed to us by this designation, was to be human, simply, completely, and to present himself thus at the central point of human history, a perfected model of humanity.

All this, to be sure, is expressed in the strange phrase "Son of Man." Historically and in the milieu in which Jesus used it, it had an infinitely more precise meaning and pre-empted an exact place in the great Messianic tradition of Israel. For Jesus' hearers this title was extremely evocative, stemming as it did from a celebrated prophecy made five centuries earlier by one of the greatest Prophets of Israel, in the time of the chosen people's great sorrow during the Babylonian captivity. In the book of Daniel, we read these words: "As the visions during the night continued, I saw one like a Son of Man coming, on the clouds of heaven; when he reached the Ancient of Days and was presented before him, he received dominion, glory, and kingship; nations and peoples of every language serve him. His dominion is an everlasting dominion that shall not be taken away, his kingship shall not be destroyed."

Dan. 7:13-14

The apocalyptic style of the Jews, here used by Daniel, may seem bizarre to us; it was in fact traditional, almost conventional, and conveyed very precise meanings, as precise as the vocabulary of modern physics or electronics. "The Ancient of Days" was God Himself, regarded as the creator of time and anterior to all sequence. The legendary being who is "like a Son of Man," he too is a being of celestial origin, he comes on the clouds of heaven. He receives directly from God the dominion over all humanity, its peoples, its nations, its languages: he is by natural right the King of all races, all governments, all cultures, all civilizations. The power of the Son of Man is eternal like that of Him who bestows it on him.

Consider now the audacity of this designation "Son of Man," which Jesus borrows directly from Daniel and applies to himself, which he renders explicit and enriches in his turn by removing from it, as we shall see, any ambiguity about the divine claim that it implies. The Jews around Jesus who recognized in the title Son of Man the highest possible pretension were not deceived; in the eyes of some of them it was blasphemous, a claim to equality with God even in eternity, equality in power over heaven and earth, in universal and incorruptible dominion, and in the judgment implied by such power. In fact, the title "Son of Man," appropriated by Jesus, bearing with it the weight of Daniel's prophecy, is as heavy with authority as the amazing declaration "Before Abraham was, I am."

Now it is easier to see that John's way of beginning his Gospel, by finding support outside time and in God Himself, is by no means a personal interpretation, a deliberate magnification of his hero. It is Jesus' own view of himself. This awareness that Jesus had of dominating time, of being the equal of God, of being clothed by Him in universal power and incorruptible judgment over the whole human race, is something we find expressed again and again throughout the Gospels. It is striking even to the point of paradox by reason of its glaring contrast with the historical and temporal career of Jesus, which, from a political point of view, for example, is banal and mediocre. Nevertheless, it is this extraordinary claim of Jesus for himself that gives the Gospels their own light, without which they fade away in incoherence and darkness.

However strange this claim on the part of a man may appear to us, once it is established and proclaimed it can be only true or false; there is no middle ground. If it is false, that means that Jesus was deceived about himself or has deceived us. In the case of Jesus, the hypothesis of a lie appears untenable: he surely believed himself to be what he said. There remains for the historian but a single choice; either Jesus was deceived, himself a victim of Messianic and religious fanaticism, or matters must be taken quite straightforwardly as they present themselves, and Jesus' view of himself must be accepted. My purpose is to prove, insofar as I am able, the credibility of this second hypothesis.

Here the difficulty begins. How can one write the history of a man who claims to dominate time? If the history of a man is the inscription of his personality on his time, what will be the history of a personality who embraces the whole of time because he is anterior to time and creates it? In order for such a history to be true the historian must, in some manner, embrace the whole of time. The first proof that Jesus' view of himself is incontestably true is that it is in fact impossible to write his history without rising above the entire unrolling of time.

Thus, at the very first step we venture to take in this history of Jesus Christ, it turns out that the idea of history itself must be altered; we are obliged to make it flexible and to give it an unfamiliar extension to the point where it can be made to bear a possible and precise relationship to eternity. The relationship of Jesus to his own time is essentially ambivalent: as heir to the Ancient of Days, he dominates time and consequently dominates his time. As a real man, he belongs to his time. Of course, in the mixed nature of concrete events nothing is so clearly divided. Very often Jesus' words and gestures appear to us ambiguous and even inconsecutive, like that sentence "Before Abraham was, I am," which breaks the sequence of tenses. This ambiguity, this apparent caesura, is nothing perhaps but the effect of superhuman clairvoyance, not clearly expressible in our human language, which is essentially limited by time. The personality of Jesus penetrates eternity and time, as a stick thrust into water penetrates two optical media.

We shall see how this phenomenon of refraction, once it is uncovered, illuminates the Gospels and aids our understanding of them.

CHAPTER II

Prophecy Regarded as Tragedy

MATTHEW wrote his Gospel about the year 44, that is, a dozen years after Jesus' death. He wrote it in the place where the events occurred, amid witnesses who could easily have contradicted him. He wrote it in Aramaic, the common language of the country. A Jew, he wrote for the Jews. It is not surprising that he was especially intent on proving Jesus' Messianic mission and the fulfillment in him and through him of the prophecies.

He begins his Gospel by giving a genealogical account of Jesus. This family tree, typically and essentially Semitic, is composed in a fashion at once bizarre and touching—bizarre by reason of its geometrical perfection, like that of a set piece; touching because of all it brings to mind of the human adventure. Matthew obviously strove not to make it exhaustive but to make it perfect. He contented himself with points of reference throughout the generations, selecting them with care. Each generation is reckoned at forty years, a perfect number. Counting from Jesus backward to the Babylonian captivity, he records fourteen generations, a doubly perfect number. Ascending from the Babylonian captivity to David, fourteen generations. From David to Abraham, fourteen generations. There the genealogy stops. Thus fourteen is repeated three times, three being another perfect number. And so this whole genealogy gives an impression of perfection and fulfillment; undoubtedly this was the impression Matthew wished to create through this astonishing presentation.

What moves us, however, is not the fine, slightly artificial architecture

11

but the way Matthew has deliberately shattered it by introducing into
the long series of masculine names the names of five women, at a period
when, in Semitic countries, women did not figure in genealogies. These
five women are: Tamar, daughter-in-law of Judah, son of Jacob, who
prostituted herself to him; Rahab, a prostitute of Jericho who betrayed
her city; Ruth, a heathen, who offered herself to Boaz and induced him
to marry her; the adulterous wife of Uriah, King David's captain, whom
David, after stealing his wife, arranged in cowardly fashion to have
killed; and finally, Mary, the mother of Jesus.

Incest, prostitution combined with treason, adultery combined with
the murder of a faithful servant—on this dungheap arises that dazzling
flower of purity the Virgin Mary, of whom Jesus Christ was to be born.
From the first page of his Gospel, Matthew, the repentant publican,
fixes his calm and lucid accountant's gaze on human ordure. This is the
line of Jesus Christ. The contrast between the arithmetical perfection
of the genealogy and the moral decay to which it expressly alludes is
one of the most astounding effects in all literature. At the end, to be
sure, come the Virgin Mary and Joseph her husband. But just as a mata-
dor in the center of the bullring traces around himself in the sand with
his sword the narrow circle from which he will not move, so Jesus has
made narrow the circle of purity around him. He is indeed of our race.
His compassion for sinners is a family sentiment. Here once more we
are vividly aware of the veracity of the Evangelists: an invented genealogy would have been very different.

Far too often the feeble apologetics of today simply pictures the infant
Jesus between Mary and Joseph as a member of an attractive young
family, such as the motion pictures and television present in millions
of sentimental clichés. Let us be grateful to the Apostle Matthew who,
from the first page of his Gospel, places Jesus in a fresco of ancestors
John 1:14 worthy of Bosch or Rouault at his cruelest. "And the Word became
flesh," John has said; completely though it was purified in the precious
body of the Virgin Mary, here nevertheless is the flesh that the Word
assumed, flesh that had had a millennial experience of sad and violent
sin.

It is to be noted that Matthew divides his genealogy into three sec-
tions, marking the great stages of the Messianic Promise of the covenant of God with His people: Abraham, who was the first to whom the
Promise was made; David, to whom this Promise was solemnly confirmed and the further promise made of the dynasty from which the
Messiah should be born; the time of the Babylonian captivity, during
which this Messianic Promise was precisely defined in the words of the

great prophet Daniel concerning the Son of Man. Finally comes Jesus, in whom the Promise was fulfilled.

The religion of Abraham cannot be better defined than by saying that it was at once carnal and mystical; profoundly carnal, for it was essentially racial, like the Promise itself; profoundly mystical, because it was entirely dependent upon direct promptings from God and like the Promise was based uniquely on the solemn word of God. Abraham was the first to receive the Promise, which, through thousands of years, was to keep alive the Messianic hope of the people that was to spring from him. He believed in that Promise; he received it and treasured it, without reservation and to the point of sublime heroism. He believed in it, and his eternal sanctity consists in having believed; it is for this that he is so rightly called "Father of the Faithful." God said to him one night, "Look at the heavens and, if you can, count the stars; so shall your seed be." And again: "In your seed shall all the nations of the earth be blessed." $\qquad$ Gen. 15:5 Gen. 22:18

Your seed, your seed, your seed . . . This phrase keeps recurring in the words of God, not only to Abraham but through the whole of the Old Testament. It is the *seed* of Abraham that, through the centuries, is to be the vehicle of God's infallible Promise. Throughout the generations, the prophetic longing of this people was directed toward the body of Christ, just as the Eucharistic longing of the Church today is directed toward that same body. The precious body of Christ was, by anticipation, the common property of this people, as today it is the common property of the Church. What a difference here from that shocking modern sentimentalism for which the transmission of life has lost its sacred character!

Impermissible though it is to hope for catastrophe, we may, alas, thanks to modern science, frame terrifying hypotheses that are not by any means fantastical. A hypothesis of this kind occurs to me, one that would make a good subject for a motion picture or a play. As the result of a global atomic cataclysm, the whole human race is stricken with sterility, with the single exception of one couple, a pair of young people lost in a distant desert. At one stroke our inheritance, our treasures, our civilization, all those goods for which we are so ready to kill or to be killed, would have lost all meaning—except in relation to that couple.

What price then would the seed of that man and the womb of that woman have in the eyes of all? His seed would carry the future of the entire race; her womb would be its only cradle. Consider the pressures on this young couple; propaganda, fanaticism, and temptation, all bent on survival, would assail them. No doubt in the end they would be killed through an attempt to force them into our nightmares. And that would be the end of the world, a quite possible end when one considers what men are.

For Abraham, the Promise made by God concerning his seed was of greater price than the whole human race and its future. He was right: a salvation far above this world was already contained in his seed. This hypothesis gives us a better understanding of the religious racism of the Old Testament and also of that benediction at the threshold of the New: "Blessed is the fruit of *thy womb.*" *Your seed, your womb*—across the millennia the faith of the Virgin Mary responds like an echo to the faith of Abraham. A daughter of his seed is greater than he, it is she who contains in her body the fulfillment of the ancient Promise. It is in her own name, to be sure, but also in the name of all her people and in the name of Abraham as well that this daughter of Israel humbly answers the angel: "Be it done to me according to thy word."

Luke 1:42

Luke 1:38

Abraham could not doubt that God Himself was committed. In a scene prefiguring the annunciation of the birth of John the Baptist, God had promised Abraham, already almost a centenarian, that he would beget a son on Sarah his wife, herself well stricken in years. What was impossible in nature was possible for God, and Isaac was born of this miracle. And not Isaac alone but the whole of Jewish Messianism was born of that miracle. This Jewish Messianism is a unique historical and sociological phenomenon, so extraordinary, so constant over the millennia, that it constitutes in itself a kind of miracle, more impressive, when closely considered, than the conception and birth of Isaac.

No more could God doubt Abraham's fidelity. In a scene prefiguring the burnt sacrifice of Jesus Christ on Calvary at the will of his Father and through his own sublime but terrifying obedience, Abraham resolved to sacrifice the adolescent Isaac, child of the Promise and of the miracle; it was not until his knife was upraised over his son that he was restrained by the angel of the Lord. Clearly the prophetic action here goes far beyond the words of the prophecy: on this unknown mountain, Abraham and Isaac foreshadowed the Passion of Christ. This scene was lived, narrated, and written down thousands of years before the death of Christ: how can one fail to be struck by a correspondence such as this, which reveals through His work the Master of time itself?

It would take too long to pursue one by one all the prophecies that, in the course of history, brought confirmation of God's Promise to Abraham. Let it suffice to say that two generations later the Promise is defined in the benediction Jacob pronounces over Judah. This time it deals with a person, a leader who will fulfill the Promise: "The scepter shall

Gen. 49:10

not depart from Judah nor shall he want a leader drawn from his stock
until the day when that One shall come who is to be sent to us: And
he shall be the hope of the nations."

Let us observe, too, the terms in which the Promise is transmitted to
David through the pronouncement of the Prophet Nathan: "And when
thy days shall be fulfilled and thou shalt sleep with thy fathers, I will
raise up thy *seed* after thee, which shall proceed out of thy bowels, and
I will establish his kingdom. . . . And thy house shall be faithful, and
thy kingdom forever before thy face, and thy throne shall be firm forever."   2 Kings 7:12, 16

Henceforth the essential characteristics of the Messianic Promise
stand revealed. It has to do with an altogether special benediction of
God on the race of Abraham, on his *seed*. This benediction at first
specifies the descendants of Judah, then the dynasty of David. He who
will completely fulfill the Promise is to be an individual, "that One who
is to be sent," "the hope of the nations"; he will possess the scepter and
the kingdom. This kingdom is universal in character: all the nations of
the earth will be blessed in the seed of Abraham. The kingdom has also
the characteristic of eternity: it will have no end. From century to century a multitude of prophecies will fill out this canvas. Some of them
are startling in their precision, such as those relating to the Passion of
the Servant of God.

And yet even more startling is the fact that the Jewish people, in
general and from century to century, were faithful to the Messianic
Promise; no more than Abraham did they doubt the Word of God.
Assuredly, there were eclipses of this fidelity. Assuredly, all did not
properly understand it, and at times there was mixed with the hope a
furious appetite for triumph and for vengeance. But in the end this
stubborn people safely transmitted the Promise from generation to generation all the way to its sublime consummation.

The Church attaches special importance to the prophecies of the Old
Testament; it quite rightly makes them one of the principal arguments
for the divinity of Christ, who fulfilled them. On the other hand, modern rationalism is particularly set on destroying their probative value.
True to its methods, it tries to isolate each prophecy, that is, so the
explanation runs, to re-establish it in its historical context, where the
light of criticism, it is believed, will annul it or at least enfeeble it. This
is tedious work, often misleading and sometimes laughable when one
sees how certain prophecies, twisted every which way, retain their
sharp-edged trenchancy.

Christian exegetes, wishing to follow the rationalists step by step on their own ground, have sometimes been enticed into partitioning their own subject and, in their attempt to prove too much or to prove matters not in debate, have ended by proving nothing at all except their own good faith in the face of every provocation. An air of severe constraint is often perceptible in their weighty discourses on the subject of credibility, that is, on everything that can justify faith when confronted with the demands of reason. The argument of credibility drawn from the fulfillment of the prophecies is very strong; nevertheless, to realize its full force one must know in what perspective this credibility lies. Too often there is an attempt to make the prophecies conform with a materialistic exactitude, an almost mathematical rigor, to the events. But the dialectic of the prophecies is of an order altogether superior to the material one: for analogies, one must look rather to the artistic order of poetry and especially of tragedy.

The great classical tragedies indeed are where one finds the same dialectic of indirection, that equilibrium between word and deed that seems to elude fate and that irrevocably precipitates it, that distant awareness that charges the smallest action, the least gesture, the littlest word with prophetic significance at once obscure and agonizing, a significance which one does not immediately comprehend but which, in an aura of inquietude, one feels to be absolutely necessary and which the denouement alone will fully reveal and, simultaneously, justify.

Aeschylus, Sophocles, Shakespeare, Racine—all dominate their theatrical worlds of space and time, and for the effective movement of tragedy it is absolutely necessary for the author to dominate the space and time of the theater, for him to have a single view, from a fixed central point, whence he directs everything toward its end. From that superior, fixed point flow the diverse vicissitudes, strictly marshaled in an admirable sequence, that lead finally to the inescapable denouement. Why talk of the conflict between the hero's free will and the foreknowledge of the author? If there is conflict, this conflict is essential to tragedy. The wonderful thing, the thing that touches us and that we feel to be true in this theatrical credibility, is precisely that Macbeth *is* free, that he wants and does not want to kill the king, that he even wants constantly to escape, but that he is constantly brought back by an infallible hand to choose, freely, his inevitable destiny.

It is said that the whole of Hebrew literature is inferior to the Greek because it has no tragedy, it has only prophecies, which are usually classified as lyric poetry. This is because people do not know how to read the Prophets and because they fail to put themselves in the right position to judge them. Here the author is not Ezechiel, Isaia, David, or Moses; he is God. The acts of the tragedy extend over thousands of years; indeed, the play has not yet ended. The theatrical space and time of this tragedy are real time and space. The first cycle of the tragedy begins with time and the creation of the world, and ends with Christ. There is a second cycle, in which we are now participating; it begins with Christ and will end with the world, the Last Judgment, and time itself.

Here, for the moment, I am speaking of the first cycle. The protagonists of this cycle are God and His people: *Your seed, your seed.* God is at once the author and the hero. It is not really so exceptional for an author to place himself on the stage. But now that we know the denouement of this first cycle—which is, precisely, the life and death of Jesus —the history of the Jewish people and the prophecies take on a striking unity and clarity. But, after that, to take apart this history and these prophecies, to subject each passage separately to criticism, refusing to place it in the great tragic movement that carries the whole toward its conclusion, is as ridiculous as to attempt to judge a scene from *Phaedra* or *Othello* without balancing it properly against the denouement of the play of which it is a part.

It is in the light of this steady forward movement of Jewish prophecy that the Old Testament must be read; then it becomes resplendent in its art and in its restraint. No longer can it be charged with lack of full explicitness. Quite the reverse: we admire its reserve, its dramatic effects —so abrupt in themselves and yet prepared for so far in advance—its repetitions, bearing a double meaning, and again the indirection of its language, the pantomimes and mirror play, the reversed symbols and the parables unmistakable in their fateful reach. Then all the objections of the rationalist are seen to be beside the point, like the requirements of a sterile and tasteless academicism.

Thus we return to the central theme of this history. The conflict between time and eternity is the conflict appropriate to tragedy. It dictates the plot, which we call destiny. It is essentially a poetic conflict, proper to every creation, including that of God. The tragic writer creates his own time and his own space, but he finds his support in, and makes his start from, a point below the level of this time and space: in the beginning there is the poet. The denouement itself must return to the starting point and, by rising into the universal, that is, into the eternity of the theater, transcend the space and time that have filled the stage.

"In the beginning God created the heavens and the earth. . . ."

"In the beginning was the Word, and the Word dwelt with God, and the Word was God. . . ."

Thus the rationalist's criticism of the prophecies inevitably collapses because it refuses to look at them in this third dimension of tragic time, which alone gives them their tension and their purpose, and without which there is nothing left of them but non-sense.

Everyone who knows the ways of the theater is aware that the first requirement of a true denouement, true in the sense of possessing complete dramatic credibility, is to surprise the spectator with the very thing he has been expecting, the thing he has been made to expect. Here everything bears the imprint and the style of the denouement: it is this that makes it impossible to foresee the event; it is the stroke of genius that overwhelms with astonishment, once it has been accomplished. For Christians, the redemptive Incarnation, the God of Sinai incarnate and dying with a great cry on the cross, is the denouement of the entire Old Testament. Saint Paul tells us that this denouement is a scandal to the Jews. What can that mean except that the Jewish people have been surprised by what they awaited, the event they did nothing but await, the event they had been made to await? However great this scandal and this surprise, these are also in a sense a sign of the perfection of the tragedy.

The essential requirement of the theater is, precisely, credibility, especially the credibility of the denouement. But the credibility of the denouement is necessarily linked to everything that has gone before from the rising of the curtain. It is understandable, then, that the Church should be attached to the Prophets, to all the Prophets, even the most remote, even the least; the Church clearly takes the author's point of view, it shares his intentions and his intransigence. "What's wrong with my last act?" a playwright asked. To which a critic replied, "Your first act." But it is equally true that if the last act is good it is so from the very first lines of the first act.

Thus the credibility of a tragedy is at once internal and total. It begins with the rise of the curtain and exhausts itself in the denouement, but in between it advances with each word and each gesture, for the value of each word and gesture lies in their being aimed at the denouement and pressing toward it with all their weight. But every tragedy has a credibility of its own: there are no two dramatic situations exactly identical, even when they appear so. To judge the credibility of a work, it is necessary not to go outside it.

In short, the golden rule of tragedy is that the denouement must *justify* everything that has gone before and paved the way for it; it justifies itself in all the characters, definitely settling the fate of each. This justification must be perfect at the level of theater; otherwise the tragedy is a failure. *Justification*—there in a word is the master key of tragedy. Nothing better can be said; Saint Paul saw this so clearly that he found Abraham's justification in the same denouement that can justify us all.

Commonplace minds imagine that in the world of the spirit, especially in the world of religion, there is no rigor, no structure, no hierarchy, no precise gradation; that everything is a vast realm of shadows and vague phantoms. This is the reason they have so much difficulty in believing that theology is a science—which nevertheless it is, and a very rigorous one. I am acquainted with enough theologians to know that they habitually hold similar prejudices in respect to poetry and art in general. They believe that this is a domain of dreams, as inconsistent as dreams. However, as Cocteau has said, the poet does not dream, he counts. My analogy between the movement of prophecy and the movement of tragedy will not convince the theologians; nevertheless I believe it is true, provided the idea one forms of a tragic poem is the rigorous and precise idea that corresponds to its true nature.

Having said this, I will readily admit that analogy is not proof. Here it is not a question of mathematical proof. My whole procedure, on the contrary, is intended to demonstrate that the credibility of the prophecies is of an entirely different order from that of mathematical proof. I cannot *prove* to you that *Hamlet* is a great tragedy if you absolutely refuse to admit it. I cannot even demonstrate the dramatic credibility of *Hamlet*; it demonstrates itself on the stage, just as movement is demonstrated in the act of walking. The credibility of a play is a fluid that comes across the footlights; if nothing comes across, it is because there is no fluid, no credibility. This dramatic credibility demonstrates itself in the degree to which the spectator finds, not that the spectacle is believable, but quite simply that he believes it. Nevertheless it is only just to say that dramatic credibility exists in the tragedy itself; it is not the spectator who creates the credibility: it is there, overwhelming in its conviction, beneath the lights that flood the scene, but it is truly effective only insofar as the spectator finds himself trembling for Hamlet, raging and suffering with him.

Most assuredly the work of criticism, exegesis, the study and comparison of texts, is of the utmost usefulness in understanding the Bible, but there is a setting for the prophecies that needs to be constructed—this, moreover, is done in the liturgy—a setting that arranges them all in relation to the denouement. It is in such a setting that they give forth their full radiance.

Tragedy, in short, would be nothing without the contagious emotions it evokes. The Greeks believed that the two emotions proper to tragedy are pity and terror. To these, the Prophets added hope. They did not have the same conception of fate as the Greeks. It is interesting from this point of view to compare the Greeks with Shakespeare: Shakespeare is a Christian; his denouements are never altogether without hope. Each time one feels that all will start afresh. In Shakespeare, fate is larger than in Sophocles. Through this margin of difference, hope slips in.

This enlargement of destiny took place across the sea when, beneath the terebinths of Mamre, God spoke to Abraham as one friend to another, and above all in that amazing scene in which, doubtless for the first time, man experienced the power he holds over God's heart, when Abraham besought God to spare the accursed cities: "If there be fifty just men in the city, will you then destroy the place and not spare it for the sake of the fifty just men within it? . . . What if there be five less than fifty just men . . . ?" And so on down to the ten that could not be found. Oedipus, for his part, does not bargain with the oracles; God, however, yielded each time at Abraham's entreaty. Fate is no longer empty and blind, expressing itself in obscure, irrevocable oracles. No, fate is God. In the beginning He created the heavens and the earth in order that man should have dominion over them; He numbers the stars of the sky and probes the loins and hearts of men. Assuredly He chastises, and that harshly, but always with justice and with discernment. But He loves, too, and He allows Himself to be touched by prayers and by tears. Little by little, the Prophets will reveal His love even more clearly in the poems which form the substance of the Church's prayer.

Gen. 18:24, 28

Thus through the millennia the drama of Old Testament prophecy unrolls. It is essentially a proclamation of hope, whose setting is prepared by God Himself. Terror, to be sure, is not lacking, nor the thunder, nor the lightning. But hope dominates. And all converges on that unheard-of dramatic height where the author of the tragedy Himself, the author who is at the same time God and fate, dies on the mountain between heaven and earth. Thus ends the tragedy which will forever evoke compassion, since Christian love is directed primarily toward Christ on the cross; it has by its very nature the qualities of reverential fear, of compassion, and of hope, which are the elements of tragic emotion.

The Creator of heaven and earth, the Master of time, combines in Himself time and eternity: on one day of all days, when the tragedy has reached fruition, he immolates Himself, in His own seting, in eternal testimony to His love. Pierce the heart of the Son of Man and there we read our own destiny.

CHAPTER III

The Miracles, or the Seal of the King

"GOD perceptible to the heart," Pascal writes. This is true of Jesus Christ, in whom more than in any other man our hearts perceive divinity. But it is not simply a question of our hearts. The obstacle encountered by modern man at the very threshold of the history of Jesus Christ comes not from the heart but from the mind. This God, who is still perceptible to the heart, seems to be drawing farther and farther away from the modern intellect until it no longer perceives Him.

It was not always so. Many of the Jews contemporary with Jesus Christ no doubt understood perfectly well the argument for his divinity based on the miracles and the fulfillment of the prophecies: their hearts revolted at the very idea that God could demean Himself so far as to become incarnate, suffer, and die. For us, on the contrary, it is just this that is most moving.

Later on, certain heretics denied the reality of Christ's human nature, maintaining that his body was only a paradoxical and tangible appearance, which veiled a nature at once glorious and impassive. As for us, the natural bent of our minds inclines us to deny the invisible and to recognize in Jesus Christ only a man like any other.

Very likely, in those eras that are called "theological" in the jargon of the positivists, miracles, angels, and demons—the whole realm of the miraculous—far from detracting from the credibility of such a history, were massive arguments in its favor. It is just this that disturbs us most.

But even during his mortal life Jesus never ceased to cause scandal.

Men were scandalized because he drank wine, spoke to women, dined with sinners, healed the sick on the Sabbath, performed miracles or did not perform them. Since then, the scandal surrounding the story of his life has not ceased. People are scandalized because he was too human or because he was too divine, because he suffered and died or, equally, because he arose from the dead, because his actions and appearance were too natural or because they were too supernatural. But the scandal that is peculiarly our own concerns most of all the miracles, which instead of edifying us cause us embarrassment. Whereas they have traditionally been considered a proof of Christ's divinity, we see in them evidence that the Gospel is a fairy tale; in our minds they reduce the whole story to the imprecise proportions of a fable. What ought to hold us in restraint frees us from all restraint: we no longer feel ourselves obligated to an integral faith in the Gospels—because of the miracles. In any case those of us who believe in the historical truth of the Gospels do so in spite of the miracles, and as for those who do not believe in their historicity, it is very often because of the miracles that they do not believe. Has the sheet anchor of our salvation failed us?

Since today one can treat the Gospel as one likes without risk of being sent to jail, it is possible to write a life of Jesus, as Renan did, eliminating all elements of the miraculous. In doing this one asserts that the Gospels are not wholly worthy of belief. Or one can interpret the miracles symbolically, taking them as unreal representations in the singularly credulous popular imagination, a more or less poetic transposition of facts that were actually very different from those reported to us. Once again, this is to assert that the strictly historical value of the Gospel is nil. A cause of intellectual unease among believers, an insurmountable intellectual scandal to unbelievers, the miracles of the Gospel pose an unavoidable question at the very threshold of this book, a book that I wish to be honest.

———

In Stockholm, in his acceptance speech for the Nobel prize in literature, Saint-John Perse defined the position of poetry in relation to modern science. I here quote from that speech because—in those circumstances and in that place and before the audience there assembled—it gives with unsurpassable perfection and with a rigorous and indisputable precision a brief geography of knowledge, now universally accepted, at least by those who understand the subject, but profoundly revolutionary in respect to what was thought to be definitely known one hundred years ago—precisely at the time of Renan.

When one considers the drama of modern science discovering its own rational limits, even in pure mathematics; when one sees, in physics, two great, controlling doctrines, presenting on the one hand *a general principle of relativity,* and on the other *a quantitative principle of uncertainty and indeterminism, which would limit forever the attainable precision of physical measurements;* when one has heard the greatest scientific innovator of the century, the originator of modern cosmology and the guarantor of the vastest intellectual and mathematical synthesis, *call intuition to the aid of reason* and proclaim that "the imagination is the true seedbed of science," going even so far as to claim for the scientist the advantage of a true "artistic vision"—does one not have the right *to consider the poetic instrument as just as legitimate as the instrument of logic?*

I hope that school children will be given this speech to learn by heart instead of being fed on positivistic inanities, with which our textbooks are still stuffed.

It is hard indeed to imagine a more authoritative announcement of the bankruptcy of positivism than this. The positivistic postulates of last century's science, on which such brilliant men as Taine, Renan, and Michelet took their stand so firmly, so comfortably, and so insolently, have crumbled. At the end of their investigations, the mathematicians and scientists of today discover, not more and more certainty and determinism, but more and more mystery and indeterminism, and what appears to be the enigmatic face of Freedom. Within the space of a hundred years a prodigious upset has taken place in the intellectual sphere.

In the same speech, the same poet denounces modern philosophy for having retreated from the threshold of metaphysics. This retreat has caused a sickness in us all. While modern science, in order to come closer and closer to reality, has accustomed itself to humility and to mystery, philosophy has taken pride in turning its back on reality and sinking into a narcissism that is simply an egregious ossification of the mind. Nothing is more pitiable than the thing we have grown accustomed to call by the name of philosophy.

But it is this modern philosophy on which our minds have been formed and from which we have gained our customary ways of thought. It is this philosophy of certainty, too certain of itself and of its false insights, this imperious philosophy disdainful of reality, this really paranoid philosophy, drunk with determinism, that still dictates our reaction to the very word "miracle." Modern science, for its part, has become much too humble, much too attentive to business, to dare pronounce ostracisms.

In my childhood when I was being instructed in the catechism I learned that the world would one day end. This proposition was taught to me as a dogma on the authority of the Gospels and the Church. Positivism sneered at this dogma, as it did at all the others. Well and good; since the Hiroshima bomb it no longer laughs; on this subject it no longer laughs at all. It has been forced to swallow its sarcasms. The end of the world has come down from the heavens of dogma to the terra firma of scientific possibility, where it possesses a dreadful likelihood, and its descent made a great noise. That such a truth, so long held only on the strength of divine revelation, should suddenly take on the character of an immediate scientific menace constitutes an intellectual fact of overwhelming grandeur. I cannot see that many people have taken note of it. Obviously, for believers, evangelical and apocalyptic prophecy have no need of this scientific illustration, but for those believers who have two cents' worth of judgment the terrible demonstration at Hiroshima should at least be a means of disembarrassing them of their inferiority complexes. Their faith assured them of something that neither science nor philosophy in the nineteenth century dared envisage. It was my little country *curé*, he who taught me the catechism, who was up-to-date—and what a date!—not the Sorbonne. It was the science and the philosophy of those times that were in error, not he.

In the nineteenth century, scientific knowledge recognized that it had limitations, but considered them temporary. It had absolute confidence in its totalitarian authority over reality and in its methods and its unlimited potentialities. It was commonly thought that in time the conquest of nature, undertaken in the sixteenth century, would be completed and that mystery would be done away with. Today—and this is what Saint-John Perse emphasizes—science knows that it is uncertain and limited, efficient to be sure, but incomplete; and man knows that he is introduced into this world like "one born blind," as Saint-John Perse again puts it. Henceforth science knows that it will never tell all because it will never know all, that it will never snatch the profoundest secret from "primeval night," and that to try to assign fixed frontiers to an expanding universe is absurd.

And what if the primeval night were inhabited? When, on behalf of the scientist, one summons intuition and artistic vision "to the aid of reason," one has entered upon a path where the words "prayer" and "grace" regain meaning—a meaning which is not, by the way, necessarily a religious one. It is, to be sure, vain to hope that scientific instruments can ever prove the existence of God; the retreat of philosophy from the threshold of metaphysics is here unavoidable. But at least it is not fantastic to believe that the "free thought" discussed by Claude Bernard, that daughter of methodical doubt and the experimental method, by proceeding no longer from certainty to certainty but from question to question, may without being untrue to itself kneel on occasion as a mendicant at the threshold of that primeval night. Then the scientist, without abandoning his human duty of standing upright and pressing forward among the shadows, will be able, in his moments of repose and contemplation, his most fruitful moments, to invoke without blushing those higher sources of aid whose name he does not know but from whom the light comes.

By renouncing its claim to be the absolute mistress of reality, science leaves a place for a different seigniory from her own, a seigniory that holds absolute sway over being in its most authentic essence—the realm of mystery and of primeval night. In other words, a universe of discourse that leaves no place for poetry has by the same token no place left over for religion. On the other hand—and it is here that Saint-John Perse's statement is of importance to me—if you leave the door open to poetry you can no longer close it upon religion. And I challenge anyone at all of intelligence and good faith to contradict me. The huge windbag of positivist philosophy is permanently punctured.

Once more, I do not want to say that modern science furnishes any proof whatever of the existence of a supernatural world; that is definitely beyond the reach of science. I do not even say that a little science alienates one from God and that much science brings one back. It is not science that leads to God. Philosophy does that, on condition that it does not desert the threshold of metaphysics, and I even believe that modern philosophy knows this and that it has withdrawn from the threshold of metaphysics simply in order not to find itself suddenly in that Presence. But through this desertion it has denied itself. By another road, purity of heart also leads to God. I say that nothing in modern science keeps us from believing in God but that it is absolutely certain that a determinist philosophy, which accepts as a postulate the absolute rationality of the universe, is completely incompatible with the modern scientific view of the universe. Religion has been called upon often enough to bow before science; it has not done so. Hiroshima and the nondeterminist scientific concept of the universe have proved that it was right. Why should not the official philosophy of our bizarre era be called upon to revise its dogmas and to bow, not to science, but to the startling proofs of its own past errors? For the habits of thought we have derived from that philosophy must, after all, be revised; certainly not in its name can we accept or reject anything whatever; it is no longer in a position to command. No longer in its name, then, can we deny the possibility of the miraculous.

By what right today, during the latter half of the twentieth century, would a poet, a scientist, or a philosopher deny the existence of that "primeval night" of which Saint-John Perse speaks? By what right would a poet, a scientist, or a philosopher declare with complete certainty that this primeval night is not inhabited? It is, on the contrary, a point of honor for human intelligence to question itself on this subject. And if that primeval night were really inhabited, by what right would we deny the Lord of that night the power to emerge from the darkness and reveal Himself? If He wished to reveal Himself to men, He would do so in his own fashion, possibly enigmatic and indirect, but unequivocal and lordly.

I shall take care, to be sure, not to present Saint-John Perse's Stockholm speech as a profession of religious faith. It is quite the reverse, since he suggests that poetry might perfectly well be the successor to religion, to "mythologies," as he scornfully says. Mythology, yes, religion is no more than that, if "the primeval night" is inhabited only by man, the congenitally blind. I would simply ask Saint-John Perse to note that if he is forever alone in the night he can never encounter anything but shadows.

For my own part I believe that man, at least in his natural state, is not blind at all but that he is plunged in night. I believe that the illumination of the poet as well as the inspiration of the scientist are gifts from "the Father of light," even if they are not recognized as such. Poetry is neither religion nor a substitute for religion; I believe nevertheless that there is no authentic poetry without a higher gift; I believe in addition that there is no authentic religion without poetry. God is a poet, which is no more than another way of saying that He is the creator.

This is what the Epistle to the Hebrews declares in the famous prologue where the appearance of Jesus Christ on earth is presented as the end and fulfillment of a long poem in which the original Word, who created all things, finds His final form of self-expression, personal, complete, living, human, and within our grasp: "God, who at sundry Heb. 1:1-3 times and in divers manners spoke in times past to the fathers by the prophets, last of all in these days has spoken to us by his Son, whom he appointed heir of all things, by whom also he made the world; who, being the brightness of his glory and the image of his substance, and upholding all things by the word of his power, has effected man's purgation from sin and taken his seat at the right hand of the Majesty on high."

Jesus is the perfect metaphor of God.

It remains nevertheless true that we moderns would like it better if Christ had not resorted to miracles in order to inspire belief in himself. What resistance is possible to the words of a man who raises the dead? This seems like a violation of conscience; one feels a kind of extortion, unworthy of God, unworthy too of any creature that is rational and free.

Well now, let us try to look more closely at the nature of Christ's miracles.

They can be classified in three categories. The first is well represented by the resurrection of the son of the widow of Naim.

Luke 7:11-16   And it came to pass soon afterwards, that he went to a town called Naim; and his disciples and a large crowd went with him. And as he drew near the gate of the town, behold, a dead man was being carried out, the only son of his mother, and she was a widow; and a large gathering from the town was with her. And the Lord, seeing her, had compassion on her, and said to her, "Do not weep." And he went up and touched the stretcher; and the bearers stood still. And he said, "Young man, I say to thee, arise." And he who was dead, sat up, and began to speak. And he gave him to his mother.

But fear seized upon all and they began to glorify God, saying, "A great prophet has risen among us," and "God has visited his people."

Each of us, in similar circumstances, has had bitter experience of his own impotence. And who among us has not on some occasion, in the secrecy of his heart, wished that he had the power to reverse a cruel fate, to restore a child to its mother, to relieve the suffering of an innocent, to possess, secretly and for one brief instant, the gift of working miracles in order to set right some too glaring injustice of fate? Each of us knows that to say to another at certain moments, "Do not weep," and not be able to accompany this advice with a miracle is an imposture. That is why some misfortunes evoke nothing but silence.

Jesus could say, "Do not weep," and accompany his order with a miracle. Having asked this woman not to weep and, furthermore, being able to perform the miracle, he would have been dishonored had he not done so. Moreover it is not this kind of miracle, miracles of pure compassion, for which we criticize Christ; rather, we envy him for them. They are precious, for they reveal, in addition to Christ's supernatural power over life and death and nature, a piteous tenderness which makes him human and very close to us. The same emotions that disturb us disturbed him too. On many an occasion in his life it would seem that this man, who was so heroic, so intent upon his goal, was yet unable to resist pity.

The second category is perfectly illustrated by the healing of a paralytic.

And after some days, he again entered Capharnaum and it was reported   Mark 2:1-12
that he was at home. And many gathered together, so that there was no longer room, not even around the door. And he spoke the word to them. And they came, bringing to him a paralytic, carried by four. And since they could not bring him to Jesus because of the crowd, they stripped off the roof where he was, and, having made an opening, they let down the pallet on which the paralytic was lying. And Jesus, seeing their faith, said to the paralytic, "Son, thy sins are forgiven thee."
Now some of the Scribes were sitting there and reasoning in their hearts. "Why does this man speak this? He blasphemes. Who can forgive sins, but only God?" And at once Jesus, knowing in his spirit that they so reasoned within themselves, said to them, "Why are you arguing these things in your hearts? Which is easier, to say to the paralytic, 'Thy sins are forgiven thee,' or to say, 'Arise, and take up thy pallet, and walk? But that you may know that the Son of Man has power on earth to forgive sins"—he said to the paralytic—"I say to thee, arise, take up thy pallet, and go to thy house."
"And immediately he arose and, taking up his pallet, went forth in the sight of all, so that they were all amazed and glorified God, saying, "Never did we see the like."

If you believe that the miracle is all that was at stake here, it is not true that the Jews had never seen its like. They had seen many miracles in the course of their history. It is rather the *ambiance* of this miracle that is entirely without equal. The narrative gives the most perfect illustration of a method peculiar to Jesus and constantly used by him, and is more important than the miracle. This is the structure of his method:

A question is put to Jesus;
on the level of the question, he replies indirectly by putting another question;
thus he creates "suspense."
Finally, in a forward movement, he links the two questions together, the one put to him and the one he has put, and replies simultaneously to both questions, on both levels at once, but in doing so he causes the whole subject to explode under the force of the stupefying revelations contained in this final reply.
Here a paralytic is brought before him, obviously for the purpose

of being cured. The question in the minds of those present, unvoiced but obvious, is: "Will he heal him? Will he not?" Jesus leaves this question in the air; he simply forgives the sick man his sins, something that no one has asked of him. Thus he calls forth from those present a new question, still unvoiced but more important than the first: "God alone having the power to forgive sins, by what authority does this man claim to forgive them?" Jesus understands very well what is at stake. He does not retreat one step. On the contrary, he advances boldly to the extreme limits of defiance—and then pushes those limits farther back. Once more he asks a question: "Which is easier: to forgive sin or to heal a paralytic?" Just as when he said to the widow at Naim, "Do not weep," he solemnly obligates himself to perform a miracle. The miracle will clinch irrefutably the effect of his demonstration. He has healed a man, but above all he has proved that he has the power to forgive sins.

But in his reply, Jesus pushes his challenge even farther—to the point of claiming for himself equality with God, with "the Ancient of Days." According to the Gospels of Mark and Luke, this is indeed the first time that Jesus has claimed for himself the title "Son of Man," the prodigious prerogatives of which we have seen. For my part, I do indeed believe that it was in these precise circumstances that Jesus for the first time took this title and thus solemnly affirmed his divine nature. This is the reason, even more than the miracle, that the Jews present were seized with stupefaction.

This second series of miracles is of great importance for our instruction; they throw decisive light on the very personality of Jesus, who claims for himself divine prerogatives, the supernatural omnipotence of God, the direct power to deliver souls as well as bodies. In the second place, they throw a no less decisive light on Jesus' mission itself.

Jesus did not come primarily to heal bodies but to deliver souls and to forgive sins. We are by nature extremely sensitive to the ills that afflict the body—suffering, sickness, and death. Jesus tries to convince us that there is a more serious ill, the ill that afflicts the soul, that wounds and kills it. It was first of all to heal this sickness of the soul that he came among us, less for the just than for the sinners. His power is always ready, accessible, open, if it is a question of healing souls. To heal the body will never be more than secondary and is not always appropriate even at the level on which Jesus places himself. But it is always appropriate, necessary, urgent, and possible that the soul be delivered from its sins and that it recognize, together with the source of its pardon, the source of its life.

Finally, there is a series of miracles against which our modern minds are likely to revolt because they have the appearance of being performed simply to amaze the spectator. This kind of miracle shocks us all because of an air of charlatanism that we are likely to attribute to it. Among these the most famous is without question the Transfiguration. What purpose is served by these miracles? Apparently none. Unless, that is, they are profoundly interwoven with the drama of Jesus' temporal adventure itself and are therefore most necessary for the revelation of the meaning of this adventure in all its dimensions.

That is what I think. Certainly Jesus' temporal adventure has a meaning beyond the human one, a cosmic meaning. It is possible, not to understand it (who can boast of understanding it completely?), but at least to divine and respect all its dimensions, on condition that one does not limit oneself in advance to the boundaries of time. He who said, in the most natural way in the world: "Before Abraham was, I am," could do and had to do things that have only a supratemporal, that is to say a prophetic, meaning.

Christ was fully conscious that he was fulfilling the prophecies; most of the time he was the only one to know that he was doing so. He also made prophecies. At every instant his presence inserts itself smoothly into a drama already outlined, or outlines the plot for a happening still to come. And the reality, once it supervenes, is always astounding, as the full-blown flower is always astounding in relation to the bud, which was nevertheless its promise and its prophecy. But Jesus controls his future with equal ease, and sometimes he has occasion to prefigure it. It is not until after the event that one can establish its relations and admire once more the perfect fulfillment of an enigmatic enactment.

As for us, we move along our ways like ants, within horizons narrowly confined by our daily lives—their duties, labors, pleasures, pains —and by the way we organize them, which is often as vain as it is meticulous. It is very rare that we take an over-all view of our past or that we picture our future. Moreover, what power have we over our own destiny? Our past is weighed down by "I could have, I should have." These words, which are indeed terrifying, have no meaning whatever when applied to Jesus—an immense privilege over all men. One can be sure that this man never said to himself, even apropos of Judas, even apropos of Jerusalem, the holy city he loved so well, "I could have, I should have." No, what he should do he was always able to do and he always did it. His words, as ever characteristic of him and as usual forming a question, "Who among you will convict me of sin?" mean just that.

He even had sovereign freedom in respect to the future—when he prefigures the future, it is without fear of being betrayed by the event. He simply says to the blockheads who were his disciples and who were one day to become his witnesses: Give heed to what you have just seen, remember it well. Do not speak of it yet, but when the corresponding event has occurred, then let this be evidence to you that I knew in advance what would happen, that I willed it so, and that I have always dominated the outcome.

Why, then, are we scandalized by Jesus' miracles, even the most magnificent, even the most gratuitous? Like all Jesus' other actions and gestures, like all his words, they are borne along in the great movement of his life which progresses from eternity to eternity, toward the total fulfillment of his destiny, a joyous flotilla, following the course of a great river toward its mouth, a flotilla that nothing will stop. Moreover, why give to Jesus' miracles more importance than he himself gave them? In his thought, in his words, and in his actions, they are always sharply subordinated to a superior significance. As Saint Thomas Aquinas says, they are the seal of the king that marks the sovereign message with the impress of his omnipotence. Seals of the king have chanced to fall into the hands of collectors, who admire them for themselves, but that was not their primary destination, the only destination that counts in my eyes; the true purpose of the king's seal is to be broken so that we may read the message authenticated by that august signet.

The miracles are no more than a sign of the power of Jesus Christ. That power, as he spent his life in telling us, was completely mobilized in the service of the spiritual salvation and the spiritual resurrection of men. The miracles would be ambiguous if they were not symbols; they would simply be saying, "Let those follow me who love power." Their meaning, actually, is this: "Let those who desire *spiritual* salvation— spiritual salvation, moreover, of the body as well as of the soul—come to me; I have power to save them in the only manner in which I have pledged myself to do so: through spiritual salvation."

When one rereads the Gospel, Pascal's comment stresses an obvious fact. First of all, he emphasizes the need of the miracles in respect to Jesus: "But for the miracles, to have disbelieved would have been no sin," and he cites John 15:24. But he subordinates the miracles to the fulfillment of the prophecies. The miracles of Jesus were, then, supremely important for his contemporaries; for us the miracle of miracles, fully self-sufficient, is the fulfillment of the prophecies in Jesus. "Jesus Christ performed miracles," says Pascal, "and so afterwards did the Apostles and the early saints in great numbers because, the prophecies not yet being accomplished, but being in process of accomplishment through them, miracles were their only witness. It was foretold that the Messiah would convert the nations. How could this prophecy have been fulfilled without the conversion of the nations? And how could the nations have been converted to the Messiah if they had not seen the final outcome of the prophecies which prove him? Therefore until he had died, risen again, and converted the nations, all was not fulfilled; and so miracles were necessary for all this time. Now they are no longer needed against the Jews, for the fulfillment of the prophecies is an abiding miracle."

It is striking to see that the official teaching of the Church has adopted this view and makes reference to the miracles principally in regard to the divine origin of the Christian religion. Not that miracles are no longer possible today, but we do not have the same need for them. It is reported of the King Saint Louis that when he was informed that a miracle was taking place in his palace chapel he did not go there, saying that he had no need of a miracle to believe in the corporeal presence of Christ in the Eucharist. Miracles, to be sure, are always possible; they still occur now and then; and the Church demands them of its saints as a prerequisite to canonization. There is nothing astonishing about them; what is astonishing is the total obedience of a man to God and, inversely, the obedience of God to a man. In this sense Simone Weil is quite right in considering as miraculous any three steps taken by a saint, whether those steps be taken on water or on dry land.

———

Nothing in this line of reasoning will eradicate modern man's prejudice against miracles. I think, in fact, that the roots of this prejudice do not lie in reason or in scientific progress, as is generally thought.

The truth is that we modern men love order, we love it with all our hearts, with all our souls, with all our strength; we love it above everything, we idolize it. We do not want this order disturbed, even by a missive from the King of Kings. And our conception of order is the meanest possible one, the most avaricious, the most stingy, the most materialistic, the stupidest. In all domains, even that of the spirit, it is a police regime that we venerate, a totalitarian order, the order of rigid and precise mechanical devices, like a Swiss watch: tick-tock, tick-tock, tick-tock, century after century.

This rigidity and monotony are reassuring to us; no surprise is possible, no mystery. By instinct we hate anything that might come to interrupt the monotony or break the rigidity, anything that might escape inflexible rhythm established once and for all. The conquest of nature, that dream which man has feverishly pursued since the Renaissance, was thought of until now simply as a steady advance by the forces of intelligence, that is by order, against the shrinking domain of chaos and absurdity. And anything was chaos except to the extent that human intelligence had taken effective possession of it through science. Once a new section of chaos was liberated by science, order reigned there, human intelligence guaranteed a perfect police state, nothing could any longer escape, tick-tock, tick-tock, everything was in order.

In this conception of universal order, acquired or still to come, there is not the tiniest place for miracles. In it a miracle is a scandal, an attack on the interior security of the universal order and of every man's knowledge, an intolerable indecency, an illusion and absurdity, against which all the forces of order, all the champions of intelligence, must be mobilized, against the offensive return of chaos.

The miracle is even an impiety. For, in this mechanistic conception of the universe, one can still imagine a place for God, that of the Great Clockmaker, as Voltaire put it. But how can one picture the Great Clockmaker Himself disturbing the fundamental tick-tock and thus voluntarily interfering with the proper working of His masterpiece, universal mechanism? In a mechanistic universe, a miracle performed by God could be only the result of absent-mindedness. This is what I was told in my youth.

This conception of a meticulous, totalitarian order in the universe is profoundly rooted in the modern mind. It is substantially the same in Descartes, in Newton, in Voltaire, in Monsieur Thiers' ordering the Parisian workmen to be shot down *en masse*, in Lenin, and in Hitler. In this conception nothing is more detestable than anarchy, which claims it can escape from this blind, mechanical, infallible order.

In the world as it is, this conception could not have triumphed in politics except by pretending to be "scientific." Science was charged with the duty of establishing order in the universe; it was the authorized police force, responsible for cosmic order. Under these conditions the wonder-worker is the anarchist par excellence, enemy number one, who puts all things in question, who must be denied free citizenship in this universal harmony and be deprived of his rights like the poet, but who is infinitely more dangerous than the poet because the poet defies the mechanical order by using words, with which an accommodation is always possible, whereas the wonder-worker is a poet in action who sets out to refashion in his own way and according to unexpected designs the already permanently established scheme of things. The wonder-worker puts himself permanently beyond the law in order that he may be crushed by it.

The fundamental cause of our resistance to miracles is the same as that of our resistance to poetry, an ontological laziness, conspiring with all the customs, all the conformities, all the blind tick-tocks, a pharisaism of laws that claim to be scientific, as fierce, as puritanical, as limited as the pharisaism of those doctors who long ago, in the name of the Law, crushed the Lord.

But it is just this scientific pharisaism, defender of a totalitarian determinism and of the rigidity of scientific law, that is henceforth indefensible. The blow that not only proved mortal to it but that disgraced it intellectually forever was not inflicted by theology—as I have said, the theologians do not know their own allies and do not love poetry. The decisive blow, the unexpected thrust, was administered by scientific knowledge itself, which shattered the iron framework of determinism at the same time that it became aware more and more acutely of its own limitations and of the mystery that surrounds it.

In proportion to its advance, not only in knowledge but in effectiveness in dominating nature, science humbled itself and abdicated all claim to tyranny beyond its own order and even within that order itself. In the age of relativity and of a curved universe in process of expansion, science no longer dares call itself infallible or claim total dominion over reality. It has learned to remain silent on matters of which it is ignorant, matters that lie beyond its probings. It will be careful not to exile the poet, and even the wonder-worker is no longer an object of ridicule; he is no longer outside the realm of the possible, the realm whose frontiers no one any longer dares to fix. There is no longer talk of the Great Clockmaker, for the rhythm of the world has ceased to be a tick-tock. What God has to say about Himself takes on a new resonance: that He is liberty, that He is wisdom above our wisdom, that He is love, and that the prayer of a child pure in heart can move mountains and uproot worlds. Whereas only fifty years ago, it was fashionable to laugh at such assertions, today there is not a scientist worthy of the name who would not say: Why not?

In the perspectives now revealed by scientific research, there is no longer a dividing line between the miraculous and the natural, facts themselves having become fluid. The atomic bomb would have been a miracle for Newton, but for many living men of science the question arises whether Christ's miracles may not be natural phenomena. The physical power of the soul over the elements is perhaps by nature more extensive than we imagine. The healing of the paralytic is not as obviously miraculous as was once thought. The fact that science recognizes large areas of mystery does not mean that all mysteries have a strictly supernatural and divine character. But the Church has never asserted the contrary.

The fact that the dividing line between what is certainly a natural phenomenon and what may be miraculous has become more and more imprecise has no more than secondary importance for our subject, at least in my opinion. The important thing is that Jesus Christ was in truth a miracle-worker, and to prove this a single miraculous act is sufficient—for example, the raising of Lazarus, the restoration to life of a man dead for four days and already in a state of decay. Not to speak of his own Resurrection.

But even this is not the ultimate. The thing of highest importance is that the miracles of Jesus have a precise meaning, imposed by himself, a meaning that is a revelation about his person, his doctrine, his mission; it is very often a prophetic meaning, too, in relation to some event to come, which the miracle more or less clearly prefigures, but which, once the event has taken place, appears in radiant clarity. In Jesus the wonder-worker is identical with the Prophet.

The striking thing is the fashion in which Jesus acts as master of nature, of the visible and the invisible world; his sovereignty is even more intelligent than it is free. He makes use at will of nature; his gestures and his actions, miraculous or otherwise, are metaphors that suggest a development beyond themselves. In Jesus the miracle-worker is identical with the poet.

To a greater degree than any poet, he destroys custom and conformity; he does so even more in his actions than in his words. He thrusts back horizons or transposes them at will. He superimposes one order upon another, not allowing himself to be confined by any one of them. He is free, and this sovereign freedom is the miracle of miracles. For all that, he is in no sense an anarchist, for it is to establish his own order, which is that of love, that he so freely transgresses all inferior orders. Unforeseeably and supremely intelligent, endlessly astonishing, he steadily eludes all determinism and every law. He is the antithesis of the mechanical order, free like his Spirit, which comes no one knows whence and which blows where it listeth, hovering over chaos, and chaos is clarified and becomes organized.

How well one understands that the representatives of the established order, of inflexible law, of the deterministic tick-tock, would have hated him, beaten him, trampled upon him. And the third day he arose from the dead, as he had foretold. It was he who had the last word. But, like a true poet, he spoke that last word so softly it is heard only by those who have ears to hear.

Part Two

The Life of Jesus Christ

CHAPTER IV

The Annunciation

IN THE SPRING of 1959 Chinese armies invaded Tibet. The ruler of that country fled. After the usual confusion and protests, the whole affair concluded with newspaper articles. The American magazine *Time* published a remarkable account of the life and adventures of the Dalai Lama, religious and political ruler of Tibet. This Dalai Lama is still alive, a refugee in India; at the moment when I am writing he is barely thirty years old. And so his origins are not yet obscured in the night of time.

The beginning of his life was accompanied by strange phenomena—let us call them supernatural if not miraculous—such as oracles, visions, divinations. Naturally, the prudent and conscientious journalist is careful not to commit himself concerning the veracity of all the facts he reports. He even makes use, a bit prematurely in my opinion, of the word "legend" in connection with events the witnesses to which are not yet dead. But in his whole narrative there is at least one historically incontestable fact. It is the four-year journey undertaken by the Wise Men of Tibet into a distant country in search of a child whom they did not know but who was to be both their God and their king.

The writers for *Time* do not connect this historical event with another, two thousand years old, which the Gospels report to us and which they present as historical; that is the journey of the Three Kings, who had come all the way from the Orient to Judea in order to worship a child, whom they were seeking on the strength of portents. Renan thought that the journey of the Magi was a fable. The social and religious organization that held sway in Tibet until the Communist inva-

41

sion was possible in the twentieth century only because of the isolation of that country. That isolation has been violated forever. We must fix the date: two hundred years from now the history of our contemporary, the Dalai Lama, will be as hard to conceive and to understand in the social circumstances of that future time as the history of the Three Kings was for Renan.

This is the point I wish to make. By what right do we attribute more straightforwardness and more veracity to *Time* journalists than to the four Gospels? We are limited by our experience. There is, however, no wisdom, no true knowledge without a certain discretion, a certain humility. We know much; we do not know all. A great many things remain possible which are beyond the reach of our imaginations for the trivial reason that we have never seen them.

And so let us not be hasty in pronouncing the word "fable" or "legend" to qualify the extraordinary and miraculous phenomena that surrounded the appearance of Jesus Christ in this world. Let us at least leave the door open. If Jesus is God, nothing is more natural than that his Incarnation should have been surrounded by miracles for the purposes of authenticating his divine origin. If he is not God, there is obviously no reason why his birth should not have been as prosaic as that of any one of us, granted, of course, that no birth is ever altogether prosaic.

Moreover, we happily recognize the poetry of the story in what is called the "Gospel of the Childhood" and we savor it; Christmas is the most popular of all our holidays. It is the truth of this account that we have some trouble in admitting. Whereas, if this infant born two thousand years ago in a stable in Bethlehem is in truth the Messiah foretold by the Prophets, then the poetry of the narrative is for me a sign of its veracity.

This, then, is the outcome of that long prophetic expectation that was mingled inextricably with the history of the Hebrew people; it is the opening of the final flower, of which the long poem extending over thousands of years was only the root, the stem, and the bud. That whole stem and that whole root were designed to bear this flower, and its opening is a poetic phenomenon more amazing than anything that preceded it, more so than the whole preparation for it, which was in itself so profoundly poetic. What more miraculous in the world than this prophetic wait, except its fulfillment? From the prophecy to its realization, one discerns a consistency of style that reveals the hand of the unique author. We remain within a dynamism, the dynamism of miracles, of prophecy, a dynamism which I have tried to show is analogous to that of a poem. This is the poem of God, the poem of His revelation and of the salvation He brings to the world.

Thomas Aquinas, the austere Saint Thomas, incomparable master of divinity, explains in the prologue to his *Summa Theologica* that, from the moment that God wanted to make men understand Him, He had to employ metaphors, not only in His words but in His actions. If it is true that God is a poet, there is no difficulty in agreeing that His means of expression are infinitely more extensive, numerous, and particularized than those of any other poet in the world. Why should He not employ them in their variety and their plenitude, especially at the moment when He decides to descend and live among men like one of them? Rimbaud says, "This gentleman does not know what he is doing: he *is* an angel," to which the civil servant replies, "There are no angels. If there were any, I should be the first to know about them, and I would be able to give you a complete report of them."

When the Son of God became incarnate, the heavens and earth were shaken, angels came and went as they did in Jacob's dream, a new star appeared in the sky and moved silently from east to west, men followed it night by night across the deserts, the angel Gabriel appeared in the temple at Jerusalem close to the sacrificial altar, and appeared again in a humble house in Galilee.

A young woman is traveling along the roads toward the mountains of Judea to visit her cousin who, in spite of her advanced age, is carrying a son in her womb. The same young woman, herself miraculously pregnant, is going far from her own home to give birth in a stable in Bethlehem, the city of kings, and there she is delivered of a son, who is God in person. Angels tell the nearby shepherds, and they proceed toward the stable to adore the newborn child. The angels in heaven sing.

The Three Kings with their sensational caravans pass through Jerusalem, pay a courtesy call on King Herod, who consults his doctors of the Law. For their part, the doctors of the Law, firm in their lore and with fingers to lips, remain seated on their rugs; however, the response they give is adequate. And then the Three Kings continue on their way toward Bethlehem, deposit their sumptuous gifts at the feet of the child, dream their dreams, and depart by a different route from the one by which they came.

The child is taken to Jerusalem, to the Temple, where he is prophetically recognized by two old people. Herod, who like the doctors of the Law has made no move, is seized by sudden hatred and sends soldiers to kill all the young children in Bethlehem and the surrounding country. The soldiers carry out the massacre, but the child for whom they are searching has already escaped, carried by his parents into exile in faraway Egypt.

Herod dies, heavy with crimes. The child and his parents return to Nazareth in Galilee and—aside from a journey to Jerusalem when Jesus is twelve years old, in the course of which his parents lose him in the Temple for three days—everything returns to the tranquillity and monotony of an existence without change. The angels remain in heaven. The Three Kings have returned to their homes. The miraculous star has disappeared, or perhaps has taken its ordained place among the constellations. The shepherds continue to watch over their flocks. Nazareth is a peaceful village, far from the great roads. Joseph, Mary, and her son constitute a family not distinguishable in any way from the others.

All the excitement, all the hurrying to and fro, all the marvelous and terrible things that have happened recede in time, as the memory of a dream grows dim, to a point where one could ask whether anything had really happened. Joseph dies. Mary alone retains all these things in her heart and ponders the future. For the calm and obscurity that follow are as prodigious as the confusion that went before. The excitement was a sign of the grandeur of this birth, but it is perhaps the subsequent tranquillity that constitutes the lesson.

———

The setting in which this narrative begins is highly significant. It is the Temple at Jerusalem.

The Jewish religion of today is completely centered on the Torah, the Scriptures. This seems to me a marked impoverishment of the ancient religion of Israel. The Temple at Jerusalem was the center of gravity of that religion; it was the visible sign, like a monumental sacrament, of the special Presence of God in the midst of His chosen and well-loved people.

Greek temples, with their columns, are marble groves in which the Greeks used to search for imaginary deities, as beautiful and charming as they were illusive. The multiplicity of these temples on the hills and on the seacoast is a reflection of Greek polytheism. The Jews, for their part, had but one Temple, on the acropolis of Zion. This Temple was intended as a substitute not for sacred trees but for the tent of a desert nomad. A nomad's tent, however, is not a Boy Scout tent: it is a mobile home, sometimes huge, sometimes sumptuous, that gives shelter to a whole family.

During the long sojourn of His people in the desert after the Exodus from Egypt, God shared their encampments, their comings and goings, dictated by chance of pasturage, their wars that resembled raids; always ready, like His people, to strike His tents and flee before an overpowering enemy, to disappear, leaving behind Him no tracks save those of the camels and the asses, quickly obliterated by wind and sand. Thus God had adopted the nomadic customs of His people; He never lost them, and His Spirit is still like the wind that blows no man knows whence or whither. In the deserts, God had lived beneath a tent, in His Tabernacle, and often during the night a column of fire stood above that tent among all the others, revealing to every eye the glory of His reassuring and terrible Presence.

When His people were settled in the Promised Land, God continued for a long time to be satisfied with a tent, close to the palace of the king and to the houses of men. It was only with regret, as it seemed, that He left His tent for the magnificent Temple that Solomon built. And however beautiful that Temple, it was in truth no more than a tent made of cedar and stone.

And so there is an intimate connection between the beginning of the Gospel of Luke, set in the Temple at Jerusalem, and John's prologue, which announces the mystery of the Incarnation by declaring: "Yes, the Word was made flesh, and *He pitched his tent among us* and *we have seen His glory,* the glory of the only begotten Son, received from his father." In the mind of the Evangelist it is quite certain that this was the same glory that the Hebrews had seen long ago in the desert, towering over another tent, the Tabernacle, in the form of a column of fire.

John 1:14

It is quite possible that in the eyes of a hasty reader this interplay of symbolic equivalents may appear frivolous or farfetched. I implore the reader not to be hasty. In literature I have no respect at all for obscurity or for deliberate complication. On the contrary, I am making an enormous effort to be accessible. But the subject is difficult, and it is reality itself that is sometimes complicated. What can I do? The only reason this book is being written, and I imagine the only reason it will be read, is in order to gain a better understanding of the Gospel narrative and, in the first instance, of Jesus' view of himself. Now this play of equivalents was enacted by Christ himself. For him that same glory of God that had accompanied the people of Israel throughout their whole history, that had at first rested on the sacred tent of the Tabernacle in the desert, transmigrated to the Temple in Jerusalem in order to dwell finally and permanently in the precious body born of the Virgin Mary.

It is, precisely, in this Temple that the scene takes place, after Jesus has driven out the money-changers. "The Jews therefore answered and said to him, 'What sign dost thou show us, seeing that thou dost these things?'. In answer Jesus said to them, 'Destroy this temple, and in three days I will raise it up.' The Jews therefore said, 'Forty-six years has this temple been in building, and wilt thou raise it up in three days?' But he was speaking of the temple of his body. When, accordingly, he had risen from the dead, his disciples remembered that he had said this, and they believed the Scripture and the word that Jesus had spoken."

John 2:18-22

Such, then, was the testimony of Jesus concerning himself; God had moved from the Temple at Jerusalem into the human nature of Jesus, as formerly He had moved from the Tabernacle into the Temple of Solomon. Once more, the Gospel cannot be properly understood except from within and by the light of the traditions of Israel. Once more and even more clearly, our Christian religion, wholly centered in our tabernacles, in the adoration of the Eucharistic body of Jesus, in his Real Presence in the Sacrament, is joined in perfect continuity, yes, a continuity without break, to the devotions of the Hebrew nomads in the desert when, upon their return from the hunt or from war, they approached their camp and saw from afar in the failing light—with what exultant pride—the column of fire descend on the tent of their God, amid the tents of their people. The Jews no longer have a Temple, but the Eucharistic body of Christ is the temple in Jerusalem, henceforth indestructible among us.

There was a priest named Zachary, engaged on that particular evening in burning incense in the Temple at Jerusalem. He was alone in the sanctuary but "the multitude of the people was without the Temple and they were praying." Suddenly "terror seized upon" Zachary: an angel was standing upright at the right hand of the sacrificial altar. It was the angel Gabriel, and he had a message to deliver.

Luke 1:10, 12

Zachary was old; his wife was equally advanced in years. The angel promised that in their old age they should bring into the world a male child. This child was to be called John, and one day he would walk before God "in the spirit and power of Elias," greatest of the Prophets of Israel, whose return was expected, even before the advent of the Messiah, to make ready a people well disposed toward the Lord. This would be a renewal of the miracle of the conception of Isaac, son of the aged Abraham and his aged wife Sarah.

Luke 1:17

Zachary doubted the angel's word. The New Testament opens on this old priest, who is afraid at first, then dubious of the divine news of his own good fortune, and whom the angel strikes down in anger. When Zachary emerges from the sanctuary, he has lost the power of speech. At this sign the people understand that he has had a vision. What the angel has said, moreover, is fulfilled; a short time later the aged Elizabeth becomes pregnant and, in the excess of her joy, remains shut up in her own house. This was the manner of the conception of the last Prophet of Israel, John, later surnamed the Baptist and the Precursor.

The people—that is, those who were present, the neighbors, the idlers, those whom it was impossible to keep from being there, from talking, from giving advice, from commenting on events, those who throughout the whole history of Jesus play the role of chorus in classical tragedy—the people then "took counsel in their hearts and said: 'What will this child be?'" Luke 1:66

Then, when Elizabeth was six months with child, "the angel Gabriel was sent from God unto a city of Galilee named Nazareth, to a virgin espoused to a man whose name was Joseph, of the house of David, and the virgin's name was Mary." She was related to the aged Elizabeth. The angel, when he had entered her house, said, "Hail, thou that art highly favored, the Lord is with thee: blessed art thou among women." The angel then announced to Mary that she would conceive a son, whose name was to be Jesus. In the prophetic tradition of Israel there was nothing more explicit or more evocative than the angel's message on the subject of this child who was to come: "The Lord God shall give unto him the throne of his father David: and he shall reign over the house of Jacob forever; and of his kingdom there shall be no end." He was to be king, priest, and judge of the tribe of Israel. This was the nature of the kingdom that all pious Israelites were expecting for the Messiah. And so the angel was announcing to Mary that she should be the mother of the Messiah. Luke 1:26-27 Luke 1:28 Luke 1:32-33

But even for this great dignity Mary would not have sacrificed her virginity, and she let this be clearly known. Not that she had an unhealthy fear of men; she was married to Joseph, and her vow of virginity can be understood only as religious homage to God, joined with the same vow of virginity on Joseph's part. The promises of the angel therefore, like Mary's vow of virginity, vastly exceed the strictly traditional Messianic conception. Moreover it is always so with divine promises: the realization fulfills the promise to the uttermost and exceeds it.

Mary would retain her virginity, she would not "know" man, for the child she was to bear would be not of man's seed, but of the Holy Ghost,

Luke 1:35 that is, directly of God. "Therefore," the angel said, "he shall be called the Son of God" in a full sense: he will have that title, name, right, nature, and personality.

To become the mother of the Messiah, it was sufficient for Mary to be daughter of David, but in order to become the mother of God it was necessary that she should be and should remain a virgin. She was "of the seed of Abraham" and through her the Christ would be the actual son of Abraham and of David, but this child she was to bear would be directly of the seed of God. In the womb of a virgin, God's millennial Promise to his chosen people would be fulfilled superabundantly: the Messiah, whom that people was awaiting, would be simultaneously and most truly the son of David and the Son of God.

CHAPTER V

The Visitation

THE ANGEL has also given Mary the news that her cousin Eliza-
beth is about to give birth, "For," the angel added, "with God all things   Luke 1:37
are possible." Mary leaves for the mountains to pay a visit to Elizabeth.
In her salutation to Mary, Elizabeth repeats the salutation of the Angel
and completes it: "Blessed art thou among women and blessed is the   Luke 1:42
fruit of thy womb." The whole of the ancient alliance, the whole history of the Promise, are enclosed between God's words to Abraham and
Elizabeth's words to the Virgin Mary.

God's Promise to Abraham was ambivalent. On the one hand, God
established an alliance with Abraham and his descendants, his race, his
seed, to whom He would give the Promised Land and who were to become a great nation; on the other hand, all the nations of the earth were
to be blessed in Abraham. It is obvious that the first part of the Promise
is racist and limited to Abraham's descendants in flesh. But the second
part is no longer racist, for it predicts, from Abraham's time onward, a
benediction upon all the nations of the earth without distinction. Since
Saint Paul, Christians have resolutely claimed their share in this benediction. The meaning of the benediction, in fact, can be only a spiritual
extension of the Promise.

The motherhood of Mary fulfills the first part of the Promise: in the
fruit of her womb the alliance between God and His people, according
to the flesh, is consummated. But this motherhood fulfills, in addition,
the second part of the Promise: in the fruit of her womb all races are
blessed, all tribes, all nations. This is what the aged Elizabeth implies

49

when she says: "Blessed art thou among women, and blessed is the fruit of thy womb."

Instantly Mary adopts the same perspective. She replies with the *"Magnificat,"* which refers explicitly to Abraham and to the origin of the Promise: ". . . for, behold, henceforth all generations shall call me blessed; because He who is mighty has done great things for me, and holy is His name. . . . He has given help to Israel, His servant, mindful of His mercy—even as He spoke to our fathers—to Abraham and to His seed forever." What a moment in time when, for the space of nine months, the womb of a virgin, a descendant of Abraham, contains in its single embrace the realization of the ancient alliance and the ancient benediction, the carnal body and what Christians call the "mystical body" of Christ. For this mystical body of Christ is simply Abraham's benediction extended to all nations. For nine months Mary was the point of convergence and realization of all past promises and prophecies and of all benedictions, past and future.

From Abraham to the Virgin Mary and to all those generations which now call or will hereafter call her blessed, it is this same religion that is expanding and developing, and this is why Pope Pius XI said of us Christians—and he said it at the moment when it needed to be said by him—"Spiritually we are Semites." Christians are sons of Abraham according to the flesh and the benediction, just as Mary was his daughter according to the flesh as well as according to the benediction.

The temporal adventure has begun, the history of Jesus Christ is under way. The uniqueness of this history is that it is not only the continuation of a race—in that there would be nothing original—but is the culmination and perpetuation of a millennial Promise and benediction that go back all the way to Abraham and to God Himself. At this moment we are at the interface of time and eternity, the point of refraction of the rod thrust into water.

As I have already emphasized, this phenomenon of refraction is always present when one is dealing with the history of Jesus Christ. That history never really begins at the point where we take hold of it; it has already begun in eternity, and we have but a meager idea of its former direction; at first glance it might appear that there had been a deviation and a caesura. The religious conflict between the Christians and the Jews bears exclusively on the interpretation of this phenomenon of refraction.

At what moment did Bonaparte begin to be Bonaparte? From the womb of his mother, no doubt. He was not preceded by anything that related to him personally. But Jesus Christ was preceded by a Promise,

Luke 1:48-55

relating to him personally, that was two thousand years old and had been unceasingly renewed. He was preceded by himself in eternity, where he exists as a person, as the only Son of God. He enters into time while remaining in eternity, like a rod that is thrust into water without being fully immersed.

At the time when Bonaparte is still in the womb of his mother Laetitia, he has no past, and no one can foresee his fabulous destiny. His mother has only hopes and ambitions, but no promise. If she is congratulated, the congratulations remain as vague as the maternal hopes and ambitions. The obscure beginning of every human being has an intoxicating flavor of adventure, but no one can know in advance the essence of that adventure. Even if it be a king's son, the adventure is only a presumption.

Here everything is different. These two women, the aged Elizabeth and the young Mary, already know the essence of the adventure. They know first of all that the adventure which is commencing is an extension of eternity, of the millennial Promise and of the prophecies. They know furthermore the identity of these seeds of men whom they bear in their wombs, and they know that those they bear are already greater than they who bear them. Elizabeth cries, "Whence comes this honor   Luke 1:43-44
that the mother of my Lord should come to me? When the sound of your salutation touched my ears, my own infant leaped with joy in my womb." Yes, they know the essence.

Elizabeth knows that the fruit of her womb has quivered with the inspiration of the Prophets and that her young cousin bears within her "the Lord," the Yahweh of her fathers, the same God of Sinai who appeared in the flame and lightning. The fruit of Mary's womb is already King, he is the Lord. His coronation and the unction of that coronation were the unction of the Holy Ghost at the moment of his human and carnal conception. Here for the first time the ancient alliance, represented by the aged Elizabeth and her son, salutes with exultant courtesy and perfect reverence the new alliance of God with His people and bows before the fulfillment of God's Promise.

There are many other memorable aspects of this story. The whole beginning of Jesus' temporal adventure is in the nature of a plot. An exacting choice is made of the very dissimilar persons who are to be made privy to the secret: an aged priest and his aged wife, a young woman. Soon the circle will be enlarged to include Mary's husband Joseph, then, after the birth of Jesus, the shepherds, the Three Kings, the two old people in the Temple; and it continues to widen until it extends to us and all those who wish to be initiated into the flock and, having been initiated, wish to live and die as part of this flock, participating in the mysterious adventure which the ancient Jews called, still in the manner of a political conspiracy, the founding, the coming and the establishment of the Kingdom of God.

Thus it was that these two women knew at that moment—and they were the only ones to know—that in them and through them the Kingdom of God had begun. This is why their jubilation at the loftiness of the event infinitely surpasses all the enthusiasms of the mothers of future emperors. When the Shah of Iran has a son, the whole Persian empire rejoices. But here, even before the birth of the heir, the whole Kingdom of God exults. This Kingdom is an hourglass that has just been inverted. The upper vessel is infinite like the heavens and eternity; the Virgin Mary is the narrow passage through which the Kingdom of God begins to infiltrate time with eternity, like fine gold dust, covering bit by bit the beaches of all the centuries to come. Elizabeth's salutation and Mary's *Magnificat* are the first crystalline echoes made by the Kingdom of God as it descends from heaven to the earth: "Our Father, Who art in heaven, . . . Thy kingdom come. . . ." And then, when the hourglass has been turned and the Kingdom has finally arrived: "My soul glorifies the Lord and my spirit has trembled with joy in God my Savior."

And so when one examines in detail the narratives of the history of Jesus Christ, there is such a quantity of correspondences, not only of one Gospel with the three others, but between the four Gospels and the whole history of Israel, and these correspondences are so perfect and of such organic precision and are so closely interlinked that it is impossible to imagine that they were born of the poetic genius of the Evangelists. These correspondences were necessarily in the events themselves that the Evangelists relate. The Evangelists did not put them there, and, if one wants to go back to the source of all these relationships, to the luminous center where they must be brought together to be altogether intelligible, it is to the poetic genius of God Himself that one must turn, for He alone dominates simultaneously the unrolling of time, the universe of nature and the universe of souls. He alone has the power to compose all these relationships on the enormous keyboard of history and, like a poet, to interlink the analogies within the same poem.

There is, then, an independent source of credibility added to all the others, a source that emerges from the simple narrative of the Evangelists when it is read as a continuation of the Old Testament. It is to this particular form of credibility that I attach especial importance because it imparts to this singular history, the history of Jesus Christ, its plenary

Matt. 6:9

Luke 1:46-47

meaning. The thing that seems to me prodigious and unique in this history is the complete identification, at every moment, of the concrete and the spiritual. What is there more concrete and more spiritual, what more dramatic and more mystical, what more objective and at the same time more subjective than the sacrifice of a God made man, nailed to a cross, on the summit of a mountain between heaven and earth? This is the origin of our Christian religion, but the Hebraic religion was the same.

In the history of Jesus Christ, therefore, it is the concrete event that is poetic, in advance not only of all interpretation but of all narrative as well. The miraculous fruit that already pulsates in the womb of a virgin, he it is who is already bringing to fulfillment a Promise made by God two thousand years ago. It is not we who establish this connection, it is not even the Evangelist himself; the connection exists in the millennial unrolling of acts that acquire their meaning through this connection, exactly as one says, "A thing promised, a thing owed, a thing fulfilled." When the thing thus promised and thus owed is finally realized, then from the Promise to its fulfillment there emerges a special order, a particular luminous order, which is that of honor. If in the *Magnificat* the Virgin Mary recalls the Promise and glorifies the Lord for its fulfillment, it is this indeed that she proclaims: the God of Israel is a God of honor.

When Saint John, in the prologue to this Gospel, assures us that the only Son of God is His Word and that this Word became flesh in order to pitch his tent among us, he is at one with the *Magnificat*. In giving us His Son, God has given us His word of honor, the fulfillment of an ancient hope and the dawn of a new one. The Word, then, is among us, like one of us; henceforth he is of the same band as we, of the same caravan, of the same wandering tribe, of the same nomadic clan, for it is very clear that we are nomads and wanderers: "We are not of this world," Rimbaud says, just as Saint Paul has said: "We have no permanent habitation here below." Heb. 13:14

But if the Word is among us, he is not here with regard to conditions: he is among us on the terms of honor. His honor is ours, but our honor is his. This is the source of great quarrels. We can betray him, and this often happens, but there is no treason in him, though indeed there is jealousy. He is the Hero-God of whom Isaia speaks. In truth he reveals and at the same time dignifies the honor of human nature. It is no negligible thing to be a man, it is not to be despised, for God Himself submitted to becoming one, and each of us, in virtue of his own humanity, is the companion of this God.

CHAPTER VI

Noel

THERE are musical silences.

When the liturgy presents the birth of Jesus Christ, it makes use of a poem from the Scriptures that dwells upon a silence of this kind: **Wis. 18:14-15** "For when peaceful stillness compassed everything and the night in its swift course was half spent, your all-powerful Word from heaven's throne bounded." Before the symphony of liberation takes its triumphal start, there is this perfect silence full of nocturnal quietude.

When one looks up the context from which this poem is taken it becomes clear that the original is a description of that tragic night when the Angel of Death struck down all the first-born of Egypt, both man and beast, sparing Israel alone. A dreadful punishment that caused Pharaoh's hatred to flinch and allowed Israel to march out of the Egyptian concentration camp.

Christian liturgy takes Pharaoh as the symbol of another enemy power, bearing, in this instance, a different kind of threat to all mankind, and it takes the Egyptian captivity as a metaphor for the prison of sin. But the liturgy nevertheless retains all the imagery of war and liberation, giving these a different meaning from the historical one, applying them directly to the Incarnation of the Word, and it is supported in this by the text of Wisdom itself, which identifies the Angel of Death and Liberation with the very Word of God.

The continuation of the poem is highly significant and gives to the **Wis. 18:15-16** feast of Christmas a warlike resonance: "A fierce warrior, into the doomed land, bearing the sharp sword of your inexorable decree. And

54

as he alighted, he filled every place with death; he still reached to heaven, while he stood upon the earth."

The Christian liturgy goes all the way with this text—that is, it accepts the strong words in their full and literal meaning. Since the text personifies the Word of God, one cannot imagine that this all-powerful Word could be better or more completely personified than by this infant, the son of Mary, who is God in person, treading the earth for the first time, without ceasing to touch heaven. But, at the same time, the historical context of this birth is reversed in relation to the escape of Israel out of Egypt. On that first Christmas Eve there was, in the sky, only a band of angels singing the glory of God and proclaiming, not death and annihilation, but peace on earth to all men of good will.

The original historical context is not entirely eliminated for all of that. The peace of Christmas is a victorious peace. It is the assurance that the enemy of man and of God, the pensive Pharaoh who reigns over the empire of shadows, will be liquidated, and that the days of his reign are numbered. This tiny baby, bedded in a manger, is a warrior, already victorious, who will raise to its pinnacle the glory of God; he will extend his domain farther than the domain of the angels, beyond annihilation and death, even to the re-creation of the universe. "For all creation, in its several kinds, was being made over anew, serv- Wis. 19:6 ing its natural laws, that your children might be preserved unharmed."

Saint Paul took up the same magnificent conception of a deliverance in Jesus Christ not only of humanity but of the entire universe: "For Rom. 8:19-23 the eager longing of creation awaits the revelation of the sons of God. For creation was made subject to vanity—not by its own will but by reason of him who made it subject—in hope, because creation itself also will be delivered from its slavery to corruption into the freedom of the glory of the sons of God. For we know that all creation groans and travails in pain until now. And not only it, but we ourselves also who have the first-fruits of the Spirit—we ourselves groan within ourselves, waiting for adoption as sons, the redemption of our body."

One must take these texts with complete literalness; they bear their own light with them and our hope. The fault of mediocre Christians is not to hope enough. Sons of God through Jesus Christ, we are integral parts of the universe, we bear it with us in the same salvation. But I have no illusions: I know very well how far the majority of Christians in my time can understand such a hope. At best they watch it go by like cows watching a train pass. This is not altogether their fault. The spirit of Christianity is a spirit of conquest and victory, and for three hundred years Christians have been apologizing for their own existence; they are on the defensive. To be responsible parts of the universe, as the poet feels himself a responsible part of the universe, of the flowers, the wild animals, the trees, the mountains, the dawn, the rain and lightning, integral parts of the universe through the birth, the death, and the Resurrection of Jesus Christ, that is what the word Catholicism means, but only the poets can feel this sort of solidarity, which is indeed poetic by nature.

I firmly believe that the Holy Scriptures considered as a poem are more profoundly true and, in a very real sense, more binding, than when they are considered solely as law, but how many Christians take the trouble to consider the Holy Scriptures? Nevertheless it is they that give form and expression to our faith and to our hope. They give us knowledge even of the universe that no science will ever be able to give. It is when the clouds conceal from the enemy the camp of Israel, when the Red Sea divides to let the chosen people pass, when the whole of nature protects the friends of God and obeys them, that the Scriptures are most profoundly true. It is the miraculous that is the rule since it is the rule of God.

By becoming the Son of Man, the all-powerful Word of God subjugated the whole of sensible nature to men of good will; it is all men of good will that nature protects under the clouds of his luminous Presence, it is all men of good will who can henceforth traverse dry-shod the Red Sea of sin, of suffering, and of death. It is therefore fitting that this birth should be celebrated with song. The benediction promised Abraham is no longer limited to his race: it extends to infinity in space and time, to every point where there is a man of good will.

———

There was, then, this nocturnal silence, and afterward the event, at once carnal and spiritual, of the birth of the Son of Man, which brought to fulfillment not only the gestation of a woman among women, but the millennial expectation of Israel. It is an essentially poetic event which sings by itself. The Word of God takes on a unique body, destined to glory and to incorruptibility. It is, in fact, the most essentially and completely poetic event that has ever taken place in the whole history of the world. In this newborn infant, the Old Testament rises to ecstasy and reaches its consummation in a single Word, the most concrete, the most moving, the most definite Word that ever has been, a Word with an infinity of resonance.

In this infant the entire universe, too, is delivered. True that in the beginning was the Word, but henceforth He is also at the final end of all things. The entire universe has no other conceivable destiny than to be conclusively expressed in Him, for, in Valéry's admirable words to Bergson, "The future is the cause of the past"; otherwise prophecy and even poetry would no longer have any meaning.

It is here, in this stable in Bethlehem, that the disagreement between the Jews and the Christians begins. There are a great many ways of evaluating and weighing this disagreement. To me personally it seems that there is between the Jewish interpretation of the Scriptures and an authentically Christian interpretation of them the whole of the abyss of difference that separates prose from poetry.

It is significant that the Jews call the holy books that are both theirs and ours the Law par excellence. A law is written in a practical language, that is, an abstract language, which searches for brevity of expression and interchangeability of terms; it is prose, which can be read only in the rhythm of prose, without one's "being forced to raise one's voice in song," to quote Paul Valéry once more. The Christian reading of these same Scriptures compels the voice to sing. But the poet is even more rigorous and precise than the jurist; he dances instead of walking. The poetic intelligence is more comprehensive; the juridical intelligence stops short at the surface of reality and substitutes for it a coherent dream.

The law brings order among things and into the affairs of men; it regulates, it directs, it determines, it limits, it opposes, it concludes, it makes pronouncements about what already exists without it and before it. But it does not produce things or human actions. Poetry acts and creates according to strict laws, to be sure; but an art of poetry by itself never made a poem. We do not deny the legislative character of the Scriptures, which is necessary and restrictive; on the contrary, we think that this restrictive necessity goes farther and deeper than the Jews themselves believe, but we always place the poem above the art of poetry. We believe that God's rhythm in His revelation is the rhythm of a song, and that the Law was made only to regulate that song down to the time of its masterpiece of expression, Jesus Christ.

———

Christ himself spoke of the mystery of human birth. It is significant that he spoke of it in the solemn discourse he gave on the eve of his death, as though, for him, birth and death had the same meaning, that of escape from imprisonment, liberation, the passage of a being already alive but bound in shadows into the unfolding of his real life in the light. "A woman about to give birth has sorrow, because her hour has   John 16:21

come. But when she has brought forth the child, she no longer remembers the anguish for her joy that a man is born into the world."

We believe, we Christians, that our temporal life is the gestation of our eternity and that death is our birth into eternal life. We also believe that there is the possibility of miscarriage, that the fruit of our life may not come successfully to term, that having failed in our life here below we can also fail in our death, that is, our real birth into eternal life.

I am speaking of individual immortality, I am not speaking simply of the immortality of the soul. Immortality of the soul is a philosophical notion. In the Christian perspective one does not picture immortality without the body's being associated with it: "I believe in the resurrec-

Rom. 8:23 tion of the flesh," what Saint Paul calls "the redemption of our body." It is for this reason too that suffering and corporeal death are, in Christianity, so intimately associated with our participation, through Christ, in the divine nature: *"Consortes divinae naturae."*

Birth is an escape from the mother's womb. But for the Son of Man who is Jesus and who is to be born in Bethlehem, city of kings, of a virgin daughter of David, temporal birth raises more questions than it answers. Like every human destiny, that of Jesus is made up of decisive thresholds that must be crossed. For every man there is the threshold of birth and the threshold of death. The exceptional nature of Christ's destiny is that there is still another threshold before birth and one after death, which he has already crossed.

For an ordinary man, conception cannot be considered a threshold, except through misuse of language: the threshold between nothingness and temporal existence. But nothingness does not exist; one does not pass from nothingness into being, one begins to exist absolutely. For Jesus, what went before his temporal existence was not nothingness, nonexistence; it was his existence as a divine person in eternity. For him conception is a threshold, the passage into temporal existence in the womb of a woman. His birth is a new threshold, from the obscure maternal womb of the Virgin Mary into existence beneath the sun. His death is a new threshold and a mysterious one as well, for his dead human body never ceased to be united hypostatically with the divine person, his cadaver *was* that person. Finally, for Jesus there is one more threshold, the threshold of bodily resurrection; he is the first to have crossed it, but the door has remained open behind him for us all.

Thus from threshold to threshold Christ's destiny proceeds likewise from eternity to eternity. This is what he himself says to Nicodemus:

John 3:13 "And no one has ascended into heaven except him who has descended from heaven: the Son of Man who is in heaven." Strange words, if one considers that he who spoke them was a man among men, seated face to face with another man, on a night like other nights beneath the obscure skies of Galilee. We must believe that the Son of Man was simultaneously on earth and in heaven and that if his destiny goes from eternity to eternity it is nevertheless never separated from eternity; it is contained in it like a sphere in a larger sphere. Through his incarnation, by becoming a man, Jesus did not immerse himself in time, he drew time into his own eternity.

Precisely because of the fact of his immersion in eternity Christ's temporal life is very different from the ordinary human life, and even more different from animal life. In passing through birth and death, an animal goes from nothingness to nothingness. In passing through birth and death man goes from nothingness to eternity. In passing through birth and death, Jesus goes from eternity to eternity. Each one of the great vicissitudes of the temporal destiny of Jesus, what I have called the several thresholds, has an analogical equivalence with all the others. Saint Paul, preaching to the Jews, said, "So we now bring you the good news that the promise made to our fathers, God has fulfilled to our children, in raising up Jesus, as also it is written in the second Psalm, Thou art my son, this day have I begotten thee." One would expect this citation to be applied to Christ's birth in Bethlehem or even to the eternal generation of the Word. But no, Saint Paul applies it directly to Christ's resurrection, to the final threshold of his destiny, to the passage from temporal death to life eternal and glorious. Acts 13:32-33

And it is true that in Christian tradition there are analogies between these various thresholds in Christ's temporal adventure—and even analogies with his eternal generation—as though they were symbols of one another. This is why the liturgy for Christmas celebrates at once the eternal birth of Christ in the bosom of his Father, the temporal birth of Christ from the womb of the Virgin Mary, and the spiritual birth of Christ through the Holy Ghost in the soul that is in a state of grace. But the analogy is always centered on the filiation of Christ with God, a unique filiation, complete and entire from the beginning and for all eternity. It is, however, a filiation that manifests itself gradually and attains the full refulgence of its revelation in the Resurrection and the Ascension, when Jesus redeems the visible world, when he is solemnly consecrated Lord of time as he has always been Lord of eternity.

Jesus Christ is youth itself, perpetually welling forth and perpetually renewed. In him eternity swallows up not only the years but the whole of time entire. Each event of his life has the new, unexpected character of lightning flashing down from heaven and instantaneously returning. For every man, natural birth is the end of a period of maturation of nine months, it is the fruit that detaches itself naturally from the tree. The birth of Jesus is that too, but it is above all the appearance in our shadowy and miserable world of the sweetness and the smile of God: *"Apparuit benignitas. . . ."*—"The goodness and kindness of God our Savior appeared. . . ." Each man's death comes by accident or through exhaustion of the body's vigor. Jesus' death is a violent accident that puts an end to his temporal life, but it also is an offering in which Jesus, at once priest and victim, freely immolates himself at the will of his Father in expiation of our sins. Born of a woman, he has human weakness and vulnerability; born of God, he revives himself and assumes once more the authority of his place at the right hand of his Father. But this time he conquers it not only as a divine person but as a man among men. And this is the prodigious reversal. For us, if Jesus Christ were not God, he could not heal and save our human nature, and if he were not man, he could not serve as our example. He is a triumph of condescension and compassion.

Titus 3:4

When Saint Leo, the Pope, wished to define for the faithful the significance of Christmas, he gave an urgent exhortation which has not, alas, lost any of its timeliness: *"Agnosce, o Christiane, dignitatem tuam. . . ."* "Christians, be on your guard, be conscious of your dignity. You have been made participants in the divine nature. Do not, through your conduct, fall once more to the level of your former decadence."

Since the optimism of the humanist and of the philosophy of enlightenment has sunk in ridicule and dismay under the impact of the experience of two world wars, in which the nature of man revealed itself as even more disquieting than had been imagined, we are witnesses to a vast plot to defame humanity and particularly the image of God in man. For some thirty years literature, motion pictures, and even philosophy, not to mention political and economic theories, have been trying to convince us that we emerge from nothingness and return to nothingness after a fugitive career in which our loftiest motives of action hardly rise above the level of the most elementary appetites and instincts—I might almost say the level of tropisms. If man in truth is nothing but that, what good is man? And if that is the case I say very seriously that it is an insult to the noblest animals, such as cats and horses, to put man in the same class with them.

May those Christians who have allowed themselves to be swept away by this vogue bestir their intelligence, pluck up the courage of their convictions, and recapture some insolence of contempt toward images of human nature that are so false and so degrading. And may the light of Christmas, rising on our night, put to flight all such timorous hobgoblins.

CHAPTER VII

The Circumcision

THE JEWS did not invent circumcision, but it must be recognized that they gave it so eminent a place in their religion and their social life that today the word "circumcised" is practically synonymous with the word "Jew"—and bears, moreover, a pejorative coloration; whether there is any justification for this, we shall see presently. Nevertheless the Jews made no change in the basic meaning of the rite of circumcision itself, a rite which, in a primitive society, indicates membership in the clan. In the most primitive form of society, in which the clan was the supreme reality, both religious and social, outside which no one was entitled to be born, live, or die, it was through circumcision that the clan officially recognized a male of its race and took possession of him.

From Aristotle's time up to that of the modern ethnologists, careful studies have been made of the primitive social structure known as the clan, a structure that antedates that of the city and is quite the opposite of it. Aristotle considered the clan (*genos*) an inferior and barbarian form of society; for him the city alone gave shelter within its walls to reason, civilization, and law. Today we are witnessing the liquidation of the clan, apparently final, throughout the whole world —in Yemen, for example, in Tibet, in Africa. The clan is no longer anything but the detritus of social and historical evolution, which appears to be wholly irreversible.

Nevertheless, for those who study it, the social structure of the clan has always been fascinating. It is barbarian, to be sure, for the clan is essentially racist: the source of order in it is not human reason or law but the will of the chief alone. The purpose of the clan is primarily biological; it is to ensure the survival of the race, its firm establishment, and its expansion. To describe and symbolize it, the figures of speech that come naturally to mind are the elementary ones drawn from the vegetable world, a tree with its roots deep in the earth and its array of branches reaching into the sky, all unified on a single trunk.

In my opinion the clan is not exclusively racist; it is essentially mystical as well, in the sense that its entire activity, its whole life, is connected to an unseen source, which is deified and adored. In the clan there is no clear distinction between religion, family discipline, collective honor, the glory of its name, the solidarity of its blood, the biological interest of the race, and the collective ownership of the earth, the flocks, or the tent. The source of the clan is adored—that is, the ancestral origin of the race. The living patriarch or in his absence his eldest son is at once the priest, the leader in war, the king, and the judge.

All things of value to the clan—religion, honor, earthly goods, armed defense—are transmitted in racial continuity through procreation. Within this elementary society, where all things are intermingled, the tomb of the ancestors, the seed of each male, the maternal womb of each woman has a character at once interchangeable and sacred: here is the root, the seed, and the soil of the magnificent tree of the clan.

In this particular context, circumcision, which places a mark on the sex of the newborn as a sign of his membership in the clan, certainly has no taint of coarseness. It is our modern societies, at once puritanical and obsessed by eroticism, that no longer have any deep understanding or any respect for the realities of sex and the holiness of the act of procreation.

A barbarian society, Aristotle called it, because it is not regulated by laws but by the will of a single individual who, being human, is not necessarily subject to reason. What Aristotle did not foresee was that God would make Himself chief of the clan. Whereupon this primitive and barbarian society, while remaining what it always had been, was elevated by God to His own level, an intrinsically supernatural one, far above all human clans and all human cities and all civilizations, because the justice of God takes precedence over even the justest law and His wisdom takes precedence over all civilizations, even the finest. This is exactly what happened. This is what God said to Abraham, chief and founder of the Hebrew clan: "I will establish My covenant Gen. 17:7 between Me and thy seed after thee in their generations for an everlasting covenant, to be a God unto thee and to thy seed after thee."

This covenant amounts to a substitution: God becomes chief of this clan, its true patriarch, its acknowledged and adored ancestor; His holy will is the only law of survival for the clan, obedience to its chief the only law of honor. This will of God, this obedience to the true God, becomes the supreme interest of the clan, to which everything must be sacrificed; it becomes the clan's common good, its protection, its defense, the thing that holds it together as the people of God. God had said "from generation to generation," and it is indeed through procreation that all the clan's material and spiritual goods, its religion and its honor, are transmitted together with life. Now membership in the clan, while still racist, has become purely, simply, and truly mystical.

In truth, this belonging to God through the clan of Abraham is much more authentic and profound than is imagined. It is clear that it was the seed of Abraham that conveyed the Word of God, His Promise, His summons, His appeal, from generation to generation, so that this Word is the generator as much as, or rather simultaneously with, the act of procreation. One sees that the Incarnation of the Word of God, without help of any male parent, but directly through the Holy Ghost in the womb of a young woman of Israel, is strictly in the line from the founding of the clan. The Word, borne along on this river, paused one day and pitched his tent on the bank. From that time on, if any male of Israel and of the clan of Abraham required to be circumcised, it was indeed Jesus more than any other. None more than he, who was the Word in person, belonged to this clan.

In every clan there is an identity between its religion and the honor of its race; Christ is simultaneously the honor and the religion of his race, he is so substantively. Each clan walks with its god. But before Abraham no clan had claimed that its god was the only true God, creator of heaven and earth and of the whole human race, and that all other gods of all the other clans were false gods, blind and deaf and impotent, dead gods, gods of deceit.

Here I should like to put a question to the Orthodox Jews. Like you, I believe that the God of the clan of Abraham is the one true God and that there is no God beside Him. Is it not likely that at a given moment in human history the essentially racist character of this religion, which is yours, should blossom out or, rather, should transpose itself into the spiritual sphere? This transposition to a universal level is, moreover, in conformity with the benediction bestowed on Abraham, for all the nations were to be blessed in him. The Word of God is the seed of salvation for all men of all races. It is true that your race alone possessed this Word of salvation through millennia. It still possesses it, alone, but this time for the entire world, since Jesus Christ is that Word incarnate, but nevertheless through his body, which we Christians adore in the Eucharist, he remains a member of your race and of your clan.

That the tribe of Abraham, however, after its solemn covenant with God remained a clan, with the primitive and barbarian significance that the *genos* had for Aristotle, there is no doubt whatever. But in the hierarchy of objective and concrete values, it is of infinitely greater worth and honor to belong to the clan of the true God than to the city of Solon. Abraham had placed directly in the hands of God all the prerogatives of chief of the clan, in particular the supreme prerogative, which is the power of life and death and forgiveness over each member of the clan. This is the meaning of the famous sacrifice of Abraham, at least in its immediate and literal significance.

That Israel was always to remain a clan is evident from the constant references made throughout its history to the God of the Patriarchs, the God of Abraham, of Isaac, and of Jacob. To the best of my recollection, despite Moses' eminent place as Prophet and as lawgiver, there is no mention in the Bible of "the God of Moses." Insofar as he was a lawgiver, Moses was already a city dweller, but the founders of the clan are and remain the Patriarchs. When Israel invokes the God of the Patriarchs, it goes outside the city and its laws; it invokes its deepest kinship and its highest honor, its prime and earliest honor of being the clan of God. And that is what it was, before so much as a single line of the Torah was written. For this reason it seems to me that to center the whole religion of Israel on the Torah is, again, an impoverishment of the ancient religion of Israel.

Christianity has kept this aspect of authentic and barbarian rite, derived from Israel, in which the one true God is at once king, priest, and judge of the clan. I believe it can be said that from Judaism to Christianity there is a change in the city and in the law, but no change in the clan.

I may be pardoned for underlining so heavily the tribal, barbaric, and primitive character of the Judaeo-Christian religion. Consider the number of books on apologetics that present contrary evidence of the moral, civilizing, legislative, administrative, humanitarian, democratic, and even socialistic or socializing character of Christianity. I recognize Christianity's contribution to civilization, but it is not a bad thing sometimes to show its other visage, nocturnal and somewhat terrifying. For after all, from Abraham's sacrifice on the mountain to the sacrifice on the cross and the Last Judgment, this religion does not present a consistently tranquilizing and sedative appearance.

Let no one tell me that this tribal and primitive aspect has no present-day importance and, moreover, that civilized humanity long ago outgrew the stage of the clan. I wish to make a distinction. I admit that our modern societies no longer have the clan's social structure. Nevertheless we have seen with our own eyes the ravages that racism can still inflict by virtue of the mystique of the clan. The patriarchal father image is still able to impress people, as we clearly observe. But the question is less one of society than one of the intimate structure of man. I believe that poetry and authentic artistic invention can have no other source in man than that which from time immemorial has served to nourish the mystique of the clan. And I am sure that in order for the spiritual and religious life of man to expand or even to be defined, it is necessary for it to be supported on every side by the clan's strict hierarchy and tragic code. The great religious orders, with the mystic importance of the patriarch established in every particular, have retained the clan structure.

As a marginal note let me say that I am struck by the fact that the methods of psychoanalysis use so many notions and so many power images from the world of the clan. I am equally struck by the fact that it was a Jewish doctor who perfected these methods and was indeed their discoverer. His racial tradition had naturally initiated him into the profoundest realities of the clan. I know very well that psychoanalysis touches upon the deepest and most inalienable aspects of man, and I should like to see a psychoanalyst who is also an ethnologist draw the parallel between the realities of the clan and those discovered by psychoanalysis. I know equally well that to those wretched people exhausted by the absurdities of modern cities, rendered lonely and bewildered in those cities, who spend their lives in search of a father, who try to find him sometimes even through suicide—to those people it is necessary to give an image of God different from that of a commissioner of police issuing regulations and maintaining public order, an image different from that of the chairman of the board of a corporation distributing dividends, an image different from that of a crony, credulous through being our accomplice, to whom it is permissible to say anything at all after having been permitted to do anything at all and in any fashion whatever.

The Evangelist Luke tells us, then, that, in accordance with the traditions of Israel, the child was circumcised eight days after his birth and that he was given the name of Jesus, as the angel had decreed.

Thus the son of Mary officially entered into the clan of the Patriarchs, the clan of Abraham, of Isaac, and of Jacob, the clan of the God of Israel. In this way he chose to assume all the responsibilities of the clan, its honor, its tradition, its history, its religion, its unique and jealous God, and that on which the clan of Abraham was founded, the covenant with that God. Jesus also chose completely to accept his race and, what is no less important, be accepted by it, to call himself, and to be recognized as, a son of Abraham.

On the day that he was circumcised, Jesus was, in the eyes of men, simply another Jew. This particular Jew, among all the sons of Abraham, would demand the right to carry further than all the others the vocation of his people, to the point of complete fulfillment in himself of the covenant of God with his people. He would claim for himself the supreme prerogatives of chief of the clan; the power of life and death carried much further than ever before, since he would raise the dead; the power of pardon such as no one had ever exercised; and the power of supreme judgment.

Historically, the circumcision marks the beginning of Jesus' earthly life within an Oriental clan. It is a definitive engagement in this clan and it takes possession of the child, who in turn seizes it and assumes this new destiny in the continuity of his race and its honor. This solemn act of initiation into the clan of Abraham poses a question about the whole life, death, and activity of Jesus. This life, this death, this activity belong first of all to the clan. Was Jesus ever apostate to his clan? Was he ever unfaithful to it? If he remained faithful, then in what sense? If he neither betrayed nor broke with the clan, in what sense did he serve its honor and maintain its solidarity? How did he become chief of this clan, the Hero-God of whom Isaia spoke?

CHAPTER VIII

The Presentation in the Temple

"ALL the males belong to me."

It would be easy to devise a parlor game by asking a group of educated people the following riddle: "These words are from a famous book; who said them and what did he mean by them?" It is possible of course that there might be a scholar present who would instantly know the right reference, but it is unlikely; this is not one of those Biblical sentences that are in constant use. Well, then?

No doubt the first idea to come to mind is that the author of this proprietary remark, so limited, precise, and universal, is a horsebreeder talking about all the stallions in his stud, of which he is not a little proud. Perhaps someone will imagine that Hitler at the summit of his racist madness might have said this about the boys of Germany, and perhaps in fact he did, why not? A more cynical imagination might attribute these words to one of the great hetairae: it is easy enough to picture an Aspasia or a Phryne in ancient Athens, a Cleopatra in the Egypt of the Ptolemies or a Catherine II of Russia making a declaration of this kind corresponding with her unquestioned power and insatiable appetite. No, that is not it. The sentence was pronounced by God and is to be found in the Law of Moses, the famous Torah, dictated by Yahweh to the lawgiver of the Jewish people.

Ex. 13:12-15   When the Lord, your God, has brought you into the land of the Chanaanites, which he swore to you and your fathers he would give you, you shall dedicate to the Lord every son that opens the womb; and all the male firstlings of your animals shall belong to the Lord. Every first-born of an ass you shall redeem with a sheep. If you do not redeem it, you shall break its neck. Every first-born son you must redeem. If your son should ask you later on,

"What does this mean?" you shall tell him, "With a strong hand the Lord brought us out of Egypt, that place of slavery. When Pharao stubbornly refused to let us go, the Lord killed every first-born in the land of Egypt, every first-born of man and of beast. That is why I sacrifice to the Lord everything of the male sex that opens the womb, and why I redeem every first-born of my sons."

A magnificent text, of superb clarity and savagery, the most revealing text one can imagine on the religious truth of Israel, the clan of God. The birth of every Israelite is assimilated to the escape from Egypt, the maternal womb, to a house of bondage from which one must be delivered by the might of God. Every man is born a slave and must be ransomed, for this is the primary meaning of the word ransom, *redemption*: a payment made to liberate someone who belongs not to himself but to another.

Here we come to the heart of the Old Testament, and it is a cause for trembling. Here before us we have what Saint Paul calls "the elements of the world"; one can try combining them in a thousand ways, but one will never come out with anything except servitude. For let us reread attentively this text in Exodus: it pictures man as emerging from one servitude only to fall into another. The people of Israel do not escape the slavery of Pharaoh except to fall under the slavery of the Law— Saint Paul will say "the curse of the Law"; man is delivered from the maternal womb only to fall under the necessity of being ransomed. And if he is in need of being ransomed, it is because he is a slave.

Gal. 4:3

Gal. 3:13

"The males belong to Yahweh." It is impossible to put in clearer terms God's ownership of this race. God reserves to Himself alone the whole seed of Israel, He treasures it, He confiscates it, He does not permit a single drop of that seed to escape Him. When the Old Testament speaks of the jealousy of God, it is perfectly clear that this must be understood first of all in an elementary sense—real jealousy, sexual and deadly. This is not my interpretation, that is how it is. That is the starting point.

Later on, to be sure, the Prophets and the New Testament will transpose this divine racism to the spiritual plane, but even on that level they will never mitigate the ardent jealousy of God, His demands for blood sacrifice, ransom, burnt offering and, in the words of Céline, "death on the installment plan." The Christian revolution will take place not through a reversal of all this apparatus or elimination of it but by giving it a new inner meaning, through a forced maturation, a miraculous blossoming, by virtue of the sole fact of the presence of Jesus Christ within this biological and sacred system.

The Law affirms the unrestricted power that God exercises as chief of the clan, the power of life and death over all members of the clan. "You belong to me, therefore you must die, therefore die." This logic leads to the total extinction of the clan for the purpose of proving conclusively that it belongs to Yahweh, and the persecutors of the Jewish people have clearly recognized that people's holy inclination toward self-extermination. It is ignoble of them to have profited by it.

Nevertheless, in order that the clan may survive, God accepts—as He has already done in the case of Abraham's sacrifice—a provisional substitution of one victim for another. The first-born foal of a she-ass can thus be "ransomed" by the less valuable life of a smaller creature. But if the Law admits of attenuation, it does not admit of any exception: "If you do not ransom it, you shall break its neck."

The eldest son of a woman has equal need of being "ransomed" by a *provisional substitute*. This implies: if he is not ransomed, his neck too must be broken. By being born we deserve death; in living we are all on reprieve from death. But within Yahweh's clan death has a different meaning from that of biological dissolution; it is the payment of the debt that every man owes to Yahweh. In the measure in which one lives, one lives only through pardon, and that pardon can be nothing but the result of a ransom, a redemption.

This is the context in which Saint Luke's account must be read where he speaks of Mary and Joseph in these words: "And when the days of her purification were fulfilled according to the Law of Moses, they took him up to Jerusalem to present him to the Lord—as it is written in the Law of the Lord, 'Every male that opens the womb shall be called holy to the Lord,' and to offer as sacrifice, according to what is said in the Law of the Lord, a pair of turtledoves or two young pigeons." To enable us to understand completely, Luke makes three explicit references in these few lines to the Law of Moses. The Law of Moses codifies the rules of Yahweh's clan, but it is also the law of a city and of a people. It is clear that the Christ desired to belong to this city as well as to the clan; he knew himself to be the only Son of God and a son of Abraham, he wished in addition to be the brother and fellow citizen of all the Israelites.

Through the legal purification of his mother and his own official presentation in the Temple at Jerusalem for the purpose of being "ransomed" by a pair of turtledoves, the infant Jesus enters definitely into the cycle of God's official ownership, of redemption and of grace, of which he will become the hero, from which he will never depart, which he will renew from within, and into which he will cause all humanity to enter in his footsteps for time and for eternity.

Luke 2:22-24

To be a human being is to deserve death; ultimately, it means some day to die. At an earlier time it meant, in the first instance, to have been culpable along with all others and then to be punished together or, eventually, to be ransomed one by another. The little time that we are given to live is through ransom and through grace, "on the install-ment plan," and on condition that another living being should die in one's place. It is finally necessary to die less because man is a corruptible being than because he belongs to God and to discharge this bondage nothing is adequate but death. "If you do not ransom him, you shall break his neck."

The whole foundation is guilt in the sight of God. At bottom death is such an injustice to man that he cannot imagine dying without being guilty: it is through sin that death entered the world, and sin soils the origins of life itself. This life-for-death is a guilty life from its incep-tion: sin, even if it has not been personally committed—and how could it be in the case of a newborn infant?—has been universally and per-sonally contracted. To be a human being is to be born a sinner. How eliminate death except by eliminating sin? How eliminate sin except through a ransom, a redemption, but a more profound and efficacious one than that of the Old Testament and of the Law, which was no more than a substitution, and a provisional one at that?

By entering the Temple at Jerusalem to be offered to God, the infant Jesus accepts in its entirety this whole world and its implacable logic— the whole world except for its elementary principle, sin. He is the only innocent among the first-born of women, he enters the Temple as con-queror, since he is free from all stain and in virtue of his innocence will conquer death and will give to redemption and to ransom a plenary meaning of innocence restored. Everything is there. The innocence of this child fulfills the Law by completely paying the ransom of man, which the Law strove to exact without being able to. The Law defines perfectly the condition of man; it clearly explains to him that he is from the outset the slave of sin and of death. But it recognizes its own impotence to deliver him from this double bondage.

Christianity will accept entire this conception of the condition of man, but it will affirm that Jesus through his victory over sin and death has liberated man from sin and death. However, when one reads Saint Paul one sees how much before he is a Christian he is a Jew when he proclaims that "All the world may become guilty before God." Saint Paul is profoundly Jewish only because the Christian conception of the universe is fundamentally Jewish, not simply through the accident of Christ's birth—we know very well that it was not an accident—but

Rom. 3:19

through an understanding of life and of death, of sin and of the necessity for ransom, which is absolutely common to Jews and to Christians.

Rom. 11:32 To have this in common is to have much in common. "God hath come through to them all in unbelief that he might have mercy upon all."

Rom. 3:4 "Let God be true, and every man is a liar." And once more: "If our

Rom. 3:5 unrighteousness can mend the righteousness of God, what shall we say?"

This strange and violent universe, this universe of race and blood, of sin and benediction, of broken necks and of redemption, of guilt and of pardon, this elemental universe that may appear to us a fierce imbroglio because we are complex, vain, and easily lose sight of the basic reality—this is the universe that Jesus Christ has claimed to crown, develop, explain, and justify as the flower crowns, develops, explains,

Rom 3:31 and justifies the stem that bears it. "Do we then make void the Law through faith [in Christ]? God forbid: *yea, we establish the Law.*" Only the rule of faith in Christ permits the Law to attain the goal it has always aimed at, the justice and the holiness of man.

But if faith establishes the definitive value of the Law, let us recognize that for a Christian the study of the Law is an essential means of entering into an understanding of faith. Christians say that one cannot properly understand the Law without considering the final event that gives it meaning, Christ, who is the flower of that root. To them one might reply that it is impossible to understand the flower properly if one does not know the root. Both come from the same organism.

Nevertheless when the infant Jesus, borne by his mother, entered for the first time the Temple of Jerusalem, this event was in the eyes of God and of His angels the revelation of an extraordinary pleonasm. The Presence of God in the Temple was an extension of the Presence of God beneath the desert tent in the midst of His people. But the infant Jesus was that same Presence of God beneath the tent of humanity in the midst of His people. An old man approached and recognized him, and his joy burst forth in a poem. Thus the earthly origins of Jesus Christ were adorned by songs from earth and heaven. There was much poetry around him.

Giotto has made an admirable painting of this meeting of the aged Simeon and the infant Jesus; their interchange of glances is unforgettable. Here is the poem Simeon addressed to God as a supplication for death:

Luke 2:29-32 Now thou dost dismiss thy servant, O Lord, according to thy word, in peace; because my eyes have seen thy salvation, which thou hast prepared before the face of all peoples: a light of revelation to the Gentiles, and a glory for thy people Israel.

CHAPTER IX

Original Sin

IN THE LIGHT of the preceding chapter, it will now no doubt be easier for the reader to understand the harsh dogma of original sin.

Would to heaven that all orthodoxies admitted and defined their dogmas straightforwardly. Philosophy, modern science, history, not to mention politics and economics, are encumbered with orthodoxies that never tell their real names, that never admit what they are, and with dogmas that are never defined.

There is not, there never has been, there never will be "free thought"; I mean human thought without belief, human thought totally freed from every dogma. A human thought cannot call itself free except in respect to this or that set of dogmas: but then my free thought is equal to yours, I am a freethinker to you, just as you are a freethinker to me. Now let us sit quietly together and chat in the friendly fashion of fellow theologians. Are you sure, sure, sure of never having condemned Galileo?

As soon as we reflect on the place of belief in our lives, we see that it is involved in all our activities, from the simplest to the most exalted. When we cross a street on the green light, the car coming on the right is supposed to stop because it has a red light: *we believe* it will stop and we risk our lives on the strength of that belief, for after all we do not *know*. You will say that this belief is entirely reasonable—and that is precisely the heart of the matter: the honor of human thought does not consist in eliminating all belief, it consists in withholding belief until there are reasonable grounds for granting it.

Here we come upon a quite different kind of credibility from that about which I was speaking in connection with tragedy. The theologian cannot bestow faith, but he has the duty to prove that the revealed truth and the dogma of which he is the custodian are not absurd, can be believed without dishonor to human reason, are not and cannot be in contradiction to science, philosophy, or the natural conclusions of reason—on the condition, be it understood, that these conclusions are not other dogmas in disguise.

For truth is one and can be only one, but is not therefore uniform, for there is a scale of values in truth and there are means for attaining the truth: no microscope has ever discovered God or the immortality of the soul, but by the same token no microscope ever discovered the genius of Einstein, which nevertheless was a fact. God, being the creator of nature as well as the revealer of mysteries, cannot contradict Himself by revealing on the level of mystery a truth that nature would contradict. This is not possible and does not happen, provided, on the one hand, that the assertion of natural science is properly proved and assured and that the theologian, on his part, remains carefully within the strict limits of dogma and does not force upon revelation meanings it does not contain.

This harmony between the assured truths of revelation and the conclusions of reason can have only a negative value, and nothing is more futile than to seek at the level of science for positive confirmation of dogma: we have no need of it, but we have an absolute need to know that what we believe by divine faith is not absurd. Faith should not shatter the unity of the mind, but rather should enlarge infinitely the field of the intelligence. The theologian does not bestow faith, but it is his duty to prove the credibility of dogma and of revelation. This credibility should be objective, accessible to the scientist and to the philosopher, though they be nonbelievers, accessible to the honest, reflective mind, though it be that of a nonbeliever, in such a way that this nonbeliever should be obliged at least to say: "I do not believe it, but it is possible to believe it and it is not absurd, the honor of reason is not destroyed if one believes it."

It is, to be sure, important to distinguish carefully what is simply hypothesis from what are established and irrefutable certainties of which one can say with absolute confidence that tomorrow they will not be thrown into question again by some new hypothesis. It is important to distinguish even more carefully the level of scientific explanation, which is essentially a description of phenomena, from the level of formal causes and sufficient reason, which is the level of philosophy. There is one more level to distinguish, which is the level of revelation and theology, where the spirit advances by reliance, no longer on evidence, but on authority and in the first instance on the authority of God the revealer. Theology is not alone in being based on authority and testimony; the entire domain of history has the same foundations. Theology has the advantage that its first witness is God, who can neither deceive Himself nor deceive us.

But above all, perhaps, it is important not to let oneself be intimidated by the mass media of publicity which send all the intellectual tourists rushing in the same direction at the same time. Neither theology nor philosophy nor experimental science nor even scientific hypotheses should be the business of publicity, fashion, or tourism; each in its own degree should be the business of truth. Truth, however, depends on a judgment of the mind, and the honor of the mind, I say, is not to let itself be intimidated. We know very well that this is rarely the case, and that if one were to annihilate at one stroke all the books in the libraries written at the behest of fashion, publicity, and intellectual tourism, the shelves would empty themselves to a dismaying degree and publishers would be ruined.

In her teaching the Church attaches no importance whatever to publicity for tourists; when everyone else turns up in one place, she on the contrary shows a tendency to retire to the desert and say her orisons. Tourism, fashion, publicity are entirely immersed in time; they have no truth beyond that of succession and change, but at the source of her teaching the Church transcends time: because she holds fast to truth, even to those humble truths of which she is not in direct charge, the Church holds unshakably as well to the distinctions of knowledge and the different orders of certitude. She refuses to let herself be intimidated or to clothe herself according to the dictates of the latest fashion.

In the complex problems raised by modern science about the origins of man and of life the Church holds fast to the transcendence of revealed truth on this subject and she resolutely maintains that this revelation cannot contradict in any particular the certainties established by science, provided that they are indeed established and not simply fashions or orthodoxies that will not tell their names and will not furnish proof, or dogmas that are disguised and transitory to boot. The Church is responsible only for her own orthodoxy, her own dogmas, and she owes no accounting except to the truth.

———

If the naturalists are open to criticism for not taking into account in their attack upon the prophecies the time dimension I have referred to, the reverse of this criticism can be leveled against them in their treatment of the origins of life and of man. The evolutionary hypothesis is used by them to brush aside every objection to their dogma. This dogma consists in denying the qualitative uniqueness of life and of the human soul compared to brute matter. Since this dogma is a little difficult to sustain against so much contrary evidence, they stretch out the difficulty over thousands of centuries in accordance with Descartes' famous rule that one must "divide up each of the difficulties into as many parcels as he can and as shall be necessary to best resolve them." The unfortunate thing is that certain difficulties do not admit of division.

Supposing the evolutionary hypothesis to be true—something that has not yet been proved—there is in all natural evolution a limiting factor, a stoppage in various directions, that can be imposed only by a cause external to the series. The naturalist is completely unable to answer this question: If the mite can become an elephant, why should he stop on so promising a path? In the whole series, mite to elephant, there is no reason to stop at the elephant.

Now the two major obstacles in the path of the theologians of naturalist dogma are the sudden appearance of life and, within the animal series, the sudden appearance of man. These are two qualitative leaps that stare one in the face. Even if it is claimed that the process extended over thousands of centuries, the appearance of life and the appearance of man belong in the qualitative domain, whereas temporal continuity, of whatever length one likes, is a matter of quantity and cannot be a sufficient cause for the appearance of something qualitatively new. These two sudden apparitions demand a cause that transcends quantity and time. There is nothing commensurate between what existed before, even if this "before" extended over millions of centuries, and what existed afterward, even if this "afterward" is as brief as a thousandth of a second. In those millions of centuries over which the evolution of the world extends, there were at least two privileged moments, thanks to a cause, transcending time and continuity, that introduced into the world by direct creation first life and then man. This is the only reasonable explanation of these two qualitative leaps.

The evolutionary hypothesis is no embarrassment whatever to the Church. The Church is interested only in the truth. So long as it is simply a question of hypotheses, she is indifferent as between evolutionism and the theory of the immutability of species, just as, on the political level, she is indifferent as between the monarchical and the republican forms of government provided that both serve justice. Evolutionism can accommodate itself to the revelation contained in Genesis and to the teaching of the Church just as easily as the doctrine of the immutability of species. In evolutionism indeed one finds a special harmony with the ways of God who, like all artists, rejoices in preparing by progressive and successive touches a sudden emergence on a higher level. Here once more it is artistic creation that furnishes us with the best analogy to divine creation.

Henri Poincaré said, "Poets have the advantage of us. The accident of a rhyme can make a whole system emerge from the shadows." Cocteau quotes these words, adding, "It's true, while searching the earth for a pebble that resembles another but not altogether, you run the risk of discovering a treasure." Our naturalists, bending over their pebbles, have counted them so carefully and so exhaustively that when they finally find the treasure they are overcome with fatigue and fail to recognize it. "We were expecting it," they say. "See how the whole preceding series of stones was leading up to this discovery." And they refuse to be astonished by the miraculous advent of a whole system that "emerges from the shadows."

They even refuse to see it as a qualitative leap. Just as those doctors of the Law condemned the Messiah, whom nevertheless they had awaited for centuries, because they were unwilling to receive Jesus in his different and unforeseeable character, so our naturalists would rather kill man and life than accept the miracle of their difference, the treasure. If humanity must perish some day, involving in its catastrophic end the destruction of life, as henceforth it has the power to do, that will be thanks to the mindless stubbornness of the naturalists. To protect man and life, it is first of all necessary to recognize and respect their inherent dignity. Lenin has already put the question: "Liberty? Why have it?" It is not at all fantastic to believe that someday people will ask themselves: "Life? What for?"

We do not, to be sure, deny that in the extremely long history of the universe there may have been a prior promise, an old testament of life and of man, but we will not permit that the Promise, once it has been superlatively fulfilled, should be killed in the name of the outdated law. Then indeed there would be nothing left but pebbles.

All this is sadly lacking in poetry, that is, in true understanding of creation. If one admits that the evolutionary hypothesis is true, how can one remain insensible to the flowing epic of the evolution of the world, which repeats its rhymes, rhymes that are all alike and yet not altogether alike, and does this over millions of centuries? Then suddenly, at two unique instants, when the attention has been lulled to sleep by the monotony of the interminable poem, at two instants brief as the wink of an eye, the accident of a rhyme causes the stately emergence from the shadows of a completely new adventure. For the scientist, this is indeed only the accident of one rhyme among the billions of rhymes in the long poem; a cause proportionate to this qualitative leap is beyond the reach of his science, completely beyond the world of phenomena which are the subject matter of that science. In his capacity as scientist he should at least recognize the majesty of this miraculous system, which, beneath his very eyes, emerges from the shadows, and should recognize too that the nature of this amazing phenomenon, as well as its cause, escapes him completely.

There is a third poetic rupture in creation: the Incarnation of the Word. The sudden appearance of life is a definitive ascent in relation to inanimate nature. The sudden appearance of man is a definitive ascent in relation to the animal world. The Incarnation of the Word is a definitive ascent of human nature to divine personality. These three poetic turning points are of an ascending order in relation to one another, but all three bear the character of a qualitative leap, of an abrupt and definitive passage into a superior order and, whatever the prior preparations, of a total event, irreducible to anything that went before it or prepared its way, of detachment, and of flight toward an adventure of a completely new kind. The motive force behind a poem does not explain it; the poem is beautiful in itself, complete, miraculous in the totality of its soaring flight above the earth and above those contingencies in which perhaps the poet himself is enmeshed.

In the same way, nothing that precedes it explains the Incarnation. It justifies itself; it is indeed the source of all justification. There was a motive for it, nevertheless, and the Scriptures as well as the Council of Nicaea tell us what that motive was: "It was for us men and for our salvation that He descended from heaven." The salvation of the human race is therefore the real motive of the Incarnation: the human race, then, was in danger of perdition.

"My soul was born wounded," said Lamennais. This is true of each one of us, and psychoanalysis is very well aware of the fact, though it tries to remove the evil without having any conception of its nature.

The evil is more extensive even than a wounded soul: it is the whole of human nature—body and soul—which is conceived and born in corruption. A rabbi quoted in the Mishnah has perfectly expressed the human situation: "Learn whence you come, whither you are going, and before whom you must render your account. Whence do you come?

From a putrid drop. Whither do you go? To a place of dust and worms. Before whom shall you render your account? Before the King of Kings of all the Kings, the Holy One, may He be blessed." A strange people, a strange religion, for which the seed of man is a putrid drop and nevertheless capable of transmitting the Promise of God. It all goes together. If one takes but a single side of things one falls into pride or abasement. Modern literature has told us often enough that we come from a putrid drop and that we go to dust and worms. But it has forgotten the tribunal of God and the Promise which are in the other scale of the balance.

After having spoken of the Promise, transmitted by the seed of Abraham, I must speak of original sin, transmitted by the seed of Adam. It is a dogma I must briefly present, for it is less uncouth than Hugo pretended to think when he wrote:

> Henceforth all things in equilibrium stand
> Upon the balance of an apple's theft
> Against God's murder.

We are dealing with a dogma, that is to say, a truth that is not self-evident, though one can easily perceive its effects, a truth, not directly demonstrable, that has been revealed to us by God and is taught by the Church. Let us add that of all dogmas this is perhaps the one most decried by, and most distasteful to, the modern mentality. It is important to see whether the opposition to it is based on evidence that actually contradicts it or whether that opposition rests on other dogmas, disguised and without authority, scientific or otherwise, but not a whit less rigid and savage on that account—even to the point of Inquisition.

What I call a disguised dogma is, for example, the belief in the inevitability of human progress, that is, that the members of mankind who preceded us were of necessity worse than we are, and those who follow us will of necessity be better. To stretch this dogma over thousands of years alters nothing if it is false. This is not of course to deny material progress: everyone knows that we have electric refrigerators, television, atomic bombs, and penicillin, things that the preceding generations did not have. But, in the first place, material progress is ambiguous. And then it is worth inquiring whether the men of today are in fact more valuable than those of yesterday. Contemporaries of Hitler and of the concentration camps are, perhaps, entitled to doubt it. Confronted by the dogma of necessary and indefinite human moral progress, however, it is clear that the Christian dogma of original sin loses its meaning.

Evil is a fact; physical evil is obvious; moral evil, a disorder of the will itself, which affects the quality of the spiritual person who is its author, is also a fact. Everyone suffers and dies. Everyone is subject to the fascination that evil holds for evil. There is something deranged in the human being, something that must be constantly repaired. Nature is not by right subject to man, he has to conquer it and, as a matter of fact, he has not done badly in that conquest. But what does it profit him so long as man's spiritual unity is imperiled in every human being? Feeling does not willingly obey superior force. The spirit and the will do not always get along together. In short, man as a whole finds it difficult to submit to his destiny. There is nothing mysterious in this: these are observations that all of us make every day about ourselves and those around us. Nor is this where the dogma of original sin comes to bear. It is on the cause of this universal disorder.

This dogma can be stated very simply: The whole human race, those now alive and those known through history, are descended from a first couple, called in the Bible Adam and Eve. This first pair, as man and woman, were directly created by God. They were created not only in a state of innocence but of completely supernatural grace and were endowed with amazing privileges, such as bodily immortality and many others.

This first couple sinned, that is, they were gravely disobedient to God. Through this sin Adam and Eve lost at one stroke everything they owed to the supernatural gift of God, not only the state of grace, incompatible with sin, but their bodily immortality and all the other privileges inherent in their original state. Here the real mystery lies: they involved the whole human race in their fall and, in a certain sense, in their sin. After them, we are all born in corruption; human nature, though not destroyed, is marred; the essential will in that nature is sinful from the beginning by reason of the original sin, not personally committed but personally contracted. This contamination occurs through the simple fact of procreation: "Your seed, your seed." This is the dogma, based on the account in Genesis; it retains the essence of that narrative, all its historical and didactic value both moral and religious.

Although we know very well that all men are sinners and that there is every evidence that they inherit sin together with their human nature, this dogma shocks us. Since our experience proves that all men are mortal and that we bear in us the anguish of approaching death, how can we imagine that we might all have been born immortal? Our sense of justice revolts at the idea that we participate in punishment for a crime that we have not committed. It revolts even more at the idea that little babies are culpable of a crime that they have obviously not personally committed but that they have nevertheless personally contracted. This dogma of original sin is difficult to admit because there is no analogy to it to be found. It embraces historical facts that we know only through revelation, cases that remain forever unverifiable.

And so, even if science should definitely adopt a polygenetic hypothesis to explain the origin of man, I do not see that such a hypothesis could contradict the fact that the first human couple were created by God; it would simply mean that the animal ascent toward humanization went on in several places at once but that it did not succeed in achieving the qualitative leap from animal to man except on a single occasion and in a single couple. It could have been otherwise, but this fact, attested by the sole authority of God the revealer, stands assured.

The dogma of original sin is at the base of Christianity. Bernanos believed and repeatedly said that this dogma is as important for the Christian life as the simple belief in God, without which no religion at all is possible. Moreover the dogma of original sin is at the base of the redemptive Incarnation; it is at the base of all Christian heroism. If it is true that we are born sinners with a nature wounded and shrouded in darkness, and yet not altogether lost, the task of salvation is to start at the beginning with each generation, with each individual. Nothing is ever definitely won, nothing is ever definitely lost, no one should ever be definitely abandoned, the law of each person is heroism. At the start every man is the captain of a sinking vessel which he must nevertheless bring safely into port. Every man is faced with the inevitable choice either to suffer shipwreck, body and goods, or to struggle against the tempest and save his vessel.

Nothing is more dangerous, there is no more cowardly lie, than to persuade men that they are, instead, caught in the mechanism of inevitable progress. This is the way to break the mainspring of heroism. And, besides, it is not true. We know perfectly well that everything begins over again each day, because everything that is human is constantly in peril: to be human, fully human, is the work of a whole lifetime, for it is accomplished little by little, day by day, it is built up one stone at a time from foundation to pinnacle. With each man, the tragedy begins all over again from the rise of the curtain to its final descent on the last act. We acquire human nature in essentially the same state of decay in which Adam left it; each one of us should raise it to the state of glory to which Christ elevated it.

It is only by placing oneself squarely in this position, upright and open-eyed, that one can understand why the Word became flesh, why he chose to dwell among us. It is because the task of each man is so far beyond the strength of our wounded nature that no one could ever accomplish it without the puissant aid, from without and within, of God Himself, who furnished the example and who, in order to show that He is allied with us in precisely this task of restoring human nature and exalting it in glory, began by clothing Himself in this human nature, protecting it with the buckler of His might and elevating it above the skies even to the throne of glory.

For just as Jesus Christ by adopting the strange title "Son of Man" both affirmed his solidarity with the entire human race and laid claim to a personal dominion over time, so he proclaimed his personal power to remit sins, including of course original sin. But he could not remit sins except by being above time and man. Not only before Abraham was, but before Adam was, he is. This is why, with each man, he is able to begin all over again from the beginning, and no ship comes safely into port except with him as pilot.

Every human being, with his own resources and the grace of Jesus, has been placed, and will be placed, between a paradise forever lost and a paradise within reach of hope. Jesus' grace is something that can be refused, but it is offered. In the passage of thousands of years nothing has changed, nothing changes, nothing will change in this immutable condition of the human being on earth. It is a condition of heroism, because it is a condition of all or nothing for each individual man. And what *all*? Paradise. And what *nothing*? Damnation. This condition constitutes the dignity of man, his tragic destiny. Nothing will change in this situation: each one retrieves it entire or loses it entire.

On this fact, too, is based the profoundest human fraternity. And, first of all, the fraternity of all men with the second Adam, Jesus Christ. The Council of Trent insisted strongly that, however deeply wounded human nature might be by original sin, it remained substantially intact, free, and capable of good. In its essence this human nature is the same in every man. Just as it was in essence before Adam's fall, so it remained after his fall, simply diminished and deadened. Human nature in Adam in his terrestrial paradise, human nature in each one of us, human nature in Christ, human nature in the damned in hell, human nature in the saints in paradise remains essentially the same. Adam did not cease to be a man after his sin. Christ, being God, is not for that reason less a man.

The first men may perhaps have resembled monkeys, why not? This is not flattering from the point of view of the canons of high fashion; human nature is not a matter of fashion. These first men bore within them the spark of reason: in their actions and through their discernment of good and evil they joined time and eternity, they took upon themselves completely the responsibility for their destiny, differing essentially in this from even the most highly evolved animal. In their fashion and according to their lights, they had to confront in their minds the same destiny as ours. It may have been, too, that it was because these first men resembled monkeys that Jesus agreed to be their brother. He agreed to be Hitler's brother. He agreed to be even my brother, for as Bernanos said to me one day, "The good Lord, who endures me, proves by doing so that He endures all." And the last man at the end of time will find himself too in the same basic situation.

Although it is completely fanciful since the hypothesis did not come true, the other side of the dogma is fascinating: the situation in the event that Adam had not sinned. Then he would have transmitted all the marvels of his state through procreation—"Your seed, your seed." There must indeed be immense power in human reproduction for it to be capable of transmitting even the grace of God, immortality, just as it now transmits original sin and its consequences, as it transmitted the Promise that God made to Abraham.

Abraham, like any primitive with a profound sense of life's richness, would not have been especially surprised that God's Promise should be linked to the seed of man; what surprised him was that God's election should light on him. We have lost this order of knowledge. In our civilizations, the sacred is submerged by the phenomenological observations of science. The assertion of the dogma of original sin and the persistence with which the Church defends it force us out of that narrow circle of scientific observation, impoverished as it is, and direct our attention to more obscure secrets, not to be measured, even less to be defined, but secrets nevertheless which we feel touch upon the sacred, upon a realm more profound and more real than that revealed by our powerful microscopes.

Here we arrive at a mysterious island that is not well marked on any map. It is situated far beyond the realms of science and the law, at that juncture where the visible world participated directly in the causality of God and matter itself is articulated with eternity. This is the root from which rise sacramentalism, poetry, metaphor, parable. Everything that grows from this root is superior to the whole scientific order, just as all the Christmas toys in a big store are not equal in worth to the wondering smile of the child who looks wistfully at them through the windowpane.

It is at this profound juncture point that human nature has received its wound; that is what makes it limp. The poets are aware of this when they intermingle innocent diversions with incalculable melancholy. What consolation can there be for the lost paradise? It sometimes happens, too, that this deep injury reveals itself suddenly to anybody—in sensual pleasure, for example, when he realizes that what he most desires is not so much satisfaction as the disillusionment that lies at its bottom. The law of original sin is hard. Every child of man is born to pain, death, and sin, which is the death of the soul. We may seek what distractions we will, evil is in us. Courage consists first of all in recognizing it where it is. How much time men waste in assailing fate while carrying their own unhappiness within themselves!

Man also bears within him his hope. He cannot, it is perfectly true, escape all alone and through his own resources, from the corruption native to him; here again is a scandal for modern minds, so proud of their knowledge and of their strength. We always believe that everything is reparable and that order will re-establish itself. But sin is first of all a break in the connection that harmonizes the creature with his God. Man alone cannot re-establish this link; it has gone adrift. The only way it can be re-established is from God's side. That has been done, and done perfectly, in the redemptive Incarnation.

This is why Luke, when he comes to write his genealogical essay on Jesus, goes farther back than Abraham, all the way back to Adam, who was, he says, "the Son of God." Behind this expression lies the whole story of Genesis, in which we are told of the creation of the first man and the first woman and of their fall, the punishment for which we all bear.

Luke 3:38

Thus Luke emphasizes the solidarity of Jesus Christ not only with the people of the Promise and with the prophets but with the whole human race from the first man to the last. At the top of the ladder Adam, "who was the Son of God," at the bottom of the genealogy Christ, who gives this designation, Son of God, a new sense, unique and unforeseen. Speaking of Adam, Luke insists on his original quality of Son of God, just as during all his life on earth Jesus will insist on his own individual quality of Son of Man. It is a fine thing to reflect on the interchangeability of these words. In this exchange lies the whole hope of humanity.

CHAPTER X

Subject to the Law

THE WHOLE purpose of the Mosaic Law is redemption from sin and from death, which is its consequence. Even the strictest observance of that Law, however, never accomplishes this purpose. Christ alone completely fulfills the purpose of the Law; he is the supreme example of the "ransomer," the redeemer, the liberator—he who ransoms the slaves once and for all. The result of this ransom is that men, who were slaves in bondage to sin or to the Law, are definitely set free, and yet are not completely delivered over to themselves—in which case they would be more thoroughly lost than before—but become sons and consequently heirs of God. Of course this slavery must be defined as well as this liberation or redemption, this sonship and inheritance. I now address myself to that task.

How was Jesus Christ, whose original and natural condition is that of Son of God, able to bring about the ransom of the human race? By becoming incarnate. "Who, being in the form of God, thought it not robbery to be equal with God: but made himself of no reputation and took upon him the form of a servant, and was made in the likeness of men"—apart from sin. According to Saint Paul, there were two conditions attached to this incarnation: on one hand, the only Son of God became in literal truth the son of a woman: on the other, he voluntarily made himself subject to the Mosaic Law. If all preachers quite rightly insist upon the truly human state of Christ, son of Mary, they very often fail to speak of his being subject to the Mosaic Law. This second condition of the Incarnation, however, seems to me equally essential, and I should like to analyze it.

Phil. 2:6-7

85

Gal. 4:4-5   Here the Vulgate seems deliberate in its forthrightness: *"Misit Deus Filium suum, factum ex muliere, factum sub Lege, ut eos qui sub Lege erant redimeret."* "God sent forth His Son, made of a woman, made under the Law, to redeem men that were under the Law, that we might receive the adoption of sons." Saint Paul expresses himself in concrete terms, using the vocabulary of the workshop, somewhat as one might say of the "Hermes of Olympia" that it was made by the chisel of Praxiteles, according to the classical Greek canons of beauty, of which, at one stroke, it became the masterpiece. Thus Jesus Christ is indeed the son of Mary, who bore him, but he is also the masterpiece of the Mosaic Law, of which he was the fulfillment.

For the proper understanding of the origin and full development of Christ it is useful to know about the woman of whom he was born, but it is also important to know about the Law of which he was the masterpiece, since he was first of all its fulfillment. For Jesus Christ was an exemplary subject of the Mosaic Law, which the Jews still call the Torah. His relations with this Law were, to be sure, exceptional and unique, as was his personality; that, however, is only a further reason for defining them.

Of all the Evangelists the one who seems to me to emphasize most insistently the subjection of Christ to the Law is, paradoxically, the only one among them who was not a Jew—Luke, a Greek, who wrote in Greece, for the Greeks, a short time before the destruction of Jerusalem. It has been said of his Gospel that it is par excellence the Gospel of the Virgin Mary, so attentive is he in making note of all that concerns the mother of Jesus. But, unquestionably for the same reasons, he applied himself as well to observing Jesus' obedience to the Mosaic Law to such a degree that one might call his Gospel the Gospel of Jesus' subjection to the Holy Torah. Very likely Luke knew Jesus' mother, but he was also the disciple of Saint Paul, the Pharisee, who imparted to him his own royal understanding of the Mosaic Law.

At the beginning of his Gospel, Luke says, speaking of the parents
Luke 1:6   of John the Baptist: "And they were both righteous before God, walking in all the commandments and ordinances of the Lord, blameless." Naturally these pious Israelites had their son circumcised according to the Law. We have seen that the same was true of Jesus. He, too, was presented in the Temple and his mother was "purified." It is Luke
Luke 2:39   who notes that "when they had performed all things according to the Law of the Lord, they returned into Galilee, to their own city Nazareth." In Luke, once more, we read that, like the most devout among the Jews, the "parents" of Jesus used to go each year to Jerusalem for

the Feast of the Passover. It was in fact in the course of one of these pil-
grimages, "when they had gone up to Jerusalem after the custom of
the feast and when they had fulfilled the days," that they lost track of
the child and found him in the Temple, "sitting in the midst of the
doctors of the Law, listening to them and asking them questions."
Here indeed is an ardent student of twelve. What was the subject of
his questions, his study, his attention, his passion? The Holy Torah of
Israel. Luke tells us, moreover, that all those present were amazed at
his intelligence and his replies.

Luke 2:42-43, 46

We have, of course, the case of Blaise Pascal. Nevertheless it is rare
for a child of twelve to be so absorbed in his studies that he will play
hooky in order to stay in school. The truth is that this child drank in
love of the Law with his mother's milk, that he was raised in strict
obedience to the Law and profound respect for it, that he himself observed the Law faithfully, and that he had a passion for it, as the child
Blaise Pascal had for geometry. It is not uncommon for a child of this
age to dream of being Alexander or Napoleon, these are commonplace
dreams within reach of anyone who dreams at all, but nothing is rarer,
finer, or more sacred than the passion for understanding at an age
usually devoted to games and candies.

This is less rare in Israel than elsewhere, for the Jews are the people
of the Book. This people, reputedly so ambitious for the goods of this
world, has a taste and a passion for knowledge. How often have we
seen Jewish families, emigrants from the worst ghettos of Eastern
Europe, barely established in the United States and still living like
beggars, nevertheless from the first generation begin to deprive themselves, setting aside five pennies a day in order sometime to pay the
tuition of the most talented of their children so that he can go to Yale
or Columbia? I consider this very fine. You do not see the same zeal
and respect for knowledge among the other minorities in America, a
country so vast, so free, and so various that everyone, in one sense or
another, belongs to a minority.

That is how I picture the Virgin Mary, a young Jewish mother, poor
and economical, severe when necessary, absorbed in her observance of
the Law, inculcating her love of the Law in her son, depriving herself
of all manner of things in order that her son may study while continuing to work at the trade of carpenter, which was Joseph's trade. Moreover, among the doctors of the Law it was traditional to practice a
manual occupation. Saint Paul, the Pharisee, doctor of the Law and
citizen of Rome—at a time when that title denoted the aristocracy of
the Empire—had a trade too, that of tentmaker. It is a coarse jest to

pretend that Paul, the weaver, or Jesus, the carpenter, were members of the proletariat in the same sense as assembly-line workers in a big factory of thirty years ago. The preaching of the Gospel is not always free from all taint of political demagoguery.

In emphasizing Jesus' subservience to the Torah, I am now speaking chiefly of his childhood and adolescence. His faithful obedience seems to me unmistakable. It remains to be seen whether in the course of his public life, in his teaching and in his conduct, Jesus retained this attitude. The contrary is what is currently thought and said. The question deserves closer study, but the field is too vast to be covered in a single chapter. Throughout the remainder of this book I shall have occasion to return to it repeatedly.

It is certain that Jesus died the victim of an Inquisition, as Joan of Arc did. But exactly why did his enemies oppose him and ally themselves against him? Was it because he rejected the Law, which it was their mission to defend? That would be too simple. I believe rather that Jesus and they were opposed because he and they held irreconcilable interpretations of the Law. If this hypothesis is true, their divergence implies an equal devotion to the Law on the part of Jesus and on the part of his adversaries. In sum, Jesus would have wished not to abolish the Law but to give the doctors of the Law a lesson to prove to them that his way of interpretation was the true one and theirs the false. Thus arose a theologians' quarrel, of all quarrels the fiercest and most implacable. And so Jesus would have been condemned not as a blasphemer and a rebel but primarily as a heretic—exactly as Joan of Arc was.

Saint Paul's position on this subject would have to be the same as that of Jesus. He does not contest the validity of the Law of Moses and the Old Testament; he maintains that it is necessary to read with eyes illuminated by the heart and that the majority of the Jews, his contemporaries, have a veil before their eyes that keeps them from reading. "But even unto this day, when Moses is read, the veil is upon their hearts. Nevertheless when it shall turn to the Lord, the veil shall be taken away." He is careful not to say that there is no further purpose in reading Moses.

Cor. 3:15-16

I do not mean to minimize the religious conflict between the Jews and the Christians, but I do not wish to exaggerate it either; I would like to place it precisely and define its limits. Christ recognized the books of the Jews as sacred; he quotes them often, giving them their full authority as the revealed Word; but he always maintained that he knew how to read these books and interpret them more precisely and

better than the doctors of the Law. In this contention, his own authority was all the greater inasmuch as he had studied the Law, had observed it always, and was, like Zachary and Elizabeth, "just before   Luke 1:6
God, walking in all the commandments and observances of the Lord,
blameless."

In what fashion, then, was Christ subject to the Law? It is impossible to imagine for an instant that he simply gave it servile obedience.
It is equally impossible to imagine that he was subservient to the Law
through hypocrisy. The answer therefore is clear: if Christ chose to be
subject to the Law, it was because he respected it, because he loved it,
because most of all he had a sovereign understanding of it, for he knew
that it had been made for him. It is again as Saint Paul says: "For the   Rom. 10:4
Christ *is* the end of the Law, or righteousness to everyone that believ-
eth." How then shall we Christians dare to misprize what Christ so
greatly loved?

Catholics have always directed their affectionate meditations toward
the role of the Virgin Mary in relation to Jesus; she was the means of
the Incarnation of the Word. But the Law too had an essential role in
relation to Jesus; it was the chief instrument of his obedience to God.
Catholic theologians criticize Protestant theologians for not giving the
Mother of God her rightful place, and I think this criticism is justified.
For, after all, Jesus was not the child of chance, and it is no inconsequential matter that he was the son of such a woman rather than of
some other.

But all modern Christian theologians, Catholic and Protestant alike,
are open to criticism for not giving the Law its rightful place. It was
not by chance that Jesus was born "subject to the Law," that he lived
after his fashion in conformity with what Saint Paul calls "the curse
of the Law," and that he was raised from the dead in fulfillment of the
Scriptures.

Essentially the Law played the same role in relation to Jesus that the
angel of the Annunciation played in relation to the Virgin Mary. Mary
said in reply to Gabriel's message, "I am the servant of the Lord,   Luke 1:38
be it done to me according to thy word," the word of the angel being
the form of Mary's obedience to the Lord. Confronted by the Law and
His message, Jesus made himself the Servant of Yahweh: it is through
his obedience to the Law that he made good his claim to the Messianic
title "Servant of Yahweh" and fulfilled it. In his whole life and in his
death, he did nothing other than the will of his Father, but it was his
wish to accomplish that will in accordance with the living word of the
Law.

He wished to fulfill all the prophecies, he wished to enclose himself in the Law as though in a prison so as to take upon himself the whole curse of the Law, due to sin, for the purpose of delivering men both from sin and from the curse of the Law. He achieved, no longer figuratively or by substitution but in reality and forever, the ransom of his people and of all the nations. After him what purpose was there in continuing to sacrifice turtledoves and rams? He was the seed of Abraham par excellence ("All the males belong to Yahweh") to whom all blessings had been promised beyond the servitude and the "curse" of the Law. As would be said by John the Baptist, the last Prophet of Israel, he is forever the Lamb of God who takes away once and for all the sins of the world.

Gal. 3:13-14 Christ hath redeemed us from the curse of the Law, being made a curse for us: for it is written, cursed is everyone that hangeth on a tree: that the blessing of Abraham might come on the Gentiles through Jesus Christ; that we might receive the promise of the spirit through faith.

I shall have occasion to return to this text by Saint Paul. In ending this chapter I leave it as a subject of meditation for the reader, like a cry suspended in the limpid night.

CHAPTER XI

The Precursor

"JERUSALEM, thou who killest the prophets!" Matt. 23:37

It was Christ who uttered these terrible words; he placed upon his own generation responsibility for all the innocent blood spilled from the time of Abel up to the time of Zacharias, "whom you killed between Matt. 23:35 the temple and the altar." The immediacy of the language and the use of the word *you* in connection with a murder committed many centuries earlier make one tremble. A vast quantity of blood, a heavy burden to bear!

A nation that kills its prophets . . . And what nation does not kill its prophets? The English would never have been able to burn Joan of Arc if the French had not surrendered her to them. In the circumstances, the Englishmen who did burn her are less vile than the Frenchmen who surrendered her and judged her and condemned her. Joan of Arc was condemned by a French bishop, assisted by judges all of whom were French. This girl, not yet twenty years of age at her death, must have had in her heart a certain image of France, for which she died, and this image surely was not the same as the one held by Bishop Cauchon, who later became Bishop of Lisieux, where he is buried in the Cathedral not far from the tomb of another saint, or that held by the honest canons of Rouen and the good Dominicans of Paris, her judges. For all the judges were as honest as could be, and no one of them for the rest of their lives was ever in disgrace for having condemned Joan. Dishonor was cast upon them much later as a posthumous judgment, just as glory was for Joan of Arc.

91

There is not a nation, there never has been a nation in the world, that is not capable of killing its prophets, and that has not done so in the long run. Nations would assassinate the wind and the fire, so great is their hatred of what is pure.

Enough of this. I simply wish to say that if Christ had the right to accuse Jerusalem of killing its Prophets, what right do we have to bring the same accusation against Jerusalem? The extraordinary thing is not that Jerusalem killed its Prophets, the miracle is that Israel throughout the whole of its history had such a multitude of them, so many that one could say of prophecy that it was an "institution" in Israel, somewhat like the monastic life in Christendom.

The "Bible of Jerusalem" in its general introduction to the Prophetic Books has the following note: "The fundamental idea that emerges from the complex facts relative to Prophecy appears to be this: the Prophet is a man who has an immediate experience of God, who has received the revelation of His Holiness and of His wishes, who judges the present and sees the past in the light of God, and who is sent by God to remind men of His requirements and to lead them in the way of obedience to Him and to His love. Understood thus, Prophecy is a phenomenon peculiar to Israel, one of the ways of Divine Providence in its direction of the Chosen People."

I have said that what is miraculous is that Israel had so many Prophets, so many bearers of the Word of God. These Prophets are also ours, for true religion has no limits in time; it extends from the creation of man to the Last Judgment and the end of the world. During thousands of years Israel was alone in bearing the weight of God's Word, that is, the explicit and authentic revelation. That the Prophets were persecuted is true because the Word of God upsets human plans and human interests and, in the case of Israel, often enough thwarted the policies of her shortsighted leaders.

What is admirable is that the Prophets exercised such an ascendancy over their people that the kings used to do anything in their power to obtain from the Prophet statements that would be favorable to them. The Prophet would refuse to make his message conform to the policies of the prince. Since the prince was the stronger, in the end the Prophet died. John the Baptist was not to escape this general rule; it was not through the people that he was killed: he was murdered through the baseness of a prince, the resentment of a queen, and the caprice of a beautiful young dancing girl.

Among all the Prophets, it is he who is called the Precursor, the fore-runner, the messenger who precedes the king and who, when he comes in sight of the people, opens his mouth and cries, "Behold him!" Orthodox Jews, even the Jews of today, cannot fail to recognize John the Baptist as theirs. The last of the Prophets—the greatest, according to Jesus—was a Prophet of Israel in a manner so exemplary, so extreme, so expressive, that he seems to have been placed there at the threshold of the Gospel like a classical statue of Prophecy.

Elected, summoned, chosen and purified from among all, John was, even from the womb of his mother, atremble with joy at his vocation. Still young, he retires to the desert to imitate in his own person the long pilgrimage of his people around Mount Sinai and to merit the fellowship of God. He separates himself from everyone and everything to make clear assertion of his exceptional vocation. Like a bear, he feeds on wild honey and grasshoppers; he clothes himself in the hide of a camel; and then, suddenly opening his great mouth, he begins to cry aloud in the desert, and his voice disturbs all Israel, it resounds in every heart, evoking a familiar echo. What a terrifying figure! And what would be our surprise if we were to see him appear suddenly in the pulpit of one of our cathedrals. . . .

We must believe that the Israelites were similarly surprised. Luke writes: "The people were in expectation, and all were wondering in their hearts about John, whether perhaps he might be the Christ." An admirable expectation, an admirable speculation! What Christian heart would not be moved? Let us not believe that our modern peoples are incapable of a similar Messianic expectation; they simply do not know where to look. Between the two wars and even during the last war, millions of Communist workers, French, German, Spanish, Italian, Serbian, and many others looked from afar on Russia as the fatherland of their hearts, more noble and more highly placed than their real earthly fatherland and, in their eyes, more worthy of devotion. They were deceived no doubt, but why should their real fatherlands not have offered them what they had to search for elsewhere? As for me, I feel very much in sympathy with the people of Israel of twenty centuries ago who were in expectation and were wondering about John the Baptist whether he might not be the Christ.

Far from implying that Jesus Christ arrived in a society that was hostile to him from the start and impenetrable to the true Messianic hope, the statements of Luke would make one rather believe that he came into a society well prepared to receive him. Since the exile and the last Prophets, the religion of Israel had been much refined and freed from many of its too earthly hopes as well as being deepened in its love of Yahweh. It was the religion of the true God, a God of justice

Luke 3:15

who demanded all, a God of love too but of a jealous love, in addition to a holy God, "the King of utter terror." It is this last aspect which will forever give to religion a barbarian savor in the etymological and primary meaning of that word: God is wholly other and does not speak our language in the way we speak it.

It was the true religion, in which God was honored and loved as thrice holy, reigning over the Cherubim of fire who dared not look upon his face. To this true and holy God no earthly food was appropriate but only the sacrifice of a pure heart, poverty of spirit, and inflexible trust in the Kingdom. This trembling and passionate adoration allied itself very well with the veneration of the Word of God, upon which the very existence of the chosen people depended, for that people was born of the Word—how should it not survive? This Word, while being the source of life, was also the ineffable Presence (the Shekinah, that is, the Presence beneath the tent), mobile as the presence of a nomad, reassuring as that of the leader in the midst of his clan.

The difference and even the conflicts between the Old and the New Testaments have often been strongly emphasized. I am not at all sure that any such conflict existed in the minds of the Evangelists. I am even inclined to believe that, aware though they were of the exceptional nature of their testimony, they inserted it quite naturally into the tradition of Israel, which found its marvelous fulfillment in Jesus. In the case of all of them, the relationship of style between the Gospels and the Old Testament is so evident that it is surely intentional.

After the short introduction which is called "The Gospel of Childhood," Luke begins his account of the public life of Christ in this solemn fashion: "Now in the fifteenth year of the reign of Tiberius Caesar, when Pontius Pilate was procurator of Judea, and Herod tetrarch of Galilee, and Philip his brother tetrarch of the district of Ituria and Trachonitis and Lysanias tetrarch of Abilene, during the high priesthood of Annas and Caiphas, the word of God came to John, the son of Zachary, in the desert." Now this is exactly the way that for centuries most of the prophetic books of Israel had begun: by a reminder of the historical context and of the reigning princes, by a statement of the date in relation to official history, by a clear affirmation that they dealt with the Word of God addressed to such and such a particular man, son of such and such. Among other possible examples here is a short one: "The word of the Lord which came to Michea of Moreseth in the days of Joatham, Achaz, and Ezechia, kings of Juda."

The Gospel of John is only an apparent exception to this traditional

Luke 3:1-2

Mich. 1:1

rule of composition. Since his Gospel begins, not with John, who was only a Prophet, but with Jesus Christ, it deals no longer simply with the word of Yahweh addressed to a man, but with this Word itself incarnate; therefore to place it in the context of the powerful of this world is unworthy; the only justifiable reference here is to the coexistence of the eternal Word with Yahweh and also with the creation of the world and of man, which occurred precisely through the mediation of this Word.

In this traditional prophetic style, the prologue to the Gospel according to John might be translated as follows: "In the beginning was the Word, and the Word was with Yahweh, and Yahweh was the Word. . . . And the Word became flesh, and he pitched his tent among us, and we have seen his glory, the glory that he holds from his Father, whose only Son he is, filled with grace and truth." John 1:1, 14

In short, John the Baptist is presented to us as a most authentic Prophet of the Old Testament. The Gospel itself is introduced as the Prophecy of Prophecies, in which the Word no longer has need of a Prophet as intermediary since he has decided to pitch his tent and dwell among us. The Epistle to the Hebrews will contain the same thought: "God, who at sundry times and in divers manners spoke in times past to the fathers by the prophets, last of all in these days has spoken to us by his Son, whom he appointed heir of all things, by whom also he made the world; [he], being the brightness of his glory and the image of his substance." Heb. 1:1-3

In the economics of salvation, which is coexistensive with the history of humanity, John the Baptist is therefore of considerable importance; he is the last link of ancient prophecy, joining it with the accomplishment of all the prophecies. Him whom all the others perceived and announced from afar in the mists of the future John pointed out in the light of the present day.

It is right that a Prophet should have been chosen to re-echo the Word, already substantially present. John in the presence of Christ is like a violin attuned to a master violin. No one can prevent him from vibrating to that presence. To all the people in expectation who have indeed recognized John as a Prophet—for the people, too, are attuned to their Prophets—he answers, "I indeed baptize you with water. But one mightier than I is coming, the strap of whose sandals I am not worthy to loose. He will baptize you with the Holy Spirit and with fire. His winnowing fan is in his hand, and he will clean out his threshing floor, and will gather the wheat into his barn; but the chaff he will Luke 3:16-17 burn up with unquenchable fire." Centuries earlier Jeremia had said, "What has straw to do with the wheat? says the Lord. Is not my word like fire?"

Jer. 23:28-29

Such is the image that the unerring Prophet gives us of the Savior of the world: a simple peasant on his threshing floor, in his hands a winnowing fan, one of those large wicker baskets shaped like a seashell which sifts the grain. He heaps the good grain on one side and makes a great fire of the straw and chaff. This is not a sentimental image: I prefer to cling to it rather than to the sugar-coated images of Saint Sulpice and of many so-called devotional manuals. I tremble, moreover, lest I may myself be nothing but straw.

John used to baptize in the water of the Jordan on the edge of the desert. He had certainly not invented this rite. The purity of water has always fascinated man not only because of its property of quenching thirst but also for that of washing away stains. For a Prophet of Israel, the immersion of the body in water could still evoke the crossing of the Red Sea when God saved his people from the fury of Pharaoh. A Prophet lived in the past as much as in the future: the high acts of God accomplished long ago were a guarantee of His protection in the future. In the diversity of history, God always maintains His own way of intervening with strong hand and upraised arm, on condition that His people are obedient and faithful and that they render to God love for love. Only here Pharaoh is no longer the subject. We shall see who is.

Baptism was a sacred pantomime or, if you like, a parable in action, signifying the union of the baptized with the historical destiny of his people, his interior conversion to make him worthy of theophanies, that is, of revelations of God. Thus it was that the crossing of the Red Sea preceded the revelation on Sinai. The history of the Prophets is full of these pantomimes, like the pantomime of the emigrant in Ezechiel: in the sight of all, the Prophet prepared his baggage, dug a hole in the wall, and fled by night into the desert, to signify to all that Israel itself would be vanquished, reduced to flight, and sent forth into exile. In the same way Yahweh gave John the command to baptize: this must also have been his means of recognizing the one greater than he who would baptize with the Holy Spirit.

Ezech. 12:1-7

"And I did not know him. But he who sent me to baptize with water said to me, 'He upon whom thou wilt see the Spirit descending, and abiding upon him, he it is who baptizes with the Holy Spirit.'" There was also beyond question an evocation of the story of the cre-

John 1:33

ation in Genesis when "the spirit of God was stirring above the waters." Gen. 1:2
And also when "the Lord God formed man out of the dust of the ground and breathed into his nostrils the breath of life"—that is to say, His own breath, His own Spirit, since the word "spirit" means breath. It was a total re-creation of man that produced this second baptism in the Holy Spirit, as the first breathing in of the Spirit of God had created man in the image of God. "And man became a living being," Genesis adds. That is also beyond doubt the effect of the second baptism in the Holy Spirit: it suffuses man with a new life, a supernatural life, the life of God Himself.

Of course John's act of baptism was accompanied by a sermon. The purely magic rite is not a part of the tradition of Israel, at least at this highly evolved stage of Hebrew religion. The action must be accompanied by a true change of heart. What then did John the Baptist say? He declared first of all his divine mission and the character of that mission; he placed himself then in the line of the great Prophets of Israel and applied to himself the words of Isaia: "A voice cries out: Isa. 40:3-4 in the desert prepare the way of the Lord! Make straight in the wasteland a highway for our God! Every valley shall be filled in, every mountain and hill shall be made low; the rugged land shall be made a plain, the rough country, a broad valley." It is clearly Israel's highest and most constant hope that John was evoking and of which he was predicting the present fulfillment.

And so John had created around him the confusion characteristic of Prophets; everyone went to see him and listen to him, the people and the leaders of the people. He had an appropriate word for each. From this moment he enters into violent conflict with the two governing castes, whom we shall encounter again in the course of the life of Jesus, always loyal to their own interests. Matthew writes, "But when Matt. 3:7-10 he saw many of the Pharisees and Sadducees coming to his baptism, he said to them, 'Generation of vipers! Who has shown you how to flee from the wrath to come? Bring forth therefore fruit befitting repentance, and do not think to say within yourselves, "We have Abraham for our father"; for I say to you that God is able out of these stones to raise up children to Abraham. For even now the ax is laid at the root of the trees; every tree therefore that is not bringing forth good fruit is to be cut down and thrown into the fire.'" A day of sweat beneath the sun, of heavy labor, of permanent distinctions between good and evil, of good trees and bad trees, of grain and of straw, of fire on one side and full granaries and barns on the other, this is the image that the

Gospel gives us of the coming of the Messiah, himself represented as a confident peasant on his threshing floor with his winnowing fan, or as a woodsman in the forest with his ax.

I have laid so much emphasis on the racist character of the religion of Israel that I have incurred the duty of pausing for a moment over this last text. At the period of the Baptist, the Prophets had already for many years pointed out that simply belonging to the race of Abraham did not suffice to make one worthy of his line. Israel too was compounded of wheat and chaff, of good fruits and bad. In addition to being physically of his race, one had to have what the Prophets called the circumcision of the heart, a faith and a purity worthy of the great Patriarch.

They had got to the point of saying that the salvation of God was reserved for a "remnant," for certain survivors not so much of the trials and tribulations as of moral decay and infidelity. With John the Baptist the physically racist character of the religion of Israel finally fell to pieces, since from the very stones God could raise up sons for Abraham. Christ will take up again this affirmation, and Saint Paul will define the conception of an "Israel of God," a purely spiritual family of Abraham whose propagation is accomplished through faith. On this capital point there is between the Old and the New Testaments, from the ancient Prophets to John the Baptist and then to Christ and to Saint Paul, no break or contradiction but continuity, progress, and fulfillment. For what in fact did Isaia mean when he wrote that *all flesh* would be able to behold the glory of God, if not that some day the special vocation of Israel would be extended to all mankind, and perhaps also that the glory of God would incarnate itself and become visible to the naked eye?

From the beginning the Catholic Church has claimed to be this "remnant," this band of survivors of whom the Prophets spoke, who never bent the knee to Baal but who might belong to any tribe, to any language, to any nation under the sky. Naturally this, too, must be understood in a spiritual sense. To believe that to be baptized and to belong to the body of the Holy Church is enough to insure the right of salvation would be to fall, not to the level of the Prophets, but far below that of the Old Testament, to the lowest level of coarseness in interpreting the Promise. It would be a "racism" of ritual worse than any other racism. This ritual racism has existed, it still exists; that is what has produced so many pogroms. Hitler and Eichmann were baptized. The baptism of Christ is not an automatic assurance against the winnowing fan and the ax; among Christians, too, there are straw and sterile trees condemned to the fire. Among Christians, too, there are Pharisees and Sadducees who attempt to escape from the wrath to come. The brood of vipers is universal; who can flatter himself that he has not in his veins so much as a drop of that blood?

CHAPTER XII

The Theophany at the Jordan

Matt. 3:15

THE GOSPEL tells how Jesus came from Nazareth to the place where John was baptizing and awaited his turn, lost in the crowd of pilgrims. When finally he approached John, the latter became aware of the pre-eminent dignity of the one who stood before him, and he protested his own unworthiness. But Jesus replied, "Let it be so now, for so it becomes us to fulfill all justice." These, according to the Synoptic Gospels, were Christ's first words at the opening of what is called his public life. It was addressed to the last Prophet of Israel; it is startling because of its abruptness.

This is a word of command: Jesus compels John to baptize him. It is also a word of obedience: Christ knows and wills himself to be part of a tradition. Not only does he follow the example of the other pilgrims approaching John, he follows in the footsteps of a whole people. Through this pantomime of baptism, he wishes to convey that he has crossed the Red Sea with all his people; he does not begin his ministry by a break but by a continuation, he wills himself to be one with all his people, with all its history, with its pilgrimage, its prayer, its penitence, despite his own innocence. He belongs to this people, he loves this unity and proclaims it at the beginning of the play. Here is the true prologue to his public action; it is within this unity that he will fulfill all justice.

But the baptism of Christ, as the first Christians understood, is in itself a pantomime of his whole destiny, of his whole history, and it is in the best tradition of pantomime, at once eloquent, suggestive, and elliptical. Through the Incarnation Jesus descended to humanity;

100

through his death he descended into Hell, where he overcame the Devil and death; through his Resurrection he rises triumphantly to the light; and through his ascension he returns to heaven. It is this same movement of descent and reascension that is expressed in the baptism; and in the depths of the waters he destroys the Dragon, that is, the Devil, whose dwelling place is the sea. Some painters have conceived the baptism of Christ in this way: when he emerges from the water, banner in hand like a warrior chief, he advances with the same victorious step as when he will come forth living from his tomb.

But the words of Jesus to John have another and more personal sense, as between the two men. This could be the beginning of the story of a "vendetta"; and who knows whether it may not have a little of that quality? In the background of the dialogue lurks a third person, who will, furthermore, make a shattering entrance upon the stage; he is, in fact, the Devil. The Synoptics are formal: at the very outset Jesus speaks to the Prophet, and immediately afterward the first person with whom he is engaged in conversation is the Devil. The dialogue with John thereby takes on a much stronger meaning; it is, in the plot of the play, the meeting of the two conspirators. And so the words of Jesus to John mean: "Enough of this! Are you ready? It is high time that the Adversary should be dealt with, it is high time that justice should be done and that it should be done by us." This is the decisive moment in a conspiracy, the moment at which it takes on the dignity of fulfillment, and the action that follows is the assault upon the prince.

It is less rare than one might think for conspirators to invoke heaven's authority for their action and its dazzling testimony to the legitimacy of their enterprise. What is rare is for heaven to grant them. That is what happened in the case of Jesus. "Jesus also having been baptized and being in prayer," Luke says, "[the] heaven was opened, and the Holy Spirit descended upon·him in bodily form as a dove, and a voice came from heaven, 'Thou art my beloved Son, in thee I am well pleased.'" *Luke 3:21-22*

The history of Israel is full of theophanies, that is, of dazzling revelations of God. They habitually have a solemn character to confirm a divine act no less solemn, an investiture, a vocation, a promise, the promulgation of the Law, the dedication of the Temple, or simply a declaration of God's love for one of His Prophets. Among all these, there are two very exceptional ones, the Biblical account of which I commend to the present reader. They deal with the personal appearance of God to the two greatest Prophets, Moses and Elias. *Ex. 33:18-34:9* *3 Kings 19:8-19*

It is interesting to note the differences between these two theophanies and the theophany in the presence of Jesus. One difference is immediately apparent: in the case of the two Prophets, the theophany takes place at the end of a sojourn in the desert and a fast of forty days. In the case of Jesus, it precedes this sojourn and this fast. It is not a reward. For Moses, the voice of God affirms the justice and the mercy of Yahweh; for Elias, it affirms in addition Yahweh's solicitude for "the remnant": "And I will leave me seven thousand men in Israel, whose knees have not been bowed before Baal, and every mouth that hath not worshiped him kissing the hands." The two revelations on Horeb took place amid a wild outburst of the elements.

3 Kings 19:18

This time no devouring flame crowned the mountains, there was no whirlwind or trembling of the earth, and if a breeze stirred, it was only the light air that rustled in the rushes at the river's edge. The scene is peaceful. Neither justice nor mercy for a people is at stake, but uniquely the love for, and unprecedented joy in, a single but exceptional individual. From this moment the style of Christ's human destiny is fixed, the style that Saint Paul has so well defined: obedience and exaltation, descent and reascension. These are truly the two poles of his destiny. Jesus begins by obeying the prophetic tradition of his people, and as a reward for that obedience God reveals Himself to him more completely than He has ever done before; He gives him the Name above all names, that of well-beloved Son, of Son par excellence, which indeed he was.

It was no novelty in Israel that God should be the Father. Israel had long since had the revelation and experience of that paternity. Similarly Israel was accustomed to speak of the Spirit of God. The appellation "son of God" was often used to indicate a special destiny, or simply a more elevated rank in the hierarchy of creatures. The special revelation of the theophany at the Jordan consists in the force and the precision of the words, their personal acceptation, and the link of simultaneity between the voice of the Father, the presence of the Son, and the appearance of the Holy Spirit. Here is the first wholly explicit manifestation of the holy Trinity of Persons in the unique divine nature. The Father speaks from the opened heavens, the Son emerges in prayer from the waters, the Spirit that unites them hovers above him in the peaceable form of a dove.

Directly, in the second person singular, God addresses His "beloved Son," in whom He is well pleased. This deepens and singularizes the concept of divine paternity and confers on it a personal transcendence that it had not hitherto possessed. For however much God has been considered the Father of His people or of that remnant who are faithful to Him, that means, as between God and men, no more than a relationship exterior to God, one of those multiple connections which, however precious, can exist between creator and creature.

But if there exists a unique being, who is par excellence the beloved Son, who draws to himself God's entire love, while being fully worthy of that love, if between the Father and him there exists a reciprocal and total joy, perfectly satisfying on either hand, then this relation of Father to Son and of Son to Father is also unique, coexistent with God Himself, coexistensive with God; otherwise indeed the joy would not be wholly satisfying. Pursuing this revelation to the end, one is led to say what we Christians say: the Father is God, the Son is God, the joy that unites them in a single Holy Spirit is itself God. The diversity being exclusively in the relations between these three Persons, the divine nature is common to them all.

But this means, too, that to be Father, Father in the fullest sense, to pour forth His paternal generosity and to receive in return complete filial devotion, a filial love beyond reproach—for this God has no need of men. Contrary to what the Jews and the Moslems believe about the fact of the dogma of the Trinity of Persons in God, the transcendence of God is better assured because it is total, full, and entire in itself. Even to be Father, God has no need, has never had and never will have any need of men. This detracts no whit from the marvelous reality of the divine paternity of God in relation to His creature, but gives to that paternity in relation to the creature the character that befits it so perfectly of total gratuitousness, of contingency, of a unilateral gift, of gracious generosity. In the face of certain sentimental extravagances, it is not a bad thing to emphasize that the unique paternity of God in relation to his only Son suffices to fill Him with eternal joy.

Beginning with this inaugural theophany at the Jordan, the revelation of God—Father, Son, and Holy Spirit—in Jesus will grow more precise and ample. It will be new, to be sure, but it will always remain in the direct line of the earlier revelations and of the ancient prophecy, just as the blossoming flower remains in the direct line of the stem and the root that bear it; it manifests their meaning.

It was common practice in the ancient world for kings to claim divine origin. The Church has recognized in the theophany at the Jordan a royal consecration. That is why in her liturgy she commemorates this event at the same time as the Epiphany and the miracle at the marriage feast in Cana. On an earlier occasion, in his first infancy, the kings of the earth recognized Jesus as their King; this time he received consecration from on high, the unction of the Holy Spirit itself. Thereafter his first miracle, when he changed water into wine, symbol of blood, at the same time that it revealed his power also signified that his own baptism was to be a baptism of blood, which would consecrate the liberating marriage of humanity with its Redeemer.

It is this that is expressed, in eloquently poetic fashion, by an anthem in the Dominican breviary for the feast of the Epiphany: "Today the Church is united with her Heavenly Bridegroom because, in the Jordan, Christ washed away her sins. With arms full of gifts, the Magi hasten to the royal marriage. And all the guests regale themselves with water transformed into wine. Alleluia!"

CHAPTER XIII

The Duel with Satan

THE HOLY SPIRIT had descended upon Jesus in the innocent form of a dove, thereby expressing God's peace with Himself. Nevertheless, it was this same Spirit that of old had thrust the Judges into battle to defend and deliver their people: "The Spirit of Yahweh was upon him, and he took the field. . . ." "The Spirit of Yahweh clothed Gedeon [like armor], and he blew upon the trumpet. . . ." "The Spirit of Yahweh seized upon him, and he hastened into battle. . . ." Here it was the same with Jesus. Matthew writes, "Then Jesus was led into the desert by the Spirit, to be tempted by the Devil." The Synoptics have left us an account of the decisive phase of this strange contest.

Judges 6:34

Matt. 4:1

Our contemporaries do not believe in the Devil. Fortune-tellers and astrologers make vastly more money than exorcists. To tell the truth, I'm not sure that even Christians, especially those who have college degrees or those who are embarrassed at not having them, believe in the Devil and in hell. Certainly it is not fashionable to believe in the Devil; this belief is not even taken seriously. Moreover, even in sermons, it is frequently said that the passages in the Gospel dealing with this subject are to be considered as poetic extrapolations, the symbolism of which, to make matters worse, has been misconceived. No doubt this is another of those mean tricks the Jews played on the Christians, something left over from an infantile cosmogony.

As I try to imagine the future reader of this book arriving at this chapter, I ask myself how far he will take me for a fool, or whether perhaps he will think I take him for a fool, by trying to make him swallow the Devil and hell. I do not want to make him swallow anything at all, either by surprise or by force. My purpose as a writer is twofold: first of all to explain to the reader what Catholicism is, as simply as possible and in the way in which I was taught it, the way I understand; and then to tell the reader why I believe in it—with this important corollary: this is how it is, take it or leave it, but at least know what you are taking or what you are rejecting.

The agony of Paul Valéry comes to my mind. Some hours before his death, he was visited by Professor Mondor, his friend and doctor. Valéry, who was fully conscious and master of himself, had had a very bad moment the day before, and he told his visitor about it. "Yesterday I thought I was passing away and I was afraid. . . ." Mondor, with that sawbones cynicism that I find in doubtful taste at a deathbed, even that of an agnostic, even that of an atheist, replied, "Why fear? You know very well there is nothing beyond." And Valéry: "I am afraid of the first two weeks; after that . . ." as though to say, "If they will only give me two weeks to get my bearings in the strange world where I am going, I am intelligent enough to find my way to the Academy." And, when Mondor tried to reassure him, if one can call it that, Valéry added with a smile, "I'm frightened of the Devil with his pitchfork. . . ."

This incident was told me the day after Valéry's funeral by a great friend of both Valéry and Mondor. I know the story is true and I do not believe I have distorted it in my report—besides, it should be recorded. Nevertheless I would scorn to use it as an argument in support of anything. It proves nothing, unless perhaps that even for a mind that has spent its life in banishing mystery from its field of vision, death, concretely present and personally menacing, remains a mystery that cannot be dispelled. Even animals experience the anguish of death; and an Academician has no dispensation from it. That Valéry should diffidently express this anguish in the conventional image, arising from the depths of childhood, of "the Devil with his pitchfork," touches me more than any philosophical reasoning, more than any superb dramatic phrase in his customary style.

Naturally there is no question of a literal pitchfork. But for a mind as lucid as Valéry's, death, his death, close at hand, poses a question infinitely larger than that of the physical pain about which the doctor is concerned. For the dying Valéry, the death of Paul Valéry becomes ineluctable; it is a scandal for the mind, and it raises a feeling of responsibility. "How have I managed to get into this predicament?" To this unique and personal question, the Judaeo-Christian tradition replies: It is through sin that death entered the world. And it is through the Devil, who has made man his accomplice, that sin entered the world.

No one is so innocent that he does not merit death as a sinner. This is a reply that strangely transcends clinical analysis.

We lack the actual experience of death; it would enable us to make judgments on many things, which it would show us in very different proportion and in a very different light from the usual ones. Death, too, is poetic and causes a whole new system of relationships to emerge from the shadows. On his deathbed Louis XIV, seeing his courtiers abandoning him, used this remarkable phrase: "When I was king . . ." The dying, however great they may be, are no longer of interest to anyone; they have already ceased to count. No one would have the idea of founding a newspaper for the dying or an academy for the dying. The dying are no longer of interest as voters, and even among friends there have been, alas, desertions. How can one deny that there is a curse upon death? If ever a man has need of an advocate, a champion to justify him, especially in his own eyes, it is at the moment of his death.

The dead, those truly dead and buried, are a quite different matter. They are the foundation for propaganda, for business. Sometimes they make a decisive difference in the affairs of the world. Obliterate the dead, all the dead, from the memory and imagination of men, and society would go mad. The dead, what publicity! And sometimes what profits! How you flourish, widows!

Though this is not true of all religions, Christianity at least takes an interest in the dying; it even professes itself to be a school that teaches men how to die; furthermore, it instructs both adults and children to judge everything in the light of death. This is an altogether remarkable undertaking.

———

For myself, I believe in the Devil and in hell; I believe on the authority of the Scriptures, which speak plainly of them; I know that it is not foolish to believe and I have no inferiority complex on this subject. To write a book about Christ and pretend that the Devil does not exist would seem to me as vain and dishonest as to write a life of Napoleon without ever mentioning wars, the Continental Blockade, England, or the kings, "all drawing their swords at once."

The existence and nature of the Devil are connected with the existence of evil in the world; less, however, with physical evil, which is sufficiently explained by the corruptibility of the material being, than with moral evil—that is, the corruption, seduction, and perversion of the will, which, instead of desiring what it knows to be good, deliberately chooses the opposite, evil.

The ancient Persians were so struck and so scandalized by the existence and power of evil in the world that they imagined the universe to be governed by two gods, of approximately equal power, the god of good and the god of evil, who, with alternating success, vied with each other for the empire of the world. This conception was transmitted to Manichaeism, and it survives, not at the level of mythology or metaphysics, where it is obviously untenable, but on the moral level, in puritanism. There are intellectual security and comfort for the soul in convincing oneself that one is entirely on the side of right, that the cause one supports is altogether pure, that one's adversary or even one's rival is totally bad, irredeemable, and that his unconditional surrender is synonymous with the triumph of absolute good. This conception spreads contamination in all quarters; it is to be found among intellectuals, rationalists, materialists, among politicians, among ecclesiastics, among businessmen, among military men; it is a leprosy of the soul, it is terrifying, it spells the extinction of moral judgment. The little poet Yevtuchenko, who has received so much publicity, wrote these dismaying words: "For me the whole world is made up of just two nations: that of good men and that of bad. I am a patriot of the international nation of good men." Obviously. This maxim fits the poet, it is idiotic.

The absolute unity of God, His quality as creator and absolute master of the universe and of history, was too central to the religion of Israel for the Jews to recognize an independent principle of evil, exercising a quasi-equality with God. No one can be God's rival. They recognized, nevertheless, not a principle of evil, but a hierarchy of evil and a chief of that hierarchy. A single creator, God, a single universe as his domain, but in the midst of this universe the rebellion of a free creature who pushes his revolt to the point of denying the dominion and the empire of God. And this mutiny turns everything to its purpose.

The universe is a battlefield; each one of us is a battlefield, where good and evil confront each other; everything—mind, heart, body—is a battlefield, everything in me and around me, other men and the goods of this world. Anything may serve as ammunition for one camp or the other, anything may be a cause of treason. This is so confused and violent a struggle that no terrain in the world is ever definitely conquered by one side or the other; no matter who, no matter what, may change allegiance at any moment. The camps will not be separated or defined except in the hereafter, and of that hereafter we have no experience. However bad a man may be, no one has the right to say that he is lost to the good without possibility of recovery.

The great advantage of the Jews lay in the distinctness of their moral judgment. They knew quite well what evil was. Evil was everything that was opposed to the will of God: evil was a revolt of the creature against his Lord, a revolt which could not compromise the foundation of God's dominion over the universe or His final triumph, but was nevertheless a revolt, and one that confronted God with a universal conflict, sharp, intelligent, obstinate, presenting at times the appearance of legitimate authority and of victory. In this revolt men played the part of massed troops, the infantry, whereas the barons were quite different— spiritual creatures, black, fallen and arrogant. The leader of this proud host had many names: Satan, Beelzebub, Belial, and sometimes Lucifer, the bearer of light.

The most spectacular and pernicious manifestation of Satan's hold on this world was, in the eyes of the Jews, idolatry. How could one better express one's revolt against a legitimate sovereign than by devising another sovereign? As climax, what offense could be more injurious than to adore, in the place of the true God, not even a spiritual and superior being, but a reptile, or worse still a wooden image or a stake driven into the ground? We are so profoundly detached from religious needs that we have trouble in imagining the passionate worship that, for thousands of years, humanity paid to idols, to the extent of sacrificing its sons and daughters in hecatombs to Moloch, Baal, and Astarte.

This degrading idolatry had such social weight that even the greatest minds of Greece never dared to break publicly with it. Before he died Socrates asserted that he owed a cock to Asclepius. Neither Plato nor Aristotle, who beyond any possible doubt saw the absurdity of their national divinities, ever dared to denounce the imposture: worse still, they felt no need to do so, considering perhaps that for the crowd a false religion was better than no religion at all. Saint Paul thought them "inexcusable."

Through idolatry man lowers himself to the level of what he worships. In this sense one has a feeling that behind all idolatry there is a superior and evil mind busily at work, a mind that has sworn a calculating hatred toward God and the harshest contempt toward man, a mind that rejoices in everything that can dishonor God in man. A king is dishonored when he allows his standards to be trampled underfoot. But the greatest dignity of man is to have been created in God's image, to be the mirror and standard of God in the material world. Somewhere there is a spectator who laughs and applauds every time the image of God is trampled, every time it bows down freely and prostrates itself before an image of stone or of wood or before a stake driven into the ground, giving to that object the homage which is due to God alone.

To one who believes in God, idolatry is too absurd, too irrational, for the idea not to occur to him that in this enterprise man is no more than a puppet in expert hands. He is a grotesque marionette in a sacrilegious comedy, and the manipulator is behind the curtain. But this manipulator exists; without him there would be no spectacle. Behind the idolatry, which at that time filled the world, is that manipulator, this stage manager of human marionettes, whom the Prophets of Israel denounced and unmasked at their own risk and peril.

We believe ourselves to be too highly evolved, too rational, too enlightened, too well informed, too alert to the standards of values, too worldly, to be idolaters. We claim that we do not worship anything or anyone. I think, on the contrary, that the scene has changed but that the sacrilegious comedy goes on. The plot to dishonor humanity and particularly to dishonor the image of God in man has never been promoted with more insolence. We have, after all, no right to criticize antiquity for its useless and monstrous hecatombs: to what Moloch, to what Astarte, to what Baal have we sacrificed all those youths since the beginning of this century? Perhaps to nothing? In that case we are more stupid and probably more effectively manipulated than those who bent their knees before a Baal of wood, which had at least the merit of existing.

A trial like Eichmann's leaves us with a strange uneasiness. This precise, meticulous functionary, this good family man, who revealed himself by bringing a bouquet of flowers to his wife on their wedding anniversary, this colonel who was a well-trained and obedient soldier, this man who was not only the minister of death for millions of human beings, men, women and children, but before that the minister of their ruin and degradation, gives the impression of having been no more than a straw man when he came before his judges, the quasi-irresponsible agent of a supernatural malice that infinitely surpassed his mediocre abilities and that equally surpassed the fury of his chieftains, the Himmlers, the Görings, the Hitlers. Eichmann was no more than the sacristan of hell.

But the high priest of that atrocious cult which was celebrated for so many years in the Nazi concentration camps, he who breathed in with delight the smoke of the scientific holocaust as an agreeable incense, this high priest has never appeared before a human tribunal. The unhappy Jews who were his chosen victims could read his name in their sacred books: the whole history of their people is the history of a war against Satan.

I do not say that Eichmann is irrefutable proof of the existence of the Devil, but I am perfectly sure that his commonplace personality is hugely out of proportion in the momentous setting of the atrocities of which he was the docile, if not lucid, agent. And if this disproportion is recognized, I should like to have it explained to me. Here is a bizarre hiatus that reminds me of a Greek proverb: Sometimes the devil breaks his cloven hoof; then you can detect his limp by following his tracks in the snow.

The good Father Lagrange writes, "The psychology of Satan is brief." It is limited, but not brief. There is a whole universe that escapes him, that of grace, and, I believe, that of honor. Sometimes the door is slammed in his face: he cannot violate the secrets of the heart. But among billions of men how many hearts have secrets? To be sure, people hide things, but very few of the things they so avariciously hide cannot easily be guessed provided one pays attention, and the Devil is an attentive observer: he possesses hatred but no passions. He has a thorough knowledge of what today is called the psychology of crowds, the calculus of probability, the social sciences, the art of "public relations" and of publicity. He knows all the motives of the average man. Only, as it happens, the average man does not seem to interest him, at least taken singly. For the Devil, just as for great generals, the average man is simply a unit in a troop. On the other hand, he loves to match himself against exceptional situations and persons.

Satan has always been extremely interested in Israel. During thousands of years it was the only people in the world that had never completely succumbed to idolatry. Israel was the beachhead that the Devil had never been able to conquer completely, the mystic strand where the Hero of God would one day land and where the liberation of the earth would begin. It was on this beach, as Satan knew, that sometime would dawn what for him would be "the longest day." It can be imagined how sharply he surveyed the approaches. Luke says that the whole people was in expectation; Satan too was expectant. In the air there was the scent of a great and imminent event, the foretaste of the landing of liberation.

The theophany at the Jordan was like a signal, the first rocket in the sky, marking H-hour and the launching of the attack. Certainly Jesus was an exceptional man; it remained to spy out from close quarters the quality of this newcomer before whom John had bowed, above whom the heavens had opened. The long history of Israel had seen many other theophanies and many other "sons of God": every divine selection for

prophecy or for royalty conferred the title of "son of God," which therefore had no uniqueness in the vocabulary of Israel. This time, however, God had spoken of His "beloved Son" in whom He was well
pleased. The thing to do was to inspect this personage and, if possible,
cause him to fall into a trap in which he would remain captive and
helpless. It must have happened occasionally in those days as well as
today that an elect of God betrayed his vocation and fell under the
sway of the Devil. Toward the end of his life Solomon, the sage king
par excellence, the man who had built the Temple and had seen with
his own eyes the glory of Yahweh enter the Sanctuary, had succumbed
to idolatry.

Now Jesus had taken refuge in the desert, very likely in a cave near
a spring, with no company there but the wild beasts. For forty days
and forty nights he abstained from all food. To this voluntary privation
must be added the rigors of an abode hot by day and freezing by night.

It is only fair to say that a physical exploit of this sort does not make
any great impression on us today: we have seen hunger strikes that were
more sensational. However, it has been proved that a man who stops
eating voluntarily to show that he puts his cause above his life with-
stands hunger infinitely better than the one who undergoes this test
from need alone or through constraint. Christ's long fast could not have
been intended as an exploit or even a hunger strike; this extraordinary
man was not at all interested in setting records. I believe that Christ
was praying and that he was so absorbed in his prayer that he did not
perhaps notice that he was fasting.

But after forty days he was hungry; he felt the elemental, brutal need
to eat and to fill his stomach. He whom a voice from heaven had designated as "My beloved Son" was also a man like us—that is, an animal,
for hunger is an animal appetite, one that we have in common with all
animals. It is hunger that makes the wolf emerge from the forest. What
makes a wolf a wolf is that hunger controls him; a man worthy of the
name controls his hunger, but he too can become a wolf.

Jesus, then, was hungry, and this was the moment the Devil chose to
offer decisive combat. It is a constant principle in the affairs of this world
that one must wait until one's adversary is hard pressed by hunger,
poverty, or necessity, to force him to kneel and accept injustice. This
is an abominable system. How many men and women have been sent
to ruin by this threat: "If you don't want to die of hunger, do what I
demand of you"! It is here that man becomes the wolf of man.

It is so degrading a system that it is beneath even the Devil. The
Devil has not sunk to using extortion of this kind. Seeing that Christ

had the hunger of a wolf, he did not bring him food and confront him with the choice: "If you want to eat, obey me."

Thus Jesus' temptation in the desert is as remarkable for what it is not as for what it is. The Devil offers Christ neither food nor drink nor money nor women. We are far removed from the "temptations of Saint Anthony" imagined by writers and actually quite vulgar; such temptations proceed more from the animal weakness of man than from the malice of the Devil. They can indeed lead people to Hell: I imagine that the Devil regards the innumerable troop that pours into his domain with a certain distaste. The Devil is a puritan, and an exquisite. I am sure that the Antichrist will resemble him in this point: the court of such a prince will be "virtuous," in the current and vulgar meaning of the word; the women there will knit for "charitable organizations," the men will drink milk and will have no mistresses. True complicity with the Devil in person is not at the level of ordinary sin.

"You are My beloved Son." These words that fell from heaven at the moment of the theophany at the Jordan were heard by the Devil too. He will make God's words the premise of his reasoning. The two first temptations begin with these words: "If you are the Son of God . . . ," "Since you are the Son of God . . ." The solemn assurance that Christ has received becomes the mechanism of the temptation: the Devil knows that even a gift from God can be turned to evil. **Luke 3:22**

"Since you are the Son of God," the Devil says, "command this stone to become bread." The first part of this sentence is irrefutable; it is indeed the role of a Son of God to give commands to nature. God has created this man in His image, as His Son, in order that he may control nature. The diabolical temptation, then, does not reside in this. It is strikingly illuminated by the reply that Christ makes: "It is written: man does not live by bread alone, but by all that comes from the mouth of God." These words may be considered as the charter of a Christian political economy. **Matt. 4:3; Luke 4:3**

Matt. 4:4; Luke 4:4

It would be overhasty to think that Christ is ordering us to choose between bread and the Word of God. Since it is impossible for man to choose against his daily bread, this would be a fine excuse to forsake the divine Word. Christ knows very well that man needs bread to live and that if he has no bread he dies. He knows very well that in a famished man what dies first is the mind, that is, the faculty in him that can receive the Word of God. Famine is not a good thing for human dignity or for the kingdom of God; without daily bread nothing is possible, not even Christianity, and this is why in the *"Pater Noster"* we ask for our daily bread. Political economy is a necessity.

But it is not enough. The body has need of bread, the soul has need of other nourishment. What? Christ will say later on: "My food is to do the will of my father." At this moment he says, and it amounts to the same thing: "All that comes from the mouth of God."

1 Kings 3:10

What issues from the mouth of God? A cry, a summons, a name, a Word, by which one lives. The whole history of Israel resounds with such summonses: "And the Lord came, and stood, and called as at other times, Samuel, Samuel. Then Samuel answered, Speak; for thy servant heareth." Blessed is he who, having heard such a summons, arises and says: "Here am I, Lord, to do Your will." There is a magnificent word to designate the summons of God: it is the "vocation" par excellence.

Man's need for bread is physical, natural, normal, legitimate; and those who devote themselves to serving this hunger do well. But man's profoundest hunger is for a vocation. To know oneself summoned by name, to have the courage to answer this appeal, to harness all one's life till one's last breath to the task to which one has been called in order to fulfill one's vocation, that is a life worthy of man because it answers fully to the appeal of God, and is like a prolonged echo of that appeal. This too is the meaning of that first temptation: it is directed essentially at Christ's vocation for the purpose of making him forget it, for the purpose of turning him aside. Christ replies simply that he has been sent not to change stones into bread but to do the will of his Father, to answer to his vocation. The initial strength of Christ confronted by Satan lies in defining perfectly his vocation and in holding to it.

Thus it is with all men. It is necessary, of course, to eat, but unhappy is the man who does not know why he is on this earth, who has never heard himself summoned to a task greater than himself, who has no vocation; he is in solitude. More unhappy still is he who, having heard himself summoned by name, does not listen, does not reply, forgets, falls asleep. Unhappy is he who prefers the immediate foods of this earth to that cry suspended in the heavens that has issued from the mouth of God.

It is a grave injustice to lead men of good will to believe that there is no vocation outside the ecclesiastical and religious domain. In the world there is a hierarchy of vocations. The supreme dignity of each person is a summons from God. Every man is called to union with God. Once this is admitted, the vocation to holy orders, to the immediate service of God, is the highest. But there are humbler temporal vocations that reveal divine providence no less clearly and that require no less heroism. I have seen writers die over a half-written page, compositors die over unfinished galleys, doctors die at the sickbeds of their patients, not to mention soldiers—who are not true soldiers except through vocation. It is not discipline that makes a soldier—that is a gross conception and, besides, a modern one—it is obedience to a vocation; no soldier is lost but in the absence of that.

There are no more excruciating pains for a man than those born of his vocation. A man's vocation is in fact the instrument of his crucifixion. *Verbum crucis.* For me it is a sign of the universal truth of Christianity that every authentic vocation, even that of an unbeliever, even that of one who does not wish to face the religious problem, involves conflict and crucifixion, dismemberment.

So it is with nations. Perhaps not all, but certainly some have a true vocation; in fact, they do not fully merit the name of fatherland unless they acknowledge a universal vocation. So it is with Israel, as is evident in her whole history. The vocation of a people is what one might call its soul. Joan of Arc incarnated the soul of France, her vocation. A statesman like Abraham Lincoln makes one feel what the soul and vocation of the American nation are. And no one will ever make me believe that Holy Russia has become Communist through belief in the "scientific" rightness of Marxist economics; I am sure it is through conversion of her whole self to the mystic and quasi-religious ideal of revolution. For vocations too can lead astray: this aberration, this mystic delirium, is a thousand times better and probably a thousand times more productive than the avaricious calm of wiser nations.

The legitimacy of a leader springs from his being able to recognize his nation's vocation and to lead that nation toward its accomplishment. Thus it is particularly shameful when a statesman speaks of his people as a farmer speaks of a farm animal: "If only it grows, if only it gets fat, if only it thrives, if only it puts on weight." It is even sadder to hear the whole nation applaud such language as though it alone were appropriate: such a nation is reduced by its master to the level of beasts, and it glories in that: "If only I can get bigger, if only I thrive, if only I grow fat, if only I put on weight!" Such a nation denies its vocation and its honor; it is no longer a fatherland, it deserves to die.

To this a statesman might reply that he is interested only in the country's digestion and leaves to others the care of its soul. In that case let us honor that statesman as a champion ox-breeder; he merits no other homage nor any other allegiance. As Simone Weil has said, one of the profound insights of the Apocalypse is to compare empires to hideous monsters that have risen from the sea. It is, to be sure, necessary for nations to eat, and political economy is an honorable and necessary career like that of wet nurse, but exclusive preoccupation with material economy and prosperity is one of the surest ways for a people to forfeit its honor, to abdicate its vocation, and to lose its soul.

The first temptation by the Devil to which Christ was subjected is of permanent and burning timeliness.

And then the Devil seizes Christ and transports him to the pinnacle of the Temple, the highest point on the ramparts of Jerusalem, which dominates the bed of the Cedron from a height of some six hundred feet. The Devil too can perform miracles. To appear in corporeal form, to transport a burden through the air to the top of a tower—all this is child's play. Nevertheless this episode remains one of the strangest among Jesus' earthly adventures.

Earlier his mother had swaddled him and cradled him like the baby he was, later men will lay hands on him and the executioner will stretch his limbs on the cross; now it is Satan who seizes him in a sacrilegious abduction, lifts him and carries him through the air, holding him pressed tight against himself in a terrible embrace. This physical possession by Satan must have been pushed by him as far as was permitted, as far indeed as the inferior powers of the soul. I think that those saints who have been most tormented by the demon—such as the Curé d'Ars, who, during the night, sometimes felt a hand softly caressing his face—must have derived much strength from this event in the life of Christ. Since he allowed himself to be held so close, why not they?

Matt. 4:6;
Luke 4:9-11

The second temptation begins like the first: "Since you are the Son of God . . ." The Devil adds: "Throw yourself down into the abyss: how can any harm come to you? Is it not written that He will give orders to his angels that they bear you up in their hands lest your foot should dash against the stone?"

Here I hazard an explanatory hypothesis. In Jewish cosmology angels had very great importance, and elsewhere as well, for Aristotle thought that the spheres of the universe were governed by "substances distinct from all matter." These are "scientific" theories that make us laugh to-day. Nevertheless, that is not to say they will not some day come back into fashion, nor are they on that account more "true" or more "false." One can very well imagine some great scientist, struck by the degree to which science is orienting itself more and more in the direction of indeterminism, constructing a theory that would incorporate beings of a free and spiritual nature in the machinery of the universe. This theory would not be absurd for the good reason that in the present state of science no theory is absurd.

Valéry writes, apropos of Pascal, "The progress of knowledge [he does not say of truth] in this realm, the great discoveries that have been made, the multitude of facts, the strangeness and instability of the theories, and, oddly, the more and more sensible dependency of phenomena upon the means of observation, impel modern men *to suspend all judgment on the subject of the nature of things.*" It is a strange "science" whose most advanced state consists in leaving the judgment in suspense on the subject of the nature of things, that is, of the truth. Relativity has won the day in scientific circles, and so one can quite legitimately talk about practical efficiency, but how can one speak of absolute and permanent truth in the sciences? By what right, then, do we raise our eyebrows and smile in a superior way at the scientific theories of the ancients? They are as good as ours, neither more nor less.

Simone Weil, who "grew up in the seraglio," has lucidly stated the problem of truth and modern science. She talks very well about it toward the end of her book *L'Enracinement.* "It may be said," she writes, "that the fruitfulness of a theory is an objective criterion. But this criterion only comes into play among those theories that are accepted. . . . If people had not been fascinated by the quantum theory when Planck first proposed it—and this despite the fact that it was absurd, or perhaps because it was absurd, for people were tired of reason—we would never have known that it was fruitful. . . . Thus there is a Darwinian process in science. Theories grow as though at random, and there is a survival of the fittest. Such a science may be a form of the *élan vital,* but it is not a form of the search for truth."

No one who knows Simone Weil would expect her to stop short on so promising a path. "Even the great public cannot ignore and does not ignore the fact that science, like every product of collective opinion, is subject to fashion. Scientists talk all the time about outmoded theories. This would be scandalous if we were not too addlepated to be conscious of scandal. How can one feel a religious respect for something that is subject to fashion?" We are close to the heart of the subject, for this is the question of the relation of religion to science. If it should be felt that Simone Weil, following Valéry, is not a competent authority in this matter, I can quote Einstein, who wrote toward the end of his life, "It is hard for me to understand the great role, especially in epochs of transition and uncertainty, played by fashion in science, a role only slightly inferior to that which it plays in women's dress. Man is indeed an animal very susceptible to suggestion on every subject."

In these conditions one can see how silly it is to attribute to science the prestige of truth—which, incidentally, it has ceased to demand—and how ridiculous it is to talk of a possible conflict between science and religion on the level of truth. If there is a conflict between them, it is not here. In the explanatory hypothesis I was proposing, the second temptation of Christ would define the location of this conflict. The Devil asks Christ, since he is the Son of God, to give proof of it from a scientific point of view and to bow to the prestige of the science of his time. Never forget that, like fashion, science is always of its time.

If, in the historical context of that epoch, angelology had the force of a scientific theory that explained the universe, the Devil's appeal to angels might perhaps have carried the same meaning as if he were to say today, "Since you are the Son of God, you are obviously very well acquainted with the quantum theory, the latest hypotheses about the evolution of nature, of the cosmos, and of humanity, and the methods of atomic fission; you are equipped with the whole arsenal of modern science, you are completely of your time, and I am sure that you are better able than anyone else to go to the most distant planets. Well then, go!" What, in effect, was the Devil's proposal to Jesus? To throw himself down from the High Place and, with the aid of Angels, to land at the bottom safe and sound. The question is less about Angels than about overcoming gravitation, and that is the great triumph of modern science. The interplanetary voyages that are henceforth possible are a total victory over gravitation.

What is the goal of modern science? The search less for truth than for empire over nature, the *"imperium naturae."* This empire seems henceforth within our reach. The temptation that still resides there is not in the object offered: it is no more wrong for a man to wish to dominate nature than for him to want his daily bread. That empire is his due by virtue of his having been made in the likeness of God. But there is great confusion and great wickedness in wanting from science only the power it confers, in not recognizing that the sovereignty over nature is man's due only because he is made in the likeness of God, in not recognizing that nature itself bears the hallmark of God. It is through a double obedience, of man to God and of nature to God, it is through the marriage of these two obediences that science can find its legitimation, its ultimate dignity, because then it will proceed according to truth, a practical truth that conforms to God's design when He created the universe and created man in its bosom for the purpose of dominating it.

And Simone Weil concludes splendidly and characteristically: "How should human thought have any other object than thought? . . . The goal of the man of learning is the union of his own mind with the mysterious wisdom eternally inscribed in the universe. How therefore could there be opposition or even separation between the spirit of science and that of religion? Scientific investigation is only one form of religious contemplation." No doubt this formulation is awkward and abrupt. But Simone Weil is quite right in reminding us that in ancient Greece every acquisition of knowledge had the quality of a mystical and sacred gift.

We know that all humanity is living on the brink of a nuclear catastrophe and that one unconsidered action could push it over. This eventuality is so terrific that we prefer not to think about it in order to live, but we know very well that it is completely real. Let us suppose then that one fine day all the A-bombs and H-bombs should be utilized in a universal conflagration. It would matter very little what nation or what head of state finally took that responsibility. This scientific holocaust would be the equivalent of the quasi-suicide of humanity. Perhaps there would be only a few survivors, "a remnant," to use the expression of the Prophets, which would regain a sinister reality not for one people alone but for the entire human species.

Supposing that some atomic scientists survived, I can imagine very well that they would be universally held responsible for the frightful disaster that had befallen men, that they would be hunted down, hanged or burned alive, as witches were burned in the Middle Ages. I can imagine very well that all remaining technical equipment would be destroyed as maleficent and that scientific research of any kind would be punished by death. Terror-stricken by the immensity of the cataclysm, humanity would turn away from science with horror and would exclude from its midst any unhappy person who might dare to follow that path again.

These new men, these survivors, would be making a great mistake, you will tell me, and you will prove your point by an irrefutable distinction between pure science and its practical application. Thus, by admitting that humanity is making detestable use of science to the point of provoking a nuclear catastrophe, nothing is proved against science itself.

Well and good! That proves it, that proves exactly what is in question. Science has become a dangerous mastodon, an imbecile without true judgment or responsibility, but unhappily omnipotent, capable of crushing all men beneath its feet: it is the monster in Picasso's "Minotauromachia." It is imperative to domesticate this mastodon, it is absolutely necessary to reduce it very soon, if not to impotence, at least to obedience. Instead it is we who do obeisance to it and bow before it; indeed we abdicate all judgment before it, we prostrate ourselves before it, we submit everything to it, our material security and our spiritual dignity, to the truth that we idolize—and this is abominable. Science is our Moloch, our Baal, our Astarte, we give it everything it demands, including our souls. We no longer look to God for our salvation, we look to science, we feel ourselves impotent and humble before it alone, we abdicate everything at its feet; nothing is too precious for us to convert into a burnt offering to science.

In a tone that recalls the Prophets of her race, Simone Weil writes, "We actually suffer from the sickness of idolatry; it is so profound that it deprives Christians of the faculty of testifying to the truth. No dialogue among deaf men can equal in comic effect the debate between the modern mind and the Church. Unbelievers choose manifest proofs of the Christian faith to make into arguments against that faith in the name of the scientific spirit. Christians never notice this but attempt feebly, with a bad conscience and with a distressing lack of intellectual probity, to deny those truths. Their blindness is the punishment for the crime of idolatry."

I may be told that she is too severe. Not a bit of it! Scientism in its grossest, most outdated, most laggard form is still engaged in playing havoc with the traditional teachings of our religion. In the farm near the place where I am finishing this book there is a little girl who goes to catechism class. When her mother told her that I was engaged in writing a chapter about the Devil, she exclaimed, "The Devil? But Monsieur l'Abbé has told us that he does not exist!" This child is candid and at an age at which one does not lie about a subject of this kind. I am sure that the honest vicar is intoxicated by pseudo-scientific theories: honest or not, this priest is lightheartedly sacrificing the authority of the Gospel to the authority of . . . to what authority actually? It is probable that he himself does not know. How could science possibly prove that the Devil exists or does not exist when science abstains from all judgment about the nature of the very things that it studies?

No matter! At a time when the experts have abandoned determinism and are more and more inclined to consider scientific research as artistic virtuosity rather than as the search for immutable truth, nothing keeps pious boobies from going into ecstasies before the scientifico-religious syncretisms that appear here and there each time a new theory is launched, like snails after the rain. And this at a time when it is henceforth evident that there cannot be conflict between religion and science because religion is concerned solely with God, who is immutable good-ness and truth, and with His revelation and the spiritual salvation He brings to man, and that science, just like Pilate, jeers at truth and jeers even more at the idea of saving anyone at all.

Or rather, yes, there is inevitable conflict whenever science demands unquestioning respect that is actually idolatrous. Just the same, it is high time to tell science that it extrapolates, that it exaggerates, that it exas-perates, that it is in our service and not we in its service and that, even if it is as big as Goliath, we do not recognize its right to make us bow down and worship it.

On the other hand, it is high time the theologians rescinded the con-demnation of Galileo. Admittedly they were wrong. They intruded into a matter that did not concern them. But let them once for all get over this business of Galileo, which so unhappily compromises them in regard to science, and let them speak to us once more of the great doctrine of the subordination of the sciences and the hierarchical degrees of knowl-edge which allows us to curb all wisdom and all understanding in obe-dience to Christ. Here, in this great doctrine, inherited from the Greeks and from Saint Thomas, lies the salvation of the intelligence and the hope of finally domesticating the mastodon that keeps us enslaved.

On reflection, it would be astonishing if the sin of idolatry, which has held the nations in subjugation for thousands of years, had suddenly disappeared as though by magic from the so-called civilized world. I believe that it has created other idols for itself, for it is clearly evident that we are all as weak as our ancestors, as prejudiced, as prompt to enroll in the cults that we impose upon ourselves and to bend our knees before Baal. As for the burnt offerings of children in honor of Moloch, I think that our generation should have the decency not to harp on this obvious evidence of barbarism.

In reading the Prophets and noting the violence of their language and the brutality with which they denounce the feebleness of their contem-poraries, it becomes clear that idolatry is a delicious sin, of reassuring sweetness and intimacy. What thunder is needed simply to arouse men from such a sin?

Admittedly we are moved by the material dimensions of scientific ac-complishment; the voyages of the astronauts, the atomic bomb, the hy-drogen bomb overwhelm our imaginations. In general we are incapable of understanding how all this is possible, but we believe implicitly, on the testimony of those sublime accomplishments, everything the scien-tists choose to tell us in their magical and authoritarian language, and we even believe what we are told on this subject by magazines barely better informed than we are. The accomplishments are there before our eyes; that is all that counts for us.

But we are impressed, too, by the effeminate and in some ways marvelous comfort with which science surrounds us. We can think only with terror of what might become of us without our cars, our electricity, our airplanes, our refrigerators, our vacuum cleaners, our radios, our televisions, our machines, our synthetics, our sleeping pills, our tranquilizers. What need do we still have of a Father in heaven when our space ships are conquering the stratosphere?

What need have we of Providence when modern comfort coddles us like a mother? We are inside this scientific universe like a baby still in its mother's womb who imagines the universe stops short at its mother's warm sides and who wants above all never to emerge from it. It is a dim universe of infinite sweetness and ease. What the Devil promised Christ, we believe is already ours: we are borne up so softly in such sure hands lest our foot should dash against a stone.

The third phase of the duel with Satan is the most instructive and the most disquieting. It has to do with a phantasmagoria which must Matt. 4:8-9 have been of such sumptuousness as to stop one's breath. "Again, the Devil taketh him up into an exceeding high mountain, and showeth him all the kingdoms of the world, and the glory of them: and the Devil saith unto him, All this power will I give thee, and the glory of them: for that is delivered unto me: and to whomsoever I will give it. If thou therefore wilt worship me all shall be thine."

The stage manager has left the wings, he reveals himself as the producer and claims his rights, he is willing to accept Christ as star and protagonist of this drama, which is being played on every stage in the world, on one condition, extremely clearly put: to be worshiped and recognized as God. This is a prodigious reversal of roles and situations; the Devil is not embarrassed, he is sure of himself, oh, how sure of himself he is and how he longs to be worshiped! The idolatrous meaning of this temptation is no longer an explanatory hypothesis: it springs forth from the text itself. The Gospel tells us that the world of politics is the sphere most favorable to idolatry.

Next to the personalities of the actors, the most singular thing in this whole dialogue is the calm affirmation by the Devil that all the power and all the kingdoms of the world and all their glory belong by right to him: they have been handed to him and he disposes of them to whomsoever he chooses. He affirms that he is the source of all political legitimacy and, in virtue of this, claims divinity and the honors due to divinity. If one were to believe him, all political order would belong to him, all political organization would be evil because it would be in contradiction to the sovereignty of God, the state would be hell, by serving the state one would be serving the Devil, and all obedience to political authority would be idolatrous. Obviously the Devil is a liar. . . .

This temptation is presented by the Devil in the form of a bargain: I shall give you what belongs to me, political power and the glory that goes with it, if you will give me what belongs to you, the homage of a free creature's adoration. Christ's reply is surprising because of all that it leaves in suspense. It is far from being responsive to the Devil's proposal. Christ does not enter into the bargaining, he does not even say, "It's too dear," he simply says that he cannot make the exchange, because this homage of a free creature's adoration, which the Devil demands, can be given only to God. "Then saith Jesus unto him, Get thee hence, Satan: for it is written, thou shalt worship the Lord thy God, and Him only shalt thou serve." For the rest, all the kingdoms of the world with their power and their glory, Christ refuses to take any interest in them, he will not even discuss the price, he does not lower himself to prove to the Devil that he is lying when he pretends to have this domain at his disposal. Is he in fact lying, and if so to what extent? Matt. 4:10

I am compelled to say that the first two temptations—to change stones into bread and to throw oneself from the top of a tower without being hurt—taken in their literal sense, do not seem very serious in the eyes of a man of today; we have accomplished so much more in the transformation of matter and in the conquest of gravity. That is, unless one gives these two temptations a deeper meaning than the surface one, as I have tried to do.

The third temptation, however, even in the terms in which it was offered, still remains a topic of burning interest. All the kingdoms of the earth, all their power, all their glory, ah yes, what a temptation today, just as it was then and just as it will be a thousand years from now! A temptation, moreover, open to everyone. What child of twelve with any imagination at all has not dreamed of one day being Alexander or Napoleon? The excuse for a child of twelve is that he does not know what denials of conscience are the standard price for the glory of being Alexander or Napoleon. But to deny one's conscience in order to obtain power and glory is still within reach of the average man: Ubu is a common person. Hitler was a mediocrity who carried the logic of very elementary ideas to the extremes of crime; the ideas, strictly speaking, are not really his but could have been picked up on any street corner. It was Hitler, however, who pushed them to excess.

As Simone Weil once more puts it, most men, with the exception of the saints, imagine that they are of such good faith that if they possessed power they would have enough justice to make the best possible use of that power for themselves and for the entire world. The most mediocre of men can tell himself that if he controlled rain and shine, there would never be anything but fair weather. A terrible temptation: Christ, who was wholly just in respect to himself and to the entire world, rejected it. He refused the empire of this world, offered as it was by those hands. How many men could resist such an offer?

Jefferson, the author of the Declaration of Independence, which seems to me the most perfect, complete, and well-balanced political document in the world—Jefferson, who was himself to become President of the United States, wrote, "There are three types of societies: those that have no government, like that of our Indians; those in which each one's will has a just influence on the government; those ruled by force. It is a question that my mind has not yet resolved whether the first situation is not the best." And to make it perfectly clear, he added this: "If it should happen some time that the people become inattentive to public affairs, you and I, and the Congress, and the assemblies, the judges and the governors, we will all become wolves. This would seem to be the *general law of our nature*, despite individual exceptions."

The field of politics, that is, the government of men by other men, the order imposed on the human flock by shepherds who are themselves only men—this vast field does not belong by right to the Devil. Certainly not, since everything that exists belongs by right to God. But it seems that this field is particularly open to the corrupting influences of him whom the Scripture sometimes calls "the prince of this world." It is par excellence the domain of fraud, of mental limitation, of propaganda, and of force. There is no baseness, such as that traditionally attributed to the valet in French comedies, no double-dealing in the manner of Scapin or Sganarelle that a politician, even an exalted one, is not capable of. And when success crowns their despicable efforts, it is no longer as valets that they speak but as masters, demanding from us respect that verges on adoration.

Men of my generation, who are approximately the same age as the century, have seen too many fratricidal wars, too many corrupt peace treaties, too many monstrous agreements, too many brazen perjuries, too many sullied victories, too many defeats both impure and dishonorable, too many hopes betrayed, too many vain promises, too many saviors and too many traitors, for us still to be entitled to any illusions. The English have an admirable maxim coined by Lord Acton: "Power tends to corrupt and absolute power corrupts absolutely." In politics it is perhaps the part of wisdom to change masters frequently in order at least to limit the period of their corrupt influence. What, after all, do the rapes, violence, and murders that occur in the ordinary course of events amount to in comparison with the mass murders and the enormous brigandage perpetrated by states, and this without any possible recourse, without judgment, without punishment, and generally without heed on the part of the world at large?

One phrase covers these accumulated injustices, one of the most despicable phrases in the whole human vocabulary: reasons of state. This phrase designates nothing avowable, except the interests of the state, that frigid monster, combined with power—that is, with the ability to throw into prison or to kill, in other words, the power to compel general obedience. Sometimes, too, one says "the superior interest of the state": superior to what? If by that is meant superior to material and individual interests, it is true; one must know how to die for the community. But most of the time this means that the state is not required to give an accounting to anyone, not even to God, and that it disposes of the entire citizen, including his soul, that its interest is superior to justice, and that, moreover, it derives its right from the fact that it is stronger. It is to Clemenceau that we owe the perfect formula for this ignominy, a formula that might serve as motto for all the dictators we have known, all without exception: "Render unto Caesar the things that are Caesar's . . . and everything belongs to Caesar." To cap the climax, Clemenceau is considered a champion of democracy. In this century we have indeed seen everything.

No one should be better equipped than Christians to face this century of violence and of lies. Christians were forewarned, not only by their Holy Books but more recently by a remarkable document, which is thought backward and reactionary, but in which I see—because I have read it attentively—a charter of human liberty in the twentieth century, provided of course that it be read and understood in time and, most important of all, obeyed by Christians. This is the *Syllabus*, which is known to be a catalogue of propositions adjudged dangerous to the belief of the faithful and to the survival of human society and for this reason absolutely condemned as false and pernicious. Here are some of them; I should like the reader to meditate on their historical implications:

—"The State, being the source and origin of all rights, is possessor of a right that suffers no limitation." (Proposition 39: condemned.)

—"An injustice crowned with success does no injury to the sanctity of the law." (Proposition 61: condemned.)

—"One must not condemn but rather deem permissible and judge worthy of highest praise violation of the most sacred oaths or any criminal and injurious actions whatsoever, provided they are committed for love of country." (Proposition 64: condemned.)

If the *Syllabus* had been understood and fully obeyed by European Christians, Europe would undoubtedly have been spared Hitler and fascism, Russia would have been spared Lenin and Stalin, and France would have been spared certain more commonplace but no less dishonest political experiences, and I completely fail to see how man's liberty would have fared the worse. But this generation of European Christians is a pile of bales that permit themselves to be loaded onto any ship at all for any destination whatever. In all the political adventures of contemporary Europe, Christians have served as ballast and that is all. And instead of being ashamed of themselves, they carry their foolishness to the point of being ashamed of the *Syllabus*.

In the whole political history of the world, even that of the "Christian" Occident, one gets the impression, when affairs of state are concerned, that triumphs of justice are little more than accidents, anomalies. Christians, more than others, should have been sensitive to the tyranny of reasons of state, not only because they should have paid more attention than others to justice, but also because their founder, Jesus Christ, and so many of their martyrs, up to and including the most recent, were condemned for reasons of state by judges neither better nor worse than many others, under laws neither better nor worse than ours. Reasons of state admit of no discussion; this is the idolatrous formula par excellence: it puts itself in the place of God and demands to be worshiped.

But the actual truth, beneath appearances, is this, as the third temptation of Christ reveals it to us: however great a chief of state may be, it is not he who makes history, or rather he makes it only through immediate obedience to someone else—either God, if he puts justice and honor above even the interests of state, or the Devil, if he claims to put the state above all justice and all morality. The "realistic" statesmen are also marionettes on strings. However tragic their destiny, it still retains a grotesque aspect. At the end of the war, it was striking to see in the newsreels how men like Hitler and Mussolini had taken on, even physically, the grotesque appearance of disjointed marionettes.

It is impossible that there should be a completely cordial understanding, without reticence or reservation, between the state and Christians. Insofar as Christians are Christians it is even impossible for them to take the state and its interests altogether seriously. Ancient Israel was already a "people of priests"; Christians, in the measure to which they are faithful to their vocation, are, in addition, a people of kings and a people of judges. Likenesses of God, like all men, they are, in virtue of this fact, above the whole order of nature and above the social order. Ransomed by the blood of Jesus Christ, they participate, through baptism, in his divine nature and also in his priesthood, in his royalty and in his judicature. What are all the kingdoms of the earth with their power and their glory in comparison with such supernatural dignity? Through that most intimate dignity, every Christian is above the state; he judges it. There is in every man and in every Christian an inalienable part of himself that is related only to God, and that infinitely precious part is to be governed only by God.

And then, the Gospel adds, the Devil, having exhausted all temptation, left Christ, and the angels, approaching, served him.   Matt. 4:11

This is a magnificent picture with which to close the chapter, the picture of this man, exhausted by his fast and by his combat, approaching that immense table, laden with wines and delicacies, set in the midst of the desert and served by the angels.

CHAPTER XIV

The Kingdom of God

WHEN one undertakes to write the history of Jesus Christ, that is, to produce a historical work about this man, honesty requires that nothing be added and nothing essential omitted, that what is essential be separated from what is accidental, and that the whole be presented in a light varying, to be sure, from one writer to another, but not on that account untrue to the subject.

As for me, I see the history as a *chanson de geste;* everything is there—the epic grandeur of the hero, single combats, war, love, blood, treason, glory, the heavens opening to take part in the contest, hell shuddering, mobilizing, and lamenting. It will be said that in taking this view I am obviously abandoning my historical purpose, that in the *chanson de geste* poetic interpretation generally outweighs both history and truth. To this I shall reply that here the subject is so great, the history so vast—embracing, in fact, heaven, earth, and hell—that the truth, the naked truth, is itself an epic, a truly supernatural one. Nevertheless, objectively considered, the dimensions of this person, Jesus Christ, are altogether different from those of the heroes of Balzac or Proust. There is nothing I can do. In the interests of my subject, I regret not having the talent of Balzac or Proust, but at least I shall be careful not to reduce the subject to my own personal dimensions.

With Christ's return from the desert, matters are henceforth clear. The enemy has been identified. Just as in later history young men will be knighted, so the heavens have opened above Jesus Christ and he has received his investiture as Son of God. Thereafter in the desert he has made his first trial of arms. Now war is declared between Christ and Satan; it will continue until the end of the world. This is the call to arms for the reconquest of the Kingdom: we are reminded of the Cid Campeador.

It is Mark who has best expressed the onrush and rapid sequence of these events: the first chapter of his Gospel has the coolness, the brevity, and the official precision of a wartime communiqué:

And it came to pass in those days, that Jesus came from Nazareth of Galilee, and was baptized of John in Jordan. And straightway coming up out of the water, he saw the heavens opened, and the Spirit like a dove descending upon him: and there came a voice from heaven, saying, Thou art My beloved Son, in whom I am well pleased. And immediately the Spirit guided him into the wilderness. And he was there in the wilderness forty days tempted of Satan; and was with the wild beasts; and the angels ministered unto him. Now after that John was put in prison, Jesus came into Galilee, preaching the Gospel of the Kingdom of God, and saying, the time is fulfilled, and the Kingdom of God is at hand: repent ye, and believe the Gospel. *Mark 1:9-15*

I saw this with my own eyes as a child, on the second of August, 1914, a radiant day. The tocsin sounded over the whole countryside, calling men to war. In the farm district of Auvergne I saw men leave their cattle, their wagons, and their pitchforks in the fields and run to respond to the summons that filled the sky. I saw this when I was seven years old, and I shall never forget it. When Jesus appeared on the shores of the Sea of Tiberias it was exactly the same thing that happened. His voice was like the tocsin.

Mark goes on:

Now as he walked by the Sea of Galilee, he saw Simon and Andrew his brother casting a net into the sea: for they were fishers. And Jesus said unto them, Come ye after me and I will make you to become fishers of men. And straightway they forsook their nets, and followed him. And when he had gone a little farther thence, he saw James the son of Zebedee and John his brother, who also were in the ship mending their nets. And straightway he called them: and they left their father Zebedee in his ship with the hired servants and went after him. *Mark 1:16-20*

War, as we all know, is no longer in fashion; the language of war is out of style. War has ceased to be picturesque, it has ceased to be a sport, it has ceased even to be a defense; it is collective suicide. The weapons of war have devoured war and are ruminating it in their monstrous belly. Let us leave that disquieting rumination alone. Of course the level on which Christ placed himself was an altogether different one from that of our carnal warfare, but it was nevertheless war he was engaged in, and a war capable of arousing the enthusiasm of an entire people. How, then, can I explain what happened unless I speak of what I saw in 1914, or perhaps of what the chroniclers of the French Revolution tell us; or cite the opening chapters of *Gone with the Wind*, which re-create for us the *ambiance* of the South in the War of Secession, or Tolstoi's splendid *War and Peace?*

It is custom that destroys us. The Evangelical revelation should give us souls of fire, but custom creates in us the souls of automatons. The words of religion are worn down like pebbles, they no longer clash, they no longer wound, they simply roll with the stream. When Mark writes

Mark 1:14   that Jesus "preached the Gospel of the Kingdom of God," I have trouble believing that his words resounded like the tocsin. I have always slept through sermons, never at the sound of the tocsin. I can clearly picture the throngs of young men, singing the "Marseillaise" and moving toward the frontiers, when France was proclaimed in danger. I picture with difficulty or not at all that when Christ said, "The times are fulfilled, the Kingdom of God is at hand," these words in the social context of the time stirred people's hearts as violently as "The Fatherland is in danger" stirred the hearts of France in the Year II of the Revolution. Nevertheless that is precisely what happened.

I shall be told that Jesus' preaching left no record in history of the great mobilizations I evoke. In the first place, this is not entirely true, for the Christian religion in the end took on the dimensions of history on the grand scale. But we are now at the beginning. Galilee was a very small country with scant interest in history on the grand scale. From the outset of his ministry, moreover, Jesus refused to participate in political action, and for the best of military reasons: on this level, his enterprise was a tempest in a teapot and, in the end, a complete fiasco. But this was true only on that level, and the people of Israel themselves are accustomed to consider matters from a somewhat higher one.

What is the nature of this Kingdom of God, whose coming Jesus proclaimed and for which he was commencing to recruit a band of supporters, his band? It is here, here above all, that the reading of the Old Testament and meditation on it illuminate the New. Indeed, one cannot understand the one without the other. The whole history of Israel is an attempt, with varying fortune but with constant resolution, to establish the Kingdom of God on earth. There is no prayer more absolutely, more typically Jewish than the second petition in the *"Pater*

Noster": "Adveniat regnum tuum!" Thy Kingdom come! When we pronounce these words we are profoundly consolidated with all Christians, past, present, and future, but also with the whole people of Israel from the time of Abraham.

This Kingdom of God was not imaginary. It had had its earthly preparations, the beginnings of its realization. They were the great days of Israel: the kingdom of David and of Solomon had been in truth the Kingdom of God, the kings having been no more than lieutenants of God, the government of the king being truly legitimate only to the degree to which it was exercised under the limitations and the directives of God's will. But the kings of Israel, even Solomon, had often betrayed God and their charge; the kingdom had been rent, destroyed, dispersed. In the ruin and humiliation of their nation, the Jews had seen very clearly the effect of a divine punishment incurred through their sins; despite all, even in the midst of this chastisement, they felt the solicitude of God resting upon them in sovereign fidelity to His promises. They were and they remained always the chosen people, the people chosen from among all, to whom God had given His Word, with whom He had made an indestructible covenant. From this divine covenant they expected the liberation of their people and the restoration of the Kingdom of God, in which they would find their home.

They were in expectation of this liberation and this restoration just as the European resistance to the Nazis expected the advance of the Russian troops or the disembarkation on French shores of the Allied troops. We knew very well that England, then Russia, then America were at war with our enemies; the London radio repeated it every night. Let those who lived through that dark period remember it and let those who did not try to imagine the explosive mixture of anguish and of hope that preceded the liberation of their country.

The Jews, too, knew that God, their God, was at war on their side against the same enemy; they had belief and hope in God infinitely greater than any hope that we, from the depths of our prisons, ever had in England, in Russia, or in America. They also had their BBC to sustain them and to animate that hope; it was their Holy Books and their Prophets. Ah! What a great and religious nation that was, sustained for thousands of years by the Word of God alone, assembled around that Word, like us, exactly like us, when silently bending over our hushed receivers, shutters closed, we heard above the static the voice that came to us from beyond the seas: "This is London! Honor and Fatherland! A Frenchman is speaking to Frenchmen!" The Jews listened to their Prophets: "Chariot of Israel and horsemen thereof!

This is God, your God, speaking to you!" Never has so high and so noble a hope sustained an earthly nation. . . .

In the whole history of mankind there has never been a great discovery without a prior hope. But it is also extremely rare that the discovery is exactly what was hoped for. Sometimes it is disappointing; occasionally it vastly surpasses the hope. What was Christopher Columbus looking for? Convinced that the world was round, he was searching in the West for a route to the Indies, and he discovered America: the discovery surpassed the hope. It is God's way to inspire hope and passionate desire, but His revelation necessarily exceeds the hope and the desire. The Jews, then, were hoping for the Kingdom of God.

And all at once, just as after so many weeks at sea the lookout on the *Santa María* suddenly cried, "Land!" thus after so many centuries of patient scanning of the horizon of history Jesus arrives and says, "The Kingdom of God is here, close to you, in you, in your midst! Up and on your feet! How many Prophets and kings have longed to see what you see, and have died without seeing it? The Queen of Sheba came from the frontiers of the world to hear the wisdom of Solomon: here, in your midst, is one greater than Solomon."

The Kingdom of God cannot be discussed without defining in some sure manner the sovereign of that Kingdom, who is God, the God of Israel, in relation to His people. Every Jew knew that his God was the only God, that all the others were idols, that this God was the creator of heaven and earth, that His Kingdom had by right no other boundaries than those of the earth and of the sky, that He was the Unique One, the Holy One, the Transcendent or Wholly Other, that He was the master of life and death, of existence and nothingness, that He numbered the stars in the sky and searched the loins and the hearts of men.

I have spoken of the earthly preparations for this Kingdom, of its partial, historical realizations. These realizations were begun by frightful wars, when Yahweh gave to His people the country of Chanaan, wars the account of which horrifies and revolts us. This first conquest was carried out through absolute racist terror. The city of Jericho, at Jos. 6:17, 21 the gates of the desert, was condemned to destruction: "And the city shall be accursed, even it, and all that are therein. . . . And they utterly destroyed all that was in the city, both man and woman, young and old, and ox, and sheep, and ass, with the edge of a sword." The whole primitive history of Israel is full of similar executions. A great Prophet like Elias, so profoundly intimate with God, slaughtered with his own hand four hundred and fifty prophets of Baal during the cloudburst at the foot of Carmel. In this terrible epoch the God of Israel enforced more strictly than anyone else the law of war: woe to the vanquished!

We cannot come to terms with these savage customs, but there is a good deal of hypocrisy in our indignation. Are our wars better than the ancient wars, do they kill fewer people? Do they cause less torture? Are they any less a betrayal of human dignity? Do they entail fewer lives? In truth the scandal in this instance lies less in the cruelty than in the fact that God Himself commanded these massacres and stood ready to chastise with extreme severity those who did not perform His orders. Dear Simone Weil never came to terms with this fact. In all honesty, I cannot come to terms with it either. It is quite possible that the Jews who were Christ's contemporaries were also unable to come to terms with it. For the behavior of God and the laws of His Kingdom had changed greatly between the time of Joshua and the time of Jesus Christ.

Nevertheless, however barbarous these anathemas may have been, they contain a fundamental and unshakable truth: the devouring majesty of God, His holiness, His absolute purity; He is the fire; it is necessary that He should burn and consume. His honor is incompatible with any idolatry, it is impossible for Him to divide His sovereignty, His majesty is not to be shared. Such truths have not changed and cannot change. So long as there is one spark of true religion in this world, of true worship of God, there will be anathemas.

Manichaeism is an infantile doctrine which we have long ago outgrown—in fact we have so far outgrown it that we have fallen into the opposite excess. Obviously we know very well that God is not the causal principle both of good and of evil, but after all if He is not the principle of evil at least He tolerates it; if He is not in league with it, at least He shuts His eyes. Moreover, is evil really so evil? Error, injustice, malice—all these to be sure exist, but their evaluation depends a great deal on the point of view from which they are seen. Well then, from the point of view of God, which can easily be confused with that of Sirius, all this is not of such tremendous importance. Is not God our Father, or as one might say our kind papa? Is not Christ our big brother, that is, if not our accomplice at least our complacent companion? How then can one believe that all will not be comfortably arranged between us? All this is exactly as if, in our bastardized religious mentalities, the problem of evil were to be resolved by the infinitely reassuring maxim against washing our dirty linen in public.

What place have anathemas in this scheme of things? This brand of cowardly and demagogic religion cannot be the true religion. It is even more offensive to God than Manichaeism, which gives Him a rival God. In fact, this God is made responsible for evil as well as good in a sentimental confusion as disgusting as dishwater. It is one of the grossest forms of idolatry: man ends by loving himself too much, he ends by believing that God Himself must infallibly be seduced by the quality or the style of what man does, which cannot but be well done because he, man, does it. A minute's reflection is enough to deflate this fraud.

I shall be accused, I know, of having an Old Testament conception of God, of putting the accent on "the King of Terror" described in the book of Job. It is true that I hold this conception, but I believe, too, that this conception has passed into the New Testament because it is true. It is Saint Paul himself who says that God is a devouring fire and that it is terrible to fall into the hands of the living God. In a vision, Christ says to Saint Catherine of Siena, "I am he who is, and you are she who is not." And a modern exegete, Father Louis Bouyer, opportunely reminds us of "the fundamental constant of all religion worthy of the name. It is, first of all, the sense of God's absolute sovereignty over man, which makes the latter as nothing before Him. . . . Let us clearly recognize that wherever this sentiment disappears, the just God will be no more than a face, inadequately masking a nonreligious moralism, and the God of love an idol in which man loves only himself and the world that is completely his." And he adds, "A God in whom one is interested not for Himself but solely for His gifts is automatically reduced to the level of the Baals of Chanaan."

Is idolatry any less idolatry because the idol is situated within ourselves, in our vitiated standards of values, in our sentimental egoism, in our megalomania? No longer is the anathema to be hurled against an earthly Jericho with its walls, its pinnacles, and its gates; it is the personal fortress of our idolatry that must be overthrown, burned, razed to the ground, sterilized with salt, in order that we may hope that the Kingdom of God, whose coming Jesus announced, may be established within us. Let us be sure of this: God is always ready to forgive sins, He has given us the definite assurance of that in Jesus, but just as truly as in the time of Joshua He remains jealous of His sole glory; and as for idolatry, He holds it in horror. It behooves us to search our hearts and scrutinize the quality of our personal religion.

The picture that is usually drawn for us of the Jews who were Jesus' contemporaries is exaggerated, even incoherent. They are represented

Job 18:14

Heb. 10:27, 31

as a gross people, fanatically attached to the goods of this world and to a chimerical political and military ideal, bursting for vengeance and for the blood of their enemies, hypocrites, as false in their religion as in their human relations, without any understanding of what was going on around them, materialists, and yet capable of sacrificing themselves *en masse* for the traditions of their country, as they had unambiguously proved with all the eloquence of spilled blood. One asks oneself how it was possible in such a milieu for noble figures like Mary the mother of Jesus, Jesus himself, John the Baptist, Saint Paul, or even Gamaliel to have been born and to have lived. The truth is that the canvas is too uniform, too extreme, too completely black, to be true. Human truth, even that about nations, is more of a mixture of good and evil.

The historical truth about the Jewish people in the time of Jesus is that, in the aggregate, they were an intelligent people, carrying on cultural and commercial relations with all the great cities of the Mediterranean basin, very critical but also very open to the stirrings of diverse civilizations, having lost their political independence to Rome like all the other Mediterranean peoples, regretting this somewhat more, no doubt, than the others, proud of their national tradition and past military glories, hotly resentful of the humiliation of being subject to an uncouth nation that was not their equal, but knowing without question, since the time of the exile and the brief interlude of the Maccabees, that their political independence was irrecoverable, and yet guarding jealously in an idolatrous world their monotheistic faith, their Temple, their worship, and their trust in Yahweh.

This trust in Yahweh, to be sure, always implied the restoration of the Kingdom of Israel, regarded as the Kingdom of God Himself. But what was this restoration to be? If originally the Kingdom of God had been in the likeness of an earthly kingdom—with its frontiers and its territories, an army and a commander, import duties, the Temple of God and the palace of the king, his lieutenant—by the time of Jesus all these persisted only as past splendors, abandoned splendors, perhaps, even in the souls of the Israelites, the hope of which had probably been relinquished, at least in the case of the most pious Jews. For centuries the Prophets had been engaged in putting Israel on guard against hopes that were too material and too concrete.

One thing remains sure: the restoration of the Kingdom would begin with a solemn Judgment, the Great Day of Yahweh, on which the good would be separated from the wicked, on which God would be well able to recognize His own. Amos, who lived in the eighth century before Christ, had already said that, in God's conduct, grace and punishment are complementaries.

Amos 5:18-19

"Woe unto you who desire the day of the Lord! To what end is it for you? The day of the Lord is darkness, and not light. As if a man did flee from a lion and a bear met him; or went into the house, and leaned his hand on the wall, and a serpent bit him."

It is hard to believe that a pious Israelite, reading this text, could imagine that the coming of the Kingdom of God would be a day of rejoicing for all. And in the Prophets, how many other similarly ambiguous texts there are. In reality, even within Israel, this event was to be a triumph for some—those who had kept their faith and their trust in Yahweh, who had served Him with a pure heart—and a catastrophe for the unbelievers and the impure. Moreover, even this triumph for the faithful of Israel was not by any means exempt from trials, from sufferings and tribulations. From the time of the Book of Job, it had been well known that the friends of God would be tempted by the Devil. At bottom the Jews knew very well—and a book like *The Last of the Just* proves that they have never forgotten—that the triumph of triumphs was not to conquer earthly treasures but to retain the friendship of God. The idea that an Israelite, accustomed to reading the Prophets, would form of the coming of the Kingdom of God was that of the amorous and terrifying approach of God, holy among the holy, pure among the pure, faithful among the faithful, accompanied by a decisive testing as though by fire, in which finally the Spirit of God would become all in all.

If among the best, the most religious, of the Israelites the notion of the Kingdom of God had evolved from that of a purely temporal empire to a principally spiritual sovereignty of God over men's hearts, the conception of the founder and chief of this kingdom also had undergone a parallel evolution. The image of the Messiah as a successful general had been supplemented by aspects far more disconcerting and even apparently contradictory. The Messiah was to be the Lord, but he was also to be the Servant, the Servant of Yahweh par excellence, who would suffer as so many of the Prophets had suffered before him, and his wounds would heal us. From a heart of stone, he could make a heart of flesh. He would come in all sweetness of spirit to gather his people together.

The recent marvelous discovery of the Dead Sea Scrolls proves to us how well these teachings had been understood. The complete decipherment of the manuscripts will teach us many surprising things, and we

wait for it with impatience. The portrait of the persecuted and suffering master of doctrine proves to what degree the more fervent souls in
Israel were prepared to receive a teaching and example that were to be,
precisely, those of Jesus. One cannot help imagining what the destiny
of Israel might have been if the mystical sect of the Essenes had triumphed in influence over the juridical sect of the Pharisees. And what
would the destiny of France have been if, in the fourteenth century,
the spirit of Joan of Arc had triumphed over the spirit of the jurists of
Philip the Fair, who were the begetters of that monster the modern
state?

Nothing, however, in the history of Israel or in the prophecies was
abandoned. The Israelites knew very well that God does not lie and
that He is faithful to His promises, that the Messiah would be at once
humiliated and glorious, both servant and leader in war. But every
devout Jew knew that the war of wars was the one declared against
Satan, that every foreign domination, that of Egypt, that of Assyria,
now that of Rome, was no more than the image and manifestation of
the universal domination of the Devil over this world of which he is
the prince. What the Jews expected first of all from their Messiah was
a decisive victory over Satan. All the rest would follow, but the coming
of the Kingdom of God could begin only with that. This is why the
account of the temptation of Christ in the Synoptics has a truly prophetic significance.

It is a remarkable fact that the Judaeo-Christian tradition has been
imprinted so strongly in our minds that it is impossible to give any profound explanation of our civilization, even in its aberrations, without
referring to that tradition. I believe it is impossible, for example, to
understand the quasi-mystical reality of the French Revolution or of
the Communist revolutions without relating them to what the Jews
called the Apocalypse.

The Greek word *apocalypse* may be translated as the revelation of a
mystery hidden in God, and this revelation brings with it such an explosive force of maturity, conflict, and emergence that *apocalypse* could
equally well be translated as "revolution." When one thinks of the
weight of hope conveyed by that strange phrase used by the *Interna-
tionales*, "the Great Night," one cannot but think of what the apocalyptic prophecies called "the Great Day of Yahweh." By Apocalypse,
the Jews understood, in fact, the end of a world, an epoch, a cycle, and
at the same time the grievous coming of an entirely new order, world,
epoch, cycle. It was the violent and warlike overthrow of the Devil's
reign and the triumphant inauguration of the reign of God. Christian

missionaries have wasted centuries trying to convert China; the Communist Apocalypse conquered China in a few years. This perhaps proves that the Judaeo-Christian Apocalypse, even when deviated and transposed to the natural order, has lost none of its revolutionary virtue, but it also proves that the Christian missionaries no longer understood the Apocalypse. Otherwise, perhaps it would have been they who converted the Chinese. All must be done over again.

I can do nothing about it, there is nothing anyone can do about it, the Christian religion is essentially warlike or revolutionary—the words amount to the same. Revolution, like war, is a simple art, consisting solely in execution. The preaching of Jesus, that is, his announcement of the coming of the Kingdom of God, was also a simple art, consisting solely in execution. His whole public ministry was conducted like the campaign of a great soldier, or better still like a resistance or revolution, one of those very modern enterprises of which Valéry says, "Carried out by a few chosen men, acting in teams, who produced in a few instants, at an unforeseen time and place, events of overwhelming importance." Christ's exorcisms, his miracles, his revelations, his declarations, even his appearances and disappearances, often have this sudden character of electrifying events that overwhelm the adversary, leaving him helpless, and yet they have the joyous nature of a liberation.

If the Kingdom whose coming Jesus announced had been of a purely temporal order, the enterprise would have been a failure: Jesus failed to secure the throne and lost his life in the adventure. But all his actions and all his words were calculated to strip away Israel's hope of terrestrial power of any kind and to transfer the conquest of the Kingdom to a realm beyond this world and beyond death by a victory, not over any terrestrial army, even that of Rome, but over the demons and Satan, their chieftain. The reach of Jesus' action and of his words is infinitely greater than that of earthly conquerors. His strategy and his tactics, even if they are not very different in style, have a wholly different objective from theirs. It is true that the warlike action of Christ is essentially subversive, it crosses frontiers as though by magic, and it is from within that it causes fortresses to crumble. It does not, for all that, claim to take place wholly outside time; it riddles time and history with holes that open infinite perspectives on eternity.

In our present life, we are like fish caught in a net, still completely immersed in the sea, at the moment when the fishermen begin to draw that net out of the water. The fish are still in the sea, but they are captives of an action that will inevitably end by drawing them out of it. Modern literature has a very lively sense of this captivity and of the net that imprisons us, only it refuses to be aware of the gentle motion that draws us all together toward the shores of life, or if it feels it, it feels it as a "journey to the end of the night." This is what John calls preferring the shadows to the light. I can very well understand that the fish experience anguish at having to leave the water forever. To leave the sea represents absolute death to them. And so they still prefer the anguish of the net in the sea to the anguish of the light and of the liberation which for them is illusory.

But the Gospel assures us that beyond death and the anguish of the light there is a new life, divine and also more truly human, which awaits us, even us. "For as in Adam all die, even so in Christ shall all be made alive. . . . Then cometh the end, when he shall have delivered up the Kingdom to God, even the Father; when he shall have put down all rule and all authority in power. For he must reign till he hath put all enemies under his feet. . . . And when all things shall be subdued unto him, then shall the Son also himself be subject unto Him that put all things under him, that God may be all in all." 1 Cor. 15:22, 24-25, 28

CHAPTER XV

The Church in Bud

THIS would be the place to interrupt this narrative in order to explain to the reader what Jesus taught. I would state the content of that teaching and explain its essential novelty within a tradition not renounced but consummated; I would describe the style of the teaching and speak of the literary genre that is called the parable. But an explanation of this sort would quickly take on the proportions of a book within a book. The rhythm I am trying to maintain would be permanently broken.

Although there is no one in the world who is more completely identified with his teaching than Jesus, it is nevertheless true that the history of Jesus Christ and his doctrine are two things that are perfectly distinguishable in the mind. To maintain the equilibrium and the movement of the present book I am compelled to exclude from it the exposition of Jesus' teaching, but I am prepared to return to it later in a second book which I shall entitle *The Doctrine of Jesus Christ*. If one cannot carry the whole cargo in a single voyage, two voyages are necessary. I therefore limit myself here to invoking that part of Jesus' teaching that seems to me indispensable for the understanding of the history of Jesus Christ, and so I shall avoid going beyond my present subject.

Matthew, writing primarily for the Jews, composed the Gospel that is par excellence that of "The Kingdom of God." He built the structure of his narrative around this notion, which is traditional in his country. He wished to prove that Jesus personified and crowned the hope of his nation. His Gospel is like a face turned toward the past, not in search of a vanished time but in the tranquil assurance that past time is recovered entire in its perfect accomplishment and that the past has done its work, which was to give birth to the present, which it was carrying. This Gospel is the joyful cry of that delivery.

Luke, a Greek writing for the gentiles, faces toward the future. He talks, to be sure, of the Kingdom of God because he is a historian and Christ talked of it, but without the word's ever being pronounced, his Gospel is par excellence the Gospel of the Church. It is unquestionably the one in which the architecture is the most complicated, the most harmonious, the most solid and most significant. It resembles the architecture of a Gothic cathedral. In Luke everything is in its place; the smallest detail, the least word has been weighed like fine gold; each element supports the whole and is organically incorporated in it.

It is known that the Synoptics pursue a sequence that is geographical rather than chronological: they tell first of all everything that happened in Galilee, where Jesus began his ministry, then everything that happened in Judea, where it ended. Indeed, if John had not intervened, much later on, to give the details of the chronology and the comings and the goings of our Lord, we might believe that the public life of Jesus lasted only one year and that in the course of his ministry he went up to Jerusalem only once, to die there.

But if, following the rule of the three Synoptics, Luke tells the facts in an equally elliptical manner, he selects them and arranges them with care; he puts them together most skillfully, that is, most artistically, with a view to producing a certain very pure effect, with such success that sometimes the unfolding of the most indisputable, real events is redoubled in impact through their meticulous and intentional arrangement, by the supplementary significance of parable. In the course of my narrative I shall have occasion to explain this more fully.

We have seen that John commences his Gospel with the same words that open the Book of Genesis and the whole Bible: "In the beginning . . ." Luke, by an analogous imitation, which I believe was equally conscious, when he begins his narrative of the public life of Christ, tells how he was expelled from Nazareth. The reminder here is of the vocation of Abraham, which serves as backdrop.

The Lord said to Abraham: "Leave your country, your kinsfolk and your father's house, for the land which I will show you; I will make a great nation of you. . . . I will bless them that bless you, and curse them that curse you. In you shall all the nations of the earth be blessed." Abraham went away as the Lord had commanded him. . . .   Gen. 12:1-4

Let us return to Luke. After the baptism, during which Jesus' vocation has been solemnly proclaimed, and after the temptation in the desert, in which it has been solemnly confirmed in brutal single combat, Jesus returns to the small village, the place where he grew up, the place where he has always been known, where his mother and all his relatives live. And he is brutally driven out. In fact Luke telescopes what seems to have been three visits to Nazareth. What he wants to show—and this is the thing that gives his account the force of parable—is that from the moment that Jesus received an absolutely authentic vocation from God it was necessary for him, like Abraham, to break with his natural clan. Here, then, is his account. It is a diptych: Jesus informs his relatives of his vocation; second panel, he is ejected from the clan.

Luke 4:16-22 And he came to Nazareth, where he had been brought up; and according to his custom, he entered the synagogue on the Sabbath and stood up to read. And the volume of Isaias the prophet was handed to him. And after he opened the volume, he found the place where it was written, "The Spirit of the Lord is upon me because he has anointed me; to bring good news to the poor he has sent me, to proclaim to the captives release, and sight to the blind; to set at liberty the oppressed, to proclaim the acceptable year of the Lord, and the day of recompense."

And closing the volume, he gave it back to the attendant and sat down. And the eyes of all in the synagogue were gazing on him. But he began to say to them, "Today this Scripture has been fulfilled in your hearing." And all bore him witness, and marveled at the words of grace that came from his mouth. And they said, "Is not this Joseph's son?"

Thus the first reaction was not bad. But after that first movement of admiration, the parochial family spirit quickly reasserted itself; it is a spirit that blasphemes everything that excels it. "Why, this young man is one of us, how can he amount to anything?" Luke continues.

Luke 4:23-30 And he said to them, "You will surely quote me this proverb, 'Physician, cure thyself! Whatever things we have heard of as done in Capharnaum, do here also in thy own country'!" But he said, "Amen I say to you, no prophet is acceptable in his own country. In truth I say to you, there were many widows in Israel in the days of Elias, when heaven was shut up for three years and six months, and a great famine came over all the land; and to none of them was Elias sent, but rather to a widowed woman in Sarepta of Sidon. And there were many lepers in Israel in the time of Eliseus the prophet; and not one of them was cleansed, but only Naaman the Syrian."

And all in the synagogue, as they heard these things, were filled with wrath. And they rose up and put him forth out of the town, and led him to the brow of the hill, on which their town was built, that they might throw him down headlong. But he, passing through their midst, went his way.

No matter! Jesus has performed his duty even toward his own village; indeed, he has begun by doing that. He has been completely candid; while commenting on Isaia—"The spirit of the Lord is upon me . . ."—he must have told of the theophany at the Jordan, when the Spirit descended upon him in the corporeal form of a dove. It is first of all to his own people, his neighbors, his cousins, and his childhood friends that he has explained "the good news for the poor," his Gospel of forgiveness, liberation, and mercy. They will have none of it.

Just as mothers always see their children as little ones, childhood friends judge one another on the basis of their common mediocrity. What was Jesus to them? The son of the lowly carpenter Joseph and, just as for Renan, nothing more. For them the world of social appearances was tightly closed on itself, close-knit, consistent; how were they to go beyond it? They had indeed heard rumors of the first miracles performed by Jesus at Capharnaum, and they made jokes about them while drinking their mint tea or whatever it was they used as an apéritif. Today it is at cocktail parties that prophets are executed. And then they challenged Jesus to perform in their presence some prodigy, which would not have proved any more convincing.

Of course we owe respect and gratitude to our origins. The fault of the family, the clan, the fatherland, is not that they exist; their fault lies in their closed and totalitarian character. They exist, but they want to be the only ones to exist and they want nothing else to exist outside themselves. This certainly is excessive. And that is why Jesus, immediately taking the irrefutable viewpoint of God, who sheds His sun and His rain on the unjust as well as the just, reminds his fellow countrymen that, for God, a pagan widow from Sidon may be the equal of all the widows of Israel, and a pagan leper from Syria may deserve to be cured rather than any of the lepers of Israel.

No man is a prophet in his own country; he is made to see this clearly. All these people, his childhood friends, his cousins, his relations, his neighbors, filled with fury at being told to their faces that something besides themselves exists, jostle Jesus, drag him by force to a precipice outside the town, and try to throw him down. They never question themselves, they have no inferiority complexes, for them instinct triumphs over everything, justifies everything, including murder. This scene of extreme violence at the outset of Jesus' ministry prefigures what will happen when, at its end, he will be led outside Jerusalem to be put to death. News of this must have caused the small homeland to rejoice.

As I was walking along the paths of the Père Lachaise cemetery in

Paris, on my way to pray at the graves of certain writers I admire, and even some I admire less, I was struck, not so much by that silent assembly of famous men, as by the inscriptions on their ugly and absurd stone monuments: "Family . . . Family . . . Family . . ." The family is a mortician; in the cemetery it holds its triumph and proclaims its victory at the top of its voice. It is there that it repossesses all its own, the avaricious sons along with the prodigal sons; it puts them permanently in the right order, it holds them close and will not let them go; may they rest in peace! More truly than it is the beginning, the family is the end of all.

Thus, like Abraham and for the same reason, because of his vocation, Jesus begins his public life by breaking with his native clan. "Go forth from your country, from your family, from the house of your father, go, go I tell you, go. . . ." Henceforth, poorer than the birds of the sky who have their nests, more impoverished than the wild beasts who have their lairs, the Son of Man will not own even a stone on which to rest his head. When he announces this, he speaks true as always: the stone on which he will rest in his tomb will have been loaned to him by another. On that tomb no family name will be written. Jesus will not be laid to rest either in Bethlehem, where he was born, or in Nazareth, where he grew up, but in Jerusalem, which is the center of the world.

This was how the vocation of Jesus Christ was affirmed. Just as Abraham had taken his nephew with him in his suite, Jesus takes with him in his adventure two of his cousins and, very naturally, his mother. But the gates of Nazareth were permanently closed behind him. He will never more set foot there. There are places to which one may not ever return.

—————

Once Jesus has freed himself from his own people and once the ground is cleared, he immediately sets about founding his own Church, just as Abraham had founded a new clan.

Luke composes his Gospel like a man loading a boat. He has assembled as many facts as possible, he has weighed them, verified them, judged them as though for Noah's Ark; he will put only one couple of each species aboard; those he retains he arranges in his Gospel with a view to a final equilibrium which, once it is seen, is altogether satisfying. This could be systematism. But Luke's touch is so light, his placing of each object so judicious, that one allows oneself to be borne along by the rhythm of his work.

In his narrative of the ministry in Galilee, Luke manages to give us a complete picture, a delicate and suggestive painting, of the primitive Church and its founder. For the Church arose quite naturally around Jesus, through his authority. Luke is equally careful to indicate the traditional nature of this establishment that supervened within the spiritual and carnal continuity of Israel, its novelty and its universal character, its hierarchy, its function, the solidity of its foundations, and its final purpose. But Luke is a poet and usually prefers to suggest rather than to assert. He proceeds in his narrative like one walking on water. I have a very vivid sense of this, I who am trying to follow him in my clumsy sabots.

Aside from the unhappy episode in Nazareth—which is, however, only too human, once one understands what relations are—Jesus' ministry in Galilee seems to have been a triumph. It is true that Jesus performed many miracles. But it is touching to notice that what seems to have struck the crowd most is the extraordinary authority of this man. It is this authority that gave birth to the Church, that is, to the assembly of men of good will around Jesus Christ. "And they were astonished at his teaching," Luke says, "for his word was with authority." He possessed such power that the attraction he exercised through his words, his deeds, and his gestures was mingled with dread. "And amazement came upon all, and they discussed it with one another, saying, 'What is this word? For with authority and power he commands the unclean spirits, and they come out.' And rumor concerning him went forth into every place of the region roundabout." *Luke 4:32*

Luke 4:36-37

He guarded his own liberty no less jealously. Suddenly he would disappear, he would escape into solitude in order to pray for long periods. His Church has its foundation, too, in his prayers. The crowds would search for him. When they had found him again they would listen to him avidly, never weary, never disappointed. They tried to detain him. But he, for his part, harkened only to his vocation. "But he said to them, 'To the other towns also I must proclaim the kingdom of God, for this is why I have been sent.'" Everywhere he succeeded; this was the golden age of his ministry. In the air were the joy of spring and the gaiety of betrothals. It was amid this happiness that the primitive Church was born. It is this atmosphere of delight that John, in his fashion, has tried to describe in his account of the joyous miracle of the changing of water into wine at the marriage in Cana. *Luke 4:43*

One cannot think without gratitude of these Jewish crowds—containing, of course, many pagans living in that country—who were the first to admire Jesus, to love him, who followed him, forgetful of food and drink and fatigue, who pressed upon him from all sides to touch

Luke 6:19 the hem of his garment: "And all the crowd were trying to touch him, for the power went forth from him and healed all." This naïve multitude pressed so hard upon him that one day he had to go aboard a boat in order to separate himself from them and speak to them. It is precisely in these circumstances that a miracle occurred which, in Luke's account of it, prefigures the essence of the Church of Jesus Christ.

Luke 5:1-10 Now it came to pass, while the crowds were pressing upon him to hear the word of God, that he was standing by Lake Genesareth. And he saw two boats moored by the lake, but the fishermen had left them and were washing their nets. And getting into one of the boats, the one that was Simon's, he asked him to put out a little from the land. And sitting down . . . he said to Simon, "Put out into the deep, and lower your nets for a catch."

And Simon answered and said to him, "Master, the whole night through we have toiled and have taken nothing; but at thy word I will lower the net." And when they had done so, they enclosed a great number of fishes, but their net was breaking. And they beckoned to their comrades in the other boat to come and help them. And they came and filled both the boats, so that they began to sink.

But when Simon Peter saw this, he fell down at Jesus' knees, saying, "Depart from me, for I am a sinful man, O Lord." For he and all who were with him were amazed at the catch of fish they had made; and so were also James and John, the sons of Zebedee, who were partners with Simon. And Jesus said to Simon, "Do not be afraid; henceforth thou shalt catch men."

In recounting this miracle, Luke is aiming at a precise effect. He does not, to be sure, ignore the fact that Simon Peter was not alone, but he organizes his picture around him. What interests him is the miracle itself and the revealing symbolism of Peter's mission, emphasized by Jesus himself: "Thou shalt catch men." But what concerns Luke above all is the over-all effect, which he contrives so well by relegating everything else to abstraction: Jesus, upright in Peter's boat, which is filled with fish to the sinking point, and Peter kneeling before him and confessing himself a sinner. This, in the Gospel, is Peter's first confession; there are others.

Naturally, since I am a Catholic, I perceive in Luke's way of describing this scene a preinvestiture of the first pope. Non-Catholics will not follow me that far. They cannot. The thing that is terribly disquieting about reading the Gospel today is that each reader's position is so firmly held that everything becomes a matter of controversy, a wholly Platonic controversy moreover. . . . This is trench warfare, immobilized for centuries, with symbolic exchanges of cannon fire over the heads of the combatants, who meanwhile are playing cards because they have nothing else to do. Oh, to make this war suddenly a war of surprise and movement. . . . No matter! This book is not a book of controversy, at least I would not have it so. But, having had some experience in motion pictures, I know about the composition of a scene and I know that in a well-made film a major scene is always intended to say something precise because its purpose is to reveal a persistent and increasing intent on the author's part.

To me it seems that Luke has tried to give us here the first symbolic image of the essential nature of the Church: a boat on the sea beneath the sky, not a pleasure craft for sunbathing or water-skiing, but a professional fisherman's boat, seaworthy in all weathers and all latitudes. This vessel is full of fish. Jesus is standing in it, Peter is kneeling before him, and, for the first time in this Gospel, he calls Jesus "Lord." All night Peter has cast his net without making a catch; on the sole word of Jesus he casts the net once more, with the miraculous result that is known.

One must cast his net one time more than he has thought necessary.

———————

Up to this point what has Jesus done?

He has acted exactly like a great strategist or a great statesman who has a major ambition and who employs the concrete means to achieve that goal. He has broken with his relations, who would have smothered him. He has attracted to himself sharp and questioning attention. He has confirmed his authority through miracles. He has made clear his position as the victorious enemy of physical evil—sickness and suffering—and of moral evil—sin. He has thus assured himself of the enthusiastic support of the people. He has presented himself as a revolutionary, giving to the Law a personal interpretation, thus elevating himself above the Law and its official interpreters. He has confirmed his unique and supreme legitimacy by contesting that of the others. He has put together a company of his own and arranged it as a hierarchy: in the center twelve apostles and, in the center of the center, Simon Peter. He has defined his program in a splendid discourse, the "Sermon on the Mount."

This does not go without opposition, an opposition, moreover, that he seems to cultivate in order to create around himself what we today would call increasing "suspense." And now, behold, he performs two master strokes that manifest his prodigious power and renew the popular enthusiasm: a healing at a distance and a resurrection from the dead. Here, at an unforeseen moment and in an unforeseen place are the overwhelming events that reveal the character of a strategy magnificently imaginative and of infallible efficacy.

All this, however, is no more than the outer aspect of Jesus' action; the core remains more difficult to perceive.

At a given time, in a given place, there are words that produce unanimity; it is not always possible to say exactly why. Today in the East the word "socialism" produces unanimity, and in the West the words "expansion" or "democratic freedoms" produce it. In the third world, the words "independence" or "neutralism" are very close to producing unanimity. In Israel at the time of Jesus the words "Kingdom of God" produced it. As always, it is what these words imply that creates the difficulty.

On this latter point, Jesus proceeds softly, by delicate and successive touches, in an absolutely nonoverwhelming way. There is indeed a striking contrast between the audacious strategy of his action and the cautious revelation of his message and of his personality—that is, almost cautious, in view of the vastness of his claims: to be the master of the Sabbath, to be above the Law, to forgive sins, to be called Lord, a title hitherto reserved to Yahweh, to call himself "the Son of Man" with all the celestial and apocalyptic implications that those words entail. . . . Those who were already Jesus' enemies must have taken him for a megalomaniac; it was only modesty, by comparison with his further demands.

By healing the servant of a centurion, Jesus clearly expressed his admiration for a pagan: "I say unto you, I have not found so great faith, no, not in Israel." Thus he showed that the door to the Kingdom was faith, and this door would be open without distinction to all, to Jews and to pagans. It is here that one can see how profoundly Luke is a disciple of Saint Paul. The following chapters in the Gospel of Luke are perfectly summarized by these lines from Corinthians: "For the Jews ask for signs, and the Greeks look for 'wisdom'; but we, for our part, preach a crucified Christ—to the Jews indeed a scandal and to the Gentiles foolishness, but to those who are called, both Jews and Greeks, Christ, the power of God and the wisdom of God. For the foolishness of God is wiser than men, and the weakness of God is stronger than men."

I say that this famous text from Saint Paul is a parallel to the development of the Gospel according to Luke from this point in his narrative. The text of Saint Paul gives us the true key to Luke's expert construction and development of his theme. We find once more in Luke the same balancing of ideas and of words, *miracles–scandal, wisdom–folly,*

Luke 7:9

1 Cor. 1:22-25

and, at the center of gravity of this scale, the person of *Christ crucified,* resolving these antinomies in himself: in Saint Paul, "Christ, the power of God and the wisdom of God"; in Luke, "the Christ of God." The text of Saint Paul is the outline for the narrative of Luke; it gives the latter its architecture and its full significance.

"The Jews ask for signs." There is no shadow of reproach in these words of Saint Paul. The miracles were to be the sign par excellence that would authenticate the mission of the Messiah. Any Jew attentive to his tradition could have said to Christ what Nicodemus said to him in the course of a nocturnal conversation: "For no man can do these miracles that thou dost, except God be with him." It had always been agreed that the Messiah would perform many miracles and that these would be the means by which the Jews would recognize him as having been sent by God. The Jews would have been lacking in their duty as trustees of the promises and the plans of God if they had not demanded miracles from the Messiah. Jesus was not at all offended by this demand; he answered it superabundantly: "The same works that I do, bear witness of me, that the Father hath sent me." And again: "If I had not done among them the works which none other man did, they had not had sin." John 3:2

John 5:36

John 15:24

And so the Jews were perfectly right in demanding miracles from Christ. John the Baptist, who very obviously and ostentatiously represents the tradition of Israel, the prophecy of Israel, the requirements of Israel, was compelled to take part in this game. Luke reports:

And John summoned two of his disciples and sent them to the Lord, saying, "Art thou he who is to come, or shall we look for another?" And when the men had come to him, they said, "John the Baptist has sent us to thee, saying, 'Art thou he who is to come, or shall we look for another?' " Luke 7:19-23

In that very hour he cured many of diseases, afflictions and evil spirits, and to many who were blind he granted sight. And he answered and said to them, "Go and report to John what you have heard and seen: the blind see, the lame walk, the lepers are cleansed, the deaf hear, the dead rise, the poor have the gospel preached to them. *And blessed is he who is not scandalized in me.*"

There has been much soul-searching to explain this message from John. Since John had already recognized Jesus at the Jordan, since he had already designated him as "the Lamb of God which taketh away the sins of the world," why did he now put to Jesus a question expressing uncertainty? It would seem clear to me that John believed in Jesus, that he believed in him with prophetic and theological faith, but why should John's faith be different in nature and manner from our faith?

Bernanos used to say: "Faith? It consists of twenty-four hours of doubt minus one minute of hope." And God knows Bernanos had faith. . . . Moreover, faith can take a different form in each individual. For me faith would be rather twenty-four hours of certainty minus one blazing minute of despair. As for John, I think that, in prison and facing death, he wanted to put his disciples in a situation to judge for themselves and according to Jewish requirements and Jewish tradition and orthodoxy, the Messianity of Jesus.

It is indeed in this sense that Jesus understands John's message. The striking thing is that he does not reply either immediately or directly to the message. He begins by dazzling the two messengers by a fireworks display of miracles: the Jews ask for signs—well and good, there would be a downpour of them. Then Jesus cites a Messianic text from Isaia which attributes precisely to the Messiah the gift of miracles; he even makes a montage of several texts. But chapter thirty-five of Isaia, to which he especially refers, is a typically Messianic and eschatological psalm. Finally, after this brilliant sequence of miracles and messianic citations, Jesus concludes by a solemn beatitude: "Blessed is he who is not scandalized in me." And so the opposition *miracles–scandal*, emphasized by Luke, does not come from Saint Paul, it comes from Jesus himself.

When the two messengers have departed, Jesus insists on the personality of John and defines his place in the economy of salvation. "I say to you, among those born of women there is not a greater prophet than John the Baptist; yet the least in the kingdom of God is greater than he." "Until John came, there were the Law and the Prophets; since then the kingdom of God is being preached and everyone is forcing his way into it." The line that Saint Paul will take up with so much eloquence continues to be defined: miracles, scandal, virtue or power.

It is impossible to overemphasize Christ's insistence on attaching himself—himself, his mission and activity—to this final link in the tradition of Israel, John the Baptist. This is he of whom it is written, "Behold, I send my messenger before thy face, who shall make ready thy way before thee." By solemnly joining himself to John, Jesus endorses the whole tradition of Israel, he agrees to answer the demands of that tradition: the Jews ask for signs. It is commonly said that Jesus rejected Israel and that Israel rejected him. This oversimplified view may be convenient; I consider it completely false. It is true that there was conflict, conflict to the death, between Jesus and the intellectual elite of his nation, the Pharisees and also the Sadducees. I shall return to this. But in the time of Jesus did that intellectual elite represent the whole na-

Luke 7:28

Luke 16:16

Luke 7:27
Mal. 3:1

tion? Was it the authentic representative? Was not John the Baptist a more typical representative, a more authentic and more complete representative, of his nation, of its vocation and of its living tradition?

What I believe is this, that in this essentially religious nation, all of whose national problems had to do with religion, John and his baptism, no doubt with the Essenes in the background, created a split in the nation as did the Dreyfus affair in France at the end of the last century or as did the defeat and the Vichy regime in France during World War II. Jesus says, "And when they had heard him, all the people and the publicans justified God, having been baptized with the baptism of John. But the Pharisees and the lawyers, not having been baptized by him, brought to naught God's purpose concerning themselves." *Luke 7:29-30*

And to make himself better understood Jesus tells a parable showing what he held against the men of the law: they are the *blasé,* that is, people who in the course of time have hardened their hearts even against what should touch them most. Woe unto them, for neither the muse of comedy nor the muse of tragedy can extend a helping hand to them; they are lost equally to laughter and to tears, they are lost to humanity and, since they are lost to humanity, what use can God be expected to make of them? "They are like children sitting in the market place, calling to one another and saying, 'We have piped to you, and you have not danced; we have sung dirges, and you have not wept.' " *Luke 7:32*

John's baptism was a sign by which those who held fast to the mystic, prophetic, and apocalyptic tradition of Israel made themselves known. Those who received it agreed with Yahweh. The Gospel clearly sides with them. The decipherment of the enormous mass of the Dead Sea Scrolls may well bring us wonderful surprises. In the tradition of Israel why should one feel compelled to take sides with the Pharisees and against the Essenes?

"The Greeks look for 'wisdom.' " As he had just said that the disciples of John had justified Yahweh, so Jesus now says with a certain solemnity, "But wisdom is justified of all her children." And in order to illustrate this word of Christ, Luke at once narrates one of the most beautiful scenes in the Gospel, the story of the repentant sinner who is forgiven, the sinner whom a very old and credible tradition identifies with Mary Magdalene. It is this tradition that I follow.

The place assigned to Mary Magdalene in the Gospel according to Luke makes her the exact counterpart of John the Baptist: as John represents the Messianic demand for miracles from Jesus, Mary Magdalene represents the Greek search for wisdom. The architects of the Middle Ages recognized perfectly the close relationship between these two persons. The narthex of the basilica at Vézelay is dedicated to Saint John the Baptist, and it nobly dominates the structure, but the basilica itself is dedicated to Mary Magdalene.

Tiberias was a cosmopolitan city, very thoroughly Hellenized; the court of Herod, Tetrarch of Galilee, was a copy of the court of the Greek emperors and princes at a period when fashion and snobbery were modeled on Greek customs and Greek culture. Mary Magdalene, "a sinner in the city" in the eyes of the Jews, was pagan in manner if not actually by nationality, and this fact alone would have made her a horror to the Pharisees. Jesus receives her, nevertheless, lets himself be touched by her, allows himself further to be moved by her tears of repentance and by her violent, adoring love. She breaks an amphora of precious perfume and pours it over the feet of the Lord in supreme and silent homage. In the course of this modest banquet, she is, more truly than Diotima in Plato's *Symposium,* the Daughter of Wisdom who recognizes in Jesus wisdom itself incarnate, just as John the Baptist had recognized in him the wonder-working Messiah who had received the baptism of the Holy Spirit and the investiture as Son of God.

And Jesus concludes this beautiful scene by saying to the master of the house, who is a Pharisee, "Her sins, which are many, are forgiven her for she has loved much." As Ronald Knox—whose commentaries are so profoundly intelligent, so modest, and so precise—says in this connection, Magdalene's love at this point is not yet prompted by gratitude, it is a love that comes before her forgiveness, it is a violent love like a great hunger or a great thirst: this woman is seized by a mortal need for security and for pardon and, with infallible instinct, recognizes in Jesus, as clearly as John the Baptist recognized it, "the Lamb of God who takes away the sin of the world" and who will purify her. Here is an unforeseen expansion of Greek wisdom, which had never so much as conceived of the idea of sin.

Mary Magdalene, her hands always filled with perfumes, moves throughout this Gospel with nimble step; in all the glory of royal beauty she visits garden banquets, seeking wisdom, love, and joy. As it had been formerly with the Three Kings, so now with her everything is courtesy; the whole pagan world prostrates itself at the feet of Jesus and proclaims him Master of Wisdom, as John had proclaimed him the Messiah. The parallel between Saint Paul and Saint Luke, fully expressed in these two astonishing persons, finally finds its center of grav-

Luke 7:47

ity in Jesus: "The Jews ask for signs, and the Greeks look for 'wisdom'; but we, for our part, preach a crucified Christ. . . ."

Nevertheless neither the word "wisdom" nor the idea was new, even in Israel. Their introduction, however, had been relatively recent, contemporaneous with the idea of royalty, when Israel, already established as a clan, had gone on to become a city too. The fatherland of wisdom is not the clan; it is the city. The "wisdom" of Israel began as a collection of empirical proverbs, rather commonplace in character, in the sense in which people talk about "the wisdom of mankind." But the speculative restlessness and religious preoccupation of this people could not rest there. With the kings of the earth, and particularly Solomon, "King of the Jews," being celebrated for their wisdom, the Jews quickly asked themselves whether God, their God, also had a wisdom and what might be the relationship between their God and His wisdom.

There was also the inevitable influence of Hellenism. That most advanced of human civilizations was in process of conquering the world, less through force of arms than by peaceful diffusion of intelligence and of art. It was characterized by a search for wisdom and familiarity with it: that is exactly what the word "philosophy" means. The Jews dreamt of a wisdom of their God above that of Socrates and Plato, as the heavens are above the earth. They forbade all plastic arts through fear of idolatry. The wisdom of their God became in fact the art of their God, which from the beginning had taken part in His councils in creating and organizing the universe. God had created the world through His Word, He had also created it through His wisdom: the Jews identified the wisdom with the Word of their God.

The Lord begot me, the first-born of his ways, the forerunner of his prodigies of long ago; from of old I was poured forth, from the first, before the earth. When there were no depths I was brought forth, when there were no fountains or springs of water; before the mountains were settled into place, before the hills, I was brought forth; while as yet the earth and the fields were not made, nor the first clods of the world. When he established the heavens I was there, when he marked out the vault over the face of the deep; when he made firm the skies above, when he fixed fast the foundations of the earth; when he set for the sea its limit, so that the waters should not transgress his command; then was I beside him as his craftsman, and I was his delight day by day, playing before him all the while, playing on the surface of his earth and I found delight in the sons of men.

Prov. 8:22-31

Moreover wisdom is explicitly described as issuing from the mouth of the Most High. One thing in particular strikes me in this vast context; it is that wisdom is compared to one of those liturgical perfumes poured out beneath the tent that sheltered the Presence of the God of Israel. When Luke writes that "all the children of wisdom rendered homage to Him," one can see how this silent but fragrant homage of Mary Magdalene may perhaps have had a range of adoration one cannot properly understand except in reference to a Presence that was the millennial center of Israel's worship. Mary Magdalene, like John the Baptist, went straight to what is essential in Jesus, to the flaming mystery of his Incarnation, redemptive of all sins.

Luke 8:35   What better homage to wisdom than to put oneself to school "at his feet"? The Bible of Jerusalem quite properly recognizes that to place oneself at the feet of a sage is explicitly to become his disciple and to proclaim oneself as such. Saint Paul will say later on that he had been Acts 22:3 "formed at the feet of Gamaliel." How can one fail to notice that, in this account of the sinful woman who was forgiven, Luke, at the risk of overweighting his style but with the determination to emphasize the situation, mentions the feet of Christ seven times in order to make clear that this woman has become the disciple par excellence of divine wisdom—a fact that he will repeat once more apropos of Mary at Bethany Luke 10:39 when she, having "seated herself at the feet of the Lord, was listening to his word." The Evangelists are precise writers.

———————

Now Luke goes on to develop the theme of *Wisdom–Word-of-God*, Luke 8:1-3 as he developed the theme of *Miracles*. He writes of Jesus: "And it came to pass afterwards, that he was journeying through towns and villages, preaching and proclaiming the good news of the kingdom of God. And with him were the Twelve, and certain women who had been cured of evil spirits and infirmities: Mary, who is called the Magdalene, from whom seven devils had gone out, and Joanna, the wife of Chuza, Herod's steward, and Susanna, and many others, who used to provide for them out of their means."

Twelve men, the Apostles, on the whole rather simple and poor: among them, nevertheless, a tax-collector, that is, one of those people who were particularly despised by the Jews and considered as sinners. Certain women, rather rich and privileged, certainly elegant and beautiful, accustomed to the courts of kings, and first among these Mary Magdalene. The caravan must have been a rather sensational sight. What did that matter to Christ? He had chosen his traveling companions, not for their fortunes, even if they happened to have them, not for their beauty or their elegance, even though one or other of the women in his suite might be superb, not for their intelligence or their adroitness, not even for their reputations, since those of Matthew and of Mary Magdalene had been ruined, but for their receptivity as disciples, their docility—that is to say, their faith in him, their love for him, their aptitude in being disciples of wisdom and servants of the Word.

Jesus now propounds a series of parables. The parable was a literary genre held very much in honor among the Semites, and Jesus was fond of enfolding his revelations in the enigma of the parable.

Luke here reports a parable which I shall not pass over because, as Ronald Knox has noted, it announces in veiled terms Jesus' program for a universal Church. By virtue of this fact it has the weight of a historical action as well as of a lesson. Jesus expounds the central conception of the *Word-Wisdom* of God. This parable goes further perhaps than is generally imagined. Here it is:

Now when a very great crowd was gathering together and men from every town were resorting to him, he said in a parable: "The sower went out to sow his seed. And as he sowed, some seed fell by the wayside and was trodden under foot, and the birds of the air ate it up. And other seed fell upon the rock, and as soon as it had sprung up it withered away, because it had no moisture. And other seed fell among thorns, and the thorns sprang up with it and choked it. And other seed fell upon good ground, and sprang up and yielded fruit a hundredfold." . . .

"Now the parable is this: the seed is the word of God. And those by the wayside are they who have heard; then the devil comes and takes away the word from their heart, that they may not believe and be saved. Now those upon the rock are they who, when they have heard, receive the word with joy; and these have no root, but believe for a while, and in time of temptation fall away. And that which fell among the thorns, these are they who have heard, and as they go their way are choked by the cares and riches and pleasures of life, and their fruit does not ripen. But that upon good ground, these are they who, with a right and good heart, having heard the word, hold it fast, and bear fruit in patience."

Luke 8:4-15

The explanation that Jesus himself has given of this remarkable parable is sufficiently clear. Nevertheless, if it be permitted to meditate and to seek out all its implications, one is struck by the key to the parable: the *seed*, that is the Word of God. Consider the pact of the ancient covenant in which God so strongly insists upon the *seed* of Abraham. In the first words of the parable itself, the solemnity of the repetition calls our attention to the eminent dignity of the personage placed on the stage: "*The sower* went out to *sow* his *seed.*" It is *the sower* who is in question, and not *a sower*, it is the Sower by antonomasia, that is, it is God Himself, since the seed is the Word of God, in short, Christ himself.

We have come once more to one of those points of confluence where the strategy of Jesus Christ blazes out, revealing him. He has suggested that he is the Temple, that is, the divine Presence in the midst of his people; he has suggested that he is the wisdom and the Word of God; he has assumed the apocalyptic title of Son of Man. Now he suggests that he is *the seed* par excellence, seed of God but also seed of Abraham, to whom the Promises have been made and on whom the covenant has been concluded. He, always he, he alone, at the end of all the roads of Israel's requirements, but also of the requirements of all seekers.

Through the parable of the sower, Luke gives a symmetrical image of the Church, balancing the one he has given in the story of the miraculous catch of fishes. On one side, the sea, with Jesus standing in a boat filled with fish; on the other, the unbounded land and the sower walking with great strides and casting handfuls of seed abroad with wild prodigality. It is this undefined character that Jesus has deliberately emphasized in the first sketches he gives of his Church.

The Gospel according to Matthew, in another parable, has put special emphasis on the universal, catholic, and truly epic character of the new Church. This is the parable of the field sown both with good grain and with tares: in explaining this parable Christ makes use of a sort Matt. 13:37-39 of poem of astounding scope: "He who sows the good seed is the Son of Man. The field is the world; the good seed, the sons of the kingdom; the weeds, the sons of the wicked one; and the enemy who sowed them is the devil. But the harvest is the end of the world, and the reapers are the angels."

It takes one's breath away, but it says very clearly what it is intended to say. These are the true dimensions of our religion and of the Church of Christ, coextensive with the universe, with the whole unrolling of time, and with eternity. He who has a lesser vision is not in a fair way to be a Christian.

One can notice the difference of interpretation between this parable and that of the sower. Here the sower is the Son of Man and the seed stands for the sons of the Kingdom. But the thing that is identical in the two cases is the universal perspective: the field is the world, the harvest is the consummation of time. Moreover such parables always have a polyvalent significance, one interpretation not excluding the other but, on the contrary, embracing it. What does John the Evangelist say?

"To this end the Son of God appeared that he might destroy the works ⟨1 John 3:8-9⟩ of the devil. Whoever is born of God does not commit sin, because his seed abides in him and he cannot sin, because he is born of God."

And what is the date of this grand religious vision of the world? Saint Paul explicitly refers it to Abraham. "For not through the Law but ⟨Rom. 4:13⟩ through the justice of faith was the promise made to Abraham and to his posterity that he should be heir of the world." In truth, from Genesis to the last Epistles of Saint Paul, and in all the Holy Scripture, there is nothing more consistent in its significance, nothing richer in analogies, nothing greater in intelligible virtualities than the concept and indeed the very word "seed."

When Saint Paul asserts that the entire world, time, and eternity are part of the heritage of Abraham, he is not innovating, he is in the pure Jewish tradition. The *Mekilta* says: "And thus you see that Abraham our father, through the sole merit of the faith he had in Yahweh, inherited both this world and the other, as it is said: and he believed in Yahweh, and Yahweh accounted that to him as justice." It is through faith and through the justification that follows upon it that we can claim the universe and eternity. The promised land of Chanaan was never more than a stage, a token, a springboard, with a view to the universal expansion in space and time of the benediction on Abraham, which was to be extended infallibly to all nations.

Once more in the famous passage in First Corinthians, where the Jews and the Greeks are reconciled in Christ crucified, Saint Paul concludes: "Consider your own call, brethren." Vocation is simply the des- ⟨1 Cor. 1:26⟩ tination of God's Word in a particular man. Luke here relates a counsel of Christ that says the same thing: "Take heed, therefore, how you ⟨Luke 8:18⟩ hear."

Then Luke, continuing to follow the theme of Word-Wisdom, relates an episode that is the remote conclusion of the scandalous scene in Nazareth. "Now his mother and brethren came to him; and they could ⟨Luke 8:19-21⟩ not get to him because of the crowd. And it was told him, 'Thy mother and thy brethren are standing outside, wishing to see thee.' But he answered and said to them, 'My mother and my brethren are they who hear the word of God, and act upon it.'" Mark reports: "'For whoever ⟨Mark 3:35⟩ does the will of God, he is my brother and sister and mother.'"

Thus the family persecution continues, the most persistent of all persecutions. Luke is a modest writer, who does not venture to tell us explicitly that the Apostle Matthew was a publican, nor that it was Mary

Magdalene who had been "the sinner in the city"—he prefers not to depict this scene in too harsh a light. But the other Evangelists are less discreet. John tells us, "For not even his brethren believed in him." And Mark, never one to mince words, writes bluntly, "But when his own people had heard of it, they went out to lay hold of him, for they said, 'He has gone mad.' " A charming family! What they planned for Jesus was worse than the cross, it was the padded cell. And yet this family was like many others, neither better nor worse. It is, nevertheless, of astonishing significance that it was his closest relations who dared to say of Jesus that he was mad and should be bound, he who was wisdom in person. At any rate the antitheses continue: miracles and scandals, Word-Wisdom and madness.

John 7:5
Mark 3:21

And Mary, the mother of Jesus, why was she in this crowd? Like all good mothers, when conflicts of this sort occur, she was serving as a hostage, she was inaugurating her functions as mediator and advocate in a frightful family quarrel in which the honor and the mission of her son were involved. It is to be observed that at the time of the trial and execution of Jesus, save for his mother's sister and his mother herself, the whole noisy family had disappeared. No doubt they were in their homes, gravely nodding their heads and assuring one another that they had been right and that the whole thing had to end this way. There you have families.

To the stratagems of his relations Jesus makes a liberating rejoinder, which denies forever any legitimacy to family tyranny. He refuses to recognize any other family or any other relations than those who listen to the Word of God and put it into practice, those who perform the will of God. Far from accusing his mother, he proclaims that this woman's grandeur consists less in the carnal fact of having brought him into the world than in her spiritual obedience to the Word of God from the time of her reply to the angel—"Be it done to me according to thy word" —to her anguished assent at the foot of the cross.

Luke 1:38

Luke's thought on this subject is very clear. He has known the Virgin Mary, he possesses much information about her. For him she was the precious vessel in which the Word of God became incarnate, the "Throne of Wisdom," as the litanies have it. Once more it is Luke who emphasizes this aspect of the history of Jesus Christ: "Now it came to pass as he was saying these things, that a certain woman from the crowd lifted up her voice and said to him, 'Blessed is the womb that bore thee, and the breasts that nursed thee.' " Jesus answers her and as, apropos of John the Baptist and the Jewish demand for miracles, he pronounced

Luke 11:27-28

the beatitude: "Blessed is he who is not scandalized in me," here, apropos of his mother, he ends with the theme of the quest for Wisdom and the Word: "Blessed are they who hear the word of God and keep it."

I may be accused of cherishing unnatural sentiments against the family and the small fatherland, perhaps even against the great fatherland. I simply try to read the Gospel as it is written. Jesus moreover condemns neither his family nor his fatherland. How should one condemn the air he breathes? Jesus explains to us that one must nevertheless be on one's guard against social realities whose natural bent is toward ferocity and lack of intelligence. We must distrust biological imperialisms and the gregarious instincts, the possessive instinct of mothers and the idolatries of patriotism. A mother, a family, a country are not owed profound respect except in so far as they too give ear to the Word of God, to the will of God, and respect vocations. None of the biological grandiloquence that surrounds these realities of nature should impress a Christian.

———

Luke's narrative continues. I am not following it in detail, I am simply outlining the high points. Here I pass over a number of episodes, one of which is of particular importance (I shall return to it), the miracle of the loaves and fishes. I come now to a famous scene, the one called the confession of Saint Peter. This is the way Luke narrates it: "And it came to pass as he was praying in private, that his disciples also **Luke 9:18-20** were with him, and he asked them, saying, 'Who do the crowds say that I am?' And they answered and said, 'John the Baptist; and others, Elias; and that one of the ancient prophets has risen again.' And he said to them, 'But who do you say that I am?' Simon Peter answered and said, 'The Christ of God.'"

"The Jews ask for signs. The Greeks seek after wisdom. We Christians preach the Christ crucified, a scandal for the Jews, a folly for the Gentiles, but for those who are called the Christ is the power of God, and the wisdom of God." This text from Saint Paul, which serves as blueprint for the chapter, is like a chessboard on which this section of Luke's narrative unfolds. The principal personages of the primitive Church take their places, each in precise and unique relationship to Jesus Christ. To be sure, this is only a symbolic chessboard, and the function of each piece is simply accentuated: in real life there is nothing incompatible in being at once the fulfiller of the Jewish demand

and the servant of the Word. Nevertheless, Luke's style of literary composition seems to me to become clearer if one regards the play as taking place on a chessboard.

John the Baptist occupies the square of the Jewish demand. Mary Magdalene is on the complementary square of the Greek search. Mary, the mother of Jesus, occupies, with surpassing grace, the square of the servants of the Word. Peter has a special square of his own: it is the square belonging to the man who was the first to call Christ the Lord and who solemnly recognized him as "the Christ of God."

But Saint Paul does not simply say "the Christ," he says "the Christ crucified." It is remarkable that in Luke's account the confession of Saint Peter is immediately followed by Jesus' foretelling of his Passion and by the first declaration of the cross as the sole means of becoming his disciple. Luke and Saint Paul are completely at one on the structure of the Church and the pillars of that Church.

Luke 9:22-26   Jesus adds: "The Son of Man must suffer many things, and be rejected by the elders and chief priests and Scribes, and be put to death, and on the third day rise again." And he says to all, "If anyone wishes to come after me, let him deny himself, and take up his cross daily, and follow me. For he who would save his life will lose it; but he who loses his life for my sake will save it. For what does it profit a man, if he gain the whole world, but ruin or lose himself? For whoever is ashamed of me and my words, of him will the Son of Man be ashamed when he comes in his glory and that of the Father and of the holy angels." It is true that God included the universe in the heritage of Abraham and his seed, but the condition for claiming this patrimony is to have been able "to save his soul."

Christ's strategy, in the redemptive revelation he makes to us regarding himself and his Church, that is, of the people assembled around him, always gently puts him back at the point of convergence of all perspectives. But he is not there in any guise, he is there as crucified. A great painter, in order to locate the architectonic center of a picture he is starting, begins by making a cross on the white canvas, a cross that is not necessarily in the center of the canvas. Give careful study to Goya's etchings and you will see how the architectonic center can be displaced in relation to the geometric center of the picture, sometimes displaced so far as to be outside the frame.

That's exactly it. Man is born at the geometric center of a given family framework, moral, social, national. At the beginning everything is in its place, everything is arranged for him, all that is really asked of him is that he allow himself to live and die according to the predetermined meaning—which can only be common sense—in the geometrical space of his native framework. My God, how certain everything is from the start, what oppressive certitude! Then a little cross is drawn somewhere by an unseen hand, far removed from the natural center, and everything gently reorganizes itself around that little cross in accordance with a universal gravity. That is to say, at first everything becomes disorganized from its former precise arrangement.

At this point Luke does not mince words: "If anyone comes to me and does not hate his father and mother, and wife and children, and brothers and sisters, yes, and even his own life, he cannot be my disciple. And he who does not carry his cross and follow me, cannot be my disciple." The attempt is being constantly made to persuade us that Christianity is a conservative social force, that is, essentially a force of inertia. I read and reread the Gospel. It strikes me above all that true fidelity to a Christian vocation must manifest itself by havoc. It is perfectly true that the familial context here has a wider significance than the gravitational field of the immediate social circle. Man's intimate enemy is first of all within himself. Saint John of the Cross has perfectly understood and explained this.

Luke 14:26-27

Only great artistic vocations offer some analogy, a simple analogy, to be sure, to a Christian vocation. Someone asked William Faulkner what the supreme law of art was, and he replied in three words: "Kill your darlings!" All true artists will understand very well what Faulkner meant and that it is by no means a jest. The words of Christ are not a jest either, nor are they a rhetorical exaggeration.

Clearly defined in the text of Saint Paul, you have all the integral parts of the Church. In Luke's report each one of these integral parts bears a name dear to Christian devotion. One can remain a man though lacking an arm or an eye, but to be a perfect man one must have two arms and two eyes. Similarly, I do not say that one cannot remain a Christian if he neglects one or another of the persons in the Gospel who gravitate around the transcendental personality of the Christ. Nevertheless, I believe that for a full understanding of the action of Jesus Christ and of his Church in its seed time, it is only right to place around him, each in his proper position, his mother, John the Baptist and Mary Magdalene, Peter, and the cross, as we find them in the Gospel. About Jesus they form a harmonious constellation, in which each element has its weight and function. And all of them, assembled around the Lord, are the essential core of the primitive Church.

The cross, at some unpredictable point defined by God—that is the imaginative and creative principle of a human destiny, a principle that begins by disorganizing all the rest. I have seldom seen this happening, but I have seen it: Simone Weil is an example, which overwhelmed me by its intensity. This favorite pupil of the rationalist Alain, this graduate of the French university, trained in Cartesian thought, surely needed to do nothing but live her life. What business had she in the Spanish War in the ranks of the Republicans? What was she doing in the factories, working at assembly lines? What was she doing as a farmhand in the French Midi? What brought her to London in 1942? She turned her life and death upside down under the irresistible attraction of a magnetic center—the little cross, drawn in advance, drawn before she was born, on the clean white canvas well prepared by a good middle-class family and by the venerable French university. The result was wholly unique.

And what of Tolstoi? It is perfectly possible to admire the writer of *Anna Karenina* and *War and Peace* while at the same time rejecting his explanation of the Gospels, which indeed seems to me somewhat abrupt, but who could fail to love the great and glorious old man who fled from his house like a thief in the night and endured his death agony in the waiting room of the station at Astapovo? We are told that when he left his home he no longer knew where he was going. No matter, Another knew for him and he obeyed.

At this point in the Gospel there is one of those anomalies that are, for me, signs of historical veracity. They are things that cannot be invented. Christ speaks of the cross for his disciples; he does not yet explicitly speak of it for himself. He foresees, in general terms, his Passion, his betrayal, his death and his Resurrection, but without mentioning the

Luke 9:44-45 precise means of his death. "Store up these words in your minds: the Son of Man is to be betrayed into the hands of men." Luke adds, and this is a pathetic touch: "But they did not understand this saying, and it was hidden from them, that they might not perceive it; and they were afraid to ask him about this saying." Worthy folk! We are all in the same position. There are premonitory signs, standing up right in the middle of our lives but veiled in darkness: we act as though we did not perceive them—and, at all costs, let no one lift the veil. . . .

Nevertheless it is strange that, at this moment in his life, Christ should speak so clearly of the cross for his disciples and not mention it for himself. Was he like one of those fire-eaters who order their men to charge while they themselves prudently stay behind in the jump-off trenches? The event has clearly shown his quality in this respect. Jesus Christ opens all roads, including the road to the cross. But to predict torture on the cross for his disciples is the reverse of demagogy. It is as though a leader of today were to promise his followers the guillotine, the electric chair, or hanging, depending on the country. Christ's auditors must have had very great souls to have followed him, if only a small part of the way.

On Christ's part, the strategy is always the same. And what is that strategy? Not a modern strategy which grows more and more identified with the material means of war. Not even strategy in Moltke's style, which is only "a system of expedients," but the ancient form of strategy which held sway on the battlefields from Alexander's time to that of Napoleon and which in practice is indistinguishable from the personality of the captain: the plan is the leader.

Jesus Christ's plan for the destiny of the world, for the destiny of each one of us, is he himself, Jesus Christ crucified, he, always he, no one and nothing else, raised aloft at the confluence of all the lines of force. Nevertheless he takes care to keep himself apart from this world: this, too, is the significance of the cross: "And I, if I be lifted up from the earth, will draw all things to myself." I was talking about a cross drawn on a blank canvas. In life, as in certain extraordinary paintings, the architectonic center has to be looked for outside the canvas, and so it is that human wisdom falls short when it searches within that universe for the secret of man and of the universe. `John 12:32`

"God has glory in what he conceals, kings have glory in what they fathom." Modern intellectuality has severed the umbilical cord that once attached it to the divine design, it has deliberately rejected its royal function and all ambition for true wisdom. Since Descartes, philosophy has determinedly sought the key to the universe within the universe; now philosophy knows that the universe will not give up its secret, perhaps because it has no secret but is only presenting charades. Man and the universe have become permanently opaque: the universe is a discourse without order or coherence, and man is an enigma to himself. Fair enough! I like this unconditional surrender to the absurd better than the false clarity, false perspectives, and cowardly optimism of the "philosophy of the enlightenment." Philosophy's next move should be a revolt against its present defeat, a heroic reaction against its present humiliation. `Prov. 25:2`

Christianity, to be sure, does not explain everything, and the Church of Jesus Christ is not an electronic machine designed to give in a few seconds complete formulas for man and for the universe. The Son of Man did not compare himself to a mathematician or to an engineer, or even to an expert accountant whose balance sheet is infallible; he compared himself to a peasant going forth to sow his grain. The harvest is not for tomorrow. Christianity is the religion of waiting, of patience, of hope, of a risk voluntarily accepted and sustained, of constancy in the face of hardships. The Church is the house of a laborer who has finished sowing and who waits, a house of worry and of confidence before the harvest. This waiting will be as long as history for the good reason that "the harvest is the end of the world, and the reapers are the angels."

This is not the place for an explanation of the whole redemptive value for man and for the universe contained in the cross. It is through it alone that we become heirs of the world, that the world becomes our house, made for us, not a cage, not a prison, not a desert, but our house in which we are at home. Christ crucified is at the point of convergence of all the lines making up the past. He is also the point of convergence of all the trajectories that plunge into the future. We know that he will judge the world and that his cross will then blaze in the sky. We shall adore him not for having proved us right but for having saved us.

Before ending this section of his Gospel, Luke tells of a strange and fantastic phenomenon, precisely framed by the first two prophecies concerning the Passion. This is the occurrence of the Transfiguration, which thereby gives the cross its background of glory.

Luke 9:28-36   Now it came to pass about eight days after these words, that he took Peter, James and John and went up the mountain to pray. And as he prayed, the appearance of his countenance was changed, and his raiment became a radiant white. And behold, two men were talking with him. And these were Moses and Elias, who, appearing in glory, spoke of his death, which he was about to fulfill in Jerusalem. Now Peter and his companions were heavy with sleep. But when they were fully awake, they saw his glory and the two men who were standing with him. And it came to pass as they were parting from him, that Peter said to Jesus, "Master, it is good for us to be here. And let us set up three tents, one for thee, and one for Moses, and one for Elias," not knowing what he said. But as he was speaking thus, there came a cloud and overshadowed them; and they were afraid as they entered the cloud. And a voice was heard in the cloud, saying, "This is my beloved Son; hear him." And after the voice had passed, Jesus was found alone.

The setting of this theophany is traditional. It recalls Israel's most solemn theophanies, those on Horeb. Through its magnificence, it adds to the theophany at the Jordan. Here Jesus' glory is of an insupportable brilliance: he is personally clothed in divinity. To announce that the Presence of God, which has hitherto accompanied the people of Israel either beneath the Tent of the Tabernacle or in the Temple at Jerusalem, has definitively taken up its place in Jesus, the ancient and terrible cloud that enveloped that Presence descends in majesty on to the mountain. The deferential presence of Moses and of Elias indicates the continuity of the designs of God and the reverence of the ancient covenant for the new. Jesus, Moses, Elias—all three are contemporaries in God's plan. This is one of those privileged moments when one may perceive time drinking eternity at its source, like an infant at its mother's breast. The solemn commandment which concludes this theophany, *Hear him,* re-echoes from age to age. It is this commandment that is the eternal foundation of the Church. It is so absolute, so entire, so supreme, that everything coming after it will be its echo; it is so far above time that everything that went before seems likewise to be an echo of this commandment.

Indeed it is written in the Law of Moses:

"A prophet like me will the Lord, your God, raise up for you from among your own kinsmen: *to him you shall listen.* This is exactly what you requested of the Lord, your God, at Horeb on the day of the assembly, when you said, 'Let us not again hear the voice of the Lord, our God, nor see this great fire any more, lest we die.' And the Lord said to me. 'This was well said, I will raise up for them a prophet like you from among their kinsmen, and will put my words into his mouth; he shall tell them all that I command him. If any man will not listen to my words which he speaks in my name, I myself will make him answer for it.' " Deut. 18:15-19

The Jews trace back to this dialogue between God and Moses the institution of prophecy and the definition of the Prophet's role: to pronounce in God's name the exact words that God puts into his mouth. But Jesus is the Word of God itself, he consummates and fulfills in himself all prophecy. Henceforth the whole of religion is to listen to him and to put into practice what he says.

Saint John of the Cross has very well explained the purpose of the keystone of revelation supplied by this scene of the Transfiguration. It sustains and completes the whole prophetic architecture of the Old Testament. With it the edifice of divine revelation is completed; all that remains is to place the cross above it. He shows that, under the ancient Law, it was proper, allowable, and laudable for the priests and Prophets to question God about the coming of the Messiah who was the end and the purpose of that Law. And God would reply in fragments, to the extent that was necessary at each stage of this long pilgrimage in time, and that interrogatory was the history of His chosen people. This people put questions to God on the subject of the hope they had received from Him. And God was compelled to answer them in order to sustain that hope. But since the theophany of the Transfiguration on Mount Tabor, God, having said everything in his Son, is henceforth "as one dumb."

To all solicitations that He break His silence by particular revelations, God might reply: "Since I have already told you everything in My Word, who is My Son, I have no other words that can at present say anything or reveal anything to you beyond this. Fix your eyes on him alone, for in him I have told you all, revealed all, and in him you will find more even than you desire or ask. . . . If you fix your eyes on him, you will find everything, for he is My whole word and My reply, he is My whole vision and My whole revelation; everything has already been said to you, been answered, made manifest, and revealed, when I have given him to you as brother, companion and master, ransom and recompense.

"From the day when I descended upon him with My Spirit on Mount Tabor, saying: 'This is My beloved Son: *hear him,*' I have put aside the old forms of teaching and response and I have given all to him: hear him, because I have no further faith to reveal, no further things to make manifest. If I spoke before, it was in order to promise the Christ; and if I was questioned, these questions touched always upon the demand and the hope for Christ, in whom all good was to be found as is now declared in the doctrine of the Evangelists and the Apostles."

In Luke's description, one sees that the Transfiguration is the precious buckle that joins in the person of Jesus the quest for wisdom and the demand for miracles.

The Jews ask for signs; here is one in the pure tradition of the theophanies of Israel, a miracle that had as witnesses the two greatest Prophets of Israel, Moses and Elias. It is the Miracle par excellence, the Sign of signs, the very Presence of their God beneath the terrifying and holy cloud. Just as after Jesus there is no further need for specific revelation, so after him miracles will no longer have the same importance. Up to his time their principal function was to make us wait and allow us to recognize the Messiah, but he is here, a miracle, consisting in the Presence of God among us.

The Greeks seek after wisdom; let them seek no more. It is here: it is the very Word of God, sown upon the earth. The Wisdom of wisdoms is to listen to that Word and put it into practice.

At this moment the last of the Prophets of Israel, John the Baptist, was dead. With him prophecy fell silent before the Word.

This, then, is the Church of Jesus.

For he himself is our peace, he it is who had made both one, and has broken down the intervening wall of the enclosure, the enmity, in his flesh. The Law of the commandments expressed in decrees he has made void, that of the two he might create in himself one new man, and make peace and reconcile both in one body to God by the cross, having slain the enmity in himself. And coming, he announced the good tidings of peace to you who were afar off, and of peace to those who were near; because through him we both have access in one Spirit to the Father.

Eph. 2:14-22

Therefore, you are now no longer strangers and foreigners, but you are citizens with the saints and members of God's household: you are built upon the foundation of the apostles and prophets with Christ Jesus himself as the chief corner stone. In him the whole structure is closely fitted together and grows into a temple holy in the Lord; in him you too are being built together into a dwelling place for God in the Spirit.

Saint Thomas Aquinas' commentary on this text of Saint Paul should be read. He explains that the assembly of the faithful, when considered vertically in relation to the Patriarch, the source of its life, who is God, is a true clan (*domus*). But this same assembly of the faithful, considered horizontally in respect to the relations of the various members to one another, becomes the City of the Saints. The evidences of belonging to that city are the acts of faith, of hope, and of charity.

Jesus is the King of this City of the Saints, as he is the natural leader of the clan of God.

CHAPTER XVI

The Body and the Eagles

I N FOLLOWING Luke's account, I purposely omitted an event that is nevertheless of extreme importance in the history of Jesus Christ. It is precisely because of its importance that I postponed it for fuller treatment here. This event is a miracle, the miracle of the loaves and fishes, but the significance Jesus gave it, with an insistence and vehemence that are surprising, makes it a watershed in his human adventure: before it, a rising slope; afterward, a descending one. Here it is John's account I shall follow: it has a certain dryness I admire, like the minutes of a meeting or a court record.

John 6:1-15   After this Jesus went away to the other side of the sea of Galilee, which is that of Tiberias. And there followed him a great crowd, because they witnessed the signs he worked on those who were sick. Jesus therefore went up the mountain, and sat there with his disciples. Now the Passover, the feast of the Jews, was near.

When, therefore, Jesus had lifted up his eyes and seen that a very great crowd had come to him, he said to Philip, "Whence shall we buy bread that these may eat?" But he said this to try him, for he himself knew what he would do. Philip answered him, "Two hundred denarii worth of bread is not enough for them, that each one may receive a little." One of his disciples, Andrew, the brother of Simon Peter, said to him, "There is a young boy here who has five barley loaves and two fishes; but what are these among so many?" Jesus then said, "Make the people recline." Now there was much grass in the place. The men therefore reclined, in number about five thousand.

Jesus then took the loaves, and when he had given thanks, distributed them to those reclining; and likewise the fishes, as much as they wished.

168

But when they were filled, he said to his disciples, "Gather the fragments that are left over, lest they be wasted." They therefore gathered them up; and they filled twelve baskets with the fragments of the five barley loaves left over by those who had eaten.

When the people, therefore, had seen the sign which Jesus had worked, they said, "This is indeed the Prophet who is to come into the world." So when Jesus perceived that they would come to take him by force and make him king, he fled again to the mountain, himself alone.

What need to comment on so precise an account? It is a dazzling miracle, a miracle of compassion, to be sure, because all these people were very hungry. Nevertheless it must be noted that Christ expressly made this humble feast into a liturgy through the rite of benediction and the giving of thanks, as reported by all four Evangelists. In this connection John makes use for the first time of the word "Eucharist."

Considered simply as a human being, Jesus assuredly had great genius, eloquence, and audacity of action, but no good sense. I ask myself what statesman would not envy his astonishing ability to captivate crowds, but what statesman, having won success and prestige, would have so little sense as to waste the reward all at once, as though gratuitously. To all appearances and by the standards of this world, Jesus' family—who, like all families, had good sense enough and to spare—was not so far wrong in treating him as a madman.

But since it is impossible for me to share that family opinion, I tell myself that Jesus' action, however disconcerting it may have been, was directed toward an end worthy of him and that the unfolding consequences of the action simply expressed a secret but constant intention aimed at that end. It is this intention that interests me and that must needs reconcile all the apparent contradictions. Indeed it is Jesus himself who invites us to seek a more profound meaning than "good sense" when he declares: "Blessed are those whom I do not scandalize." In what concerns Jesus, good sense is a mass-producer of scandal.

We can begin by defining the abstract trajectory of Jesus' action. We have seen what happened in Nazareth. First of all, he aroused his little village to enthusiasm, then he chose the moment of his greatest popularity apparently to ruin all. Surely it was because he attached little importance to a certain kind of popularity. In the synagogue at Nazareth he proclaims four truths, which affront his audience so violently that his partisans of the day before are ready to murder him. That is how it happened in Nazareth; the same thing is now going to happen here in the vaster theater on the shores of the lake; it will recur, exactly the same, in the following year in Jerusalem. And this time it will be for good, he will die of it. What then is the profound intention in a way of acting that cannot but seem disconcerting?

What is taking place here? The enthusiasm of the people around Jesus has visibly reached its height. By the thousands they leave the city for the desert, not simply to see him, touch him, listen to him, and then return home, but to go on seeing him, to touch him again, to listen to him to the last breath, simply to be with him, with no apparent intention whatever of returning to their homes. He has uprooted a whole population, and they follow him as a swarm of bees clusters around the queen. They distress him, he flees, they search for him, they find him, they spy on him, they keep him under surveillance, they demand an account of his disappearances: "Master, when camest thou hither?" It is the question of a lover, a jealous lover. This is beautiful, this passionate attachment of all these Jews to our Lord Jesus Christ; would we be capable of it? In short, it is one of those rare moments in history when the leader and the people are inexorably welded together, when they make but a single being. One no longer knows whether the people obey him or he obeys them.

John 6:25

Jesus justifies this passionate attachment by a sensational miracle: with five loaves and two fishes, he makes a feast for five thousand persons. This is concrete, this is spectacular, all these poor people have their stomachs filled, a marvelous boon, which, however, does not detract one whit from the sincerity of their feelings. For the touching thing about it is that they have come not to be fed but to listen to Jesus Christ: they want to make him king, but they have not mistaken him for the Salvation Army's soup kitchen.

I have said that in Jesus the wonder-worker is identical with the Prophet. This is clearly the case here. He has performed a dazzling miracle first of all because he wished to say something, something of importance. The miracle is only a prologue to sharpen the appetite of the spirit—by satisfying the hunger of the body, to arouse the questioning that is the hunger of the soul.

It is not so easy to know what he intends. Here for months and months on the shores of the lake, in the presence of these simple people who love him, he preaches the nearness of the Kingdom of God, he confirms through his miracles that he is the Messiah, he calls himself the Son of Man, he allows himself to be called "son of David": these honest folk come to believe quite sincerely that he is the pretender to the throne of Israel. And so they want to seize him and make him king. It is all well meant and undoubtedly perfectly sincere. It is nevertheless imperious. Just as the family of Jesus, considering him mad, wished to seize him, these people, judging him worthy to reign, also wish to lay hands on him. What has possessed all of them to wish constantly to appropriate him, to enslave him, to chain him to their passions? Nevertheless they are not entirely wrong: salvation indeed consists in laying hold of Jesus and never letting him go.

This time Jesus flees. John says he withdraws all alone into the mountain. Then, in the midst of the night, he rejoins his Apostles, walking on the waters.

———

And it is on the next day that Jesus, as though by whim, destroys with a single breath, as if it were a house of cards, the superb and fragile edifice of popular enthusiasm. This happens in the cool shade of the synagogue at Capharnaum. There is not, there never has been, there never will be, a political leader who would behave this way. When one holds the delirium of the crowd in one's hands, one keeps it for oneself. With an effectiveness that is without parallel, Jesus provokes this delirium through his eloquence and his astounding miracles. He encourages this delirium, he whips it up to its paroxysm as one whips up cream. Then he deflates it at one stroke by an overwhelming discourse. He will act in exactly the same fashion on Palm Sunday.

Let us get to the facts. What did Jesus say to provoke this deliberate disaster? For it is not his enemies that make his people flee, it is he. He has said that he is the "bread of life." What does that mean? Not only does this allegorical language of the Jews disconcert us, we find it cold. How could these words provoke this immense withdrawal from Jesus, a withdrawal so complete that this man, who but yesterday fled into the mountain in order to escape those who wanted to make him king, today will find himself abandoned and almost alone? Jesus simply affirmed that he was "bread of life": is there anything here to produce so violent a reaction? Let us imagine today a minister in Parliament, a professor on the lecture platform, a revolutionary leader at a popular meeting, affirming that he is the bread of life; the audience will at most be bewildered, the conclusion will be that this man is slightly mad and that what he has said means nothing at all.

Like all Jesus' most decisive sayings, this one, unless it is put back into its context, into its tradition, into its order of explication, is almost unintelligible. Read in translation, outside the historical and mystical aura of the people of Israel, it loses its savor, it lacks salt, it is without flavor. This uprooting of texts and transposing them into that atmosphere of cellophane and refrigerators known as bigotry is the source of a pious and insupportable style. Here, however, in this particular situation, when one reads the Gospel closely, one is obliged to see that this discourse of Jesus had the effect of an incendiary bomb tossed into the midst of the congregation. Simply on hearing it the people exploded with rage, perhaps with disgust. It was obviously important.

Jesus begins with a reproach, which is a good way of catching the attention of an audience. He criticizes his partisans, he criticizes his own success, he does not exaggerate its importance, still less does he take pride in it. In substance he says to them—and it must have been just as blunt as this—I know why you follow me, it is not because of the miracles I perform, it is because I have filled your stomachs. In satisfying your hunger, my poor people, you have forgotten your vocation. And what is that vocation? You, Jews, you are here to demand miracles, to inspect them, to record them, this is your calling, your predestined place in God's plan, it is your means of recognizing the Messiah. The miracle of the loaves and fishes is dazzling as a miracle, as a Messianic sign; all that it meant to you is a free feast. What then do you require?

Jesus' strategy is always the same. He centers attention upon himself, he makes himself the keystone of the arch of explanation. Having affirmed the Messianic importance of the miracle, he declares that Moses himself was a lesser wonder-worker than he is. And, since this has to do with nourishment and with loaves, he declares that he is himself the highest nourishment of man, his bread the most precious, the most substantial.

In the discussion, as John reports it, it is clear that the audience was divided and that there were several contrary currents, at least at first. In the heat of the quarrel some of Jesus' interlocutors come close to blasphemy: they minimize the miracle they have seen with their own John 6:30-31 eyes, they who but yesterday were transported with enthusiasm. "What sign, then, dost thou, that we may see and believe thee? What work dost thou perform? Our fathers ate the manna in the desert, even as it is written, 'Bread from heaven he gave them to eat.'" In human relationships, nothing is more despicable than ingratitude, nothing more revolting than to minimize the gift of him from whose hand we have eaten when we were hungry. Who among us is incapable of a similar forgetfulness?

Jesus makes a frontal counterattack. He says definitely that the miracle of the manna was no more than a pale precursor of his miracle and John 6:32-33, 35, 40 his work. "I say to you, Moses did not give you the bread from heaven but my Father gives you the true bread from heaven. For the bread of God is that which comes down from heaven and gives life to the world.

. . . I am the bread of life. He who comes to me shall not hunger, and he who believes in me shall never thirst. . . . For this is the will of my Father who sent me, that whoever beholds the Son, and believes in him, shall have everlasting life, and I will raise him up on the last day."

Without following the order in John, I have made a montage of these astonishing declarations in which Jesus affirms his celestial and truly divine origin, his nourishing value for those who have faith in him, his power over life and over the last day, when time will be consumed, and his power to raise the dead.

Jesus' plan of action is similarly always the same; it is a highly efficient plan of attack and movement, familiar to dramatic authors. Battle is fiercely joined on a limited terrain. When the enemy replies, the conflict has already been carried to a higher level and a more extended area. And so it goes until everything within reach has been engaged and perhaps pulverized. Jesus never contents himself with defending what has been challenged; he always moves beyond that, far beyond that, adding mountains of increasing claims which infinitely surpass what was originally put in question, thus creating situations that are more and more explosive and more and more exasperating to the adversary. When Jesus is reproached with drawing his bow too far, instead of relaxing it, he bends it farther still. This requires courage that constantly rises to heroism. The adversary's arguments are thus always surpassed, his range is always too long, and his barrage falls on a position already abandoned. He never succeeds in readjusting his fire. Jesus has always moved forward to a new position.

This time his maneuver is sensational and leaves one dumfounded. They say to Jesus, Your miracle is not conclusive, Moses' miracle of the manna was much more so. He replies by placing himself on a level far above Moses; he is the anointed of God. The miraculous nourishment given by Moses did not prevent people from dying. He, Jesus, presides over the resurrection of the dead and eternal life. He is himself the bread that comes from heaven and that brings the believer life everlasting: "Do not labor for the food that perishes, but for that which John 6:27 endures unto life everlasting, which the Son of Man will give you. For upon him the Father, God himself, has set his seal."

As always, he places himself at the center of all the traditions of Israel and claims for himself all the beneficent powers hitherto attributed to Yahweh. Here the Book of Wisdom must be quoted:

For you have dominion over life and death; you lead down to the gates of Wis. 16:13-14, 20 the nether world and lead back. Man, however, slays in his malice, but when the spirit has departed, it does not return, nor can he bring back the soul once it is confined.

. . . you nourished your people with food of angels and furnished them bread from heaven, ready to hand, untoiled-for, endowed with all delights and conforming to every taste.

Wis. 16:26 And here we are brought back to a fundamental theme: "It is not the various kinds of fruits that nourish man, but it is your word that preserves those who believe you!"

With this last quotation we find ourselves once more in very familiar country. It is essentially the Word of God that nourishes believers, and preserves them in the being of their spiritual vocation, since the first function of nourishment is to preserve the state of being.

The dialectic of revelation peculiar to the Gospel is very consistent in its development of metaphors and parables. Then suddenly it is no longer a question of metaphor; one's foot strikes directly against reality. It is this claudication of the metaphoric with the real whose syncopated rhythm must be seized if we do not wish to miss any part of this revela-

Luke 8:11 tion. When Luke tells us, "The seed is the Word of God"—and if we take these words in their most literal sense, as must absolutely be done when studying the Gospel—we understand perfectly well that Jesus, who has already proclaimed himself the Word of God, proclaims himself also the seed of God, as he is the seed of Abraham: Jesus' manner of being the Word of God is to have been begotten of Him, to be His Son par excellence, His own seed. Hence the precise and particular meaning, strictly personal, that the word "Father" acquires on Jesus' lips when he speaks of God. All this is closely connected and most evident. But we are no longer in the realm of metaphor, we are amid the reality of things and relations: or rather we are at the same time in metaphor and reality, in a poetry heavy and full to bursting with the weight of suggestion.

Following the thread of this dialectic, we see very clearly that the seed becomes the harvest, and the harvest becomes the bread. What reason for astonishment, then, that Jesus, who is the Word and the seed, should also be the bread and the nourishment of man, with an eschatological connotation of personal triumph over death and time, since Matthew

Matt. 13:30 has already told us also that "the harvest is the consummation of the century"?

The Jews entered easily into this dialectic and followed perfectly the thread of Jesus' discourse, as a fisherman follows the turnings of a trout among the rushes. They had always known that the Word and the wisdom of God were the nutrient bread. The doctors of the Talmud will later on call themselves "the Defenders of the Bread." Jesus' claim to be the living bread, descended from heaven and granted by the Father, found a connection at once in their minds with all his preceding claims: to be the Son of Man, to be the Word, to be he who pardons sins, in short, to be of heavenly origin and the equal of God. It can be seen how impossible it is in the Gospel to separate metaphor from reality: they are inextricable. That Jesus should be at once the seed of Abraham and the seed of God, nothing could be more real, but that the harvest should be the consummation of the century means that Jesus Christ, Son and seed of God, is in very truth Lord of time and eternity, master of life and of the resurrection of the dead. It is in this sense that I say the evangelical revelation obeys a poetic dialectic; it does not for all that obey the Cartesian one.

———

Jesus' hearers, however, were not through with surprises: there were going to be many others.

It is commonly said that the Jewish people were too carnal to understand properly the message and actions of Jesus. This is not at all my opinion. I think rather than Jesus' hearers were exactly what we are, we, even those who are baptized, even the so-called good Christians: too carnal, to be sure, to understand the message and actions of Jesus in the fullness of their spiritual meaning, but also, and perhaps above all, too "intellectual," too "cultivated," much too "civilized," to understand properly what Jesus' message and actions contained of the primitive, the concrete, and, in the present case, the carnal and the sanguinary. I should cite here the Gospel according to John without omitting a single word, without changing the order of the sentences. I simply beg the reader not to be dishonest, still less to play the expert, but to read this terrifying text as it stands, without reserve, without reticence, taking the words in their most concrete, crudest, most brutal meaning, which is their true meaning. I imagine that many readers will not be able even to make the effort but will commence to split hairs in a knowledgeable way. Then let them close this book here and give it up. Why persevere?

"I am the living bread that has come down from heaven. If anyone eat of this bread he shall live forever; and the bread that I will give is my flesh for the life of the world." The Jews on that account argued with one another, saying, "How can this man give us his flesh to eat?" Jesus therefore said to them, "Amen, amen, I say to you, unless you eat the flesh of the Son of Man, and drink his blood, you shall not have life in you. He who eats my

John 6:51-58

flesh and drinks my blood has life everlasting and I will raise him up on the last day. For my flesh is food indeed, and my blood is drink indeed. He who eats my flesh, and drinks my blood, abides in me and I in him. As the living Father has sent me, and as I live because of the Father, so he who eats me, he also shall live because of me."

Turn this text any way you will, study it from any angle, if you take it literally, as it should be taken, it is an unequivocal invitation to ritual cannibalism, to religious anthropophagy. Many of Jesus' disciples, no doubt the majority, would find such a discourse impossible to swallow. *"Durus est hic sermo, et quis potet eum audire?"* "This is too much: who can go on listening to this man?" It would show little knowledge of Jesus to believe that he then replied by retraction, excuse, or evasion, or even that he retreated a single step. On the contrary, he advances a step farther. He persists, he presses on, he gives the final touch to revelation, and no doubt to the fury of his auditors. John writes: "But Jesus, knowing in himself that his disciples were murmuring at this, said to them, 'Does this scandalize you? What then if you should see the Son of Man ascending where he was before?'"

John 6:62-63

Through this prophecy of his corporeal ascension into heaven Jesus closes the circle. It is striking that he firmly places the revelation of the Eucharist in the framework of his affirmation of his divine sonship, his Incarnation, his mission, and the announcement of his ascension. At the same time he also affirms the incorporation of the Eucharistic believer in himself, the real composition of his Mystical Body, that is, the Church. Everything is there, assembled in a few sentences. "As I live because of the Father, the living Father who has sent me, so he who eats me will live, in his turn, because of me." He has already said to Nicodemus, "And no one has ascended into heaven except him who has descended from heaven: the Son of Man who is in heaven." But here he is perfectly concrete and precise: he has descended as bread to assuage our hunger and to be eaten by us. It is through this act of "eating" that the Eucharistic believer is assimilated to the body of Jesus and will ascend with him to heaven. It is difficult, impossible indeed, for me to think that one is not obliged to take in the same concrete, corporeal, carnal sense ("And the Word became flesh"), Christ's descent from heaven and his Incarnation, his being Eucharistically eaten and his ascension. Otherwise Jesus was talking without saying anything, and that would be the gravest insult that could be offered to him.

Moreover, Jesus' auditors understood what he meant, they took his words literally. That is why there was a decisive break between him and

John 3:13

them, a break that would be incomprehensible if Jesus' discourse had not had the physical meaning that alone can explain their indignation. John concludes a few lines farther down: "After this, many of his disciples went back to their old ways, and walked no more in his company. . . ." It was to be the disbanding, the rout, of his followers; not a small rout, but, in the poet's words, "The giant rout with panic-stricken face." Jesus' bands melted away like wax in the breath of a furnace. This was the ruin of all that Jesus had done in Galilee, an enterprise that had begun under such happy auspices. Nearly two thousand years have passed. I reread this strange page and I ask: What would I myself have done if I had been there? I am not sure and I dare not answer.

John 6:67

To be sure, there are others, much more at their ease, who have already answered for me and are quite ready to relieve me of my embarrassment. Good Catholics who go to Mass will laugh at my difficulty, will find me grotesque and shocking for having dared write the word "cannibalism"; they will sternly point out to me that the sacramental manner of the Eucharist and the appearance of the bread and the wine remove from that Sacrament any suspicion of being an anthropophagic rite. I too know, as well as they do, that the Eucharistic rite removes any trace of atrocity from the eating of Jesus' flesh, but I also know that it is indeed Jesus' flesh that we eat and, substantially, nothing else. I know, too, that the institution of the Sacrament and the Eucharistic rite took place a year after this discourse. After, be it noted—that made it easier.

There are those who are partisans of allegory. They say that the body and blood of Jesus are only symbolically present in the Eucharist. They say that what we eat in the Eucharist is real bread, though symbolic of Christ's body, that what we drink is real wine, though symbolic of Christ's blood. And thus spiritually but truly we participate in the body and blood of Christ. They rely upon the explanation given by Jesus himself: "It is the spirit that gives life; the flesh profits nothing. The words that I have spoken to you are spirit and life." To be sure, when one is in communion with the body and blood of Christ, one must know what he is doing; this is what Saint Paul calls "discerning" the body and blood of Christ. The sixteenth-century general in Holland who threw consecrated Hosts to his horses to eat did not thereby make the horses communicants, incapable as they were of "discernment." But I avow that I see in Christ's words absolutely nothing symbolical.

John 6:64

All Christ's words are spirit and they are life. When Jesus, after his corporeal Resurrection, commands Thomas to place his hand in the wounds made by the nails, then once more, then above all, his words are spirit and life. To reinforce our faith in that Resurrection, these words have nothing whatever symbolical.

It is true that Jesus says in this place that the flesh is of no avail and that the spirit alone gives life. But in the whole Eucharistic discourse, it is perfectly clear that Christ is demanding of his disciples first of all faith, total confidence in his person and in his words: if he proposes his flesh, his real flesh, to be eaten and his blood, his real blood, to be drunk, he wishes them to be eaten and drunk, not to sustain the body, but through a living participation of our spirit in that act of eating to comfort and nourish the soul. Saint Paul will speak in no other fashion: "Therefore whoever eats this bread or drinks the cup of the Lord unworthily, will be guilty of the body and the blood of the Lord," and not simply answerable to a symbol he has profaned.

I Cor. 11:27

I shall pursue my thought to the end. The discoveries of modern ethnographers have taught us that in the most primitive clans where cannibalism was practiced it was essentially a religious and mystical rite. The flesh of heroes was eaten and their blood was drunk in order to appropriate their virtues. In its character as religious rite, this barbarous ceremony, which is so revolting to us, was essentially a communion with the soul and spirit of the dead hero. Nevertheless it was in fact his flesh that was eaten, his blood that was drunk. Here we find ourselves brought back to that primitive social reality, the clan, which I believe God adopted, at first to found Israel, then to found his Church, and to save the world.

Let us press on. Within the religion of Israel there had been blood sacrifices in which the flesh of the victims consecrated to God had been eaten. It was a religion of blood. Let the reader recall what I have written in connection with the circumcision and he will understand that all these sacrifices of bulls, rams, lambs, and turtle doves, these sacrifices in themselves, were symbolical. For it is not these innocent animals that merit death, it is sinful men: "If you do not redeem him, break his neck." But the religion of Israel did not stop in mid-course; it was awaiting another victim, a completely innocent victim, alone worthy of God, who would ransom once for all by his sacrificial flesh and shed blood the sins of all the people.

Ex. 13:13

What does Saint Paul, the pupil of Gamaliel, say? That there is no remission of sins without effusion of blood. He also says that it is the Christ who has ransomed us by his blood. The entire Christian religion gravitates around a human sacrifice. The Aztecs used to think that they were acting properly when they sacrificed human victims to their god on the mountains. They were considered barbarians and were massacred in large numbers because of these human sacrifices. It would have been better to explain to them that a single human victim is the Redeemer, because he alone is without sin, and that is the Christ. And that his sacrifice, accomplished once for all on the mountain, but sacramentally renewed always and everywhere in the Eucharistic liturgy, renders vain all other sacrifices. Primitive cannibal tribes felt that, in order to communicate with the soul of a hero, it was necessary to eat his flesh and drink his blood. And it is true that one must eat the flesh of Christ and drink his blood to have perfect communion with his soul and his Godhead.

It will have been noticed that I like to refer to the discoveries of ethnographers. Ethnography fascinates me. I acquired a taste for it in Aristotle and in the commentaries of Saint Thomas Aquinas. But it was, above all, the commentary of Saint Thomas on the Epistle to the Ephesians, where he asserts that the deepest social structure of the Church, the structure that derives from her unique relation with God, is that of a clan (domus), that convinced me I would be able to find in the primitive and rigid structures of the clan analogies that would be precious in illuminating the life of the Church. To be sure, there are transpositions to be made, but all theology transposes from the natural to the supernatural order. When we say that God is Father, we know that He is not so in the human fashion: we transpose. But He is Father, truly Father, to such a degree that all other paternity models itself on His, is no more than the shadow of His.

First of all by constituting Israel as His own clan, then by constituting His Church as His own clan, God has adopted this primitive and barbaric tribal structure. In His hands this structure has become purified; there is no longer anything barbaric about it because God is above and not below all wisdom and all civilization. But it remains a true clan. This is why the primitive societies, even fetishists, even animists, are closer to understanding the profound reality of Christianity than religious societies that are thought more evolved because they have more abstract notions. I speak as I think—and I know there are numerous ethnographers who think as I do. Islam with its abstract conception of God represents a regression of civilization by comparison with fetishism.

The manner in which God is Father is above the human manner of paternity as the sky is above the earth, but God is truly Father. The manner in which Christ's sacrificial flesh and shed blood are in the center of the Christian religion, this manner is above the bloody rites of primitive societies, but it is Christ's sacrificial flesh and shed blood that are truly there on the altar between the hands of the priest. To reduce this terrible rite to symbolism is to regress to the Old Testament, where a ram, a lamb, or a turtle dove symbolized the true victim, he who alone would take away the sins of the world and would ransom his people. Today we are asked to believe that it is the bread and the wine that symbolize this victim, but the victim is not truly present. "Behold Israel according to the flesh," writes Saint Paul, "are not they who eat of the sacrifices partakers of the altar?" But he says of us Christians that we are in communion not with the altar alone but with the body and the blood of Christ.

1 Cor. 10:18

It remains to discover how all this is possible. There is a theology of the Eucharist in which the essential part is contained in this word, expressly coined: "transubstantiation." By virtue of the rite instituted by Christ on the eve of Maundy Thursday and through God's miraculous omnipotence, at the moment when the priest pronounces the words of consecration—the accidents of the bread and the wine remaining intact and visible on the altar—all the substance of the bread is converted into the substance of Christ's body, all the substance of the wine is converted into the substance of Christ's blood. It is, then, substantially only the body and the blood of Christ that are present on the altar in place of the bread and the wine. And the sacrifice on the cross is thus renewed in a nonsanguinary but real way through the sacramental separation of the body and blood of Jesus Christ. This sacramental way, a miracle of poetry and compassion, thus has for its effect the wiping out of space and time because it deals with substance, not with accidents or quantity. In any place at all, until the end of the world, it is with the unique sacrifice on the cross that we hold communion in truly eating, outside space and outside time, the real sacrificial body and in drinking the real shed blood of Jesus Christ.

It is here, here above all, that Jesus the man dominates time, and we can surprise in the act that refraction, about which I have spoken, of eternity in time.

———

The few lines that follow in the history of Jesus Christ are one of the saddest pages in the Gospel. This man, so proud, so wholly generous, so heroic, so conscious of his divine origin, for the first time holds out his hands and begs for a little love.

John 6:67-71

"From this time many of his disciples turned back and no longer went about with him. Jesus therefore said to the Twelve, 'Do you also wish to go away?' Simon Peter therefore answered, 'Lord, to whom shall we go? Thou hast words of everlasting life, and we have come to believe and to know that thou art the Christ, the Son of God.' Jesus answered them, 'Have I not chosen you, the Twelve? Yet one of you is a devil.' "

The great army of Jesus' partisans has dispersed, he remains with the Twelve, one of whom has already betrayed him in his heart. The atmosphere is like that on the evening of a defeat. Peter, honest Peter, is the one who brings Jesus some of that comfort of which just then he stands in need.

As I have already said, it was not because they were coarse people that those who abandoned Jesus did so. Quite the contrary, they were the ones who judged Jesus' discourse, the bluntness of which in fact made them tremble, as coarse and brutal. The ceremony of the Eucharist as we practice it today has a peaceful appearance, almost abstract, but its content is terrible, it is the participation, at once physical and spiritual, of the faithful in the sacrifice on the Cross, communion with the body and the blood of a sacrificial human victim. It is once again Saint Paul who writes, " 'For as often as you shall eat this bread and I Cor. 11:26-29 drink the cup, you proclaim the death of the Lord, until he comes.' Therefore whoever eats this bread or drinks the cup of the Lord unworthily, will be guilty of the body and the blood of the Lord. But let a man prove himself, and so let him eat of that bread and drink of the cup; for he who eats and drinks unworthily, without distinguishing the body, eats and drinks judgment to himself." I do not believe, indeed I do not, that any heavier responsibility was ever placed on the shoulders of men.

It is also a comfort. When one knows who Jesus is, it would be a mortal grief never to have seen and touched him, to be forever separated from him by time and space. I mean physically separated, for I myself am one of those coarse creatures for whom the physical absence of one they love is the greatest of woes. Images and symbols do not console me.

It is also a hope. It suffices me to know that Jesus' body is there before me, immortal; I know that my own body, if I do not separate myself from his, will be immortal too.

This much is evident about the religion of Jesus: it is concrete, physical, corporeal, and therefore opposed to those religions that consider themselves more spiritual because they are more abstract—which is a grave mental confusion. I do not believe in the remission of sins without effusion of blood. I do not believe in a religion that does not have at its center a sacrificial victim, that is, a murdered body. The body that is the center of Christian adoration is henceforth a glorified body, but it still bears the scars of five wounds because, long ago, on one day among other days, it underwent a violent death in order to enter into glory. And the same road is left open. The task of our redemption can be completed only if our ransomed bodies participate in his glory.

The great theologian of the Eucharist is Saint Thomas Aquinas. He is, moreover, the great theologian of all parts of theology and of theology as a whole. Nothing more can be said. But he is also the great poet of the Eucharist. In his capacity as poet he is closer in nature to Mallarmé than to Verlaine—that is, he is more absolutely a poet. His "Office of the Holy Sacrament" is perfect in form and musicality, with complete identity between the harmony of the words and the harmony of the sense.

We begin with a singular fact, unmatched in the whole history of religions. This poem was written for the feast of the very holy body of Christ: *"In festo Sanctissimi Corporis Christi."* We Christians adore a human body, we have a feast to celebrate this human body, and, for full measure, we call the feast for this body by the name *Corpus Christi.* Let the professors of comparative religion consult their sources, let them search, I do not think that they will discover a single religion, even among those reputedly the most sensual, in which the center of the cult and the object of adoration is a human body and in which that body is venerated and adored with so much candor and magnificence. There have been feasts for Aphrodite and for Dionysus, in which bodies were granted extreme license, but what was adored was Aphrodite and Dionysus, not simply their bodies.

We as Christians celebrate before all else the Body of Christ, and in what precise words!

> . . . Hail, true Body, born of the Virgin Mary . . .
> . . . mystery of the glorious Body and the precious Blood . . .
> . . . fruit of the generous entrails . . .
> . . . Lordly Body . . .
> . . . O Redeeming Host . . .
> . . . sacred mysteries of your body and your blood . . .
> . . . sacred banquet . . .

And, in a prayer, Saint Thomas adds: "Oh very sweet God, grant that I may receive the Body of Your only Son, our Lord Jesus Christ, which he drew from the Virgin Mary, in such manner that I may deserve to be incorporated in his mystical Body and to be counted among his members." The whole Christian religion is expressed in this last prayer in such concrete terms: in fact all is there.

I have very often noticed that in books of theology, even in manuals of piety, there is a certain embarrassment in the language used on the subject of the Eucharist. People do not dare to talk unreservedly about it. Perhaps we resemble more than we like to believe those Jews who were the first auditors and disciples of Jesus. We avoid talking of the body of Christ in the Eucharist, we hardly dare say that we eat his sacrificial flesh and that we drink his blood. We talk of the Presence of Jesus Christ in the Sacrament, or simply of the Real Presence, a little as though it were something abstract. We talk about the Holy Sacrament in a wholly abstract way. Actually we do not like to owe our spiritual salvation to the body of a man, drawn from the entrails of a woman. There is a cellophane covering of puritanism that separates us from the realities redeeming the physical of the Eucharist. Oh, how civilized we are, how delicate! Cursed be that civilization and that delicacy that separates me from the sacred body that is my salvation!

There are innumerable conciliar texts on the subject of the Eucharist. None of them is preferable in my eyes to that of the Roman Council of 1079. It is a profession of faith imposed on Bérenger de Tours, who was the most famous professor of his times. Here it is:

I, Bérenger, believe in my heart and confess with my lips

that the bread and wine that are placed on the altar are, through the mystery of the holy declaration and the words of our Redeemer, substantially transformed into the true flesh, real and life-giving, and into the blood of Jesus Christ, our Lord;

that, after the consecration, there is the true body of Christ, who was born of the Virgin and who was hung on the cross, an offering for the salvation of the world, who sits at the right hand of the Father, likewise the true blood of Christ which gushed from his side;

that all this is done not merely symbolically and by the spiritual power of the Sacrament, but in the true reality of the nature of things and in the truth of their substance, as it is written in this note, as I read it to you, and as you understand it.

This is what I believe, and I shall give no future instruction contrary to this belief. So help me God and the holy Evangelists of God.

———

Theologians seek analogies in the order of nature to explain, not the mystery, but the conditions of the mystery which make that mystery possible. The Eucharist is a poetic masterpiece. The Body of Christ is in the Sacrament as a poem is enclosed in itself: nothing in it can be altered without the disappearance of the Presence and its grace. And as the physical—I was about to say carnal—presence of the entire poem is immediate and primary, and the meaning follows that physical presence and does not precede it, so in the Eucharist, it is the Presence of Christ's body that is immediate and primary, the soul of Christ and his divinity follow, so to speak, upon that corporeal presence. However, the words "follow" and "precede" do not have here, as with the poem and its meaning, their common significance. Everything happens in a sacramental space and time that are, precisely, the absence of time and space.

One should read the questions of Saint Thomas Aquinas on "the manner in which Christ exists in this Sacrament."

Is Christ contained entire in this Sacrament? Yes.

Is the Body of Christ in this Sacrament as though in a place? No.

Is the Body of Christ, together with its proper motions, contained in this Sacrament? No.

Can the eye see, could at least the glorified eye of a saint in heaven see, the manner in which the Body of Christ is contained in this Sacrament? No.

It has been noted that the Gospels, which are very clear about the indissolubility of marriage, say practically nothing at all about sensual pleasure, whereas Saint Paul thunders terrible condemnations against the customs of the pagans. The four Evangelists and Saint Paul, on the other hand, place the Eucharist at the center of the Christian revelation. Now I believe it is impossible for a soul, once it has entered profoundly into the Eucharistic mystery and into the kind of adoration that flows from it, still to attach any value to sensuality, not simply because of the obligation to confess, if one is in a state of mortal sin, before receiving the Sacrament, but principally because devotion to the body of Christ blots out and annihilates the fascination of any other body. *"Fallax gratia, et vana est pulchritudo."*

Prov. 21:30

A distinction must always be made between the substance and the accidents of an object. Beeswax, for example, remains wax though its color, its external form, its weight, its place, its quantity, all may change; the wax remains in substance wax. In this case what changes is what the philosophers call "the accidents," which affect the quantity and the superficial quality of the wax. The voluptuary is avid for sensations of touch, he is eager to see, to listen to, to feel his beloved's body, to be in its presence and measure its length against his own. In this the voluptuary—and sometimes he knows this very well—not only fails to reach the soul of his beloved, he does not even attain to the substance of that body. In its harsh and precise language theology would say that he touches only the accidents.

The poet writes:

> Her fair form answers to a harmony
> Too exquisite for fumbling thought
> To note or analyze its varying accords.

The theologian replies: *accidents*. What the eye sees, what the ear hears, what the sense of smell records, what the lips taste, the size, position, and movements of the body, what the hands touch—all these are *accidents*. The substance, to be sure, is not in some other place, indeed it finds its natural expression in all that denotes it, but the substance itself is not directly accessible to the senses. And it is precisely this substance that Don Juan would like to gain possession of. That is why he is in search less of pleasure than of the disillusionment that lies at its bottom. Don Juan, in his own depths, is actually in agreement with the theologian: he has understood the lie and the vanity of appearances; he knows that everything that pretends to satisfy his hunger, his most profound hunger, is no more than "accidents" and that his hunger will not be assuaged. If he were willing and if God granted him grace, he would be in a favorable state to understand the requirements and realities of the Eucharist.

In the Eucharistic rite what is seen, what is touched, what is tasted, what is measured, what is localized or divided—all that is alien to the body of Christ: these are the accidents of the bread and wine. But the body of Christ is there, substantially present, it is he whom we truly eat, it is his blood that we drink. The voluptuary seeks the accidents alone, and the substance escapes him. The Eucharistic man disregards the accidents, holds them as alien to what he desires: the very substance of the body and blood of Jesus Christ. Thus there are Eucharistic souls whose tears and joys have nothing in common with the ordinary experiences of life. Some of these souls have their motion only around the Host and the Sacrament, as a flower follows the light. A fascinated silence dwells in them, like a face that dwells in a mirror.

There is, of course, no sensualism in the Eucharistic service; the sacramental manner of Christ's corporeal presence there prevents forever any equivocation. The exquisite modesty of the Sacrament between us and this divine body, however, does not repress but on the contrary completely frees the passionate adoration that carries us toward him. How much more authentically are we entitled to use here the words the self-obsessed Narcissus addressed to his own image:

> ... dear body,
> I love you, sole barrier between me and the dead.

By citing here these lines by Valéry, the context of which is in complete opposition to my subject, I am by no means trying to create a syncretism. It is just possible—although sensuality is indeed the exact opposite of Eucharistic devotion—that there is one language and only one in which to express true devotion to a body.

I really believe that what led me to develop this idea was a Eucharistic homily by Saint Gregory the Great, included in the Dominican Breviary for Sunday in the octave of Corpus Christi. I love the candid language of this pope:

I will show you the distance between the delights of the body and those of the heart. Corporeal delights, so long as they are not attained, arouse in us a violent desire; as soon as they are tasted, satiety quickly turns to disgust. On the other hand, so long as we do not obtain spiritual delights, they fill us with distaste; as soon as they are obtained, one begins to desire them. And the more one hungers after them, the more of them one can devour. In the former, desire is the source of pleasure, experience of displeasure. In these, desire is held of no account, experience pleases the more. In assuagement, the desire for spiritual delights augments the soul, for the more one tastes their savor, the more he realizes he is acquiring a further taste for them. This is why one cannot love them so long as one does not possess them because one is ignorant of their savor. Who can love what he does not know? It is thus that the Psalmist instructs us: "Taste then," he says, "and see how delicious is the Lord." As though he were clearly telling us: At the moment you do not know its exquisite taste, place this nourishment of life under the palate of your heart: having tasted its sweetness, you will then become capable of loving it.

At the point we have now reached in the life of Jesus, all this is as yet only a sermon, a prophecy, which will not be realized until the evening of Maundy Thursday, when the Sacrament of the Eucharist will be instituted. The Eucharist is, first of all and above all, a fact as concrete as any other. Calling it a historical fact means that the institution of this Sacrament is dated and circumscribed in time. But what of the substantial Presence of Christ in the Sacrament? It is here indeed that we apprehend at its furthest point of actualization what I have called the phenomenon of refraction peculiar to Jesus, God and man, immersed in time and yet dominating it. In the Sacrament of the Eucharist, the fracture is not only apparent, it is real and total: the body, the true body of Jesus, escapes from subservience to time and space, to measure and sensation. It is free of all that and, in offering itself to us, it draws us into that freedom of which, without him, we could certainly have had no conception. The corporeal and sacramental presence of Jesus is a fact central to the world, but it is a fact that is, so to speak, trans-historical, for it transcends time.

Jesus is there, corporeally present, in the Sacrament, but under an aspect foreign to him, *"sub aliena specie."* What does that mean? The appearance of the bread and the wine persists and subsists miraculously without any ground to support them. What then is the function of these accidents, these appearances, subsisting between the body of Jesus and us? A disguise? A mask? Exactly that, and here again ethnography can be of help to us.

Bérenger, the eleventh-century professor whose profession of faith I have cited—a profession imposed upon him—had a modern mind, that is to say, a mind immersed in the profane, a mind that had lost its sense of the sacred, at least as concerns material things. And when the sacred is not concretized in matter, it ends by deserting this world. Bérenger thought it unworthy of Christ to present himself for adoration under an alien aspect, that of bread and wine. He thought that this was an insupportable lie. And no doubt that is what the mask has become in our profane societies—a carnival mask, a criminal's mask, to baffle pursuit, to mislead the search, to escape from one's proper identity. The mask is by nature essentially ambiguous, and this is what Bérenger no doubt failed to understand. Instead of baffling, it can be an infallible guide; instead of misleading, it can be an open door to the sought-for treasure; instead of concealing identity, it can confirm it.

This, in fact, is what happens in the Eucharist. The appearances are essentially ambiguous. The unbeliever is not an idiot when, trusting solely to what he sees, he says, "Here is bread and wine, and nothing more." The believer is not an idiot either when, trusting in the words of Christ, he says, "No, this is truly the body and the blood of Christ, but under an unfamiliar aspect." The believer knows that, at the moment of consecration, the body of Christ has substantially and secretly taken the place of the bread and wine. The appearance of bread and wine remains, a mask.

But this mask is veracious, it reveals as much as it hides. The appearance does not lie, for this body is here to be eaten, this blood is here to be drunk. This body is more nourishing, is more truly bread, than ordinary bread, whose place it has secretly taken. The blood is more refreshing, more intoxicating, more truly wine, than ordinary wine, whose place it has secretly taken. This is a strange and magnificent cult, efficacious and subtle, the cult that surrounds this man, silent and masked, at the center of the Christian liturgy, whose mask is only candor, sincerity, modesty, and also generosity, for this is how he can deliver himself wholly and without reserve as food and drink, under an alien and veracious appearance.

It is highly fitting that God should save us by means of a body of our own species but one without sin; however, if this body is to be the true savior of the human race, we need more than a symbol, we need the reality of the saving body. To avoid any sensual ambiguity, this body is present under the mask of other elements, but it is indeed the body of God that we eat, it is his blood that we drink, a thing that no other religion was able to imagine but that all primitive religions, possessed of a sense of the sacred, would have longed for in desperation had they thought it possible.

Here we pass over various religions styled spiritual, universal, and intellectual—moral, too, after an evolutionary and philanthropic fashion. I prefer to feel myself in the tradition of the savages who ate the bodies of their heroes in order to acquire their virtues rather than in that of all those austere fanatics who are so splendidly intelligent that they understand everything, each one more a professor than the next, and all unbearably boring. A religion of the salvation of man, if it be a true one, must be a divinely human transaction in which the body and the blood, in a divine way, are not forgotten.

If we disregard the modern, that is profane, function of the mask, which is utilitarian and embarrassing because it is in fact habitually mendacious—save in very great art—and if we turn our attention to the primitive and sacred function, we can see that the Eucharistic disguise (*aliena specie*) is a marvelous means of expressing the sacred. In primitive religious clans, the mask is essentially liturgical, it is associated with adoration, with justice, with healing, with education, with initiation, always as a function of spirits or of the divinity. The totemic ancestor materializes in his mask. Masks were invented to capture spirits. During three thousand years, the Egyptians placed on the face of their dead heroes stylized masks "so that the spirit might find his place of repose, the mask serving as the spirit's guide to allow him to regain his body." In the museum at Athens you see the gold funerary masks of the Mycenaean princes. Gold, the incorruptible metal, obviously signifies immortality, and these masks express a touching expectation and astonishment. Yes, for thousands of years, humanity groped its way, but with an amazing sense of the right direction, toward that which it could not find by itself, that which Jesus Christ alone has given it in abundance.

What is to be said of the way in which the Eucharist fulfills the hope, the explicit hope, of Israel, the people of God? Here indeed is the masterpiece of Jesus' strategy: to be present everywhere at once, instantaneously and permanently, with a corporeal presence that is an event not overwhelming but liberating. He, always he, everywhere. His presence is the exact opposite of those public appearances that also strive for universality in time and space—that of a film star, for instance, or a commercial product. It is a presence that seeks not to alienate anyone, but only to reconcile—an unimaginable presence, solemn, poetic, real.

The whole long, poetic adventure of Israel, the theophanies accompanied by cloud and lightning, the prophecies, the enigmas and the pantomimes, the resounding miracles "with strong hand and upraised arm," here recede into absolute silence, as certain symphonies, the most perfect ones, unfold only in order to create after them a certain quality of silence. And to perceive the quality of this silence, one must recall the symphony from its first murmur. To sense the musical plenitude of the Eucharistic silence, one must have perceived from its very beginning the sonorous unrolling of the history of Israel. It is an intoxicating silence that creates about it an entirely new feeling, owing nothing but to itself.

Jesus Christ is there, however, and he is the Word. In the beginning was the Word; he is also at the end of all things, and the world was created only in order to find one day its full expression in him. While waiting, he is silent, but from the depths of his silence he nevertheless directs the poem of eternity and time.

He is the seed of God—and also the seed of Abraham—physically buried in the field of the world. The harvest will be the revelation of his physical and mystical body at the moment when time, in him, attains its maturity.

He is the glory buried and concealed in the silent but active Presence. Close your eyes. Good. Forget all the accidents subject to the corrupting influence of time and space. Good. Withdraw yourself from all the vicissitudes of history and personal experience. Good. Have you forgotten everything that is under the sky? Then he is there before you, and his body has become a snare to capture your soul.

He is the Son of Man. In him and through him the prince of this world has already suffered defeat. He has already withdrawn time from under the feet of the prince of this world, as one suddenly rolls up a carpet from under the feet of a stranger. And the dominion of that prince extends only over time. But he, he sits bodily besides the Ancient of Days: all power has been placed already and forever upon his human shoulders.

He is the Paschal Lamb, the sacramental, sacrificial victim; he will bear sin away and destroy it forever in a furnace of love.

Here I should like to make perfectly clear that the purity demanded of the believer in order to have communion with the flesh and blood of Christ goes far beyond the simple ability (very rare in itself) to abstract oneself from accidents in order to attain to substance. That is only a Eucharistic athleticism. The invitation to the Eucharist is not an invitation to a performance of mental gymnastics designed to transcend accidents, it is an invitation to a banquet, to a feast, to the Feast of God.

In one of the very first and most moving of the theophanies in the long history of Israel—a theophany in which, moreover, Christians see a dim prefiguration of the Trinity—God in the guise of three angels encounters Abraham beneath the oaks of Mamre. Abraham at once offers them a meal, the best a shepherd can provide, and the three Gen. 18:8 angels accept it. During the whole repast, Abraham "stood by them under the tree, and they did eat." This bucolic meal, this little *fête champêtre* between God and the first of the Patriarchs, is narrated in Genesis, the first book of the Bible. In the Apocalypse, the last book, there is also mention of a meal. Jesus Christ, Lord and God, says, Apoc. 3:20 "Behold, I stand at the door and knock. If any man listens to my voice and opens the door to me, I will come in to him and will sup with him, and he with me." Between these two texts lies the whole gradual progress of divine revelation and of the intimacy of man with his God.

This progression is so enormous that by its end a complete reversal of situation has taken place. Abraham stands upright before his guests, he does not eat with them, he watches them eat, he adopts an attitude of reverence, ready to serve them, and it is he who gives the food. In the last text, however, it is Jesus Christ, Lord and God, who stands outside the door and knocks softly without entering. It is he who has adopted the attitude of humility, of expectation, of constant readiness to serve. The supper he comes to share with his host is the meal par excellence of friendship and of loving intimacy. Death knocks at the door in a very different and imperious fashion from that of the Master of life and death. Should we be shocked? Should we reproach Jesus Christ for having introduced courtesy into the relations of God with man and having carried this courtesy to the limit? Obviously many people when they know that they are masters feel no need to knock at a door before entering: it would be futile to resist them. But are we so grossly made as to regret that the highest lordship goes hand in hand with the most exquisite courtesy, and would we prefer that fear and the motives of fear should be greater determinants of faith in God than the delicate overtures of an attentive love?

In speaking of a pagan—the centurion (whose words the Church puts in the mouths of communicants: "Lord, I am not worthy that you should enter into my house. . . .")—Jesus has explained the faith necessary to participate in the divine banquet: "Amen I say to you, I have not found such great faith in Israel. And I tell you that many will come from the east and from the west, and will feast with Abraham and Isaac and Jacob in the kingdom of heaven, but the children of the kingdom will be put forth into the darkness outside. . . ." Matt. 8:10-12

This is one of those passages in the Gospel where we, good Christians that we are, puff ourselves up and say, "After all, these Jews—if they did not recognize the Messiah, it was because they did not deserve him. Whereas we . . ." Are we so sure of having the faith and the humility of that centurion? In view of the speed with which our Occidental societies are becoming de-Christianized, have we never felt afraid of being numbered among those "children of the kingdom" who deserve to be cast into outer darkness, while the blacks, the Patagonians or the Papuans are perhaps worthier than we of being seated at the same table with Abraham? I have seen the Indians in Mexico performing their devotions in the basilica at Guadalupe: they probably did not know how to read or write and very likely did not get enough to eat, but they had the faith of the centurion, the authenticity of which blazed out with a clarity so strong that it put superstition to shame: on that day, too, I asked questions of myself, without quite daring to reply.

Perhaps the great scandal of the Eucharist—of which Jesus himself speaks—lies here. We would not have asked so much, certainly not this much. The very grandeur and magnificence of the gift dazzle our avarice. We do not like to feel ourselves overwhelmed by such prodigality: this is something simply improper. The great celebration of the Eucharist is called the Feast of God, and we have lost our feeling for the feast, for its paroxysm and its sublime prodigality.

From the beginning, the Prophets have described the Messianic times as an immense festivity, a luxurious banquet, a table open to all at the crossroads or on the mountain: "Wisdom has built her house, she has set up her seven columns; she has dressed her meat, mixed her wine, Prov. 9:1-5 yes, she has spread her table. She has sent out her maidens; she calls from the heights out over the city: 'Let whoever is simple turn in here; to him who lacks understanding, I say, "Come, eat of my food, and drink of the wine I have mixed!" ' "

Isa. 25:6-9 And above all Isaia: "On this mountain the Lord of hosts will provide for all peoples a feast of rich food and choice wines, juicy, rich food and pure, choice wines. On this mountain he will destroy the veil that veils all peoples, the web that is woven over all nations; he will destroy death forever. The Lord God will wipe away the tears from all faces; the reproach of his people he will remove from the whole earth; for the Lord has spoken. On that day it will be said: 'Behold our God, to whom we looked to save us! This is the Lord for whom we looked; let us rejoice and be glad that he has saved us!' "

Obviously there is always a subtle variation between prophecy and reality, the same variation that exists between poetic suggestion and reality, but after the institution of the Eucharist how can one read without being overwhelmed this description of a feast abounding in rich foods and choice wines?

In the next chapter I study the conflict that brought Jesus into opposition with the official authorities of his nation, the conflict that led finally to his condemnation and death. I note at this point and apropos of the Eucharist that one of the important roots of this conflict seems to me to be that the Pharisees, too, had lost their feeling for the feast and that to all intents and purposes they no longer conceived the Messianic era as a festival and a feast. They preferred the Law to the feast. These words may seem obscure: they have, however, a very precise, explicatory meaning.

In his book *L'Homme et le Sacré,* Roger Caillois gives a highly intelligent, well-documented analysis of the feast and its significance in primitive societies and in the clans. His description is absolutely absorbing.

Ethnographers have noted that primitive societies in which the social structure and the social life are entirely dominated by preoccupation with the sacred obey an alternating movement of dispersion and concentration, of dissolution and cohesion, of decay and renewal, a diastole and systole of the social heart. This alternation coincides sometimes with that of the seasons, or perhaps even with a predominance of the sacred over the profane or vice versa. But within the sacred itself this alternation takes place.

Roger Caillois writes:

In ordinary life the sacred manifests itself almost exclusively by interdictions. It is defined as what is "reserved," what is "separate"; it is set aside from common usage, protected by prohibitions designed to prevent any harm to the world order, any risk of unhinging it or of introducing a ferment of trouble. It appears then as essentially *negative*. . . . The elimination of the waste products that accumulate in the functioning of all organisms, the annual liquidation of sins and the expulsion of the old times do not suffice. They serve only to bury the past, crumbling and befouled, *which has served its time* and which must give place to a virgin world, the celebration of which is destined to compel its arrival. The interdictions have shown themselves incapable, for the best reasons, of contributing to a restoration of their first youth. *The regulatory mechanism does not have in itself any principle capable of reinvigorating itself.* It is necessary to call upon the creative virtue of the gods and to return to the beginning of the world, to turn to those forces that first transformed chaos into cosmos. . . . Then all that exists must needs be rejuvenated. *It is necessary to re-enact the creation of the world.*

I am struck by these remarks, not because they allude to a barbarian social framework and to barbarian rites, which modern rationalism has too cavalierly cast aside, but because they define the perspectives of that eternal human nostalgia which I believe the Eucharist, with its rites, its ceremonies, and its prayers, extends and sublimely satisfies. It is the Offertory of the Roman Mass that alludes to the admirable creation of man and the even more admirable re-creation of man through the Redemption.

The feast is an explosion. It must certainly correspond to a biological need for relaxation. In connection with the Saturnalia, the Romans had an axiom that is wisdom itself: *"Semel in anno licet insanire"*—"Once a year men shall be permitted to play the fool," that is, to transgress even the rules of reason and of the social contract. This recurs in the carnival. But it would be too summary a reflection to find in this the whole explanation of the feast. In the primitive society of the clan, the feast is a magical rite that, by a return to the mystical origins of life, abolishes time, the principle of age and of wear-and-tear, and rejuvenates not only the human race but the whole of nature for a new beginning. It restores the world to its virginity and innocence, bringing it close to the divinity itself.

What a helpless and melancholy nostalgia for a lost paradise is implied in the feasts of those rough and savage peoples! They were, nevertheless, peoples who understood perfectly, often far better than we do, that the source of life is divine, that in its depths nature is mystical, that the realities most important to man belong to the sacred order: innocence or transgression, God's favor or His wrath, and decisive victory over time, over wear-and-tear and death. The precious things these peoples seek in their feasts are supplied in superabundance by the Eucharist. That is the presage, pledge, and announcement of the eternal feast of the second paradise. To the question, "Is the effect of this Sacrament to gain possession of glory?" Saint Thomas Aquinas replies with an unhesitating "Yes."

I consider it a grave misfortune, a misfortune on a global scale and probably irreparable, that the colonization by the Occident of the still mentally primitive races took place when it did. It was a time when those so-called savage peoples were living principally the conglomerate life of the clan within unevolved social structures where nevertheless all profound tendencies expressed an insatiable hunger for the mystical and the sacred. The Occident had just become secularized and could offer only a civilization that was almost entirely nonreligious. These peoples who were hungering and thirsting for God were supplied with canned goods and Coca-Cola. I have absolutely nothing against canned goods or Coca-Cola or, in a more general way, against material and mechanical civilization, still less against the necessary effort, which now seems actually to be taking shape, to save humanity from hunger and misery. I simply say that this is not enough and that it never will be enough.

In the thirteenth century, when the papacy instituted the solemn feast of Corpus Christi, there was a prodigious explosion of joy in the whole of Christendom, especially in France and England. Roger Caillois is right in emphasizing that our modern societies, however desacralized they may be, still feel the nostalgia and the need for the feast. In his opinion modern societies, just as bewildered as the coarsest of primitive peoples, satisfy this need in the mad and sacrilegious prodigality of war —and, I would add, in revolution and the arms race, tomorrow perhaps in the conquest of space. Be that as it may, the hunger of these societies remains visibly unassuaged.

In the Gospel according to Luke there is a strange statement by Jesus, Luke 17:37 which is commonly applied to the Eucharist: "Where the body is, there too will the eagles be gathered together"—some translators say "the vultures." Thus the Eucharist is represented to us as a feast and banquet for birds of prey. It is not a meal for ants or insects, it is a repast for eagles.

Humanity's true and permanent feast, perpetually open to all, is the

Eucharist. It bears the believer away from his daily cares and banal sensualities, from the wear and the disillusionment of time, it puts him in communion not only with Jesus Christ but with all the worshipers of Jesus Christ living or dead, with the angels too and with all men who hunger and thirst for this banquet without even knowing it exists. As a true rite of theophany, the Eucharist incorporates this in its immense ceremony, which transcends time and history and renews the world.

And a voice came forth from the throne, saying, "Praise our God, all you *Apoc. 19:5-7, 9* his servants, and you who fear him, the small and the great!" And I heard as it were a voice of a great crowd, and as the voice of many waters, and as the voice of mighty thunders, saying, "Alleluia! for the Lord, our God almighty, now reigns! Let us be glad and rejoice and give glory to him; for the marriage of the Lamb has come, and his spouse has prepared herself. . . ." And he said to me, "Write: Blessed are they who are called to the marriage supper of the Lamb."

With this beatitude I end the chapter.

CHAPTER XVII

The Conflict

IN HIS brief but very learned history of Judaism, from Abraham to the founding of the state of Israel, Isidore Epstein writes of the destruction of Jerusalem in the year 70 of our era: "Of all the parties and all the sects that existed at the time of the Destruction, and according to an ancient source *there were twenty-four of them, the only one to survive the national cataclysm was the Pharisees.* All the other parties failed their people in the time of dire need. The Judaeo-Christians at the very outbreak of the war hurried to the safe retreat of Pella beyond the Jordan, while the Sadducees, the Zealots, and Essenes, and all the other sects vanished gradually from the scene. The Pharisees alone stood at their post and were left to rebuild the shattered fabric of the spiritual life of Israel. The Pharisees were indeed the party eminently suited to cope with the needs of the times."

Although little is known of the circumstances in which the state of Israel was sunk at that time, the exactitude of this description can be recognized. For the subject that now occupies us, the history of Jesus Christ, such a state of affairs suggests two interesting conclusions. The first is that it is practically impossible to form an exact idea of the religious and political society of the Jews at the time of Jesus Christ, that is, before the destruction of Jerusalem: twenty-four parties, at once political and religious, of whose names we retain barely five (the Pharisees, the Sadducees, the Essenes, the Zealots, the Sicarians), before the catastrophe, and then after the catastrophe, only one, the Pharisees. This is so radical a transformation that it is extremely difficult to picture what existed before from what remains at the end.

Without making any value judgment, I suggest two parallel cases. France, between the two World Wars, seethed with parties, sects, dissensions, and discords. Let us suppose that after the Second World War she found herself with only one party, the champion of legalism and political realism, the Action Française. How could one form an idea, from the character of this single party, of what France had been like at the time of the Front Populaire? At present the United States of America swarms with religious sects. Let us suppose that, as the result of a national cataclysm, only the Baptists survived to represent the religious spirit in the United States. Who could form an idea of the religious complexity that preceded it? The same is true here: the party of the Pharisees found itself alone, and it marked the later national traditions so strongly that it is almost impossible for us to know what Israel was like before the destruction of Jerusalem.

The second conclusion is that the only party to survive the catastrophe and to take Israel into its hands, the party of the Pharisees, is that one of all the parties in Israel that had been pre-eminently opposed to Jesus Christ. In this fact lies an immense and perhaps irreparable misfortune. Retrospectively the conflict of Christ with the Pharisees would seem to extend to the whole Jewish nation. This conclusion, however, appears to me to be absolutely false. Nothing prevents us from thinking—on the contrary, there is much to make us believe, including the Gospels and above all the Synoptics—that the enemies of Christ were only a minority of the nation (socially prominent, to be sure) but that the immense majority of the Jewish people were on the side of Christ.

But there is more, and it is much more serious. I beseech my readers—and I am thinking now especially of Jewish readers—to believe me when I assert that I am speaking with extreme candor. I know very well that I may be mistaken, but when I raise certain questions I dare to assume that these questions arise objectively. It is important for all to know what questions really arise, even if it should happen that I am incapable of supplying an adequate answer; and this may well be the case with me, perhaps more often than the average. I believe that the destruction of Jerusalem, the shipwreck of the state of Israel, in the year 70, the dispersion of the nation (begun before that but now irremediable) away from its natural and sacred center, the Temple, has singularly impoverished the ancient religion of Israel and that the taking over of its destiny by the single sect of the Pharisees in no wise compensated for this impoverishment but, on the contrary, consecrated it, solidified it, and rendered it definitive. And here is the question that confronts me: since the mutation was so extensive, profound, and irreversible, since so many elements, including essential ones, were suddenly thrown overboard, is Judaism still recognizable after it? Personally I do not think so. For me there are, historically, two Judaisms, with a break between them, the Judaism from Abraham to the destruction of Jerusalem and the Judaism after the destruction of Jerusalem. Christ, however, lived and died under the first.

I know that here I am entering upon an endless quarrel similar to the one that brings Protestants into conflict with Catholics. The Pharisees have insisted on the character of Judaism as individual, spiritual (I will not say mystical), universal, and disincarnate. The Holy Torah has taken the place for them of country, Promised Land, Temple, and the Ark of the Covenant; it has perhaps even taken the place of the Promise and has concretized among them the Presence of God and His glory. They have thus saved what could be saved, which is the maxim in all defeats; they have thus enabled the nation to survive. But at what cost? They have had to abandon: the concrete reality of the Temple at Jerusalem, home of God and dwelling place of His glory; the priesthood of Aaron; the sacrifices that are the center of gravity in every authentic religion; the Apocalypse, with its eschatological tradition so profoundly connected with Messianism (I discuss this in the next chapter); and the Promised Land, heritage of Abraham.

Here are many precious things abandoned beyond recovery. Such an impoverishment of the ancient religion of Israel can be compared in fact only to the Lutheran crisis, which threw overboard the authority of the See of Rome, the corporeal Presence of Christ in the Eucharist, the priesthood of Christ and his hierarchy, the profound significance of the Sacraments and of grace.

An immense withering away! The loss of the Temple above all and the profanation of the holy mountain, which had been since Solomon's time the visible footstool of God, must have appeared to many Jews like the decapitation of their religion. It is true that the Pharisees had the merit of saving what could be saved, but how many Jews have died, by the tens of thousands, who would not acquiesce in having snatched from them what they judged to be thrice holy and irreplaceable? When Hadrian in 132 had a temple to Jupiter Capitolinus erected on Mount Zion, the Jews revolted once more, without hope of success, simply for the honor of God, under the leadership of Simeon Bar Kochba, who, Epstein says, "drew after him the greater part of the populace." A pure and heroic revolt, if ever there was one! He was vanquished, to be sure, twice vanquished, for he was killed and the event proved him wrong.

Bar Kochba, however, was only a war leader, who left behind him nothing but a few letters, whereas the Pharisees on the other hand were scribes. Those who write finally make themselves understood, their reasons persist, that is, in the end they prove themselves right. Those who are able only to shed their blood die a second time in the heart of history.

It is true, the sacrilege was there, ineluctable. Horrible Roman barbarism had erected this grotesque idol of Jupiter in the very place where the God of Israel had sat in glory. It remained there. Like the Pharisees, but not for the same reasons, I believe that the Temple was no longer necessary to the survival of Judaism. Why? Because the Presence of God had already migrated to the body of Jesus Christ, and was henceforth inaccessible to the blows of a temporal destiny. The Sacraments of the new covenant had replaced the ancient sacrifices. The priesthood of Jesus had replaced the priesthood of Aaron by its sovereign fulfillment. Reality had replaced metaphors by giving them their definitive meaning. The entire earth had become the heritage of Abraham; all races could engraft themselves onto the ancient stem of Abraham, and the benediction fell on all nations, ransomed by Jesus Christ. In Christ and Christianity the religion, the rites, and the prophecies of ancient Israel, from Abraham to the destruction of Jerusalem, are perfectly accomplished. Bar Kochba was right: one must fight and die for the Temple, but the Temple of the God of Israel is no longer where he believed it was. The Presence of God and His glory have migrated elsewhere, just as they formerly migrated from the Tabernacle to the Temple.

So it is in history: there are certain catastrophes that have the effect of irreparable amputations. Oh, no doubt they are explicable, there are ambiguities, and neither side is wholly pure—still less the third side that has remained neutral. Such was the fall of Constantinople, such the defeat of Bar Kochba. I shall remain forever inconsolable about it. There will be those who will laugh to see me attribute so much importance to Bar Kochba, whose name they have not so much as read in the course of their studies. This in fact is what I meant when I said that some of the vanquished die twice. Was the stake for which they died less important on that account? The Romans killed Bar Kochba, but in the end it was the Pharisees who triumphed over him, imposing on Judaism an amputation that would have horrified that gallant man.

This little introduction is intended to direct the present chapter toward its goal, the explanation of the conflict between Christ and his adversaries, and, in the first instance, the definition of those adversaries and the pinpointing of the conflict. For this material is full of ambiguities, and what purpose is there in writing if not to begin by dissipating ambiguities?

As I have said, it happened that, before the destruction of Jerusalem, the caste that was principally opposed to Christ was the Pharisees, the same caste that later on was to assume and confiscate the whole destiny of Judaism. But in the time of Jesus things were far less simple: the Temple, the chief priest, the priesthood of Aaron, the blood sacrifices, and the Sanhedrin existed as well, side by side with the Law, the Holy Torah. It even seems that the Pharisees had not yet succeeded in imposing upon the whole nation the authority of their oral interpretation of the Torah, a point that was still much in free dispute. It is in fact on precisely this point that the conflict between the Pharisees and Jesus was joined, and perhaps before that between them and John the Baptist. After all, the Pharisees at that time represented only one minority party in the totality of the national life. One could still refuse to adhere to their ideals and methods and yet be counted a good Jew. Since first I was able to read the newspapers, I have always profoundly distrusted the Action Française, but I did not think myself a less good Frenchman on that account. Members of the A.F., however, considered all those who opposed them bad Frenchmen; perhaps it was the same way with the Pharisees.

I absolutely refuse to believe that Christ rejected the Law, but he did violently, deliberately, and completely reject the Pharisees' interpretation of the Law. It was, however, this partisan interpretation that, fifty years after Christ and as a result of the collapse of the state, was going to achieve a definitive triumph in the heart of Judaism. The Gospel according to John was written in the context of the Pharisees' triumph, and this perhaps in part explains why this Gospel so easily identifies "the Jews" with the enemies of Christ. This is an extrapolation that is unfair to the majority of the Jews who were Jesus' contemporaries, and it is historically inaccurate. This is something that needs to be known and said because it is true.

The Synoptics, who lived before the destruction of Jerusalem, are careful not to identify the Jewish people as a whole with the enemies Mark 12:37 of Jesus. On the contrary, they constantly emphasize the fact that "the mass of the people listened to him with pleasure." They meticulously identify Jesus' adversaries in an intellectual, governing class: principally the Pharisees, the scribes, the doctors of the Law, and, to a lesser degree, the Sadducees, who exercised the highest theocratic and sacerdotal functions in the state. Unfortunately, it is necessary to dwell on this point:

the fact that, very generally, over a period of two thousand years, Christians have held all the Jews uniformly and collectively responsible for the Passion and death of Jesus Christ is one of the deepest and most tenacious roots of anti-Semitism.

Someone will tell me that Hitler cannot be considered an exemplary Christian. I reply that it is foolish to condemn Hitler if one does not repudiate from the bottom of his heart, from the bottom of his soul, absolutely and completely, the police system and the murderous machinery that Hitler set in motion. But this system, this machinery, was not invented by him. The pogrom existed long before Hitler, utilized by Christians principally against Jews. Hitler applied to the pogrom and the inquisition, which had till then been at the handicraft stage, the seven principles of efficiency that bring an undertaking to the "mass production" stage: energy, decision, economy, continuity, systematization, speed, and repetition. He organized the pogrom and the inquisition as assembly lines. The result was the death of six million Jews, brothers by race of our Lord Jesus Christ. I find it extremely hypocritical to condemn Hitler without condemning with equal horror the pogrom and the inquisition, which have sullied for so long the history of Christian peoples, and the principle of which Hitler simply industrialized, exactly as Lenin industrialized political revolution.

Anti-Semitism would not be so easy for Christians or so widespread among them if it did not have a preservative social usefulness. It dispenses us from any need to examine our consciences at all deeply about our own responsibility for the murder of God. I shall explain.

The juridical murder of Jesus Christ is so horrible a crime that we are compelled to seek out its causes and its authors. That murder stands in the center of human history, monstrous, crushing, inevitable. Who will dare to take the responsibility and say, "It is I who did that"? Our epoch is so disoriented that it has lightheartedly assumed the responsibility for killing God: "God is dead, and it is we who have killed Him." But Jesus Christ is not only God, he is also a man without sin, the innocent childhood of the race. One cannot assassinate God without at the same time killing this child of men, the only innocent. It is not the least among the consequences of the mystery of the Incarnation that we can no longer disembarrass ourselves of God without at the same time dipping our hands in the only innocent blood, and this is something that even Nietzsche was not willing to do; but it does not depend on Nietzsche or anyone else—that is how it is, no one can alter it. God imprisoned Himself in the flesh of a man, the only man without sin; one cannot kill God without immolating that sacred flesh. Who then has killed God? Who then has killed the innocent childhood of the race? These two questions eternally equal only one. The modern epoch, however, is dominated intellectually by the inquisition; it writhes as though in a poisoned snare: whether to sacrifice the innocent in order to save God or to kill God in order to save the innocent. But this *is* a snare, a false problem, like so many of our modern problems. Some day it will certainly be necessary to recognize that for the innocent there is no salvation save in God and His holy service, and that the true service of God is incompatible with the sacrifice of the innocent.

The real question is: who then killed Jesus Christ, true God and innocent man? Everyone recoils in horror, ready to attribute to anyone at all—provided it is not himself or one of his—the responsibility for this atrocious crime. Then the answer comes of itself, in all its intellectual cowardice: the Jews killed Jesus Christ. The anti-Semitism of the Christians is a way of eternally washing their hands of the blood of the just man. Provided I am not a Jew, I can be absolutely sure I did not kill Jesus Christ, I can be absolutely sure of never even being capable of killing him, since this inexpiable crime is eternally reserved to a single race, whose indelible malediction it is. Henceforth this accursed race is liable to all punishments; among them there is not a single innocent. It is impossible to describe the extent of the moral devastation among Christians, the hecatombs of innocents among the Jews, that this imposition of racial anti-Semitism on the part of Christians has caused in the course of history.

For this is a historical as well as a moral swindle. It is a historical swindle because it was not the entire Jewish people, it was not even the Jews as such, who were opposed to Jesus Christ and finally condemned him. It was certain legalistic and religious fanatics, the Pharisees, allied in this instance with a privileged class, the Sadducees. The racial anti-Semitism of the Christians is a moral swindle too. The juridical murder of Christ is a crime of the priests and the doctors of the Law, it is the crime of bigots. It is Tartuffe who killed Jesus Christ and who, today as well as yesterday, is always capable of killing him, in all tranquility of conscience.

Worst of all, the priests who judged and condemned Jesus Christ were true priests of the true God, the doctors of the Law were students of a divinely appointed Law. In the course of his trial and of the long quarrel that preceded it, Jesus Christ never contested the legitimacy of the authority held by his adversaries. What does this mean? Well, it means that one can be a legitimate shepherd of souls and at the same time capable of killing God and the innocent. Neither sacerdotal ordination nor the most legitimate and authentic spiritual mission protects one from Pharisaism and from murderous hypocrisy. That would be too convenient.

We are well aware that the priests and the monks who judged Joan of Arc and the bishop who condemned her were real priests, real monks, and a real bishop. They were not monsters, they did not think of themselves as monsters, some among them certainly thought they were doing their duty; this juridical murder of an innocent woman, of a saint, did absolutely nothing to impair their social honorability or their advancement; Bishop Cauchon is still honorably entombed in the cathedral of Lisieux, in the beautiful chapel where Saint Thérèse of the Infant Jesus made her First Communion. The judges of Joan of Arc consisted of "an honest bishop," "honest canons," and slightly fanatical monks; some of them no doubt were cowards, but all were assuredly "Pharisees" in some measure, a bit "Tartuffe" at the edges. May God have mercy on them! To make use once more of Bernanos' words, who can pride himself on not having in his veins a single drop of those vipers' blood?

The trial and death of Joan of Arc have always been a proof to me that the anti-Semitism of the Christians, based on the collective charge of deicide, is an insupportable monstrosity. When I read the documents and retreat into my own depths, weighing all the circumstances of the condemnation of Christ or of Joan of Arc, I am not sure, had I been there, on which side I should have found myself. It is so easy to slip into Pharisaism, and from Pharisaism into shedding innocent blood.

Montesquieu maintained that "we owe to the Code of the Visigoths all the maxims, principles, and views of the Inquisition of today." It would be worth while to make sure of that: in my capacity as Christian, nothing prevents me from holding the Code of the Visigoths in profoundest scorn, if it is inhuman. In the work of Francesco Pegna, a sixteenth-century Spanish theologian who undertook to justify the Inquisition, I read: "If an innocent man is unjustly condemned, he has no reason to complain of the sentence of the Church, which was based on sufficient proof and could not take account of what was hidden. If false witnesses caused his condemnation, he should receive his sentence with resignation and rejoice to die for the truth." If one sniffs this pious commentary from all sides, it is impossible not to detect the subtle scent of Tartuffe and the Pharisees.

I do not think that these reflections on the anti-Semitism of certain Christians are in any way a departure from my subject. It is my belief that the conflict that brought Jesus Christ into opposition with the Pharisees, the trial of Jesus, and his condemnation to death are at the center of the story, perpetually timely, perpetually renewed, and that it would be much too easy to think that the name of Christian and the sacred seal of baptism infallibly vaccinate a man against injustice and immunize him against any possibility of dipping his hands in innocent blood. On the contrary, this dreadful security of conscience which arms the souls of certain judges and makes them capable of condemning the innocent in the name of what they consider a superior cause, is, I believe, precisely the same security of conscience that armed the souls of the judges of Jesus Christ.

John 16:12   Jesus Christ himself was led to denounce this kind of justice: "I have told you this in order that you may not be scandalized. They will throw you out of the synagogue. Moreover, the hour will come when whoever kills you will imagine that he is rendering worship to God." Let us think carefully: it would be all too convenient to believe that it was only in the name of the synagogue that the innocents of this world have been massacred. Beyond the synagogue and a brief persecution of the Christians by the Jews (for which the Christians have since exacted very ample payment), Jesus was denouncing in advance the nature of certain juridical murders of the innocent in the name of a supreme cause, be that cause the interests of the Church and the Spanish nation against the Jews handed over to the Inquisition, or the reasons of state of Louis XIV against the Huguenots, or the sacred superiority of the German race according to Hitler, or the necessities of history and the mission of an ideal proletariat according to the Communists—one could prolong the list indefinitely. It is always Tartuffe who condemns and kills the innocent.

———————

How one would love to remake history . . . childish wish!

No matter how often it happened, when I was young and rereading Victor Hugo's account of the Battle of Waterloo, when at last the cannon thundered in the distance, I would always hope it was Grouchy: "Sudden and joyous, he said: Grouchy. It was Blücher." It made no difference that I knew in advance the battle was lost, I always believed at the decisive moment the miracle would occur and hope would not change sides.

That is where I am in my book. I cannot keep from hoping once more that the Pharisees will understand and will become reconciled with Christ, that they too will cry, "Blessed is he who comes in the name of the Lord!" Nevertheless, I know that none of this happened but that all reached its consummation in malediction.

It is true, and all historians recognize the fact, that the Pharisees claimed an oral tradition of the Law, parallel to the written Law of Moses and constituting an authorized commentary on that Law: it is this traditional, oral commentary that must, ultimately, be the source of the Mishnah and the Talmud. Without in any way claiming that the Law had no need of commentaries or that the whole tradition was misleading, Jesus Christ took sides with steady determination against the whole scholastic judicial system, which was smothering the very text of the Law beneath the commentary, which was effacing what was primary in order to throw into relief what was secondary, which was strangling the very spirit of the Law in the name of its literal observance. "You make void," he said to the Pharisees, "the Word of God by your tradition." A terrible accusation, among a people born of the Word and of the Promise of God: what would Israel be without the Word of God? The conflict between Jesus Christ and the Pharisees is therefore basic; it bears upon the foundation of things.

Matt. 15:6

Jesus does not contest the authority of the Law of Moses; quite the contrary, it is the pure, bright meaning of the Law that he defends against the Pharisees, he will not tolerate that it be obscured. He proclaims himself more faithful to Moses than the Pharisees themselves; at bottom he claims to be more a Jew than they are. "And he said to them, 'Well do you nullify the commandment of God, that you may keep your own tradition! For Moses said . . . But you say . . . You make void the commandment of God by your tradition, which you have handed down.'" Jesus then pronounces these words, at the sound of which all theologians should eternally tremble, all scholastics, all commentators, and, more than anyone else, the author of this book: "Every plant that my heavenly Father has not planted will be rooted up. Let them alone; they are blind guides of blind men. But if a blind man guide a blind man, both fall into a pit."

Mark 7:9-11, 13

Matt. 15:13-14

If I were a Jew, it would interest me, as Jew, in the highest degree to know who was the more Jew, Christ or the Pharisees. The answer is by no means self-evident, save for those who do their history with their viscera and not with a magnifying glass on the documents. Jesus proclaims the incontestable and unshakable authority of the Law of Moses: "Do not think that I have come to destroy the Law or the Prophets. I have not come to destroy, but to fulfill."

Matt. 5:17

Concerning the very nature of law there is an ambiguity analogous to the ambiguity that obscures the nature of our understanding. Is intelligence a directed function that devours the very substance of things, not consuming them but assimilating them entire, and that, through this purposeful assimilation, puts us in communion with the universe? Or is the understanding, rather, forever a prisoner of its own myth, reduced to deifying itself or to annihilating itself in order to secure the illusion of freedom? If the only purpose of the understanding is to know itself, instead of knowing the universe and through the universe God, then it is its own idol, it knows from the start the vanity and the eternal emptiness of that religion of which it is at once the idol, the priest, and the victim. What is called philosophical idealism is a Pharisaism of the understanding: the idealists are those who do not enter and who keep others from entering.

It is the same with the Law. Is it pregnant with purpose or is it eternally closed in upon itself? Is it a "means" to something else, much higher and much more precious, or is it self-sufficient, the alpha and omega of all justice? Is it "poetic," suggestive of Christian purposes, or is it instead "prosaic," expressing only itself—does it dance or is it content to walk? The basis of the conflict between Christ and the Pharisees is that he had a poetic and purposive conception of the Law, and they had a prosaic and literal one. It is striking that Jesus does not speak of the Law except in connection with the Kingdom of God, that for him the Law is a living and fecund organism and that the fruit of the Law is the Kingdom of God, and that one cannot rightly judge a tree except by its fruit. The tree is made for the fruit, it finds its fulfillment in that. It is through the fruit, its quality and its flavor, that the tree must be judged; it is not the tree that judges the fruit. Christ is never tired of insisting on the primary function of the Law, to give birth to the Kingdom of God. The Law is essentially prophetic and eschatological, poetic, suggestive, and pregnant with the Kingdom of God; it is in the Kingdom of God and in it alone that the Law finds its fulfillment and is delivered. When Jesus proclaims the coming of the Kingdom of God in himself and through himself, he proclaims at the same time that the Law has come to term, but this is not a denial of the Law, it is its ful-

Luke 16:16 fillment, as giving birth is the fulfillment of a woman. "Until John came, there were the Law and the Prophets; since then the kingdom of God is being preached and everyone is forcing his way into it." One is born to the Kingdom of God by the aid of forceps. To stay behind and refuse to move from the Law to the Kingdom is to wish to remain in the condition of a foetus.

Jesus blames the Pharisees for not seeing the relation between the
John 5:39 Law and himself, leader and fulfiller of the Kingdom of God: "You search the Scriptures, because in them you think that you have life everlasting. And it is they that bear witness to me." It is he who is the

fruit of the Law; how can they fail to see that? Justice, the fruit of the Law and promised by it—that is he, how can they fail to recognize him? "Do not think that I have come to destroy the Law or the Prophets. I have not come to destroy, but to fulfill. For amen I say to you, till heaven and earth pass away, not one jot or one tittle shall be lost from the Law till all things have been accomplished. . . . For I say to you that unless your justice exceeds that of the Scribes and Pharisees, you shall not enter the kingdom of heaven." *Matt. 5:17-18, 20*

Astonishing dialectic: heaven and earth are made for the Law, which is made for the Kingdom of God, and all this will find its consummation at once. In the same text Jesus seems to make observance of the Law the condition and the measure of the place that each can obtain in the Kingdom of God: "Therefore whoever does away with one of these least commandments, and so teaches men, shall be called least in the kingdom of heaven; but whoever carries them out and teaches them, he shall be called great in the kingdom of heaven." *Matt. 5:19*

I imagine that it was texts like these that were the justification for the founding, after the ascension of the Lord, of the Judaeo-Christian community, where for a long time the ceremonies of the old Law were observed together with the Sacraments and precepts of the new. The fruit does not detach itself from the tree all at once, the umbilical cord is not immediately cut. But finally the Judaeo-Christians themselves recognized that the Kingdom of God had come with Jesus and in him, and that through him the Law had borne its fruit: this the Pharisees will never admit. In general terms, the New Testament gives us a privileged picture of a particularly cruel confrontation between fruitful legitimacy and sterile legalism.

———

The conflict of Christ with the Pharisees ended in the most famous trial in history, as a result of which Jesus was condemned and executed. But the trial of Jesus was preceded by another trial, that of the Pharisees themselves, a trial conducted summarily and with blazing eloquence by Jesus Christ. It is this that gives the conflict its inexorable aspect of mutual excommunication. The two parties threw everything into the scale, absolutely everything—their goods, their lives, their prestige, their authority, their responsibility, their eloquence, their persons. Jesus will find himself, naked as a worm, hung on a cross on the mountain. But the chief priest will rend his garment and reveal himself naked. The veil of the Temple will be torn in two and the sanctuary will show itself bare and deserted. Judas, the traitor, will hang himself and his belly will burst open. The earth itself will be rent and will vomit forth specters. But the Pharisees, too, will be despoiled and will eternally wear mourning for this moment. All will have thrown all into the scales, all will sink in the catastrophe, the scales themselves will be engulfed.

Jesus' indictment of the Pharisees, which is reported to us in the extraordinary twenty-third chapter of Matthew, begins with a statement of the legitimate or presumed authority of the Pharisees, who in effect claimed the right to interpret the Law: "The Scribes and the Pharisees have seated themselves in the chair of Moses." From this magisterial and authoritative position, it is unlikely that they will easily allow themselves to be dislodged.

Matt. 23:2

Political power is enviable, and political ambition is one of the strongest passions in the world, the source of many injustices. For certain more sophisticated persons, power over souls is even more enviable, it is also more formidable, it extends much further. Although I have trouble realizing it, history proves to us that there is often great pleasure in being able to send one's enemy to prison or even to the scaffold. The pleasure of the Grand Inquisitor is to send you to hell. It is most remarkable that Jesus Christ never questions the authority of the chief priest and that he explicitly acknowledges a certain authority to the Pharisees. The charge he brings against them has absolutely nothing to do with that share of authority that is legitimately theirs; it has to do with the way in which they exercise their authority, with the abuses of it, with the contradictions between their teaching and their conduct—that is, he accuses them of hypocrisy, which is the natural and vicious downward tendency of authority even when it is legitimate, just as justice, compassion, loyalty, and a certain candid heroism are the ascensional and virtuous forces in authority.

Nothing could be clearer than Jesus' words, which are eternally applicable, not only to the Pharisees, but to all those who hold authority, even legitimate authority, when it is hypocritically abused. "Do what they tell you, then, continue to observe what they tell you but do not imitate their actions, for they tell you one thing and do another." If Jesus Christ had not recognized a positive legitimacy in the Law of Moses and in the teachings of the Pharisees he would never have said that.

Then come the central and massive accusations in the indictment: They teach and they do not act. They fasten up packs too heavy to be borne, and lay them on men's shoulders; they themselves will not stir a finger to lift them. They act always so as to be a mark for men's eyes.

Their hearts are set on taking the chief places, the first seats in the synagogue, and having their hands kissed in the market place. They loved to be called Rabbi. They do not enter, but they keep others from entering. They strain out the gnat, but they swallow the camel.

Who among us, possessing one particle of authority over souls, would not tremble to merit such reproaches? And I am not speaking only of priests, and I am not speaking only of the others. I am speaking of all those who are *clercs*—writers, journalists, philosophers, professors, politicians, the official dispensers of advice, the distributors of truth. Sirs, it is to all of us that this discourse is addressed.

Then criticism changes to invective. Never did anyone handle invective as Jesus Christ did. He uses it to whip up the conflict, the event rises to its paroxysm, thus leaving no alternative save a brutal denouement. It must be acknowledged that Jesus, like all the Prophets of his race, had a genius for caricature; the features that make up his portrait of the Pharisee are unforgettable. Bergson said, "The caricaturist's art is to seize this sometimes imperceptible movement and to render it visible to all eyes by emphasizing it. He makes his models grimace as they themselves would have grimaced if they had given their grimace full scope." Invective and caricature are impossible without generalization. It would be unjust to think that all Pharisees without exception corresponded to the portrait Jesus made of them; the Acts of the Apostles records the noble words of Gamaliel, Saint Paul's master, but no doubt he was the exception that proves the rule.

The discourse continues with a series of maledictions. If these maledictions had not been really pronounced by Jesus, who would have dared to put them in his mouth? Here again is one of those signs of the veracity of the Gospel. The Sermon on the Mount and the Beatitudes seem in natural accord with the personality of him who said of himself that he was "gentle and humble of heart." But opposed to the Beatitudes stand the Maledictions, just as authentic, just as eloquent as the Beatitudes. The Christian wends his way toward eternity between these two high walls, the Beatitudes on one side, the Maledictions on the other. Here nothing can replace the bare text of the Gospel.

"But woe to you, Scribes and Pharisees, hypocrites! because you shut the kingdom of heaven against men. For you yourselves do not go in, nor do you allow those going in to enter.

"Woe to you, Scribes and Pharisees, hypocrites! because you devour the houses of widows, praying long prayers. For this you shall receive a greater judgment.

Matt. 23:13-33

"Woe to you, Scribes and Pharisees, hypocrites! because you traverse sea and land to make one convert; and when he has become one, you make him twofold more a son of hell than yourselves.

"Woe to you, blind guides, who say, 'Whoever swears by the temple, it is nothing; but whoever swears by the gold of the temple, he is bound.' You blind fools! for which is greater, the gold, or the temple which sanctifies the gold? 'And whoever swears by the altar, it is nothing; but whoever swears by the gift that is upon it, he is bound.' Blind ones! for which is greater, the gift, or the altar which sanctifies the gift? Therefore he who swears by the altar swears by it, and by all things that are on it; and he who swears by the temple swears by it and by him who dwells in it. And he who swears by heaven swears by the throne of God, and by Him who sits upon it.

"Woe to you, Scribes and Pharisees, hypocrites! because you pay tithes on mint and anise and cummin, and have left undone the weightier matters of the Law, right judgment and mercy and faith. These things you ought to have done, while not leaving the others undone. Blind guides, who strain out the gnat but swallow the camel!

"Woe to you, Scribes and Pharisees, hypocrites! because you clean the outside of the cup and the dish, but within they are full of robbery and uncleanness. Thou blind Pharisee! clean first the inside of the cup and of the dish, that the outside too may be clean.

"Woe to you, Scribes and Pharisees, hypocrites! because you are like whited sepulchers, which outwardly appear to men beautiful, but within are full of dead men's bones and of all uncleanness. So you also outwardly appear just to men, but within you are full of hypocrisy and iniquity.

"Woe to you, Scribes and Pharisees, hypocrites! you who build the sepulchers of the prophets, and adorn the tombs of the just, and say, 'If we had lived in the days of our fathers, we would not have been their accomplices in the blood of the prophets.' Thus you are witnesses against yourselves that you are the sons of those who killed the prophets. You also fill up the measure of your fathers. Serpents, brood of vipers, how are you to escape the judgment of hell? . . ."

It does not matter that I have read these lines a thousand times, I am still stunned now as I transcribe them. Could he not have said these things more gently? No. Harsh things must be harshly said if they are to be effective. But what severity, what violence, what inexorable condemnation, all the more overpowering because this passage is single and unique in the Gospel! It seems—indeed it does more than seem, it is certain—that for Jesus there is only one inexpiable sin and that is hypocrisy, for it is certainly hypocrisy that is aimed at here, so accurately that the word "pharisaism" has become its synonym. Hypocrisy is the antithesis of charity, which is the form of all Christian virtues, so completely so that love of God alone suffices to render a man universally virtuous. Hypocrisy is universal disintegration not only of all the virtues, but of the vices as well, which become through it vices of vice. An analysis might well be made of the essential pharisaism of fashion in our customs. How many have allowed themselves to be swept into this or that depravity, sexual or otherwise, simply because, in the milieu where they live, that is the fashion?

These celebrated and frightening Maledictions determined once and for all the temporal destiny of Jesus. By snatching the masks from the hypocrites, Jesus signed his own death warrant. Tartuffe never forgives being unmasked. Jesus Christ was assassinated juridically and hypocritically by Tartuffe.

Several of the charges in Christ's indictment of the Pharisees seem to us outdated, and for this reason they do not move us. What do we care about phylacteries, flowing locks, the tax on mint, on caraway, on rue, and on all legumes? What is not outdated is the implacable declaration that brings Tartuffe into opposition with Jesus Christ. Pascal tells us that Jesus is in agony until the end of the world. Until the end of the world, too, and at each minute that passes and within every conscience, Christ rises to his full stature and confronts Tartuffe to unmask him. He who has never been in the closed arena of this confrontation is already, body and goods, in the camp of Tartuffe, even though he may pay lip service to Jesus Christ. Tartuffe alone remains outside the Kingdom of Heaven, beyond redemption, beyond the salvation brought by Jesus Christ; a magic threshold forever keeps him from entering, otherwise he would have to discard his mask and mantle of hypocrisy. His hopeless destiny is to prevent others too from entering. There is no greater impediment to conversion than an honest soul's fear of finding himself in the company of Tartuffe. Truth, however, demands that this fear, too, be surmounted. We are in such wretched plight that for us to wish at all costs to distinguish ourselves from Tartuffe is impossible without some measure of hypocrisy. Only with death are all masks cast away.

———

Great human errors, those that have great powers of seduction and produce great catastrophes, are the ones that start off in the right direction in the pursuit of truth but stop short in mid-course. It is certain that Jesus and the Pharisees went halfway together: together they venerated the Law of Moses and its divine origin. The Pharisees stopped there, but Jesus pressed on. He was not only taking into account the origin, that is, the efficient and formal cause of the Law; he saw beyond that its purpose. To venerate the Law in its origin, its form, and its expression, and to refuse to go further, is to make an idol of it and a murderous one: there is no heart, no tolerance, no compassion in the Law, it is abstract and it recognizes in man only an abstraction. It is a praying mantis that mimics its prey to destroy it.

Jesus had an emancipated conception of the Law; for him it was no longer an idol but a means, the instrument for the coming of the Kingdom of God, of which he was the head. It was destined to yield and dissolve in that Kingdom, once it had come. Faithful to his strategy and to his tactics, Jesus knew that the Law had an end and that he himself was this end. Jesus was the very purpose of the Law, he was aware of this fact, he proclaimed it clearly, it is in this sense that he put himself above the Law, he was its fulfillment and its fruit. He was in fact its masterpiece. The Law imprisoned each man in guilt in the sight of God, in sin, in death, which is the punishment for sin, but it also held out the hope that God would one day deliver His people. This deliverance was to be the coming of the Kingdom of God. Jesus announced that coming, he claimed to deliver men from sin and from death and to transfer them from servitude to the liberty of the children of God, in the heritage of God.

The Pharisees, on the contrary, were disposed to think that the strict application of the Law by itself would make them "just." The Law of Moses gives no such hope, it simply gives lucidity about the state of sin, the lucidity of the shadows. In reading the Gospel according to John, a comparison with the eye and with light springs to mind. The anatomical complication of the eye is certainly fascinating, as are the complications of the Law of Moses. But the eye, with all its organic perfections, is not self-sufficient; it opens and strives to see in vain, it sees nothing at all, until it meets the light, which is what it was made for, its fruit, its joy, its deliverance. Jesus was the light of that wide-open eye, the Law of Moses. Let the Pharisees explain the eye to us and celebrate its admirable anatomy; we do not contradict what they say, we simply declare that the eye was made for the light.

Throughout the Gospels nothing is more clearly or more constantly affirmed than Jesus' purpose in coming into this world. Not simply to confirm the accuracy of a legal mechanism, but to give to the eye its light, not simply to be subservient to the Law, but to bring the deliverance that the Law promises without giving: deliverance from sin and death. Not simply to be a slave but to be son and heir in the Kingdom of God. "I have not come to judge the world, but to save the world." "For God did not send his Son into the world in order to judge the world, but

John 12:47
John 3:17

that the world might be saved through him." "For the Son of Man came Luke 19:10
to seek and to save what was lost." "I say to you that, even so, there Luke 15:7
will be joy in heaven over one sinner who repents, more than over
ninety-nine just who have no need of repentance." This is the root of
the matter: the Pharisees found such security in the Law that they
believed they had no need either of salvation or of penitence. And the
Law gives neither security nor salvation; it is designed to make men
desire them passionately. It is once more Saint Paul, the converted
Pharisee, who has expressed this best: "This saying is true and worthy 1 Tim. 1:15
of entire acceptance, that Jesus Christ came into the world to save sinners, of whom I am the chief." Wonderful religion in which, in the
light of the sun of justice, it is enough to see oneself as one is in order
to be first. This does not mean that one should glory in being a sinner—
that, once more, would be pharisaical. It is not sin that saves or that
gives the glory, it is the Lord Jesus Christ alone, the Savior.

From this point all is self-explanatory. The end of the Law is the
justification of the sinner, but Jesus pardons sins. The end of the Law
is the honor of God, but the Son of Man honors the Father as He has
never before been honored by his most heroic obedience: he is, then,
the master of the Sabbath and of all observances. The end of the Law
is compassion, and Jesus came to save the world. The end of the Law
is to serve the Promise made by God to Abraham, and Jesus, at once
son of Abraham and Son of God, is the Messiah of Israel. The end of
the Law, as of all law, is the happiness of those who are subject to
it: shame upon that philosophy, that judicial system, that political
system, that authority whatever it may be, that makes light of the
happiness of men! But Jesus is the benediction promised to Abraham,
and the final beatitude of every man coming into this world, as the
light is the joy and the final purpose of every eye that opens. The end
of the Law is the common good of the people of God, and Jesus is the
substance of that common good, he is God in person.

The contest of Christ with the Pharisees calls to mind the tragedy
of a mother who, after giving birth, falls asleep under the effect of
some bewitchment and wakes up still expecting the arrival of the child
she has already borne. She pretends to believe that the infant presented
to her is not hers, she refuses to see that her womb is empty. Nevertheless, if Israel ever had a legitimate child who glorified it, this was indeed
Jesus Christ, our Lord, whom the aged Simeon had prophetically recognized in the Temple: "Now thou dost dismiss thy servant, O Lord, ac- Luke 2:29-32
cording to thy word, in peace; because my eyes have seen thy salvation,
which thou hast prepared before the face of all peoples: a light of revela-

tion to the Gentiles, and a glory for thy people Israel." The Pharisees
were the horrid midwives who convinced the House of Israel that this
child of men and Son of God was not theirs. But nothing is more
terrible for a son of man than to have doubt thrown on the legitimacy
of his birth: Jesus Christ was no exception to this rule.

This is why his invectives against the Pharisees are so cutting. The
quarrel deepens in concentric circles, like hell. You fall from whirlpool
to whirlpool. A quarrel about the Law becomes a quarrel about legitimacy: who is the son of whom? It is John who tells us of this prodigious
strife. The rationalistic exegetes who suspect him of having invented
these speeches do him the honor of attributing to him great powers of
imagination. Who could invent, after the event, such a family trial? It
is striking that in this quarrel about legitimacy the Pharisees as well
as Jesus go back beyond Moses, that is, to a period before the Law,
as far back as Abraham (to the Promise made to Abraham) and from
Abraham to God. On this point the Pharisees are flagrantly inconsequential, as Saint Paul was to demonstrate later on. The Jewish people,
in so far as they were the people of God, existed before Moses, before
the Law; but before Abraham and before the Promise, they did not exist.
To lay claim to Abraham is to lay claim to the Promise, not the Law.
The Promise being fulfilled in Jesus, the Law, which was in service of
the Promise, has, strictly speaking, no further *raison d'être*.

In this discussion, Christ, once more in his own fashion, proceeds to
the end of that compelling dialectic peculiar to the Jews, in which
everything is oriented in respect to two opposite poles. It is not a universe
of halftones. Christ goes to the very end of the Promise made to Abraham and the benediction implied in that Promise, to the end of the
universality of that benediction and of the filiation implied in the benediction. It is in this context that the revelation made by Jesus of his
unique divine filiation is inserted and becomes comprehensible, a completely personal revelation and the core of the revelation of the Trinity
of Persons in the unique divine nature. To oppose this, to take leave of
the benediction and not to recognize the unique filiation of Jesus, means
to depart from the Promise made to Abraham and to exile oneself from
the line of Abraham, it means to enter into the malediction and the
lie, it means to be a son of the Devil.

John 8:31-59   Jesus therefore said to the Jews who had come to believe in him, "If you
abide in my word, you shall be my disciples indeed, and you shall know the
truth, and the truth shall make you free."

They answered him, "We are the children of Abraham, and we have
never yet been slaves to anyone. How sayest thou, 'You shall be free'?"

Jesus answered them, "Amen, amen, I say to you, everyone who commits sin is a slave of sin. But the slave does not abide in the house forever; the son abides there forever. If therefore the Son makes you free, you will be free indeed. I know that you are the children of Abraham; but you seek to kill me because my word takes no hold among you. I speak what I have seen with the Father; and you do what you have seen with your father."

They answered and said to him, "Abraham is our father."

Jesus said to them, "If you are the children of Abraham, do the works of Abraham. But as it is, you are seeking to kill me, one who has spoken the truth to you which I have heard from God. That is not what Abraham did. You are doing the works of your father."

They therefore said to him, "We have not been born of fornication; we have one Father, God."

Jesus therefore said to them, "If God were your Father, you would surely love me. For from God I came forth and have come; for neither have I come of myself, but he sent me. Why do you not understand my speech? Because you cannot listen to my word. The father from whom you are is the devil, and the desire of your father it is your will to do. He was a murderer from the beginning, and has not stood in the truth because there is no truth in him. When he tells a lie he speaks from his very nature, for he is a liar and the father of lies. But because I speak the truth you do not believe me. Which of you can convict me of sin? If I speak the truth, why do you not believe me? He who is of God hears the words of God. The reason why you do not hear is that you are not of God."

The Jews therefore in answer said to him, "Are we not right in saying that thou art a Samaritan, and hast a devil?"

Jesus answered, "I have not a devil, but I honor my Father, and you dishonor me. Yet I do not seek my own glory; there is one who seeks and who judges. Amen, amen, I say to you, if anyone keep my word, he will never see death."

The Jews therefore said, "Now we know that thou hast a devil. Abraham is dead, and the prophets, and thou sayest, 'If anyone keep my word he will never taste death.' Art thou greater than our father Abraham, who is dead? And the prophets are dead. Whom dost thou make thyself?"

Jesus answered, "If I glorify myself, my glory is nothing. It is my Father who glorifies me, of whom you say that he is your God. And you do not know him, but I know him. And if I say that I do not know him, I shall be like you, a liar. But I know him, and I keep his word. Abraham your father rejoiced that he was to see my day. He saw it and was glad."

The Jews therefore said to him, "Thou art not yet fifty years old, and hast thou seen Abraham?"

Jesus said to them, "Amen, amen, I say to you before Abraham was, I am."

They therefore took up stones to cast at him; but Jesus hid himself, and went out from the temple.

The reader, now familiar with my book, must have recognized in this passage the importance and persistence of certain words and ideas: the seed, the word, the clan, the filiation of Abraham and of God, the Devil, the slave who is not of the clan, and the son who is part of it forever. My hope is that my book has already helped the reader to a better understanding of what is in essence a family quarrel, burning and secret like all family quarrels.

It is in the dialectic of a family quarrel that all men, even strangers, are to be summoned to take apart. Neutrality on the subject of Jesus is becoming more and more impossible—today too it is impossible— loyalty to Jesus is growing more and more dangerous, the very person of Jesus is more and more exposed, as one sees him here, very close in fact to ritual assassination by stoning. Just as in national affairs every time two parties are formed over some crucial issue—and this, God knows, we have seen happen—the flags are unfurled and each person is forced to sign up.

The Pharisees did not yet hold the position of power they were to acquire later on. They were not masters of the Temple and of the official central power. But they were the masters of the synagogues and already exercised some control and power of blackmail over the officials and the priests. I would compare the synagogues at this time to the Jacobin clubs, spread all over France at the beginning of the Revolution, which had no official power but which nevertheless, through their superior influence, dominated the official authorities. This immense strength of the synagogues throughout the whole country was thrown John 12:42-43 against Jesus. John has preserved the record for us: "And yet, even among the rulers, many believed in him; but because of the Pharisees they did not acknowledge it, lest they should be put out of the synagogue. For they loved the glory of men more than the glory of God."

If there was one sect among the twenty-four that were struggling for control of the public life of Israel at that time, that was opposed in spirit to the Pharisees, it was certainly the Sadducees. The Sadducees were recruited principally from the priestly caste, that is, they controlled the official power in an essentially theocratic regime and got their living from the Temple, which was the center of gravity of the whole nation and of the Diaspora. The Sadducees were far from being legalists like the Pharisees. They respected the Law, to be sure; how could it be otherwise? But they despised the fussy spirit and the scholastic frenzy of the Pharisees. They were in control of the power and the positions, they profited from them, they lived well and lavishly, they had no need to enforce rigid rules or a meticulous morality. They, for their part, were rich, skeptical, liberal to the point of syncretism, and extremely tolerant, provided their class privileges were not menaced. The religion of Israel, moreover, was at that time more tolerant than is generally believed. The Sadducees did not so much as believe in the immortality of the soul, but this did not prevent them from holding most of the highest priestly offices.

The Pharisees hated them, but had need of them. An alliance was arranged between the Pharisees and the Sadducees to destroy Jesus. In the circumstances it was the most formidable alliance possible; the Pharisees were masters of the synagogues and posed as the intransigent guardians of the Law, but the Sadducees were masters of the Temple, of the official religion, of the Sanhedrin, of the priesthood, of excommunication, and of the supreme tribunal. In moments of great crisis one frequently sees this sort of alliance between the extreme Right, represented here by the Pharisees, and the conservative Center to put a stop to some revolutionary movement: it always means the suicide of the Center. Confronted by the Pharisees, in spite of all the privileges of the established order, the Sadducees carried little weight, as one can clearly see in the sequel. For the moment and against Jesus, this alliance was going to prove effective.

And Jesus? Never were his qualities as Prophet and as wonder-worker, as artisan and poet of his own destiny, so dazzling, so tightly bound together in a single bundle, as in these last months of his earthly adventure. Threatened by the common front, for which, moreover, he provided the only principle of cohesion, he deliberately stood alone. He had no organization, no shock troops, no party. All he had were twelve Apostles, of whom one was preparing to betray him and the rest did not really understand what he wanted. Moreover, he felt no hesitation in treating them as idiots, although the translations of the Gospels soften that term: "Are you too wanting in understanding?" For the word "idiot" Littré Matt. 15:16 gives the definition "wanting in understanding": then why use a peri- Mark 7:18 phrasis? Certain women were devoted to him, but they were only women. And he had the crowd on his side, the immense, volatile, enthusiastic crowd, ardent in its support, but actually useless as long as it was unorganized and unstable as a flood.

He had too much genius, he knew men and the nature of their battles too well, for his isolation not to have been intentionally arranged. Moreover it was not complete isolation. As Jesus progressively forces his way into this mortal combat, not without fear but in all lucidity, with a bold heart and without ever flinching, he speaks just as a general speaks of his divisions—and he had no army—as a modern chief of state speaks of his nuclear arsenal—and he had nothing of the sort—he, Jesus, speaks of his Father. "My Father and I . . ." There is his rampart, his invincibility, his arsenal, his resources, his power of intervention and decision, capable of producing at any place and at any moment some crushing event. They say to him, "the Law," they say to him, "the Temple," they say to him, "Abraham and his seed," they say to him, "the Sabbath," they throw in his face, as a defiance and an interdiction, the most sacred observances of Israel. He always and invariably replies, "My Father and I . . ." He, once more, always he, he at the center and at the root of all, the pivot of Israel and of the whole universe, his Father and he. Not that he repudiates the Law, the Temple, the Sabbath, Abraham, and all the observances of Israel, but he knows and he proclaims that he is the eminent and living end of all these dedications and all these hopes. Whenever anyone fails to recognize him, it is because he stops halfway, and to stop halfway is to interrupt the movement of all holiness, of all religion, whose end can only be God.

But what is his immediate wish? Political power, the throne of Israel, a revolution? Friends and enemies alike rack their brains and mistake the answer to this. He wants only one thing, the will of his Father, and the will of his Father is that he should accomplish the prophecies and that, at the approaching Passover, he should be the one veritable Lamb of God, sacrificed for the sins of the world. All other Jewish Passovers from the very first, at the time of the escape from Egypt, have been celebrated only in order to prefigure this one. Jesus solemnly Luke 9:22 prophesies his death and the circumstances of that death: "The Son of Man must suffer many things, and be rejected by the elders and chief priests and Scribes, and be put to death, and on the third day rise again." Each one of us moves forward in time as though in a labyrinth, and then suddenly death surprises us at the exit of the tunnel, but for him death will be no surprise, he dominates all the labyrinths of time, he moves toward his death like a bridegroom toward his bride.

And then the miracles. From the beginning of his public life, Jesus has performed a multitude of miracles, which were the Messianic sign of the coming of the Kingdom of God. Now, at the end of that public life, the miracles become overwhelming, rich in significance, eschatological, bursting with poetry, the visible signs of the Father in His well-loved Son. To my mind, the miracles of Christ are inseparable from the revelation of the Trinity. And the action of the Holy Spirit will continue and complete in us the teachings of Jesus' miracles, performed once for all "in those times." Jesus' intentions are unmistakable when he combines his teaching, his miracles, and the Trinitarian revelation: "If I had not come and spoken to them, they would have no sin. But now they have no excuse for their sin. He who hates me hates my Father also. If I had not done among them works such as no one else has done, they would have no sin. But now they have seen, and have hated both me and my Father. . . . But when the Advocate has come, whom I will send you from the Father, the Spirit óf truth who proceeds from the Father, he will bear witness concerning me. And you also bear witness, because from the beginning you are with me." *John 15:22-24, 26-27*

At the end of this flashing life, in the full fury of this battle that will cost him his life, Jesus amasses miracles that explode like the bomb over Hiroshima, with a radioactive fallout that will cover all the shores of time until the end of the world. These miracles unique in power and significance, miracles that eternally justify our rational obedience and our faith, these are "the works that none other has wrought." One must read in the Gospel according to John the narrative of the healing of the man born blind and of the resurrection of Lazarus. The rationalist's criticism, based entirely on the rigid dogma that miracles are impossible and on the negation of God, sees in them only symbols of Jesus' claim to be the light of the world and the master of life and death. But if Jesus was in truth the master of life and death and the light of the world, what is surprising in his having performed these miracles in accordance with his own image? He acted like every artist who projects himself in his work. In any case, there will never be any explanation for the hatred, the fear, and the enthusiasm of which Jesus was the object, if these miracles did not take place. It was for them that the people admired him, it was for them that the Pharisees feared him. How can one out-match such a man? This is indeed the question that all the enemies of Christ put to themselves.

It was reasons of state that brought a pause in the conflict. John says:

The chief priests and the Pharisees therefore gathered together a council, and said, "What are we doing? for this man is working many signs. If we let him alone as he is, all will believe in him, and the Romans will come and take away both our place and our nation." But one of them, Caiphas, being high priest that year, said to them, "You know nothing at all; nor do you reflect that it is expedient for us that one man die for the people, instead of the whole nation perishing." This, however, he said not of himself; but being high priest that year, he *prophesied* that Jesus was to die for the nation; and not only for the nation, but that he might gather into one the children of God who were scattered abroad. *John 11:47-56*

So from that day forth their plan was to put him to death. Jesus therefore no longer went about openly among the Jews, but withdrew to the district near the desert, to a town called Ephrem; and there he stayed with his disciples. Now the Passover of the Jews was at hand; and many from the country went up to Jerusalem before the Passover, in order to purify themselves. And they were looking for Jesus. And as they stood in the temple they were saying to one another, "What do you think, that he is not coming to the feast?" But the chief priests and Pharisees had given orders that, if anyone knew where he was, he should report it, so that they might seize him.

And so at the end of the conflict, Jesus is solemnly excommunicated and branded in his nation as a criminal whom it is imperative to apprehend.

CHAPTER XVIII

The Christian Apocalypse

MEANWHILE I keep hearing so many irrefutable charges brought against these poems and against this poet! One day a man buttonholed me and repeated, with a kind of desperate pain and indignation: "But after all, sir, I am a doctor of letters and I don't understand any of it!" I had no answer, I who am a simple bachelor of arts. . . .

It is this anecdote of Valéry that comes to mind as I approach the subject of the Christian Apocalypse. How many before me have racked their brains over this subject! I myself have spent forty-five years of my life in reading, studying, and meditating on the Gospels. What authority could I have if the Gospels were wrong or intentionally misleading? For a long time now I have lived inside these texts; they are the home of my youth. Nevertheless, I swear it is not the comfort of habit that keeps me there: I would cease to be a Christian if I were not convinced that these texts give me a true account. It is not because they are venerable that I am attached to them, they are venerable to me only because they tell the truth. Better to sever all connections and die alone at night beside an unknown road than to die some day outside the truth. Let me add that I find absolutely no trace in the Gospels of that sentimental complicity one looks for among astrologers and soothsayers.

From the age of fourteen I read everything that came my way. At this time, it was the fashion to heap up objections to the historical truth and the authenticity of the Gospels. These objections profoundly shook my Catholic faith, as a great tree begins to tremble at the first breath of the hurricane. My doubts were surely not unconnected with my religious vocation and, oddly enough, with my decision to enter an order devoted to study and prolonged research. Life seemed to me to change its meaning completely, depending on whether the supernatural hope advanced by the Gospels was well founded or not. I wanted to be sure that it was; the stake was so important as to be well worth the gamble of my youth.

At that period—and suddenly it seems so long ago—so-called "independent" criticism (Independent of what? Certainly not of all dogma) was still dominated by the triple authority of David Friedrich Strauss, Ernest Renan, and Adolf von Harnack, who cut and slashed at the history of Jesus Christ with superb unconcern. The entire age of generalization and extrapolation was without any sense for degrees of being and of knowledge, and was completely closed to the possibility of exceptions. People did not believe in miracles, did not believe in prophecy, but did believe with an iron and unshakable faith in the determinism of physical law and in a universe at once limited, evolutionary, progressive, and to all intents and purposes eternal.

In less than half a century all these intellectual knickknacks have been thrown on the rubbish heap. But the exegesis of that generation was of no greater value than its philosophy of science: it has followed textual and archaeological discoveries no more closely than determinism has followed the work being done in the laboratories. The site of Troy was discovered, the fact has come to light that Abraham was not a myth, and, since Strauss's time, we have seen scholars assign an earlier and earlier date to the Pauline Epistles and to the Synoptics, as far back as the first generation of Christians. The Gospel according to John has served as a landmark and sometimes as a guide for archaeological researches, and the recent discovery of the Dead Sea Scrolls gives his discourse a tone contemporary with that of the Essenes, that is to say, before the destruction of Jerusalem in 70 A.D. Well, then?

Well, then, it is very simple. A pseudo-exegesis, falsely scientific, hoodwinked generations of Christians who wanted at all costs to reconcile their faith with their times—and it was their times that had gone astray, not their faith. Many lost their faith because of arguments that today would make us not only laugh but blush. But did the rationalistic exegesis of the last century fail in its purpose after all? This is a question I have often asked myself. The rationalists of the last century had a missionary spirit, they wanted to convert men to incredulity. What was a man like Renan trying to do when he published his *Life of Jesus?* Did he want to publish certain truths that he believed were historically established or did he want to cause certain defenseless minds to lose their faith? Was he a historian or a propagandist? A scholar or a peddler of slogans that were simple and effective but counterfeit?

During the Second World War, in the course of the long Nazi night that extended over Europe, it happened that I frequently discussed the Christian Apocalypse with my dear friend Albert Camus. He admitted the authenticity of these apocalyptic discourses of Christ as reported in the Synoptics. In his student days he had studied them closely while preparing a thesis on this subject. He did not doubt that Jesus had indeed pronounced these famous words about the destruction of Jerusalem and the end of the world. Indeed, he made an argument of them, irrefutable according to him, that Christ had been mistaken in his prophecy, that he had predicted the end of the world at the same time as the destruction of Jerusalem, that he had therefore not established a Church to survive him. These objections, coming from a man I loved, a man whose intellectual honesty I knew, forced me to revolve in my mind and heart these texts that are still obscure. This constant rumination had exactly the same effect on me that prolonged familiarity with the poems of Mallarmé had on the young Paul Valéry: "By reciting these verses to myself involuntarily, verses that are so hard to understand, I discovered that the enigmas grew less and understanding took form. The poet was justifying himself. Repetition made my mind stretch toward a limit, toward a perfectly definite meaning."

Matthew, a Jew writing for the Jews, writing in Jerusalem in the same language Jesus had used, writing some dozen years after the events he is describing and before the destruction of Jerusalem, is the Evangelist who reports at greatest length the apocalyptic discourses of Jesus: he was very obviously and very strongly impressed by them. It is principally to his text that I shall refer in this chapter, with occasional references to the parallel texts of Luke and Mark.

Here once more Jesus entered into a tradition that antedates him. The Apocalypse is a literary genre that the Persians had used earlier, but it was the Jews who were to give it its profound significance, its vast reach, and its masterpieces. It is a highly specialized and precise literary form, corresponding to a particular mentality and to a particular conception of the human condition. Just as I do not believe that one can fully understand and define the literary genre of ancient Greek tragedy without knowing and defining what the Greeks called *Destiny* —blind, unerring, irrefutable, irresponsible, inevitable Necessity—so the Jewish Apocalypse cannot be understood if one does not know that

God is the absolute and supreme Master of history, that He is at once its free initiator and its loving and judicial end, that He governs, from within history, each human destiny and the whole of creation, that He probes the loins and hearts of men and also counts the stars in the sky. At the same time God knows very well what He is doing and He is not blind. He also speaks—in the case of the Jews indeed He speaks a great deal, the whole of Jewish history resounds with His Word. Sometimes He enters into contest with men, He is supremely responsible even when quarrelsome, and His love for His creatures is so great that He appears to have the whims and regrets of a lover.

At one stroke the past, the present, and the future take on a significance altogether different from the one they had for the Greeks. Nietzsche and later Camus saw very clearly that the Greek conception of history and the Jewish conception of history were antagonistic and irreconcilable. Like Nietzsche, Camus opted for the Greek conception: he accused communism of having transposed the Jewish conception into a universe that was purely material and temporal. That is true. The Jewish conception of history is linear and progressive in the sense that it has a beginning, which is God, and an end, which is God, progress consisting of increasingly close approximations to that end: there is a growing maturity of history beneath the eternal sun of God. Communism retains the style of the Apocalypse, but it no longer makes time dependent upon eternity, and it replaces God by a fictitious necessity that is literally mythological.

The Greek conception of history is cyclical; it perfectly expresses the famous myth of eternal recurrence. Despite the eloquence Nietzsche has expended on this theme, I cannot help wondering whether even he ever seriously believed in the historical reality of eternal recurrence. This implies a truly gross, materialistic, and "temporal" notion of eternity as simply infinite and inexhaustible time, in the course of which the combinations of matter, which, however numerous, are necessarily finite in number (one might well ask why), must renew themselves in identical forms.

The Jews, knowing that God is the magnetic pole of history, have a different notion of eternity as supramaterial and truly supernatural. Eternity is the living heart of history, sending blood along all the arteries of time and at each instant pumping it back toward itself through all the veins. Yes, when one pays attention, at each instant of time one can feel the pulse of eternity. God is above His creation and above time, itself a created thing, since He regulates the movement of creation toward its end. Pascal's definition is well known: God is a circle whose center is everywhere and whose circumference is nowhere. The same is true of eternity, of which God is the exhaustive subject: His center is at each moment that passes, His circumference has never been attained. It is perfectly evident that the vocabulary of this "geometry" of eternity must be full of surprises and refractions compared to our Euclidian geometry of sense experience.

But even in the realm of material practicality the great modern discoveries have depended on non-Euclidian geometry. Is it then so difficult for us to conceive that the supernatural and divine universe when it expresses itself in human language does so according to the laws of an unknown geometry, laws that may give the impression of incoherence whereas their expression in our sublunary world reflects another kind of coherence, which we can only guess at? The opposite would be open to suspicion. When a straight stick is thrust into water it appears to be broken, not because it is broken but because it traverses two different mediums. The Jewish Apocalypse is based entirely on a similar phenomenon of refraction.

Here I return once more to the solemn declaration of Jesus, which indicates so clearly that eternity is a magnetic center that is universally present at every instant of time and dominates it absolutely: "Before Abraham was, *I am*." This means nothing at all or it means very clearly that this man of thirty who spoke these words two thousand years ago was veritably and certainly the contemporary of Abraham who, in turn, had already been dead and buried for two thousand years at the time of Jesus. How could this be? Well, Jesus' enemies took up stones to throw at him and kill him: they, for their part, had understood perfectly.

Poetry too, in its superior essence, is an attempt to dominate space and time, it ceases to take them into account. I am talking of a poetry that can express itself just as well in painting or in music as in words. Poetry regards all things in an intelligible light in which the sensible forms themselves become imperishable and glorious in some unexpected association and escape, as though by enchantment, from the material confines of duration and decay as easily as from those of distance. To be sure, a very great poet like Mallarmé may give a first impression of obscurity or even of incoherence. Valéry has said of him, "He consumed himself in attempting to reconcile time with the moment, a torment for all artists who think profoundly about their art." A reader worthy of such a poet has to travel the same rough road in reverse: then the incoherences disappear by dissolving into a harmony of superterrestrial correspondences.

"The difficulty experienced at first in understanding," Valéry writes in another place, "comes from an *extreme contraction of figures,* a *fusion of metaphors,* the rapid *transmutation of images* extremely compressed and subjected to a sort of *discipline of density,* which the poet has imposed upon himself and which is in accordance with his intention of keeping the language of poetry always definitely and almost absolutely distinct from the language of prose. One might say that he would like poetry, which must essentially distinguish itself from prose through its phonetic and musical form, to *distinguish itself as well through the form of its meaning."*

I can only invite any reader who is eager for understanding to meditate on these lines by Valéry. As a result of meditating myself on the apocalyptic discourses of Jesus and also on the Apocalypse of Saint John I have come to the same definitions of the literary forms necessary to express telescoped realities: contraction of figures, fusion of metaphors, transmutation of images, and, above all, an extreme discipline of density, this last word *density* understood in its literal and physical sense: *the ratio of mass to volume.* The Apocalypse condenses into an extremely small visionary volume an enormous mass of future facts that are historically disparate and vastly dispersed in time: in the present case, the destruction of Jerusalem, the Parousia or Second Coming of Christ as Lord and Judge, and finally the end of the world. This visionary condensation of history takes place at the level of divine revelation, at a junction of eternity with time, where the Word of God erupts into history. That is to say, far above the earth, above prose, above the course of ordinary events and above the banal discourse of human language.

Nevertheless between the Apocalypse, on the one hand, and a poem in Mallarmé's sense, on the other, there is an inversion of values. In the poem, the word comes first, drawing the sense after it, condensing it, so to speak, above the prose. In the Apocalypse the prophetic vision comes first, jostling words and metaphors, condensing them at a vertiginous height, above real time and grammatical time as well: "Before Abraham was, I am." The Apocalypse is the dew of history: it precipitates, on the meadows of human language, enormous events far distant from one another but condensed in eternity.

It was a question by the Apostles—a rather dull-witted one, to be sure—that set in motion Jesus' apocalyptic discourse. There is some indication that this question and the reply to it had a larger circle of auditors than just the Apostles, since the request for an explanation was made later and in confidence, as if the Apostles were frightened at the imprudence of their master's language. "And Jesus left the temple and was going away, when his disciples came forward to show him the buildings of the temple. But he answered and said to them, 'Do you see all these things? Amen I say to you, there will not be left here one stone upon another that will not be thrown down.'" Matt. 24:1-2

We can hardly imagine what a shock it was for these simple Israelites to hear the announcement of the imminent destruction of the Temple. They had confidence in their master, but such a prophecy seemed to them horrifying. At that time in Israel and for a short period thereafter, the Temple and Mount Zion, the visible residence of God and the footstool of His glory, were the very center of all religion of the living God. Jesus announced nothing less than the total destruction of this center. He had already predicted in the clearest terms that the true religion would become universal, even his own ritual, and that this ritual would be in the likeness of God, whose center is everywhere and whose circumference is nowhere. He had made this confidence casually in the course of a journey, standing at the edge of a well, and he had made it to a woman of easy virtue. It is truly astonishing to observe how Christ chose his interlocutors, and above all his female interlocutors. Mary Magdalene, the sinner, and this woman of Samaria received his most precious confidences. This should give pause to those aged bigots, as wicked as they are ugly, who spend their time slandering young women.

Jesus said to her, "Go, call thy husband and come here." The woman answered and said, "I have no husband." Jesus said to her, "Thou hast said well, 'I have no husband,' for thou hast had five husbands, and he whom thou now hast is not thy husband. In this thou hast spoken truly." John 4:16-26

The woman said to him, "Sir, I see that thou art a prophet. Our fathers worshiped on this mountain, but you say that at Jerusalem is the place where one ought to worship." Jesus said to her, "Woman, believe me, the hour is coming when neither on this mountain nor in Jerusalem will you worship the Father. You worship what you do not know; we worship what we know, for salvation is from the Jews. But the hour is coming, and is now here, when the true worshipers will worship the Father in spirit and in truth. For the Father also seeks such to worship him. God is spirit, and they who worship him must worship in spirit and in truth."

The woman said to him, "I know that Messiah is coming (who is called Christ), and when he comes he will tell us all things." Jesus said to her, "I who speak with thee am he."

Aside from the personalities of the two interlocutors, there are many striking things about this dialogue reported by John. Jesus desires to be in the tradition of Israel, keeps himself true to it and proclaims the fact, not only by announcing his personal Messianity, but by solemnly affirming the legitimacy of Israel and of the Temple up to his time, since salvation flows from the Jews as though from a spring. In addition there are these extraordinary words: "The Father also seeks such to worship him." Man is in search of God, but God too is seeking man: both seem to be in the night. Eternity is night for man, but for God time seems to be the night of night. Nevertheless it is necessary that both seek each other out where they dwell, and when they encounter each other, gropingly, it is in a "dark night." To be even more precise, what Jesus announces to the woman of Samaria is not a discarnate religion, since he reveals himself as the Messiah and since he is in the flesh, but a religion of which Jerusalem and its Temple will no longer be the unique center. An enormous reversal, which the Pharisees, and Judaism under their influence, were to accept a half-century later, but which at the time of Jesus was premature and no doubt blasphemous even to envisage. This point will become one of the most important motives for the condemnation of Jesus.

Saint Paul is not a man to stop halfway. He will go back to the very origins of the Temple, he will define the ultimate consequences for all of us of the identity in the sacred order between the Temple and the body of Christ. In an early letter to the Hebrews he explains that Jesus is at once the chief priest and the offering and that he is also this tent, this Tabernacle prior to the Temple in Jerusalem, prior even to the sacred tent constructed by Moses, since Moses constructed the tent *after an earlier model* that had been shown to him on the mountain. For Saint Paul this model, anterior to all the earthly habitations of God among His people, is Jesus: "Before Abraham was, *I am.*" But also before this first tent and the first Tabernacle of God in the desert *he is.*

Here is the text of the Epistle to the Hebrews:

Heb. 8:1-5 Now the main point in what we are saying is this. We have such a high priest, who has taken his seat at the right hand of the throne of Majesty in the heavens, *a minister of the Holies, and of the true tabernacle, which the Lord has erected and not man.* For every high priest is appointed to offer gifts and sacrifices; therefore it is necessary that this one also should have something to offer. If then he were on earth, he would not even be a priest, since there are already others to offer gifts according to the Law. *The worship they offer is a mere copy and shadow of things heavenly,* even as Moses was warned when he was completing the tabernacle: "See that *you make them according to the pattern shown you on the mountain.*"

In hot pursuit, like a hunter on the trail, Paul follows this fantastic migration of God's Presence from the model on the mountain to the tent on the desert, from the tent to the Temple in Jerusalem, from the Temple in Jerusalem to the body of Christ, from the body of Christ to the Mystical Body that is the Church, and he concludes triumphantly, like the bugle sound at the end of the chase: "Do you not know that you are the temple of God and that the Spirit of God dwells in you? If anyone destroys the temple of God, him will God destroy; for holy is the temple of God, and *this temple you are.*"

Now the Passover of the Jews was at hand, and Jesus went up to Jerusalem. And he found in the temple men selling oxen, sheep and doves, and money-changers at their tables. And making a kind of whip of cords, he drove them all out of the temple, also the sheep and oxen, and he poured out the money of the changers and overturned the tables. And to them who were selling the doves he said, "Take these things away, and do not make the house of my Father a house of business." . . . The Jews therefore answered and said to him, "What sign dost thou show us, seeing that thou dost these things?" In answer Jesus said to them, "Destroy this temple, and in three days I will raise it up." The Jews therefore said, "Forty-six years has this temple been in building, and wilt thou raise it up in three days?" But he was speaking of the temple of his body. When, accordingly, he had risen from the dead, his disciples remembered that he had said this, and they believed the Scripture and the word that Jesus had spoken.

John 2:13-16,
18-22

In this scene Jesus begins by behaving as the absolute master of the Temple by driving out the money-changers: in his Father's house he is at home. Then he identifies the Temple with his own body, a daring move that throws much light on the poetic art of the Apocalypse. His adversaries count up the years it took to build the Temple, they stay on the level of prose, but he speaks with the extreme density of the poet, with sudden transmutations that express and embrace real substitutions and replacements. At its level Jesus' language is more precise, more complete, and more exact than that of his adversaries. Prose is heavy and slack.

A contemporary exegete, Father Louis Bouyer, seems to me to show a profound understanding of the Judaeo-Christian Apocalypse in its character of revolutionary conflict without quarter. He writes:

There are two successive worlds, the one like the other made of visible and invisible elements mixed together, and one of these worlds must invade the other and supplant it. . . . At the same time, when one speaks of the mysticism of Israel, it is not as a thing of the past that the world of God lets itself be seen but as the future. More exactly, to introduce the element

of personal initiative, so essential to Yahweh, it is the world *that is coming.*
. . . The divine Presence that Israel awaits is precisely a presence that is to
make its triumphal entry in this very world as though on a chariot of war.
. . . Thus the successive opposition of the two worlds envisaged by the
mysticism of Israel appears to us finally as a very different thing from a
succession or alternation. It has to do with one of these worlds irresistibly
supplanting the other. This is why the Day of Yahweh, the day on which
His reign begins, is the Day of Judgment: a day of crisis that must unravel
present history by the overriding eruption of a sovereign power. . . . This
design of God will realize itself in a manner inconceivable to men: the
people of God will be saved by virtue of this catastrophe, and the coming
of the divine Kingdom will be realized through the crumbling of all earthly
empires. . . ."

This is the source of the ambiguity—ambivalence, in fact—that
underlies the whole Gospel and no doubt the Jewish mentality as well
at the time of Jesus. When the Apostles had heard with horror the
announcement of the destruction of the Temple they approached their
Matt. 24:3   master secretly to ask him for an explanation: "And as he was sitting
on the Mount of Olives, the disciples came to him privately saying,
'Tell us, when are these things to happen, and what will be the sign
of thy coming and of the end of the world?'" For them and no doubt
for many Jews of that period, and later on for Bar Kochba, it was impossible that the Temple should be destroyed without the entire creation's crumbling away and the world's coming to its end.

Jesus, however, had said that the Temple would be replaced by his
own body, he had said to the woman of Samaria that the worship of
the true God would henceforth have its center everywhere and its
circumference nowhere, a prophecy perfectly compatible with the
preceding one and realized to perfection in the Eucharist and in his
Mystical Body. In neither case did he talk about the end of the world;
it was the question from his disciples that brought together the destruction of Jerusalem, the Parousia, and the end of the world.

Devoted Israelites faced completely toward the future, toward the
Judgment of God, which they had always called "the great Day of
Yahweh"; they foresaw, indeed they actually knew, that their terrestrial
fatherland with its treasures, its history, its Temple, and its glory
were the announcement and presage of splendid things to come, things
worthy of God and of His promises. Just as Proust set out "in search of
time past," the people of Israel had mobilized in search of the future,
the age to come that must at all costs be gained, when everything would
be more beautiful, happier, purer, for God alone would reign then, all

in all, and He would dry the tears from our faces. The Devil would be permanently vanquished and relegated to the abyss. Entering resolutely into this tradition and this perspective, Jesus proclaimed that Israel was only the shadow of what was to come, a shadow projected by a radiant reality stationed in front of it, almost within arm's reach. So it is with the planets, half night, half day, and the half that is in night dreams that tomorrow it will belong to the light.

There had been a Temple of Solomon, which in its time took the place of a tent, but there will be another, more perfect Temple, of which the historical Temple was only the shadow. There had been a Kingdom of Israel, but there will be another Kingdom, the Kingdom that is to come, the Reign of God, the Israel of God, of which David's kingdom was only the shadow and the announcement. There had been a covenant made with Abraham and the seed of Abraham, bearer of this covenant, but there will be another Covenant no longer for time but for eternity, of which the covenant with Abraham was only the shadow, and within this new Covenant the true seed of Abraham will be spiritual, eternal, universal. There had been a historical Jerusalem, city of kings, a glorious city, the city of God, but it was no more than the shadow of a Jerusalem to come, "the holy city, New Jerusalem, com-   Apoc. 21:2
ing down out of heaven from God, made ready as a bride adorned for her husband." There had been a lamb whose blood marked with the letter Tau the houses of the Hebrews to protect them from the blows of the destroying Angel and to liberate them from their servitude in Egypt, but this lamb was only the shadow and the prefiguration of another Lamb, immolated on the T of the cross, who would wipe out the sin of the world: "'Worthy is the Lamb who was slain to receive   Apoc. 5:12-13
power and divinity and wisdom and strength and honor and glory and blessing.' And every creature that is in heaven and on the earth and under the earth, and such as are on the sea, and all that are in them, I heard them all saying, 'To him who sits upon the throne, and to the Lamb, blessing and honor and glory and dominion, forever and ever.'"
There had been kings in Israel, "sons of God" and sons of their people, but there will be the Messiah, King of the future age. The strictly apocalyptic title that Jesus appropriated for himself, "the Son of Man," will pre-empt for him all the Messianic prophecies, all the prerogatives, past and future, of ancient Israel.

It is easy to understand why, later on, in order to immunize Judaism against the influence of Christianity, the Pharisees set aside the prodigious apocalyptic tradition of Israel which, since Ezechiel and Daniel, had given meaning to Messianism and to Jewish prophecy.

Jesus was infinitely more a Jew than the Pharisees, who laced Judaism in the iron corset of their legalism, whereas before them it would seem to have been so free, so extraordinarily poetic and mystical. Jesus accepts the whole tradition of Israel, he releases its poetic meaning, including the poetic meaning of the Law; he puts nothing aside except what was human, too human, prosaic, and what stifled the Word of God; he brings all to sovereign accomplishment in a dazzling meaning, in a magnificent hope. And never was he more authentically Jew than in his apocalyptic discourse.

This apocalyptic discourse reveals in its way God's plan, as a rainbow tells us in its way that there is farther off on the other side of the mountains a watery surface that we do not see. The mistake would be to demand that this account give us landmarks and measured distances such as we expect in road maps. The Apocalypse is not a road map of the future; rather it gives us the sort of view that we have of the starry sky, in which the respective directions of the stars are exact but the distances are impossible to judge by the naked eye. And other stars have been born millions of centuries ago whose light has not yet reached us.

The Apostles' question has to do with three events, which in their minds perhaps constituted only one: the imminent destruction of the earthly Jerusalem, which had just been revealed to them; the mighty coming of the Son of Man for the Judgment, which will be called the Parousia; and the end of the world. Jesus' reply moves from one to another of these events: sometimes he distinguishes them even in time, sometimes too he seems to mingle them.

All these apocalyptic revelations, which I cannot cite here entire for the simple reason that I cannot quote the entire text of the Gospel in this book—all these revelations presuppose a fundamental truth, with which Judaism is impregnated and which Saint Paul will express 1 Cor. 7:29-32 perfectly. "But this I say, brethren, *the time is short;* it remains that those who have wives be as if they had none; and those who weep, as though not weeping; and those who rejoice, as though not rejoicing; and those who buy, as though not possessing; and those who use this world, as though not using it, *for this world as we see it is passing away. I would have you free from care.*" There is a Christian way of using the world, "as though not using it." This does not mean at all that one must abstain from everything while awaiting the future age, that one must neither weep nor rejoice, but that one must be always ready to leave everything because everything is likely to leave us at any moment and because, moreover, our profound allegiance is not to this world: earthly Jerusalems pass like beloved faces, and nothing here below is permanent except this universal flowing away. The Jews, a primitive nomadic people, have inoculated us with their nomadic metaphysics. We can quite well defend our cities and our civilizations, we know perfectly well that human courage consists in living and dying on a rampart, but we know too that the most beautiful terrestrial city is only an encampment and that civilizations too are mortal. Our age knows this better than any other.

The words of Saint Paul are an echo of Christ's words: "But take heed to yourselves, lest your hearts be overburdened with self-indulgence and drunkenness and the cares of this life, and that *day* come upon you suddenly as a snare. For come it will upon all who dwell on the face of the earth." Christ wants our whole life to be at the *qui vive*. He says again, "Heaven and earth will pass away, but my words will not pass away." Because heaven and earth belong to time, they are reflections in a mirror, but the words of Jesus belong to the immutable Kingdom of eternity.

Luke 21:34-35

Matt. 24:35

These few passages, and many others that resemble them, define a revolution in the psychological and moral order of human conduct in this world, a revolution as extensive as that of relativity in the domain of physics. It is indeed a sort of relativity that the Judaeo-Christian Apocalypse has introduced into the conception of life and the universe. This must be, I believe, at the bottom of Camus' objection to the Christian Apocalypse: for him this low world was the only reality, whereas for a Christian it is only the reverse side of a stage set, whose glorious right side we should ardently aspire to see. It happens, nevertheless, that we are taken in by the reverse side of the scene; the Jews themselves were taken in by it, of whom Pascal writes, "The Jews have so greatly loved representations, and have studied them so well, that they mistook the reality when it came at the time and in the manner predicted." Who among us is not somewhat of a Jew in this respect, not so eager to see time efface itself in eternity or the night shadow flee before the body of the light?

Just as the non-Euclidian geometries and the theory of relativity have upset the scientific legitimacy of a three-dimensional universe, it is certain that Christianity has thrown doubt on a moral universe confined to man and the present life. Henceforth everything has a double sense, and death itself is not what it seems. In connection with Camus' death, William Faulkner said, "Everyone says he was killed against a tree; he collided with God." Both are true.

Well then, Jesus announced the imminent and brutal destruction of Jerusalem: forty years later this happened, as he had said. But in the apocalyptic vision these great events are polyvalent: the end of Jerusalem represents the end of the world; the end of the world itself is not a simple and wholly isolated event. The world in which I am will truly end for me on the day when I shall die. The end of the world awaited Camus at the foot of a tree in the Ile de France; it awaited Saint-Exupéry in the sky over the Mediterranean; for each there is his own end of the world. The teaching of Jesus Christ is that each end of the world, general or particular, coincides with his coming into his own in might and in glory, it coincides with his Parousia as irrefutable judge.

It is known that the first Christians very generally expected that the end of the entire world and the return of Christ in his glory would follow close upon the destruction of Jerusalem. There are numerous echoes of this expectation in the New Testament. The passages in the Gospel where Jesus seems to fix a date are obscure and appear contradictory; the exegetes rack their brains over them. Sometimes it seems that the whole thing will happen before the disappearance of the generation contemporary with Jesus. At other times it appears that no one knows the time of the final catastrophe, no one, not even the Son, but only the Father. Venturing in my turn among the formidable snares of this revelation, I certainly do not claim to be able to explain everything and make it clear. But I do not see, either, why one should demand from a theologian or an exegete the perfectly clear and definitive solution of all problems. No one would dare address such a demand to a biologist regarding the secrets of life, or to a physicist regarding the secrets of the material universe. If one were to do so he would be very ill received: the biologist and the physicist would not fail to reply that to wish for absolute clarity on problems that are themselves obscure would cut the wings of reflection and of imagination, the moving forces in all progress in knowledge. The biologist and the physicist would be a thousand times right; I do not see any reason, either, why a theologian should have an answer to everything. Then let us leave to theology and to exegesis their fair share of hypotheses. What is hypothesis? It is in fact a question put in reply to another question: scientific knowledge has a feminine character. Women are admirably adept in the art of replying to one question with another. The Christian Apocalypse resounds with questions that re-echo and answer one another from the four corners of time.

But the admirable thing about Christianity is precisely that it plunges us, from the moment of baptism, into a universe of questioning. Jesus

Christ taught us first of all that it is part of the dignity of man to raise questions about death and the end of the world. This is not a matter of course. What I have found infinitely depressing about Islam is the lack of questioning: it is a universe of ready-made answers or, to be precise, of one general-purpose answer: "It is written," that is how it has always been and that is how it must be. The difference between this and the doctrine of eternal recurrence is insignificant. Camus, who thought himself in the Greek tradition, was certainly much more in the Moorish tradition. Christ, for his part, put everything in question: Jerusalem and his earthly fatherland, in the name of a celestial Jerusalem; the Law, in the name of charity; time, in the name of eternity; death, in the name of life and resurrection; the world, in the name of the Judgment of the world, whereas the world claimed to judge everything and not to be judged; the Devil, in the name of paradise and the eternal happiness of man. Ah, what a game was started there! Our civilization may, if it likes, pride itself on being de-Christianized and no longer expecting the return of our Lord Jesus Christ in might and in judgment, but it still lives by, and lives only by, those questions he raised and implanted forever in the heart of man. To be a true Christian will always be heroic, but above all and before all, it will never be foolish.

It seems to me that our era, the era of Einstein and the theory of relativity but also the era of Hiroshima and nuclear armaments, is in a better position than any other to understand that "this world as we see it is passing away." As I have already suggested, in my childhood people made fun of the dogma of the end of the world and of the apocalyptic revelation of the Gospels under the influence of a philosophy that was positivistic, deterministic, sensualistic, idealistic, materialistic, progressivistic, bestial, idiotic, and degenerate. Hiroshima should instantly have congealed an ironic grimace on the face of every thoughtful man. The end of the world? Why, from now on we have it within arm's reach. Just step inside, the store is full. The end of the world is at large in the ocean depths, borne in atomic submarines, it soars through the stratosphere in weapon-carriers. Carriers of what? Why, precisely that— the end of the world. We have packed the end of the world into tin cans like sardines or compotes. From now on the stage is set, the end of the world will not disappoint us. When I read in my daily newspaper, whatever the language, that the survival of the world depends on "a balance of terror," and when I open the Gospel according to Matthew at Chapter 24, I reflect that this little Jewish accountant, dead for two thousand years, has not been noticeably outdated by current events.

Matt. 24:29-31 "But immediately after the tribulation of those days, the sun will be darkened, and the moon will not give her light, and the stars will fall from heaven, and the powers of heaven will be shaken. And then will appear the sign of the Son of Man in heaven; and then will all tribes of the earth mourn, and they will see the Son of Man coming upon the clouds of heaven with great power and majesty. And he will send forth his angels with a trumpet and a great sound, and they will gather his elect from the four winds, from one end of the heavens to the other."

For there is the other side of the revelation. Just as, in the resurrection of Lazarus and in his own Resurrection, Jesus presented himself as the supreme master of death and of life, he here declares himself to be master of the end of the world. Whatever secondary causes may precipitate that catastrophe, they will be no more than secondary, the event will not assume its definitive significance except with the return of Christ in his glory as Judge, that is, with his Parousia. It is true that Hiroshima gave unimaginable credibility to Christ's apocalyptic revelation. There is no reason at all to accept only half of this revelation, the half that has received quasi-experimental confirmation.

For my own part I had no need of Hiroshima to make me believe in the certainty of the end of the world, since I had believed in it all along on the word of Jesus Christ. I was in the position of Leverrier after he had predicted the existence and the position of the planet Neptune: on September 23, 1846, when J. G. Galle in Berlin confirmed the existence and position of Neptune, Leverrier was not astounded. No more was I astounded by Hiroshima. I am a Christian and I accept Christ's word. But I accept it in its entirety. That is why I also believe in Christ's providence over his own and in the imminence of his Parousia.

In speaking of its imminence, I am careful not to mention any definite period of time. It is possible that the end of the world and the justiciary Parousia of Christ are still millions of centuries away; nevertheless they are imminent. I have said that the end of the world is at large in the depths of the ocean and in the stratosphere, that is not far from us, we hope that it will stay quiet as long as possible; nevertheless it is imminent. The madman who unleashes the end of the world will believe he is the cause, but he will be only the instrument. The end of the world is imminent in another and superior fashion: from all eternity it is contained in a free decree of God, and this decree, like everything eternal, invests time in all its parts; its center is everywhere, its circumference nowhere. This is why that Day will break upon men unforeseen, it will close over them like a trap; moreover, Christ says it will steal upon them like a thief.

On the other hand, Christ affirms that he came first of all to save the world, not to judge it, thus postponing as long as possible his justiciary return. And here Matthew inserts the parable of the ten virgins. The very remarkable thing about this parable is that, in strict justice, there is absolutely nothing with which to reproach any one of the ten virgins: all are virgins, all are in their places and waiting, all fall asleep because the bridegroom is late, no one of them would have been guilty if the bridegroom had been on time. It is not the virgins called foolish that committed a fault, it is the bridegroom who was lacking in the courtesy of kings, which is promptness. One begins to enter into a profound understanding of Christianity when one seizes the fact that God is always late, or, which amounts to the same thing, that we are always in too much of a hurry. The foolish virgins were foolish and were condemned, not because they lacked enough oil to attend the arrival of the bridegroom had he come at the appointed hour, but because they had not drawn the additional oil that would have allowed them to wait out the delay without their lamps' going out. Like beautiful, too-much-courted women, God does not allow His own tardiness to be imputed to Him as a reproach. In our relations with God, we must always keep in reserve a supplement of patience, a supplement of generosity; the weights in the scale are falsified in His favor. When we think we have waited to the extreme limit, we must still wait an hour longer; when we believe we have given all, we must still scrape the bottom of the till and give Him a little more, the skin as well as the bones to make up full weight, the heart and the last drop of the heart's blood, the soul and its final breath; He is the usurer of our lives. When He has completely ruined us, then He gives himself to us, and all is made good.

At the very beginning of this book, when I did not yet know whither it would sweep me, I wrote this: "How can one write the history of a man who claims to dominate time? If the history of a man is the inscription of his personality on his time, what will be the history of a personality who embraces the whole of time because he is anterior to time and creates it? In order for such a history to be true the historian must, in some manner, embrace the whole of time. The first proof that Jesus' view of himself is incontestably true is that it is in fact impossible to write his history without rising above the entire unrolling of time." Now I see very clearly that I am not in command of my book, it commands me.

The apocalyptic discourse of Jesus Christ does not lose itself in the

Matt. 25:1-13

clouds, it concludes with an evocation of the Last Judgment. Here too, here once more, Jesus places himself at the center of all, not only because he is the supreme Judge, but because it is in relation to himself that he establishes the standard of all values in accordance with which this terrible judgment will be pronounced. And then an extraordinary thing transpires: this judgment that is the end of history is also immanent in history and in the conscience of each one of us, consciences that can and must judge themselves on the basis of brotherly love. Saint John of the Cross has summarized it thus: we will all be judged according to our love. Jesus, who places himself at the center of the world's end and of the Last Judgment, identifies himself also with the least among us: it is simultaneously Jesus Christ and the most humble of men who occupies this center. This is the Communion of the Saints: the judgment of the greatest according to the services they have rendered to the least.

Come now, comrade Communists, you who deafen us with your assertions that religion is an opium that prevents the coming of that radiant and fraternal city "where the free development of each is the condition of the free development of all." Come and consider honestly for once this religion in which one cannot harm the poor, the weak, the humble without offending God Himself and His Christ, in which honor and service rendered to the poor, the weak, and the humble redounds to God Himself. We on our side are quite willing to admit that sometimes Christians are bad practitioners of their religion and that they often store up for themselves a terrible awakening on the Day of Judgment, but do you on your side have the generosity to acknowledge that this religion threatens no one. Make us ashamed of not being worthy of it, but do not blaspheme it: you cannot touch it without threatening the lives and the honor of the poor, the weak, and the humble.

I shall quote in its entirety this prodigious text:

Matt. 25:31-46   "But when the Son of Man shall come in his majesty, and all the angels with him, then he will sit on the throne of his glory; and before him will be gathered all the nations, and he will separate them one from another, as the shepherd separates the sheep from the goats; and he will set the sheep on his right hand, but the goats on the left.

"Then the king will say to those on his right hand, 'Come, blessed of my Father, take possession of the kingdom prepared for you from the foundation of the world; for I was hungry and you gave me to eat; I was thirsty and you gave me to drink; I was a stranger and you took me in; naked and you covered me; sick and you visited me; I was in prison and you came to me.' Then the just will answer him, saying, 'Lord, when did we see thee hungry, and feed thee; or thirsty, and give thee drink? And when did we see thee a stranger, and take thee in; or naked, and clothe thee? Or when did we see thee sick, or in prison, and come to thee?' And answering the king will say to them, 'Amen I say to you, as long as you did it for one of these, the least of my brethren, you did it for me.'

"Then he will say to those on his left hand, 'Depart from me, accursed ones, into the everlasting fire, which was prepared for the devil and his angels. For I was hungry, and you did not give me to eat; I was thirsty and you gave me no drink; I was a stranger and you did not take me in; naked, and you did not clothe me; sick, and in prison, and you did not visit me.' Then they also will answer and say, 'Lord, when did we see thee hungry, or thirsty, or a stranger, or naked, or sick, or in prison, and did not minister to thee?' Then he will answer them, saying, 'Amen I say to you, as long as you did not do it for one of these least ones, you did not do it for me.' And these will go into everlasting punishment, but the just into everlasting life."

Finally there remains to be said what is perhaps most important of all. The universe of the Christian Apocalypse, the discussion of which moves so readily from the creation of the world to the eternity of reward and punishment, has no need of justification outside itself. It is not a problem, it is the solution. It is like the universe of music in which, from the first measures of a familiar symphony, we know that all our anguish is going to be at once raised to its climax and suddenly resolved.

Part Three

The Passion of Jesus Christ

CHAPTER XIX

Christ's Hour Is Come

Now THE confrontation between Jesus and his enemies was complete. Nothing was less certain than the outcome. Suspense had reached its climax. In eight days' time, from Sunday to Sunday, all was to play itself out, with reversals of fortune and literally unheard-of situations. I think Jesus' conduct during those days should be analyzed with as much care as the Italian Campaign of Bonaparte used to be analyzed in the military academies. It is a combination of prudence and audacity—great audacity combined with a little prudence—which brought him within arm's reach of political victory and empire over the world, to an extent that could have made him the rival of Caesar and Alexander. He did not want it, he aimed higher and farther.

It was not so easy, however, to understand Jesus' goals, his intentions, his maneuvers. I believe, along with many others, that Judas was deceived and that his treason sprang from a first reaction: "This is too stupid!" Throughout that terrible week the small number of those who remained loyal to Jesus to the end did so only through love. Intelligence quickly lost its wind. Beyond lost battles there is no road at all except for love and honor. Intelligence may well follow after them, but as their captive. The miracle here is that on the morning of Easter intelligence too was recompensed. But Judas was no longer there to see that after all it had not been as stupid as he had thought. It is always honorable to follow Jesus, even in his worst humiliation, and in the end it is never stupid.

This week is called "holy," but it might also be called "the terrible

243

week," or "the black week," so strong is the feeling, day after day, of being thrust into the night of nights.

For now we come to the death of our Lord Jesus Christ. I shall say that he really wished to die a cruel death, I shall say why he wished to die thus. I shall say that they wanted to kill him, that finally they did kill him, I shall say that they wanted him to die the death of rebellious slaves, the death of blasphemers. I shall say why they wanted to kill him thus. I shall say how all this came about and why, given the situation between his adversaries and him, it could hardly have turned out otherwise. Everything is abnormal in this frightful story, and the event itself could not have taken place without abnormal accompaniments. The earth trembled in Israel.

First of all, Israel was at that time a militarily vanquished nation, oppressed and occupied. And by what conqueror? Rome, a coarse and brutal power if ever there was one. It is true that many other nations accommodated themselves to the Roman yoke: well and good, it is to Israel's honor that she did not ever accommodate herself. For a pious Jew everything in the Roman domination was insupportable, absolutely everything, but above all the idolatry, and that particularly debasing form of idolatry that has always made such ravages in men's consciences, adoration of reasons of state. Even today we are not free of that idolatry, to which Lenin as well as Mussolini succumbed.

Like Hitler in France during the last war the Romans had the adroitness to leave Israel a ghost of autonomy, a semblance of national government. By nature and necessity, this government collaborated with the occupier; its reason of state was to save what could be saved, to do everything to escape the constant danger of aggravating the situation. Although this government was theocratic and sacerdotal, its preoccupations were principally political, it was less concerned with pleasing God than with not displeasing Rome. Roman power was so evident that all revolt seemed impossible. Jewish Messianism, with its promise of national liberation, could spoil all. Those who were charged with preserving what remained of national independence instinctively distrusted any ill-considered movement that might bring about the collapse of the fragile edifice they were determined to hold upright. All this is something we in France have seen at first hand and have known well. A government of collaborators does not, for all its efforts, gain the esteem and confidence of the occupier, but, in the measure to which its own people remain proud, it draws upon itself the contempt and distrust of that people. Reading between the lines of the Gospels, one can see that it was just such a situation that existed in Israel.

Never had theological hope, like a bowstring, been stretched so tight; never on the other hand had the magnificent and solemn promises of God to His people clashed more sharply with humiliating reality. The Promise was of empire over the world. The reality was servitude. The managing, intellectual class plied its trade: it managed the nation day by day and preserved its own privileges. The people, for their part, believed that God, their God, would deliver Israel; no one knew when or how, but the hope was maintained intact. The people were deaf to the arguments of political realism; the omnipotence of Rome, based on arms and administration, seemed to them contemptible compared to the power of the true God. The conflict in which Jesus was to meet his death was a conflict between political realism (save what can be saved) and theological hope (God, even alone, especially when alone, is alone capable of saving all).

Hope says no as well as yes: there is honor in the exercise of hope. Never perhaps has any nation collectively been more loyal to the honor of theological hope than the Jewish people at the time of Jesus. But, as always and everywhere, the managing class was devoted to defeatism. "If we let him alone as he is, all will believe in him, and the Romans John 11:48 will come and take away both our place and our nation." That is the spirit of Munich. Defeatism produces a transfer of hatred: it is no longer the enemy that is detested, it is the man of honor and hope who provokes the enemy that must be detested. This too we have seen and endured.

The baptism of John, a sign of the conversion of the heart to God, a sign too of faith in the speedy coming of the Kingdom, had cut the nation in two: it had become in Israel the rallying point of hope, the sacrament of honor, against political realism and its wariness, exactly like—though on a different level—the call of June 18, 1940, which was to cut France in two. It is necessary to repeat that, if the contest was difficult for Jesus, it was far, very far, from being lost in advance, quite the reverse. The situation looked very bad for the government. To judge matters from a human point of view, the affair could very well have turned into a gigantic Saint Bartholomew's Day and all Jesus' adversaries could have been exterminated. Jesus staked his life, that much is clear, and the event proved it. But his enemies too were risking their necks, in earnest, and they knew it. Unless one sees this at the start there is danger of not properly understanding this terrible and blood-stained week.

And it came to pass on one of the days, as he was teaching the people in Luke 20:1-8 the temple and preaching the gospel, that the chief priests and Scribes together with the elders came up and spoke to him, saying, "Tell us, by what authority dost thou do these things? Or who is it that gave thee this authority?" But he answered and said to them, "I also will ask you one question. Answer me: was the baptism of John from heaven, or from men?" But they began to argue among themselves, saying, "If we say, 'From heaven,' he will say, 'Why then did you not believe him?' But if we say, 'From men,' *all the people will stone us*; for they are convinced that John was a prophet." And they answered that they did not know whence it was. Then Jesus said to them, "Neither do I tell you by what authority I do these things."

The circle is now perfectly joined: at the denouement of Jesus' temporal adventure there is a return to the starting point and to John's baptism. There is a beautiful symmetry in the fact that the question of this baptism, of its legitimacy and religious significance, returns in so solemn and so menacing a way at the beginning of this week in which "all justice shall be fulfilled."

Matt. 3:15

Read, in the Gospels, these dialogues charged with double meanings, mined with explosives, in which the plan to destroy Jesus is clear as day, but in which Jesus himself appears magnificently irrefutable and formidable. "And the chief priests and the Scribes heard it, and they sought a way to destroy him; *for they were afraid of him, because all the crowd were astonished at his teaching.*"

Mark 11:18

The context of the discussions reported in the Gospels is so far removed from us that these discussions themselves may well seem like scholastic games. They were duels to the death, like the passes in a *corrida*. Fear is there beneath every look, ready to change instantaneously into panic and flight, for the one camp as for the other or, inversely, to change into implacable cruelty at the slightest sign of yielding on the part of the adversary. We too have been afraid, and I can weigh exactly the density of these moments. That at least is not scholastic; fear belongs to all times.

For among Jesus' followers there was fear too, and with good reason. Mark writes, "They were now on their way, going up to Jerusalem; and Jesus was walking on in front of them, and they were in dismay, and those who followed were afraid." John too had noted that on the last ascent toward Jerusalem the Apostles knew that they were risking their lives: "Let us also go, that we may die with him. . . ."

Mark 10:32

John 11:16

And Jesus? For his part he has no fear, at least as yet. He knows in advance the fatal issue, he no longer makes a mystery of it, he speaks openly of it to whoever will listen. Henceforth all precautions are futile. At the very moment when his enemies believe themselves on the verge of defeat and despair of victory, he predicts their victory, joined, however, with certain consequences that they do not perceive. He no longer so much as considers the possibility of reconciliation, still less of compromise. He concentrates his eloquence, which has never been so piercing, on clarifying definitively, before he dies, his personal position and that of Israel. He solemnly affirms the end of religious racism and religious nationalism. He proclaims the enlargement, the bursting forth of the ancient religion. Taking up a celebrated metaphor of the Prophets, who liked to compare Israel to a vineyard, Jesus speaks more generally of the inheritance of God, the Kingdom of God, as a vineyard turned over to renters in a distant country. As the master is far away, the vinegrowers come to consider themselves the owners of the vineyard and behave as such. Then the master sends his servants to demand an accounting and to receive the owner's share of the vintage.

"There was a man, a householder, who planted a vineyard, and put a hedge about it, and dug a wine vat in it, and built a tower; then he let it out to vine-dressers, and went abroad. But when the fruit season drew near, he sent his servants to the vine-dressers to receive his fruits. And the vine-dressers seized his servants, and beat one, killed another, and stoned another. Again he sent another party of servants more numerous than the first; and they did the same to these. Matt. 21:33-41, 43

"Finally he sent his son to them, saying, 'They will respect my son.' But the vine-dressers, on seeing the son, said among themselves, 'This is the heir; come, let us kill him, and we shall have his inheritance.' So they seized him, cast him out of the vineyard, and killed him. When, therefore, the owner of the vineyard comes, what will he do to those vine-dressers?"

They said to him, "He will utterly destroy those evil men, and will let out the vineyard to other vine-dressers, who will render to him the fruits in their seasons." Jesus said to them, ". . . Therefore I say to you, that the kingdom of God will be taken away from you and will be given to a people yielding its fruits."

At the bare announcement of this possibility, Jesus' adversaries exclaim, "May God forbid!" Admirable protest! Admirable debate! Admirable nation! Even those who were making ready to assassinate the well-loved Son were unwilling to renounce the Kingdom of God and Israel's highest vocation, which was to serve as the earthly basis and bridgehead for that Kingdom. Go today and threaten the great of this world, the governors of America, of Russia, of France, of England, or of the Chinese People's Republic by telling them that the Kingdom of God has been taken from them. They will laugh heartily at the Kingdom of God. They will not become enraged about that, they will Luke 20:16

not kill a man for that, even if the man is Jesus Christ. The Kingdom of God has ceased to interest the nations; at any rate, it interests them far less than oil and uranium or even butter and margarine.

Perhaps, however, it is not so simple as that? To feel itself alive, a great nation needs something more than a prosperous economy. This can be seen by certain signs. Go and say to the British that they are no longer the country of habeas corpus and of the Magna Charta, to the Americans that they are no longer the country of liberty and of the Declaration of Independence, to the French that they are no longer the country of the Rights of Man, to the Russians that they are no longer the country of the Revolution—all will take this very ill, for nations are susceptible. What one has a right to demand of all and each, nation or individual, is that he practice the vocation he proclaims and that it produce fruits.

To predict that the Kingdom of God would be taken away from Israel was to predict the very end of that nation, or at least a change so profound that the nation would be unrecognizable. "Your house shall be left empty and deserted." "May God forbid," reply the leaders of that nation. They know very well that the nation was made only for the Kingdom of God, which is the highest vocation any nation was ever given: the nation in the service of the Kingdom, not the Kingdom in the service of the nation.

By affirming that "the Kingdom of God will be taken away from you and will be given to a people yielding its fruits," Christ creates a revolution. He permanently separates true religion from nationalism and racism. Here we find ourselves on very familiar ground, the context has not changed very much. Christ died a victim of racist and nationalist fury. It is part of the logic of the nation to demand from its citizens a total and literally religious devotion. The fact that Jesus fell a victim to nationalism makes him a very modern martyr. Not that the nation is bad in itself, but to give it everything, the body and the soul, to adore it and love it above all things, is an idolatry like any other, worse than one other whose ravages we have seen.

The Apostles, Christ's first disciples, must have been powerfully impressed by this decisive separation between the Kingdom of God on the one hand and nation and race on the other. They were the first generation of leaders in the Catholic Church. It is remarkable that on the morrow of the Ascension of the Lord all the members of the Catholic hierarchy, absolutely all without exception (pope, Apostles, bishops, priests), all were Jews, Jewish by race and by nationality. Fifty years later the hierarchy of that same Catholic Church was entirely in the hands of non-Jews, from the top of the ladder to the bottom. Historically this is to be explained by various causes. It remains nevertheless true that this first generation of Christian bishops and priests, all Jews, gave to the centuries to follow a brilliant and unique example of racial disinterestedness, of internationalism and generous universalism. They did not consider themselves owners of the Kingdom of God; it sufficed them to be its first servants, the pillars of the Church. These Jews, whose race has been called so avaricious, so greedy, held very firmly the entire leadership of the Catholic Church; they opened their hands and freely abandoned this leadership to non-Jews.

I say that this is a unique example, for in fact it is so in the two thousand years of Christian history. It is true that for a long time nationalistic solidarity had little weight in the choice of the bishops and of the pope. But at the end of the Middle Ages France broke that tradition: when she had the disposal of the papacy, she kept it as long as she could. When Italy in her turn had it, she did the same thing. Today she retains it still. And it is only in our time that we have seen the white race give up some of its historical privileges in the Catholic hierarchy. At bottom, even when it is a question of religion and of the Kingdom of God, we naturally believe that God himself cannot do without us, as though His Spirit could not blow where it listeth.

The Apostles and the first bishops profoundly understood the teaching of their master. Like him they were not nationalists, otherwise they would have so managed things that the Catholic hierarchy would have remained Jewish as long as possible and perhaps forever. The Apostles did not believe in the exclusive superiority of their race and their nation, they believed that the Kingdom of God and the authority of the Holy Spirit were truly transmitted by the laying on of their holy and venerable hands which had touched the Lord. And so they laid those hands, without regard to race or nation, on the heads of all those they judged worthy of continuing the work of the Kingdom of God. Blessed be they! It is thanks to them that the Church is catholic. And it is no fault of theirs that the Church is not in fact as universal as it ought to be.

———

In a few months Jesus had succeeded in what is perhaps the most difficult thing of all in any great political career. He had become the cynosure of the whole nation. People talked only of him, what he was going to say; what he was going to do or not do was, day by day, each day's event. At the approach of the Passover, Jerusalem seethed with people. There were not only the inhabitants, preparing for the feast, but pilgrims by the thousands come from all over Palestine and from the whole Diaspora. The streets and squares were never empty. Everyone knew of the excommunication of Jesus by the priests, everyone knew of the unprecedented miracle at Bethany, where Jesus had raised a dead man who had been for four days in the tomb, everyone knew that after this miracle—whether from prudence or design—Jesus and his small band had once more disappeared. A single question flew from mouth to mouth: would Jesus or would he not profit by the assembly of the whole people around his Temple and his God to celebrate in their midst the greatest festival of that chosen people and, who knows, to cause himself to be consecrated King of Israel—and to what use would he put his victory?

Thus only a few days before his death Jesus completely dominated the situation. He was the opposite of one vanquished. The strange aspect of his position is that he seems to have been the only one to foresee for himself a speedy and ignominious death. Enemies, friends, the crowd—all believe in his triumph. He alone is the secret of the outcome, already ripe.

Not wholly alone, however. Close to him is a woman who has divined what is going to happen, not through political genius, of which she appears to have none, but through love. She loves the Lord. Long before the lance of the centurion, she has laid bare this heart, king and center of all hearts, she has read there inexorable destiny. She has seen, inevitable, his love death who some hours later is to say, "This is the greatest love a man can show, that he should lay down his life for his friends." While all the others marvel at the miracles and talk about them, this woman wonders at the love and her heart contracts, she remains silent. The miracles are a demonstration of power, and the law of power is to impose itself when it is strongest. This woman knows as well as anyone that Jesus is the strongest, that he is literally invincible, but she knows, and she is the only one to know, that that is not the question, absolutely not that. This woman knows that the supreme law of the Kingdom inaugurated by Jesus is not power but love.

This woman has understood in advance Jesus' destiny because she has understood more clearly than the others, and at this moment practically alone, that the miracles were only a means and a demonstration in the service of the Kingdom of God, but that love was the very essence of that Kingdom. And it is here that this woman is tragic, unique, extreme; she has understood that the supreme and irrefutable demonstration of love is death, grievous death, conscious, freely offered, given

John 15:13

for nothing, without recompense. In the midst of the preparations for feasting and of the popular tumults and rumors, in the midst of the conflict of enthusiasm and hate, this woman, for her part, thinks only of love and of its miraculous flower, death. Beyond the wonder-worker, even beyond the poet, she sees in Jesus a conqueror, to be sure, but in a unique manner of conquest in which he is at once sacrificer and victim. She knows the nature of the victory for which this conqueror was born: that victory is death through love, and he will enter into it with assured step and wide-open eyes.

This woman measures in advance the enormity of the event. The Lord, creator of heaven and earth, absolute master of eternity and of history, who has become incarnate through love in order to be a Man among men, in order not to dazzle us by his divinity, knows that he is King, but he has never envisaged any other conquest than the conquest of our freedom, and he knows that the human freedom he has created does not yield except to love. He knows that our freedom leads us through love into his Kingdom; this is the very salvation and consecration of that freedom. And so he is about to put the final touch on the masterpiece of his Kingdom by his loving death, the paradigm of all extreme love.

This woman who has gone so far in understanding the heart of Jesus and in compassion, this unique woman—at that moment far above the Apostles—is Mary Magdalene, the sinner of the Gospel of Luke, forgiven by Jesus because she has loved much, the woman possessed of seven demons in the Gospel of Mark, delivered from them by Jesus, the heroine of the Gospel of John, sister of Lazarus whom Jesus raised from the dead.

At the threshold of this black week, during which occurred the redemption of our sins, the defeat of Satan, and the salvation of the world, stands this woman with an amphora of precious perfume in her hands. Like Diotima in Plato she appears in the course of a banquet. Just as John the Baptist baptized the Lord by pouring on his head the water of the Jordan, she is about to anoint the Lord in preparation for his burial by pouring on his head this perfumed and royal oil. Like Ezechiel she has an eloquent and mute pantomime to play before the King of Paradise and in the sight of the House of Israel, at the center of the nascent Catholic Church, a pantomime rich in significance to the end of time. I have already cited Ezechiel's pantomime, which I find so expressive of the terrible destiny of Israel: "You shall bring out your baggage like an exile in the daytime while they are looking on; in the evening, again while they are looking on, you shall go out like one of Ezech. 12:4-6 those driven into exile; while they look on, dig a hole in the wall and pass through it; while they look on, shoulder the burden and set out in the darkness; cover your face that you may not see the land, for I have made you a sign for the house of Israel." He who has tasted exile cannot fail to savor the bitterness of this tragic mime.

But whoever has been present at the death of someone he loves cannot fail either to be sensible to the solemn sadness of the ceremony performed by Mary Magdalene on the eve of this holy and terrible week. John writes, "Mary therefore took a pound of ointment, genuine nard of great value, and anointed the feet of Jesus, and with her hair wiped his feet dry. And the house was filled with the odor of the ointment. Then one of his disciples, Judas Iscariot, he who was about to betray him, said, 'Why was this ointment not sold for three hundred denarii, and given to the poor?' Now he said this, not that he cared for the poor, but because he was a thief, and holding the purse, used to take what was put in it. Jesus therefore said, 'Let her be—that she may keep it for the day of my burial. For the poor you have always with you, but you do not always have me.'" Matthew completes the words of Jesus: "'For in pouring this ointment on my body, she has done it for my burial. Amen I say to you, wherever in the whole world this gospel is preached, this also that she has done shall be told in memory of her.'" As for me, who am among those who have received the mission of preaching the Gospel, I take care not to forget.

John 12:3-8

Matt. 26:12-13

This extraordinary and solemn promise, which forever links the destiny of the Gospel with the memory of this young and beautiful woman, a woman made for love, who never in her whole life has understood anything except by love and through love, thus proves that it is enough to love in order to enter deeper than anyone else into the Kingdom of Jesus. To be sure, when one reads the Gospels attentively, the predictions of Jesus concerning his Passion and his death are so numerous, so explicit, so detailed, that one might be tempted to think Mary Magdalene deserves no great credit for having thus prophesied the burial of her Lord. It would have sufficed for her to listen to what he said again and again and to have retained it in order to reveal it now in a silent and solemn mime like a good pupil interpreting a lesson learned from his master.

But it is precisely she who seems to have been the only one to have heard, understood, and remembered. As for the others, they took the easiest course; Jesus' predictions about his Passion and his death were drowned out by the noise of the miracles, the acclamation of the crowds, the roar of approaching triumphs. He spoke to them like a man speaking beside a waterfall—one had to be very close to hear him at all. Mary Magdalene was the closest. Her exceptional merit, from one end of the Gospel to the other, even her loyalty to herself, her deep consistency, was to have listened, understood, remembered by heart everything Jesus said. The prophetic gift of this woman springs from her quality as an exceptional disciple of Jesus Christ. Her prophetic mime recalls and underlines the prophecies of Jesus himself, as counterpoint underlines the principal melody; she is a prophet in the way a violin attunes itself to a master violin.

Among many other predictions, Jesus had said, "I am the good shepherd . . . and I lay down my life for my sheep. . . . For this reason the Father loves me, because I lay down my life that I may take it up again. No one takes it from me, but I lay it down of myself. I have the power to lay it down, and I have the power to take it up again. Such is the command I have received from my Father." How many others, under the impulse of a generous or paranoiac imagination, offer their lives, only to die peacefully in their beds years after that offering. For the sincerity of his words, Jesus died on a cross between heaven and earth. On the very eve of his death he will say as a reminder, "But he comes that the world may know that I love the Father, and that I do as the Father has commanded me." This command was aimed at his breast as the rifles of an execution squad are aimed at the breast of the man they are about to execute. In this situation everything that is said is serious. Mary Magdalene alone understands the situation. *John 10:14-15, 17-18* *John 14:31*

At the very moment, then, when all is joyous, when the Apostles, and no doubt Judas in particular, are evaluating the political chances of their master, seeing them as more and more favorable, when they are betting on the revolution, thinking of the throne of Israel, already perhaps distributing their posts, the ministries and the portfolios, this woman appears in deep mourning in the midst of the festive repast and, by anointment with a precious perfume, announces that the fairest body among the children of men will soon be no more than a cadaver stretched out beneath the earth. For all the times that Jesus has spoken of *his hour,* it was reserved for this somber and beautiful messenger to appear and announce, amid a solemn silence, that the hour has finally struck.

———

At the beginning of this book I considered prophecy as a tragedy. In the whole temporal adventure of Jesus, God, always supremely faithful to His promises, remains supremely faithful to His own style, and this style is the style of tragedy. Beginning with the funerary and royal anointment of Jesus by Mary Magdalene, the unfolding of the Passion of Christ strictly conforms to the laws of classical tragedy. In this so-well-known story, the "suspense" is of the same kind as the "suspense" in a Greek tragedy. This to be sure can only be an analogy, but all theology is a matter of analogies. An analogy of this sort can aid me in attempting in my turn to recount this sorrowful week, it will aid me in placing the accent here or there, as each orchestra conductor "recounts" in his own fashion and according to his own personality the same symphony.

Of all Shakespeare's tragedies, *Macbeth* is, no doubt, if not the most moving at least the most perfect from the point of view of dramatic architecture. After the first three scenes, Macbeth knows that he will be king:

> All hail, Macbeth, that shalt be king hereafter!

But we do not know, nor does Macbeth, how this will come about. The "suspense" is in the manner of the inexorable accomplishment of the prophecy.

It is the same for all the guests at the banquet in the house of Simon the Leper. After Mary Magdalene has poured her perfume on the Lord's body and after Jesus has explained the meaning of her gesture, all should know that Jesus is going to die, that he will be placed in the earth, that he knows this in advance, and that he accepts his fate in advance. This is clearly expressed, as clearly as Macbeth is told that he will be king. It remains to find out how Jesus will arrive there. This is why Holy Week really begins with this banquet, with this anointing of Christ by Mary Magdalene. Because there is the beginning of the "suspense" of the whole ineluctable tragedy.

John, who has given us the most precise account of the Passion of Jesus, with the dry objectivity of a law-court record, is also the one among the Evangelists whom I shall most faithfully follow. He has noted the reactions of those present at the anointing by Mary Magdalene and particularly the reactions of Judas. He emphasizes the avarice of Judas, whom Jesus—with an ironic sense of administration—has made the treasurer of the little band and to whom he had entrusted the common purse. In everything John says about Judas one can detect deep animosity against the traitor. Many characteristics of the Evangelists, moreover, indicate that harmony was not perfect within the community of the Apostles. But between John and Judas there may also have been a special rivalry, each considering that he had a claim to be the first among those near Jesus.

Having personally reflected a great deal on the character of Judas and the motives for the betrayal, I imagine that he was a sort of Richelieu or Talleyrand—that he felt he had the qualifications to be a great prime minister and that he profoundly believed in the political future of Jesus, whereas John was simply "the disciple Jesus loved." Judas dreamed of assuring the deliverance of Israel from Rome and its infamous collaborators in the same fashion that she had already been delivered from Pharaoh, whose army had been swallowed up in the Red Sea. Jesus' miracles, his omnipotence as a wonder-worker, seemed to Judas exactly the right instrument of prestige and effectiveness to overturn everything, engulf everything, carry everything before it, unleash the revolution and bring it to a triumphant issue.

Personally I cannot believe that greed alone determined Judas' betrayal. Thirty pieces of silver are a trifle: an avaricious man would have demanded higher payment. Moreover, Judas did not even keep the thirty pieces of silver. He did not act out the role of miser to the end.

When Bernanos was a child he could not help feeling great pity for the miserable Judas. How could a man who had seen Christ so close, who had heard and touched him, who at one moment had loved him enough to leave everything and follow him, how could such a man have been able to betray him and deliver him up to his enemies? The overwhelming of this soul in darkness remained a dreadful mystery to Bernanos. He could not believe in the damnation of Judas—about which, by the way, no one knows anything. While still a young boy, then, Bernanos from time to time took his savings to the village curé to have masses said for Judas. Since he did not dare pronounce this name, he would simply say to the honest priest, "For a soul in pain." Thus at the end of the last century in a little village in France masses were said for the repose of the soul of the man of whom Jesus had said that it would have been better for him not to have been born. It is traits like this that make it impossible not to love Bernanos, who in this resembles Saint Dominic, the saint who dared extend his charity even to those damned in hell: *"et usque ad in inferno damnatos extendebat caritatem suam."*

Judas was of this world, terribly so. He knew that grandeur in this world is born of power, "the final argument of kings"—*"ultima ratio regum."* Jesus' incredible miracles had roused his enthusiasm, he marveled at the exercise of this power that extended even over death. He had rightly discerned in it an instrument of revolution and political domination, infallible and irresistible, capable, in any circumstances, of swinging the balance in Jesus' favor. What would Lenin have done if, in addition to his genius for revolution, he had had the gift of miracles? Judas perhaps had the revolutionary genius of Lenin and Jesus the gift of miracles: between them they would possess the world. "We shall conquer because we are the stronger"—that is the law of human warfare, it was Judas' law. Especially after the raising of Lazarus, a dazzling miracle that had thrown consternation into the enemy's camp, Judas had felt victory within arm's reach: why not stretch out one's hand and pluck the marvelous fruit of which conquerors dream? Judas did not go beyond that: he dreamed of the empire of the world for Jesus. Those who know the laws of this world know that it is not on love that empires are founded. Judas had come to the point of hating love.

The misunderstanding between Judas and Mary Magdalene had nothing to do with the empire, nor the conquest, nor the victory. It had to do with the content of these words and the means of achieving the empire. Jesus had always declared that he had come into this world to reign, as fire is made to burn. And from the time of her first encounter with him Mary Magdalene had recognized him as the King of hearts and had crowned him as such. But power constrains bodies, it is love that controls souls, and the only empire Jesus strove for was that of souls, and, through the soul, of the body too, which participates in the virtue of and the glory of the soul. This in itself was a very novel ambition. But the newest thing of all was the road opened by Jesus to this conquest and this empire, a road altogether heroic and grievous, on which one receives nothing but gives all. It is through love and love alone that Jesus reigns. The empire of this world is not beyond his powers, not at all; it is beneath his ambitions. It is clear that Jesus, from the time of his meeting with the Devil in the desert, has always aimed higher than earthly kingdoms: what use had he for mortal realms, who had the disposal of celestial kingdoms?

Non eripit mortalia
Qui regna dat coelestia.

Judas grasped none of this, he thought it a dream. To have the empire of the world within one's grasp and not to want it, that was too stupid. From the moment when he finally understood, he began no doubt to hate Jesus, and Mary Magdalene, who seemed to him a most dangerous accomplice in this ambition of love. For political realism, the supernatural ambition introduced into this world by Jesus is a vain dream, and therefore despicable. But for Jesus political realism is an equally vain enterprise and still more despicable. It is as Saint Augustine was to say so eloquently: two loves have built two cities. Self-love to the point of disregard for God has built the City of the Devil. Love of God to the point of disregard of self has built the City of God.

Fundamentally Judas belonged to the same world as Jesus' adversaries; he was, like them, a political realist. But whereas Jesus' enemies feared and respected the power of Rome, Judas for his part believed that Jesus, with his wonder-working powers, could sweep all away, including Rome and its legions. He was not mistaken. But he could not imagine that one might be in possession of such powers without in fact using them to sweep away Rome and its detestable collaborators. When Judas committed treason and changed sides, he was only joining his own. Nevertheless he was greater than his new masters, and he knew it very well. He died of it. It was he who committed suicide. They did not.

CHAPTER XX

Palm Sunday

POLITICALLY the decisive day was Palm Sunday. That day confirmed Mary Magdalene in her somber presentiment, saw the launching of Judas' treason, disheartened and dispersed Jesus' followers, and brought back hope to his enemies. Nevertheless, at first sight no day had ever dawned for him under better auspices. He held the offensive and almost the victory, he had cornered his enemies. For Jesus the day began like Austerlitz and ended like Waterloo. But whereas Napoleon did everything possible to win the battle, his own battle, Jesus did everything possible to lose it. He wanted to prove something quite different from the questions that can be settled by human battles. All the events of that deadly week will be used by Jesus to define what is at stake for him—the truth. When later on Jesus speaks of truth to Pilate, the latter will say, "What is truth?" The question does indeed arise, and I shall return to it; moreover, not the least merit of Christianity is that it obliges skeptics, realists, and the blasé to put that question to themselves.

The day began gloriously, with cries of joy, acclamations, fanfares, streamers, dances, fifes and tambourines, improvised triumphal arches covered with flowers, mantles flung before the graceful steps of an ass, palms torn from the trees and made into a roof above the conqueror, like the drawn swords over the head of a victorious general. The conqueror was Jesus, the crowd that provided this triumphal entry was the people of Israel, who had not felt such joy since the exodus from Egypt and who shouted his glory till the echoes rang.

Now the next day, the great crowd which had come to the feast, when they John 12:12-19
heard that Jesus was coming to Jerusalem, took the branches of palms and
went forth to meet him. And they cried out, "Hosanna! Blessed is he who
comes in the name of the Lord, the king of Israel!" And Jesus found a
young ass, and sat upon it, as it is written,

> Fear not, daughter of Sion;　　　　　　　　　　　　　　　Zach. 9:9
> Behold, thy king comes,
> Sitting upon the colt of an ass.

. . . The crowd therefore, which was with him when he called Lazarus from
the tomb and raised him from the dead, bore witness to him. And the
reason why the crowd also went to meet him was that they heard that he
had worked this sign. The Pharisees therefore said among themselves, "Do
you see that we avail nothing? Behold, the entire world has gone after him."

John explicitly notes that the immediate cause of Jesus' triumph was
the raising of Lazarus from the dead, an unheard-of miracle, rich in
significance if any miracle ever was: before dying Jesus has proved
superbly that he is the Lord of death as well as of life, and he has
prefigured his own Resurrection. Luke, who does not mention the
raising of Lazarus, also specifies the miracles as the cause of Jesus'
triumph. The Jews ask for signs, that is what the Jews are there for,
it is their providential function, the Messiah is to make himself known
to them by this sign. Well and good, on that particular day, without
any shadow of doubt the Jews recognized in Jesus the Messiah; the
triumph they celebrate is a literally Messianic one.

. . . Throwing their cloaks over the colt they set Jesus on it. And as he went, Luke 19:35-40
they kept spreading their cloaks upon the road. And when he was drawing
near, being by now at the descent of the Mount of Olives, the whole company of the disciples began to rejoice and to praise God with a loud voice
for all the miracles that they had seen, saying, "Blessed is he who comes
as king, in the name of the Lord! Peace in heaven, and glory in the highest!"
And some of the Pharisees from the crowds said to him, "Master, rebuke
thy disciples." He said to them, "I tell you that if these keep silence, the
stones will cry out."

We too have seen a similar occasion, an unforgettable one. On
August 26, 1944, in liberated Paris amid a people delirious with joy,
when the leaders of Free France and of the Resistance, with de Gaulle
in their center, came down the Champs Elysées, how many among
them were pariahs, men sentenced to death, banished men, the rebellious, the excommunicated? They had triumphed, and all the rest was
swept before them. When Jesus entered Jerusalem in triumph, he too
had been excommunicated and condemned to death, and his enemies

trembled in impotent rage. At this moment he could achieve anything he wished.

In communion with that Jewish crowd from all parts of Palestine and the Diaspora, which now ascends the slopes of their acropolis, accompanying Jesus toward the Temple of the living God, never, never, never, will we grow weary of proclaiming the Messianic glory of Jesus Christ, revealed by his miracles, never will we allow ourselves to be intimidated by Tartuffe, who always thinks that too much of a fuss is being made, never will we give in to the Pharisees, rationalistic, scientific, realistic, and opportunistic, with their bleary eyes that cannot sustain the brilliance of miracles, never will we allow ourselves to be "brought to reason." And if anyone asks me why I have written this book, I so little qualified even to approach such a subject, I shall boldly reply that on one day of days even the stones of the streets were allowed to cry out.

The triumph celebrated for Jesus on Palm Sunday is proof that the Jewish people in general were on Jesus' side, since on that particular day they recognized him as the Messiah. By what right could the Pharisees represent the Jewish nation more authentically than this crowd of people who were singing and shouting praises?

Thus far all is perfectly comprehensible. Jesus finds himself in exactly the same situation in which he was once before, in Galilee after the miracle of the loaves and fishes, when the crowd searched for him to make him king. But this time he does not withdraw; on the contrary, he takes part in the play. Granted there is nothing brutal about this triumph, Jesus does not enter into Jerusalem on a chariot, surrounded by soldiers and followed by captives in chains; nevertheless he presents himself as king, the heir of David. Through his miracles he has shown the Jewish people his letters of credit, and that people recognize him for what he is: the envoy of God, the Messiah, King of Israel. Jesus accepts these titles and these acclamations as his due. At this moment even Judas must believe that before the day ends Jesus will be seated on the throne of Israel.

What would Jesus do? His enemies were helpless, the crowd deliriously obedient. In such circumstances, if what one really wants is political power, one must strike while the iron is hot, there is not a minute to lose. In the sequel the Jewish people fought so heroically and so long against the Romans that one must believe that on that Palm Sunday, if Jesus had wished it, he could have galvanized that people and thrown them into any warlike adventure whatever. It is not at all unlikely that he would have emerged victorious; after all, he had the gift of miracles, and that represented "the absolute weapon." On the other hand, however, matters were so far advanced and so clear that Jesus now had no other choice but the throne or the gibbet. If he did not achieve the first, he could no longer escape the second. Jesus had crossed the Rubicon.

Then a truly remarkable thing happened.

Nothing happened.

Jesus talked. He talked for hours in the outer sanctuary of the Temple. This inexhaustible eloquence had the effect of dispersing his partisans—the same effect that the rain had on Robespierre's troops in the Place de l'Hôtel de Ville while they wearily waited in the night for orders that never came. Many did not understand; those who did understood that, through audacity and ambiguity almost beyond belief, Jesus was accepting the gibbet in advance, but was claiming at the same time that the gibbet was the one true throne to which he must aspire: "And I, if I be lifted up from the earth, will draw all things to myself." The universal Kingdom that he claimed would not burst upon him except on the cross. Here is the résumé that John gives us of that astonishing discourse: *John 12:32*

But Jesus answered them, "The hour has come for the Son of Man to be glorified. Amen, amen, I say to you, unless the grain of wheat falls into the ground and dies, it remains alone. But if it dies, it brings forth much fruit. He who loves his life, loses it; and he who hates his life in this world, keeps it unto life everlasting. If anyone serves me, let him follow me; and where I am there also shall my servant be. If anyone serves me, my Father will honor him. Now my soul is troubled. And what shall I say? Father, save me from this hour! No, this is why I came to this hour. Father, glorify Thy name!" There came therefore a voice from heaven, "I have both glorified it, and I will glorify it again." *John 12:23-36*

Then the crowd which was standing round and had heard, said that it had thundered. Others said, "An angel has spoken to him." Jesus answered and said, "Not for me did this voice come, but for you. Now is the judgment of the world; now will the prince of the world be cast out. And I, if I be lifted up from the earth, will draw all things to myself." Now he said this signifying by what death he was to die. The crowd answered him, "We have heard from the Law that the Christ abides forever. And how canst thou say, 'The Son of Man must be lifted up'? Who is this Son of Man?" Jesus therefore said to them, "Yet a little while the light is among you. Walk while you have the light, that darkness may not overtake you. He who walks in the darkness does not know where he goes. While you have the light, believe in the light, that you may become sons of light."

These things Jesus spoke, and he went away and hid himself from them.

It was finished. Jesus put an end to that day of triumph by disappearing. In Jesus' whole life this is one of the events that give greatest cause for reflection on his conduct and true intentions. Why accept the triumph if only in the end to disappear? If Caesar after crossing the Rubicon had deserted his own troops, he would forever have been branded a coward.

We know that Jesus was not a coward; he was to prove that throughout the whole sinister week. Judas was so feverishly eager for physical victory that no doubt in his impassioned judgment he went to the extreme of considering the return to Bethany a shameful flight, as it had every appearance of being. Jesus was so courageous that he was indifferent to being thought a coward, and that indifference on that point is the extreme of courage.

Then what? What did Jesus want? It is easier to say what he did not want. In the conversation he will have with Pilate on the morning of Good Friday, it is clear that Jesus does not wish to be either Caesar or Alexander. All the hurly-burly of the conquerors of this world, with their armed troops arranged in platoons, companies, battalions, regiments, divisions, and corps, all these men and all this matériel, together with their battle plans, everything that flashes, moves, and stops en masse, everything that kills and is killed, all this hardware called war and its instruments—with this Jesus will have absolutely nothing to do. His reply to Pilate shows very clearly that he was entirely capable of being a Caesar or an Alexander: " 'My kingdom is not of this world. If my kingdom were of this world, my followers would have fought that I might not be delivered to the Jews. But as it is, my kingdom is not from here.' Pilate therefore said to him, 'Thou art then a king?' Jesus answered, 'Thou sayest it; I am a king.' "

John 18:36-37

It is as if Jesus were saying to the proconsul, "If I were on the same level as you and your legions, you would not amount to much and I would take a certain pleasure in making you run. Only, you see, you and I do not belong to the same world. I know that my life is at stake. I will not for that reason compromise myself in a world that is absolutely not my world." There you have the thing that Judas has not understood. But we, reader, why should we be insensible to such heroism, a heroism containing so much elegance? That is the place where the spirit of chivalry was born, a spirit that was to form a race of soldiers more sensible to the elegance of loyalty than to the drunkenness of victory.

God defend me from wishing to judge Him who will judge me. I am simply trying, with all the respect of which I am capable, to understand Jesus' character, his style of humanity. One cannot deny that his attitude on Palm Sunday would provoke in us some embarrassment if, after his acceptance of the Messianic triumph, his flight to Bethany at nightfall had involved the loss of lives. A coup d'état that fails brings with it casualties; this event did not. The tragic week will cost only two lives—Jesus' own, which had been offered up in advance, and that of Judas. But it was not because of Jesus that Judas died. The law of honor, which obliges the captain to be the last to leave a sinking ship, which unites the leader with his men and compels him to confront the greatest perils in order to save them to the last one, this law of honor was observed by Jesus to the end. What a disgrace for the leader of a plot to extricate himself personally while his subordinates pay with their lives for their loyalty to him! We have seen that, too, happen and we have seen that some individuals survive shame very easily.

Jesus was not of this world, true enough! Nevertheless he was on his guard to see that the honor of this world should have nothing to reproach him with. In his last prayer, when he is recapitulating his earthly activity, he speaks proud words on the subject of his Apostles: "Those whom thou hast given me I guarded; and not one of them perished except the son of perdition, in order that the Scripture might be fulfilled." John 17:12

Nevertheless, if one evaluates the whole position from the point of view of human politics, even after the fiasco of Palm Sunday the people have not yet lost confidence in their Prophet, which proves how completely prepared those people were to receive the most heroic, the most supernatural teaching. Judas, for his part, has understood that, politically, the affair could only turn out badly, since Jesus is accepting in advance the horrible torture of the cross: he no longer feels at one with that man and he changes camps. To recapitulate Jesus' action in these last days the Evangelists write: "Now in the daytime he was teaching in the temple; but as for the nights, he would go out and pass them on the mountain called Olivet. And all the people came to him early in the morning in the temple to hear him." "Now Judas, who betrayed him, also knew the place, since Jesus had often met there together with his disciples." Luke 21:37-38 John 18:2

But whatever the favor of the crowd, the bets were down. Jesus' enemies had regained their courage. To their great astonishment they were to discover that Jesus did not wish to engage them in a proof of strength. If he himself was withholding his power, then they felt themselves little by little becoming the stronger. In the course of that week there was a single casual miracle, that of the fig tree, which was cursed and instantaneously blasted: it is on that familiar and peaceful tree that Jesus hangs up his miraculous power, as a village musician before dying hangs up the guitar that hitherto has led the merrymaking. Henceforth Jesus is like Samson after Delilah cut his hair. He will not recover his power until he wishes to do so, and he will not again desire it until after he has tasted death.

Judas has secretly made contact with the chief priests and is seeking an opportunity to hand over his master. The net is drawing close around Jesus. Despite this he acts and speaks with marvelous freedom, all the more moving because he knows himself betrayed and lost. Death alone will close his mouth. It is in these days that Jesus makes his great apocalyptic discourse and brings to its climax his conflict with the Pharisees. He fans the very flame in which he will perish.

CHAPTER XXI

Maundy Thursday

J OHN the Evangelist tells us that "Jesus was to die for the nation; John 11:51-52 and not only for the nation, but that he might gather into one the children of God who were scattered abroad." This is the supernatural foundation of ecumenicism which strives to gather together in good will all Christians throughout the world. Therefore much may be expected of this universal ferment of ecumenicism. But I personally do not believe that ecumenicism can bear abundant fruits without having general and explicit recourse to the sources of Christianity—that is, to Israel.

No example is clearer than that of the Last Supper. Since the Protestant Reformation, Christians have been quarreling about the significance and the implications of this repast. During the last century criticism saw in the account of the institution of the Eucharist the influence of Hellenistic initiation rites. On the other hand it was asked how the ritual of the Mass, which is obviously complicated and ceremonial in nature, could claim to continue and commemorate this last reunion of Christ with his Apostles on the eve of his death. Would a man who is going to die and knows it occupy himself with observances and with ceremonial? Well, yes, exactly that, if he is a man worthy of the name. He occupies himself in this way more than ever before.

When the delegates from the National Convention had come to the prison and informed Louis XVI that he had been condemned to death, the former King took three steps backward, which, according to the protocol of the French court, was the sign that the royal audience was at an end; the delegates understood him, took their leave, bowing deeply, and withdrew backwards, all in accordance with the ceremonial

265

of the court. Indeed, Louis XVI was more a king in prison and on the scaffold than when he sat on the throne.

This example is no more than an analogy, not meant to belittle my subject, an example of conduct in no way equal to that of Jesus Christ. But if poor, ordinary human beings concentrate all their heroism on dying in a certain fashion—for the essential thing is not the dying but dying well—how can one believe that Jesus did not to the very end remain true to himself in each of his gestures, in each of his words? He was born "subject to the Law"; he wished to die "subject to the Law." The Law, however, was a closely woven net of gestures, purifications, prayers, ablutions, and benedictions, a universal and precise ceremonial which left no place for chance or for sentimental improvisations. It was a detailed and sometimes fussy setting for one's entire life. And this was true for each day and each meal: how much more for a feast day, how much more for the greatest of all feasts which was the feast of the Passover, and for the Paschal meal?

Only Jesus, "subject to the Law," is also the purpose of the Law: he forces it to its maturity and delivers it of a meaning that it bore within it and prefigured, but which, once it is realized and the umbilical cord cut, is a new being, just as an infant is different from its mother. One must go back a very long way in the history of Judaism to discover the outlines of the structure of the primitive Church. Christianity is the revelation, the coming of God's plan for the salvation of men; it is also the conclusion and the crowning of a religious society which is older than it by two thousand years, the Jewish society. The vine of Christianity comes from Heaven, but it was planted in this earth; moreover, the vintage retains a strong flavor of this soil.

When Picasso interprets in his own fashion a celebrated painting by Velásquez, everyone recognizes Velásquez' theme, but the thing that overwhelms us with aesthetic pleasure is the surprise of seeing this well-known theme treated by Picasso: nothing is more characteristically Picasso than his "In the Manner of Velásquez." But we would misjudge the work and we would not have the same surprise if we had never in our lives seen the Velásquez in question or a reproduction of it.

Something analogous is happening here, and not for the first time in the Gospel. First one enters on the ground level into a traditional Jewish social structure, in a traditional Jewish ceremonial, congealed, fixed, and routine, described in detail in the Law and the Mishnah. Provided one knows the Law and the Mishnah and the Jewish customs of Jesus' time—as a painter knows Velásquez—one advances on solid ground, perfectly described by the surveyors, one knows where one is and where one is going. Or rather one thinks he knows this, for all of a sudden he perceives that he is somewhere else: this is no longer Velásquez, it is Picasso. The ceremonial has been subtly rearranged with a view to an entirely new significance, the design of the social structure has been inflected into a new fashion and a new perspective.

And then it becomes of extreme importance to locate exactly, to notice and underscore what has been curtailed or added, or changed, or modified, the precise spot at which routine was definitely swept off its feet. But to perceive what is new it is necessary to know what the preceding custom, tradition, and institution were: it is against this background that the Christian revelation—or revolution—appears in its true light. Hence the importance for the study of the Evangelists of the Old Testament in general and even the later writings such as the Mishnah, and now the Dead Sea Scrolls. The great painters are just the ones who know all this better than anyone else. How can one talk of Christ without defining his relationship to his milieu? Like the great artists, Jesus Christ broke an automatism: it is at the points of breakage that his revelation bursts through.

In studying Jewish society at the time of Jesus it has become clear that the group, consisting of him and his twelve disciples, whose leader he was, was certainly not an original social phenomenon. Such groups existed in great numbers in Israel: they were called *chebroth* (*chebrah* in the singular), which we translate by "religious community," "fraternity," "congregation," or even "club" or "society," if these last words do not have too profane a connotation. For these were essentially associations, comprising a small number of men and having a common religious purpose of charity, piety, the study of the Law, and leading a communal life like that of an ambulatory monastery. They were associations closed in on themselves, centered in a master, whose common bond was normally no special interest or ambition but essentially friendship and fraternal love. The universal Catholic Church, with its organization and its hierarchy, found its origin, its seed, its essential characteristics, in this first *chebrah*, of which Jesus was the center and the chief, as he has remained the center and chief of the Catholic Church.

We know something about the customs of such groups. The group as such evinced itself principally in the course of a weekly supper: that was its chief public demonstration of existence. Such repasts habitually took place on the eve of the Sabbath, or on the eve of feasts. Jesus' *chebrah* must have followed that rule and, whatever the diverse occupations of the Apostles, they must have arranged to reassemble together around their master for the weekly supper of the *chebrah*.

Thanks to the Mishnah we also know perfectly the arrangement of these suppers, particularly that of the Paschal supper. They were not conducted casually in the manner of our modern meetings of friends in a restaurant. Besides, among the Jews, nothing was carried on casually: everything was liturgy, a strict series of actions and benedictions. In passing it might be noted that this condemns those modern liturgists who believe they can recover the primitive spirit of the Last Supper by adopting a manner of easy-going informality: no grosser mistake could be made.

This Jewish liturgy served as the framework for the primitive Catholic liturgy. The Synoptics and Saint Paul, who tell us about the Last Supper, do not report the details of that liturgy. Why should they? Those details were well known at the time, as well known as the painting by Velásquez now is which served as Picasso's motif. But their accounts cannot be properly read except against the background of the Jewish liturgical tradition for such suppers. Only the Synoptics and Saint Paul emphasize precisely what, in that Last Supper, has suddenly broken the traditional automatism.

And what is this break? It is the point at which the new covenant is founded, which gives an entirely new meaning and contour to the ancient rite and to the very structure of the Christian *chebrah*.

———

Thomas Aquinas, with his precise sense of the truth and his precision of language, calls the Eucharist "the memorial to the death of the Lord." This is exactly what Jesus instituted within the framework of the fraternal and traditional repast of a small Jewish *chebrah* on the occasion of the feast of the Passover. Here I explicitly acknowledge my debt to Dom Gregory Dix, the Anglican Benedictine who wrote *The Shape of the Liturgy*.

In the course of the Last Supper, Jesus profoundly modified the very meaning of the Jewish ritual, introducing into this ritual completely new elements. He oriented everything in this Last Supper, in word and act, toward an augural and inaugural significance: within the ancient rite, he founded a new rite of his own, simpler and fuller than the old one; in a word, he instituted the Sacrament of the Eucharist, and that institution would not be so remarkable and so famous, so solemn and so memorable, had it not deliberately broken with the ancient rite. It was precisely at the points of cleavage that Christ introduced what he wanted to establish.

If one wants to make a gesture or a word unforgettable, it must not be tossed up into the air. A good method is to set an automatism going and then suddenly to interrupt this automatism; then and only then one may make the incredible gesture, utter the unheard-of cry. Then indeed everything will be unforgettable, as on that occasion when all the radios of the world, all of them at once, interrupted their mutterings to announce in the ensuing silence, *"War has been declared."*

Jesus has arranged this scene with care in order to engrave the event deeply into the minds of the guests. He has made use of the traditional Paschal supper, which faced principally toward the past, in commemoration of Israel's deliverance out of the land of Egypt, but he has disarranged the traditional ceremonial, giving henceforth to his *chebrah* a new spirit and a new rule, centering from now on the whole life of this *chebrah,* no longer in a commemoration of an ancient deliverance but in the Eucharistic commemoration of his personal sacrifice and of his imminent death, of which the sacrifice of the Paschal lamb was simply the annunciation. O Church of Jesus Christ, you have borne witness well, and yours are living memorials, including the Real Presence.

When the moment of this Paschal repast had come, Jesus announced the unique solemnity of the hour. John writes, "Before the feast of the Passover, Jesus, knowing that the hour had come for him to pass out of this world to the Father, having loved his own who were in the world, loved them to the end." And Luke: "And when the hour had come, he reclined at table, and the twelve apostles with him. And he said to them, 'I have greatly desired to eat this Passover with you before I suffer; for I say to you that I will eat of it no more, until it has been fulfilled in the kingdom of God.' " *John 13:1* *Luke 22:14-16*

And then Jesus inaugurates the Jewish repast in the Jewish manner by offering a cup, which he blesses and which then passes from hand to hand. But in offering this cup to his friends, he recapitulates his whole temporal destiny: the shadow of death hovers over this repast, but the repast also illuminates the now imminent hope of victory and of the Kingdom.

"And having taken a cup, he gave thanks and said, 'Take this and share it among you; for I say to you that I will not drink of the fruit of the vine, until the kingdom of God comes.' " This is not as yet the Eucharistic rite; it is simply, according to the ancient ritual, wine in a cup. But what poetic condescension, what courtesy on the part of our Lord, that the wine that laughs in our glasses should henceforth and for every one of us be a symbol and reminder of the Kingdom of God *Luke 22:17-18* on account of which we have been created and put into this world below.

The Paschal meal was a feast, and each of the guests drank at least four cups of wine. Psalms were sung, children questioned the old men, who answered them, the Paschal lamb was eaten, what had been done by God for His people in the past was recalled, the coming of the Kingdom was evoked in which the election of Israel would find its full consummation in glory. Jesus undoubtedly followed tradition. There is no doubt that his Last Supper, despite the shadow of the cross, was a joyous repast, with abundant wine and with songs. The youngest, no doubt Saint John, puts the ritual question: "How does this night differ from other nights?" And Jesus replies, "It is because of that which the Lord did for me when I came forth out of Egypt. Therefore are we bound to give thanks, to praise, to glorify, to honour, to exalt, to extol, and to bless Him who wrought all these wonders for our fathers and for us. He brought us out from bondage to freedom, from sorrow to gladness, and from mourning to a festival-day, and from darkness to great light, and from servitude to redemption; so let us say before Him the Hallelujah." For traditionally, in each generation, each Jew must consider himself as having personally escaped from Egypt: everything that God has done for his fathers has been done for him individually.

Why is this night so different from other nights? The Christian Easter, to be sure, continues and extends the Jewish Passover. Each Christian, too, escapes from Egypt and passes out of the shadows into the great light and out of servitude into redemption. But all this is even ·more true of the Christian Easter than of the Jewish Passover. For the Paschal lamb and the escape from Egypt are only prophetic prefigurations of Jesus, who wipes away the sin of the world, they are prophetic of the salvation he brings. Now, now only, are we in the reality of redemption. That is why this night is unique.

After the benediction and the passing of the first cup, even before he institutes the Eucharist, Jesus, who has a clear and decisive mind and always does precisely what he intends, defines unequivocally the spirit that is thereafter to animate the hierarchy of his Church, his *chebrah*. The Synoptics state precisely that up to this moment there had been a contest among the Apostles to know who was first among them. It is at this point that Jesus begins to disarrange the classic ceremonial by a mime of his own, a parable in action.

In the banquet halls there was always a basin and a ewer for the cleansing of hands. Sometimes it was the host himself who washed his guests' hands. Now Jesus rises, takes off his tunic, girds himself with a

towel, and washes, not the hands, as the custom was, but the feet of the
Apostles. Then he reveals the meaning of his action: "Do you know
what I have done to you? You call me Master and Lord, and you say
well, for so I am. If, therefore, I the Lord and Master have washed your
feet, you also ought to wash the feet of one another. For I have given
you an example, that as I have done to you, so you also should do.
Amen, amen, I say to you, no servant is greater than his master, nor is
one who is sent greater than he who sent him."

John 13:12-17

Even more explicitly Mark indicates not only the difference but the
opposition between the imperious spirit of the princes of this world and
the spirit that should animate the *chebrah* of Jesus. "You know that
those who are regarded as rulers among the Gentiles lord it over them,
and their great men exercise authority over them. But it is not so among
you. On the contrary, whoever wishes to become great shall be your
servant; and whoever wishes to be first among you shall be the slave of
all; for the Son of Man also has not come to be served but to serve, and
to give his life as a ransom for many."

Mark 10:42-45

Not to be ministered unto but to minister, to give his soul, his life,
as a ransom for others: these are the jewels in the diadem of Christ the
King. To my mind, the washing of the Apostles' feet is as important as
the entrance of Jesus into Jerusalem on Palm Sunday: it too is a
Messianic event and it forms a pendant to the earlier one. Through
this pantomime and his explanation of it Jesus here defines the nature
and the meaning of the Messianic Kingdom that had been accorded to
him by the people of Israel. Just as the bath is designed to cleanse, the
effect of this Kingdom is to purify souls. Jesus washes the feet of his
disciples, and this is indeed a menial service reserved for the lowest
slaves, it is also a maternal service; mothers wash their babies. Jesus'
monarchy is at once a monarchy of service and a maternal monarchy.
Moreover, this maternal service is demanding in the highest degree,
for it requires the giving of his life as ransom for the purification of the
multitude. All this is made clear through light, positive touches—as a
painter composes a picture by juxtaposing colors but obviously not at
random. However it is clear that, while pagan priests so often express
themselves through cruelty, including human sacrifice, the man who
is invested by authority derived from Christ, if he wishes to remain true
to the spirit of Christ, must make himself the servant of all, as Jesus
has made himself the servant: he entered voluntarily into all servitude
(of suffering, of tears, of death, of the tomb) to deliver us from slavery
to sin, the single slavery that need be feared, for it separates us from the
Kingdom of God.

On the morning of Palm Sunday, Jesus took public responsibility for a whole series of prophecies that promised Israel a glorious Messiah. Now, before his Apostles, Jesus takes upon himself the realization of a different series of prophecies—which until he came seemed incompatible with the first—foretelling a redemptive but suffering Messiah. I must here quote the fourth song of the servant of Yahweh, written by Isaia more than half a millennium before the Passion of Jesus. I quote this astonishing text in its entirety, because it puts what is happening here in its proper light:

Who would believe what we have heard? To whom has the arm of the Lord been revealed? He grew up like a sapling before him, like a shoot from the parched earth; there was in him no stately bearing to make us look at him, nor appearance that would attract us to him. He was spurned and avoided by men, a man of suffering, accustomed to infirmity, one of those from whom men hide their faces, spurned, and we held him in no esteem.

Yet it was our infirmities that he bore, our sufferings that he endured, while we thought of him as stricken, as one smitten by God and afflicted. But he was pierced for our offenses, crushed for our sins; upon him was the chastisement that makes us whole, by his stripes we were healed.

We had all gone astray like sheep, each following his own way; but the Lord laid upon him the guilt of us all. Though he was harshly treated, he submitted and opened not his mouth; like a lamb led to the slaughter or a sheep before the shearers, he was silent and opened not his mouth.

Oppressed and condemned, he was taken away, and who would have thought any more of his destiny? When he was cut off from the land of the living, and smitten for the sin of his people, a grave was assigned him among the wicked and a burial place with evildoers, though he had done no wrong nor spoken any falsehood.

(But the Lord was pleased to crush him in infirmity.) If he gives his life as an offering for sin, he shall see his descendants in a long life, and the will of the Lord shall be accomplished through him.

Because of his affliction he shall see the light in fullness of days; through his suffering, my servant shall justify many, and their guilt he shall bear. Therefore I will give him his portion among the great, and he shall divide the spoils with the mighty, because he surrendered himself to death and was counted among the wicked; and he shall take away the sins of many, and win pardon for their offenses.

I leave it to the reader to meditate on this strange and startling text. Nietzsche used to jeer at Christian sweetness and humility. It is easier to make fun of these qualities than to practice them. Here, on this night of Maundy Thursday, face to face with Judas, Jesus' sweetness and humility are the fruits of truly heroic self-control and love. One of the most striking traits of Jesus' personality is that, with him, love is never blind. In order to love, Jesus does not deliberately close his eyes, as we so often do. At the very moment when he is giving Judas the most touching proofs of his friendship and his humility, Jesus denounces the betrayal and the traitor. Jesus loves us all, even the most miserable and the least worthy of that love, but he loves us with eyes wide open to what we are and to what we do. No greater hope has even been given us: whoever we are we will never impose upon him. We are discovered, and at the same time every way of escape is closed to us, his heart is our only refuge. This is the truth of our human condition. And the greatest braggarts among us know this, too, and who knows what happens in the heart of a braggart at that ineluctable moment when he knows that he is going to die?

In a few hours Jesus is going to die, and Judas' feet, which he has just washed, will dangle under a tree above the ground. Jesus knows this. "'The Son of Man indeed goes his way, as it is written of him; but **Matt. 26:24-25** woe to that man by whom the Son of Man is betrayed! It were better for that man if he had not been born.' And Judas who betrayed him answered and said, 'Is it I, Rabbi?' He said to him, 'Thou hast said it.'" Then Jesus holds out to Judas a morsel of bread dipped in the sauce, according to the Oriental fashion of singling out the guest of honor. "When, therefore, he had received the morsel, he went out quickly. **John 13:30** Now it was night."

Here is the first catacomb. Night, hatred, violence, and treason are outside. The primitive Church, gathered in its entirety around its founder and leader—and in heaven, the Father bending over it—is ready for the institution of the marvelous Sacrament of Jesus' love and death, the pledge of eternal life.

"The accident of a rhyme causes a system to emerge from the shadows." But here nothing is accidental. Since the escape from Egypt and the first Passover, with the first sacrificial lambs, there has been one Passover after another in Israel, all of them exactly alike in their immutable ritual. But why are this night and this Paschal repast so different from all the others? On two occasions, very distinctly, very solemnly, once at the beginning of the repast, with the breaking of the bread, and a second time at the end of the repast, with the sharing of the wine, Jesus deliberately breaks the ancient ceremonial of Israel and, in purposely breaking it, gives it a new and definitive meaning.

Saint Paul writes, "For I myself have received from the Lord (what I **1 Cor. 11:23-26** also delivered to you), that the Lord Jesus, on the night in which he was betrayed, took bread, and giving thanks broke, and said, 'This is my body which shall be given up for you; do this in remembrance of me.' In like manner also the cup, after he had supped, saying, 'This cup is the new covenant in my blood; do this as often as you drink it, in remembrance of me. For as often as you shall eat this bread and drink the cup, you proclaim the death of the Lord, until he comes.'"

Matthew is specific about the consecration of the wine as the blood of the Lord: "All of you drink of this; for this is my blood of the new covenant, which is being shed for many unto the forgiveness of sins." And thus it is here that the obsession of the ancient covenant and the ancient Law expires, an obsession that has tormented this people for thousands of years—sin, which all the blood of bulls and heifers, of lambs and goats, has never been able to wipe out. Here is a blood so pure that it instantly effaces the sin of the world. Tomorrow Pilate will ask, "What is truth?" which also means, "What is a lie?" Some of the others say, "What is sin?" which also means, "What is grace?" But the Jews, for their part, knew and still know what a yoke had been placed on the neck of man. It is this implacable yoke that Christ breaks by his death and the shedding of his blood. As the Evangelist John has said, "For the Law was given through Moses; grace and truth came through Jesus Christ." It is incomprehensible to me that the Jews did not precipitate themselves head first into the redemption of sins thrown open by Jesus Christ. Perhaps they were too accustomed to vain contrition and preferred their own guiltiness to their deliverance.

Psychoanalysts will know that what I am saying here is true: an education can be so puritanical and so rigid that the victim of it, once he has become an adult, can no longer escape the mental categories that have been imposed upon him, even though he may wish to. A habit can be so inveterate that one will sacrifice everything to preserve it and to conform to it. In different words, this is what John calls preferring "the shadows to the light." At that point it is perhaps vain to raise the question of individual responsibility.

Jesus' solemn injunction, "Henceforth do this in memory of me," cannot refer to the feast of friendship of the *chebrah* or to the Paschal repast which had been celebrated for centuries and which in any case will continue to be celebrated in the Judaeo-Christian communities themselves. This injunction can refer only—otherwise it has no meaning—to what is entirely new in this Last Supper of Jesus with his Apostles, to the rupture with the ancient rite, to the sacrifice of blood, marking the new covenant, and to the remission of sins, to the com-

Matt. 26:27-28

John 1:17

John 3:19

munion with this sacrifice under the aspect of bread and wine, themselves transubstantiated into the body and the blood of Jesus. Thus Jesus gives to his Apostles the order and the power to celebrate indefinitely the Eucharistic sacrifice, as he himself has just celebrated it. The fact that this sacrifice is celebrated for the first time on the occasion and in the setting of a repast of the *chebrah* and of a Jewish Paschal feast has only relative and secondary importance. Henceforth, what alone will count are the new covenant in more precious blood and the remission of sins, which was the avowed purpose of the Law, a purpose it could never accomplish.

At the same time and by the same injunction Jesus institutes the Sacrament of the Order; he establishes a new priesthood, his own, completely fulfilling the prophecy of Jeremia, a prophecy which, after the destruction of Jerusalem, Judaism will cease even to remember: "For thus says the Lord: Never shall David lack a successor on the throne of the house of Israel, nor shall priests of Levi ever be lacking, to offer holocausts before me, to burn cereal offerings, and to sacrifice victims." On Palm Sunday, Jesus had caused himself to be recognized by the people of Israel as the King-Messiah and the son of David. On this night, through the Eucharist, he secures forever the descendants of David on the throne of the true Israel of God and at the same time perpetuates his own priesthood by transmitting it indefinitely. Jer. 33:17-18

I am very well aware that the word "institution" has taken on in modern times a pejorative connotation. People will not fail to insist that every institution that endures becomes involved in routine, machinery, aging, inertia, sclerosis. By "instituting" the Eucharist, Christ broke a thousand-year-old automatism. Well and good! Did he not inaugurate another, now twice a thousand years old?

Saint Thomas Aquinas—as always, giving fresh offense to fools—tells us that the Church of Christ "was *fabricated*, beginning with the Sacraments that flowed from the pierced side of Christ as he hung on the cross." What, essentially, was he doing on the cross, this Jesus of Nazareth? What had he been doing earlier during that somber vigil from Maundy Thursday to Good Friday? Like a skilled artisan he was laying out and fabricating his Church. A structure depends on art. The institution of the Church reveals art and poetry. This is the very reason that it is immune to all automatism, like the *Iliad*, like a great eternal poem. One finds one's way into the Church and into its Sacraments not with the aid of a mariner's compass but through silence, prayer, and faith.

The Church's teaching concerning the Mass rigorously insists that it is a true sacrifice, but an "intentional" sacrifice, so to speak, referring entirely to the unique sacrifice on the cross. People believe they have the same thought twice at two different moments, but even the order of the understanding transcends time and space: every authentic thought is as new as a birth, even if it contains the same weight of truth about the same object, which it can represent to itself indefinitely. So it is with the Mass, the unique sacrifice of the cross, indefinitely and truly ("sacramentally") re-presented. Through the creative words of Christ-God, on that night of Maundy Thursday a few hours before the historic event, the sacrificial reality of the death of Christ on the cross even now descends definitively into those deep waters where it escapes forever from time and space, from the material world and its categories. These deep waters are the sacramental order in its entirety. How should the sacrifice of the cross "repeat itself" in the innumerable Masses that have been celebrated, since it renews itself only in the order of sacramental reality and since that sacramental reality escapes through its essence from the conditions of repetition? There is no true repetition except in time and space.

Georges Braque used to say that when he stood in front of a white canvas he knew that the picture was already there. Between him and that picture there was only the screen of the white canvas. To make the picture, to "fabricate" it, consisted in progressively effacing that screen, brush stroke by brush stroke, and, when the white canvas had been completely effaced, the picture existed, irrefutably present. Jesus Christ, who dies with a great cry at the separation of his body and his blood, is there, he is present behind every Mass. The sacramental gestures and words of the priest suddenly efface the screen, and we hold true communion with the sacrifice of our Lord.

It is noteworthy that in the primitive Church Maundy Thursday was commemorated according to two absolutely distinct traditions. Just as it is possible that the disciples of Socrates commemorated their last reunion with their master who was about to die, Christians commemorated the last repast of the *chebrah* of Jesus, that final vigil of the master with his disciples. This is what the Greek Christians called *agape,* and the word *agape* is perhaps a translation of the Hebrew *chebrah*. But in an absolutely different tradition, Christians have celebrated the Eucharist. They have abstracted from the Last Supper of the Lord (which was also the Paschal repast of the *chebrah*) what had been particular to Christ personally and to that night of all nights which was the night of Maundy Thursday. Everywhere Christians commemorated what Christ had especially commanded them to commemorate, that is, the consecration and breaking of the Eucharistic bread and the consecration and sharing of the Eucharistic cup. This Eucharistic celebration is to be found everywhere, from Syria to Spain, with its four principal stages (whereas the Paschal repast had seven), which are still the four essential stages of the Mass: the offertory, the prayer of thanksgiving, the breaking of the bread, the Communion (Dom Gregory Dix, *The Shape of the Liturgy*, Chapter IV).

All this is to indicate that the Church has a good memory, a seamless one, and that this memory does not change.

There is nothing in any literature, religious or otherwise, absolutely nothing, comparable to the account of that evening of Maundy Thursday in the four Gospels, particularly in John. Plato, in the *Phaedo*, has narrated the death of Socrates, and his account will remain eternally beautiful. It is splendid to see a man who is going to die and who knows it dominate the event, affirm not only the immortality of the soul but its mastery over the body, even rejoice in death as a deliverance, because of the hope of greater goods earned here below by the constant practice of philosophy. Socrates dies surrounded by disciples, all of whom remain loyal to him. It is a peaceful death, without conflict, without fear, without anguish. Socrates quits his body like a man discarding a soiled tunic before the bath.

For Jesus Christ everything seems to start the same way. He too is surrounded by his disciples, he too talks of immortality, he too talks of his departure, he too talks about the body. But in the reality of things everything, absolutely everything, is different, in fact reversed. I think of Simone Weil, who had so great a love for Jesus Christ that she could spend hours in adoration before the Eucharistic Host, I think that if she did not take the decisive step of baptism it was principally because of her intellectual intoxication with Platonism, which is at bottom irreconcilable with the fundamental facts of Christianity.

And so Jesus, just like Socrates, begins that evening surrounded by all his Apostles. But what strikes one immediately is a difference of reality. The group in the *Phaedo* is perceived as though through a screen of intelligence and serenity, like Chinese shadows; the group at the Last Supper is revealed in the crude light of tragedy; everything there possesses the three dimensions of anguish, lucidity, and death. The institution of the Eucharist is narrowly framed by two prophecies of Jesus, prophecies of extreme cruelty which come true in the few succeeding hours. Jesus predicts that Judas will betray him and that   Matt. 26:30

Peter will deny him thrice. Jesus also quotes the prophecy of Zacharia:

Zach. 13:7 "I shall strike the shepherd that the sheep may be dispersed. . . ." This is what Jesus' disciples were like, he knows it, he says it, he insists upon it in order that all may be clear in advance; he knows them well: a traitor, a renegade, all the others fugitives. Jesus, before entering into

John 16:32 death, enters into solitude: "Behold, the hour is coming, and has already come, for you to be scattered, each one to his own house, and to leave me alone." Nevertheless he alludes to the refuge he still has with his Father, and this is heart-rending because tomorrow the door of that refuge too will be closed against him. Tonight he can still say with

John 16:32 truth, "But I am not alone, because the Father is with me." Tomorrow

Matt. 27:46 on the cross he will say, "My God, my God, why hast thou forsaken me?"

After predicting Simon Peter's denial, Jesus nevertheless adds,

Luke 22:31-32 "Simon, Simon, behold, Satan has desired to have you, that he may sift you as wheat. [Here the *you* is a plural, designating all the Apostles.] But I have prayed for thee, that thy faith may not fail; and do thou, when once thou hast turned again, strengthen thy brethren."

We have no better testimony than the Gospels for the actions, gestures, and words of the Lord Jesus. For a Christian nothing counts, or nothing should count, more than the actions, gestures, words, and wishes of the Lord Jesus. It is impossible for me personally, when confronted with these last words of Jesus addressed to Peter and pronounced at this solemn moment, not to see a special investiture and a solemn testament. A redoubtable investiture, the mark of extreme confidence, at the very moment when the denial and the crowing of the cock are foretold; and for us, who are all called one day or another to pass through the sieve of Satan, the sign of a permanent refuge and a total security. The primacy of Peter for me is not simply a habit of thought accepted since childhood, an intellectual comfort, a laziness of the mind, it is above all a life preserver on a ship pitching dangerously in a raging sea: this ship may stand as an appropriate image of the modern mind.

It is to Peter that Jesus confided permanent authority and supremacy of council in his *chebrah,* his Church. None of this can be explained except in relation to a long future. If the world was to come to an end day after tomorrow through the triumphal return of Christ, for what purpose was the institution of the Eucharist and the primacy of Peter, for what purpose, to use the expression of Thomas Aquinas, was the "fabrication" of a Church, a priesthood, or a hierarchy? All this was obviously arranged to endure through time and, in its way, to transcend time.

It was the custom for the repast of the *chebrah* to end with a long nocturnal conversation. When the leader of the *chebrah* was a rabbi, this consisted principally of the master's religious teaching to his disciples. Here once more it was the same. But this night was not like other nights, and all the words of Jesus carried the enormous resonance of death.

Jesus spoke at length about his Father, to whom he was returning, about the Spirit, whom he would send to inspire and sustain his Church, about the works he himself had performed, about his blind adversaries, about the Devil, who was already vanquished; but above all it rested on his heart to make clear that death would not separate him from his own because he was offering his death to love and love transforms life and death. "Greater love than this no one has, that one lay down his life for his friends." "Let not your heart be troubled. . . . And if I go and prepare a place for you, I am coming again, and I will take you to myself." "I will not leave you orphans; I will come to you." In his prophetic view time no longer counts, or rather it is prodigiously elastic. "A little while and you shall see me no longer; and again a little while and you shall see me." There is good reason to ask oneself, as the Apostles did, what this means.

John 15:13; 14:1-3; 14:18; 16:16

In reality this "little while" has not the same sense, the same dimensions, even the same standard of measurement as in our everyday language. Here it means just as much the three days that separate Jesus from his resurrection as the "little while" that separates us from the end of the world and the triumphal return of Jesus to judge the living and the dead. Even though this world we live in should still endure some millions of centuries, the whole unrolling of time is no more than "a little while." If this "little" is long, it is only because of our impatience, the impatience of creatures immersed in time.

Who will deliver Christians once and for all from Platonism, from Hinduism, from all the meaningless nonsense of metempsychosis and from contempt for the body? Hatred of the body is even more than a heresy, it is a misconception of man, and, if the body has absolutely nothing to do with religion, then we are being asked to love God with what we do not possess. Our soul is the form of a body: we must do it that much justice.

It is to Plato that we owe the first theory of the totalitarian state. It is to Plato's influence that we owe gnosticism and Manichaeism, which in turn served as the metaphysical foundation for the puritanism that infects our modern societies, whether Christian or Communist. In any case, there is nothing like Platonic influence to enfeeble and enervate Christianity.

In the *Phaedo* Socrates says, "That the impure should enter into contact with the pure, let us be on our guard against believing that this is permitted." Who would not subscribe to so fine a statement? It remains to be seen what is pure and what impure. For Plato the impure is the body—abominable and ridiculous confusion. It is on the body that Plato heaps all the most contemptuous epithets: the body is a folly, it is an infection, the body is a malfeasance that hinders the understanding, that equally hinders philosophy and the salvation of the soul. Moreover, the soul alone is capable of understanding, of philosophy, and of salvation. Death is therefore the supreme purification, which liberates the soul from its one evil, the body. At any rate, death definitely saves the soul of the perfect philosopher, for the vulgar soul, which is not totally detached from the body, which has the misfortune of being attached to it, is menaced with horrible reincarnations. No authority in the world can convince me that this philosophy is not at once false, hypocritical, extravagant, and pernicious.

Long live Aristotle, who tells us that the soul is the form of the body and that no understanding is possible for man that does not have its origin in the senses and sense perception. Long live Valéry as well, who wrote:

> . . . dear body,
> I love you, sole object that defends me from the dead.

But here we are concerned with the history of Jesus Christ. Yes, precisely so, on this evening of Maundy Thursday, just like Socrates at the moment of his death, Jesus talks of the pure and of the impure. John 13:10-11 Having washed the feet of his Apostles, Jesus adds: "'He who has bathed needs only to wash, and he is clean all over. And you are clean, but not all.' For he knew who it was that would betray him. This is why he said, 'You are not all clean.'" In this language of parable, the bath symbolizes the total purity of the soul. But among these souls one is impure. Is it the soul of an adulterer, a fornicator, a leper? No, it is the soul of a traitor. Treason, there you have it: for Jesus the impurity of impurities is treason. And treason is first of all a matter of judgment, of the will, that is, of the soul. The seat of purity and impurity in Christianity is the soul, even in the case of sins of the flesh. And let Plato get out of the way. . . .

In as much as I am a Christian, I am ready to admit that there is in the world only one human body that is pure through its own merit, that is the body of Jesus Christ, but it is a body: *"Ave verum corpus natum de Maria Virgine."* And Plato would not agree that a body could be pure. I am equally ready to admit that only one human soul is pure through its own merit and that is the soul of Jesus Christ. This Plato would not agree to either; for him a soul is pure in the measure in which it is itself, nothing but itself, separated from its body. All this fine Platonic philosophy is certainly directly opposed to the last article of our Credo: "I believe in the resurrection of the body."

To be sure, we Christians know as well as Socrates and Plato that one must not mix the impure with the pure. But for us the body can be pure, it is not necessarily an infection and a malfeasance. But the soul, on the other hand, can have its impurities—even the soul entirely separated from the body and its passions. After all, the Devil is spirit, nothing but spirit, and he is impure. And the body of Christ in the Eucharist is body, true body, born of a woman, and it is pure, it is beneficence, it is wisdom, it is the instrument of salvation for the soul. If Plato is right, we are sacrilegious, but if we are right, Plato is insane.

Granted, the greatest Christian saints have all desired to die, but they have not desired death for its own sake, they have desired it as a means of rejoining Christ, and all, beyond death, have hoped still more for the resurrection of the flesh. But let us not forget that Christ has transformed and reversed the meaning of human death: it is no longer punishment. After his own death, it became essentially a means of rejoining him and of identifying ourselves with him on the cross. These are not theological speculations. One may have spent one's life in distracting oneself from the thought of death, but the moment will nevertheless come when one must die. I know very well how hard it is to announce to some wretched man that he is about to die, and I myself am very cowardly on this point. When it is a question of another man's death, the majesty of death takes my breath away. Nevertheless, a higher majesty stands behind that of death; it is the majesty of Christ on the cross, and it prepares a welcome for the dying man. Many men live without having had the privilege of even knowing what Eucharistic communion with the body and the blood of Jesus Christ is. But it suffices to be a man and to die to have opened to him who dies communion with the death of Jesus Christ.

But on this Maundy Thursday, the eve of his death, Jesus is alone; no one before him can extend to him, across the gulf of death, a helping hand. He sees death approach. He sees it as it is, the violent separation of his soul from his body, a dreadful misery. And for the first time since the fall of Adam, this body and this soul are so well made for each other that they have no cause to reproach each other. Oh, how unjust that impious action that is going to separate them! Yes, what a frightful misfortune, since death is a malediction, since it is a punishment for sin and precisely in Jesus there was nothing but innocence, nothing to censure, nothing to punish. Here is the one man without sin, and he begins to tremble at the approach of death.

Judas has long since departed to look after his business. It is now some time since the repast ended. Jesus and his Apostles have left the Cenacle, they have gone past the ramparts and have left Jerusalem, they have descended into the ravine of the Cedron and climbed the other side; they are now in the Garden of Olives, and already some of them, wrapped in their burnooses, are lying down under the ancient trees for a good night's sleep.

Matt. 26:38 But Jesus is seized by anguish. He says to his Apostles, "My soul is sad, even unto death. Wait here and watch with me." And he withdraws to pray.

But what he had foreseen takes place; he is alone, no one of his group resists sleep. On that first night of their investiture, of their sacerdotal ordination and of their First Communion, these first bishops of the Catholic Church all fall fast asleep, the first pope as well, while their master prepares to die in anguish. This Maundy Thursday ends in the profound slumber of the Church Militant. Judas alone among the Apostles has no desire to sleep.

CHAPTER XXII

Good Friday

AND NOW, within this history of Jesus Christ, we come to the history of the Passion of Jesus Christ, which, from century to century, has never ceased to stir men's hearts and arouse heroic imitation. It is the history of an innocent man betrayed by one of his own disciples, condemned to death and executed by infamous and cruel torture.

What then? Men of my age have only to think back. In the space of our adult lives have we not seen traitors and betrayed, innocent men judged and condemned, men tortured in infamous and cruel ways?

Admittedly Jesus Christ died by crucifixion, and this is a particularly horrible torture. But some forty years later, after the destruction of Jerusalem, the Romans crucified Jews by the tens of thousands: there were not enough trees in the country to make crosses.

Let us see things as they are. Cruel though this torment was, the death of a man of thirty-three, even though innocent, as Jesus was, produces in us less revulsion, less pity, less horror, than the death of thousands of children crammed into crematory ovens. After so many atrocities committed, after such torment inflicted and endured, after the torture of such a terrifying number of victims, after everything we have seen with our own eyes and everything the cruel history of mankind tells us, does the Passion of Jesus Christ still retain something absolutely singular, unique, and exceptional?

To gain an understanding of the meaning and scope of the Passion of Jesus Christ we must withdraw a little, even from our own experience of human sorrow and our wholly legitimate compassion. When Saint Paul wants to explain to the Corinthians the exact significance

2 Cor. 6:12-14

and dimension of Christ's Passion, he takes the precaution of telling them, "In us there is no lack of room for you, but in your heart there is no room for us. Now as having a recompense in like kind—I speak as to my children—be you also open wide to us *[dilatamini et vos]*. Do not bear the yoke with unbelievers."

I know very well what may be said to this. If I call upon faith, it is because I am incapable of explaining in everyday language what the Passion of Jesus Christ is. Nevertheless what can one do? It is true that in its external aspects the Passion is simply the account of the juridical murder of an innocent man, a rather commonplace event, especially in our times. But it is not only that; it is the manner in which God, in the blood of this man, who is His Son, reconciled the universe to Himself and, at the center of the universe, reconciled to himself man, us, all of us, whoever we are.

But these two aspects of the Passion are the face and the reverse of the same coin, the one would not exist without the other. If Christ had not died in accordance with the Law, there would have been no redemption from sin, no reconciliation with God. But, on the other hand, if there had been no God, there would have been no need for redemption from sin, there would have been no sin, sin being an offense committed by man against God. In that case the remission of sins would be no more than an imaginary concoction, and the juridical murder of Jesus Christ would have had no more importance than the killing of a fly. But in that case why attach more importance to the holocausts at Auschwitz and at Buchenwald, where in fact men fell like flies, than to the disinfection of a room with insecticide? If God does not exist, the Passion of Jesus Christ has no more than a literary and sentimental importance, that is to say, none at all.

"Man should never fall into the mistake of believing that he is lord and master of nature. . . . In a universe in which the planets and the sun follow circular orbits, in which the moons revolve around their planets, *in which force reigns everywhere and is sole mistress over weakness, which she forces to serve her docilely or which she breaks, man cannot count on special laws.*" When Hitler wrote these considered and pointed sentences in the fashion of a good pupil, he was in fact simply being a good pupil. His thinking did not differ from that of Monsieur Taine or Renan or Michelet, it did not differ from that of so many shapers of thought from the most illustrious to the most elementary, not only in the German universities but in all the great universities of the Western world. In point of fact he was the avowed disciple of just such masters, he pushed their teaching to the extreme. But in this he was, like them, in complete rupture with the Judaeo-Christian tradition and with the *Syllabus,* which solemnly condemns the following proposition: "No other forces need be recognized in the world than those contained in matter" (Propositions 58 and 59). Does man depend on special laws? That is indeed the problem. The natural order is cruel; every motion picture about animals shows us that in intolerable fashion. If man is totally immersed in the natural order, why become excited about the massive extermination of the weak by those who are stronger?

I know Jean-Paul Sartre writes in all seriousness, "The retrospective illusion is in smithereens; martyr, salvation, immortality; all this is collapsing, the edifice is in ruins. I have come to grips with the Holy Spirit in the cellars and I have driven him out; atheism is a cruel enterprise and of long duration: I believe I have carried it to the end. I see clear, I am disabused. . . ."

He sees clear? What does he see? Nothing. He admits it, he "no longer knows what to do with his life." A marvelous result of obstinate lucidity. When one has read Sartre from the beginning, one knows very well that he had to come out where he did. From the start he denied all significance to man's essence, he did more than deny, he hated it. We, for our part, say that man is created in the image of God, that he is its mirror. Sartre at the start broke that mirror. What cause is there for astonishment in the fact that all he now holds in his hand is the empty frame? But then what use is man? And what difference is there between throwing men in batches into a crematory oven and throwing live lobsters into a boiling pot? If one, why not the other?

This is where the materialist shoe pinches our intellectuals. What is the difference between a man and a lobster? I shall be told that man is distinguished from animals because he himself produces his means of subsistence and production. In the course of history man modifies his own life through collective labor, which presupposes a social mode of life. Is this all there is to say—this feeble platitude, more etymological than philosophical—in favor of man and his uniqueness? Is this the whole price of man? The employment of crematory ovens is a social mode too, why not? If Marx has a certain grandeur and truth, it surely comes from his having proved and brilliantly demonstrated that the social sphere is within, and not above, the over-all cycle of nature. Hitler thought the same thing. But if the truth of things lies in this, man has no special importance, he is definitely and completely trapped in nature.

Our era is cruel, but it is also stupid—cruel because it is stupid. We must locate, recognize, and proclaim the infinite difference between man and the mere animal, the individual superiority of man over the entire order of nature, including the social order, the singularity of man, the spiritual dignity of the human person, in order simply to begin to be able to respect man. What is called "morality" is not a matter of course, it can only be a conclusion whose premises are metaphysical, that is to say, outside the world of nature. There is no human dignity, there is no true human solidarity, there is no communion, without a basis above this world. That is how it is, the rest is idle fancy or hallucination, monkey-shines or illusion.

———

I detest modern sentimentality, and in the account of the Passion it is more than anywhere else detestable. I know too that "the word *I* is detestable." If I happen to say "I" in this book much more often, no doubt, than is proper, it is because the subject is so vast and oppressive that I feel lost. This book, alas, is only my book. And so, like a photographer who takes care to include in his picture a little ass at the foot of the pyramids in order to indicate their scale, I sometimes say "I" so that the reader will not think that having read my book he has "exhausted" the subject. It is the subject that is completely exhausting me. The day when I finish this book I know I shall have come to the end of my strength, and all will still remain to be said.

Arriving at the Garden of Olives, Jesus leaves his band of Apostles to make their customary encampment and goes forward under the trees to pray. He takes with him only Peter, James, and John: these three are the most privileged of all, they who, at the moment of the Transfiguration, have already seen the prophetic glory of Jesus and his Messianic consecration between Moses and Elias and who now are about to be present at the agony of their master. They have seen him glorious and transfigured on the mountain, they are going to see him stretched on the ground, sweating blood in his torment. Nothing is less "mythological" than this man, nothing less contrived, manufactured, "harmonized," than our Lord Jesus Christ.

Luke's narrative continues:

Luke 22:40-46   But when he was at the place, he said to them, "Pray, that you may not enter into temptation." And he himself withdrew from them about a stone's throw, and kneeling down, he began to pray, saying, "Father, if thou art willing, remove this cup from me; yet not my will but thine be done."

And there appeared to him an angel from heaven to strengthen him. And falling into an agony he prayed the more earnestly. And his sweat became as drops of blood running down upon the ground.

And rising from prayer he came to the disciples, and found them sleeping for sorrow. And he said to them, "Why do you sleep? Rise and pray, that you may not enter into temptation."

The word "agony" here does not mean that final struggle that the body puts up against the menacing seizure of death, but extreme anguish. Only one who has felt, under the influence of fear, humiliation, bereavement, shame, or simply the sadness of existence, the inexorable grasp of an iron hand in the hollow of his own body, between heart and stomach, will have learned what anguish is. Modern medicine, especially since Freud, has gone a long way in the study and therapy of anguish. We know that nothing can more easily alienate a man from himself, we know that at the moment of an acute crisis of anguish the most convincing reasons, those that are most clear and obvious, have no effect upon the patient because what is needed is to revive the will to live and because the patient is detached from his own life. We know that anguish at its climax is, even for souls tempered like steel, the antechamber to madness and suicide.

In this dark garden Jesus Christ became acquainted with anguish at its peak. He did not yield to its temptations, but he knew them. This must be said clearly for the comfort of all miserable beings who struggle at the edge of the abyss. If there was ever a moment when the enterprise of our redemption was on the point of failing through the weakness of a human nature, surely this is the moment. That enterprise is so far above human strength that Jesus three times, feeling himself weakening, pleaded with his Father to let "this cup" pass from him. Nevertheless, with prodigious energy, he added each time: ". . . yet not *my* will, but *thine* be done." Like a knight close to being unhorsed who still has the courage and the strength to take up behind him one stronger than himself, who will spur his horse and bring him to the goal. For in truth what must be done will be done, and the cup will be drunk to the lees.

The Gospel says that God sent an angel to comfort Jesus Christ. The interior collapse of this man was so imminent that he needed the aid of an angel to escape from it and outface it. Medical specialists know that in the whole Gospel there is no account that rings truer than this one. The same doctors assert that this moment of agony was surely the hardest in the whole life of Jesus Christ, even harder than crucifixion and death. Catholic doctrine assures us that each of us is accompanied by an angel: surely it is in the hour of anguish that we have greatest need of him, in the hour when the armor of the soul may break. Let the poor inmates of psychiatric hospitals know that prayer attracts angels, and that in their worst moments if they call for aid an angel will be present at their bedsides. We are never completely alone.

What were the causes of the prodigious prostration of this man who was so strong, so heroic, so much master of himself? Strong he was, but not rough or coarse. On the contrary, he was of extremely sensitive and delicate stuff that vibrated at the least touch like a Stradivarius. In front of Lazarus' tomb, when Jesus had seen the great and beautiful Mary Magdalene weep, his spirit quivered like a tall tree in the wind and he was troubled within himself: *"infremuit spiritu et turbavit semetipsum."*

John 11:33

The Day of Palms had been an equal drain on Jesus' sensibilities, through the contrast, which he alone perceived, between the triumph that was being held for him that day and the gibbet that would be erected for him on the morrow. In the gray of the dawn when the crowd came to look for him in Bethany to make him king, when he descended the slope of the Mount of Olives on the ass, and when he saw the City of David, rose and gold beneath the sun, he broke into tears at the thought of the frightful siege which, forty years later, was to destroy that city and, as it were, uproot it from the world.

On that same Day of Palms, while the crowd was responding to his charm and drinking in his words, he interrupted his discourse to make a harrowing confidence, which no one understood at all: "Now my soul is troubled. And what shall I say? Father, save me from this hour!" Panic was dawning, but on that day it was easier for obedience to take precedence. Jesus added, "No, this is why I came to this hour. Father, glorify thy name!"

John 12:27-28

Thus publicly and in the midst of his triumph he had nevertheless cried out for aid. Let each one look back over his past. How many times in an adult life does it happen that one is forced to cry out for help, to open one's mouth and physically cry for help? Twice in that sinister week Jesus was reduced to that. On Palm Sunday a voice came from heaven to reassure him. On the night of the Garden of Olives no one replied to him. The "hour," that mysterious "hour," for which he had come and from which he would not escape, stooped upon him as an eagle stoops on a poor afrighted hare. He had desired to be immersed in time like one of us, so he was inexorably caught in the snare, he who had been made for the free spaces of eternity.

That last night of Jesus was a condemned man's night. Such nights are all the same. Never does the pendulum of the soul oscillate in wider arcs between wild hope and sad lucidity, between luminous courage and blind panic. The whole man is carried to extremes, and to the most violent contradictions. Horrified, to be sure, to the point of terror; heroic also to the peak of courage. Oh, how that man, cast to the ground and sweating blood, that man who cries out for help, how he resembles us, how close he is to each one of us! All this happened as it is written, yes, as it is written, even the speeches in John, previously quoted, which they would have us believe are only edited reminiscences, embellished, inflated, embroidered. The years pass—I speak in the light of my own experience—one does not embellish one's memories of the last night of a man condemned to death. What one has seen and heard at such moments leaves in the memory a precise mark, indelible, sharply defined, deep, like the mark of the fleur-de-lis branded by the executioner on the criminal's shoulder. Observe, for example, in the text of the four Gospels, including that of John, how often in the course of that night the hour is mentioned. The last night of a man condemned to death is passed in asking what is the time.

Nowhere in the Gospels perhaps is it so clear that the eyewitness and earwitness account of John completes that of the Synoptics. Thanks to John one perceives the whole amplitude of the oscillation of Jesus' soul, that diastole and systole of a destiny so immense that it finds its perfect contraction in a single hour, the hour of hours, and its dilation embraces all the shores of eternity: "before the world was."

"Behold, the hour is coming, and has already come. . . .These things I have spoken to you that in me you may have peace. In the world you will have affliction. But take courage, I have overcome the world. . . . Father, the hour has come! Glorify thy Son, that thy Son may glorify thee, even as thou has given him power over all flesh, in order that to all thou hast given him he may give everlasting life. Now this is everlasting life, that they may know thee, the only true God, and him whom thou hast sent, Jesus Christ. . . . And now do thou, Father, glorify me with thyself, with the glory that I had with thee before the world existed. . . . Father, I will that where I am, they also whom thou hast given me may be with me; in order that they may behold my glory, which thou hast given me, because thou hast loved me before the creation of the world." *John 16:32-17:5; 17:24*

After these sovereign words, less than an hour after, Jesus, seized by panic and twisted by the pain of his anguish, drags himself over the rocks, calling aloud for help, and there is none to answer him. No man, on the night before his execution, has pushed to such an extreme the victory of the spirit and the defeat of the body.

What is the cause of this anguish that expresses itself in bloody sweat? Matthew says "sorrow and prostration." Mark adds dread: *"pavere et taedere."* But the cause proportionate to this dread and to this sorrow— this they do not tell. The Christian who should enter into the secret of *Matt. 26:37* *Mark 14:33* that anguish would never emerge, held "prisoner of the holy Agony," as Bernanos has said. It is perhaps Saint Paul who has penetrated most profoundly into this secret, to such a point that one ventures only to transcribe his words, which, if he had not written them, no one would have dared invent.

2 Cor. 5:19-21   Saint Paul explains to the Corinthians the meaning of the Passion of Jesus Christ. His words are of a dazzling clarity and strength. "For God was truly in Christ, reconciling the world to himself by not reckoning against men their sins. . . . We exhort you, for Christ's sake, be reconciled to God. *For our sakes he made him to be sin* who knew nothing of sin, so that in him we might become the justice of God." Saint Paul, of course, does not at all intend to say that Jesus ever personally committed any sin but that he had identified himself to such a degree with the destiny of man that he had taken on this destiny with all its consequences of sin—in the first instance death, suffering, and shame—he had assumed this costume like a mantle of ignominy precisely for the purpose of rending it once for all in order that we in our turn by taking off sin and putting on Jesus Christ might become in God justice and holiness.

Here I must quote from what is called "The Mystery of Jesus" by Blaise Pascal. How could this little bourgeois from Auvergne, this geometrician and physicist, enter so profoundly into such a mystery? Simone Weil, graduate of the Ecole Normale Supérieure and pupil of Alain, and Blaise Pascal are clear evidence that the Spirit assuredly blows where it wills.

In his Passion Jesus suffers torments caused him by men; but in his agony he suffers torments caused by himself: *turbare semetipsum*. It is torture by a hand not human but omnipotent, but only omnipotence can sustain it.

Jesus seeks some consolation at least from his three dearest friends, and they are asleep; he begs them to watch with him a little, and they abandon him with complete neglect, having so little compassion that they cannot even for a moment keep themselves from falling asleep. And thus Jesus was left alone to the wrath of God.

Jesus is alone in the world, not only in experiencing and partaking of his pain, but in knowing about it: heaven and he are alone in this knowledge.

Jesus is in a garden, not of delights like the first Adam, who there lost himself and the whole human race, but in a garden of tortures where he saved himself and the whole human race.

He suffers this pain and this abandonment in the horror of the night.

I believe Jesus never complained except this one time; but then he complained as though he could no longer contain his excessive sorrow: "My soul is sad unto death."

Jesus seeks company and solace on the part of men. This is unique in his whole life, as it seems to me. But he receives nothing of the sort, for his disciples are asleep.

Jesus will be in agony until the end of the world: one must not sleep during this time. . . .

Jesus has pleaded with men, and he has not been satisfied. . . .

"I was thinking of you in my agony, I shed those drops of blood for you. . . . Do you wish always to cost me the blood of my humanity without giving me your tears? . . .

"If you knew your sins, you would lose heart. . . .

"I love you more ardently than you have loved your defilement: *ut immundas pro luto.*"

———

Now the mechanism of human justice goes into operation. Everything will happen very fast.

To read the Synoptics alone one would think that the Pharisees had no part in the trial and death of Jesus. That is what Isidore Epstein maintains in his history of Judaism. But this is improbable; surely the truth is quite different. John, who was there, mentions the presence of the Pharisees at the place of Jesus' arrest. As to the juridical evolution of the trial, it was not in the hands of the Pharisees *as such* but in those of the Sanhedrin, composed of priests, elders or notables, and scribes, most of whom, not to say all, were actually Pharisees. The sentence of death was the prerogative of the Roman procurator, but in this case his victim was handed over to him. Such was the juridical procedure in a nation of jurists, jealously preoccupied with formalities. But to say that the Pharisees had no part in the death of Jesus would be like maintaining that the Jacobins had no part in the execution of Louis XVI, on the pretext that juridically the Jacobin Club was distinct from the National Convention, which alone had authority to vote the death sentence of the king.

The torment of anguish, of fear, and of blood is past, it lies behind. The pendulum swings to the other extreme, that of heroism and honor, which will prevail to the last. Now it is heroism that will reign without flinching to the very end, pure as diamond. Like a bearer who has had a moment of weakness and lain down beside the path but who finally gets up, adjusts the heavy burden on his shoulders, and resumes the march with firm step to the finish, so Jesus arises, and henceforth he confronts his mortal destiny with sovereign courage. How one must admire him, who had been so low, for standing upright once more! Those who invented the distinction between moral and physical courage are intellectuals who had to justify themselves for being cowards. There is only one kind of courage, and it arms the body as well as the soul in steel. "Are you trembling, carcass? You would tremble far more if you knew where I am taking you." This speech by Turenne is a soldier's speech, it is as applicable here as on the field of battle. Now Jesus is on his feet and even his body no longer trembles. It is his valiant soul that has begun the march, but the carcass will follow, it will follow without failing, obedient, submissive, even to death on the cross.

Jesus says to his Apostles, and on his face there is the smile of a conqueror, which explains the apparent contradiction between his first sentence and his last: "Sleep on now, and take your rest! It is enough; the hour has come. Behold, the Son of Man is betrayed into the hands of sinners. Rise, let us go. Behold, he who will betray me is at hand." The three Synoptics have noted that he did not have time to finish what he was saying. Judas was there, quite close to him. All battles begin like that, with an unfinished sentence. The first shell that falls, the first bullet that whistles past interrupts a speech and leaves it hanging in the sky.

Mark 14:41-42

Here everything starts in confusion, as it had at the time of Christ's birth. But whereas Bethlehem had seen, beneath a sky sown with stars, the assembly and alliance of the Magi, the shepherds, and the angels, here in this dark garden the Passion of Jesus Christ begins face to face with a quite different coalition. Mark writes, "And while he was yet speaking, Judas Iscariot, one of the Twelve, came and went with him a great crowd with swords and clubs, from the chief priests and the Scribes and the elders."

Mark 14:43

If Christ "is in agony till the end of the world," he is also arrested, betrayed, mocked at, and executed till the end of the world—and, whatever the official appearances, *by the same people*. If, between 1940 and 1945, one wanted to rediscover Christ in history, I imagine it would have been better to look for him among "the last of the just," that is, among the Christians or Jews who were suffering and dying a slow death in masses in the death camps, than among those—almost all of them baptized, by the way—who were furnishing the camps with their victims.

It is true, however, that the great mass of society escapes the rather summary classification of victim or executioner. There was a crowd that night in the Garden of Olives, but the great majority of the inhabitants of Jerusalem were sleeping peacefully in their own homes. When innocent people are being arrested, the general rule is not to be there, in any case to be silent, and in order to be sure of being silent to be as sound asleep as possible. If on that night in Jerusalem anyone cried out in favor of Jesus Christ, it was the cry of one dreaming.

Very little is actually known about the motives for Judas' betrayal. The little that is said of it excites curiosity rather than satisfies it: "The Devil entered into him." How? Why? And what did the Devil cause him to do that he should appear that night at the head of a troop in that somber garden? What a strange and sinister convention to identify Jesus to the police spies by kissing him! Still the fact remains that Judas was there. The night must have been as black as ink. Judas called to Jesus, "Master! Master! It is I! Hail!" both to make himself known and in order to recognize Jesus himself. And gropingly, in the shadows, he gave him a kiss. Jesus said, "Judas, dost thou betray the Son of Man with a kiss?" And Matthew notes that he called Judas "my friend." Luke 22:3

Matt. 26:49

Luke 22:49
Matt. 26:50

In the Orient people embrace frequently, and it is probable that Judas' gesture was customary with him. But this is the only time the Gospels are at pains to note that Jesus received a kiss on the face: it has become eternally "the Judas kiss." Mary Magdalene had only kissed Jesus' feet. In any case, this kiss from Judas is the last that Jesus will receive before dying. After that fatal kiss, men, his brothers, will give him nothing save spittle and blows.

What a poignant solitude, that of these two men embracing each other in the night! In a few hours both will be dead, and by a supreme mockery the one like the other hung from the wood, fruits of the tree, fruits of malediction. In connection with the crucifixion of Jesus, Saint Paul returns to the terrible sentence in the Law, which prescribes the malediction of God on whoever is hung from the wood. Miserable Judas, having delivered up his master and now devoured by remorse, tries nevertheless to join him, but too late and in malediction. The ambiguity of Judas' destiny is terrible: did he love Jesus? Did he love him to the end after his fashion? No doubt—with a twisted love, impotent and desperate, forever sterile, as our love, alas, can be, to such an extent is the heart of man "crooked and full of filth," to such an extent do we excel in turning to evil that which should save us.

Immediately after Judas' kiss the police spies seize Jesus. The disciples put up some weak show of resistance. Peter even cuts Malchus' ear; Jesus touches and heals this ear which the first pope has so awkwardly wounded. Jesus does not protest against his arrest. Nevertheless, he underlines its grotesque aspect: Why so vast a mobilization? Why this expedition with staffs and swords as though to capture a dangerous brigand, when it would have been so easy to lay hands on him in full daylight in the Temple? He is speaking ironically; it would not have been easy. His enemies wanted to seize him in complete security and without risking an uprising. Now that the danger has come, Jesus no longer has the slightest fear, but his enemies will be afraid of him until the end. They cannot get over having so easily outmatched such a man. And, beyond death, they will fear him still to the point of setting a guard over his tomb.

Seeing him seized, all the Apostles, with the first pope in the lead, abandon him and flee. Something altogether astounding will have to take place to turn these runaways into martyrs.

———

And now what is to be done with this man, bound, jostled among the soldiers, who, amid the tumult of arms and in the light of the torches, is stumblingly reascending the slopes of Cedron? The ramparts of the Temple raise their enormous mass in front of him in the night already beginning to pale. No doubt a liaison agent has been sent ahead to inform all Jesus' enemies, at need to awaken them. As on Palm Sunday, but in a very different mood, Jerusalem awaits Jesus Christ. They take him first to Annas, former high priest and brother-in-law of Caiphas, who is still powerful. This brief episode is what I call "a veridical incoherence" in the Gospel. Why would anyone invent it, for apparently it is completely pointless? But it took place and, as a conscientious chronicler, John has reported it.

Isidore Epstein asserts that at the time of Jesus there were not one but two Sanhedrins in Israel, that is, two Supreme Courts, one dominated by the Pharisees and specializing in religious law, the other more strictly engaged in criminal, civil, and political law. If this assertion is true and if I may be permitted to make a hypothesis, it is possible that Annas was presiding over the strictly religious Sanhedrin and that he immediately handed Jesus' case over to the other one. Why? Because the case of Jesus interested neither Annas nor the Pharisees? I do not believe it. It is just as possible that it was because only cases judged by the Great Sanhedrin, presided over by the high priest responsible to Rome, could later be referred to the procurator. For, from the start, it was necessary that Jesus' case should come before the procurator, if a death sentence was to be procured and executed.

Only someone who has never been involved in a lawsuit, who has never heard a lawyer talk, could be ignorant of the fact that in a given situation what interests the man of law is less to find the most legitimate procedure and follow it than to discover the most effective procedure, the one that will be most likely to lead him to the goal he has set himself, the one that will produce practical results and will prove him right—right in the eyes of the law.

Now that Jesus is under lock and key, what is the next problem? Obviously the first thought to come into the mind of a villain would be to murder him and throw his body into a pit. But the enemies of Jesus were absolutely not villains and murderers. They were the intellectual, social, religious, and political elite of Israel; they were the people who fill the academies, the social clubs, the official tribunals, the salons—in short people with whom it is an honor to be invited to dine. They were, moreover, men too intelligent not to be accustomed to weigh all the possible consequences of their acts. They had succeeded in laying hands on Jesus; now it was not simply a question of killing him, it was necessary to send him to hell. They did not want simply to disembarrass themselves of Jesus, they needed above all to mark him with infamy in the eyes of the whole people, and not with just any infamy, but, in that theocratic and religious nation, with the ordained and ritualistic infamy.

Saint Paul, raised in the strict school of the Pharisees, is of all Christian writers the one who has best defined the decisive motive behind the trial, condemnation, and execution of Jesus. What he says throws an icy light on the infernal machination of Jesus' enemies. He writes to the Galatians: "Christ redeemed us from *the curse of the Law, becoming a curse for us;* for it is written, Cursed is everyone who hangs on a gibbet." Gal. 3:13

Now if we refer to the text of the Law to which Saint Paul alludes, we read: "If a man guilty of a capital offense is put to death and his corpse hung on a tree, it shall not remain on the tree overnight. You shall bury it the same day; otherwise, since God's curse rests on him who hangs on a tree, you will defile the land which the Lord, your God, is giving you as an inheritance." It is with this frightful text that Christ's enemies began, and it is by starting from this text ourselves that we too can follow link by link the chain of their intentions and their acts. Deut. 21:22-23

Raised as we are in desacralized societies, it is hard for us to picture the taboos of primitive societies. More than that, the very conceptions of honor, infamy, and ceremony are profoundly alien to us; we perceive only the outer surface. The privilege accorded an English gentleman, for example, of being hanged with a silk cord instead of a hemp rope, this privilege makes us laugh; hanged is hanged, what price the rope?

But the society of Israel was far from being as gross as our modern societies. Its taboos were rigorous and terrible; the Supreme Judge of that society was God Himself: it was He who disposed not only over life and death, but also over each man's membership in the clan of Israel or his expulsion from it. The enemies of Jesus Christ wanted to make his murder a ceremony that would proclaim in the face of heaven and earth not only the death of this man but above all his defilement, his infamy, his expulsion for time and eternity from the house of Israel, that he had been forever damned of God, that he had been cursed by God Himself.

With that to start with, it remained only to picture the procedure and liturgy of this murder.

In order for Jesus to be considered by all of Israel as damned and cursed of God, it was necessary that he should be put to death and hanged from a tree. The Law could not err. If God permitted Jesus to be hanged from a tree, it was because Jesus was the enemy of God, cursed by Him.

Therefore it was necessary that Jesus should be condemned to death, and to death by hanging.

However, in the political situation of Israel, a country occupied by Rome, the sentence of death could be pronounced only by the Roman procurator. It was impossible to indict Jesus under the common law as a brigand or murderer. Therefore it was necessary to find some accusation that would arouse the procurator, and that could be only of a political nature.

On the other hand, the situation had a certain advantage. The Romans did not, properly speaking, practice hanging, but executed their criminals publicly by decapitation if they were Roman citizens and by crucifixion if they were slaves or foreigners. But Jesus was not a Roman citizen. If, therefore, they could succeed in having him condemned to death, he would necessarily be crucified on a gibbet of wood, which in the eyes of all would be equivalent to being hanged from a tree, and would be more particularly cruel as well.

Once this plan was elaborated, all that remained was tactics and procedure. One could rely on Jesus' enemies: they knew all about that.

In the account of that atrocious day, on which the immolation of the fairest of the children of men took place and the reconciliation of the universe with God, it would be easy to emphasize only the traits of human baseness. There was baseness, the Gospels have recorded it, and it cannot be forgotten. There was something else as well.

To the very end Christ's enemies were the instrument of a purpose that transcended them; they too were caught in the great prophetic surge that permanently raised the human destiny of Jesus to eternity and that, through this destiny, supremely fulfilled the Kingdom of God. What I am saying here may seem somewhat literary, somewhat emphatic, somewhat rhetorical. It is the absolute truth.

Jesus asserts his identity and enters into his role with as much precision as heroism, but his enemies give him the cue, the play would not be complete without them. Even when they lie or mock, a double sense attends their words and gestures, like shadow play. They, too, are accomplishing the Scriptures, they cannot choose but do so, they are forced to enter into the game. Above them is a Director whom they obey, unwittingly but punctually. In the Passion of Jesus Christ, the realization of the prophecies is as conspicuous as a dazzling stage set. Moreover, it is analogous to that. One can refuse to perceive the setting of a tragedy, nevertheless it exists and, as Paul Claudel used to say, that man has a poor understanding of his art who finds anything lacking in the art of God. It is this setting, with eternity and the Old Testament as backdrop, that I would like to try to illuminate.

First of all there was a trial. Jesus had been born "subject to the Law," he would die "subject to the Law." It is here that Caiphas proved himself great. Would to heaven that all innocents unjustly accused might be given a legal trial, that they might always have the opportunity of speaking for themselves: it is easier to die if you have had the opportunity of solemnly declaring the cause for which you are dying. Caiphas was the chief priest, he conducted the trial of Jesus, perhaps he insisted upon it. There could have been no lack of hirelings around him to urge that a murder in prison, disguised as suicide, would be more expeditious and safer. Jesus had his trial, and he was judged according to the Law of his God and of his people.

The Sanhedrin had met in the house of the chief priest, and the examination began at once. John, who is the only one to give an account of these preliminaries of the trial, is not absolutely clear about the comings and goings of Annas and Caiphas. Perhaps the two chief priests, the former and the present one, lived in two wings of the same palace, connected by an interior patio. It is not at all clear either if it was Caiphas or Annas who began the examination.

The high priest therefore questioned Jesus concerning his disciples, and concerning his teaching. Jesus answered him, "I have spoken openly to the world; I have always taught in the synagogue and in the temple, where all the Jews gather, and in secret I have said nothing. Why dost thou question me? Question those who have heard what I spoke to them; behold, these know what I have said." *John 18:19-23*

Now when he had said these things, one of the attendants who was standing by struck Jesus a blow, saying, "Is that the way thou dost answer the high priest?" Jesus answered him, "If I have spoken ill, bear witness to the evil; but if well, why dost thou strike me?"

Here, before a judge and pontiff of his nation, Jesus consecrated freedom of speech—he did not institute it, for, to the honor of humanity, it had existed in one place or another at all times, but he consecrated it for Christians. He also gave it sharp and unforgettable expression, of which we can make use to confront anyone: "If I have spoken ill, bear witness to the evil; but if well, why dost thou strike me?" The situation is worth further analysis. Jesus is not an anarchist: at no moment does he question the competence of the court, and he replies to the questions of the chief priest. Jesus is not a plotter: his teaching is public, given publicly, in public places, where by tradition anyone has the right to teach, for the freedom to teach was of incredible extent among the Jews. Jesus knows his rights as a Jewish citizen and does not relinquish them; he rejects all special pleading: the whole trial, accusation and defense, must be based on public testimony. One can abstract from this scene a Christian penal code, in which the honor and liberty of the defense must be respected because they have been claimed and defined by Christ, who was himself in the tradition of his nation. It is in the Gospel according to John that we find the principles of this code, not in the traditions of the Visigoths.

Jesus eternally furnishes the example. At no moment does he contest the legitimacy or the authority of the chief priest of his nation. But by his example he maintains that there is no authority, spiritual or temporal, in the world, however legitimate it may be, that can dispense with the laws of justice or with respect for the defense, no authority that cannot be summoned to render account: "If I have spoken ill, bear witness of the evil; but if well, why dost thou strike me?" Blessed be John, who has preserved these words for us.

Moreover—and this detail has its importance—it is not the chief priest who strikes Jesus. It is an attendant of the chief priest. Nothing is worse than a courtier behaving zealously. They are an abominable crew under all regimes, in all hierarchies, in all human organizations, in all countries. Jesus is struck and will be struck to the end of the world: this sort of blow, without explanation, without justification, inflicted on a man who cannot defend himself, is one of the most cowardly actions possible and dishonors him who perfoms it. It is true that Jesus is patient, and because of his example we must be so too; but he is not timid: he looks the wretch in the eye and replies without fear. We too must be careful not to confuse patience and cowardice. Jesus did not return the blow, but he put a question, he demanded a reply, which of course never came: men of violence in positions of power do not have to answer those who are bound and defenseless.

This blow from a courtier, from an "attendant," as the Gospel says, initiated the whole vile action. Nothing is more contagious than the blusterings of cowardice. All who have been in enemy hands know this. "And some began to spit on him, and to blindfold him, and to buffet him, and to say to him, 'Prophesy.' And the attendants struck him with blows of their hands."

Mark 14:65

During this time, in a courtyard of the same palace, Peter denies his master three times. And this triple denial on the part of the prince of the Apostles was worse than a blow from a lackey. Jesus was not different from us. To be abandoned by one you love is harder to bear than an injury from one who hates you. Jesus, having crossed the courtyard amid the guards, looked at Peter, and at that moment the cock crowed. Then the first pope broke into sobs and fled into the brightening dawn. Those bitter tears redeemed him in the eyes of Jesus, they redeem him in ours. Poor first pope, so close to each one of us . . . Whereas, more than his treason, the dry despair of Judas permanently separates him from us and us from him. Judas inspires fear, Peter touches us. I think it is admirable that the first pope was not a stoic hero and that he was acquainted with tears of shame.

———

A strange trial, but we ourselves have seen similar ones, in which the principal and pre-established point is, first of all, that the accused must at all costs be legally condemned to death, then that he must in fact be executed, and, finally, that he must not be executed no matter how but painfully and infamously.

Furthermore, there were in fact two entirely distinct trials, with—for the good of the cause, as one might say—a different indictment in each. The first trial is a transaction interior to Israel and it runs its course according to the Jewish Law. It ends in a sentence of death, a sentence which, however, in view of the privileges of the Roman procurator, could not be carried out. Hence the second trial, "for the gallery," the "gallery" being the aforesaid Roman procurator. This second trial ends in a sentence of death on grounds more closely connected with the preoccupations of a Roman functionary: this time the sentence could be executed, it was executed, it was executed by a death of infamy, in accordance with the wishes of Jesus' accusers.

The unity of the two trials was in fact constituted by the person of Jesus, accused and condemned in both instances, but also by the identity of his accusers, who were also the same in both courts. The strangest fact is that in each of the two trials the accusation was different and both times it was nevertheless correct—though not altogether in the sense in which it was introduced. Stranger still, instead of pleading not guilty, Jesus in each instance laid claim to and reinforced the titles which were used to incriminate him and which served as basis for the indictment. But he carefully defined the meaning of those titles. In both cases, however, the sentence was supremely unjust. The height of strangeness was that the execution of the sentence eternally confirmed Jesus in the two titles, Son of Man and King of the Jews, which had been used against him, which he had claimed to the very end, and for which he was in fact condemned in the Jewish court and in the pagan court.

Let us turn now to the first of these trials, that before the Sanhedrin. First of all, what was this Sanhedrin before which Jesus was summoned Mark 15:1 to appear? Mark is very precise: "And as soon as it was morning, the chief priests held a consultation with the elders, the Scribes and the whole Sanhedrin." A solemn and venerable assembly if there ever was one: the high clergy, the high aristocracy, the high magistrature of Israel, a kind of estates general. I am not speaking lightly when I say that this assembly was the most venerable in existence. I do not share present-day conformism, according to which everything that is socially accepted as distinguished and superior, everything that is invested with high authority and important functions, must of necessity be rotten. I believe, on the contrary, in the virtue of social and even hereditary tradition.

But I know, too, that human assemblies are human, and there are dangers and weaknesses in everything human. The privileges of caste, instead of reinforcing the sense of responsibility, can also engender an incurable frivolity. The highest functions, spiritual or temporal, can in fact fall into frivolous and cruel hands. Cruelty is born of an excess of frivolity, just as diabetes is born of an excess of sugar in the organism. The sad thing was that in Jesus' time the Jewish people, probably to a greater degree than ever before in their long history, was worthy of the high vocation of Israel. But the governing classes were congealed in pettifogging and ferocious juridical conservatism.

The trial was begun by the calling of witnesses, but they contradicted one another. Two of them reported one of Jesus' parables, which they

interpreted in a crude, literal sense. The judges, themselves so well acquainted with the language of parable, were discouraged. Jesus had,
poetically, identified his own body with the Temple, the seat of the
glory and the Presence of God, and in doing so he had predicted his
own Resurrection. It is a remarkable fact that this parable should be
recalled at the very moment when the point in question was of Jesus'
death. But it was clear that the interrogation was losing itself in incoherence.

The chief priest feels this. To escape from it, he rises. Mark and
Matthew have noted that the chief priest rose. When a supreme judge
rises, it is a momentous event. Exegesis forfeits a great deal when it
emphasizes in the Gospel and in the Holy Scriptures in general only
the words, often to the neglect of the gestures. And so the chief priest
rose in order to interrogate the accused himself. A solemn moment,
when the prime minister of the ancient covenant rises in order to look
into the eyes of the heir of that ancient covenant, the fruit of that covenant, the seed of Abraham par excellence—*your seed, your seed*—in
which all the nations of the earth were to be blessed.

The stakes were mortal, for Jesus certainly, even more so for Israel.
Perhaps there were a few seconds of hesitation. The chief priest approached Jesus, looked at him fixedly, scrutinized him, and, quite literally, *he did not recognize him.* Like the Patriarch Isaac he had become blind, he was unable to recognize his own heir. A pathetic situation: if at that moment, by a sudden illumination, which did not come,
the ancient tradition of Israel had recognized as its own this ultimate
and glorious offspring, the face of the world would have changed. It is
a situation more tragic than that of Priam, whose son is returned to
him and is recognized by him as his own, but he is dead. And behind
that father and son the city flamed under the torch of the conquerors.
Here the son is still alive, but Priam does not recognize him, and because he has not recognized him, he is going to condemn him to death.
And nevertheless it is his son. Forty years later, Jerusalem will go up
in flames behind them.

I have said, and I shall never tire of repeating, that the great misfortune of Israel is that its destiny fell into the hands of men of the law,
instead of falling into the hands of poets. Poets perceive signs and connections. Legalists imprison themselves in the letter, which becomes
their tomb. But they do not bury themselves alone: those in question
dragged with them into their sepulcher a whole world, the glorious past
of Israel.

As Jesus remained silent and did not reply, the chief priest, standing, said to him, "I adjure thee by the living God that thou tell us whether thou art the Christ, the Son of God."

Matt. 26:63

This solemn adjuration, made in the name of the God of Israel by His appointed representative, could not be evaded by any son of Israel; no son of Israel worthy of his race would fail to answer with the very truth. It is inconceivable that in so solemn a situation a subject of the Law, as Jesus was, would have lied to the chief priest. I do not consider myself an especially good example, but I know very well that if the pope in person solemnly summoned me to tell him the truth, not even the idea of lying to him would arise. If I knew the truth I would tell it to him, even though that truth might result in my head's being instantly struck off. What other authority is there in the world comparable to that of a sovereign pontiff? And that is what Caiphas was.

On many occasions in the course of his life Jesus had been asked who he was. Usually he had evaded the question or had replied only by enigmas. But now, to the chief priest, he replies clearly and straightforwardly. What, then, was Caiphas' question? The same as that of John the Baptist and of so many others: was Jesus the Christ, the Son of God, the Messiah promised to Israel, yes or no?

I know very well that present-day Judaism, at least in the case of its intellectuals, has practically abandoned the hope of a personal Messiah and that Jewish Messianism today has been confused with the consciousness of the universal sacerdotal vocation of the Jewish race as mediator between the whole of humanity and the true God, the God of the Hebrew clan. But Judaism, after the destruction of Jerusalem, abandoned so many things—among them its most precious possessions—that one has some trouble in recognizing its continuity. At Jesus' time, it was a Messiah in the most personal sense that Caiphas and all the other Jews were awaiting.

To the solemn question of the sovereign pontiff, Jesus replied that he was the Messiah. If he had stopped there in his reply, the trial might have gone on forever. Such an assertion was not an offense, since the Messiah was in fact to appear and make himself known by his miracles and the fulfillment in him of the prophecies. On a single previous occasion, in the course of a tête-à-tête with the woman of Samaria, Jesus had clearly affirmed his Messianity. But here, before the Supreme Court of Israel, Jesus claims his Messianity so clearly only because he is before the chief priest of his people, who is questioning him on this subject. Jesus therefore recognizes the competence of the court, he remains to the end "subject to the Law." But he has decided to speak clearly on this subject because no further ambiguity is possible. He is a man in the hands of the enemy, a prisoner, defeated in the eyes of the world, alone and abandoned by his own people, betrayed by one of them: thus his declaration of Messianity cannot mislead or suggest a wish on his part for temporal power like that of a Caesar. If he is a glorious Messiah, he hides it well. And so he can say that he is truly the Messiah: one must take him at his word, have confidence in him, have faith. This declaration of Messianity on the part of this accused man, situated as he was, touches me more deeply than all the miracles, because it actually puts Jesus' Messianity on a quite different level from that of force and constraint.

Contrary to what might be imagined, the tribunal would not have been shocked by such a claim. It would simply have prepared itself for the long procedure of testing the validity of this man's title to what he said he was. Up to then Jesus was not liable to a capital sentence. The supreme title "Son of God" itself remained ambiguous and had been used without blasphemy by the kings of Israel. The witnesses to the charge were floundering, the accusation was sinking in quicksand, it was Jesus himself who refloated the trial, for, to his own destruction, he did not stop there.

In fact, he added, "Thou hast said it. Nevertheless, I say to you, *here-* Matt. 26:64 *after you shall see the Son of Man* sitting at the right hand of the Power and *coming upon the clouds of heaven.*" Had lightning struck in the midst of the court, it would not have produced a greater stupor. Here, in full Sanhedrin, before the Supreme Court of his nation, face to face with the chief priest, this humble Galilean, his face already covered with spittle, had given voice to the most extravagant of pretensions, claiming for himself not only Messianity but eternity, empire over the centuries, the Last Judgment, omnipotence, in a word, equality with God Himself. For this indeed is what Jesus' words meant. Before the chief priest he dares call himself "Son of Man" and evoke unmistakably before all these notables the great prophecy of Daniel: "As the visions Dan. 7:13-14 during the night continued, I saw one like a son of man coming, on the clouds of heaven; when he reached the Ancient One and was presented before him, he received dominion, glory, and kingship; nations and peoples of every language serve him. His dominion is an everlasting dominion that shall not be taken away, his kingship shall not be destroyed."

I try to understand what has happened. The history of Jesus Christ is unintelligible in the social context that is ours. To understand it one must transcend that context and try to imagine the Jewish society in

Jesus' time. In one of our modern democratic tribunals, an accused who called himself the "Son of Man" and talked about "clouds of heaven" would immediately be sent by the judge to a psychiatrist. But the Sanhedrin had absolutely nothing democratic or modern about it. Jesus' declaration had the effect of a bomb. At one stroke all these people became crazed with rage. Their system of thinking and judging exploded. Each and every one of them knew by heart the prophecy of Israel: Jesus' few words, "Son of Man," "clouds of heaven," had set in motion all the mechanism of memory and exegesis. They all knew very well that the prophecy of Daniel could designate only a being who was literally divine. It was monstrous to think that this man, whom they had before them and at their mercy, claimed to be a divine being.

I have dwelt sufficiently, at the beginning of this book, on the prophecy of Daniel not to have to enlarge upon it here. This monumental declaration by Jesus, in such total contradiction to appearances, threw the assembly into confusion and everything ended abruptly. Matthew reports, "Then the high priest tore his garments, saying, 'He has blasphemed; what further need have we of witnesses? Behold, now you have heard the blasphemy. What do you think?' And they answered and said, 'He is liable to death.'"

Matt. 26:65-66

The Law reserved its most severe and infamous punishment for blasphemy, the crime of crimes, *lèse-majesté*—the single and unique majesty, in that religious nation, being the majesty of God. Caiphas believes he is immolating Jesus in accordance with the Law. And yet, as John has noted, since he is chief priest for that year, it is not within his power, while applying the Law, not to fulfill the prophecy at the same time. To the very end Jesus remains "subject to the Law," and it is within the limitations of that subjection that he fulfills the prophecies, all the prophecies, and the promises made to Israel. But Caiphas, too, is subject to the Law, subject and prime minister of that Law, and furthermore a Prophet, since he is chief priest. Nothing is finer, nothing more splendid, nothing more tragic in the world, in the whole history of men, and in all literature, than this confrontation, in the persons of Caiphas and Jesus, of the old and the new covenant, of the Law and its prophetically designated and obedient victim, of the prophecy of Israel and its supreme consummation.

———

And so Jesus has now been condemned to death according to that Law of his people, condemned for the gravest crime, according to that Law, blasphemy: the personal and direct offense committed against the living God.

In antiquity, to be sure, nothing was commoner than the deification of mortals. Rome itself deified its emperors. But that is precisely the point; all these nations that multiplied their gods were idolatrous. Israel alone—and this is its glory—proclaimed the uniqueness of God. Even under the yoke of Rome, Israel did not recognize and did not practice the cult of the emperor. Great and insolent nation! It is here, here above all, that it is important to see and to recognize that Jesus was at one with his nation and remained so to the very end. Caiphas and he had exactly the same conception of God and of His absolute unity. This is why their encounter is so charged with meaning. In an idolatrous nation Jesus' pretension would have been in bad taste. In Israel it was considered blasphemous, and this was possible only in Israel.

From time to time one hears that a court of Jewish lawyers has met, in Israel or elsewhere, to retry the case of Jesus according to the Law, and to pronounce an acquittal. Such staged performances seem to me absolutely pointless. As far as the Law of Israel is concerned, I have more faith in the competence of Caiphas than in that of modern rabbis. Jesus was condemned to death for blasphemy, less because he called himself "Son of God" than because, by solemnly laying claim to the title "Son of Man," consecrated by the prophecy of Daniel, he claimed to participate with the unique and very holy God in the empire, the power, the judgment, and eternity. He claimed to be God in person.

This pretension, once voiced before the tribunal, could only be false or true. If false and mendacious, then Caiphas was a thousand times right, Jesus had blasphemed and, according to the Law of Moses, he deserved the death reserved for him; he also deserved infamy and malediction. But if it was true, then Jesus had not blasphemed, since God cannot deny Himself. But then Jesus, because he was God in person, was above the Law of Moses, above Moses himself: over him the Law no longer had any power, for him it no longer served any purpose, the Law expired at the feet of this defendant. The Law could do all except judge God. God being above the Law, in Jesus Christ and through Jesus Christ we were all freed from the Law, being dependent henceforth only on God's good pleasure and that of his well-loved Son, good pleasure that we call "grace."

Saint Paul, the Pharisee, spent his whole life in retrying the case of Jesus. There is no other way than his of retrying the case of Jesus and arriving at an acquittal without at the same time proclaiming the Law of Moses forever incompetent and void. Eternally incompetent and void, a Law murdered with him whom it put to death.

But modern Judaism, born after the fall of Jerusalem and under the influence of the Pharisees, has, quite to the contrary, abandoned all of ancient Judaism, everything—the priesthood, the Temple, the sacrifices, the prophecy, personal Messianity, the Apocalypse, the Promise—everything except the Law and the human traditions with which the Pharisees have, in practice, overloaded the Law. That Law, inflated by these traditions, is a terrible yoke, which the greater number of Jews have shaken off as they evolved, for it condemns in advance all development and extends its fanaticism even into realms that have nothing religious about them, such as the art of cooking. Maimonides went so far as to place Moses definitely above Abraham and the Patriarchs; Maimonides was intelligent: he understood that this is the sole means of eclipsing the Promise by the Law, but this substitution of Moses for Abraham in the founding of the religion of Israel is a sort of blasphemy.

This is why Christianity is and remains more "Jewish" than modern Judaism. In Jesus, in a fashion both sacramental and real, we have retained the Temple, the priesthood of Aaron, the Sacrifice, the prophecy, personal Messianism, the Apocalypse, and above all the Promise. Moreover, in an effable but concrete (spiritual and carnal) Eucharistic fashion, we Christians have even safeguarded, in a single body that we adore, Jewish racism—an open and avowed racism, without inferiority complex—for it is truly Jewish flesh and Jewish blood (*Your seed, your seed*) through which we gain salvation. In short we have retained everything of ancient Judaism; we have retained it in a sacramental and spiritual blossoming of itself—everything save the Law, which eternally disqualified itself by failing to recognize "the desired of the nations."

In the solemn judgment of Jesus by the Sanhedrin, after the shattering declaration on the part of the accused, it seems to me noteworthy that the first exclamation of the high priest should have been, "He has blasphemed!" By no means did he accuse Jesus of wanting to inaugurate an idolatrous cult, but rather of having pronounced a blasphemy. Moreover, even today the Jews—I mean the Orthodox Jews, the only ones pertinent to my subject—do not in any way accuse Christians of idolatry because they adore the body of Jesus Christ, but of prolonging a blasphemy. This is a reaction more puritan than mystic: that God should have become incarnate in the body of a man, even though a man of their race, is inconceivable to them: it is as though God had defiled Himself.

Jesus in fact greatly simplified the problem for the Sanhedrin. No one could have dared hope for a more cooperative accused. His personal claims went far beyond the original accusation. In fact, he left his judges no choice but to condemn him to death for blasphemy or to kneel down before him and adore him. Where, when, how has one seen judges kneeling before one accused? The insolence of the Jewish nation was total by reason of its monotheism in the midst of all other nations, but within this monotheism the insolence of Jesus was no less perfect. He was confronted with the Law of God, and he laid claim to nothing less than sharing with God the sovereignty, the Kingdom, the eternal empire, and the adoration of the nations. One can say that Jesus truly dominated the situation.

"He deserves death"—that was the sentence of the Sanhedrin. The exegetes cite several texts from the Mosaic God in support of this sentence. The one that seems apt to me is from Leviticus. There had been a quarrel in the camp between a Hebrew and another man, the son of an Egyptian and an Israelite woman. In the heat of the argument the second blasphemed the name of Yahweh, which the text through antonomasia calls *the Name*. "So the people brought him to Moses, who kept him in custody till a decision from the Lord should settle the case for them. The Lord then said to Moses, 'Take *the blasphemer* outside the camp, and when all who heard him have laid their hands on his head, let the whole community stone him. Tell the Israelites: Anyone *who curses* his God shall bear the penalty of his sin; *whoever blasphemes the name of the Lord shall be put to death*. The whole community shall stone him; alien and native alike *must be put to death for blaspheming the Lord's name*.'" Lev. 24:11-16

The Jewish conception of the blasphemy is so alive, so concrete, so blinding that it is like an electric discharge that flashes back and forth between the blasphemer and God. The blasphemer curses God in order that God may curse him in turn. The sign and sanction of this countermalediction is lingering death, infamous death, inflicted outside the camp and by the whole community. The essential thing is that the blasphemy be considered a malediction against God which returns like a boomerang upon the head of him who hurled it. In this oscillation, one must take sides. The community takes God's side by expelling the blasphemer from its bosom and inflicting a painful death upon him. This painful death was by stoning, but another text of the Mosaic Law will come to complete the first one: the text in Deuteronomy that expresses the malediction of God by hanging from the tree.

It is Saint Paul who has best defined this dialectic into which I have been trying to enter here. Let there be no doubt, Caiphas reasoned exactly like Saint Paul. One, like the other, was inside the same dialectic, but they drew opposite—that is, irreconcilable—conclusions. Caiphas, supreme judge according to the Law of Moses, considered Jesus a blasphemer and, applying the Law, condemned him to death outside the city; he invoked on the guilty man the malediction of God through hanging from the wood. Saint Paul affirms that Jesus did not blaspheme because he is God, as he said: it is, then, the Law that blasphemed by condemning him. By counterstroke, Saint Paul picks up the malediction—like a soldier picking up an unexploded grenade to hurl back at the enemy—and turns it back complete at the Law, no longer in the name of the Law, which blasphemed the Lord, but in the name of Abraham and the Promise.

I am inventing nothing: this is the clear and explicit meaning of Abraham's vocation accomplished in Jesus Christ. God said to Abraham:

Gen. 12:2-3

> "I will make a great nation of you. I will bless you,
> And make your name great, so that you shall be a blessing.
> I will bless them that bless you,
> And curse them that curse you.
> In you shall all the nations of the earth be blessed."

Through the mouth of Caiphas the Law had the misfortune to curse him who is par excellence the seed of Abraham and the seed of God. By virtue of the Promise made to Abraham, God must needs curse the Law. He does so. This malediction is directed against the Law, obviously not against the Jewish people. The Jews, like all the other nations, can enter into the benediction promised to Abraham, made concrete in Jesus and extended by him to all the clans of the earth. But they must strip themselves of the Law which, by assassinating the Holy One of God, has incurred the malediction. It might have been otherwise, but this is the way it is, and what is done is done.

For Saint Paul, then, Jesus did not blaspheme, he was what he said he was, Son of God in a unique and personal sense, Son of Man, according to the prophecy of Daniel and in the light of that prophecy. And therefore if the Law condemned him, it is the Law that was to be condemned, because in Jesus it condemned and vowed to malediction the very seed of Abraham, to which had been promised, in the most solemn and irrevocable fashion, all the benedictions. Let the Law be accursed in its turn. The Law and its legitimacy terminated with Caiphas. Through Jesus' death, the Promise and the benediction are perpetuated in him and, through him, are conveyed to all the nations. Here again we Christians are more "Jews" than the modern Jews. Our reasoning is exactly like that of Caiphas. By condemning Jesus the Law blasphemed *the Name*: let it be driven out of the camp, branded with malediction and infamy, let it die the death of a malefactor.

So long as one remains within the Law one is enmeshed in malediction. One must get outside it. As a lightning rod attracts, receives, and disperses the lightning, so Jesus concentrated upon himself the whole malediction of the Law in order to release us from it once for all and in order that we may all, through him, hung from the wood, emerge into the universal benediction anterior to the Law and promised to Abraham and to his seed. There is a continuity between this seed of Abraham, forever blessed, and that tree of the cross on which Jesus was hung. Jesus is the spreading tree of that seed. What unbroken consistency there is everywhere in the Old Testament, the four Gospels, and Saint Paul!

Here I must cite at some length Paul's Epistle to the Galatians:

For I through the Law have died to the Law that I may live to God. *With Christ I am nailed to the cross.* It is now no longer I that live, but Christ lives in me. And the life that I now live in the flesh, I live in the faith of the Son of God, who loved me and gave himself up for me. I do not cast away the grace of God. For if justice is by the Law, then Christ died in vain. . . . Even thus "Abraham believed God, and it was credited to him as justice." Know therefore that the men of faith are the real sons of Abraham. And the Scripture, foreseeing that God would justify the Gentiles by faith, announced to Abraham beforehand, "In thee shall all the nations be blessed." Therefore the men of faith shall be blessed with faithful Abraham.

For those who rely on the works of the Law are under a curse. For it is written, *Cursed is everyone who does not hold to all things that are written in the book of the Law, to perform them.* But that by the Law no man is justified before God is evident, because "he who is just lives by faith." But the Law does not rest on faith; but, "he who does these things shall live by them." *Christ redeemed us from the curse of the Law, becoming a curse for us; for it is written, Cursed is everyone who hangs on a gibbet;* that the blessing of Abraham might come to the Gentiles through Christ Jesus, that through faith we might receive the promise of the Spirit. . . .

For all you who have been baptized into Christ, have put on Christ. There is neither Jew nor Greek; there is neither slave nor freeman; there is neither male nor female. For you are all one in Christ Jesus. And if you are Christ's, then you are the offspring of Abraham, heirs according to promise. . . . But when the fullness of time came, God sent his Son, born of a woman, born under the Law, that he might redeem those who were under

Gal. 2:19-21;
3:6-14, 27-29;
4:4-7

the Law, that we might receive the adoption of sons. And because you are sons, God has sent the spirit of his Son into our hearts, crying, "Abba, Father." So that he is no longer a slave, but a son; and if a son, an heir also through God. . . .

I know very well that to our Western minds, trained, more's the pity, on Descartes, this dialectic may seem frivolous, anyway not compelling. Compelling? Assuredly not in the sense that two and two make four. Why should it be? Among the dialectical instruments that can help us in our search for truth, arithmetic is the lowest. Here we are in an order of reality infinitely superior to that of numbers, of bodies, and even of minds. It is the order of prophecy and of divine revelation—of charity, as Pascal would say. It is an order of sacred realities, literally super-natural, into which one cannot enter without illumination on the one hand, without our own free choice on the other.

In any case, here we are above the juridical dialectic of *yours* and *mine,* even above the dialectic of morals. It is, rather, the dialectic of poetry that offers some analogy, with its subtle requirements of parallel-ism and identification, its echoes of rhymes and allusions. Perhaps an even more humble dialectic, the dialectic of facts, that of chemistry, for example, would provide us with a kind of analogy: you bring two sub-stances together in the expectation that this decisive meeting will pro-duce a disproportionate and irrefutable result.

Here, in Jerusalem two thousand years ago, in the growing dawn, the decisive confrontation took place in the assembly of the Sanhedrin be-tween Christ and the Law of his nation. That confrontation had the effect of an explosive catalysis. It literally produced a "catastrophe," as the denouement of a tragedy is called. It was in that catastrophe that the legitimacy of the Law crumbled, and it is that catastrophe that eter-nally frees us both from the Law and from sin, which was the occasion of the Law but for which the Law had no remedy.

I am speaking of the poetic denouement of a tragedy. But, as Edgar Allan Poe says in "The Philosophy of Composition": "Nothing is more clear than that every plot, worth the name, must be elaborated to its *dénouement* before anything be attempted with the pen." That God had elaborated His plan from before the Promise, before the existence of the Jewish people, before Abraham, and *a fortiori* long before Moses and the Law, with a view to this precise and particular denouement, with a view to this "catastrophe" that saves us all, in which Jesus is im-molated as an expiatory victim on the mountain, of this we read the proof and the poetic sign in Genesis:

After these events God put Abraham to a test. He said to him:

GOD: Abraham, Abraham.

ABRAHAM: Here I am.

Gen. 22:1-13, 15-18

GOD: Take your only son Isaac whom you love and go into the district of Moria, and there offer him as a holocaust on the hill which I shall point out to you.

Early in the morning Abraham harnessed his ass, took with him two of his servants and his son Isaac, and cut wood for the holocaust. Then he set out on his journey to the place which God had indicated to him. On the third day he looked up and saw the place at a distance. He said to his servants:

ABRAHAM: Stay here with the ass while the boy and I go there to worship; then we shall come back to you.

Abraham took *the wood* for the holocaust and put it upon his son Isaac while he himself carried the fire and the knife. As they walked together, Isaac said to his father Abraham:

ISAAC: Father.

ABRAHAM: Yes, son!

ISAAC: You have the fire and *the wood*, but where is the sheep for the holocaust?

ABRAHAM: *God himself will provide the sheep for the holocaust, my son.* And they went on together.

When they arrived at the place of which God had told him, Abraham built an altar there and *arranged the wood on it.* Then he *bound his son Isaac and laid him on the wood upon the altar.* Abraham stretched out his hand, and took the knife *to kill his son.*

But an angel of the Lord called to him from heaven:

ANGEL: Abraham, Abraham!

ABRAHAM: Here I am.

ANGEL: Do not lay a hand on the boy; do nothing to him. I know now that you fear God, since you have not withheld your only son from me.

Abraham looked about and saw a ram caught by its horns in the bush. He went and took it, and *offered it as a holocaust in place of his son.* . . .

Again the angel of the Lord called from heaven to Abraham and said:

ANGEL: *I swear by myself, says the Lord,* since you have done this and have not withheld your only son, I will indeed bless you, and will surely multiply your descendants as the stars of the heavens, as the sands on the seashore. Your descendants shall possess the gates of their enemies. *In your seed all the nations of the earth shall be blessed, because you have obeyed me.*

Here all is admirable, but it becomes poignant when one looks at the scene as a transparency superimposed on that of Calvary: it is its poetic mirror. And Calvary itself is henceforth the poetic mirror of the whole heroic sacrifice exacted by God from an obedient soul filled with good will. Here it is a ram that takes the place of the well-loved son. On Calvary it is the well-loved son who takes the place of the goats and the lambs, the poor sinners. And in the destiny of each one of us it can happen that the ram is lacking and the sacrifice must be carried through to the end. But in a mirror, too, we notice that the image is reversed; this is why I speak of the poetic mirror.

The historicity of Isaac's sacrifice may be contested. It seems to me improbable that it should have been invented. And if it were invented, no one could deny that Genesis was written centuries and centuries before the death of Jesus on Calvary. There is not a dramatist in the world worthy of that name who would contest the poetic relationship between the sacrifice of Isaac and the sacrifice of Jesus Christ. To be sure, there are differences and, as I have said, the reversed image of the poetic mirror. But what poet would not see the necessity of these differences and the truth of the parallelism? This is what is called surprising the reader or the spectator with what he expects, with what he has been made to expect. The sacrifice of Christ *does not copy* that of Isaac. But if it had been a servile copy, then one might doubt the veracity of the account of the Passion. The fact that it was not a copy but an analogy proves the authenticity of the report. Caiphas was surely not thinking about the sacrifice of Isaac when he sent Jesus Christ to his death; that is why he was a "Prophet," infallible but blind. Someone above him was thinking for him. It is necessary to be the master of historical time, as Shakespeare was the master of theatrical time, in order to establish such a prodigious parallelism in the actual unrolling of real historical time.

In explaining the prophecy of the sacrifice of Isaac, Christian exegetes usually consider that first Isaac and then the ram took the place of Christ and that Abraham took the place of God the Father, whose commandment Christ fulfilled in his Passion. As Saint Paul will say, "He humbled himself, becoming obedient to death, even to death on a cross." And obviously they are perfectly right. But I believe that one can also say that, in the accomplishment of the prophecy, Caiphas, chief priest for that year and Prophet of the people of God, performed the function of Abraham. Jesus, son of that people to the end, subject of the Law, seed par excellence of Abraham, allowed himself to be bound and sacrificed on the wood by the chief priest, the patriarchal sacrificer: and that time there was not to be a ram to take his place, there could no longer have been a ram because, just as he had come to take upon himself the malediction of the Law, Jesus had also come in order that through his sacrifice he might eternally replace and render superfluous the rams, the bulls, the sheep, and the doves whose sacrifice had been only the pro-

Phil. 2:8

phetic metaphor for his sacrifice. Furthermore, Jesus, by his forever exemplary obedience, at the very moment at which he was prophetically condemned took the place of the chief priest and of all the priests who had preceded Caiphas back to Aaron and Melchisedech, as the unique mediator between God and men, and as the eternal and unique sacrificial priest. It is here that the whole of the Old Testament—not only the Law but also the Promise, the priesthood, the prophecy, the tent and the Temple, the whole cult of the old covenant—finds its fulfillment and accomplishment, its appropriate and real "catastrophe."

Everything is reversed, the right becomes the left, as in a mirror. Caiphas accuses Jesus of having blasphemed *the Name* and condemns him to death for blasphemy. By entering voluntarily into this sacrificial death and the malediction on the wood, Jesus reconquers through his blood this *Name* which is his from the beginning.

It is once more Saint Paul who says this, in a sort of hymn, which perhaps the very first Christians sang even before Saint Paul took the pains of transcribing it:

> Who though he was by nature God, Phil. 2:6-11
> Did not consider being equal to God
> A thing to be clung to,
> But emptied himself,
> Taking the nature of a slave
> And being made like unto men.
> And appearing in the form of man,
> He humbled himself,
> Becoming obedient to death,
> Even to death on a cross.
> Therefore God also has exalted him
> And has bestowed upon him
> The name that is above every name,
> So that at the name of Jesus
> Every knee should bend of those in heaven,
> On earth and under the earth,
> And every tongue should confess
> That the Lord Jesus Christ
> Is in the glory of God the Father.

It is true that Christian children by reading the account of the Passion of Jesus Christ become anti-Semites, just as little Frenchmen become anti-English by reading about the death of Joan of Arc. There is, to be sure, much sociological comfort in all this, comfort of the sort that the psychoanalysts call "projection." Mentally we whip the Jews for the murder of Christ, just as Xerxes whipped the Hellespont: the Hellespont was Xerxes' scapegoat. In the atrocious murder of Jesus Christ, a culprit must indeed be found; the essential thing is that we should not be involved. A symptomatic anxiety: it is in fact a revelation about ourselves that this story, two thousand years old, is of such concern to us that the question actually presents itself to each one of us whether he may not be personally implicated. The Passion of Jesus Christ is fearfully searching, indiscreet, and harrowing, it puts us all to the question. In order that we may not feel personally responsible for it, we are ready to assign this crime the crime of crimes to any culprit at all who falls into our hands. And beyond question historically it is the Jews who have fallen into our hands.

In vain. Anti-Semitism will only heap one guilt on another, it will not relieve us of our first and inalienable responsibility. Caiphas, the Pharisees, the implacable priests, Herod the man of the world, Pilate who washes his hands, Judas who counts his silver, Peter who denies before the cock crows, the soldiers who cast dice at the foot of the cross—but they are we, all of us, absolutely all, Christians or Jews, believers or unbelievers. This history is our own. Once we have put a foot inside, the door closes behind us, whether we like it or not, we are embarked on the frenetic toboggan of individual responsibility—so much the worse for us if our hearts fail. If Jesus Christ died as he died, I am surely in some measure involved. I have his blood on my hands. No recourse is possible, not even to the perfumes of Arabia.

It is no less symptomatic that, in this affair, the Jewish historians and the Christian historians resemble each other so much that they are as interchangeable as twin brothers: they bat the ball back and forth to one another. It is true that the Christian historians, beginning with John, have accused "the Jews" without using proper discrimination. But it should be noted also that the Jewish historians accuse the Romans, most of all Pilate, who, like Bishop Cauchon, is no longer here to defend himself.

As for the so-called "Biblical" films produced in Hollywood to meet commercial demands, their purpose is not to recount the Passion of our Lord Jesus Christ in authentic images but, first of all, to fill the theatres without giving the slightest offense to anyone, not the slightest offense to the Jews, not the slightest offense to the Christians. Such films are dishonorable, they impudently blaspheme the holy truth of history, they corrupt to an incredible degree the sensibilities of Christians and the understanding of the facts. For the fierce guardians of Christian morality, there would seem to be a more urgent task than applying calipers to the braziers and evaluating the thickness of the tulle that veils the facile Venuses of Hollywood. That task would be to disavow and denounce these cinematographic mythifications, which are attacks on the truth and decency of history a thousand times more scandalous than any adultery. It is frightening to realize that in a domain as important as the cinema puritanism is extending its ravages by distracting the attention of Christian people from those vitally important values that must be maintained at all costs.

In the Passion of Jesus Christ the supreme value, which controls all, lies in the facts, the irrefutable, unchangeable, irreversible facts, the sacred, saving facts. But these are not saviors except insofar as they cast back to us our own image, our own responsibility, not the faults of others. These facts have been written and described not to assure us all of a clean conscience but to awaken our consciences before our appearance at the tribunal of God.

———

Once Jesus' condemnation to death had been achieved in the Sanhedrin, it remained to have it ratified by the Roman procurator, who alone had the right to order its execution. And so Caiphas referred Jesus to the tribunal of Pilate. In principle, this was a great good fortune for Christ: how often, in colonial times in North Africa, have I seen natives choose French justice in preference to that of their alcaides. Not that French judges were necessarily more just, but they were not involved in local quarrels. Such seemed indeed to be the position of Pilate; Jesus' enemies were under no illusion about it. For them the game was far from won. And so they followed Jesus, but in front of Pilate they changed their tune. They were in fact undertaking a new trial more difficult than the first.

It was perfectly evident that they could not hope to obtain the execution of Jesus if they brought before the procurator the same indictment as before the Sanhedrin: "Son of Man"—what meaning could that have for a high Roman functionary? Pilate had not read Daniel and probably cared nothing about him. The customs and religion of the Jews, Jewish ceremonies and interdictions, including the word "blasphemy" taken in its strictly Jewish sense—all this must have appeared to Pilate as strange, foreign, frivolous, cruel, and fanatical as the customs of the Aztecs do to us. Pilate very likely possessed the elegance and nonchalance, tempered by moments of exasperation, indifference, and arrogance, of a British governor in Zanzibar under Queen Victoria. He could not have been completely satisfied either with his post or himself, still less with those whom he administered—a clever, quarrelsome lot, in his eyes, intriguing in high places, even with the emperor, obstinate men and litigious. Moreover this province of Judea, the most turbulent in the whole empire, was also the poorest. For a high Roman functionary the post of procurator of Judea was at once a trap and a semi-disgrace.

It was barely day when the throng invaded the outskirts of the Praetorium. I say the outskirts, for these incredible people brought their taboos into everything, even their passions and their hatred. They accepted the Roman procurator as a judge for a son of Israel, since they were taking Jesus to him, but for nothing in the world would they on that particular day have set foot within the limits of a pagan praetorium, so as not to defile themselves on the eve of the Passover. Such was their attitude: there is in religious observances a certain logic that makes them stray from their goal, that leads them straight into Pharisaism. It never entered the minds of Jesus' enemies that by demanding that innocent blood be shed they were incurring a greater defilement than by violating an imaginary line with their feet. Nevertheless they pushed Jesus in front of them into the Praetorium, Jesus, who was, like them, "subject to the Law." In that now sacred space, between his judge and his accusers, Jesus is alone, untouchable. It is strange that no painter has ever attempted to represent that throng of Jesus' accusers, crowded together and yet without any real obstacle, immobilized at the imaginary line of legal purity. Jesus is already on the other side, "delivered over to the pagans" as he had predicted. I firmly believe that the most cruel and unjust crimes in history have been committed by puritans. It is significant that the totalitarian hecatombs were called "purifications."

The dialogue about truth now takes place. Pilate has been roused from his bed by the noise. He is still half asleep, which further incenses him against his interlocuters. What possessed them to wake people so early with a demand that someone be put to death?

Luke 23:2   MEMBERS OF THE SANHEDRINS We have found this man perverting our nation, and forbidding the payment of taxes to Caesar, and saying that he is Christ a king. . . .

John 18:29-31   PILATE: What accusation do you bring against this man?

MEMBERS OF THE SANHEDRIN: If he were not a criminal we should not have handed him over to thee. . . .

PILATE: Take him yourselves, and judge him according to your law.

MEMBERS OF THE SANHEDRIN: It is not lawful for us to put anyone to death.

That is what was said. In five exchanges the criminal trial has been begun. To be sure, only those accusations against Jesus are retained—a mixture of truth and falsehood—that are calculated to influence a high functionary, whose ambition it is to maintain order and whose motto is "No fuss!" Obviously, if the Sanhedrin had had the power to execute a condemned man, Pilate would not have been disturbed. From now on, all is favorable to their bringing the procurator to give the order of execution which he alone has the power to endorse. But Pilate, for his part, will do everything possible to get out of this wasp's nest.

Pilate therefore again entered into the praetorium, and he summoned Jesus, and said to him, "Art thou the king of the Jews?" Jesus answered, "Dost thou say this of thyself, or have others told thee of me?" Pilate answered, "Am I a Jew? Thy own people and the chief priests have delivered thee to me. What hast thou done?" Jesus answered, "My kingdom is not of this world. If my kingdom were of this world, my followers would have fought that I might not be delivered to the Jews. But, as it is, my kingdom is not from here." Pilate therefore said to him, "Thou art then a king?" Jesus answered, "Thou sayest it; I am a king. This is why I was born, and why I have come into the world, to bear witness to the truth. Everyone who is of the truth hears my voice." Pilate said to him, "What is truth?"   John 18:33-38

And when he had said this, he went outside to the Jews again, and said to them, "I find no guilt in him."

Pilate is visibly on guard, careful not to exceed his authority. What would happen if judges tried to understand the inner life of an accused? Jesus had said of himself, "I am the truth." And here he is before Pilate, who shrugs his shoulders and asks aloud, "What is truth?" One has an impulse to say to him, "Watch out, look closer." But the dialogue is a dialogue of deaf men. At least Pilate is deaf, and blind as well. His function limits him. The man himself is not wicked, but he obeys the functionary. And the functionary in turn obeys . . . what? whom? Caesar, to be sure, but, above all, fear.

When Caiphas, calling upon God in his capacity as chief priest, solemnly interrogated him, Jesus replied. Here it is the same; when Pilate, exercising his authority as governor, interrogates him, Jesus once more replies. Nevertheless, Jesus shows the ambiguity and the subordination of authorities. In the case of Pilate, as in that of Caiphas, he judges his judges, he judges their jurisdiction, he claims a higher jurisdiction and a more decisive instance than theirs, he subordinates justice to truth, he affirms that he is King above this world—all this, astounding and literally prodigious though it is, in a tone infinitely simple, natural, and free of all insolence.

At one moment in this trial, which will last throughout the whole morning, Jesus is accused of having claimed to be "the son of God."

Pilate, who must have been at once skeptical and superstitious, as is often the case with souls religiously at low ebb, is frightened:

John 19:9-11 PILATE: Whence do you come?
[But Jesus makes no reply.]
PILATE: You do not answer me? Do you not know that I have power to set you free and power to crucify you?
JESUS: You would not have any power over me if it had not been given you from on high.

Pilate was thinking perhaps of Caesar, but it is of God that Jesus was speaking. This will lead Saint Paul to say that all authority derives from God. That statement by Saint Paul will be used and misused. Here Jesus declares to this official—and no one could be more detached from his own trial—that all authority descends more or less directly from God, that all authority therefore must render an accounting to God Himself, whatever other accounts it may feel called upon to render in this world. This is very comforting for simple citizens, for the justice of this world has often gone awry: after all, what accounting, during their lifetime, did Hitler and Stalin render and to whom?

Jesus steadily raises the level of the debate. The frightful thing is that his adversaries steadily lower it. This appeal to Pilate was frightfully degrading for them. Why? These chief priests, these notables, these scribes, wrapped in their knowledge and their dignity, claim to represent not only the single people elect of God but God Himself, the only God, their God, Him of the Law and of the covenant. And then, in front of this pagan, this proconsul, whom they despise but on whom they depend, they descend by degrees into abjection, to the point of denying before him everything that constitutes the honor and the pride of their nation. They submit to every mortification, they swallow every insult, in order that their prey may not escape them. Throughout the whole length of the Gospels, one is ashamed for them. The Devil has sounded the tally-ho, and the dogs await their quarry.

Pilate hesitates, shuffles, gains time, takes evasive action. Learning that Jesus is a Galilean, he sends him to the tribunal of Herod. Who was he, this Herod? If he had been born in our century—and this type of man exists always, just like Pilate, just like Caiphas, just like the Pharisees—I would swear that Herod had been born at a masked ball in a Pierrot's hat, so completely does he incarnate the frivolity of a certain class that would dance on volcanoes or beneath black atomic clouds. Proust has made himself the chronicler of that court.

Josephus tells us about Herod. He was the son of Herod the Great but he was far from having the latter's scope. He was crafty and, when in his cups, cruel. This can be clearly seen on the occasion when, under the influence of sensuality and drunkenness—on a point of honor, too, for he had imprudently given his word—he put John the Baptist to death in order to please his wife Herodia. In his eyes all this no doubt was of small consequence. What mattered to him was that he, the son of a king, was only tetrarch of Galilee and Pereas, a paltry fragment of the paternal empire. He was not king and he suffered from this fact, although people called him king nevertheless to flatter him. Even the little that he possessed—by the favor of Tiberius and surely far beneath his deserts in his own eyes—this little was to be taken from him by Caligula. Herod will finish his days, accompanied by Herodia, in exile, supplanted in his own realm by his brother-in-law, the brother of Herodia, a more elegant and able man. What a miserable old age this Oriental prince must have had, with his worn-out companion, in a small town in Gaul that later on was to be called Saint-Bertrand de Comminges. Exile is hard for anyone but hardest of all for a worldly wretch who lives only to occupy a place of honor and, above all, to be seen there.

For the moment he is still in a place of honor and enjoying it, a prince royal and regnant, surrounded by his court, on a pilgrimage to Jerusalem, where he maintains a palace. And now they bring him Jesus of Nazareth, a Prophet who had been active in his territory, whom he desired to know because he had heard a great deal of talk about him. If Jesus had really wanted to extricate himself from this affair, this was his opportunity, within easy reach. Herod too had risen early, but in circumstances that were harder for him than for Pilate: to rise at dawn is a more extraordinary event, I was about to say a more heroic one, for a prince than for an administrator. No matter! Herod got up willingly. He was enchanted to receive Jesus. Luke reports:

And Pilate said to the chief priests and to the crowds: "I find no guilt in this man." But they persisted, saying, "He is stirring up the people, teaching throughout all Judea, and beginning from Galilee even to this place." But Pilate, hearing Galilee, asked whether the man was a Galilean. And learning that he belonged to Herod's jurisdiction, he sent him back to Herod, who likewise was in Jerusalem in those days.

Now when Herod saw Jesus, he was exceedingly glad; for he had been a long time desirous to see him, because he had heard so much about him, and he was hoping to see some miracle done by him.

Now he put many questions to him, but he made him no answer. Now the chief priests and Scribes were standing by, vehemently accusing him. But Herod, with his soldiery, treated him with contempt and mocked him, array-

Luke 23:4-12

ing him in a bright robe, and sent him back to Pilate. And Herod and Pilate became friends that very day; whereas previously they had been at enmity with each other.

I have spoken of Proust. Among the Evangelists, Luke is Proust: he has the same keenness of observation and preciseness of description, though not of course the elaboration. For reasons I can only guess at, he was fascinated by everything connected with the court of Herod, as Proust was by everything connected with the Hôtel de Guermantes. I myself would love to have Proust's knowledge of the worldly carnival in order to disentangle all the implications of this astonishing confrontation between King Herod and Jesus.

The first thing to observe: When Caiphas, the chief priest, interrogates Jesus, the latter replies to him directly by proclaiming his divine origin and eternal judicature. When Pilate, the governor, interrogates him, he replies no less directly by affirming his true and supernatural royalty. But Herod will not succeed in extracting one word from Jesus, not one single word.

Now Jesus has talked a great deal in the course of his life, and the least one can say is that he was not at all fussy about the social standing of his interlocutors, he truly talked to anyone at all. He talked to the poor, he talked to the rich; he talked most of all to the Jews, but also to pagans, when occasion arose, and to Samaritans, those brother enemies of the Jews; he talked to men, he talked to women; he talked to his mother, who was without sin, he talked, with equal courtesy, to women of the streets; he talked especially to the ignorant, but sometimes he chanced to talk to men of learning; he talked to the fishermen on the lake and to soldiers; he talked to John the Baptist, the Prophet, but he also talked to the Pharisees, he inveighed against them, but he talked to them; he talked to Judas, and to the very last called him his friend. On the cross he will talk to a thief. To Herod alone he had nothing to say. To those who are called "worldlings" Jesus has nothing to say.

What people call "the world," is it damned here below? Not even Jesus could communicate with it. Oh, I distrust social geographies with too clearly marked frontiers! It is true that a real duchess is naturally inclined to frivolity. It can happen, too, that a certain appearance of frivolity is her form of modesty and, on occasion, of heroism. The frivolity in question here, although it is more common in a certain social class, is not by any means the prerogative of that class; this frivolity obliterates all sense of responsibility in men. In this sense, Cain's reply to God—"Am I my brother's keeper?"—is a frivolous reply, a reply in the manner of Proust. I know grave ecclesiastics, soldiers covered with medals, gilt-edged academicians, who are even more frivolous than the most hardened and worldly dandies. I shall even say that ecclesiastical dignitaries, beneath their formal exteriors, are more inclined than others to frivolity.

Frivolity is a blinding of the soul and a deafening of the heart, whose first effect is to wipe out the existence of others. If Jesus says nothing to Herod, it is because Herod cannot hear anything. During that long and atrocious day one can easily feel that something happened between Jesus and Caiphas, between Jesus and Pilate; but between Jesus and Herod nothing, absolutely nothing, took place. There was not even a contact. Worldliness imprisons the mind in an extremely narrow circle of reference with extremely limited and superficial interests. The *quality* of Jesus was necessarily outside this magic circle: how could Herod have had even a vague idea, the vaguest suspicion, of what Jesus was? In simple truth and literally speaking, for Herod, Jesus was no more than an occasion, though an exceptional one, for amusing himself.

Luke writes that Herod hoped to see Jesus perform a miracle. But what idea could this worldly prince have of a miracle? Worldliness degrades the heart, but it also debases the intelligence. For Herod a miracle was some astonishing feat that could distract him for a few moments, and it was nothing more. For the single misfortune, the single sin, the single calamity that people of the world recognize is boredom: they are puritans of boredom. Let anything, even the end of the world, come, but in no circumstances let them be bored. However, to avoid being bored, they are capable of moving heaven and earth: one must not underestimate the prodigious energy of people of the world or their indomitable determination.

It is true that in the course of that interminable morning Jesus was never closer to obtaining grace ("grace" for him?) and escaping death. Had he consented to become Herod's buffoon, his official wonder-worker, all the courtiers would have rallied around and supported him. People of the world are in fact incapable of so much as questioning themselves about the innocence or guilt of a man, but anyone who can amuse them is sacred, they will never let him drop. Even the ferocious Pharisees, those dogs hot on the scent, would have been forced to let him go, if Jesus had only consented to become an entertainer.

And Jesus, in the midst of all this? He continues to be silent. The Gospel tells us that the king put a good many questions to him: he does not trouble to answer any of them. Perhaps he does not even hear them. His silence is a double silence, one silence through absence of response, but silence as well to the question that does not reach to him.

In his whole life on earth this is the single occasion when one feels that Jesus is absent. This man, so intensely present to his time, to his people, to the awareness of each of his interlocutors (and we are among them), to the whole history of the world and to eternity, this man here before Herod is absent; it is prodigious, more than human. Whose fault? It takes two to create an absence. A trifle, then, suffices to cause Jesus to be present; Herod does not possess this, he does not weigh that much. I picture Jesus' look fixed on this shoddy king, moving from part to part and seeing no more of his person than the back of the throne on which he sat.

The courtiers must have murmured at this unheard-of insolence. Someone saved Jesus from an imminent outburst of anger by suggesting that perhaps he was mad. Then everything came to an end very fast. Derisively they clothed Jesus in brilliant cast-off clothes, they sent him back to Pilate, and they passed on to other diversions.

If I have lingered over this episode, perhaps it is because it fascinates me as a personal warning. I, in my turn, am journeying word by word toward old age, the traditional age of frivolity, and I too catch myself adopting solemn airs. Although I am not inclined to fear, this frightens me: that Jesus Christ may become absent to me, that he may not even hear my questions any longer, and that one day his gaze will pass through me without seeing me.

Frivolity is not taken seriously enough; it consumes everything it touches. It can lead to the most sordid blasphemy. King Herod shares with Jesus' relations—is not frivolity, however, a custom in families?—the horrible distinction of having treated as a madman him who is Wisdom itself. He is Wisdom, and he was treated as a madman. He is the Word, and he is silent. He is a wonder-worker, too: in the course of his whole public life, God knows what miracles rained around him, they poured. Here, total dryness, a brazen sky. Let us be careful how we ask for miracles—and everyone does, even unbelievers. A miracle is never granted to frivolity. Let this be understood! The refusal by Jesus of Herod's demand gives us a unique and precious insight into what Jesus meant by miracles. A miracle is the King's seal. You do not entrust to impertinent and futile hands the seals of the Kingdom.

Now Jesus is once more before Pilate. The play grows tenser, and Pilate can no longer evade it. Nevertheless, before entering into it, he struggles wretchedly. Luke says, "And Pilate called together the chief priests and the rulers and the people, and said to them, 'You have

Luke 23:13-15

brought before me this man, as one who perverts the people; and behold, I upon examining him in your presence have found no guilt in
this man as touching those things of which you accuse him. Neither
has Herod; for I sent you back to him, and behold, nothing deserving
of death has been committed by him.'" Up to this point no objection
can be made: Pilate speaks the language of an honest, scrupulous judge,
of a man devoted to duty. Why did he not stop there? Now, however,
he makes his first slip. What he says, in effect, is this: "And so, after   Luke 23:16
having him chastised, I shall set him free."

Why does he have him chastised if he is innocent, and why set him
free if he is guilty? With this first concession to injustice, everything
will become possible. Like a man who has finally lost his hold, Pilate
is going to fall headlong into the abyss.

To be frank, any kind of cynical *Gauleiter*, any simple, unscrupulous
political brute who, for reasons of state and in order not to be bothered,
would have proceeded at once to the extreme of injustice, who would
have had Jesus executed without hesitation or evasion by an arbitrary
decree, would have been less contemptible than this Pilate, a man who
each time commits a lesser injustice to avoid a greater one, to save, as
he thinks, what can be saved, who finally, from one concession to another, comes to sanction and commit the injustice of injustices and then
washes his hands of it. We know this Pilate too well, we have had
rather too much experience of him, we know too well that, under the
pretext of saving what can be saved, all is lost, with honor in the lead—
we know all this too thoroughly to retain any indulgence whatever for
this vile fellow.

If Pilate had feebly given in at the start and had surrendered everything at once, Jesus would have been crucified, but in the course of that
long, atrocious morning he would have been spared the flagellation and
the crown of thorns, the parallel with Barabbas and all the insults, all
the affronts, of the soldiery and the populace, everything that must now
be told and that, in the whole Passion of the Lord, gives rises to the
greatest shame and remorse.

Pilate, then, has said, "After having him chastised, I shall set him
free." Why this punishment? Pilate himself would not have cared to
be questioned about his reason: authority does not like to give reasons;
simply to be asked for them seems to put its legitimacy in doubt. Why
is Pilate going to chastise Jesus? To teach him a lesson, of course, as
people say. A lesson, and to teach him what that he does not already
know? Well, to teach him that he, Pilate, is the stronger, that he is
proconsul of Rome, that one does not wake up a proconsul so early in

the morning for a trifle, that it is necessary that he, Pilate, vent his irritation on someone, that this whole affair enrages him, that he cannot stand either disorder or noise and that, as fools say, noise does no good and nothing good comes of it. It is true that Jesus has made a good deal of noise in his short life. And on this particular morning there has been decidedly too much hullabaloo around the proconsul. That is a sufficient reason for whipping this poor wretch, the center of all this uproar; it will teach him. . . . What is he to learn from it? Not to begin over again, but to hide himself in a hole and make sure he is forgotten. And he, Pilate, will have peace, a just and sovereign peace, for those in power cannot easily imagine that justice is not synonymous with their tranquillity.

In this case the lesson was harsh: flagellation. Pilate did not use half-measures. When its own tranquillity is in question, authority never uses half-measures. This torment makes one shudder even after our most modern methods of torture. The victim was stripped, his hands were tied in front of him to a low post, and he was beaten with redoubled blows in cadence with straps of leather, sometimes ornamented with strips or balls of metal. Occasionally a man of weak constitution succumbed and died at once beneath the whips; that was considered just an accident. But Jesus was of particularly robust constitution. In my youth a rather celebrated nun, who obviously was herself perpetually ill, loved to repeat that "grace does not reside in healthy bodies." What did she know about it? In Jesus, grace resided in a body that was exceptionally vigorous and healthy. Jesus survived the punishment of flagellation; he was not for that reason in a less pitiable state: a man streaming with blood, his flesh deeply lacerated, is not a pretty sight.

Jesus has become an object, worse than an object, a plaything for the people's amusement, worse than a plaything, a poor, defenseless animal, tortured by sadistic children. His body passes from hand to hand, while he can do nothing, nor can anyone imagine that he might have a word to say. And in fact he says nothing. He, through whose word heaven and earth were created, is completely passive. He lets things happen to himself. Those who have been in the hands of the enemy know that at certain moments a man's sole physiological ambition is to submit, to deaden the blows, to survive. Jesus survives and suffers. Little by little there is created between this tormented body and its torturers that frightful complicity which is the inverted image of sensual pleasure and which constitutes the extreme horror of concentration camps and chambers of torture. Granted that the soul and will of Christ are dominant over his torment, nevertheless his body enters into the game, being entirely dominated by violence.

Never have the words "abnegation" and "martyrdom" had more meaning than here. He who has never set foot in this nightmare universe, though he be a doctor of theology, how should he have any idea of it? I write all this about Jesus Christ and the torture of flagellation because it is necessary that it should be said. Either concentration camps and torture chambers will return, and then it is needful that those who enter them should know that they enter together with Jesus Christ—Jesus Christ will be flagellated until the end of the world, let us not find ourselves on the side of the torturers—or all this will never return, and then it is needful for us to know the extent of our Lord's torment. This, however, is a false alternative: men being what they are, it will return, and in worse form, by virtue of "progress."

Pilate is personally responsible for the flagellation of Jesus; it is he who had the idea and who gave the order. The worst of it is that he did not do this through wickedness. It is essentially the crime of a careless administrator. "After having him chastised . . ." Pilate thus catches his fingers in the cogwheels of injustice; he will be dragged into them entire. Society and men are such that the mechanism "crime-punishment" is easily reversed. It is true that in simple justice every crime deserves punishment, but it is no less true that in commonplace minds punishment ends by creating a presumption of guilt. The idea does not easily occur to men that a punishment might be undeserved. Socially speaking, the man punished is always wrong. "Throw enough mud," people say, "and some of it is sure to stick." "Inflict enough punishment," one might say, "and the man punished will end by becoming guilty, even in his own eyes." And this is how slanders, accusations, exiles, blows, and executions end by requiring no justification: punishment pays its own way. Kafka has told us all about this subject, and so has Freud; it is also the drama of many children with their parents, of many underlings with their superiors.

And so Jesus Christ accepts it all and does not protest. Nevertheless, the final surrender was never wrenched from him, the admission in the end that he was guilty. In this his courage was great. By his example, when we are overwhelmed by injustice, we can submit and be silent, but nothing in the world should make us confuse the just with the unjust. Guilty? We are always in some measure guilty before God, even if we are not conscious of it: *"Ab occultis meis munda me!"* But to admit guilt, before men, for something we have not done, simply to have peace and to satisfy their tyranny, is not humility but mendacity and cowardice. Our Master never set us any such example.

———

Then a great disturbance takes place: something new is going on. Everyone's attention—that of the Evangelists as well—swings toward another pole of attraction. For a moment history abandons Jesus in the hands of his torturers in order to concentrate on a new hero, who, moreover, is known only through the role of antagonist that he plays here: Barabbas. Matthew writes, "Now at festival time the procurator used to release to the crowd a prisoner, whomever they would. Now he had at that time a notorious prisoner called Barabbas."

Matt. 27:15-16

Who was this Barabbas, whose first name, according to Matthew, was Jesus? John does not mince words: he was a brigand. Luke states that he had committed a murder during an uprising in the city. The two facts are not incompatible. When one has had the honor of being thrown into political prison by the Germans during the occupation, one knows what a marvelous mixture of good types and bad went to make up this rabble that laid claim pell-mell to the resistance. The occupation of a territory confuses all values because it justifies everything: murder, theft, incendiarism, assassination coexist with the purest heroism and the most disinterested sacrifices. And so Barabbas was a brigand, and his detention was perfectly justified. One can conceive, however, that for the Jewish crowd he may have become the symbol of resistance to the invader.

John 18:40
Luke 23:19

This gracious liberation of a prisoner was a rite practiced elsewhere in the empire as well. According to the Jewish way of dividing the days, the feast of the Passover would begin that day at nightfall. Thus it was normal at daybreak for the crowd to assemble at the palace of the governor and claim its due. Pilate and the members of the Sanhedrin had the same thought: why should not Jesus profit by this liberality? Pilate saw in this an occasion to escape from his duties as judge, but the members of the Sanhedrin, on the contrary, saw in it the danger that their prey would escape from them, probably for good. They were much disturbed. Then one sees them, like ants bustling to reinforce the structure of a damaged ant heap, spreading through the crowd, urging the name of Barabbas in the place of that of Jesus. At such moments imagination and quick action are needed.

In that crowd, Jesus, for his part, had no friends. I can well imagine that Mary Magdalene, who was a great lady, Joseph of Arimathea, and Nicodemus were active in the background and were perhaps even interceding with Pilate's wife. But it was in the crowd that the issue was being settled, and in that crowd there were neither the Apostles nor any one of those who had been cured by Jesus' miracles. How could it happen that such a man should find himself so completely alone so suddenly? Alas, when one has had some experience of life one knows that such things do happen! Jesus' friends, then, were not present; his enemies had a clear field and they profited by it. Crowds are malleable; if you approach them in the right way, you can make them say what you wish. In short, within a few minutes Barabbas becomes the national hero who must be freed at all costs and who must be freed at once.

I shall not speak ill of Barabbas, he was no nonentity: it is not within a nonentity's capacity to become a brigand. To be more precise, if, at that moment, he was put in the scale with Jesus and if the balance tipped in his favor, Barabbas had nothing to do with it. Deep in his prison cell he did not even know that his fate was being decided before Pilate's tribunal. His whole good luck consisted in the fact that Jesus was so fiercely and so effectively hated that Barabbas, by contrast, came to seem supremely lovable. The scene in which Pilate tries to save Jesus and in which the members of the Sanhedrin cling desperately to the person of Barabbas is a scene of hysteria. You rub your eyes to see whether you are not asleep, but I think, too, that it is impossible for such a scene to have been invented: human folly is not invented. "And the crowd came up, and began to ask that he do for them as he was wont. But Pilate addressed them, saying, 'Do you wish that I release to you the king of the Jews?' For he knew that the chief priests had delivered him up out of envy. But the chief priests stirred up the crowd to have him release Barabbas for them instead. But Pilate again spoke and said to them, 'What then do you want me to do to the king of the Jews?' But they cried out again, 'Crucify him!' But Pilate said to them, 'Why, what evil has he done?' But they kept crying out the more, 'Crucify him!' "

Mark 15:8-14

It is true, human folly is not invented, it exists. Have we not seen with our own eyes Christian peoples turn their backs on their ancient traditions to acclaim—whom? Why, brigands and those who have the minds and customs of brigands, the haughty dictators of this century of enlightenment. Until the end of the world it will happen again and again that Barabbas is preferred to Jesus Christ, and among the crowds that acclaim Barabbas there will always be chief priests and scribes.

Meanwhile the soldiers, judging no doubt that the lesson they had been giving Jesus was, if not understood, at least sufficient, stopped whipping him, and, as they had heard that the reason for all this torture was that the poor wretch was the king of the Jews, they parodied the ceremony of coronation. Matthew says: "Then the soldiers of the procurator took Jesus into the praetorium, and gathered together about him the whole cohort. And they stripped him and put on him a scarlet cloak; and plaiting a crown of thorns, they put it upon his head, and a reed into his right hand; and bending the knee before him they mocked him, saying, 'Hail, King of the Jews!' And they spat on him, and took the reed and kept striking him on the head." In the Orient there are great thorns, longer than a man's hand, and reeds as solid as cudgels. This indicates how serious the game was. And thus to the "chastisement" they added derision. No Christian can read these lines without feeling his heart burning with compassion and indignation. There comes back to my mind the exclamation attributed to Clovis when he first heard the account of the Passion: "Why was I not there with my Franks?"

Over this atrocious scene, however, there hovers a higher irony, an irony à la Kafka, so marked that one wonders once more who it is that is directing the play, for Jesus was in fact King of the Jews and remains so eternally. Jesus does nothing, he lets things happen. Obviously he is no more than a toy in the hands of the Roman soldiers. Nevertheless a moment comes when you wonder whether the soldiers themselves are not playthings of a higher will that compels them to perform gestures of triumphal significance. It was the Army that claimed the right to create emperors: *"Ave Caesar, Imperator."* And these are Roman soldiers who have proclaimed Jesus King. This is like a reverse image of what happened in Bethlehem: after the homage of the Jewish shepherds came that of the pagan Magi. Here, after the insults in the court of the chief priest and the derision in the court of Herod, it is the Roman Army that mocks. Saint Athanasius has clearly seen the ambiguity of the situation; he explains it to us in a text cited in the Dominican Breviary for Wednesday of Holy Week:

They condemn him to death as a man, and now that he is going to die they adore him as a God. They reduce him to less than nothing, then they proclaim him King. They take off his common clothes to clothe him with purple. They do not know Who it is they are heaping with abuse; but in spite of themselves they call him Prophet. And while they are mocking him and striking him, they nevertheless are according him the trophies of victory: the chlamys of purple, the crown woven of thorns, a scepter of reed. It is true that they do all this in derision, and yet, without their knowing it and in spite of themselves, this results only in his receiving from them what is his rightful due.

Obviously, if one refuses to understand what I am here trying to explain, this whole parallelism will prove nothing, except from the viewpoint of subtle and superior staging, which is precisely the level on which prophecy moves.

John has reported this scene for us, a scene of astounding violence and rage, between Pilate and the members of the Sanhedrin:

Pilate therefore again went outside and said to them: John 19:4-17

PILATE: Behold, I bring him out to you, that you may know that I find no guilt in him.

Jesus therefore came forth, wearing the crown of thorns and the purple cloak.

PILATE: Behold, the man!

When, therefore, the chief priests and the attendants saw him, they cried:

MEMBERS OF THE SANHEDRIN: Crucify him! Crucify him!

PILATE: Take him yourselves and crucify him, for I find no guilt in him.

MEMBERS OF THE SANHEDRIN: We have a Law, and according to that Law he must die, because he has made himself Son of God.

Now when Pilate heard this statement, he feared the more. And he again went back into the praetorium, and said to Jesus:

PILATE: Where art thou from?

But Jesus gave him no answer.

PILATE: Dost thou not speak to me? Dost thou not know that I have power to crucify thee, and that I have power to release thee?

JESUS: Thou wouldst have no power at all over me were it not given thee from above. Therefore, he who betrayed me to thee has the greater sin.

And from then on Pilate was looking for a way to release him. But the Jews cried out:

MEMBERS OF THE SANHEDRIN: If thou release this man, thou art no friend of Caesar; for everyone who makes himself king sets himself against Caesar.

Pilate therefore, when he heard these words, brought Jesus outside and sat down on the judgment seat, at a place called Lithostrotos, but in Hebrew, Gabbatha. Now it was the Preparation Day for the Passover, about the sixth hour.

PILATE: Behold, your king!

MEMBERS OF THE SANHEDRIN: Away with him! Away with him! Crucify him!

PILATE: Shall I crucify your king?

MEMBERS OF THE SANHEDRIN: We have no king but Caesar.

Then he handed him over to them to be crucified. And so they took Jesus and led him away. And bearing the cross for himself, he went forth to the place called the Skull, in Hebrew, Golgotha.

How one wishes that this page had never been written, or rather that the facts it describes had never taken place, that the words it reports had never been spoken. . . . Even in the trial of Joan of Arc, the hatred of the priests never went so far, their villainy never descended to such depths. Along with their rightful vocation, these men were denying the most ancient, the most glorious vocation of Israel. Once more they were involving only themselves in deicide. I do not believe that the Catholic Church, as such, was compromised in the cruel judgment of Joan of Arc or in the folly of the Galilean judgment; why should we any more wish to involve the Jewish people in the frightful animosity of their chief priests against their innocent victim?

Yes, their animosity was horrible. They descended from denial to denial, even to the point of apostasy. Matthew adds a bit of dialogue that makes us shudder:

Matt. 27:24-25   PILATE: I am innocent of the blood of this just man.
THE CROWD: His blood be on us and on our children.

All these people have clearly lost their heads. Hatred at its paroxysm is a singular intoxication, a strange blindness. An event occurred there which, after two thousand years, arouses in the heart of every normal human being both shame and sorrow. And yet, from the moment that we—you, the reader, and I, the writer—are engaged in this story, we must surely follow it to the end, seeking out the details and relating them to one another.

Here, first of all, is the solemn apparition of Christ, clothed in purple, crowned with thorns, with a reed for a scepter, his face covered with spittle and blood. Pilate says, *"Behold the man"—"Ecce homo."* The priests and their acolytes answer, "Crucify him!" Yes, behold the man, tottering, haggard, such a one as we have so often seen coming from the hands of the torturers, on the threshold of concentration camps, of torture chambers, of prisons; behold the man whose image will haunt us until our final agony, behold the man who, from being a victim, draws himself up as the accuser of our so-called civilization, materialistic and despiritualized. Even though he were a criminal, this man is clothed for us in the whole majesty of human pain, of the infinite patience of the poor. Since that day of all days, when Jesus Christ was offered as a spectacle in the humiliation of his suffering and of the derision heaped upon him, God and man hold communion in pain, as in a sacrament offered to all, believer or unbeliever, baptized or pagan, sinner or innocent. What man is not vulnerable to suffering and to being mocked? Here we are at the secret heart of Christianity, a Christianity without frontiers, a Christianity known to God alone, the God who sounds the loins and hearts. "The misery of man," writes Bernanos, "is the wonder of the universe."

Pain, patience, the end, death, henceforth open to all the miserable a secret door to the Communion of the Saints in Jesus Christ: thus they have access to a nocturnal sky in which unknown constellations gravitate around this black sun of human pain, which Pilate on a day revealed to a crowd delirious with hatred:

"Behold the man!"

"Crucify him!"

They will not be satisfied with his pain and his humiliation, they want his blood to the last drop, they want to see him die, raised above the earth, nailed against the sky, like a bird of prey nailed to a portal.

———

All religions have their moral codes; most of them have their revelations and their dogmas; Christianity alone goes farther, to the point of deifying human pain. In Jesus, God himself has sat down beside us to break with us the banal and universal bread of suffering. We have seen and met atheists, the streets are full of them, we have heard them deny so much as the possibility of revelation and the legitimacy of all religions, they have held up to scorn before us all miracles and prophecy, but to deny the whole of Christianity one must go farther still, one must deny this sacred sign, placed henceforth upon the miserable, one must deny the supreme majesty of pain. For human pain—not revolt, but pain—the patience of the poor, their end, their death, henceforth have the majesty of the outraged Christ.

I do not pretend to explain this scene, I do not even pretend to understand it. Its image, after two millennia, imposes itself on me as it has imposed itself on so many painters who endured it before depicting it. I so greatly wish that all this had never happened and, at the same time, I am choked with gratitude that it did happen. It is true that the enemies of Christ descended to the depths of degradation, but he, he descended to the depths of human pain and humiliation. And because nothing could touch him without becoming sacred, behold this human torment henceforth raised to the skies on a shield of glory. There is only one misfortune, and that is not to be among the saints, but it is incontestable, too, that henceforth there will never be sanctity that is not marked with the seal of sorrow. Henceforth, thanks to Jesus Christ, there is a revelation of God in simple human pain, there is the Presence of God in simple human pain, even in its torments and its grimaces.

This is a secret that can well be discovered in the depths of a dungeon or on a hospital bed. Rouault spent his life bringing together in a single countenance two expressions that seem contradictory only if one has never meditated on the outraged Christ: the expression of the derided clown and that of the victim of torture. He succeeded in reconstituting that holy face, alight with divinity, in which humiliation and suffering glow with an incomparable majesty.

I know, I know, we have gone through romanticism and sundry other literary movements in which poets were all more or less accursed. There are stupid sorrows, sterile torments, and sacrilegious despairs that are the antechamber to hell. Hell itself is pain without ransom. The ambiguity of everything human touches the sorrow of man too. Just so. It is here, in this pagan Praetorium, at the feet of this man, who is King of the Jews and Son of God, that human pain and humiliation reach the limit of their ambiguity; it is here that they permanently emerge from neutrality to become either positive or negative, like electricity, either redemptive or damning—there is no more middle ground. The sorrow of man can only be sacred or sacrilegious. But who, except God Himself, can judge? The wretch who dies with a blasphemy on his lips horrifies us, but who among us knows all the ways of communion with the outraged Christ?

I am by no means a specialist in ancient mythologies. Nevertheless I am sufficiently acquainted with them to know that centuries before Christianity men held communion in the death of their gods. Let us be on our guard, however, against too easy analogies of the sort that aroused the indignation of the Church Fathers. It is true that nothing is finer, nothing more peaceful and in a sense more touching, than the funerary steles preserved in the museum at Athens. Nothing is more diametrically opposed, either, to the image of *"Ecce homo"*: these are two wholly contradictory conceptions of life and death. In the "mystery religions" it is clear that the initiate does not have access to divinity until after being "carried out of the circle of pain and sorrow," that is, out of our present life, and that, with the same contempt for the body as in Plato, he must "divest himself of mortality to arrive at the divine." But in Christianity it is actually within this same pain, this same sorrow, and this same mortality that one holds communion, in and through Jesus Christ, with the life eternal and Divinity itself.

Assuredly we must not abandon any of those things that Jesus Christ left in our custody, and we do not abandon any of them: not the revelation, the dogmas, the Sacraments, the papacy, the visible character of the Church, the rites, the disciplines, the miracles, the prophecies—we abandon none of these, we retain them all, but in those things that are more external it is possible to discover misleading analogies with other religions. When one goes deeper, however, one perceives that all analogy is impossible. More even than a religion of the forgiveness of sin, Christianity is the religion of grace and of love; it is, then, the religion of freedom, for grace is the freedom of God, and man himself cannot love except freely. Then, in contemplating the outraged Christ, one perceives that Christianity, even more than being the religion of freedom, is the religion of sanctified and sanctifying pain. The more freely a Christian enters into pain and death, the greater and more valorous is his love. Ancient religions incorporated human terror and even human sensuality: no religion, either before or after Christianity, has incorporated the misery of man, which has in fact become the wonder of the universe.

Pilate is going to make a last, determined effort to save Jesus. A futile effort, for it is misdirected. From the beginning he should have proclaimed the innocence of the accused, have acted accordingly and not departed an inch from that position. After the unjust flagellation, Pilate was bound to slip into injustice. However, he is obstinate. He goes on repeating, "I find no guilt in him." Then why have had him scourged? John 19:6 But Christ's enemies are even more obstinate. Lord God, how implacable are the wars of Your religion and how inflexible cruelty becomes when it disguises itself as zeal and piety! For it is very clear that all these people are pious, devoted people, pillars of the sacristy, as we would say today. "We have a Law, and according to that Law he must die, because John 19:7 he has made himself Son of God."

At these words Pilate was even more terrified, not simply because he was superstitious and, for a pagan, there was nothing so astonishing about a Son of God wandering around among men, but because, if this was the case with Jesus, what a blunder to have had him scourged. But then, too, as a statesman Pilate judged that Jesus had aroused the hatred of the bigots, and he knew his world well enough to be sure that such hatred considers everything permissible and never lays down its arms. And so Pilate was terrified. He did not for that reason stop trying to release Jesus. But the attack of the accusers did not abate. They wanted the hide of the accused, they wanted it very much, and they were men of character. Then there came to Pilate's ears the insinuation he must have dreaded from the beginning, the ultimate argument that made every Roman functionary flinch, the clear threat of a denunciation to Caesar—at that time Tiberius, a suspicious and jealous tyrant. "If thou John 19:12 release this man, thou art no friend of Caesar; for everyone who makes himself king sets himself against Caesar." A word to the wise.

The threat struck Pilate point-blank. A word to him was sufficient. He must have blanched. And then his heart became inflamed with rage at these priests and Pharisees, whose hypocrisy revolted him. How so? For years, day after day, in the administration of the state, these people had opposed to him, Pilate, the representative of Caesar, their nation's autonomy, the immunities of their religion, which forbade them to recognize Caesar's divinity, the privileges of their cult, which obliged him to set down the imperial eagles outside the Temple, and today these same fierce defenders of Israel's traditions are taking Caesar's rights to heart and accusing him of not being Caesar's friend because for some obscure and unavowable reason they want the hide of one of their fellow citizens, which he does not want to give them. All this is going pretty far, and we are going to see what we shall see. Henceforth the fate of Jesus is decided; there is no longer any question about him, he is batted between the two camps like a tennis ball. They have said, "Whoever makes himself king . . ." Well and good, Pilate is going to take them at their word.

Pilate leads Jesus outside and presents him to them anew, arrayed as he now is as a King of Carnival.

John 19:14-15   PILATE: Behold, *your king!*
THEY: Away with him! Away with him! Crucify him!
PILATE: Shall I crucify *your king?*
THEY: We have *no other king but Caesar.*

This is what Pilate has been aiming at, this admission on the part of the chief priests. "Paris is well worth a Mass," as the heads of state say. For Pilate, no doubt, such a denial of the national pretensions of Israel John 19:16-17   was well worth the life of an innocent man. "Then he handed him over to them to be crucified. And so they took Jesus and led him away. And bearing the cross for himself, he went forth. . . ."

The chief priests have renounced everything: the Kingdom of God, the dynasty of David, the honor of the cult of the one God—for they knew very well that to recognize Caesar as their king was to adore him —even their Law, everything that constituted the glory of their nation, its predestination. But their hatred was satisfied: Jesus left the city excommunicated, he was going to be hung from the wood. Oh, when hatred enters your heart so as to govern it completely, be silent, flee, hide yourself, disappear, play dead, or be ready in advance to forswear all that you hold most precious, with honor in the lead!

It is almost thirty years since I have visited Vienna. One of the strongest reasons that make me want to return is to see once more the great
painting by Brueghel the Elder entitled "The Carrying of the Cross."
So far as I recall, one would say from a distance that it is an immense
bouquet of flowers. Approaching, one perceives that each of the "flowers" is a medallion, a separate scene treated in miniature. Then one
proceeds from discovery to discovery. I do not remember the details, or
rather I have lived so much with this picture in my heart, it has accompanied me so consistently, that I have surely invented details: there
are a man attacked by thieves, a woman abandoned, a man stabbed in
the back, a mother holding on her knees the body of her little child,
a leper with his bell, a woman giving birth in pain, a man in agony on
his deathbed, an accused before his judges, a condemned man about to
be hanged—I omit as much as I invent—but the significance of the picture I remember very well: it is an inventory of human pain. However,
among all those medallions, treated like any other, not even in the center of the picture, but placed at random in the mass, there is Jesus Christ
bearing his cross.

Brueghel understood that there is no longer any anguish, no longer
any distress in the world, in which Jesus Christ may not have his part,
he is one among us in our common misery, but it is not within the
power of any of us to prevent Jesus Christ from being, in fact, the companion of our misery. He has entered into the misery of man to such
a degree that there is, in truth, no longer any human sorrow in this
world that is altogether solitary. He has destroyed the solitude of our
sorrow. In Jesus Christ bearing his cross God has forced His way into
each one of our miseries. The ancient Jews had indeed divined that
there is no god closer to men than their God, but they had not divined
to what point that was possible, nor how it would be done. The ancient
mythologies, too, had divined that divinity seeks the association of men,
and it had invented this association through human passion, sensuality,
or anger. But that God holds communion with men in pain and in death
could be only a divine invention—it is so for me, it is the supreme seal
of the true religion, the sign of a love that is literally divine, the sacrament of divine freedom and invention in its love for us.

Thus God's plan for the establishment of His universal Kingdom was
accomplished, but so, no less, was the plan of Jesus' enemies. It is here
that Brueghel's painting obsesses me. Excommunicated, Jesus leaves
Jerusalem to die, but definitively and for eternity he founds a new Jerusalem, which, before being a Jerusalem of glory, is a Jerusalem of pain,
a new and solemn communion of God with men, the communion of the

miserable, by and through the unlimited interchange of his holy Passion.

The Gospels report that on this *via dolorosa* Jesus was accompanied by two malefactors, likewise condemned to death, who, like him, were carrying their crosses. These crosses were heavy. Since Jesus was exhausted by the anguish of the preceding night, the outrages of his trial and the torture of flagellation, it was feared that he would not last to the end, and on the way the services of a man returning from the fields were requisitioned. It is thus that Simon the Cyrenian came to aid Jesus in carrying his cross: this humble peasant, requisitioned by the police because of his physical vigor and inconsequential social position, has become the image of all Christian mystics. For the Passion of Jesus Christ has two meanings: it is true that through it God entered by force into our human misery, but it is also possible for us through love to enter, in our turn, into the Passion of Jesus Christ, to partake in it through our compassion. Christian holiness is, first of all, this compassion experienced in regard to the suffering and death of Jesus. The primary gesture of Christian sanctity will always be that of Simon the Cyrenian: to aid Jesus in carrying his cross.

I am certainly not going to make out of the communion of the miserable, which gravitates around the outraged Christ, a second Catholic Church to duplicate the first. I simply affirm that the significance and the grace of the Passion of Jesus Christ extend to all humanity, without regard to person: this sanguinary event, the death of Jesus, is the business of every man born of woman. What would the Catholic Church itself be without the Passion and death of Jesus, from which it was born? I simply wish to say what every child knows from his catechism—that even the catholicity of the Church is pierced with secret doors, that no destiny can become fully Christian without a return to the source of the Church, which is Christ on the cross. Who, for example, can measure what the prolonged, painful, and heroic death agony of John XXIII added to the pontificate of John XXIII? From a juridical point of view, nothing, nothing at all: he had been baptized, become a priest, bishop of Rome, pope, like any of his predecessors. And yet when, on his deathbed, he invoked with great cries the Ecumenical Council and the unity of the Church, that prayer, at that moment and on his lips, carried vastly farther than any encyclical.

Moreover, at this moment when Jesus, condemned to death, is ascending the slopes of Calvary, who is this man at his side, helping him carry his cross? It is neither the pope nor a bishop. The first pope, the first bishops, except for John, are not there. Where are they? The Gospels do not say, but the fact is they are not there. A few years later when the first pope himself will also be condemned to be crucified and when he will indeed by executed, head down, this death will add nothing to his pastoral jurisdiction, to his executive powers, to his authority as pope. It is not in the capacity of pope, or even as one baptized, that a person suffers and dies. It is in one's capacity as a human being and through the most common, the most universal, I was about to say the lowest, aspect of human nature, for, after all, animals too suffer and die. But the martyrdom of Saint Peter, the first pope, caused him to enter gloriously into his exalted place in the profound communion of woe and of the miserable, consecrated by the Passion of Jesus Christ. The first pope was not at Golgotha; he lost nothing by waiting. The supreme and most intimate dignity of man is to hold communion with Christ on the cross. And so Simon the Cyrenian was not pope or bishop, but he was at Calvary and on the right side—by chance, moreover, and perhaps in spite of himself. I cannot keep from believing that he is the leader and the representative of an innumerable multitude throughout the centuries who aid and assist Jesus in his Passion without even knowing who he is. It is easy to make a list of all the bishops in the world and even of all the priests, but the name of Simon the Cyrenian is not written in any register. He is content to aid Jesus in carrying his cross. It is this privilege, open to all, that has made possible my understanding of the painting of Brueghel the Elder.

Luke relates:

And as they led him away, they laid hold of a certain Simon of Cyrene, coming from the country, and upon him they laid the cross to bear it after Jesus. Now there was following him a great crowd of the people, and of women, who were bewailing and lamenting him. But Jesus turning to them said, "Daughters of Jerusalem, do not weep for me, but weep for yourselves and for your children. For behold, days are coming in which men will say, 'Blessed are the barren, and the wombs that never bore, and breasts that never nursed.' Then they will begin to say to the mountains, 'Fall upon us,' and to the hills, 'Cover us!' For if in the case of green wood they do these things, what is to happen in the case of the dry?" Now there were also two other malefactors led to execution with him.   Luke 23:26-32

Who were these "women of Jerusalem"? Disciples of Jesus? Perhaps. Or perhaps they were simple women touched by the misery of this man. More likely, however, they were a sisterhood of mourners whose custom it was to accompany these sinister processions of the condemned. In these circumstances it seems as though the whole honor of humanity rested in the hands of women. For after all, aside from Simon the Cyrenian, aside from Saint John, and aside, presently, from the good thief, one of the two malefactors condemned with him, men are there only as executioners or out of curiosity; as for the chief priests and the scribes, they are there to rejoice in the defeat of Jesus Christ and triumphantly reap the last breath of their vanquished adversary.

These women, for their part, are here through compassion, for the purpose of weeping. Since his brief exchange with Pilate, Jesus has been silent. He breaks his silence to speak to them. He warns them of the catastrophe that is going to fall upon Jerusalem and he adds, so natural with him is the genius for parable, "If green wood is treated thus, what will become of dry wood?" This means: the innocent no more deserves punishment than living wood, full of sap, is meant to be burned. Only dry wood is destined for the fire, like a culprit sent to his punishment. But if one goes to the extreme of punishing the innocent and burning green wood, what will happen to dry wood—and to sinners? Obviously in the first instance Jerusalem is meant, but beyond Jerusalem, all of us. Jesus positively did not come to eliminate misery, suffering, and death from human destiny, but only to give them the meaning of a supreme communion, of which he is the center of gravity. He, an innocent, voluntarily endured misery, suffering, and death, whereas he merited none of this. Why should we be amazed at having to submit to them, we sinners? The marvelous thing is that, since Golgotha, we can give them a meaning.

Jesus says to the women, "Weep for your children." I understand very well that the death of an infant makes the soul revolt. There are no considerations of reason to pit against such a revolt. Here one is beyond reasoning. Nevertheless an infant, however innocent he may be, is less so than Jesus Christ, he is of less green wood. But it is not a question of explaining and "justifying" the death of innocent infants. Jesus Christ does not explain his own death either, still less does he revolt against it. We feel, nevertheless, that if there is a lost secret that might, without betraying justice, without denying the honor of human solidarity, allow us—not to understand, that is impossible—but to accept without blaspheming the death of a little child, it is on the road of the cross that we can recover it, precisely, perhaps, because Jesus did not content himself with tracing out this *via dolorosa* on the map and indicating its stages, but opened it and trod it himself with his heavy burden; he entered upon it with a firm step, he traversed it to the end.

To the mind confronted by the whole problem of evil on the occasion of the death of an infant, there is no adequate answer, because in this world there is no adequate consolation for such a woe. There is only this man whose path intersects ours and who carries his cross. He has no answer either to our misery: he does not forbid us to weep; instead he recommends it: "Weep for your children." But, at least, what is called the problem of evil has become his cross, he will die on it. Christianity is not a harmonious and complete panoply of ready-made answers, it is a harassment of questions implanted in the living flesh. It is true that the cross of each one of us has the form of a question. Perhaps we are not required to find the answer but to submit honorably to the question until our final breath. The answer lies beyond this world.

And so here is Jesus on the road to Calvary. This man who has spoken so much now barely speaks at all; his hour has definitely come. He is going to seal with his personal and sacred misery the highest message of heroism and patience that men have ever heard. Has he been wrong? Has he been right? At least he is paying with his own person. And it is this, beyond the reasonings of our minds, that inclines our hearts to hope that he has been right.

The immense procession had reached its goal, and the crowd covered the hill. The execution began. In our modern societies trials are longer, but usually the execution is quick: the guillotine, the garrote, the electric chair, hanging, a bullet at the base of the skull, or a volley aimed at a man tied to the stake—all this is rapid as a dream. But execution by crucifixion has no end. This one will last for three hours and will be considered exceptionally short; crucifixion is the death of a man presented as a spectacle, and the spectacle should be prolonged. The cross is the gibbet, it is also the pillory; the proof of this is that at the top of the cross a notice is nailed, explaining the reason for the execution:

And Pilate also wrote an inscription and had it put on the cross. And there was written, JESUS OF NAZARETH, THE KING OF THE JEWS. Many of the Jews therefore read this inscription, because the place where Jesus was crucified was near the city; and it was written in Hebrew, in Greek, and in Latin. The chief priests of the Jews said therefore to Pilate, "Do not write, 'The King of the Jews,' but, 'He said, I am the King of the Jews.'" Pilate answered, "What I have written, I have written." *John 19:19-22*

Pilate is annoyed. Not because his hand has been forced and he has condemned an innocent man; after all, he is a statesman, and for him an injustice is better than disorder. What he cannot forgive the chief priests is their threat to appeal against him to Caesar. They have gone so far as to say: "We have no other King but Caesar." Thus the old story of a Jewish kingdom that will also be the Kingdom of God, this story that has been haunting the imagination of the Jewish people for two thousand years, ends here, liquidated, with the death of this ridiculous pretender. So let the King of the Jews be put in the pillory that one and all entering Jerusalem or leaving it may know that the King of the Jews has died the death of a criminal and that henceforth in this little corner of the earth there is one sole ruler, Caesar.

I know that as soon as we begin to explain the other aspect of this story unbelievers will accuse us of romancing. Just the same, it is no romance that Jesus had wished to die by crucifixion, that he had founded his universal Empire on his crucifixion ("When I shall be raised from the earth, I shall draw all to myself"), that, on Palm Sunday and even before Pilate, he had claimed the title King of the Jews and that he had always maintained he was instituting on earth that Kingdom of God that had in fact been promised to the Jews for two thousand years. The fact that Pilate, acting from the practical motives of a vindictive administrator, had underscored Jesus' claim by his notice, this fact more than Jesus' claim, more than his affirmation, reveals a conjuncture that is inexplicable except by the direct intervention of the Master of history, at a level of historical stage direction that dominates history and the unrolling of time.

In the light of the Jewish prophecy we are going to see more and more that the crucifixion proclaims and accomplishes the Kingdom of Jesus, that it is his consecration. The notice nailed to the summit of the cross by order of Pilate says so in its manner. Without knowing it, Pilate *prophesies,* as Caiphas had prophesied, "that Jesus was to die for the nation, and not only for the nation, but that he might gather into one the children of God who were scattered abroad."

No, all this, even though in a double meaning, is absolutely not a fable, and, at the moment, the literal sense is frightful. Jesus Christ was really crucified. Here my courage extends only far enough to copy what that honest exegete Father Lagrange has written:

The first Christians had a horror of representing Christ on the cross, for they had seen with their own eyes those poor bodies, completely naked, attached to a rough stake surmounted in the form of a T by a transverse bar, their hands nailed to this gibbet, their feet also affixed by nails, their bodies sagging under their own weight, their heads bobbing, dogs, attracted by the odor of blood, devouring their feet, vultures wheeling above this field of carnage, and the victims exhausted by torture, burning with thirst and calling for death in inarticulate cries. It was the torture of slaves and of bandits. This was what Jesus endured. . . . And so they crucified him, first nailing his hands to the gibbet, which they then raised on the upright stake, callously jostling his tormented body. The Fathers were not

John 12:32

John 11:51-52

at all scandalized by complete nudity. Nevertheless, since the Jews spared even those they tortured from this, it is to be believed that the Romans respected their custom. When they began to crucify Jesus, it was barely past midday. . . . Then the two bandits were likewise crucified, one to the right, the other to the left. This was the soldiers' final mockery of the King of the Jews: these highwaymen were given the places of honor beside him. Isaia had announced that he would be counted among the wicked.

Thus the double meaning continues. The prophecy alluded to is at the end of the Song of the Servant of Yahweh, which I have quoted in connection with the washing of the Apostles' feet by Jesus. There is no doubt that this Messianic song had at once the meaning of a universal redemption from sin, of a supreme humiliation of the suffering Messiah and at the same time of his final and supreme triumph: the cross of Jesus is his throne. ". . . through his suffering, my servant shall justify many, and their guilt he shall bear. Therefore I will give him his portion among the great, and he shall divide the spoils with the mighty, because he surrendered himself to death and was counted among the wicked; and he shall take away the sins of many, and win pardon for their offenses." Isa. 53:11-12

Here then, planted in the middle of the world, is the tree of the cross, with its fruit come to maturity. It is here that we must see the result of Jesus' whole life and of his words as well, in the first instance the culmination of the parables concerning the seed. Here we must see, too, the issue of the whole tradition of Israel that goes back to the Promise made concerning the seed of Abraham and, no doubt, as far back as the story of the terrestrial paradise, where the tree of life was planted in the midst of the garden, and where, after the fall, emnity was declared between the seed of the serpent and the seed of man. The seed of Abraham is now the tree of life planted in the new garden, it is the natural development of the Kingdom of God: "What is the kingdom of God like, and to what shall I liken it? It is like a grain of mustard seed, which a man took and cast into his own garden; and it grew and became a large tree, and the birds of the air dwelt in its branches." Luke 13:18-19

Let us forget that we are Cartesians or mathematicians, let us forget our realistic logic, let us enter into a dialectic more profound and more true, the dialectic of life. It is true that the grown oak is contained, virtually, in the acorn and that the most majestic oak is only the acorn, plus the whole of heaven and of earth, the acorn plus the adventure of that living seed. The oak cannot deny its origins, but it cannot deny, either, the earth that bears it or the sky that embraces. Such is Jesus on the cross, planted in the soil of Israel and embracing the sky. The garden, the seed, the tree, these are the real symbols that haunt all of Jewish history, from the first garden, where Adam sinned, to this present garden, where the second Adam is going to die, ransoming through regeneration the whole human race, by virtue of the cross that is planted here and here becomes the axis of the universe.

> And in this dream of his Boas beheld an oak
> Rooted in his own belly, its summit reached the sky;
> Up it there climbed a race of men, chain-like,
> A King sang at its foot, on high a God was dying.

The poetical and mystical identity of Israel with a tree, like that with the miraculous (divine) seed of Abraham, has always been proclaimed by the Jews, even by the great rabbis of the Middle Ages, at least those of them who had not (like Maimonides) too far rationalized their religion. Judah ha-Levi, prince of eleventh-century Jewish poets, thus explains the Diaspora, without seeming to perceive how far his text is applicable to the assembly of humanity around the cross: "It is a secret and sage design of God; thus it is with the wisdom hidden in the *seed*, planted in the ground, where, invisible to sight, it seems to unite with earth and the water; but in the end the *seed* transforms the earth and the water into its own substance, purifies the elements and bears *fruit*. . . . Thus the nations pave the way for the expected Messiah who is the *fruit*, for all serve his *fruit*. And if they recognize him, all will be but *a single tree*." I have never read a more beautiful definition of the ideal catholicity of the Church: it is the Tree of the Cross, identifying itself with the nations and redeeming them through its fruit.

Hatred, envy, and jealousy are immersed in time, they live only on a short-term basis, from day to day. Prophecy and poetic genius transcend time and its reversals. The enemies of Jesus Christ believe they have triumphed: their miserable and shabby plan, the plan of jurists and tabbycats, this plan has succeeded, here is Jesus hung from the wood, in accord with the malediction of the Law. And nevertheless, in the same real occurrence, precisely the same one, the prophecy and the Promise are being fulfilled at the same time. The *seed* of Abraham, in which all nations are eternally blessed, here has become the *tree* on the mountain, spreading in the sky and bearing *fruit*, according to the famous anthem of the time of the Advent: "O Root of Jesse, planted as a standard for the people, the Kings look upon you and raise their hands to their lips, the nations come to supplicate you." Yes, the Tree of Israel, in which, according to the poem of Judah ha-Levi all nations should unite in order to share in the benediction of its fruit, this tree is Jesus Christ on the cross. It is this that we Christians know and confess: God has kept His word, given to Abraham, and we are all, Christians, Jews, men, women, believers and nonbelievers, yes, all, blessed, if we wish to be, in Jesus crucified.

This is what Saint Paul in his magnificently precise language calls "the Israel of God":

But as for me, God forbid that I should *glory* save in the cross of our Lord Jesus Christ, through whom the world is crucified to me, and I to the world. For in Christ Jesus neither circumcision nor uncircumcision but a new creation is of any account. And whoever follow this rule, peace and mercy upon them, even upon the Israel of God. Henceforth let no man give me trouble, for I bear the marks of the Lord Jesus in my body.   Gal. 6:14-17

Since in this section of my book I have decided to reconcile myself to quotations, here again is Claudel's invocation to the Tree, in which I hear a thousand echoes of the ancient prophecy:

O Tree, receive me! It was all alone that I went out from the protection of your boughs, now it is all alone that I turn back to you, O my unmoving father!

Then take me again beneath your shade, O son of Earth, O wood, in this my hour of need! O murmurer, inform me

Of the word that is I, whose dreadful effort stirs in me!

You, you are one continuous effort, the drawing forth of your own body steadily from lifeless stuff.

How you, old man, suckle at the earth,

Forcing deep your roots, subtle and strong, scattering them this way and that! And the sky, how you hold on to it! How you bind yourself entire

To its aspiration in one huge leaf, Form of Fire!

The inexhaustible earth in the embrace of all your being's roots

And the infinite sky, with sun, with stars in the procession of the Year,

Where you cling fast with that mouth made of all your arms, with the bouquet of your body, seizing it with all in you that breathes,

The earth and sky in their entirety, these needs must be that you may stand erect!

So may I too stand upright! That I lose not my soul! This quintessential sap, this moisture within myself, this effervescence

Whose subject is the person that I am, may I not lose it in some trifling tuft of grass and flowers! May I grow large in my own unity! . . .

Here the poet goes astray, and his tree is still pagan. In the whole world there is only one true way of holding oneself upright without pride and without rigidity; that is to be nailed to the same cross with Jesus crucified. It is the Law that dies for having nailed God to the wood. God does not die.

Gal. 2:19-21 For I through the Law have died to the Law that I may live to God. With Christ I am nailed to the cross. It is now no longer I that live, but Christ lives in me. And the life that I now live in the flesh, I live in the faith of the Son of God, who loved me and gave himself up for me. I do not cast away the grace of God. For if justice is by the Law, then Christ died in vain.

Did Christ die in vain? To this question, in so far as they raise it, traditional Judaism and the modern world reply that he did in fact die in vain. Under the influence of the Pharisees, Judaism in the time following the destruction of Jerusalem attached itself fiercely to a Law that had murdered the Messiah God. It preferred the servitude and the guilt of the Law to the freedom from sin and the grace brought by Jesus on the cross. The modern world, too, prefers the Old Testament to the New; modern literature is full of avowals of the guilt of man. But, no less, it denies the grace of God. At bottom men easily lose their taste for liberty: I have known men in the depths of hideous prison cells who, when presented with a chance to escape, have refused to do so. "What's the good?" they said. They also feared the risk. For an escape always involves risks, and the escape from sin by means of the cross of Jesus Christ is man's supreme risk. He who does not see this understands nothing about Christianity.

Jesus, nailed to the cross, speaks in the face of heaven. He has spoken to Judas, he has spoken to Caiphas, he has spoken to Pilate, he has just spoken to the daughters of Jerusalem, and now, raised up from the earth,
Luke 23:34 his first words are for God: "Father," he says, "forgive them. They know not what they do." The first words of Jesus on the cross are in fact for the purpose of freeing man from the burden of his guilt. One cannot fail to admire the grandeur and the generosity of this prayer. So long as it is only a question of himself, Christ's prayer remained conditional: "Father, if it is possible, let this cup pass from me!" Now that it is a question of his enemies and his executioners, Christ's prayer becomes imperative: "Father, forgive!" We will never know—because habitually we are not very much interested in learning—the good that we can do our enemies simply by a prayer of command to God. Christ adds this judgment, which is a judgment not only of mercy but of truth, for it admirably expresses the sadness of the human condition: "They know not what they do."

This is literally true: these people did not know what they were doing.
Acts 3:17-18 Saint Peter underscores this afresh after the Resurrection: "And now, brethren, I know that you acted in ignorance, as did also your rulers. But in this way God fulfilled what he had announced beforehand by the

mouth of all the prophets, namely that his Christ should suffer." Still the double meaning. Thus the wicked plan of men coincides very precisely with the merciful design of God. Christ's enemies were criminals, but they believed their crime was commonplace, they were ignorant of the sublime correspondence that raised it to the level of the implementation of prophecy. Blind as they certainly were, they did not know, nor did they want to know, that Jesus was the Lord of Glory. This unawareness and this ambiguity are tragic: even in the midst of their crime they are the instruments of a necessary and infallible prophecy, but a prophecy that is beyond them. This does not, of course, excuse them, any more than it excuses all those who persecute the saints, the poor, the defenseless and unhappy in order to teach them a lesson.

As for God, the first supplication of Jesus on the cross is that He should pardon these criminals. By what prodigious aberration, in clear contradiction to these solemn words, will Christians in the succeeding centuries persist in persecuting the Jewish people on the pretext of avenging the murder of Jesus Christ?

Blessed be this imperious supplication of Jesus to his Father, blessed be it for the Jews, blessed be it for all of us, even and above all if we prefer our guilt to our deliverance! We hardly know what we do and we are in great need of forgiveness. The peoples gaze upon Christ on the cross, raised like a standard on the mountain, the kings raise their hands to their lips, but God, too, looks upon His Son hanging from the Tree of Israel. In the name of the Law He is required to curse him, but He cannot curse His well-loved Son; it is the Law that is dishonored, and all those who lay claim to Christ can henceforth survive without the Law.

Nor will God curse Israel, either, that is His elected seed, that is His tree, that is His vine; He will judge the tree by its fruit, and, however grievous it may be, this fruit is Jesus Christ. It is God Himself who planted the Tree of Israel, He will never forget it, even if He persists in His age-old quarrel with the race of Abraham. May we not, before the cross, that bears the weight of His Son, who is also a son of Israel, place in God's mouth these tragic words?

> At last, it grew, and grew, and bore and bore,
> Till at the length,
> It grew a gallows, and did bear our son,
> It bore thy fruit and mine. . . .

This heartbreaking plaint of a father in Kyd's *Spanish Tragedy* ends with an imprecation: "Oh wicked, wicked plant!" But the cross, on the contrary, reverses all maledictions. This tree is forever blessed by its fruit.

John 19:23-24   John continues his account: "The soldiers therefore, when they had crucified him, took his garments and made of them four parts, to each soldier a part, and also the tunic. Now the tunic was without seam, woven in one piece from the top. They therefore said to one another, "Let us not tear it, but let us cast lots for it, to see whose it shall be. . . . These things therefore the soldiers did."

The Gospels speak only of the division of his clothes by lot among the soldiers, but this obviously implies that Jesus was first stripped. Christian piety is deeply moved by this moment when Jesus was publicly unclothed; it has been made into a Station of the Cross. Actually it was a matter of course. The condemned were undressed before being crucified.

Thus, just as he had been born naked in Bethlehem, Jesus will die naked. Nakedness can be the occasion for sensuality and pleasure; we are so obsessed with eroticism that we think of that first of all. On reflection, nakedness is rather the sign of a solemn efficacy: athletes wrestle naked in the stadium; the patient is placed naked on the operating table, as is the victim on the altar; it was naked that the miserable victims of the death factories were herded pell-mell into the gas chambers; and, if the procreation of a man takes place in nakedness, body to body, the implantation of a man's seed and the transmission of life are nevertheless a great and solemn event, a fine and sacred thing. Nature denudes herself before the vital upsurge of spring. Jesus is naked like a wrestler, confronting Satan in one final contest, and the oil that anoints his body is his own blood. He embraces the cross and procreates a new race, "a new creature," Saint Paul says: he remodels and recreates the universe. And it is true: Jesus' Passion and his crucifixion, this terrible embrace of Jesus, body to body with his cross, are the instrument of reconciliation of the universe with God through the recreation of that same universe.

The stripping naked of Jesus has another analogy, foretold by Jesus himself. On the threshing floor, the flail strips the grain of its husk. It is naked that the grain is ground to make bread, it is naked that the grain is cast into the ground to die, and to give birth to new harvests. Thus it was with Jesus Christ: here the chaff is definitively separated from the wheat.

The spoils of the condemned man belonged traditionally to his executioners. Christ's robe being seamless and for that reason of special value, the soldiers drew lots for it, not wanting to tear it. This, then, was Jesus' ordinary garb, his everyday dress: a robe of such value as to make the soldiers covet it and to awaken their respect. It follows that Jesus, during the course of his life, was not dressed in rags like some poor outcast: this needs to be said because it is true.

The primitives and the Byzantine painters have represented Christ on the cross between the sun and the moon, ordering the whole sky and its constellations. To the very end, in fact, he remains who he is, master of the universe, infinitely dominant over time by reason of his eternity, and to the end he will be at pains to manifest this sovereignty—to which I shall return. Jesus, then, controls the necessary revolutions of the stars, but at the same time, at the foot of the cross, the soldiers are throwing dice: it is strange to see him thus governing the play of chance as well. The Church Fathers considered that the seamless robe symbolized the unity of the Church, which must not on any account be torn. Did they push the analogy further still to the thought that this unity of the Church could be left to chance? I think not. But I believe that to preserve the unity of the Church, or to re-establish it, it is also necessary to love and respect it just as the soldiers appreciated and respected the seamless robe enough not to want to tear it. They preferred chance to exact justice. The law of "to each his due" would have required division of the robe, and this division they did not want.

John continues: "Now there were standing by the cross of Jesus his mother and his mother's sister, Mary of Cleophas, and Mary Magdalene. When Jesus, therefore, saw his mother and the disciple standing by, whom he loved, he said to his mother, 'Woman, behold, thy son.' Then he said to the disciple, 'Behold, thy mother.' And from that hour the disciple took her into his home." John 19:25-27

Aside from the miracle at Cana three years before and one brief appearance when she seems to have been involved, rather against her will, in the actions of a stupid and turbulent family, little has been seen of Jesus' mother since the beginning of his public life. Now she is here at the foot of the cross. And John, the only one of the Apostles, the only one of the bishops of the primitive Church, quite alone—he has regained his self-possession, he is there too. As for Mary Magdalene, she would move mountains to remain with her Lord. Mary, mother of Jesus, is accompanied by a relation, a sister or cousin, named Mary, too, and married to Cleophas. That is all. The little group of fearless and faithful ones huddles together at the foot of the cross.

Yes, one can truly say that the Virgin Mary has not encumbered her son's career. She was not even present on Palm Sunday, but she is here, intrepid and upright, in sorrow, at the foot of the gibbet.

> *Stabat Mater dolorosa,*
> *Juxta Crucem lacrymosa,*
> *Dum pendebat Filius.*

Jesus' birth and his death on the cross, these are the two occasions on which the Gospel assigns to Mary a place of the very first importance. As for his birth, that is altogether natural, he could not do without a mother. But the presence of Mary at the foot of the cross takes on all the greater importance. Christian piety has meditated profoundly and assiduously on the destiny of this woman, seeking out all its implications of joy and sorrow, of heroism and glory. One can say that, at the foot of the cross, Mary's spiritual and literally divine motherhood triumphs definitively over the ties of biology. I shall explain.

What Christians venerate in the mother of Jesus is, of course, the physical and natural fact of her motherhood, which reached its term in the very Person of the Word incarnate. She is truly the mother of God, through physical and natural maternity. She bore in her womb the Seed of God, she was heavy with God, she brought God into the world. But this motherhood is not limited to its biological function, it blossomed into a spiritual maternity, and through this Mary deserves even greater admiration and honor. Indeed, motherhood that remains merely biological quickly takes on the possessive and tyrannical characteristics of all things biological. There is nothing honorable in this. Every day we see destructive and ignoble aspects of motherhood, the scourge of "mama's boys," who are even more contemptible than "papa's boys." Modern medicine has documented the horrible consequences of this excessive motherliness. An American magazine recounted a highly significant case history, which I have carefully preserved. Here is a summary of it.

One day, in a Minnesota clinic, the specialist in treating and re-educating those crippled by polio was shown a poor wretch in a wheel chair. He was thirty-seven years old. Since the age of fifteen he had been paralyzed in one position, bent over, his knees under his chin. For twenty-two years he had not changed this position. His mother, who had looked after him with unwearying devotion for all this time, claimed that the paralysis was the result of poliomyelitis. There followed medical examinations, treatment, massage, therapeutic baths—with no result. The account of the attack of poliomyelitis appeared suspect. One day a doctor pointed out that this man of thirty-seven, otherwise in good health, maintained exactly the posture of a fetus in its mother's womb. This had not been noticed before, but, once it was, the results were startling. The patient was given treatment by hypnotism. General amazement: insofar as the muscular habit of twenty-two years permitted it, his limbs began to loosen and extend. His mother was furious.

This is what had happened. Separated from his mother for the first time at the age of fifteen, the boy had suffered an attack of nervous bronchitis; then suddenly his body had contracted and become rigid in the position of a fetus in the maternal sac. No less instinctively, his mother entered into the game and devoted her life to caring for him— with a devotion, moreover, that excited the admiration of all those near her. "I like him just the way he is," she kept repeating. To the last moment she was opposed to medical treatment—in the name of absolute maternal love, of course. She was indeed a mother and she was nothing more. Nevertheless, thanks to the authority of a chaplain (a Catholic, by the way), the doctors succeeded in curing this thirty-seven-year-old baby.

I know of no story better calculated to deflate the literature of maternal love. Biological motherhood, to be sure, has a nourishing function that is necessary in the first stages of life, but if it is not transformed later into disinterested love, it becomes simply and completely monstrous.

It is here that we again encounter the Virgin Mary, mother of Jesus Christ, and discover her whole incomparable grandeur. One might be tempted to deplore the Gospels' extreme reticence about her. To me it is the brilliant proof of the infinite respect she had for her son, for her son's liberty, for her son's mission, and for the manner in which he expected to accomplish that mission. She was the very first to understand who he was. She knew that the primitive umbilical connection did not confer upon her any permanent authority over him, that the commands of his Father in heaven would always be stronger for him than any human ties. The wonderful thing was that the bonds, uniting Jesus Christ with human nature (the first of which was in fact the umbilical cord) became the very channels of divine grace and of our redemption. It is through his mother that Christ is primarily united with that human nature which he came to purify, heal, sanctify, and save.

During the whole of Christ's public life his mother practically disappears from the scene. She does not reappear until Calvary: it is here that she completes and fulfills her own mission, that of divine motherhood. It is not a son curled up on himself in the crouching posture of a fetus, in desperate need of the warmth and protection of the maternal womb, that Mary gave to the world; it is man erect, planted straight, his arms extended, identified with the tree that embraces the sky. It is so rare that a mother voluntarily transcends biology that one might ask whether the Virgin Mary is not even more precious here than in her original dignity as Virgin Mother. She has surmounted the maternal instinct of biological possessiveness, she has entered into the talent and generosity that are Christ's. She gives her son freely, like a beautiful fruit; the cross replaces her in the maternal task of supporting that fruit. She has relinquished all biological ownership in her son in order to enter into the poverty of the Kingdom of God. To none more than to her does the first of the Beatitudes more perfectly apply: "Blessed are you poor, for yours is the Kingdom of God." She is bereft of her son, and for this the Kingdom of God is hers to such a degree that she holds its seals and is its doorkeeper.

Luke 6:20

Unbelievers naturally refuse to admit the virginal motherhood of Mary. Nevertheless, what have they to object to this miraculous motherhood? Nothing, except the habit of relying on law and the belief that law cannot be transgressed. There is a secular, millennial, universal way of making children, and it must not be derogated. This is a juridical attitude, most basely juridical, almost that of the police state, absolutely unphilosophical. For, closely observed, the anatomical structure of the eye or even the natural process of conception is not less marvelous than a virgin birth: chance does not create these things. It is noteworthy that the minds most opposed to miracles are the most commonplace, the least poetic, the least sensitive to the marvels of nature, to its perpetual renewal: for, after all, each day is the world's first day. Does not the void encircle all things today as yesterday, are all things any more explicable today than yesterday?

The Virgin Mary, through the miracle of her motherhood, had understood that this child of hers did not, despite that motherhood, belong to her and that the destiny of this man transcended her to an infinite degree. Now she is here at the foot of the cross, where in fact the destiny of this miraculous child is being fulfilled. "When Jesus, therefore, saw his mother and the disciple standing by, whom he loved, he said to his mother, 'Woman . . .'" This is one of those passages in the Gospel that have caused pious commentators the greatest embarrassment. It is true that among the Semites this mode of address—"Woman!"—is simply normal and courteous, too formal, perhaps, in these circumstances. What mother, attending her dying son, would not want to be called "Mother" by him for a last time? Moreover, anyone familiar with battlefields and field hospitals knows very well that the cry that comes of itself to the lips of a young man faced by death is, precisely, "Mama!"

But, observe, Jesus Christ does not die crying "Mama!" It is, rather, the contrary that happens.

For what follows is still harsher. Jesus selects for his mother a substitute for himself. He selects one among his disciples whom he loves most, the only one of his disciples, in fact, who is present. "Woman, behold your son!" Whatever the virtues of Saint John, when one has been the mother of Jesus Christ this cannot but mean a great fall. Jesus could certainly have said these things more gently, but he chose to say them thus. It is a harsh testament. He truly wishes to cut the umbilical cord and to die free of all purely biological bonds. This represents unheard-of heroism and, to me, is the most sublime expression of virginity. Moreover, for Mary Magdalene, who, true to her custom, remains prostrate at the feet of her master, Jesus Christ has not a single word. Only a few minutes of life remain to him: he is not going to give up these supreme minutes to the tenderness of women. However harsh it may have been, there can be no doubt that the Virgin Mary has fully accepted her son's testament. She has understood its meaning perfectly. She too has cut the umbilical cord. She has not wanted to monopolize or hold back her son, to draw him once more to her maternal bosom; on the contrary, she is reconciled to seeing him grown to the full stature of a complete man, extended on the cross (yes, truly the opposite of the uterine position) upright, crucified, bent like a bow with its arrow and already breathed in by the sky. Here the Virgin Mary emerges definitively from the whole biological dialectic to enter herself into the heart of her son's mission. Here, more even than in Bethlehem, she is the model for all Christian motherhood: her motherhood becomes all heroism.

By wholeheartedly accepting the harsh testament given her by her son, Mary enters more deeply than she has yet done into her own function of divine motherhood. She accepts in her own heart what is closest to the heart of her son. By adopting as her own son the disciple that Jesus loved, Mary, in concert with Jesus, gives birth to the very work of our redemption. She is the mother of God, and she becomes even more so, if one may speak thus, by adopting into her spacious motherhood poor, sinful humanity. She sees her son dying, but she understands what is happening on the cross: the reconciliation of the universe with God, through the purification and the re-creation of that same universe. Her motherhood grows wider, taking on the very dimensions of the supreme work of her son, the redemption from sins. True that her son did not call upon her as he died, he deliberately left her available for each one of us. This is why it is possible for us, all of us, to call upon her with complete confidence: "Holy Mary, Mother of God, pray for us poor sinners now *and at the hour of our death*. Amen."

Jesus speaks. The little group of the faithful beneath the gibbet does not. Not a sound comes from the lips of the young man or the three women. In view of the malediction of the Law, horror chokes their breath at the spectacle their eyes contemplate. John, who will die a very old man, will preserve these tragic memories to the end of his life. With him they will have the clarity that memories of youth have for old men. This is why his Gospel has the preciseness of a police-court record.

Around the cross, Jesus' enemies have no such reason for being silent. They are triumphant, they cannot get over their victory over this man. They cannot suppress their satisfaction, their sarcasm, and their joy. To insult those condemned to death at the very moment of their execution is rare, but it can happen, for we too have seen it with our own eyes. In reality the execution of Jesus follows so close upon his condemnation that it has almost the violent, hysterical, mad atmosphere of a lynching. One is forced to recognize how thoroughly Jesus has upset the society around him, interfered with its interests, threatened its privileges, insulted its fanaticisms, to be so fiercely and so consistently hated even on his gibbet, even at the moment of death, when hatred ordinarily lays down its arms.

Mark 15:29-32   Mark recounts: "And the passers-by were jeering at him, shaking their heads, and saying, 'Aha, thou who destroyest the temple, and in three days buildest it up again; come down from the cross, and save thyself!' In like manner, the chief priests with the Scribes said in mockery to one another, 'He saved others, himself he cannot save! Let the Christ, the King of Israel, come down now from the cross, that we may see and believe.'" This is truly a case of "Woe to the vanquished!" Alas, it is human!

I am struck by the fact that at this supreme moment there occurs once more spontaneously—this time with derisive intent—a reference to the prophetic parable in which Jesus symbolically identified his own body with the Temple, traditional seat of the glory of God and sacred dwelling place of His Presence. Jesus' enemies believe they are mocking him; they have never spoken more accurately. The double meaning continues. Yes, it is precisely this parable, so obscure to us but so clear in the Jewish milieu as to seem blasphemous, that is recalled here, at the foot of the cross, in an attempt to convict Jesus of imposture. This shows that it had been understood and that people saw the claim to personal intimacy with God on Jesus' part implied in this analogy of his body with the Temple. But what superior power forces those scribes and priests to recall precisely this prophecy of Jesus when it is on the point of realization? Ought not elementary prudence have counseled them to wait until the "three days" he spoke of were in fact over? They cannot keep from experiencing a presentiment of the immense surprise in store for them. Over this insult addressed to Jesus the very day of his death, as over all the torments that were inflicted upon him, there hovers irrefutable irony.

They add: "Let the Christ, the King of Israel, come down from the cross, that we may see and believe." Jesus has performed enough miracles in his life to be able to perform this one too: it would not have convinced his enemies any more than the others. Moreover, for him it is no longer a question of performing miracles and proving his power. He has performed all those miracles so that people may go on believing in him even when he no longer performs them, and the moment for no longer performing them has come. For Jesus it is now a question of giving meaning to his death and proving through it not his power but his love. "Christ and King of Israel," this he is. His Kingdom is of love. The great portal of this Kingdom is suffering and death. The cross of Jesus is his throne; were he to descend from it now, it would mean that he was abdicating, together with his own mission, the Kingdom of God which is his.

The Gospel goes on to describe the episode of the two thieves crucified with Jesus:

Now one of those robbers who were hanged was abusing him, saying, "If thou art the Christ, save thyself and us!" But the other in answer rebuked him and said, "Dost not even thou fear God, seeing that thou art under the same sentence? And we indeed justly, for we are receiving what our deeds deserved; but this man has done nothing wrong." And he said to Jesus, "Lord, remember me when thou comest into thy kingdom." And Jesus said to him, "Amen I say to thee, this day thou shalt be with me in paradise." *Luke 23:39-43*

This is the last conversation Jesus had during his mortal life, here is the last testimony to his divine majesty, the last profession of faith in his title of King of a realm that transcends death. And who is the man who renders our Lord this ultimate and sublime homage? The pope? No: Saint Peter is weeping for his denial, he is hidden and silent. The Apostles? No: aside from Saint John they are not there either, and, in the sequel, we shall see clearly enough that the first bishops have lost heart. This final, clear, and public homage comes to Jesus from a man whom, three hours before, he had never encountered. What sort of man? A brigand, crucified with him, who receives the ransom for his crimes and who, at the same time, confesses those crimes, the justice of his punishment, and the royal divinity of Jesus Christ. It is he whom Christian piety has tenderly named "the good thief."

There is no evidence in the Gospels that Jesus spent much time with bandits: there was no occasion for it. And now in a half-day, the last day of his mortal life, his destiny becomes intimately involved with that of three brigands: Barabbas and the two thieves crucified at the same time as Jesus. This is a great deal in a few hours. Jesus has taken Barabbas' place on the cross, or, if you like, Barabbas has taken Jesus' place in freedom. At any event, it is Jesus who is here, crucified like an outlaw, with two other outlaws. Another man would have protested against such company; Jesus accepts it, and his last conversation is with one of these two wretches. He did not have conversation with his mother or with Saint John: he alone spoke, they were silent. But with the good thief there is a real exchange, and of what sort? Of a kind to bring hope to the farthest fallen among us:

> *Qui Mariam absolvisti,*
> *Et latronem exaudisti,*
> *Mihi quoque spem dedisti.*

This hardened bandit suddenly experienced an illumination of the heart. He saw clearly. From the height of his cross everything suddenly became visible before him, as after a long night there comes the immense enlargement of the dawn. He saw the other side of things. His own torment, that of Jesus, the supreme derision of this execution and this pillory, the obvious defeat of all temporal glory, the infamy of this gibbet—none of all this kept the good thief from perceiving in his companion in misery the King-Messiah promised for millennia to Israel and proclaimed, ironically and truthfully, in the notice written by Pilate.

There is a privileged familiarity in sharing in the same torture. Never are lovers in the same bed or friends at the same table closer to one another than two soldiers sharing the same danger or two condemned men executed at the same time. Obviously this sad communion can be refused, and that is what the bad thief does, brazenly unrepentant even on the cross. But the good thief, who must know him well, calls him to order. In a supernatural moment of illumination—and such moments are more frequent than is thought—the good thief perceives that his opportunity, the opportunity of his whole life, is here, in this place of torture called Calvary, or, in Hebrew, Golgotha. He sees, clear as day, that he was created, put into this world, that he was born and has lived, only for what is happening now, to be, in the supreme agony, in torture, in dishonor and death, the companion of God and to render testimony to this fact.

He understands that this unawaited and sublime companionship transforms his shameful situation into glory. This companionship makes him a Prophet: truly so, for the good thief speaks like Daniel of the "Son of Man" who is dying on the cross at his side, he speaks as the angel Gabriel himself spoke to Mary at the moment of the Annunciation: "The Lord God will give him the throne of David his father, and he shall be king over the house of Jacob forever; and of his kingdom there shall be no end." Yes, between the angel who spoke to Mary in the little house in Nazareth and this brigand who speaks familiarly to Jesus Christ on his cross, like one soldier speaking familiarly to another in the smoke of battle, the continuity is perfect. In the tone, at once tender and imperious, that soldiers actually use under fire the brigand says, "Lord, remember me when thou comest into thy kingdom." He does not beseech, he commands. This imperial right is his because of his companionship with Jesus on the cross. After all, there will never be any but him to exercise this special right.

Luke 1:32-33

Luke 23:42

It is in this fashion that the last shall be first. This bandit has understood what neither Caiphas nor Pilate understood, that Jesus is truly King, that his Kingdom is not of this world, that the coming of this Kingdom is suffering and death, that the cross of Jesus is his throne, and that this same Jesus, in accordance with what the Prophets have said, will return on the clouds of the sky to judge the living and the dead. It is to be noted that this convicted criminal did not choose the time of miracles and public acclamation to confess the royalty of our Lord. He laughs at the opinion of the chief priests, of the scribes, and of the cautious pedants of all times, those who, with their feet solidly planted on the ground, blaspheme Jesus Christ. No, he chose the moment of the most extreme humiliation and total abandonment of our Lord. How close this bandit is to our heart: it is not our desire, either, to believe in the divine royalty of Jesus because of his miracles. Actually at this moment the good thief is alone, absolutely alone, in confessing the royalty of Jesus. This fact represents such a reversal of apparent values that the good thief seems to me the paragon of nonconformism and of the revolutionary spirit. The most remarkable thing is that he should be right. Jesus is King through his cross, sign of his devoted love, more than through his miracles, the sign of his power.

In connection with this bandit I have something on my heart. In the course of two thousand years of Christianity and the liturgical cycle, it seems to me that a feast day might well have been dedicated to the good thief. The Virgin Mary of course has her feasts. Mary Magdalene has one, too, and it is well merited, despite her persecution by the exegetes who have cut her into fragments. Saint John has his as well. Even the other Apostles and first pope, who at this moment are hiding like moles, have their feast days on the calendar—and this is proper, they are the pillars of the Church. But for the good thief, not a thing, the year has not enough days to include him. It must be that he makes the parish priests uncomfortable and frightens the panegyrists. The man who enters the parish only for his last hour is not a model parishioner. He is obviously not the sort of fellow that one would like to encounter on a dark road. The Romans eliminated him, and it is altogether likely that our modern societies would do the same. Furthermore, he is of the same opinion, he considers his own punishment just. In short, he is not proper company, no feast day for him.

He, of course, laughs at this: it suffices him to be the companion in misery of Jesus Christ, his first martyr, he who is the first to receive the baptism of blood and of desire. This brigand has retained enough sense of justice to be indignant, not at his own torture, which he accepts, but at the torture inflicted on Jesus Christ. I find that he is exemplary after all. He has no social connection with Jesus, absolutely none, not of friendship, not of apostolic or sacerdotal mission, not of papal authority, nothing except the chance companionship of this crucifixion and, then, this profession of the faith of the miserable in their Lord, the redemption from sins granted to this profession of faith, and finally the promise of paradise made by him who is King of paradise.

In his long confidences of the preceding night Jesus said, addressing God: "Now this is everlasting life, that they may know thee, the only true God, and him whom thou hast sent, Jesus Christ." Just so, the good thief on his cross has truly recognized Jesus Christ for who he is. It is his eternal glory to have confessed him at this moment. His reward was immediate: "This very day you will be with me in paradise." He entered paradise on Good Friday, before any of the other saints, his feast day is Good Friday: obviously it is impossible to celebrate that day. But in paradise, where he is, he remains the only saint canonized by Jesus Christ himself, even though he is not in the calendar. On reflection, moreover, we realize that we do not even know this man's name, he has not so much as been introduced to us, how can one give his name to a child at baptism? He is a smuggler in paradise.

John 17:3

And yet what Christian worthy of that name would not give all the kingdoms of the earth and their glory to receive from Jesus on the cross the promise that this man received, the promise of paradise? Moreover, what wretched outlaw, rejected by everyone, would not give his life to be in the place of this brigand and, like him, to make his profession of faith in Jesus, Prince of the tortured and king of paradise? Mary Magdalene, she who also received from those same lips the forgiveness of her sins, was there at the foot of her master's cross. She heard the confession of the good thief and Jesus' promise: if she ever envied anyone in the world, it was surely this bandit on his cross, at that moment.

One day, at the time of Jesus' great triumph, amid the miracles, when all the people were crying "Hosanna!" a woman approached him and made, on behalf of her two sons, almost the same request that the good thief made on his cross. "Then the mother of the sons of Zebedee came to him with her sons; and worshiping, she made a request of him. He said to her, 'What dost thou want?' She said to him, 'Command that these my two sons may sit, one at thy right hand and one at thy left hand, in thy kingdom.' But Jesus answered and said, 'You do not know what you are asking for. Can you drink of the cup of which I am about to drink?' They said to him, 'We can.'" Oh, those presumptuous ones! Matt. 20:20-22

Another possessive mother who had understood nothing, another impertinent mother, as almost all mothers are on the subject of their sons. "Say that my two sons shall be seated one at your right hand, the other at your left, in your Kingdom." Oh, no! Poor idiot, the place on the right has already been reserved for a bandit of the highways.

Obviously the guillotine or a bullet at the base of the skull is more expeditious. Jesus would not finish dying. But that was exactly what was wanted; his enemies regaled themselves with his slow agony. As for the little group of those who loved him, everything became intolerable for them. To understand them, one must have seen with his own eyes one of those terrible agonies in which the lookers-on cry out in their hearts, and the dying man himself cries out aloud, for death to come to the rescue. Just as at certain moments the whole physiological ambition of a man is to endure, at others it is to be finished as quickly as possible. Despite all our diversions and the comedies we enact for one another, how fragile and how miserable we are. . . . Death is harsh, it is literally scandalous: useless to think only of death, it remains unforeseeable; useless to seek distractions from death, it remains no less inescapable. I love Jesus Christ, I love people who do not lose heart at death. For all his miracles, all his innocence, all his virtues, even for all his divinity, he would be of no use to me if he had found means to escape death. I would still owe him, to be sure, all the duties of natural religion, but I am not much moved by that. Whereas, with Jesus Christ, religion is not so much a duty as a passion *(pati divina)*, like friendship or love, like a soldier's fidelity, like the taste for justice, like honor, like all those things that constitute the leaven of life.

Whereas the man who dies, were he my worst enemy, at the moment of death is simply my brother and I am disarmed before him. There is far greater reason to feel thus if, as here, it is a man I never met, who died two thousand years ago, and who nevertheless died of his own free will, and for me, even more than that, in my place. It sometimes happens in war that a man throws himself between you and death, and if this happens to you, you do not forget him.

Mark 15:33-36   Mark says: "And when the sixth hour [noon] came, there was darkness over the whole land until the ninth hour. And at the ninth hour Jesus cried out with a loud voice, saying, *'Eloi, Eloi, lama sabacthani?'* which, translated, is 'My God, my God, why hast thou forsaken me?' And some of the bystanders on hearing this said, 'Behold, he is calling Elias.' But someone ran, soaked a sponge in common wine, put it on a reed, and offered it to him to drink, saying, 'Wait, let us see whether Elias is coming to take him down. . . .' "

Toward midday the sirocco had risen. This wind, coming from the desert, raises black dust devils that tower like funerary columns in the sky and suspend a tent of night over the land. The Gospels have noted the intensity of the phenomenon as a sign of the sorrow of all nature. It is truly terrifying. When I used to go walking near the little hermitage in the Sahara where I lived, I was on occasion, in full daylight and within some ten seconds, enveloped in a great black winding cloth so that in order not to lose the path I had to feel my way home.

This ominous three-hour night deeply impressed those present. One can sense the voices growing lower and the sneerers continuing to sneer only to give themselves courage, like boys whistling in the dark. That wind is searing. The wretched victims, already drained of blood from their wounds, were suffering frightful thirst. Jesus had the humility to admit it: "I am thirsty!" he said. A soldier took a sponge that was serving as stopper in a gourd full of sharp, bitter wine. He put the soaked sponge on the tip of a spear and brought it within the reach of Jesus' lips. John notes that here again a prophecy was being fulfilled: ". . . in my thirst they gave me vinegar to drink." This whole psalm deserves to be read in connection with the account of the Passion: it is a lamen-

John 19:28

Ps. 68:22

tation, foretelling the abandonment and the sufferings of the Servant of Yahweh.

It is another psalm, however, that must be quoted here entire, Psalm 21, whose first verse Jesus intones: "My God, my God, why hast Thou forsaken me?" Mark notes that Jesus cried this aloud in the night. When you have heard the prayers of dying men, you know very well how they start some familiar prayer in a loud voice, only to continue it, lips closed, in the intimacy of their souls. This is what happened here. The people did not understand at all, and they simply caught a similarity in sound between this invocation to God in Aramaic and the name of the Prophet Elias, who was expected by everyone to return and prepare for the coming of the Messiah. And so they mocked Jesus' Messianic dream, at precisely the moment when this dream was being realized. In truth Jesus by his death founded the Kingdom of God.

But the scribes and the priests must have blanched in the dark. They knew the Scriptures well and they knew by heart this psalm intoned by Jesus. If any one of them mentally went on with the recitation together with Jesus, he must have recognized the astounding parallel with what was happening before his eyes. I have translated this hymn from the Vulgate, a text that suggests a more poetic rhythm than any other translation. It must be said that there are minor differences between translations. But it is not detail by detail that it should be compared: the thing to compare is the setting of the prophetic poem with the setting of this tragic but true event.

My God, my God, why hast Thou forsaken me?
Far removed from salvation, the clamor of my crimes,
I shall cry by day, and Thou wilt not hear.
I shall cry in the midst of the night, and no echo of my folly will return to me.
My God, my God, why hast Thou forsaken me?
Yet Thou art there, ancient Glory of Israel,
It was in Thee that our fathers trusted,
Thou didst reward their trust by liberating them,
They cried to Thee and rescue came, they were not confounded.
My God, my God, why hast Thou forsaken me?
But I, poor worm, have no manhood left;
I am a byword to all, the laughing stock of the rabble.
All those who catch sight of me fall to mocking;
Mouthing out insults, while they toss their heads in scorn,
"He committed himself to the Lord, why does not the Lord come to his
     rescue and set him free?"
My God, my God, why hast Thou forsaken me?
What hand but Thine drew me out from my mother's womb?

Who else was my refuge when I hung at the breast?
From the hour of my birth, Thou art my guardian;
Since I left my mother's womb, Thou art my God!
Do not leave me now, when trouble is close at hand;
Stand near, when I have none to help me.
My God, my God, why hast Thou forsaken me?
My enemies ring me round, packed close as a herd of oxen,
Strong as bulls from Basan; so might a lion
Threaten me with its jaws, roaring for its prey.
My God, my God, why hast Thou forsaken me?
I am spent as spilt water, all my bones out of joint,
My heart turned to molten wax within me;
Parched is my throat, like clay in the baking,
And my tongue sticks fast in my mouth; Thou hast laid me in the dust to die.
Prowling about me like a pack of dogs,
Their wicked conspiracy hedges me in.
My God, my God, why hast Thou forsaken me?
They have torn holes in my hands and feet;
I can count my bones one by one; and they stand there watching me.
They divide my spoils among them,
They cast lots for my garments.
My God, my God, why hast Thou forsaken me?
Then, Lord, do not stand at a distance;
If Thou wouldst aid me, come speedily to my side.
Only life is left to me; save that from the sword,
From the power of these dogs;
Rescue me from the very mouth of the lion,
The very horns of the wild oxen that have brought me thus low.
My God, my God, why hast Thou forsaken me?
Then I will proclaim Thy renown to my brethren;
Where Thy people gather I will join in singing Thy praise:
"Praise the Lord, all you that are His worshipers;
Honor to Him from the seed of Jacob,
Reverence to Him from the seed of Israel!
He has not turned his face away from me;
My cry for help did not go unheeded."
My God, my God, why hast Thou forsaken me?
Take what I owe Thee, my song of praise before a great assembly.
I will pay my vows to the Lord in the sight of His worshipers;
The poor shall eat now, and have their fill.
"Glory to the Lord from all those who seek Him!
Their hearts shall be alive eternally!"
My God, my God, why hast Thou forsaken me?
The farthest dwellers on earth will bethink themselves of the Lord,
And come back to him;

All the races of the heathen will worship before Him;
To the Lord royalty belongs,
The whole world's homage is His due.
My God, my God, why hast Thou forsaken me?
Him shall they worship, Him only, that are laid to rest in the earth,
Even from their dust they shall adore.
My God, my God, why hast Thou forsaken me?
I, too, shall live on in His presence,
And my seed shall serve Him.
A generation yet to come will proclaim the Lord's name;
And the heavens will announce His justice to a people that must yet be born,
And what the Lord did.
My God, my God, why hast Thou forsaken me?

There are several reasons for repeating throughout the poem, as I have done, its initial invocation: "My God, my God, why hast Thou forsaken me?"—in order to divide the poem into stanzas and to emphasize its cadence. But also—for here I am in the Gospel and not in the Old Testament—to keep in mind throughout the psalm the words that Jesus cried out in a loud voice. For these words have given offense. Now let us see. Even when constantly repeated, these words, which might be called despairing, do not have the effect of erasing the triumphal and Messianic meaning of the poem. Clearly the whole Passion of Jesus Christ issues in the glory of God, the universal homage of the nations to God, their reconciliation in His praise.

Thus Jesus, by intoning this splendid psalm aloud, remains to the end within that stage setting where eternity governs time and parcels it out, and where reality echoes its pronouncements. The double meaning continues. But the realization of the prophecy does not lessen at all the frightful reality of the literal meaning. It is true that Jesus, by dying in the way he does, is fulfilling the most treasured prophecies of Israel. Nevertheless he dies, and he feels himself truly abandoned by God, for he says so.

Let me quote here the commentary of dear Father Lagrange. It seems to me that no one could be more honest than he is. And the first requirement of the whole story of Jesus Christ must be honesty. There is no salvation without strict truthfulness.

. . . He was suffering. Rejected by the leaders of his nation as a blasphemer and abandoned to strangers, treated as a malefactor by the Romans, conspued by the populace, railed at by a thief, abandoned by his own, there remained only one further pain for him to endure in his soul, the most cruel of all, abandonment by his Father. We must believe this, since the Evangelists have said it. *They have said it and it is unquestionably the most in-*

contestable proof of their veracity. Jesus' enemies had just mocked him for his confidence in his God: "No! he is deceived, God has abandoned him!" The Christians must have considered this insult a blasphemy to the object of their devotion, Jesus Christ, Son of God. *Then why admit that it was true? Why have Jesus himself admit it by crying in his distress: "My God, my God, why hast Thou forsaken me?" Was this not to invite their readers and all the ages to shake their heads along with the doctors of Israel in evidence of incredulity? They dared say it, without attenuation, without explanation of any sort. In this case, as in the others, they said what they knew.* And it is also the most shining example of the good reasons they had to believe in Jesus. They knew this sentence, but it could not shake their firmly grounded conviction. It was mysterious; that was no reason at all for rejecting the evidence of the miracles and of the Resurrection.

The mystery continues for us. Even at the moment when Jesus' soul is about to leave his body, we must not suppose a sort of division of his personality in two. It is always the Son of God who speaks. But the human voice expresses the feeling of his humanity, of his soul in desolation, as though God were withdrawing from it. . . . Saint Paul alone has the authority to make a statement about Jesus that seems even stronger and that in part explains the cry uttered on the cross. Burdened, on his gibbet, with all the sins of the world, Jesus had become a malediction. But he was delivering us from the malediction by taking it on himself, and the desolation burst forth in joy in the last verses of the psalm whose first words he pronounced. The afflictions of the just man, the true Messiah, issue in the glory of God. The psalm reproduced in advance the ironic challenge of the doctors: "He committed himself to the Lord, why does not the Lord come to his rescue and set him free?" And, in fact, the abandoned man abandons himself. He knows that for this price the farthest parts of the earth will turn toward God, and all the family of the nations will prostrate themselves before his face.

Saint Paul was certainly right. The abandonment by God that Jesus experienced on the cross is connected with the very malediction of God whose object he was. For, after all, it was not for himself that he was dying this shameful death of slaves, it was for us and in our place, to free us from all our slavery and from death itself. That is costly; it is extremely costly to concern oneself with the fate of others, far more costly to concern oneself with the fate of all. Either the dogma of universal redemption in Jesus crucified has no meaning at all, or this is its meaning.

When the wine has been made, how can you distinguish one cluster of grapes from all the clusters that went into the making of the wine? How, when the bread has been baked, can you still distinguish one grain of wheat among all the grains that have been ground up to make flour? It is here on Calvary that the wine press and the mill are to be found. A single cluster of grapes will save the whole grape harvest which was bitter and ruined, and will purify all the wine; but first that cluster of grapes must be mixed with the whole grape harvest and it must be trodden out together with it. A single grain of wheat will save the whole wheat harvest which was lost and rotted, and it will purify all the bread; but first that grain of wheat must be mixed with the whole harvest so that it cannot be distinguished from the rest, and it must be threshed and ground with that harvest.

Will we finally understand? It is not so difficult, it is as simple as life and death. This malediction of the Law, on which Saint Paul so strongly insists, this malediction that has fallen upon Jesus as he hangs on the cross and that he experiences as abandonment by God Himself— this is the first turn of the mill that is beginning to mix the grain and to crush it. It is the first stamping in the wine press that will crush the whole grape harvest. All humanity must pass through it. In fact it is the whole of humanity (all men insofar as they are men) that is the grape harvest and the wheat harvest. When the wine is made and the bread baked, all the wine and all the bread will be pure that come from this press and this mill. Only those will become wine and bread who, in their time, have freely entered into the same wine press and the same mill that are being set in motion here on this murderous threshing floor.

Here the Communion of the Saints has its beginning. It commences in atrocious suffering, in the malediction of the Law, in the experience of abandonment by God and by all creatures, in the agony and death of the fairest of the children of men. The good wine and bread begin at this wine press and this mill. Thus commence the redemption and salvation of humanity. Jesus is at the moment when no one can distinguish him from the whole mass of sinful humanity, this is why he feels so abandoned.

Of a certainty he is God, the Second Person of the Trinity, even on the cross he remains King of Paradise; this he has just solemnly affirmed to the good thief. Yes, it is the same man, the very same, agonizing on a cross like a malefactor, who promises paradise to his companion in misery for that same evening, and who now reproaches God with having abandoned him.

We accept all sorts of contradictions in those we love, we even maintain that their contradictions bring out their personalities more clearly. We must accept the contradictions in Jesus; here they beautifully reveal a single and unique personality, subsisting in fact in two contradictory natures. One of these natures is divine and eternal—paradise belongs to it by right; the other, the human one, is obscure and mortal and subject to all the weaknesses of mortality.

What can be said and ought to be said is that Jesus has played his human role without any kind of trickery to the very end. He has identified himself with his human nature to such a degree that at certain moments—as here—it would seem that in order to stay with us, to be altogether on our side in this adventure, he has burned his bridges behind him. This man is clearly of the same character as those captains who go down with their ships, and not like those ship's officers who, when they feel their vessels sinking, swim away like rats.

There is no distress—I was about to write despair—lying in wait for us, in which we cannot feel his fraternal hand on our shoulder.

———

Now it is truly the end. From his mother's womb Jesus has had no other goal but God. Like an arrow still quivering, he is now planted in the target. The hour for which he had come has almost passed. On all sides at once death rises around him. He knows that his mother has remained at his feet, but he no longer sees her. It is good that she is there, at the foot of the cross; she is the point of departure, as the cross is the end, of Jesus' human destiny. The encounter of Mary with the cross recapitulates in elliptical fashion the whole of that destiny. In the serene light of death, abstract and pale, Jesus sees that destiny entire with the eyes of the spirit, he can follow its unfaltering trajectory. This destiny is indeed what was meant to be: there is nothing superfluous, nor anything lacking. As soldiers say: mission accomplished.

This is the meaning, I am certain it is the meaning, of the words now pronounced by Jesus, *"Consummatum est!"* before which translators hesitate. It is the statement of a soldier who has done his duty. I must record this before people have entirely forgotten what a soldier is, and what David was when he returned to camp after defeating the monster Goliath. Yes, Jesus returns to eternity as the young David returned to the camp of Israel. He has vanquished Satan, he has freed humanity from sin, from fear and from shame. Mission accomplished; never will the triumph of a victorious general be better merited than by him.

John 19:30

Then Jesus uttered a great cry: a war cry, a cry of victory, the roar of a lion leaping on its prey, for the vanquished do not cry thus. That cry rolls through the centuries, it shatters all walls. It is a summons, as well, a rallying cry, the cry of a man who is the first to plant the flag on a citadel taken by assault, or on "the roof of the world." I have spent my life studying and discussing religion, I know all that can be said for and against it, but in the end the best of arguments never puts a man on his feet. That great cry uttered on the cross sets in motion, like a cannon shot, those immense multitudes who will always claim as their chieftain this man who dies with a great cry, embracing the heavens.

Then Jesus said, "Father, I return my spirit into Your hands!" After that he bowed his head. He was dead. Luke 24:46

Let us dare to lift our eyes toward him. He is indeed God's standard planted in the midst of the world. He is also the Son of God in a unique and personal sense. As Joan of Arc will die asserting, "My voices did not deceive me," these last words to God are to assert that God is his Father. There is no ostentation in this assertion, but his last words are for his Father and not for himself. He dies freely, he abandons his body to the earth whence that body came. But he returns his soul to Him whose it is by right, to God. After him, however, all of us can, in death, make those final words of Jesus our own, for he has opened to all the divine paternity which, until then, he alone embodied. The communication between God and man, cut off by the Devil and by sin, has been re-established. You can call; henceforth God will hear. What Jesus returns to the hollow of God's extended hand is the first human soul to be wholly obedient and filial.

The ancient Greeks placed an obol in the mouths of the dead to pay Charon for their passage across the river Styx. The soul of Jesus Christ is the precious obol that has paid, once for all, everyone's fare, and Jesus himself has become the ferryman across all the rivers of death, no longer to the shadowy Elysian Fields, but to the bright Kingdom into which he enters first as a conqueror and sovereign.

The analogy goes further still. The obol for the great passage is called "viaticum," and the priest places it between the teeth of the dying Christian; it is the Eucharistic body of Jesus Christ, now glorified and re-united in substance with the soul of Jesus Christ, as it is united with his divinity. Jesus is the ferryman and the obol.

Jesus has just died. Matthew notes that the earth trembled, tombs broke open, and, in the following days, there were ghosts in Jerusalem. Although I have never met one, I have nothing against ghosts. After so many miracles, why not this one? What seems clear is that Jesus' death inspired fear. The three Synoptics have noted that the immense veil in the Temple, which hung from the top of the vault to the floor and shut off the Sanctuary, was torn—a terrible sign, as though the

God of Israel were deserting His dwelling. It is the Synoptics too, writing before the destruction of Jerusalem, who have made note of Jesus' prophecies concerning the approaching ruin of the Temple. To them this tearing of the sacred veil was a premonitory sign.

On Calvary those who were still present were struck with consternation. Like the soldiers who were to burn Joan of Arc, the centurion publicly recognized the holiness of Jesus, and those present departed, beating their breasts. The little group of faithful women, with Saint John, had drawn somewhat apart in sign of mourning. Except for the centurion, it would seem that no one spoke: not a cry, not a sob; silence and stupor.

Those who have seen a death sentence carried out know what a heavy cloak of silent guilt falls on the shoulders of all those present at the moment of the condemned man's death, even though he may have been a murderer. Here, after two thousand years, one cannot evoke that moment when Jesus died without one's heart's being constricted with the anguish of one's own responsibility. And what if it were true that, in the osmosis whereby eternity breathes into itself the whole sequence of time—what if it were true that each one of us is personally implicated in some precise way in the murder of Jesus Christ?

To the end there will be around Jesus an alternation of calm and agitation. The morning of this day was filled with comings and goings and with uproar; then, after he had been crucified, for a period of three hours everything was quiet. Now all is once more in agitation. There is reason for this haste. Jesus died about three o'clock in the afternoon. At nightfall the Sabbath will begin, and then it is forbidden to perform any action whatever. In addition there is the commandment in Deuteronomy that before night a body hung from the wood shall be buried "in order not to defile the earth, well loved of the Lord."

And so everything began to seethe, as though in an ant heap. Joseph of Arimathea was a rich and powerful man, a member of the Sanhedrin, but the Gospels note that he held himself aloof from the trial of Jesus. He was, then, a notable who was certainly not conspicuous for his courage. But in an urgent and dramatic situation like the death of Jesus and the necessity of his burial before nightfall those close to the dead man could not be too particular but had to make use of any means open to them. He alone could do something effective and quick. By whom was he informed? Perhaps he acted of his own accord, for in secret he was a disciple of Jesus. He and Nicodemus, another notable, another rich man, another secret disciple, made proper arrangements for the burial.

Joseph of Arimathea went to see Pilate and claimed Jesus' body. Pilate was not likely to refuse this favor to someone of the importance of Joseph. Why had not this Joseph intervened earlier? That is the way things are. There are people of this sort who do things for their friends only after those friends are dead. A dead body is reassuring. The risks are always limited. But if Joseph of Arimathea reasoned this way, his reasoning was wrong in the case of this dead man. In any case, people's show of sorrow is not to be trusted. Those who wear their mourning most ostentatiously are not those who most loved the deceased.

Pilate was astonished that Jesus was already dead. To be on the safe side, he sent a centurion and soldiers to verify the death, and to put an end to the two others who were being tortured. The soldiers arrived; they broke the legs of the two thieves and thus effectively ended their lives. The soul of the good thief went to paradise. The soldiers saw quite well that Jesus was dead. For safety's sake one of them gave him what is called a *coup de grâce*: he pierced his heart with his lance. And at once blood and water welled out. This event—the *coup de grâce* followed by the flowing forth of a little blood and water—impressed itself upon the sensibilities and imagination of John to an altogether extraordinary degree. He witnessed it and reports it to us with a solemnity that is not customary with him. He even calls as witness to the veracity of his account our Lord Jesus in heaven. This wound in the side will indeed play a part in the future life of Jesus; after his Resurrection he will make use of it to identify himself in the body to his disciples. It still plays a role today.

John does not claim that the fact of blood and water issuing from the wound constituted a miracle, and probably it was not one, for Jesus had only just died. What struck John with amazement was a conjunction of circumstances, which seem less impressive to us because we are not as fascinated as he was by such portents. The thing that moved John, as the last testament of Jesus, the last expression of his will and love, was the almost exact simultaneity of Jesus' final breath, in which he rendered up his spirit, and this flowing of water and blood from his pierced side. To the end of his life John will meditate on this conjunction of circumstances: it seems to him that in it he has seized, instantly and permanently, the essence of Christianity. He will speak of it again in his first Epistle, where he sums up in Jesus the whole of the Old Testament, from the account of the creation, when the Spirit brooded over the waters to fecundate them, from the sacrifice of Abel, murdered by his brother, from the covenant with Abraham, down to the sacrifice of Jesus on the cross which is the culmination and fruition of this long story.

I am going to quote at some length this first Epistle of John, for it raises anew, in a sweet and subtle harmony, the principal themes of this history of Jesus Christ:

1 John 3:1, 9, 16, 20; 4:10; 5:1

Behold what manner of love the Father has bestowed upon us, that we should be called *children of God;* and such we are. . . . Whoever is *born of God* does not commit sin, because *His seed* abides in him and he cannot sin, because he is *born of God.* . . . In this we have come to know his love, that he laid down his life for us; and we likewise ought to lay down our life for the brethren. . . . Because if our heart blames us, God is greater than our heart and knows all things. . . . He has first loved us, and sent His Son a propitiation for our sins. . . . Everyone who believes that Jesus is the Christ is *born of God.* And everyone who loves *Him who begot,* loves also the *one begotten of Him.*

And finally it is here that John comes to the recollection of what he saw with his own eyes on Calvary.

1 John 5:4-8, 10

Because all that is *born of God* overcomes the world; and this is the victory that overcomes the world, our faith. Who is there that overcomes the world if not he who believes that Jesus is *the Son of God?* This is he *who came in water and in blood,* Jesus Christ; *not in the water only, but in the water and in the blood. And it is the Spirit that bears witness that Christ is the truth.* For there are three that bear witness: the *Spirit,* and the *water,* and *the blood;* and *these three are one.* . . . He who believes in the Son of God has the testimony of God in himself.

I always hesitate to use the word "mystery," a word that serves so often as an excuse for the laziness of theologians. "That is a mystery!" And they shut their books, descend from their seats, and take their departure, slamming the door behind them. Even if I do not pretend to understand everything, let alone explain everything, I am trying at least to follow and describe from outside a biological process like that of an egg becoming a chicken. Here is a question of the evolving life process of God Himself within humanity. The true religion, that of the single and most holy God, was in the first instance racist, born and transmitted from generation to generation by people of flesh and blood, the clan of Israel. To this carnal race God made a Promise, the Promise of universal and eternal empire, the Kingdom of God. But from the very beginning it was made clear and explicit that all nations, all races, absolutely all, would be blessed in that Promise, would enter into that Kingdom, and would participate in some way in that seed, which was at once the seed of Abraham and the seed of God. The manner in which all this would take place, particularly the change from a single race as bearer of the benediction to all races as participants in that benediction—this was not said and remained to be seen.

It is in Jesus, seed of Abraham and seed par excellence of God, that the decisive transmutation has taken place. This was accomplished by the sacrificial death of Jesus on the cross. From that tree and the fruit of that tree is born the Israel of God. The whole racist vocabulary remains within Christianity, and we can see it clearly in this Epistle of Saint John. But this racism no longer has anything material or carnal about it, in the narrow sense of a clan perpetuating itself. This "race" of the new covenant, which henceforth bears the Promise made to Abraham, is born of the water, the blood, and the Spirit, it is henceforth propagated by the water, the blood, and the Spirit, and it can incorporate into itself all the nations.

How was it created? By faith in Jesus, Christ and Son of God. This faith is the true seed of God (seed also of Abraham, the believer, as Saint Paul asserts elsewhere). The Church remains as "racist" as was the clan of Israel but the means and instrument of this racism are faith in Jesus Christ and the Sacraments. It is truly from the wounded side of the Lord that the Church was born, as Eve was drawn from Adam's side. The Church is the fruitful bride of Jesus Christ crucified. She carries in her generous womb all the children of God who were until then dispersed among the multitude of races and nations. Henceforth there is a baptism of water, there is a baptism of blood, there is a baptism of desire, in which the Spirit of Jesus takes possession of believers and begets them anew in the seed of benediction. Such is the essence of the universal and eternal Kingdom of God. It is in truth in Christ crucified and transpierced that the benedictions, promised to all the nations through Abraham and his seed, are once for all concretely realized.

If John was so struck by this flowing of blood and water from the wounded side of Jesus, conjoined with the last breath, which rendered up the Spirit of Jesus, it is because he saw in them the same flowing of the seed of Abraham and of the Promise made to Abraham, thenceforth to be borne to all the nations by means of baptism.

In recounting what happened immediately after the death of Jesus, John refers to two prophecies, whose fulfillment he recognized. How did it happen that the bones of the two other crucified men were broken and those of Jesus were not? In the part of the Law describing the precise ritual of immolating the Paschal lamb, it is decreed that the bones Ex. 12:46 of the lamb shall not be broken. It was thus with Jesus, veritable Paschal Num. 9:12

lamb, for which all the other lambs sacrificed since the escape of the people of Israel from Egypt have been only the image and the annunciation.

But the lance wound in Jesus' side recalls to John another prophecy, an eschatological and apocalyptical one, made by the Prophet Zacharia. It is an altogether extraordinary poem, full of blazing contradiction, more gripping than any other poem surrealist, pre-surrealist, or post-surrealist. Its subject is at once the misery of Jerusalem and its final triumph, the end of the institution of prophecy and the fulfillment of the prophecies, the eternity of Israel as the people of God and yet, within each tribe of Israel, the permanent separation of the men from the women. It is a wild poem, full of torches that sow fire in the night and of mad horsemen who mount on blind and fiery steeds. In the course of this poem these verses occur, which seize the attention when they are read in connection with the Passion of Jesus Christ:

Zach. 11, 12

Zach. 12:10

They shall look on him whom they have thrust through,
And they shall mourn for him
As one mourns for an only son,
And they shall grieve over him as one grieves over a first-born.

Zach. 13:6

And this again: "What are these wounds on your chest?" (The Vulgate translates this: ". . . in the palms of your hands.") "With these I was wounded in the house of my dear ones."

The body of Jesus was taken down from the cross in some haste, but with respect. Fortunately Joseph of Arimathea owned a garden that adjoined Calvary. In this garden he had a superb tomb built for himself, carved into the rock; it had thus far never been used. Nicodemus came, too, with a mixture of myrrh and aloes weighing some fifty pounds. Joseph had brought a magnificent winding sheet. All this for the best, if one may speak so; the burial would not take too much time, for the hour was decidedly advanced, and each had to return to his own house for the celebration of Passover.

Thus Jesus was prepared for burial in the Jewish fashion and was placed in the tomb. In Judea, as in Greece, fine tombs had two chambers, a large empty vestibule and a very small chamber inside the rock, where the body was placed on a stone bench, like the tomb of Agamemnon in Greece, although the tomb of Joseph of Arimathea must surely have been smaller than that of the king of Mycenae. A heavy stone was rolled against the outside door to close the tomb.

Because of their anxiety to finish this task as quickly as possible, the interment was only a temporary one. The women counted on returning the day after the Sabbath with aromatics to complete the funeral rites. But for the moment the minimum was done and well done. The men rolled the stone against the tomb, and everyone departed.

Not quite everyone. In this story of blood and death, the women always form a little band apart. Mary Magdalene and Mary the mother of Joses still remained there seated in front of the sepulcher, not able to tear their eyes from that stone that imprisoned their well-beloved; they could not resolve to leave this terrible place.

I note in passing, for it goes to my heart, that Matthew says apropos of these two women: "Mary of Magdala *and the other Mary*." He positively does not say: "Mary of Magdala and *another Mary*." Besides the Virgin Mary, always clearly distinguished in the Gospels, and Mary of Magdala, there has never been any "other Mary" around Jesus except the one of whom we are told that she was the mother of Joses and James and sister or cousin of the Holy Virgin. No other Mary, positively no other. "Mary of Bethany"—an appellation never used in the Gospels—someone different from Mary of Magdala, is an invention pure and simple of the exegetes, who are greatly embarrassed by the personal grandeur of Mary Magdalene and by the immense role she played close to Jesus. Matt. 27:61

At the very moment when the first star appeared in the sky the distant trumpets in the Temple sounded the first call, announcing that Passover was about to begin. Mary Magdalene and her companion finally quitted the tomb and returned to their homes to celebrate the Jewish Passover. But the true Passover had already been celebrated: the Christ, our Passover, had been immolated: *Pascha nostrum, immolatus est Christus.* And yet all was not over. Matthew writes:

And the next day, which was the one after the Day of Preparation, the chief priests and the Pharisees went in a body to Pilate, saying, "Sir, we have remembered how that deceiver said, while he was yet alive, 'After three days I will rise again.' Give orders, therefore, that the sepulcher be guarded until the third day, or else his disciples may come and steal him away, and say to the people, 'He has risen from the dead'; and the last imposture will be worse than the first." Pilate said to them, "You have a guard; go guard it as well as you know how." So they went and made the sepulcher secure, sealing the stone, and setting the guard. Matt. 27:62-66

Matthew was writing in Aramaic on the very scene of the events he described and only some dozen years after them. His testimony would have been laughed to scorn if it had not been true. If I am told—as I have been—that it is improbable that a corpse should be guarded, I can reply that, after the Liberation of France and at the time of the great purification trials in 1945, I saw details of voluntary but very zealous guards posted in the cemeteries to watch over the burial plot of those who had been shot and to prevent anyone from approaching. And that was kept up for more than three days.

Throughout the whole of the Passion, Jesus' enemies had kept in mind the symbolic identification, made by Jesus himself, between the Temple and his own body. He had prophesied, and everyone remembered it, that he would raise the Temple anew in three days. On another occasion he had been even more explicit:

Matt. 12:38-40   Then certain of the Scribes and Pharisees answered him, saying, "Master, we would see a sign from thee." But he answered and said to them, "An evil and adulterous generation demands a sign, and no sign shall be given it but the sign of Jonas the prophet. For even as Jonas was in the belly of the fish three days and three nights, so will the Son of Man be three days and three nights in the heart of the earth."

In their hearts Jesus' enemies were only partially reassured by his death. And so, from their point of view, two precautions were better than one.

CHAPTER XXIII

Easter Eve

THROUGHOUT my whole life, I have been asking myself about
the future of Christianity in our modern civilization, its timeliness, its
effectiveness, its usefulness. For a younger generation which, as recent
investigations show, is fascinated by comfort, money, security, invest-
ment, cars, television, refrigerators, and washing machines, for these
young people, who admittedly believe neither in love nor in politics
(they barely believe in pleasure, certainly not in passion), who still take
an idolatrous attitude toward science and for the most part accept
indifference in matters of religion as good mental hygiene and economy
of the heart, for such young people what can the Passion of our Lord
Jesus Christ still represent?

Has a religion that teaches that man's misery is a sacred mark of predestination and that death may become the instrument of his redemption—has such a religion still any meaning in a society that has lost even
the notion of sin, that is, moreover, intent on eliminating suffering,
that considers death as no more than a natural consequence of man's
materiality, his final wearing out, his discard on the rubbish heap
because of failure of function? Besides, it is easier to replace one man
by another than to change cars. The so-called infinite value of the
individual seems a trifle ridiculous within a society threatened far more
by the population explosion than by any other disaster, except perhaps
a nuclear catastrophe.

In our society of tranquilizers, sleeping pills, alcohol, more or less
openly admitted euthanasia, and insurance of all kinds, suffering and
death are truly awkward incidents, still inevitable perhaps, but in any

case indecent. Suffering is no longer the thing. As for dying, it is an asocial act, annoyingly useless and disagreeable for everyone. We are no longer far from those primitive societies where the dying were carried outside the community so as not to defile the confines of the camp.

Our stage setting for death, the laying out, the obsequies, stink of lies. This stage setting is so riddled with reticence, allusions, euphemisms, omissions, grandiloquence, puritanism, and ugliness that in the end one has to ask oneself just what it is meant to be. As a matter of fact, it is an attempt to divert people from death, to divert them up to the last moment so that its coming, for each one of us, may be as discreet as possible, like a final distraction to which one submits mechanically, as a man might pick out the wrong coat in a cloakroom. We have emptied death of its great and solemn interrogation, we avoid the cold eye it fixes upon us.

Under these conditions, the Christian religion seems to have only one place to claim for itself, a place that is willingly resigned to it among the other funeral enterprises—as insurance, free insurance, of course, against death and the hereafter, a hypothetical hereafter. Its priests are so dismally clad that they seem actually to wish to place themselves in the social category of undertakers' assistants.

Such is the case in our Occidental societies, which still lay vague claim to Christianity. What is to be said of the Communist societies, where the state religion is atheism? One is left speechless by the declarations of the worthy Russian cosmonauts who, because they are quite certain they did not encounter God in their stratospheric excursions, conclude therefore, in perfect good faith, that He does not exist.

Under these conditions, what meaning can be assigned to the Passion of Christ, whose purpose was the reconciliation of the universe with God? We do not deny that the universe needs to be reconciled, but it is with man alone that we think it must be reconciled, and science is accomplishing this reconciliation under our eyes, it is giving man the empire over nature: *imperium naturae*. This conquest is reconciling the universe with man, but in this family celebration one sees no place for God. Surely the most timely question in the whole Bible is that of Saint Paul: has Christ died in vain?

In the course of this book I have sufficiently emphasized the ambiguity of science, its limitations, and its very low intellectual watermark, not to need to deal at length with this subject here. The truth is that science does not reconcile anything or anybody. The control of nature may fall into any hands; this is something we must realize. Whom did the Hiroshima bomb reconcile and with whom? It is true that the Japanese became reconciled with the Americans, but that was despite the bomb and surely not because of it. If Hitler had had the atomic bomb, he would not have hesitated to drop it on London and Paris: what reconciliation would he have obtained in that way? The reconciliation of the dead. Science can do much good and has done so at its level. It can do much evil, for unlike religion it is purely utilitarian, it does not concern itself with final ends. The control of nature that it gives us produces as much terror as adoration. When shall we be able to escape from both this terror and this adoration, when shall we be in a position to look science in the eye without flinching? Science is neither salvation nor apocalypse, it is no more than a (barely) domesticated animal, which should always be kept on a tight leash.

Let me repeat, Christianity does not pronounce condemnation on the control of nature, which has in fact been promised to men since Genesis, but it asserts that the control of nature is not an end in itself, that the use to be made of it remains to be defined. Everything I am saying here must be clear as day to our contemporaries, for, from the beginning of this century, one can add up the devastation caused by natural catastrophes (floods, earthquakes, volcanic eruptions, tempests and shipwrecks, lightning), and the sum of all this havoc is absolutely nothing, compared to the ravages caused by the malice of men, using against one another this celebrated control of nature for their mutual ruin, their mutual destruction, their mutual extermination. This experience—irrefutable to me, for it has happened in my time—throws serious doubt on science as an enterprise of universal reconciliation.

Moreover, what do we really know, even in our laboratories, about the nature of gravitation, of the various radiations, or of electricity? We know how to use them, how to calculate their approximate behavior, their directions, their intensity, but of their true nature we know nothing. Then by what right, by what right indeed, does the meanest academic underling speak in the name of science and, in the name of science, feel free to sneer at the Gospel story? Vulgar pedants, what certainty have you to give us in exchange, and what hope?

The teaching of the Apostles and the Church on the subject of the Passion of Jesus Christ is of astounding intellectual audacity. What now? Can it be possible that the infamous execution of that obscure Jew two thousand years ago, the result of a judicial blunder, could be at the center of the universe, the principle of its renewal and instrument of its reconciliation with God? Could it be true that the gibbet on which this man died is the central pivot of all the constellations, the living heart behind all the pulsations of history? Let us proceed softly, honestly. The most profound revelation brought to us by the Passion of Jesus Christ is, perhaps, that the essential rhythm of the universe, which sets it in motion and directs it to its goal, is love. Saint Augustine had a presentiment of this in the equation he made between love and gravitation: *amor = pondus*. Physicists and mathematicians continue to debate the nature of gravity. And what if it were love?

Such an assertion is, no doubt, impossible to prove directly or to demonstrate by even the most precise electronic means. But we do not claim that this assertion is based on laboratory proof. It is based on revelation. It is, moreover, a view of things that cannot be disproved, either, and that, if it were true, would give us the key to man and to the universe.

Yes, and how can one fail to be aware of it? If the nature of gravitation is love, then the nature of the universe, its law and its profoundest destination are love as well. Everything is transfigured, everything becomes wonderful. Oh, there is, to be sure, love and love. The love that links a planet to the sun is different from the love that links an infant animal to its mother's nursing breast or a saint to God. But in all orders and according to their degrees, it is love that binds the universe together, that makes it work, that suspends it entire from God as a suckling is suspended from its mother's breast. The Christian vision of the world is that this intimate circulation of the universe and this attachment of the universe to God had been broken by sin and that the Passion of Jesus Christ restored them, repaired them and remade them at their most vital and most secret point, the point of tangency between the universe and God. Within its most intimate depths the universe recovered its equilibrium by redirecting its gravitation to God, by grace of the cross of Jesus Christ, the axis and pivot of the universe: *Stat crux dum volvitur orbis*. There is, then, a key that was lost and that has been recovered; it will open for us the true secret of the universe, it is a golden key, a key of love, it is the cross of Jesus Christ.

But then Jesus' words on the eve of his death take on a singular resonance, that of a universal law of gravitation: "This is my commandment, that you love one another as I have loved you. Greater love than this no one has, that one lay down his life for his friends." The death of devotion, of love, the sacrificial death, the death of a burnt offering becomes identical with the greatest weight. At the death of Jesus Christ the world tipped in the direction where it had suddenly become heaviest. Until then death was the great divider, the great

John 15:12

separator, the great devourer, the great unraveler. Through the weight of love that Jesus' death was able to reintroduce into the world, it became the great reconciler, the great peacemaker, the great reuniter and communicator. It reconciles the universe with God in love, it reconciles man to God in love, it reconciles man with himself and men with one another in love.

We have eloquent proof that this has been the Christian vision of the universe from the very origin of Christianity (it is also the fulfillment of the revelation in the Book of Genesis and in the Book of Wisdom) in the Epistles of Saint Paul. Saint Paul, addressing himself to the pagans, tells them:

... you were at that time without Christ, excluded as aliens from the com- Eph. 2:12-22 munity of Israel, and strangers to the covenants of the promise, having no hope, and without God in the world. But now in Christ Jesus you, who were once afar off, have been brought near through the blood of Christ. For he himself is our peace, he it is who has made both one, and has broken down the intervening wall of the enclosure, the enmity, in his flesh. The Law of the commandments expressed in decrees he has made void, that of the two he might create in himself one new man, and make peace and reconcile both in one body to God by the cross, having slain the enmity in himself. And coming, he announced the good tidings of peace to you who were afar off, and of peace to those who were near; because through him we both have access in one Spirit to the Father. Therefore, you are now no longer strangers and foreigners, but you are citizens with the saints and members of God's household: you are built upon the foundation of the apostles and prophets with Christ Jesus himself as the chief corner stone. In him the whole structure is closely fitted together and grows into a temple holy in the Lord; in him you too are being built together into a dwelling place for God in the Spirit.

This is obviously not a page of literature in the current meaning of the word. It is prose that is hard to translate, jarring, forged by great blows of the hammer on the anvil, with insistency, repetitions, and oppositions that are underscored and accentuated. The unity of mankind in Christ Jesus alone is proclaimed as a victory won in high combat, as a settled and joyous peace: there was somewhere in the universe a "wall of shame" that has permanently collapsed because it was stormed by force and because love is the strongest of forces. With the scattered stones of this wall of shame, the immense and eternal Temple is being built to the glory of God in the body and spirit of Jesus, who serves as the cornerstone of that Temple. The universe is the huge building-yard of love. The true Temple of Jerusalem is henceforth the body of Jesus Christ and the entire human race which is incorporated in him through the same spirit of love. This architectural doctrine of the universe occurs again in the Apocalypse and in the Epistles of the other Apostles in perfect continuity with the Gospel and Old Testament. One has only to read them to see it.

There is a striking similarity between the spiritual, or rather de-spiritualized, condition of the pagans addressed by Saint Paul and our own condition: *Spem non habentes et sine Deo in hoc mundo.* "Devoid of hope in a world without God." That is indeed our situation.

For the men of our time to hear, if only with the ear of the heart, the news of salvation, they lack both God and any true hope. To those people who consider themselves "cheated," that is, who find no absolute in existence, no fixed point to which to anchor their destiny, one can nevertheless reply, with strict philosophy, that if there is no absolute, there is no relative either, all is absurd, that is to say, all is chance: the flower I smell is pure chance both in structure and in perfume, but my eye and my olfactory system are also accidental, and I am accidental, and the weight of my body is an accident that keeps me in an accidental place. In reality you cannot circumscribe the role of chance any more than you can circumscribe the role of God. Beyond doubt one must go further and say positively that the universe is no longer neutral, that it alternates between love and hate; whoever refuses love sooner or later encounters universal hatred. It may be said that I digress. I do not digress at all. Since Hiroshima we know very well that from now on the human race has the power to destroy itself. The end of the world will be the inevitable offspring of a hideous copulation between control of nature and universal hatred: one begins to perceive very clearly the attraction that these two monsters exert upon each other. We are condemned to love simply in order to survive. It would be just as well to love, not by decree, but freely as free men. If Christianity bestows a meaning on man and the universe, this is certainly it. I am very proud that the tradition of my ancestors had placed me in a position to hear these truths when I was no more than a small boy. I have grown up, and it all seems to me more than ever true.

It is unbelievable how sensitive Catholics are to intellectual bluff. They are always afraid of not being up to date. The thought never strikes them that their sacred books are more interesting and have more true things to say than the most recent fashionable philosophy. They have a taste for ambiguities, for compromises between fire and water, for the no man's land of the intelligence. Luck be with them. . . . How many times have I seen them bow with respect before the most absurd slogans, hold their peace in the face of the most ridiculous blasphemies and behave as though God were, after all, a convenient hypothesis that should be kept in place among the panoply of accepted ideas.

Of what consequence are accepted ideas? The truth is that absolutely nothing in the world justifies itself so completely as God, or, rather, everything must find its justification in Him, once it is understood that we call *God* precisely the universal center of gravity of all intelligible justification. It should be added that universal chance poses infinitely more problems for the intelligence than God, God being the opposite of a problem: He is the necessary and inevitable solution, the center beyond the world where all intelligible perspectives of the universe come together. At the limit of its researches, provided these are at once methodical, honest, and persistent, the intelligence knows that it is moving toward God, even if it discovers at the same time its natural inability to attain and enjoy Him.

But at the same moment that the intelligence discovers God as inevitable it recognizes its obligation to adore Him and render thanks to Him for all that exists. It is this that the modern mind refuses to do; it would rather turn around and retrace its steps than find itself confronted with this necessity so repugnant to its pride, it will prefer to resign itself to universal chance, that is, to deny itself and give up completely. How can I possibly feel any respect for such a craven retreat before the most elementary responsibilities of the mind?

For it is true that if the intelligence wishes to emancipate itself from God and behave as though He did not exist, nothing remains to it but the hazards of chance, not even enterprise, for enterprise always retains a meaning, and there is no enterprise without character: the ventures of an earthworm are one thing, those of a being created in the image of God are another. The addition to a creature's nature of the enlarging factor of enterprise is what is called his history. History of what kind? Not of phenomena, but of universal vocation, of his obedience to what is higher than himself, or his disobedience.

When I say that the Passion of Jesus Christ is the center of gravity of the universe, it means, first of all, that it is the pivot of universal history; all obedience and all disobedience will be measured by that standard. If Christianity is true, this is easy to understand. In the whole history of the world there is no event more important or with more universal resonance than the redemptive Incarnation. That the Creator of heaven and earth, the founder of all being and the Master of history, should personally bury Himself within his creation, that He should become

Himself a human being among all His other creatures, that He should take part within the history of the world like a seed cast into the earth, and that the supreme fruition of this unique adventure inside the universal adventure should be the tree of the cross against which God Himself expires with a great cry of love for the whole of His creation—this means that it is the blood of God that gushes forth eternally over the whole of that transfigured creation.

What I am explaining here is the Christian faith. No one can be forced to believe in it. But, as Saint Paul says, if it is never expounded and proclaimed how could one believe it? Personally I am doing my best to announce and explain to the people of my time in their own language the good and extraordinary news of Jesus crucified. It is, once more, Saint Paul who has best expressed the significance and scope of the redemptive Incarnation. I shall indulge myself here by translating him in my own fashion. He is speaking of God, the Father, and he says:

Col. 1:13-23   He has rescued us from the power of darkness,
He has transferred us to the Kingdom of His Son's delight.
In this Son of God, in his blood, we find the redemption that sets us free,
And the remission of sins.
It is he, the Son, who is the visible image of the invisible God,
He is the first-born of all creation, because in him all things took their being,
    in heaven and on earth,
Visible and invisible,
The Thrones, the Dominions, the Principalities, the Powers,
All, absolutely all, were created by him and in him.
This is why he takes precedence over all things, and in him all things subsist.
He too is the head and the body of the Church, it begins with him since his
    was the first birth out of death,
Thus in every way the primacy remains his,
Because in him the whole plenitude has found its exquisite habitation,
To him belongs the reconciliation of all things in himself.
He has made peace among all things, whether on earth or in heaven, through
    his blood, shed on the cross.
You too were once estranged from him, your minds were alienated from him
    by a life of sin,
But now you are reconciled by him in the body and the flesh through his
    death,
So as to bring you into his presence holy and spotless and unreproved,
If at all times you remain true to your faith,
Grounded in it, firmly grounded in the faith that comes from the Gospel
That you once listened to,
A Gospel that is preached to all creation under heaven
And in whose service I, Paul, have been made a minister and instrument.

There is a man who can speak out. And so there is a reconciliation, a harmonization, a communication, and an intimate circulation, orderly and peaceful, established throughout the whole universe (angelic, human, and physical) by the fountain of blood that streams from the cross.

Obviously such a vision of the universe has nothing to do with scientific views or even metaphysical ones; they are not even in competition, although the Christian vision of the universe does presuppose a metaphysical vision of the same universe. One must know that God is the creator of heaven and earth before one can attach any importance to the way in which the universe finds its way back to God, whence it comes. For this is indeed the point. The Christian vision is a historical, apocalyptic, and eschatological view of the universe. The Word of God, through whom the universe was created, becomes its shepherd through his blood sacrifice; he reassembles the whole universe beneath the crosier of his cross, all things become members of his purified flock, angels and men, the planets that swim in the sky and the fish in the seas, the birds and the worms, he reassembles them all and brings back the flock complete to the paternal fold.

What chance has such a vision of winning the souls and imaginations of our contemporaries? Marxism, as a matter of fact, has won over many of us, and it too is a "theology" of history, an apocalypse and an eschatology, shorn, it is true, of all origin and metaphysical end. It is an apocalypse whose credibility is founded, not on miracles, but on supposedly scientific dogmas which are a part of the obsolete rubbish of the nineteenth century, founded as well on the myth of progress, which is blindly followed—as a dead dog follows the river, Bernanos used to say, by being carried downstream—founded, finally, like the Christian apocalypse, on prophecies, but prophecies all of which have been proved shamefully wrong by the facts during the last hundred years. No matter! This caricature has made a conquest of hundreds of millions of hearts, and the names of Marx and Lenin are today known, celebrated, and venerated by more men, women, and children in the world than the name of Jesus Christ.

Never in the whole history of Christianity has there been a more appropriate time to meditate on the burial of our Lord Jesus Christ. We have seen God die, we have seen him placed in the ground, we have seen the great stone rolled against his tomb, we have seen the supercilious legalists place seals on the sepulcher. And is it in this tormented body, now heaped with aromatics, that we are asked to keep our faith? In the medieval litanies of the Dominicans there is this surprising invocation to the Virgin: "By that Easter Eve when you kept the faith!" We are in the Easter Eve of the world.

Why deny it, why not see things as they are? We have against us the appearances, prejudices, myths, propagandas, concupiscences of this world, time seems to be working against us, and the festivals that are openly celebrated are no longer ours. One after another we have retired all our banners. Laws and customs are no longer Christian. Art and literature are no longer Christian. The exceptions prove the rule, and very often we have to blush at the sight of what officially bears the name of Christian. The architecture of our modern churches is the ugliest in the world. To us belong mourning, solitude, scorn, shame, and fear. But to us too, if we have the courage and the grace, belong prayer, faith, and love offered up, through the rock, to the wounded body of the fairest of the children of men.

Yes, Jesus Christ, our Lord, is dead, quite dead, and buried. And here are the soldiers standing guard before his tomb. Those exceptional beings who loved him in this world are now in their houses, which seem empty and immense. They weep and meditate in their hearts on that absence which stupefies them and on which they wound themselves as one wounds oneself on barbed wire when trying to get through it. This absence lacerates them in all their members, they cannot free themselves from it: the more they move, the more they wound themselves.

He whom Saint Paul superbly calls "the visible image of the invisible God," is laid in the earth, himself invisible in the night of the tomb. How believe in him in that darkness? Does one believe in the existence of a mirror in a darkened room? He was the mirror of God among us, and God seems to have disappeared from the world now that Jesus Christ is no longer there to reflect Him in the light of day. This actually is what was laid in the earth: the visible image of the invisible God. He was and he remains the sublime example among us of the whole human race and of the whole universe.

Man was created and forged in the image of God. Even the material universe bears some vestiges of God and a faint resemblance to Him. It is in this exemplarity, rather than in the laws of physics or in universal gravitation, that the universe finds and demonstrates its unity. Who knows whether even the laws of physics and gravitation are not a vague reflection and an imperfect expression of that original resemblance that gives to each being its form and the soil of its destiny? This is why Jesus Christ, the Word of God incarnate, is at the center of the universe: in him the whole universe—and man above all—recognizes it in its native clarity, recognizes the image of its metaphysical origin.

Indeed man was not created and forged according to the abstract canons of Greek beauty or Japanese beauty or beauty of any other kind; he was not forged in the image of an abstract moral law; he was not even forged according to the Law of Moses, which is of much later date. He was created and forged in the image of God, who is eternally anterior to him, and forged to dominate the universe, which is no more than the footprint of God, whereas he, man, is His image.

The essential mission of Jesus Christ, by nature Son of God, was to restore man and the universe to conformity with their original exemplary character. That this prodigious return to the original exemplarity of man and of the universe had to be accomplished through the suffering, death, and burial, through the sacrificial immolation, of Jesus Christ, Son of God, is a fact; if one looks into this mirror, this fact is seen as the central and determining fact of universal history. There it is, the very truth of God; there is every reason to speak it.

It is certainly correct to sum up the teaching of Jesus Christ in the fact that he revealed to the world the fatherhood of God. But this revelation came long before Jesus Christ; it is recorded in Genesis, it is the most ancient tradition of the Jewish people. For God, having created man in His image, is his father through creation, and the material universe itself, the vestige of God, participates in this sonship. But the vague sonship of the universe, which becomes more particularized in man, is suddenly illuminated and made resplendent in a unique and sublime burst of light, in Jesus Christ, well-loved only Son and man as well. Through his blood, the blood of the cross, he has cleansed the image of God tarnished by sin, he has even purified the vestiges of God scattered through creation. As flowers turn toward the light, everything divine in the universe, everything that bears the seal of that sublime origin, turns instinctively toward Jesus Christ and recognizes in him the fulfillment of its initial splendor.

I am sorry if these words have the ring of eloquence; how else would you have me speak of this miracle of light, the appearance of Jesus Christ in this world? Obviously one can always choose the shadows in preference to the light.

For if the light naturally attracts us, the shadows too have a power that keeps us enslaved. Since we were forged in the image of God and not in the image of the moralists, the legalists, the sociologists, the psychologists, the journalists, or that of noncommissioned officers, the enemy of God is our personal enemy, he is the Devil. There is someone in the universe who seeks to defile, wherever he finds them, the images and vestiges of God. This too we have seen very clearly: there are human hatreds that seem to go through a man and far beyond him. They can be recognized by the fact that they aim not only at destroying the man—which is strange in itself—but most of all at debasing him.

Let us have no doubt about it, the ancient Serpent was there, too, in the crevice of the rock, restless, cold, and yet attentive to the solemn silence that filled this tomb.

And so the Passion of Jesus Christ has reconciled the universe, and within the universe man, to God, in the way a mirror is reconciled to the light by opening wide the windows and cleansing the mirror of all impurity. This is what redemption from sin is, this is the restoration, the recreation of the universe in the blood of Jesus. Thanks to this purifying blood, the universe again finds in itself traces of the divine, and man, looking at himself, recognizes his profoundest sonship.

When I was young I had as my master of novices a very good and violent man, of sweet memory to me, who made us learn by heart the Epistles of Saint Paul in Latin. I found this effort wearisome. Despite the eloquence of the master of novices, I did not understand Saint Paul; nevertheless, I was aware of his poetic cadences. But today my gratitude goes out, beyond death, to that master of my youth; the small understanding that I have of the Kingdom of God was sown by him.

Here, then, is Saint Paul, explaining to the Christians of Rome how the Passion of Jesus draws to itself all the weight, all the obscure aspiration of the universe toward the revelation of the divine sonship, which is the deep truth of this universe:

Rom. 8:14-24 For whoever are led by the Spirit of God, they are the sons of God. Now you have not received a spirit of bondage so as to be again in fear, but you have received a spirit of adoption as sons, by virtue of which we cry, "*Abba!* Father!" The Spirit himself gives testimony to our spirit that we are sons of God. But if we are sons, we are heirs also: heirs indeed of God and joint heirs with Christ, provided, however, we suffer with him that we may also be glorified with him. For I reckon that the sufferings of the present time are not worthy to be compared with the glory to come that will be revealed in us.

For the eager longing of creation awaits the revelation of the sons of God. For creation was made subject to vanity—not by its own will but by reason of him who made it subject—in hope, because creation itself also will be delivered from its slavery to corruption into the freedom of the glory of the sons of God. For we know that all creation groans and travails in pain until now. And not only it, but we ourselves also who have the first-fruits of the Spirit—we ourselves groan within ourselves, waiting for the adoption as sons, the redemption of our body. For in hope were we saved.

This hope makes a fitting close to this chapter on Easter Eve. The entire universe, the stars and the angels, the mountains and the rivers, are in expectation before this tomb that hides itself in the night. Our physicists do not know the nature of energy. Perhaps it, too, is an expectation, an inarticulate and obscure hope. The universe is in suffering, it is in the birth throes of a prodigious transfiguration. We Christians know what is taking place. Through our sufferings, through death accepted in union with the Passion of Jesus Christ, we are the lookout at the bow, on the very point of hope, scanning the dark waters for sight of the first gleam of dawn on the sea.

Part Four

The Glory of Jesus Christ

CHAPTER XXIV

The Resurrection

Each time I have embarked on an important chapter of this book I have said to myself that this was the most difficult one and that, once it was finished, the book would go its own way, slowly but surely. However, each chapter has turned out to be harder than the one before, and now that I am coming to the end of this exhausting book, there stands before me the most difficult of all the difficult chapters. There is only one thing to do: dive off the cliff into the river and swim across, stroke after stroke, or drown in it. Naturally one can always give the impression that one has gained the farther shore, and I know very well that this chapter will contain a number of precise and definite passages. It is an entirely different matter to make quite sure that I am treating the subject without trickery. Trickery is so easy in a book.

And so let us plunge into this forbidding chapter. Everyone knows what it is about. Having suffered under Pontius Pilate, Jesus Christ died and was buried; then comes the subject of the present chapter: on the third day he rose from the dead. Resurrection from the dead? Does this idea come naturally to us? Let us put the question to ourselves honestly. Supposing this idea occurs to us, what real credence do we give it? In such a matter one can hardly refuse to let each person answer for himself. Well then, for once in this book allow me to question myself and reply for myself, alone.

All my life I have seen people die around me. When I was young, death stupefied and scandalized me. Now it is life that astonishes and dazzles me. Nothing would seem more natural to me, nothing more normal, than that I should die before reaching the end of this page. I know very well that life is a gift that can be withdrawn at any second. I am an offshoot of a source of energy, and my connection with it does not depend on me. Moreover, it does not seem possible to me that this interconnection depends only on chance. Chance is no explanation for anything as consistent as my life, and yet so fragile. Chance does not make fragile things, it makes coarse and brutal things. No one has ever seen chance make a Chinese porcelain.

It is not so much death that I fear as the circumstances of death: the avenues that lead to death are often humiliating and soiled. I have always thought the most elegant death is that of the soldier on the battlefield, stretched out on the ground underneath the sky. But one chooses neither one's death nor its circumstances.

More formidable even than death is old age, decrepitude. I know that the older we become the tighter we hold on to life: this fierce attachment of a human ruin to the debris of his life seems to me most disgusting of all. The Christian religion teaches us that at its outset death was a punishment, but the worst punishment, in the present state of our existence, would surely be not to die at all. What a dreadful torture, surpassing the imagination, to survive everything, to survive indefinitely! Can you see what Louis XIV would be like, or even Napoleon, if they were still alive?

Death, moreover, is a deliverance from this present life. It can stupidly break up a grand enterprise, destroy a hope, blast a great love, but it also puts an end to what would inevitably degenerate if it lasted. This means that our present life, precious and honorable though it is, is a completely relative good which does not deserve to be clung to.

There remains the far side of death, "the first fortnight afterward," as Valéry cautiously put it. It is strange that this question arises. Why should it? I cannot say, but the fact is that it does arise. What is there beyond death? Is there anything at all? The question is really strictly personal. When I shall be dead, will everything be over *for me*? Shall I still exist somewhere and in some fashion, and yet be substantially identical with myself, possessing a connection with my past as a human being, a memory, a responsibility to the past, the capacity to suffer and to enjoy? Or shall I rather have totally ceased to exist? The question arises for everyone. Perhaps it characterizes the human condition, for it would appear that it does not occur to animals. But there is no adequate answer, for it would be necessary to die in order to answer with authority. The certainties on this subject are beyond our natural powers. They are exterior to earthly man, exterior to his experience, exterior to his reason. And this is true, moreover, for all certainties.

Those who assert that man survives death know it from another source. But those who assert there is nothing beyond death, what is their authority? As a matter of fact, those who answer in the affirmative are not so sure, and those who answer in the negative are not so sure either. When it is a question of the beyond, one ends by doubting doubt itself; skepticism behaves dogmatically, but its certainty depends on a hypothesis.

Retracing my path, I ask myself another question. So far as I am concerned, do I want a future life, survival after death, or do I not? Taking the word *want* in the usual sense, I am not even sure that I do. I am not so well satisfied with myself that the prospect of having to put up with myself indefinitely can ravish me with enthusiasm. Anyway, if that desire exists, it is mixed with fear. There are moments when I would be just as glad to have everything finished for good. But, still on a nonreligious plane and at the purely natural level of my character and of my experience of what I am, I know that, if the choice were given me of surviving death or of extinction, I would choose at the last moment to survive. One thing about myself I am sure of is my insatiable curiosity. Whatever risks might be involved, I would want to see. And so at bottom I want to survive and persist in being.

As I continue to question myself at this level, another certainty becomes clear: the imagination has no hold on the beyond. The truth is that in current conversations the very notions of survival, a beyond, immortality, and nothingness are too often simply imaginary projections. If there is one thing that must be guarded against in talking about what lies beyond death and about nothingness, it is surely the imagination. On this subject the imagination is only the mistress of error and a terrible encumbrance. It crushes everything. The anticipations of the imagination are of no value whatever in connection with the beyond, whether they lean toward nothingness or immortality. The imagination is far too closely tied to the categories of space and time; if death signifies anything, it is surely that these categories are permanently transcended and abolished.

The imagination is incapable of conceiving the beyond. All the pictures it supplies, whether terrifying or reassuring, insofar as they are simply the product of imagination, are absolutely worthless and without meaning. There is no area of reflection and discussion in which the imagination plays more tricks than in that of death and the beyond. The imagination, daughter of anxiety, gives birth to anxiety or to phantoms of security, all equally vain. The way most people talk about nothingness makes me think that the conception they have formed of it is simply their way of dismissing the problem before going to sleep.

So far I have been talking only of my death and my beyond. I am at an age when I have experienced a hundred times the death of another, the cruel mourning, the dreadful separation from a beloved being. No matter how often this experience is repeated, it remains frightful for some persons—not for all, alas! More than my own inevitable death, that of others confronts me with questions. What do I think on this subject? Is a being I have greatly loved and who has died still alive somewhere with a life of his own? Where? How? Can I rejoin him? Shall I see him again? And if I see him, shall I recognize him? Will he recognize me? What shall we talk about, and shall we talk? And what about all these questions that crowd in upon me, are they reasonable or a product of delirium? Am I myself a wise man or a madman to ask them? Do I really want to see those I have so much loved? Is not this desire itself mixed with fear? And if I were given the choice, what would I do? Would I see them again or not? Have they not changed in identity to such an extent that to see them again would be a dreadful disillusionment?

In point of fact I know very well that, in the case of each one of them, what I desire is not so much a common life in the future as to go back, to set back the clock, to begin the story over, to alter its course, to reverse fatality, to relive a sweet past that will never end. The death of others is precisely this absolute impotence of ours to live the past over and to remold it. "I could have, I should have"—frightful words!

But the idea that some friend who is dead should suddenly stand before me again in his full spiritual and bodily identity and that he should talk to me as he used to do—this idea never occurs to me. A hypothesis of this sort embarrasses and even frightens me. I know there are many women who have no dread of it. But for my own part I feel a repugnance toward revenants, and, even if I were confronted by the fact, I would not believe in it. The large role played by the imagination in anything of this sort makes it suspect.

What can be concluded from all this? Not a great deal except what I said at the beginning of the chapter: the brutal and ineluctable fact of death, death for others as well as for oneself, leaves a man at a loss because this fact goes beyond all his experience and the reach of his imagination. At least it was not idle to ask these questions for the purpose of eliminating all traces of imagination from a discussion in which it could only increase confusion.

In making a motion picture, what takes longest is not the filming of a scene but the prior lighting of the set. In the same way, before coming to the Gospel accounts themselves, I should like to banish as many as possible of the ambiguities on the subject of the Resurrection of Jesus Christ. What I am explaining here is the Catholic faith as I was taught it and as I understand it. It is in its light that I read the texts of the Gospel. Many objections would fall of themselves once the lights were suitably arranged.

There is a basic ambiguity concerning the Resurrection of Jesus Christ, an ambiguity from which many Catholic sermons and explanations are not exempt, and it is necessary to banish it. It is all the more dangerous because it is connected with the words themselves, "resurrection from the dead." The first necessity for the banishment of an ambiguity is to define it.

Well then, the words "rose from the dead" have two different meanings; I do not say completely opposed meanings but very different ones, the one being as superior to the other as the sky is to the earth. Actually the meaning that comes first to the mind is an earthly meaning: in it "rose from the dead" means to return to the life one has lost, as a man returns to his house after being away for a time. In this earthly sense, resurrection is a way of setting back time as one sets back a watch. It is a strange withdrawal: one takes the step backward into life that one has made forward into death. One has passed the threshold of death, and one passes it again in the opposite direction, finding oneself alive and ready to take up things again where they were, regaining one's identity in the place where one was. In the Gospel this was the case with Lazarus, raised from the dead by Jesus: he did not become immortal through it. For him death was only an appointment postponed.

It is worth noting that this kind of resurrection recalls the bewitchments in children's fairy tales in which the beautiful princess falls deeply asleep to awake either at the end of a hundred years or at the touch of Prince Charming. No problem is solved by this, not the problem of life or of death or of this magic sleep. Our modern sensibility is offended by these children's stories, and I have already more than sufficiently pointed out how much it is offended by miracles. But I am not talking here about the resurrection of Lazarus, I am talking about the Resurrection of Christ.

For the words "raised from the dead" have another meaning, a "celestial" meaning if you like, and this is the only meaning applicable to the Resurrection of Jesus Christ. For him it was a question not of taking a step backward but, once he had passed the threshold of earthly death, of thrusting forward, without withdrawing an inch, over a new threshold and making a prodigious leap in advance—no longer to set time back, but by a victorious act of violence to penetrate into eternity, which is beyond time and death. Christ has not set foot again in his terrestrial house; he has entered complete, body and soul, into his home, eternity. His Resurrection is in no sense a withdrawal, it is a prodigious move forward, entirely new, at least for his body. His resurrection is not a return to our terrestrial life, it is a triumphal progress beyond terrestrial life, beyond terrestrial death, beyond the tomb: he does not return, he escapes, he passes through a door that has hitherto been hidden from us, he permanently escapes both from our present life and from death. He is beyond, he is free, he moves joyously on the eternal plains of his original fatherland.

There it is, the wonder of wonders! A prisoner has got away, a man has escaped from our terrestrial condition; henceforth he is beyond the reach of the executioner and the judge, of the legislator and the preceptor, of the familial clan and the cruel fatherlands of this world, of the doctor, of the nurse and the undertaker, beyond the reach of *yours* and *mine,* of commerce and of money, of party walls, of syndicates, of the police and the insurance companies, of calumny and of anguish, in short beyond the reach of daily life and of death, its ineluctable end point; for him death is no more than a doorway to pass through, and he has passed through it toward another adventure. Henceforth he is free with an inconceivable freedom before him, and he has left behind him the lighted road that enables us to rejoin him through death. In him and through him our own escape is already assured. Ours is that liberty, his and ours! When the angel rolled the stone away, the whole prison house of mankind trembled on its foundations: henceforth the breach in it is so large and so deep that it will never be repaired.

For this joyous and victorious Resurrection of Jesus Christ permanently changes the meaning of life and death, of the life and the death of each one of us. Jesus Christ has opened the way, he has breached the bulwark, he has forced the rampart; who loves him will follow him; after him and through him the city is ours! What city? The celestial Jerusalem, life eternal for our souls and for our bodies. Tombs are no longer shut, the carapace of steel that enclosed man's destiny in death has been shattered to bits. This indeed is the meaning of the Resurrection of Jesus Christ, or it has no meaning.

Yes, body and soul, complete, Jesus Christ passed into eternity, the other side of the world. Or rather he carried eternity by storm, he conquered it in high combat, and he did this for us as well as for himself, for our poor souls and for our poor bodies, all at once. The bodies of Gandhi and of Nehru were burned and their ashes scattered on the sacred river, their souls were congratulated on being finally freed from those bodies. . . . Poor Hindus, poor Plato! I prefer Jesus Christ. Man will never be perfectly free unless he recovers his body and that body is also free:

> . . . dear body,
> I love you, sole object that protects me from the dead!

What a great and marvelous religion is ours, which assures us that even our bodies will participate in life eternal, in beautiful, incorruptible innocence. "I believe in the resurrection of the body and the life everlasting. So be it!"

It would be inconceivable, naturally, that this passage from time to eternity, this radical change of state, should not entail some modification in the soul and in the body also. For the human soul, access to eternity implies true immutability: it is the elimination of enigmas, mirrors, divisive truths, uncertainties. The soul bathes in truth and knows all things, just as it is itself known.

What does it mean for the body? It is here that one grasps the profound optimism of Christianity in contrast to the pessimism of Plato and the Hindus. The revelation peculiar to the Resurrection of Jesus Christ is that the human body, that humble and necessary instrument of the soul, can follow the soul even into eternity and participate in that eternity. What happened once for one individual can happen for all. We Christians expect the "resurrection of the body," its promotion to eternity. A prodigious adventure!

Here, too, to the extent that we are modern men, we are scandalized; it is too splendid. We are quite willing to give in to our bodies, we abandon ourselves to them, we put up with their whims, their pleasures, their greeds, their sensuality, but we give in with a sense of shame. We become obese, decrepit, hideous. But at bottom we do not love our bodies, we do not respect them, we distrust them, we despise them; how could we believe they are worthy of becoming the temple of the Holy Spirit? We think them not only unworthy, but incapable of drinking of the cup of eternal life and unworthy, too—these bodies of ours—of enjoying God, yes, enjoying God, how else am I to say it? That is what has been promised us. Eternal life is the embrace of God. God, to be sure, is Spirit, and it is our minds, our wills, our souls that He directly seizes, He breathes them in and embraces them in an irresistible transport of love. How would it be possible, once the body is reunited with the soul, that it should resist such an embrace? In that all-powerful clasp, the body too will be overwhelmed, it will exult from top to toe, it will quiver with joy. That is what happened to Jesus Christ on the morning of his Resurrection.

And if we believe that is not possible, it is because we have been brought up at ground level, in the most abject timidity, devoid of all ambition and all pride. We reason like tramps. All this is much too fine for us, much too grand. Through total lack of spiritual heroism we prefer to believe that we are made to squat and rot forever in the mud, out of which we have been raised once for all. At the moment when we should fall on our knees and cry, "I am not worthy!" a demon whispers coarsely in our ears, "It is not true! This cannot be true!"

The Resurrection of our Lord Jesus Christ sweeps away this miserable and servile philosophy: we are made to enter, body and soul, into eternity, to enjoy God, to feast upon Him as the beautiful fruit of our appropriate destiny.

———

Mark, the Evangelist, the disciple of Peter, was unquestionably a simple man. His Gospel reveals a feeling for the concrete, a concern about brute facts, without embellishment, without interpretation, without adornment, without embroidery, the honesty of a chronicler whose coolness might make one think that the facts he is recounting do not concern him at all. In his story of the Passion, there is not a word, not an accent, that expresses his own feelings. From time to time one knows what Tacitus thinks, what he feels, what judgments he makes, what arouses his indignation. Mark tells the facts, names the actors, explains who they are, what they do, what they say, always writing as briefly as possible, and he leaves it at that. He is the least literary writer imaginable.

Indeed, he barely deserves the name of writer. He has assembled the statements of witnesses, he has certainly collated and criticized them, for he is far from stupid, but in the end he says what he knows in the simplest possible way, without the least apologetic concern, the concern that is so evident in Matthew. Mark recounts the facts and lets them speak for themselves. It is exactly the kind of testimony that, during a heated trial in a court of law, arouses the respect of the public and the prosecution and makes an impression on judges skeptical of the defense, for it simply opens the shutters and lets the light in so that each can see things as they are.

Mark himself is not involved, he espouses nothing, he testifies; let each one see with his own eyes and judge with his own understanding. Obviously the facts he recounts are sometimes astonishing—what can he do about that? Is it his concern that they are astonishing? His concern is to say what happened. Above all, do not ask him to theorize, you will get nothing from him: not the tiniest morsel of ideology to chew on.

The facts recounted by Mark are almost two thousand years old, but Mark's recital of them has not aged. What makes it hard for us to read it as it is is the two thousand years of discussion, controversy, victories, and defeats of Christianity. Are we still capable of forgetting what we know, of learning ignorance, so that we can read Mark as candidly as he wrote? Assuredly not. We are immersed in our century like fish in water: a fish that decided to leave the water would not understand the world better, it would die. Ignorance cannot be learned, the critical spirit cannot be unlearned either. All right, so much the better! But why reserve the exercise of our critical intelligence for the text of the Gospel and why not *also* criticize our century, its erudition and even its skepticism? Skepticism without the critical spirit is another form of credulity.

It is true that we do not naturally believe in the resurrection of the body or in immortality. Are we so sure we are right? In history there was a sect called "Docetism": the Docetes did not believe in the reality of the Passion and death of Jesus Christ; for them, he only apparently suffered and died. Were they more or less absurd than we? For us, on the contrary, the Passion of Jesus Christ, his death, and his burial are a reassurance: up to that point his destiny does not escape the common lot, it does not escape us, it does not embarrass our habits of thought and experience. But suppose the essence of this destiny of Jesus Christ was precisely to escape from the universal and "normal" law?

In addition to being foremost in all things, Jesus Christ is assuredly an original. And we have a horror not only of all primacy but also of all originality. Is this reasonable? To be raised from the dead, to prolong a human destiny actually into eternity, what extravagance and, perhaps, what a scandal! It is surely improper, it is the sort of thing that is not done. If this should happen, where would we be going? But this is exactly the question that Jesus Christ raises: where are we going? Why should we want so desperately to prevent the question from being raised?

This is Mark's account:

And when the Sabbath was past, Mary Magdalene, Mary the mother of James, and Salome, bought spices, that they might go and anoint him.   Mark 16:1-8

And very early on the first day of the week, they came to the tomb, when the sun had just risen. And they were saying to one another, "Who will roll the stone back from the entrance of the tomb for us?" And looking up they saw that the stone had been rolled back, for it was very large.

But on entering the tomb, they saw a young man sitting at the right side, clothed in a white robe, and they were amazed. He said to them, "Do not be terrified. You are looking for Jesus of Nazareth, who was crucified. He has risen, he is not here. Behold the place where they laid him. But go, tell his disciples and Peter that he goes before you into Galilee; there you shall see him, as he told you."

And they departed and fled from the tomb, for trembling and fear had seized them.

And they said nothing to anyone, for they were afraid.

The exegetes, including even the prudent Father Lagrange, admit that the first version of the Gospel of Mark ends here. What follows is an extension, written later either by Mark himself or by someone else, and is, moreover, only a summary of the other Gospels.

In reading this altogether simple and candid narrative by Mark, we discover that we, perhaps, are as similar as brothers to the first witnesses of this event. For these women assembled in the gray of the dawn at the tomb of Joseph of Arimathea, the most improbable thing in the world, something of which they would never have dreamed, is that Jesus should be alive again. However great the love they bear their master, for them he is dead and buried, quite dead, definitely dead, but inadequately buried. Now it is simply a question of performing for this wounded body the rituals of embalming, unction, and sepulture which there had been no time to complete on the eve of the Sabbath.

If one reads this account by Mark like any other text, what emerges? The honest women who loved Jesus are on their way to the cemetery to complete the embalming of a body precipitately laid to rest. Their only preoccupation is to gain access to the tomb, for the boulder at the entrance is too heavy for them. They arrive: the tomb has already been opened. Let us put ourselves in their place. Various possibilities occur to them. Perhaps there has been a profanation of the tomb? Perhaps some of the Apostles have come before them to perform the same duties they are preparing to perform? On the other hand, perhaps the enemies of Jesus have stolen his body? In any case their surprise and concern are great. But not for a moment does the idea of a resurrection cross their minds.

Nevertheless, these women want to know what has happened: and so they enter. They come upon a young man completely unknown to them, clothed in white, who tries to reassure them, points out that

Jesus is no longer there, asserts that he has risen from the dead and that he has made a rendezvous with his disciples in Galilee. This young man speaks to them with extraordinary naturalness, in the tone a valet might use in announcing to a visitor that his master has had to go out but has made a new appointment.

And the effect produced on these courageous young women by the announcement of the resurrection of Jesus: joy? tears of joy? eloquence? enthusiasm? No, quite the contrary: stupor, consternation, dread, and wordless flight! These women are mute and they will not talk right away; when they do decide to, it will result in their being treated by the Apostles as crazed. For the moment they are afraid, they touch themselves, they rub their eyes, they cannot get over the event, they are frightened to death. Are these the reactions of credulity? It seems to me they are quite the opposite.

What I love about the Gospel accounts, not simply that of Mark but all of them, is that they indicate with blinding clarity that the first reaction, the repeated reaction, the constant reaction, to the *hearsay* of Jesus' Resurrection was incredulity—and this among the disciples, those who loved Jesus most, those who tomorrow by virtue of the experience of their own senses, a renewed and critical experience, will be transformed into witnesses to the fact of that Resurrection. The women do not believe the angel, the Apostles do not believe Mary Magdalene, they do not believe the two disciples from Emmaus, and this chain of incredulity goes on. Thomas will not believe the unanimous testimony of the other Apostles.

The skepticism of modern man can find precedent in the very earliest apostolic tradition, but not among Jesus' enemies. They, for their part, as we shall see, believe in the Resurrection of Christ more quickly than his friends do. It is true that, because of the seals placed on the tomb and the guards stationed there, they are at first in a better position than the Apostles to know the facts.

It is at least clear that the skepticism of the Apostles and their inability even to imagine the fact of the Resurrection of their master were just as solid as the skepticism and inability of any modern man. Their heads were made of just as solid wood as ours. They did not give in except under the bombardment of incontestable appearances—incontestable to their senses. I prefer that. I too have a horror of being a dupe, I do not go along easily. But it is one thing to hate to be duped and quite another to remain impervious to facts on the pretext that what is exceptional cannot be true.

Here it is Mark's account that interests me. He was writing before the Judaeo-Roman War, which was to lead to the destruction of Jerusalem; he was writing no doubt in Rome, and he was familiar with the accounts of Peter and the teaching of Paul. He had conscientiously informed himself. On the other hand, he is incapable of stage-setting, he wants to tell what he knows, he does not want to prove anything. His account is that of a man who has taken notes and who presents them without modification or even rearrangement. In the language of the cinema we would say that his account of the Resurrection of the Lord is a "synopsis," no more than adequate because it is so concise and elliptical. If we had only this account we would barely know what had happened—that is, we would know only the strictly essential: the discovery of the empty tomb and the assertion by the angel of the Resurrection of the Lord.

Here, however, is the continuation of the Gospel of Mark:

Mark 16:9-14   Now when he had risen from the dead early on the first day of the week, he appeared first to Mary Magdalene, out of whom he had cast seven devils. She went and brought word to those who had been with him, as they were mourning and weeping. And they, hearing that he was alive and had been seen by her, *did not believe it.*

After this he was manifested *in another form* to two of them, as they were walking on their way into the country. And they went and brought word to the rest, and even then *they did not believe.*

At length he appeared to the Eleven as they were at table; and he upbraided them for their *lack of faith* and hardness of heart, in that *they had not believed* those who had seen him after he had risen. . . .

If the fact of the Resurrection of Jesus Christ was invented out of whole cloth and if the Evangelists wrote for the purpose of making people swallow this more or less conscious swindle, it must be admitted that there never was a more maladroit story than the Gospel of Mark. It is impossible to emphasize more than he has done in the little space the incredulity of Jesus' friends: when Mark alludes to the appearance before the disciples of Emmaus, which Luke on the other hand tells in greater detail, he, who is always so hurried, takes time to underscore the fact that Jesus was seen in a different appearance from his ordinary one; this circumstance does not seem to trouble him in the least. Then he continues his account at full speed, imperturbably telescoping it. If we did not have the other Gospels, we would not be able to determine the time interval between the Resurrection and the Ascension; one might believe that it all happened in one brief day. Mark is in a hurry to come to the final affirmation: Jesus in heaven, on the right hand of

God, and the Apostles on earth, preaching the Word everywhere with his miraculous assistance.

I think there is nothing paradoxical in maintaining that such obvious awkwardness is proof of good faith. All those whose responsibility it is to reconstruct events that have happened—policemen, detectives, judges, historians—know that the complex of circumstances around a given fact is not without dissonances. The best testimony is rarely the most "harmonious." Quite the contrary, too perfect "harmonization" throws doubt on the veracity of the witness. This is the place to quote a sentence from Heraclitus that Father Lagrange cites with satisfaction: "Better tacit concord than explicit." I mean to say, when one is inventing or conniving in an invention, then one manages to do better than Mark, better than the four Gospels. If this is an imaginary story, it is deplorable. But if it is the truth, then the dissonances are natural enough.

In my opinion there is another reason for the apparent disorder of the different accounts of the Resurrection. That is the confusion caused by the extraordinary, unique, prodigious, and profoundly joyous nature of the event. The great and joyous occurrences in human history explode and in doing so create confusion. I was very advantageously placed to witness the Liberation of Paris twenty years ago. I am sure of certain important facts. But I would have the greatest trouble today in writing out in proper order the exact chronology of the details. It was overwhelming and it was also bewildering. I do not believe that any four of us would relate the events in exactly the same way. This does not mean that the Liberation of Paris never took place or that General Leclerc was a myth.

The first testimony on the subject of the Resurrection of Jesus Christ, however, is not a Gospel but the Epistles of Paul—most important, the first Epistle to the Corinthians. I quote the entire passage:

For I delivered to you first of all, what I also received, that Christ died for our sins according to the Scriptures, and that he was buried, and that he rose again the third day, according to the Scriptures, and that he appeared to Cephas [Peter], and after that to the Eleven. Then he was seen by more than five hundred brethren at one time, many of whom are with us still, but some have fallen asleep. After that he was seen by James, then by all the apostles. And last of all, as by one born out of due time, he was seen also by me.
1 Cor. 15:3-8

I borrow from Father Braun's critical commentary on this text:

The authenticity of this piece is beyond question. When Paul wrote the above, he was at Ephesus, about the year 55. His account of the facts of which he reminds the Corinthians repeats the oral teaching he had given them during his stay in their city in 51–52. This teaching itself is given under the name of *paradosis* (tradition). This term, of rabbinical inspiration (we must not forget that Paul before his conversion belonged to the sect of the Pharisees), means the communication of an unchanging doctrine by means of simple repetition.

In summarizing the account of the appearances, Paul was aware of repeating what he had himself learned in Jerusalem in the course of his journeys at intervals between the years 36 and 50. It can be affirmed with certainty that he is reproducing one of the major elements of the apostolic catechesis, at its earliest stage. Through the intermediation of Paul, then, we go back to the first Apostles, at a moment very close to the event in question. Saint Paul feels no need to prove anything at all. The subject of his testimony had already been accepted in all the communities. He limits himself to mentioning it in order to resolve a specific difficulty relating to the resurrection of the dead in general.

Thus Saint Paul, when he wrote this, was aware of transmitting, without changing one iota, the Christian faith, the apostolic tradition, based on three historic facts, already considered indisputable: the death of Jesus, the burial of Jesus, the Resurrection of Jesus from the dead. Some twenty years separated him from those events: he stood in relation to them as I stand, at the moment of writing this book, to the events of the French Resistance and the Liberation of Paris.

And these three historical facts—the death, the burial, and the Resurrection of Jesus—had already taken on a significance that strangely transcends the temporal and spacial framework of their occurrence. Paul twice notes that they were accomplished in conformity with the Scriptures, thus explicitly connecting the destiny of Jesus with the whole of the Old Testament, which was the preparation for that destiny. To whom is Paul talking about these already historical facts, facts known and accepted, moreover, by his correspondents? Not to the Jews in Judea, but to the inhabitants of Corinth in Greece, a great seaport, with connections in the whole Mediterranean basin. The triple fact of the death, burial, and resurrection of the Lord, already connected in the Jewish Scriptures with the most ancient and venerable religious past of mankind, had become an international event, more than international, universal. I mean that it affected the destiny of every person in the world. This is also the way the question presented itself to Saint Paul and his correspondents; in my opinion it is exactly thus that it should present itself to us.

We should be less astonished than other generations at this explosion of significance—suddenly reaching to the confines of the known world—of a strictly localized historical event. Relatively few men were the agents or the witnesses of the bombing of Hiroshima: the significance of that event was no less sudden and universal. Every man, throughout the world, felt personally involved. Henceforth man *knows* that the end of the world and the end of humanity are possible, whereas on the eve of Hiroshima he did not know. Henceforth man must live with that personal menace. In short, the bomb dropped on Hiroshima was nothing but a historical fact, narrowly localized in time and space. But its significance immediately became universal, even metaphysical.

The same thing is true of the Resurrection of Jesus Christ. It is a historical fact, localized in time and space, but its significance was immediately revealed as universal. Thenceforth every man knew that the resurrection of the dead was possible and the access to eternity was open to all, body and soul. Thenceforth every man had to live with this hope. The incomprehensible and infinitely sad thing is this: behind the passion expended in trying to destroy the historical validity of the fact of Jesus' Resurrection one is aware less of scientific honesty than of hatred of hope, of this particular hope.

Yes, the Resurrection of Jesus Christ exploded in the world for the salvation of all, as the Hiroshima bomb exploded in the world as a menace to all. It is hard to understand what happened unless one perceives the unique and exceptional character, and also the prophetic and universal character, of the event. Paul continues:

Whether then it is I or they, so we preach, and so you have believed. Now 1 Cor. 15:11-21 if Christ is preached as risen from the dead, how do some among you say that there is no resurrection of the dead? But if there is no resurrection of the dead, neither has Christ risen; and if Christ has not risen, vain then is our preaching, vain too is your faith.

Yes, and we are found false witnesses as to God, in that we have borne witness against God that he raised Christ—whom he did not raise, if the dead do not rise. For if the dead do not rise, neither has Christ risen; and if Christ has not risen, vain is your faith, for you are still in your sins. Hence they also who have fallen asleep in Christ, have perished. If with this life only in view we have had hope in Christ, we are of all men the most to be pitied.

But as it is, Christ has risen from the dead, the first-fruits of those who have fallen asleep. For since by a man came death, by a man also comes resurrection of the dead.

I love Paul's rabbinical manner of striking home, of hammering, of defining the questions. One cannot say more clearly that Christianity is an imposture if the fact it asserts of the Resurrection of Jesus is not historical, if it did not really happen, on one day of days, in the garden of Joseph of Arimathea. One cannot say more clearly that there is no happiness for man except within the truth, including humble historical truth—in this instance, the historical truth of the corporeal resurrection of Jesus. One cannot say more clearly that if this fact of the Resurrection of Jesus is not historically established, Christianity, based entirely on the objective and historical reality of this fact, is adding to its imposture malediction and insult to the happiness of man. "If the Christ was not raised from the dead, we are the most unhappy of all men," and we are also frightful idiots to sacrifice the unbridled enjoyment of the present for an eternal life that does not exist. It is as clear as that, and it is a good thing to say it clearly.

Yes, things are clear, the frontiers are marked: the fact of the Resurrection of Jesus from the dead—pledge of the general resurrection of the dead—is the line of demarcation, depending on whether one accepts or rejects it. How closely we resemble those first Christians of Corinth, incoherent and frivolous as we! They were Christians, baptized, converted by the most eloquent of the Apostles; they explicitly denied nothing in their catechism, but they did not believe in the resurrection of the dead, they *could not* believe in it. And yet they had already accepted the Resurrection of Jesus Christ, no doubt as a mythological, poetic, even religious and mystical event, for they loved Christ and their new religion, but the idea did not occur to them that each of them, yes, each one of them and each one of us, everyone that they had known, everyone that we have known, each of us, you, my reader, I who am writing, each one, will be raised, identical to himself in body, as in soul and mind. This was beyond them, as it is beyond us when we fail to keep ourselves steadfastly within the fortress of our Christian faith.

This greatly needs to be said. For three centuries there has been a frantic effort afoot to dismantle our fortress and steal away our faith.

Let us discuss this subject.

———

For a proper understanding of the facts and the Gospels which record those facts, emphasis must be laid on certain circumstances relating to the death, burial, and Resurrection of Jesus Christ:

The Evangelical accounts are in perfect accord with archaeology and modern discoveries. For example, the structure of the tomb of Joseph of Arimathea, as it is sketched in the Gospels, corresponds exactly with the structure and arrangement of many tombs of the same epoch in that region.

The Evangelical data correspond with Jewish customs and laws at the time of Christ, as well as with the customs and laws of the Romans of the same period—for example, the fact that the sentence of death was reserved to the Roman procurator, the custom of releasing a condemned man as a boon to the people on a feast day, the torture of crucifixion, the practice of ending that torture in time for the dead to be buried before nightfall, the handing over of the body to a powerful friend who claimed it, the necessity of hasty burial in view of the closeness of the Sabbath. We know this epoch infinitely better than Strauss or Renan did: it is they who have been outdated by recent discoveries, not the Gospel.

I have already noted that in the space of a single lifetime we have seen archaeological discoveries and scientific textual criticism reassign the Synoptics to their traditional date, that is, before the destruction of Jerusalem, less than forty years after the death of Jesus Christ. I have also noted that the Dead Sea Scrolls show such a literary similarity to John that this Gospel, itself reputedly the most recent, is beyond doubt much earlier than had been thought, and it is not at all improbable that it was written by an eyewitness to the events. In fact, this Gospel has served as the basis for valuable archaeological discoveries.

The Apostles took no part in the burial of Jesus, save for Saint John, who was young and could probably do nothing. The other Apostles were not there; they were in hiding, for they were afraid. Nevertheless it was certainly their duty to be there. Their attitude in fact was lamentable. The Evangelists have noted these circumstances. It would seem that the "apologetic" interest of the Apostles, the interest of the growing Church, governed by those same Apostles, would have been to hide these circumstances, or to omit them, or to attenuate them. But no, the Evangelists have told these things, as they have told all the rest, because they are true. Why give them credence on this subject and not on the rest? The Gospels are constructed not at all like a special plea or a lawyer's brief, but in the manner of objective chronicles, conscientious and—as one often feels—disinterested.

The Apostles were not present at the burial of Jesus. On the other hand, two personages are introduced there by the Synoptic Gospels and by John: Joseph of Arimathea, the owner of the tomb, who had obtained Jesus' body from Pilate; and Nicodemus. They were two notables: Mark says expressly that Joseph of Arimathea was a member of the Sanhedrin. At the time when the first Christian catechesis was being constructed, the one on which Mark relies and which he simply recorded, Joseph of Arimathea was no doubt still alive; in any case, his name was socially known and important. A circumstance of this gravity, which puts in the limelight a Jewish notable in touch with Pilate, a notable belonging to the Sanhedrin, the owner of a garden and a tomb at the gate of Jerusalem—such a circumstance could not have been invented for the excellent reason that it would have been too easy to deny it, if it were false, not only for the interested parties but for anyone at all.

Rationalistic criticism has made a distinction between the Christ of faith and the Christ of history. The purpose of this distinction was obviously to leave to Christians and to their Gospels responsibility for the Christ of faith, while at the same time contesting the historicity of the Christ of history. The phrases, "the historical Christ" and "the mystical Christ," have also been used; they amount to the same thing. Thus the Resurrection of Jesus Christ would be considered a religious and mystical fact completely outside the orbit of history. This distinction impresses many novices. In reality it is a fraud and a false dichotomy, such as are frequently to be found here and there in the books. History by its very nature is the establishment of a fact of the past through the sole means of testimony and documents. Because of the fact that history rests on testimony (which, moreover, it is its duty to criticize) it is a matter of faith. No one of our contemporaries has seen with his own eyes Alexander, Caesar, or even Napoleon: we *believe* that they existed through *faith* in documents. The Alexander, the Caesar, the Napoleon of history are also and adequately an Alexander of faith, a Caesar of faith, a Napoleon of faith: it could not be otherwise from the moment that history makes its inevitable appeal to testimony. A fact of history is necessarily a fact of faith, but the opposite is not true: a fact of faith is not of necessity a historical faith. The Apostles, however, and the Evangelists claim to be testifying to a historical fact when they testify to the Resurrection of Jesus Christ: it is the historicity of this fact that is still the foundation of our faith, which is not only a religious faith but basically a historian's faith. We believe in Jesus Christ, Son of God, but we believe also and first of all in Jesus, in his death, in his burial, in his Resurrection, as any specialist believes in the past existence of Alexander, Caesar, and Napoleon.

The Church was not born in the void or in a laboratory retort. It was born in the open air, in the very locality where Jesus was born, lived, was judged, died, was buried, rose from the dead, and was seen and touched after his Resurrection. The Church was born of the historical fact of the Resurrection of Jesus from the dead. How can one imagine that such a fact could have been publicly affirmed, in the very locality and shortly after the event, without being contradicted at a time when it so seriously disturbed established interests, customs, and passions? What a boon to the enemies of Jesus and of the growing Church to be able to convict the Apostles of imposture or of madness simply by confronting their accounts with the facts. This confrontation for the purpose of contradiction never took place, simply because both camps were too close to the facts for it to be possible for either to contest them. The immediate point at issue was the significance of these facts and not the facts themselves. In the same way today former President Truman, the English pacifists, and the victims of Hiroshima would certainly not be in agreement over the dropping of the fateful bomb.

In fact, when one reads the Acts of the Apostles and Saint Paul—the latter a highly desirable witness because he was at first an enemy—one perceives that the contradiction has to do not with the facts but rather with the responsibility for and the consequences of them. Friends and enemies of Christianity were in agreement about the facts, forced into agreement no doubt by the proximity of those same facts, still warm and irrefutable. What did the enemies of the infant Church hold against the Apostles? The fact of being saddled with responsibility for the death of Jesus. In addition, they reproached the Apostles with upsetting the traditions of Moses, preaching in the name of Jesus, asserting the Messianic and divine nature of Jesus' personality, and, most of all, with daring to assert that Jesus was henceforth at the right hand of God. It was on account of this last declaration that Saint Stephen was murdered—in the presence of the future Saint Paul, who at that time approved the murder.

Strange though it seems, the enemies of the infant Church appear not to have denied even the fact of the Resurrection and appearances of Jesus, still less his death or the circumstances of his burial and Resurrection. The hatred of the people who were the enemies of Jesus and, later, of the Apostles, bears witness to the veracity of the Gospels, for that contemporary hatred never disputes their veracity.

It is true that the Jewish historian Josephus, also a contemporary, devotes little space to Jesus and to Christianity. Certain passages in which he mentions this subject seem to be Christian interpolations. What can reasonably be said is that Josephus—who is not considered overly scrupulous, who at the time of the war joined the Roman camp in suspicious circumstances, and who, moreover, belonged to the sect of the Pharisees —perhaps says *a little too little* about Jesus and the origins of Christianity for his silences to be altogether candid. However unimportant it may have been politically, the execution of Jesus had given rise to a juridical action which, among a legalistic people, must have left traces. The open tomb and the disappearance of the body must have given rise to an inquiry. Nothing of this remains. The archives of Jerusalem were destroyed along with the city.

Then, too, the Pharisees very quickly took into their hands the destiny of Judaism. They were intelligent and subtle politicians, and perhaps they understood that silence was the best means of dealing with an affair that was in every respect beyond them. Chancelleries, especially ecclesiastical chancelleries, know the strength and weight of silence. Just the same, one could not expect Jesus' worst enemies to become the chroniclers of the facts. The Pharisees wrote nothing on the subject of Jesus. But they did not write anything, either, to contradict the history that was being written without their consent and sometimes against them. How could they have been ignorant of the writings and the preaching of the Apostles? But how could they contradict them if they knew they were irrefutable? The best thing for them was to remain silent.

Like certain great and sudden historical events the resurrection of Jesus Christ had a liberating meaning for some and a crushing meaning for others. It is obvious that for Christ's enemies it was crushing, more than crushing, disconcerting and embarrassing. They were the people who held political power, and this event did not jibe with their interests or with their expectations. In similar circumstances the tendency of every government is to disguise the facts or to suppress them, at the very least to minimize them. Sometimes an official truth is successfully imposed on the whole of public opinion.

Our generation, on one particular occasion, has had a strange experience. On November 22, 1963, President Kennedy was assassinated in Dallas, Texas. After almost a year, what more do we know? What precise information can we expect to have in the near future, or even in the remote future? This brutal murder disarranged so many things, and perhaps rearranged so many things, that it may be better for us to know nothing.

How can one fail to believe that the historical fact of the resurrection of Jesus Christ threw the government responsible for his death into confusion? The fact that we do not know very much about how that government reacted disproves nothing about the fact; it is rather an added proof of its veracity.

After all, when almost two thousand years have passed, it is a little late to try to cast doubt on the very existence of Jesus (as some have had the effrontery to do) or his death on the cross, or his burial in the tomb of Joseph of Arimathea, or even the existence of Joseph of Arimathea and of his tomb, or of the guard over the tomb, or of the tomb open and empty on the third day and the appearances of Jesus that followed. Rationalistic criticism is not rational, everything is grist to its mill, all means are legitimate. It constructs the most extravagant hypotheses with an air of imperturbability.

It has represented the Apostles as fire-eaters, as experienced plotters, full of courage and imagination, who spirited away Jesus' body in order to support the story of his Resurrection. Whereas, during those black days, the Apostles were cowards; they were certainly not fanatics filled with exaltation but poor creatures clinging desperately to their own skins and interested only in keeping out of sight.

Whether it speaks in the voice of Renan or in that of some illustrious professor, rationalistic criticism cannot escape from its own unreal epoch: it possesses all the doltishness of romanticism. "Expectation generally creates its object," Renan writes gravely. "The interior travail of their enthusiastic souls could suggest to them the vision of what they hoped for," writes Alfred Loisy. "In external circumstances, which we cannot precisely describe," Maurice Goguel writes more prudently, "the Messianic faith of the Apostles was not only restored but exalted. This resurrection of their faith became confused in their minds with the resurrection of the Lord himself." And Charles Guignebert: "This sort of tension between desire and faith in minds and hearts of men at once crude and mystical, exalted by moral suffering and in a state of anxious expectation, has only one logical outcome—visions."

I am sorry to be lacking in respect toward all these academic and university authorities, but their conception of men and their experience of life seem to me altogether puerile. I took part in the Resistance— curiously enough with the son of Professor Guignebert; I have been in prison; I have belonged to groups "at once crude and mystical," as the elder Guignebert calls them. False rumors certainly abounded, the fruit of our desire rather than of events. Prophecies, too. We passionately longed for the liberation of our country, we awaited it with fervor or despair, depending on the day; but all that atmosphere of exaltation did not advance the liberation by a single hour.

All the combatants in the Resistance, the prudent and the daring alike, are in agreement on the date and the fact of the Liberation of Paris in August 1944. If that Liberation of Paris had never taken place, it is very probable that we would have known that, too, and despite our private quarrels and our exaltation, while awaiting death in a concentration camp or at daybreak against a wall, we would have been in agreement, too, that Paris had not been liberated. To which one of us in prison would it have occurred to say: "Expectation generally creates its object?" I prefer the Pharisees, who, having nothing better than such nonsense to say, did not have the heart to write it down and in fact said nothing at all. If this preposterous stuff is all you have against the historicity of the Gospels, then hold your sententious mouths.

Before tracing the course of events and undertaking a more detailed analysis of the text of the Gospel, permit me to pause here briefly and gather together the general conclusions about the Resurrection of Jesus Christ to which I myself have been led through slow and richly rewarding meditation on the Gospels.

First of all, the Resurrection of Jesus Christ is a historical fact. It is not a legendary or symbolic fact or simply "a mystical and religious" one, as has been insinuated for the purpose of denying its historical reality. It is a historical fact whose authenticity, like that of every historical fact, depends upon testimony and the critical examination of that testimony.

The Resurrection of Jesus Christ is, nonetheless, a miraculous fact, absolutely inexplicable through the simple operation of natural forces.

It is not only a miraculous fact, but a fact absolutely unique up to this time (apart, according to the Catholic faith, from the resurrection of the Virgin, which is later in time and consequent upon it). There had been other miraculous resurrections, recounted in the Bible and the Gospel itself. That of Jesus has a completely different character. It is a change of state and condition. Through his Resurrection Jesus did not make a return into our time and our earthly condition, but entered bodily into eternity; he permanently opened the access to eternity for man, body and soul. His resurrection is not a retreat, it is a forward motion, this time irreversible: the risen Christ dies no more.

The Resurrection is a unique fact, but of irreversible and universal significance, like the creation of the world, like the fall of Adam, like the invention of fire or of the wheel, like the liberation of atomic energy. This Resurrection involves the whole of humanity in a solidarity that is in fact universal; it is a new point of attraction at the center of gravity of the human universe; it disarranges and rearranges the movements of all human destinies, whether we wish it so or not.

My task now is to attempt a more circumstantial account of the Resurrection, drawing principally on Matthew, Luke, and John, who complement one another. It is clear that the Evangelists, here more than anywhere else, are less interested in harmonizing details than in firmly establishing their testimony about the essential fact. Sometimes one Evangelist talks of a single angel where another mentions two; Matthew speaks of the women disciples of Jesus in general, whereas John mentions only Mary Magdalene; one puts the emphasis on the appearances in Galilee, the other on those in Judea. For his part, Paul does not speak of the finding of the empty tomb, but he never dissociates the burial of Christ from his Resurrection. On the essential fact, the Acts of the Apostles, Paul, and the Gospels all are in accord: the burial of Jesus Christ, proof of his death, his bodily appearances, proof of his Resurrection from the dead. It is indeed the same man whose body was laid in the tomb of Joseph of Arimathea who appeared to his disciples three days later and had them touch that body, henceforth living and glorious. This is the essential, prodigious fact on which the testimony of the Apostles is concentrated.

It remains no less certain that around this essential fact the various accounts of the circumstances remain disordered and difficult to harmonize. That is the way it is with every event that is exceptional, amazing, sudden, and brutal. Even in our own time the immediate testimony about the murderous attack in public on President Kennedy was inconsistent except on the single fact that he had been assassinated in Dallas, Texas, in November 1963. This means that any reconstruction of the secondary facts carries with it a margin of hypothesis and personal choice among a number of possibilities.

Matthew, who wrote in Aramaic in Jerusalem itself and not long after the event, is the only one to mention the episode of the guard at the tomb. This episode ends in comedy. I have often noticed that every great event carries with it an element of drollery: this seems to be a mark of its authenticity. We are, of course, accustomed to consider with utmost gravity anything that touches our religion. But as for Jesus Christ himself, who had spent that day on the other side of the world, why should he be forbidden a little amusement on precisely that day? Amusement at the expense of those who were his enemies, perhaps even at the expense of those who were his friends. After all, he had risen from the dead, he saw things differently thenceforth, his style was not altogether the same. What is there astonishing in that? The behavior of any man is different in the midst of battle and after the victory has been won. And what a victory for Jesus! This day is his. In their times of utmost glory, the greatest captains retain a trace of humor. Risen from among the dead, Jesus Christ does not cease to be a man, a great man and a great captain.

And so he did not disdain to throw the purple of ridicule over those who had driven him to death. They, however, really believed they had bested him; finally and for the first time they were at ease; Jesus was dead, thoroughly dead, discreetly and permanently stretched out on a stone bench in the obscure inner chamber of a tomb. Let the seals of the chief priest be placed on that tomb and, for greater security, let a guard and sentinels be stationed before that tomb!

Matt. 28:2-4   Matthew says, "And behold, there was a great earthquake; for an angel of the Lord came down from heaven, and drawing near rolled back the stone, and sat upon it. His countenance was like lightning, and his raiment like snow. And for fear of him the guards were terrified, and became like dead men. . . ." Those who lived through the last war know what the breath of a big bomb is like, not even to mention the atomic bomb. Obviously something of the same sort happened here. The soldiers were thrown to the ground, then groped about to discover whether they were still alive, felt their limbs, tremblingly reassembled their arms and their equipment, glanced, cautiously perhaps, into the interior of the tomb, for after all duty came first, only to discover with terror that the tomb was empty. Dumfounded at this, they withdrew to take counsel at a distance and decide what must be done. Since there was nothing else to do, hanging their heads, they returned in a column of twos to Jerusalem to give an accounting to the chief priests. They would look fine after letting a dead man escape. There was no chance of their escaping court-martial. What a disaster!

Their reception by the chief priests was surprising. The latter did not fall into a rage; they did not denounce the guard to Pilate for desertion of their post, but accepted what had happened with amazing readiness. In fact—and this is what I find striking—when the guard, overcome and confused, came to find them and told them that an angel had knocked them down, that the tomb was open, and that the body had disappeared, the chief priests did not doubt for an instant that they were in the presence of a new prodigy on the part of him whom they called "the Seducer." They, the enemies of Jesus, at this moment believed in his continuing miraculous power, they believed more promptly than most of his friends. Hatred has its own form of clairvoyance. . . . In their minds this man would always be a serpent, whose head they thought they had crushed, but who suddenly rose up again more dangerous than ever.

What were they to do? The chief priests thought it over and decided to bribe the soldiers. Matthew finishes his account: "And when they had assembled with the elders, and had consulted together, they gave much money to the soldiers, telling them, 'Say, "His disciples came by night and stole him while we were sleeping." And if the procurator hears of this, we will persuade him and keep you out of trouble.' And they took the money, and did as they were instructed; and this story has been spread abroad among the Jews even to the present day." Matt. 28:12-15

The stubbornness of hatred does not recoil before anything and does not fear to heap one absurdity on another. At the moment when the disciples, filled with consternation at the shipwreck of all their hopes and sick with dread of being arrested in their turn, have shut themselves up in a house, not venturing to set foot outside, they are accused of having made a surprise attack of most improbable daring. This is like those hunting stories in which the unhappy hare, finally tired of flee- ing, turns and pursues the hunter. To crown it all, the guards, instead of being thrown into prison for negligence of duty and desertion of their post, are given money so that they can go into the taverns and tell everyone the story of their unpardonable failure. They would buy round after round to the health of the chief priest and to the fabulous dead man who could go through walls.

I have often observed that the behavior of women in the presence of a corpse is different from that of men. For them the corpse of a beloved being is still the beloved being: they embrace it, they wash it, they dress it in its best clothes, they cover it with perfume and with flowers: they would like to keep it as long as possible before entrusting it to the earth. Then later it is women who generally visit cemeteries, except on those occasions when such visits are beyond their strength.

As for men, it is quite different. The best of them are capable of great sacrifices, the sacrifice of life itself, for the safety of a friend, but once death has supervened, the corpse embarrasses them; let it be given the final honors, and let that be that. There is nothing simpler, nothing more expeditious, nothing more honorable either, than the burial of a comrade on the battlefield. And life goes on.

This time it was exactly that way. One can feel it between the lines of the Gospel. Among Jesus' disciples the women and the men behave in opposite fashions. For the men it is all over, their hope is broken, they are overwhelmed by the blow, they resent it but in the end they adjust to it. What else is there to do? Life goes on: tomorrow each will return to his former trade, the fisherman to his boat, the peasant to his plow. The two men who are known as the disciples of Emmaus illus-

Luke 24:19-21

trate this situation. They are speaking of Jesus of Nazareth: "Concerning Jesus of Nazareth, who was a prophet, mighty in work and word before God and all the people; and how our chief priests and rulers delivered him up to be sentenced to death, and crucified him. But we were hoping that it was he who should redeem Israel. . . ." But what now? He is dead, and this hope lies at their feet like a broken vessel to be thrown away. And so they return to their homes to take up their daily tasks, pensioners of a splendid dream and a great conquest, demobilized soldiers of a revolution that began well and then miscarried.

But the women? Ah, with the women it is quite different! They do not adjust to anything. They know very well that Jesus is dead, they have seen him laid in the earth, they were there. But, even more than being their hope, Jesus was their love; beyond death he remains so. This love has not broken: the death of the well-beloved has only hardened this diamond-like love. These young Jewish women, rocked from infancy to the marvelous strophes of the Song of Songs, have intuitively recognized in Jesus the prince of that Song. They know by heart the splendid verses:

Can. 8:6-7

> Set me as a seal on your heart,
> As a seal on your arm;
> For stern as death is love,
> Relentless as the nether world is devotion;
> Its flames are a blazing fire.
> Deep waters cannot quench love,
> Nor floods sweep it away. . . .

We have no idea of the importance of perfumes in ancient civilizations. In the Song of Songs there is as much talk of perfume as of beauty or of love. Is there in the whole history of men anything more moving than the preparations made by these few women who, with the Sabbath over, at daybreak busy themselves exclusively with perfumes and would be capable of moving heaven and earth to obtain them? Once the Temple trumpets have announced the end of the great Sabbath, they leave their houses and begin hurrying through the narrow streets, they visit the perfume stores, pounding for admittance, and, loaded down with precious amphorae, they proceed in the brightening dawn toward the garden of Joseph of Arimathea. Perhaps this was the beginning of the first fine day of spring, when the birds were awakening and there was a lightness in all of nature, as all these women, shod in sandals, hurried along the roads.

It is not known whether they all arrived together. Probably Mary Magdalene, younger and more agile—more greatly in love, as well—

than the others, was the swiftest. The guards had already left when she arrived at the tomb. Her despair was great to find it open and empty. Like some unwearying gazelle, she began to run again, back to Jerusalem and straight to the house where she found John and Simon Peter. She entered, shook them, awakened them, and, breathlessly, cried into their ears: "They have taken the Lord from the tomb, and we do not John 20:2 know where they have laid him . . . !" The idea that Jesus might have risen never crosses her mind, not even hers. But she does not say "the body" or "the corpse," but "the Lord," and this personalization is splendid.

Then in the early morning there is a bewildering series of comings and goings by diverse roads: people meet or, more often, miss one another, see angels, and then do not see them any more; everyone seems to be playing hide and seek with everyone else. This has indeed the air of a stage effect, improbable, unbelievable, but true, ineluctably true and real. What an admirable stratagem on the part of Jesus, who remains as always the poet. It was necessary first of all to arouse the disciples from their torpor, from their prostration, from their despair, from their mourning, and to plunge them to the ears in disquietude and questioning.

For after all, at the beginning of that fantastic morning, there was a moment—a moment that may have lasted for several hours—during which everyone wondered just what had happened. Everyone, I say, friends and enemies, the chief priests as well as the Apostles. During this long moment, in those few houses in Jerusalem where it was known that Jesus' tomb was open and empty, there was the sort of solemn unrest that reigns in a country on whose frontiers a decisive battle is being fought, with the fate of the country at stake and the outcome as yet unknown. How heavy and how agonizing is the wait! What had become, yes, what had become, of that body that had disappeared as though by magic?

While Mary Magdalene, in desperation, was hurrying along the roads, the other women arrived at the tomb. They perceived an angel (Luke says there were two) who assured them that Jesus had risen. Mark and Luke speak of the Angels as unknown men, clothed in dazzling white tunics, who went before these much intimidated young women. The two Evangelists have the angels say that Jesus *will precede* his disciples to Galilee. But in the sequel Jesus appears in Judea before appearing in Galilee. Perhaps it is here that the Vulgate has misled the translators: for the corresponding Greek word can mean not only "to precede" but also "to escort," "to take with one."

For my own part I can think of another explanation as well. We strive to project our rational consistency into the mind of Jesus Christ. According to the rules of rational consistency, Jesus could not have said to his angels that he would precede the disciples in Galilee, since he had the intention of appearing to them first in Judea. But why not attribute to this man who is Jesus the impulses of the human heart as well? Why should he not have changed his mind? Why should not his impatience to see his friends and to be recognized by them—after the terrible separation of death—why should this not have upset his original plan? The precipitancy of his heart prevented him from waiting and postponing his meeting with those whom he loved and for whom he had died. And so there was a failure of communication between Jesus and the angels: what did the angels matter? On Easter morning they were no more than servants, it was the disciples who remained his beloved friends. Men were what principally interested him that morning, not angels; it was toward men that the weight of his heart irresistibly drew him. For even the omnipotence of God seems incapable of resisting love.

The women return to Jerusalem, overcome with terror. Peter and John, informed by Mary Magdalene, rush to the tomb. John, who is younger, arrives first. Out of respect for his elder, he waits so that the latter may enter before him. This waiting on John's part is a beautiful thing, in which respect for authority restrains the impatience of love. Each of them is now altogether awake. Like responsible men, they want to know and take into account the smallest details. One detail does, in fact, strike them: the bands which had been wound around the corpse lie on the ground, and the shroud with which it had been covered has been carefully folded and placed in a corner. If the body had been stolen, it would have been taken away as it was, with the bands still around it, and no one would have troubled to straighten up the tomb. It was then that John knew he was in the presence of a new miracle by his master. *He believed.*

Important testimony, that. Such scenes are not invented. Men capable of devising the story that Jesus had been raised from the dead— and the disciples were certainly incapable of it—would not have paid any attention to the bands and the winding-sheet; it would never have occurred to them to turn such things to their advantage. Something of the sort could find a place in Arthur Conan Doyle, but only in the cases of crimes planned well in advance. The death of their master struck the Apostles like a bolt of lightning, not allowing them time for any premeditation. A detective who arrives at the scene of a crime just committed—as Peter and John arrived at the tomb—knows that at the very first moment, when everything is still in place, any detail may open a path to the truth.

A Strauss, a Renan, a Loisy has nothing of the detective about him. They are intellectuals bent on theorizing, where all that is needed is to open one's eyes and observe minutely.

Peter and John return to their homes. Overcome with anguish, Mary Magdalene goes sadly back to the place where she has lost—permanently, she believes—all trace of her beloved. What follows is fragrant with love as a garden in the twilight of a hot summer's day is fragrant with the scent of flowers. Here John must be quoted:

But Mary was standing outside weeping at the tomb. So, as she wept, she stooped down and looked into the tomb, and saw two angels in white sitting, one at the head and one at the feet, where the body of Jesus had been laid. They said to her, "Woman, why art thou weeping?" She said to them, "Because they have taken away my Lord, and I do not know where they have laid him." John 20:11-18

When she had said this she turned around and beheld Jesus standing there, and she did not know that it was Jesus. Jesus said to her, "Woman, why art thou weeping? Whom dost thou seek?" She, thinking that he was the gardener, said to him, "Sir, if thou hast removed him, tell me where thou hast laid him and I will take him away."

Jesus said to her, "Mary!" Turning, she said to him, "Rabboni!" (that is to say, Master).

Jesus said to her, "Do not touch me, for I have not yet ascended to my Father, but go to my brethren and say to them, 'I ascend to my Father and your Father, to my God and your God.' "

Mary Magdalene came, and announced to the disciples, "I have seen the Lord, and these things he said to me."

On a visit to Vézelay I chanced to hear the discourse of a worthy Benedictine who was doing the honors of the place. I blushed for him. In that marvelous basilica, constructed in honor of Mary Magdalene, this poor man persisted in explaining its architecture and history as though Mary Magdalene had never existed. But that is how it is: this woman has always exasperated certain kinds of people. Today she exasperates the puritans, the intellectuals, and the exegetes, as formerly she exasperated the Pharisees and, among the Apostles, Judas. She is too great, she is too near to Christ, she understands everything too well, she loves too well, and yet she says nothing or almost nothing, but she intrudes, she gives scandal. However, she not only scandalizes Pharisees and traitors, above all she gets on the nerves of the mediocre. She has great vision and great love, she raps only at those portals whose knocker is at a horseman's height through her beauty alone, through her style, through the boldness and precision of her gestures; she is too spectacular. She is provocative. She provokes admiration, and, on the side of the shadows, anger.

The apostolic testimony on which the Church is founded deals essentially with the burial and the Resurrection of Jesus Christ. Now, Mary Magdalene was the first involved in this double event. Through her anointing of Jesus at Bethany she and she alone predicted the coming death and burial of the Son of Man. With Jesus' mother and John she was at the foot of the cross. She was also at the tomb and she stayed there after all the others had left. Now she is here on Easter morning, she returns first to the tomb, and the first appearance of Christ recounted in the Gospels is to her. It is then that Jesus takes her, before any of the others, into his confidence in regard to his ascension to the Father. It would seem that he did not want to enjoy his full glory without first admitting her to the secret.

I have insisted as strongly as I could on the distinction between a resurrection that is simply a drawing back into our present life and a resurrection that is a movement forward, an access to life eternal: Mary Magdalene was instructed, and by Jesus himself, concerning the manner of his Resurrection. From the moment that it was a question of his returning to his Father, he no longer belonged to our earthly world except through his human solidarity with all of us: "My Father and your Father, my God and your God." To Mary Magdalene, Jesus reveals the whole dimensions of his Catholic, that is to say, universal Church. His sitting beside the Father is the pledge and guaranty of the Communion of Saints: it is there that we are to rejoin him, it is there that he appoints the meeting through the intermediation of Mary Magdalene, there lies the ultimate term of our human destiny. What a great saint is she who was judged worthy of being incorporated immediately and so profoundly into the mystery of our salvation! The liturgy which, with modesty and daring, goes so deeply into the secret of the Scriptures applies to Mary Magdalene the praises written for the Beloved in the Song of Songs. Truly and poetically, she is that Beloved.

Highest of all is assuredly the Virgin Mary, the door through which the Word entered to dwell among us. The Virgin Mary is within the "hypostatic order," as theologians say, since her maternity reaches its term in the personality of the Son of God himself. She is the Mother of God, the "Theotokos" acclaimed in the Councils. No human being

is more closely associated than she with the adventure of the redemptive Incarnation. On these grounds she well deserves, in relation to
Jesus, the second Adam, the title that has been bestowed on her of
second Eve, through whom salvation came to us, as through the first
Eve we met shipwreck.

But in another fashion Mary Magdalene also deserves this title of
second Eve. It is not I who say so. I am going to quote here in its entirety an objection and a reply from the *Summa Theologica*. Thomas
Aquinas raises the question whether it was proper that the Resurrection of Jesus Christ should have been made manifest to a few rather
than to all. The third objection is typical misogyny: whether it was
made to all or not to all, if there was any class who should not have
entered into the secret of the resurrection, it was women. Here it is:

The resurrection of Christ was made manifest to those who were to bear
witness to it: they were to deliver their testimony through public preaching. However this is an office that is not proper for women. Saint Paul
formally commands, "In the assemblies let women be silent!" And once
more: "I do not permit women to teach." It seems, then, that it was not the
right procedure for the risen Christ to appear at first to women rather than
to gatherings of men.

Aquinas replies:

It is true that woman is not authorized to teach publicly in the Church.
It is, however, permitted to her to give instruction and counsels in private
and to members of her family. It is Ambrose who says, "Woman is given
the mission with those who belong to her household." She is not given the
mission of bearing to all the people the testimony of the resurrection.

Nevertheless the Christ first appeared to women in order that woman,
who first delivered to man a message of death, should also be the first to
announce life in the glory of the risen Christ. This is why Cyril explains,
"It was woman who was formerly the minister of death, it is she too who is
first to perceive and announce the venerable mystery of the resurrection.
It was there that the female sex obtained absolution from the ignominy
and rejection of the malediction."

I think that this Cyril, quoted approvingly by Aquinas, is Saint Cyril
of Alexandria, the ardent champion of the Council at Ephesus, who
proclaimed the divine maternity of Mary. It is important to note that
these lines quoted by Aquinas are taken from a commentary by Cyril
on the passage in the Gospel of John that I am now explaining and that
recounts the appearance of Christ to Mary Magdalene. The parallel

between Eve and Mary Magdalene goes very far back in tradition: it must not be lost.

Thomas Aquinas concludes:

By this one can see as well that, insofar as the state of glory is concerned, there is no disadvantage in being a woman. If they are animated by a greater charity, women will enjoy a greater glory, flowing from the divine vision. It is evident that these women loved the Lord in a closer and more intimate fashion [*arctius amaverunt*] since at the time when the disciples themselves withdrew from the tomb, they did not leave, and it was they who were the first to see the Lord rising in his glory [*in gloria resurgentem*].

Yes, they caught him in the very act of his glorious Resurrection.

Thomas Aquinas, like Matthew, is speaking of holy women in general, where John speaks only of Mary Magdalene. It is possible indeed that Jesus appeared twice, to Mary Magdalene and then to other women separately. But Mark is explicit: "He appeared first to Mary Magdalene, out of whom he had cast seven devils." What a long road this woman has traversed from the day when, prostrate at the feet of Jesus and bathing them with her tears, she obtained forgiveness for her sins because of the quality and intensity of her love, to this garden where she once more seizes the feet of her Savior and covers them with kisses. In order to express this tenderness and this joy we may properly draw upon the Song of Songs: "My lover belongs to me and I to him; he browses among the lilies."

I know the misgivings that may come to mind. These misgivings are unclean and they are false: they rise from the most shadowy and infected regions of our being. Why should they be a cause of fear? They cannot stain the glow and the tenderness of this meeting in the shining garden of Joseph of Arimathea. Certainly this woman has been a courtesan, "a woman of the streets," but it is not her past, forgiven and wiped out, that disposes Jesus in her favor. It is the fact that she has been lifted up, entire, through the violence of her love for the glorious risen body of her Lord. And in that transcendence even her own body begins to be transfigured into a languor of love that is above this world. There is nothing here but what is pure and holy: through death the body of Christ is restored in glory, but through the glowing furnace of charity the body of Mary Magdalene, too, has become a delicate metal precious and wholly pure.

Once more it is Saint Paul who puts this most plainly: "I speak in a human way because of the weakness of your flesh; for as you yielded your members as slaves of uncleanness and iniquity unto iniquity, so now yield your members as slaves of justice unto sanctification." For

Mark 16:9

Can. 2:16

Rom. 6:19

Paul's text is as direct as that. Mary Magdalene, the former daughter of joy, is now the daughter of a joy that is divine.

I know very well the source of our suspicions and of the uneasiness that Mary Magdalene causes us. The shame is entirely ours. Our era is abominably puritan; the minute we think of the body we think of evil. We believe that the body is damned in advance, that it belongs by right to the Devil, that it is impossible for it to be pure, and that everything that comes of it can only be bad. Well now, that is simply not true. The body too can be purified, it can be transfigured by the grace of Jesus Christ, it too is worthy of entering into glory. If this moving encounter between Jesus, arisen and disguised as a gardener, and Mary Magdalene, overwhelmed by love—if this encounter means anything, that is certainly what it means. Mary Magdalene should be the great saint of modern times. Let us beseech her to cleanse us from our puritanism and from the stains it has put even on our judgment, which is bold only in evil. In matters of the good, our judgment is timid indeed.

I shall speak even more clearly, for any ambiguity that lingers around Mary Magdalene and her relations with Jesus Christ is a proper cause for exasperation, and of no further importance. Personally I am careful to be true to the teaching of the Church and I attempt to free myself from all puritanism, at least in my judgments. The natural relation of the male and female sexes does not shock me at all. On the contrary, since this relation happens to be the means for the transmission of life, I consider its character sacred in nature, and this inspires nothing but respect. But after all, despite the ridicule that has been heaped upon chastity in our modern civilization, nothing will force me to depreciate it. Courage, too, and heroism, have been turned to derision. Less than chastity, perhaps, but to some extent, and even that is too much.

Obviously, like everything that is connected with the body, chastity is ambiguous. Not all that is materially chaste is for that reason virtuous: there is a chastity of stones, a chastity of dry hearts, a chastity of those who are misers of themselves, and a chastity of those who are impotent, and there is a chastity of cowardly bigots, who are afraid of hell. All these forms of chastity are rotten.

But I say that there is a heroic chastity, which is the consummation of love, for it is the most sublime consecration to God of the moral and physical generosity of a human being—yes, Pharisees, even of that being's beauty and physical generosity. Jesus and Mary Magdalene, what a fine couple for the cinema, one thinks. . . . Not at all, it is by no means what you believe, certainly not through lack of love or mutual inclination, but on the contrary through such an excess of love that it cannot be expressed except by silence. And if you do not perceive that this is possible, it is because you are totally lacking in poetic imagination.

Between the ordinary relations of a man and a woman who love each other and the kind of heroic chastity of which I am speaking, there is a difference of the same order as between a friendship that expresses itself in conversation, frequent meetings, customary services, and, on the other hand, death voluntarily accepted, in ineluctable circumstances, to save one's friend. Would you say that a death of this sort is the end or the negation of that friendship? Quite the opposite, it is its seal and consummation. Such is the chastity of Mary Magdalene: that beautiful woman was so perfectly made for love that love has drawn her into the total immolation of herself. "Do not touch me!" Jesus says to her, and this means, "Let me go, cease to hold me back!" Mary Magdalene lets her Beloved withdraw, and this relinquishment is the fairest homage of love that a woman ever paid a man.

If you do not see that, you will be forever unable to understand any of the grandeur of the individual, nor will you ever know to what degree the Lord Jesus is lovable, to what degree he demands to be loved, to what degree it is at once sweet and hard to love him, to what degree he is jealous of our bodies as well as our souls. It is at the cost of this precious love that our bodies themselves, to use the words of Saint Paul, can become temples of the Holy Spirit. Could ambition for this give rise to contempt for the body, contempt for love, to puritanism? On the contrary, it could only arouse respect for the body and for love.

Mary Magdalene has many things to teach us, which we can learn simply by meditating on her example. She was made patroness of the Crusades and of Frankish knighthood because of her prediction of the burial of Christ, because of her fidelity at the tomb of Christ, and also, perhaps, because, before the fact, she conceived of courtly love. She has been the great patroness of the Dominican Order, the Order of Preachers, who call her *"Apostola Apostolorum"*—"Apostle of the Apostles"—for it was she who was the first to announce to the Apostles themselves the news that, through their mouths, was to encompass the earth: Christ is risen.

What happened? The Apostles did not believe her. They thought she was raving, that the violence of her grief had driven her mad. To love to the point of madness has never been socially well thought of, and that was the state of Mary Magdalene. It is Luke who takes note of it:

"And having returned from the tomb, they reported all these things to   Luke 24:9-11
the Eleven, and to all the rest. Now, it was Mary Magdalene and Joanna
and Mary, the mother of James, and the other women who were with
them, who were telling these things to the apostles. But this tale seemed
to them to be *nonsense, and they did not believe the women.*" The holy
Church began well. One cannot say that the Catholic hierarchy has
been from its beginnings afflicted with an excessive inclination toward
credulity. And this continues to be so: no one is harder to convince than
an ecclesiastical superior. Quite automatically he prefers to think you
mad rather than to believe your word. That was what happened to poor
Max Jacob. When he went, trembling, to see his curé in order to tell
him that he had been having visions, the curé said, "Do not worry, my
friend; there is a treatment for that, and people get over it!"

May Mary Magdalene teach us patience and humility as well! But
the Apostles would pay for their conduct. Jesus Christ never allowed
lack of respect for Mary Magdalene to pass unrebuked: this is one of
the constant elements in his behavior from one end of the Gospel to
the other. And the Benedictine of Vézelay, what lies in store for him?

Mark notes that, later the same day, Jesus "appeared to the Eleven   Mark 16:14
as they were at table; and he upbraided them for their lack of faith
and hardness of heart, *in that they had not believed those who had
seen him after he had risen.*" While the encounter in the garden between the risen Christ and Mary Magdalene is wholly steeped in tenderness, when Jesus finally sees his Apostles, he begins at once to up-
braid them harshly. And serve them right!

After the appearance to Mary Magdalene, there is an appearance to
Simon Peter, about which nothing is known except that it took place.
Then there is the appearance on the road to Emmaus, depicted with
such unobtrusive piety by Rembrandt.

Here is Luke's account:

And behold, two of them were going that very day to a village named   Luke 24:13-32
Emmaus, which is sixty stadia from Jerusalem. And they were talking to
each other about all these things that had happened. And it came to pass,
while they were conversing and arguing together, that Jesus himself also
drew near and went along with them; but their eyes were held, that they
should not recognize him.

And he said to them, "What words are these that you are exchanging as
you walk and are sad?" But one of them, named Cleophas, answered and

said to him, "Art thou the only stranger in Jerusalem who does not know the things that have happened there in these days?" And he said to them, "What things?"

And they said to him, "Concerning Jesus of Nazareth, who was a prophet, mighty in work and word before God and all the people; and how our chief priests and rulers delivered him up to be sentenced to death, and crucified him. But we were hoping that it was he who should redeem Israel. Yes, and besides all this, today is the third day since these things came to pass. And moreover, certain women of our company, who were at the tomb before it was light, astounded us, and not finding his body, they came, saying that they had also seen a vision of angels, who said that he is alive. So some of our company went to the tomb, and found it even as the women had said, but him they did not see."

But he said to them, "O foolish ones and slow of heart to believe in all that the prophets have spoken! Did not the Christ have to suffer these things before entering into his glory?" And beginning then with Moses and with all the Prophets, he interpreted to them in all the Scriptures the things referring to himself.

And they drew near to the village to which they were going, and he acted as though he were going on. And they urged him, saying, "Stay with us, for it is getting towards evening, and the day is now far spent." And he went in with them.

And it came to pass when he reclined at table with them, that he took the bread and blessed and broke and began handing it to them. And their eyes were opened, and they recognized him; and he vanished from their sight. And they said to each other, "Was not our heart burning within us while he was speaking on the road and explaining to us the Scriptures?"

Here is Jesus, arisen, searching for his own along the road. Obviously he recognizes them, but they do not recognize him, at least not immediately. First he wants to warm their hearts and win over their minds before revealing himself completely. This is splendid courtesy on his part. It is also a lover's game. In all times lovers have made use of disguises and surprises with one another, especially in happy circumstances. After a dreadful contest, Jesus has won, he finds his own again, he cannot refrain from astonishing and surprising them: this is not deceit, it is the poetry of love. Perhaps he has appeared to many others who, because their hearts and minds were not preoccupied with him, were not worthy that he should make himself known to them. This is the place to quote Pascal's words: "You would not have sought me, had you not already found me."

It is true that as we travel along the roads of this world we do not truly meet any fellow wayfarers save those affected with our own concerns. If we reflected on this a little, how many "relationships" would we not immediately discard, relationships that we keep up only through frivolity? These two simple peasants, returning home, on horseback no doubt, after that terrible week, were not talking to each other about their business, or their pleasures, or their money, or their families. They were talking about Jesus, about his very cruel death, about the hope he had awakened in them that their country would be liberated, about their dreadful disillusionment at the news of his death, about the sadness of their hearts. . . . Oh, those good men!

Jesus, also on horseback, joins them and gently begins to take part in their conversation, principally because it is a conversation in which he is completely at home. What real chance have we of ever meeting Jesus, if he is not already the subject of our concern? And then, very shortly, he is speaking with authority. What does he speak about? He quotes and explains the Scriptures, invokes the prophetic argument, he summarizes the prophecies in a phrase that is the essence of his temporal destiny and at the same time the golden rule of all Christian life. "Did not the Christ have to suffer these things before entering into his glory?" There is the core of the Christian revelation: yes, the misery of man is the wonder of the universe, because it opens up to him life eternal.

As we love him or do not love him, so there is no other means for us to enter in our turn into the glory and the company of Jesus Christ except by the road of suffering and through the door of the cross. As a very ancient orison has it: "May we, through his Passion and his cross, be led to the glory of his Resurrection"—"Per Passionem ejus et crucem, ad Resurrectionis gloriam perducamur." Suffering is the necessary price for the companionship of Jesus Christ: and as Saint Teresa of Avila said to him straightforwardly, "From the way you treat your friends, it is easy to understand why you have so few."

What Scriptures did Jesus quote on the road? No doubt those that are in the tradition of the Church and in its liturgical prayers, the very ones I have cited here and there in this book. However commonplace we Christians may be, when we talk with respect and some understanding of our religion, we simply resume and prolong this peaceful conversation that warmed the hearts of these three mounted men on a road in Judea in the lengthening shadows of evening.

Arrived at their destination, the two travelers cordially invited the unknown to spend the night. And, since neither sorrow nor theology keep men from being hungry, they set themselves at table with excellent appetite. Then they recognized Jesus by his benediction and the breaking of the bread. And immediately afterward Jesus disappeared.

But joy, unlike sorrow, banishes hunger; joy kept them from resuming their repast. They rise immediately from the table and remount their horses, to the bewilderment of the servitors, who now see only two diners where a moment before there had been three.

With their hearts full of lightness at the great news, they gallop through the night toward Jerusalem, where they were told that Jesus has appeared to Peter. Then, since, after all, they have not eaten, they sit down again at table with the Apostles, who are only ten in number, Judas being dead and Thomas absent.

Luke continues:

Luke 24:36-43   Now while they were talking of these things, Jesus stood in their midst, and said to them, "Peace to you! It is I, do not be afraid." But they were startled and panic-stricken, and thought that they saw a spirit. And he said to them, "Why are you disturbed, and why do doubts arise in your hearts? See my hands and feet, that it is I myself. Feel me and see; for a spirit does not have flesh and bones, as you see I have." And having said this, he showed them his hands and his feet.

But as they still disbelieved and marveled for joy, he said, "Have you anything here to eat?" And they offered him a piece of broiled fish and a honeycomb. And when he had eaten in their presence, he took what remained and gave it to them.

Here we must pause a moment over the manner of these appearances. On the one hand, Jesus wishes to prove his identity ("It is indeed I!") and the reality of his body: he shows the wounds of the nails in his hands and feet, he causes himself to be touched, felt, as one feels an animal or as a doctor palpates a patient, he actually eats a bit of fish no less palpable and real, he insists that he is not a phantom, a ghost, and he produces material and tangible proofs. On the other hand . . . well, his body behaves in a strange fashion, positively not like our bodies. He passes through double-locked doors, as he had passed through the stone of the tomb, he changes his appearance at will: Mary Magdalene herself and the disciples at Emmaus did not at first recognize him. She recognized him by his special way of pronouncing her own first name, and they recognized him by his breaking of the bread. He appears and disappears, equally at will.

Rationalistic criticism, to be sure, sees in all this nothing but inconsistency, which is not even worth the trouble of discussing. And yet to me it would seem that our experience as men of this modern age should inspire us with more prudence in our judgments about the possible transmutations of matter.

Only fifty years ago who could have suspected that twenty pounds of crude uranium, "that soft metallic element, dense, hard and of a whitish color like nickel," contained and could deliver energy equivalent to that contained in three thousand tons of oil? Three thousand tons of oil would be approximately the amount that could be transported by two trains of sixty cars each. One can see, can one not, the fantastic mobility of this phenomenon? What economy of space and time and energy in transportation! What a prodigious source of energy and what astounding mobility! This is something that the generation preceding mine could not foresee. I can take an airplane at Orly, with twenty pounds of crude uranium in my suitcase, and find myself next day in Tokyo as though I had transported in a few hours from Paris to Japan a source of energy equivalent to two trainloads of oil. This is literally fabulous. We do not dispute the facts, we believe them with perfect assurance. I say that we believe them simply on hearsay, for the scientists who are able to understand this subject and make practical use of it are few in number. As for myself, I read about it in the *Encyclopaedia Britannica*, a work of unquestioned honesty in such matters. But why should I take the *Encyclopaedia Britannica* at face value and not believe the Gospels?

I shall be told that in order to release its energy uranium must be subjected to a process that consists essentially in the fission of its atoms under intense bombardment by neutrons. This procedure is difficult, exceptional, and very costly. Granted! But the Resurrection of Christ, the passage of a human body from the state of a corpse to the state of participation in life eternal, is that not too an astonishing shock, an exceptionally vigorous and effective "process"? A surprising transmutation of this body? Before Jesus Christ this had never been seen; moreover, the Apostles themselves could not get over it. But before 1938, when Otto Hahn and Fritz Strassmann succeeded in their experiment in producing nuclear fission of uranium, no one suspected the resources of uranium either. Renan, in his time, still had some excuse for being skeptical about the possible transmutations of matter, but we? Seriously, no! When a coarse mineral like uranium contains such surprises, why should we be amazed that a human body, so much further evolved than a mineral and, moreover, spiritualized by its very form, should behave in unforeseen ways under the shock and "bombardment" of eternal life? Frankly I refuse, I refuse absolutely, to find this inconsistent.

It is the opposite that would be inconsistent. Our sluggishness of mind is so great, even when confronted with the phenomena of nature, that if the accounts of these appearances had been fabricated out of whole cloth, they would certainly have been very different: care would have been taken to show that the body of Christ was in no way different from what it had been before his death, save for the wounds. The same weight would have been attributed to it, the same needs, the same density, the same limitations. He would not have gone through walls, he would have climbed the stairs and rapped at the door, like everyone else. The miracle is not the agility, the subtlety, the lightness with which Christ's body seems endowed after his Resurrection, the miracle is the Resurrection of this body and its passage into eternal life. Once this is admitted, nothing astonishes me, all the phenomena that dumfound us seem to me normal. We are the last to be able to dispute the surprising virtues hidden in matter which a prodigious shock can suddenly release.

I am no less impressed by Jesus' insistence that the materiality and solidity of his body should be confirmed by the senses. He is embodied in flesh and bone, living flesh and solid bone: all this is palpable, firm. He can eat if he wishes to, and he eats real food. He insists upon the fact that it is he, he himself, in his own identity, spiritual and bodily. He has forgotten nothing, he recognizes his own, he is able to make them recognize him, he is not abrupt about it, to be sure, and he re- mains the poet, but he is not dreaming, he dissipates all dreams, he makes a point of not being taken for someone else, above all not for a phantom. How well these appearances of the Christ answer the ques- tions I raised at the beginning of this chapter. We, too, one day shall be like him, and God himself will wipe the tears from our eyes.

I can easily detect, even in the case of certain Catholic writers, some embarrassment at these very concrete words of the Gospel. How much these prudent writers would have preferred all this to have taken place in dimness. But no, Jesus Christ had a horror of dimness. He is there in full daylight, open to the inquisitorial hands and eyes of these men who are going to be his witnesses. It is essential that their experience of his physical reality should be fairly made. At bottom, the academic minds of the aforesaid writers are afraid of admitting the double evi- dence: first, the omnipotence of God displayed in Jesus resurrected, secondly, the wonderful surprises inherent in matter. Plato and puri- tanism have injected their venom. For me, on the contrary, the most amazing thing would have been for this body, henceforth a participant in eternal life, to have remained as dense as any other sublunary body. It is no longer dense, but it is just as real as any other sublunary body.

All the Gospels are in accord. John adds the account of a marvelously convincing scene:

John 20:24-29 Now Thomas, one of the Twelve, called the Twin, was not with them when Jesus came. The other disciples therefore said to him, "We have seen the Lord." But he said to them, "Unless I see in his hands the print of the nails, and put my finger into the place of the nails, and put my hand into his side, I will not believe."

And after eight days, his disciples were again inside, and Thomas with them. Jesus came, the doors being closed, and stood in their midst, and said, "Peace be to you!" Then he said to Thomas, "Bring here thy finger, and see my hands; and bring here thy hand, and put it into my side; and be not unbelieving but believing."

Thomas answered and said to him, "My Lord and my God!" Jesus said to him, "Because thou hast seen me, thou hast believed. Blessed are they who have not seen, and yet have believed."

The latter case is our own, we who believe without having seen. But our faith would be less sure had it not been for the obstinate skepticism of honest Thomas; it is to Thomas, too, that we owe the finest profession of faith in Jesus Christ: "My Lord and my God!"

It remains difficult to form an idea of the ambiance that reigned among the disciples during the forty days that separate the Resurrection from the Ascension of Jesus Christ. Jesus was alive, he had been seen repeatedly, he had been seen, touched, felt, palpated; they had thoroughly assured themselves of his personal identity and his physical reality. Prodigious though it might be, he was again alive, who had been dead and buried.

At the same time he was very careful not to resume the course of his daily life with his Apostles. He would appear, and this was on each occasion a great joy; then he would disappear, leaving everything once more in suspense in their minds and hearts. More than ever he was acting like a poet, creating expectation and then surprising his friends with exactly what they had been waiting for. I think that one can say it was an atmosphere of love, in which the presence of the beloved overwhelms the heart and his absence oppresses it, in which his presence reduces one almost to silence and his absence stirs regret at not having said and done what one should have said or done.

Forty days is a fairly long while. Friends and enemies have time to raise questions. It seems to me impossible that the chief priests, who were certainly in touch with the police, had not heard talk of the appearances. But what could they do? These appearances were not disturbing the public peace, they were limited to a small group of men who seemed to want to disappear from sight. The best thing, no doubt, was to act as though nothing were happening. There would always be time to take counsel. These forty days, then, seem like a truce: it is the Apostles who, on the day of the Pentecost, will break the truce by proclaiming their testimony to the Resurrection of their master. The Pentecost was a thunderclap in a sky that Jesus' enemies had hoped would remain serene. The interval had been a privileged moment, unique in the history of the world, like the silence and limpidity of a summer morning before the first cannon shot of the battle.

For the Apostles it was a withdrawal. Who knows whether at this moment their great temptation was not to remain content and return to their daily lives, with the consolation of the events they had lived through? Their relationship to their master had changed profoundly: henceforth everything was clearer, and in retrospect everything that had happened before became clearer too. It was in these days that the Apostles finally knew without any possible doubt that their master was not only their leader, a wonder-worker, a Prophet greater than the others, the Messiah himself, but also God in person: "My Lord and my God," as Thomas had said to him. This revelation was so enormous that they must have needed some time to assimilate it, to digest it, to make it their own.

The fact of Jesus' Resurrection was an enormous consolation to his Apostles. But the event was limited in its scope to the little group of those who were already linked to Jesus through their affection and their loyalty. It is very possible that at first the Apostles saw no more in it than that. Jesus was alive once more, he had triumphed over death; extraordinary though this was, it was true, they were relieved of the whole weight of their sadness and their mourning. The story was as moving as any that could be conceived, with a "happy ending," as though at the conclusion of the *Iliad* Priam had been given back not Hector's corpse but his own living son. Like the pious Israelites that they were, the Apostles kept in their hearts the certainty that God had visited them, and their eyes retained the splendor of that illumination. It was an objective, real experience, of course, but it was also a mystical experience absolutely without parallel: neither Moses nor Elias nor Abraham himself had been on terms of such intimacy with God as they had been; they found their lives transfigured by the certainty of that intimacy.

How many great saints have been visited by God and have died unknown! They died, bearing in their hearts the sweetness of that visit and the secret of their peace: "You wanted my peace?" the saint cries. "Come and take it." These are the final words of Bernanos' *Under the*

Sun of Satan—thrown defiantly at "the illustrious man who had come so far to find him."

But Jesus quite obviously did not mean to stop there with his Apostles. It was not for them alone that the Word had become flesh, that he had lived among us, that he had suffered under Pontius Pilate, that he had died, that he had risen on the third day, that he had been touched by their hands, and that they had seen his glory, the glory of an only Son of the Father, full of grace and truth. And John adds: "No one has at any time seen God. The only-begotten Son, who is in the bosom of the Father, he has revealed him." John 1:18

As always with his Apostles, Jesus is striving to enlarge their field of vision. Now time presses. They are still under the impact of the amazing events of the preceding week. They must be made to understand the range of those events, a range that is universal in both space and time. Yes, it is not for them alone, it is for all men, for the whole human race in all its generations, that Jesus died, that he was buried, that on the third day he rose from the dead before ascending to God, his Father and our Father, his God and our God. It is precisely in this universal extension of the significance of narrowly localized historical events that the mission of the Apostles lies. Jesus had chosen them for just this purpose: to be his privileged witnesses and, in particular, the witnesses to his Resurrection. It is this that they have to comprehend definitely and in a very short time. Each one had been, as Saint Paul will say, *"segregatus in Evangelium Dei"*—"especially qualified for the Gospel of God."

Jesus Christ himself had completely fulfilled the mission with which he had been charged by his Father: the Kingdom of God had been founded, sins had been forgiven, God had been reconciled with the universe, and Jesus had left the door to glory and eternal life wide open for all. What remained was to forge solidly the final link between this salvation, achieved and universal in its scope, and each one of those who were to benefit by it and were to enter into it. This link is traditionally called the institution of the Church. "Then he opened their Luke 24:45-48 minds, that they might understand the Scriptures. And he said to them, 'Thus it is written; and thus the Christ should suffer, and should rise again from the dead on the third day; and that repentance and remission of sins should be preached in his name to all the nations, beginning from Jerusalem. *And you yourselves are witnesses of these things.*'"

It is clear that the foundation of the Church is the apostolic testimony. This the Apostles themselves understood very well. When, some weeks later, the question arises of co-opting another Apostle to take the place left empty by Judas and to complete the number twelve, Peter will say, "Therefore, of these men who have been in our company all the time that the Lord Jesus moved among us, from John's baptism until the day that he was taken up from us, of these one must become a *witness with us of his Resurrection.*" The essential duty of Christian apostleship is, above all, the testimony to the Resurrection of Jesus Christ. This testimony is the foundation of our Christian faith. It is useful to note that this Christian faith depends on our judgment, which accepts firmly established testimony *("rationabile obsequium")*; this faith is, in essence, not a matter of the emotions. On the contrary, on this subject emotion is as suspect in our eyes as in those of anyone else; we are not disposed to leave our judgment at the mercy of our emotions. I have already said that if Christ did not truly rise from the dead I consider myself, with Saint Paul, the most unhappy of men—and in addition an imbecile. Our faith is based on historic and authentic testimony; it has nothing whatever to do with credulity.

Acts 1:21-22

On the strength of ancient documents we quite readily admit (that is, we believe) that Alexander conquered Suza and Ecbatana; emotionally, however, that does not matter to us one way or the other. The fact that Jesus Christ should have risen and should have entered bodily into eternal life raises a personal question for each one of us; it is indeed the question of our definitive personal destiny, the question of salvation. Pascal maintained that if the elementary truths of mathematics were linked with the question of salvation, they too would inevitably have been disputed. Quite possibly so. But I know, also, that Christian faith is not pure unless it is first stripped of all credulity. Read Saint John of the Cross and you will see how necessary it is to surmount all human emotions as well, emotions that are all too human.

It is the Church that transmits the apostolic testimony. The problem was simple, it was in fact a problem of transport and communication, like the building of a canal to carry water, or a pipeline to carry oil, or a high-tension cable to transmit electric energy or, better yet, a radio or television network to transmit sounds and images. That is what the Church is, a canal, a pipeline, a high-tension cable, a network to transmit the good news of salvation, or rather perhaps an umbilical cord through which pass the nourishment, the blood, the life, the understanding of the Kingdom of God. We are in the womb of the Church like the unborn child in its mother's womb. The Church carries us even to eternity, where Jesus has preceded us.

As Bossuet said, the Church is nothing other than Jesus Christ propagated and shared. I shall say, more concretely, that the Church is Jesus Christ continuing to incorporate within himself the universe, absolved and reconciled. One can even say that the Church is the mystery of Easter propagated and shared, to such a degree did the repeated and physical evidence of that living and glorious body dazzle the Apostles, render concrete their faith, hope, and love, to such a degree did this mystery of a risen body imply and summarize all the other mysteries of our religion and prove to be the very foundation of the Church.

There is something perhaps even more precise. The Church is the transmission of the Gospel to all men. What is the Gospel? Great confusion has arisen in our minds from the fact (perfectly reasonable in itself) that the four books which tell the story of Jesus Christ are called Gospels. The word "Gospel" is linked in our minds with a written book. But in the New Testament, the Greek word *"Evangelion"* means primarily not a written document but essentially *"the good news* of the salvation that is brought you by Jesus Christ and whose center he is." It is the coming of the Kingdom of God, awaited by the Jews since Abraham, that took place through, with, and in Jesus Christ. The beginning of this Kingdom of God is the Incarnation, the accomplishment of this Kingdom of God is the Resurrection of Jesus Christ from the dead and his bodily return to the glory of his Father. The total extension of the Kingdom of God, the Church, is the announcement of this extraordinary news to all men through the preaching of the apostolic testimony.

The fulfillment of the Kingdom of God will come at the end of the world when Jesus Christ, definitively triumphant, will return the Kingdom to his Father, and God will be all in all.

Let us recall the extraordinary epic poem which I have already quoted and which belongs in this place:

He who sows the good seed is the Son of Man.   Matt. 13:37-39, 43
The field is the world;
The good seed, the sons of the kingdom;
The weeds, the sons of the wicked one;
And the enemy who sowed them is the devil.
But the harvest is the end of the world,
And the reapers are the angels. . . .
Then the just will shine forth like the sun in the kingdom of their Father.
He who has ears to hear, let him hear.

Now the grain that begins to grow is the risen Christ. Christ himself has made the comparison between the grain that died in order to rise in the harvest and his own death, his own burial, and his own

Resurrection. Saint Paul will explain that, for the Christian, baptism is a burial with Christ, in which the neophyte, buried with Christ, rises with him. Yes, the grain grows in the field, which is the world, that is the great and good news of Easter morning to which the Apostles bear witness to all generations. The Church is nothing other than the proclamation, at all the crossroads of history and through all the loudspeakers of the pulpit, of this great and good news: the grain grows, for Christ is risen—the Christ, premise of the whole universal harvest.

The Church continues the service of Jesus Christ. It too is the sower. Through baptism it buries the neophyte with Jesus Christ in order that he may rise with him. For all generations and in the entire field of the world, thanks to the Church of Jesus Christ, the sowing will continue, the grain will struggle upward in the night of faith toward the light, the great and good news will continue to be proclaimed: Christ is risen!

To whom, then, but to Jesus Christ can the solemn promise made to Abraham refer? "I will indeed bless you, and will surely multiply *your descendants* as the stars of the heavens, as the sands on the seashore. *Your descendants* shall possess the gates of their enemies. *In your descendants all the nations of the earth shall be blessed, because you have obeyed me.*" That was said to Abraham after the "sacrifice of Isaac" on the mountain, the prophetic metaphor of the sacrifice of Christ on Calvary. Well then, this seed of Abraham (likewise the seed of God) was cast into the earth in perfect obedience at the moment of the burial of Jesus Christ, and this seed has sprung up to be the benediction of all nations: Christ is risen. And if this first grain has sprung up, it means that the whole harvest will spring up. Jesus Christ is the premise: in him and through him we know that the grain will spring up—there you have the good news. This defines the two functions of the Church: like the Son of Man it is a sower through baptism and the Sacraments. But it is also the announcer of the good news through its "preaching."

There again is a word that has an ill sound because we have rather too often fallen asleep during sermons. Whose fault? Quite clearly it is the fault of the one who falls asleep, but perhaps, too, it is the fault of the preacher. Since evangelical preaching can be summed up as the announcement of the good news, today when means of communication are so numerous, so varied, so far advanced, so powerful, it is unforgivable that the announcement of the good news should not make use of all these to their fullest extent. It is not the message that needs to be modernized—that is always timely—it is its expression and means of transmission.

Christ is risen! This good news that concerns everyone who comes

Gen. 22:17-18

into the world must be announced incessantly by word and by pen, by telegraph, telephone, and radio, through books and through the theater, from the heights of the pulpit and through the microphones of popular assemblies, in the cities and on the highways, by television and in the darkened halls of the cinema, on the eight continents and in all languages, in verse and in prose, through didactic teaching and the evocative medium of poetry, in all varieties of literature and in all forms of artistic expression, in order that no man may escape from the huge uproar of this news: Christ is risen!

After all, that can be done, for it once was done. At the time of the cathedral of Chartres, the glassmakers, the tapestry workers, the fresco painters, the sculptors, the architects, as well as the preachers, the theologians, and the poets repeated, each in his own language, this good news. What has happened? Well, we have no talent, and the exceptions that will certainly be mentioned to me simply prove the general rule. Why have we no talent? I do not know. We talk of Christianity as though it were true, but do we really believe in it, I mean with that faith that moves mountains? Perhaps too we are afraid of being taken for imbeciles? But it is precisely this fear that is imbecile. We are the custodians of the highest message of hope ever addressed to men. Is this not truly reason enough for us to make the walls come tumbling down?

Let us, then, return to Saint Paul, who, for his part at least, never grows old and has never put anyone to sleep. Not that he is, properly speaking, a writer; that talent was granted him as overmeasure. One might call his language that of a chemist in his laboratory, of a surgeon in the amphitheater, of an architect in his building yard or a gardener, talking about grafts and cuttings in his garden.

> For if thou confess with thy mouth that Jesus is the Lord,
> And believe in thy heart that God has raised him from the dead,
> Thou shalt be saved.
>
> For with the heart a man believes unto justice,
> And with the mouth profession of faith is made unto salvation. . . .
> For whoever calls upon the name of the Lord shall be saved!
>
> How then are they to call upon him in whom they have not believed?
> But how are they to believe him whom they have not heard?
> And how are they to hear, if no one preaches?
> And how are men to preach unless they be sent? . . .
>
> Faith then depends on hearing,
> And hearing on the word of Christ.

Rom. 10:9-10, 13-15, 17

Need I recall here the equivalence stressed in the Gospel between the Word and the seed? "The seed is the Word of God." The same themes keep recurring and remain constant in Christianity. Sower and messenger, such is the Church.

In a certain way, Christ and the Church are all one. Moreover, Saint Paul speaks of the Church as being "the body of Christ." And he goes on:

Col. 1:24-27   . . . the Church; whose minister I have become in virtue of the office that God has given me in your regard. [What is this office?]
For I am to preach the word of God fully—
The mystery which has been hidden for ages and generations,
[And what is this mystery?] . . .
Christ in you,
Your hope of glory!

Further on:

Col. 2:9-10, 12-13   For in him [Christ] *dwells* all the fullness of the Godhead *bodily*,
And in him . . . you have received of that fullness. . . .
For you were *buried together with him* in Baptism,
And *in him also rose again*
Through faith in the working of God who raised him from the dead . . .
He *brought to life along with him*,
Forgiving you all your sins.

Speaking of the dangers that threaten the faith of believers, ever-present dangers—ascetism, fascination with the law, false ideologies, so-called scientific extrapolations, horoscopes and magic—he concludes with a play on words (as one might say: "Do not mistake the shadow

Col. 2:17   for the substance"): "These are a shadow of things to come, but *the substance is of Christ*." There is no speech that better confirms the eminent and central place of the Eucharist in the Christian religion.

And at the end he draws the consequences of that supernatural magnetism whose field is the world and which polarizes man toward the risen Christ:

Col. 3:1-4   Therefore, if you have risen with Christ,
Seek the things that are above,
Where Christ is seated at the right hand of God.
Mind the things that are above, not the things that are on earth.
For you have died
And your life is hidden with Christ in God.
When Christ, your life, shall appear,
Then you too will appear with him in glory.

Nevertheless it is very extraordinary that the highest message of hope that humanity has ever received is summarized by saying to us, "You are dead," and "Hide yourselves!" To feign death and to hide oneself can be cowardice; this simply means that true life lies elsewhere. And we feel this very clearly.

But it is the whole of Saint Paul that should be quoted here. Happy would I be if I could influence some readers to go back to Saint Paul and meditate on him. Saint Paul is splendid, his writings are as honest and strong as sunny wine, they say just what he wanted them to say. The more one reads him, the less complicated he becomes. How can one squander time on cosmico-theological books, as inflated in thought as in style, when it is open to everyone to read Saint Paul?

———

The gravest imprudence that can be committed in reading the Gospels is to detach them from the rest of the Bible, from the revelation, and from the tradition of Israel. It is impossible to imagine how completely faithful to the past the tradition of Israel was—and still is in Orthodox circles—faithful with inflexible fidelity. The rest of us, on the other hand, take pride in being uprooted. Our words are loose, our definitions extremely vague. The debacle into which Romanticism dragged our language has eroded it, the steady inflation of words, which is the rule in newspapers, radio, television, and conversation, has profoundly devaluated modern language. We have no idea of the richness of the words used in the Gospel, nor of their precision. The words employed by the writers of the New Testament were hard money, the best in the world, in contrast to our flimsy currency.

And so what meaning do the words "glory," "glorified body," "glorious body" convey to us? They sound fine, and we ask no more. We pass on. That is to say, we pass by the capital truths of religion. When John says of Jesus, "We have seen his glory," we think he is speaking John 1:14 as a marshal of the empire used to speak of Napoleon, or as one of Alexander's generals spoke of that greatest captain of all times. Whereas for an Orthodox Israelite to speak of "the glory" of Jesus Christ means literally to confess that Jesus Christ is God. In the Jewish tradition the word "glory" (*kabod* in Hebrew) is strictly reserved to God. My task here is to try to understand what is written, and my responsibility, alas, is not to depreciate the meaning. I say "alas," for I know very well that my abilities are limited.

Like the words "presence," "tent," "temple," "word" and, in my opinion, also like "seed" and "kingdom," the word "glory" is one of the essential pillars of the whole of the Scriptures, one of the capital words in the whole divine revelation to the Hebrew people. As soon as one hears it one should prick up one's ears and pay attention, for it is never used at random. On the three levels, theological, metaphysical, and physical, this word "glory" has a precise meaning. On the theological level, the glory is an essential attribute of God, which manifests his privileged Presence. On the metaphysical level, the glory designates a manifestation of absolute transcendence, a phenomenon holy in the highest degree. On the physical level, the glory is accompanied by certain fairly constant signs: an incandescent fire, a blinding burst of light, energy that is dangerous, even deadly in itself, a cloud or column of radiant smoke and also on occasion the presence of seraphim and cherubim, those blazing creatures who serve as throne for the divine Majesty. Throughout the millennia this has been the style of God's manifestation of Himself to Israel. The glory is an essential element of a theophany.

It is necessary for this book to reach an end, and so I cannot quote everything. But I shall at least cite a few of the most celebrated theophanies—first of all, that on Mount Sinai:

Ex. 24:15-18

After Moses had gone up, a *cloud* covered the mountain. The *glory* of the Lord settled upon Mount Sinai. The *cloud* covered it for six days, and on the seventh day he called to Moses from the midst of the *cloud*. To the Israelites the *glory* of the Lord was seen as a *consuming fire* on the mountaintop. But Moses passed into the midst of the *cloud* as he went up on the mountain; and there he stayed for forty days and forty nights.

And again:

Ex. 40:34-38

Then the *cloud* covered the Meeting *Tent*, and the *glory* of the Lord filled the Dwelling. Moses could not enter the Meeting *Tent*, because the *cloud* settled down upon it and the *glory* of the Lord filled the Dwelling. Whenever the *cloud* rose from the Dwelling, the Israelites would set out on their journey. But if the *cloud* did not lift, they would not go forward; only when it lifted did they go forward. In the daytime the *cloud* of the Lord was seen over the Dwelling; whereas at night, *fire* was seen *in the cloud* by the whole house of Israel in all the stages of their journey.

Six centuries later, the book of the Prophet Ezechiel is the epic of the glory of Yahweh. This amazing book should be read; it marks the beginning of the Jewish apocalyptic style.

Ezech. 10:4, 3-4,
18-19, 22-23

The *cherubim* were stationed to the right of the *temple* . . . as the man entered, the *cloud* filled the inner court, and the *glory* of the Lord rose from over the *cherubim* to the threshold of the *temple; the temple was filled with the cloud,* and all the court *was bright with the glory of the Lord.* . . . Then the *glory* of the Lord left the threshold of the temple and rested upon the *cherubim*. These lifted their wings, and I saw them rise from the earth, the wheels rising along with them. They stood at the entrance of the eastern gate of the Lord's house, and the *glory* of the God of Israel was up above them. . . . Then the *cherubim* lifted their wings, and the wheels went along with them, while up above them was the *glory* of the God of Israel. And the *glory* of the Lord rose from the city and took a stand on the mountain which is to the east of the city.

The astounding thing about this prophecy is that the mountain to the east of the city is the Mount of Olives from which Jesus, risen and glorious, will ascend to Heaven in a cloud.

These citations, which could easily be multiplied, are enough to prove what I have been trying to show throughout this book, that Jesus was born, that he lived, died, was buried, and arose again in a precise context a thousand years old. Jesus' Resurrection and the apostolic foundation of the Church find their specific place in the tradition of the Old Testament theophanies. During these forty days, while their master, already corporeally present in eternity, appears to them and speaks to them, the Apostles have had the certainty of renewing for themselves the experience that Moses had formerly had on Mount Sinai, when for forty days he was enveloped in the glory of Yahweh and God spoke to him. It was in this experience of familiarity with the glory of their master that the Apostles saw the confirmation of their vocation as messengers of God and of the Good News. Isaia before them had had a like experience:

In the year king Ozia died, I saw the Lord seated on a high and lofty throne, with the train of his garment filling the temple. Seraphim were stationed above; each of them had six wings: with two they veiled their faces, with two they veiled their feet, and with two they hovered aloft. "Holy, holy, holy is the Lord of hosts!" they cried one to the other. "All the earth is filled with his glory!"

At the sound of that cry, the frame of the door shook and the house was filled with smoke. Then I said, "Woe is me, I am doomed! For I am a man of unclean lips, living among a people of unclean lips; yet my eyes have seen the King, the Lord of hosts!"

Then one of the seraphim flew to me, holding an ember which he had taken with tongs from the altar. He touched my mouth with it. "See," he said, "now that this has touched your lips, your wickedness is removed, your sin purged."

Then I heard the voice of the Lord saying, "Whom shall I send? Who will go for us?"

"Here I am," I said; "send me!"

Isa. 6:1-9

And he replied: "Go . . ."

The difference, and it is great, was that the glory of God was no longer blinding, terrifying, or brutal. *"Apparuit benignitas . . ."* Henceforth it is in the sweetness and beauty of a perfected humanity that the glory of Yahweh resides.

For the Apostles—at least for three of them—this Paschal experience of the glory of God in the body of a man, that of their master, had another context, closer and more personal than the ancient theophanies. For Peter, James, and John it was the experience of the Transfiguration of Jesus. I am not inventing the connection between the Transfiguration and the Resurrection, it was Jesus himself who explicitly pointed to it.

Here is Mark's account, and I think it important to emphasize that, in the three Synoptics (John does not mention the Transfiguration), the story of the Transfiguration is closely bracketed, on the one side, by the announcement of the coming of the Kingdom of God within the course of one generation and, on the other, by the very clear prophecy of the Resurrection of Jesus from the dead.

Mark 8:39; 9:1-9   And he said to them, "Amen I say to you, there are some of those standing here who will not taste death, till they have seen the kingdom of God coming in power." [Matthew says: "the Son of Man coming in his kingdom."]

Now after six days Jesus took Peter, James and John, and led them up a high mountain off by themselves, and was transfigured before them. And his garments became shining, exceeding white as snow, as no fuller on earth can whiten. And there appeared to them Elias with Moses, and they were talking with Jesus.

And Peter addressed Jesus, saying, "Rabbi, it is good for us to be here. And let us set up three tents, one for thee, and one for Moses, and one for Elias." For he did not know what to say, for they were struck with fear.

And there came a *cloud* overshadowing them, and there came a voice out of the *cloud,* saying, "This is my beloved Son; hear him."

And suddenly looking round, they no longer saw anyone with them but only Jesus.

And as they were coming down from the mountain, he cautioned them to tell no one what they had seen, except when the Son of Man should have risen from the dead. And they kept what he said to themselves, discussing with one another what the words, "When he shall have risen from the dead," might mean.

In describing the same scene of Jesus' Transfiguration Luke is even Luke 9:32   more precise: "Now Peter and his companions were heavy with sleep. But when they were fully awake, they saw his *glory* and the two men who were standing with him." It was, then, indeed a theophany.

And so the three Apostles were debating the meaning of the words "when he shall have risen from the dead." They would not truly understand these words except through the fact of the Resurrection of Jesus Christ: thus it is with all prophecy, one can understand it properly only after the event has occurred. But here, at the Transfiguration, the three Apostles learn through their own concrete experience that their master is greater than Moses and Elias and that the *glory* of Yahweh is upon him. The Transfiguration is a prefiguration and a prophecy of the Resurrection. That is why I speak of it here.

I speak of it for another reason as well. The account of the Transfiguration, in each of the three Synoptics is begun by a verse that has provoked an enormous amount of controversy:

[Matthew:] "Amen I say to you, there are some of those standing here who will not taste death, till they have seen the Son of Man coming in his kingdom." Matt. 16:28

[Luke:] "But I say to you truly, there are some of those standing here who will not taste death, till they have seen the kingdom of God." Luke 9:27

[Mark:] "Amen I say to you, there are some of those standing here who will not taste death, till they have seen the kingdom of God coming in power." Mark 8:39

These words were certainly spoken by Jesus. In fact, it is rare to find such precise agreement among the Synoptics. And the words must have been said with a certain solemnity for them to have been remembered so exactly. They constitute one of the principal foundations of the famous theory of "consistent eschatology," proposed by Johannes von Weiss and popularized by Albert Schweitzer. According to this theory Jesus believed that the end of the world was imminent, he believed it would occur during the period contemporary with himself. Consequently he surely did not intend to found a lasting Church, and his morality is an "interim" morality for the single purpose of preparing men to meet the death throes of the world, which would be brief and would come soon. But the world endured. The Church was born from this continuance that had not been foreseen in the program; and by the same token one can understand the unreasonable demands of Christian morality, which are so impractical in daily life. I know that this theory can have a hold on men's minds, even men well versed in the text of the Scriptures.

I believe I understand very well why such unbelievers are irritated at what they call "the bad faith of the Catholic apologists," who have decided once for all that they are right and have decided, with equal firmness and also once for all, to ignore the difficulties and find in the text of the Gospels only clarity, harmony, and musical pauses. This is not my case. I find the texts of the Gospels difficult, and I have gone to the extent of undertaking a big book to explain my view of them.

But I think I am entitled to feel some exasperation at the attitude, which I consider systematized and *a priori,* of those unbelievers who are in such a hurry to talk about the irreducible contradictions within the Gospel texts. I shall point out to them, in my turn, that these texts are difficult, that, when one wishes to resolve the difficulties without staying at the surface level, long study and assiduous meditation are necessary, and that to become involved in inconsistencies is not astonishing if, from the outset, one sees in Jesus Christ only a human being like others and refuses to admit not only the existence but even the possibility of miracles and the supernatural. To my mind, the key to the consistency of the texts that have caused the most difficulty lies in the double nature, divine and human, of Jesus Christ, or, if you like, these texts find their consistency only at the unprecedented height of that personality. A prism breaks up light; for a personality that emerges by nature into eternity, time too "breaks up" certain affirmations. Once this is said, I have no difficulty in admitting that if Jesus Christ is not God in person all these accounts concerning him collapse in chaos. He who said, "Before Abraham was, I am," cannot have altogether the same notion of temporal succession that we do, who are submerged in that succession.

There is absolutely no excuse for pretending to ignore the fact that the famous eschatalogical verse under discussion is, in the three Synoptics, introductory to the theophany of the Transfiguration. In Mark it is the first verse of the chapter. In Luke and Matthew it also immediately precedes the account of the Transfiguration, but it comes at the close of the preceding chapter. Everyone knows, however, that the division of the Gospels into chapters and verses was not in the originals and is of no importance except for the convenience of the reader; it has absolutely no bearing on the meaning.

There are several theophanies in the Gospels, all directly connected with the person of Jesus. One can even say that the revelation of Jesus' personal divinity was made by successive stages, from theophany to theophany. The first Gospel theophany took place at the baptism of Jesus by John the Baptist: it is noteworthy that Saint Paul makes the apostolic testimony go back to that. The second was the theophany of the Transfiguration, itself prophetic, according to the word of Jesus, of the theophany of the Resurrection. The third and most important, in which the revelation of the personal divinity of Jesus culminates, is the theophany of Jesus which he himself foretold to Caiphas, when he will return on the clouds of heaven to judge the living and the dead. It is called "the Second Coming," at the end of the world, the Parousia.

Those who cling to the theory of "consistent eschatology" identify the last theophany, that of the Second Coming and the end of the world, with the coming of the Kingdom of God. This identification is gratuitous, it is a sleight-of-hand trick. Why limit the coming of the Kingdom of God to the Second Coming? There is no authority for doing so in the text. It is possible that some of the first Christians were misled by this and that they expected the end of the world in the immediate future. But Jesus himself was not misled, and he did not mislead us on this point any more than on any other. When he said, "There are among those persons present some who will not taste death until they have seen the Kingdom of God coming in power," why limit this to a single Christological theophany, the last one? This coming of the Kingdom can equally well mean the theophany of the Transfiguration, which is going to be described immediately afterward; but, above all, it must apply to the Resurrection and the Ascension, which are the theophany of theophanies, in which the Kingdom of God is finally and completely realized and of which the Second Coming is simply a far-off consequence. It is true, then, that among Jesus' auditors on that day there were at least three who would not taste death without having seen the glory of Jesus in the Transfiguration, and there were many others who would be witnesses of his Resurrection.

Once this is said, all the theophanies are seen to be linked together; they are signs and guaranties one of another. The Transfiguration foretells and guarantees the Resurrection soon to come. And we shall see that the Ascension of Christ foretells and guarantees the Second Coming. In the same way the theophanies of the Old Testament, above all the one witnessed by Moses in which promise was made of a Prophet who must be "listened to" in the name of God, foretell and guarantee the theophanies of the baptism of Jesus and the Transfiguration when the voice of God is fully inaugurated by the Resurrection of the Lord. The nearness of this Kingdom is certainly also the meaning of the preaching of John the Baptist and of all Jesus' early sermons, in which no reference is made to the end of the world. Why then introduce this reference when it does not exist in the texts?

The angel had made a rendezvous in Galilee. After eight or ten days in Jerusalem, following the glorious morning of their master's Resurrection, the Apostles went there. Thus they found themselves on the very grounds where it had all begun for them. They also found things there "even more the same than before." Had they been dreaming?

The lake, their lake, was still as gay as a Mediterranean. The rhythm of life in the villages was the same. Two and a half years, three years, what was that? People had not even had time to grow old. There was still the same palavering on the shores of the sea, the same twittering of women around the fountains. The Apostles had been involved in an amazing adventure, granted! But everything here inclined them to forgetfulness, to a prudent return to the old paths of habit traced by their ancestors. I find it admirable that Christ desired, before totally uprooting them, to confront the Apostles for a last time with the temptation of daily life, the well-beaten roads, the mediocrity and security of the material world, and, on these shores, the sweetness of life. Why go to the ends of the earth when it was so comfortable in their own homes? Far from the Holy City, with its intrigues and its passions, they would thus have the opportunity to rub their eyes and feel themselves once more in contact with everything that constituted for them the humble reality that does not lie.

Indeed it seems that daily life immediately regained its hold on them. They were there, alone, left to their own devices, without work; what were they to do? One evening Simon Peter, weary of waiting and of John 21:3 inactivity and no doubt still fascinated by his life's work, said, "I am going fishing." The others replied, "We also are going with thee." And there they were again, joyous and busy, rigging the boat, preparing a meal to take with them and a gourd of wine, the lantern, the nets; then, when night fell, they set out once more on the lake. This is always a moment of silence: a boat full of men, leaving the dock at midnight to go fishing, makes no noise save the dull and regular splash of the oars striking the surface in cadence. The night passes quickly under the stars, the boat lowers its nets into the sea in a wide circle and then, after a time, hauls them in again with the fishes.

If there are any. This time there were none. Peter must have been saddened: his trade, the trade of his youth, his livelihood, seemed to be betraying him. The return was even more silent than the departure. At that season mornings are still fresh, but no one paid any attention to the golden light that streaked the horizon and dissipated the mist trembling over the lake. They approached the shore. There, in addition to the cats, patiently seated at a distance from one another, as though they had never been introduced, and awaiting the return of the fishermen in the hope of any small fish that might be tossed to them, stood a man on the shore.

From afar he cried out, "Young men, would you have fish to eat?" John 21:5-6 And his voice carried over the sea. They responded in the same tone but with the taciturnity of men discontented with themselves, "No!"

The man shouted to them once more, "Cast your net to the right of the boat and you will make a catch."

Just as a gambler after a night of losses is always ready to place a final bet, believing it will change his luck, the true fisherman always believes that a final cast of the net will be the lucky one. And so they lowered their net, which took some time. But when they started to haul it in they found they could not lift it, it contained so many fishes: and yet the net did not break. Peter's professional honor had been saved.

John looked at the unknown man on the shore, and suddenly the memory of the miraculous fishes of the year before returned to his mind. Peter, too, was looking at that man who was so well acquainted with the ways of fish. John bent toward Peter and said to him, "It is the John 21:7 Lord!"

Peter's reaction was instantaneous. "Simon Peter therefore, hearing that it was the Lord, girt his tunic about him, for he was stripped, and threw himself into the sea." How characteristic of him: he throws himself into the sea first and does not reflect until afterward. And so he quickly arrived beside Jesus and found nothing to say to him. He felt the chill of the water and his own fears: "But the other disciples came John 21:8 with the boat (for they were not far from land, only about two hundred cubits off), dragging the net full of fishes."

John, who describes this scene, goes on:

When, therefore, they had landed, they saw a fire ready, and a fish laid John 21:9-13 upon it, and bread. Jesus said to them, "Bring here some of the fishes that you caught just now." Simon Peter went aboard and hauled the net onto the land full of large fishes, one hundred and fifty-three in number. And though there were so many, the net was not torn. Jesus said to them, "Come and breakfast." And none of those reclining dared asked him "Who art thou?" knowing that it was the Lord. And Jesus came and took the bread, and gave it to them, and likewise the fish.

In the whole of human literature I know of no scene in which the magic of love is so present, so fateful, and, as it were, so overwhelming. It reduces the Apostles to silence: excess of joy here has the same effect as excess of sorrow. In what other way can one conceive the reuniting of love after a long and cruel separation? Only the simplest actions and words, shorn of all eloquence, can express the inner violence of that joy. Each one can feel his own heart beating within his breast, and each one is silent. Jesus alone speaks, but barely. What does he say? "Bring here some of the fishes that you caught just now. . . . Come and breakfast." All the rest is conveyed through action. And what acts? He breathes on the embers; he carefully supervises the cooking of their modest but delicious meal of fish fresh from the lake; he breaks the bread and gives to each his food. It is here that Christianity has found its most authentic manner of sanctity, devoid of all ostentation, compatible with the banality of daily acts and words. For sanctity is the love of Jesus.

Here, on this nameless beach in the joyous light, how well Jesus veils his glory, how careful he is not to dazzle, how far he is from wanting to terrify. How one would have loved to be there; what a lovable man he must have been! Each of them knows very well who he is. The contrast between his true majesty, triumphant over sin and death, and the obliging modesty of his manner provokes a feeling so beautiful and so acute that tears of emotion rise to their eyes and each one feels himself pierced by a deep wound. Even better than he knows the ways of fishes, Jesus knows how to touch the hearts of men. . . .

Now the sun is high in the heavens, and its light floods the peaceful shores of the lake, the boat barely sways on the surface of the water. All around, the cats respect this intimate solemnity. Jesus fixes his eyes on Peter:

John 21:15-19   JESUS: Simon, son of John, dost thou love me more than these do?
PETER: Yes, Lord, thou knowest that I love thee. . . .
JESUS: Feed my lambs. . . . Simon, son of John, dost thou love me?
PETER: Yes, Lord, thou knowest that I love thee. . . .
JESUS: Feed my lambs. . . . Simon, son of John, dost thou love me?
Peter was grieved because he said to him for the third time, "Dost thou love me?"
PETER: Lord, thou knowest all things, thou knowest that I love thee. . . .
JESUS: Feed my sheep. . . . Amen, amen, I say to thee, when thou wast young thou didst gird thyself and walk where thou wouldst. But when thou art old thou wilt stretch forth thy hands, and another will gird thee, and lead thee where thou wouldst not.
Now this he said to signify by what manner of death he should glorify God.

There it is; the temptation of daily life has been wiped out. The adventure begins again, and there will be no more stopping. For Peter the cross looms on the horizon. How escape from the sight of Jesus Christ?

In a quite different sense this appearance seems to me just as convincing as the one when Jesus made Thomas touch his wounds. Here it is unmistakable recognition in the precise area of memory and of love. Jesus takes care to make himself known through the infallible tact of his intuition. Yes, it is indeed he, it cannot be anyone but him, the Jesus of the miraculous fishes of the preceding year, their companion on the journeys along the shores of the lake, the same Jesus, too, that Peter denied three times before the crowing of the cock in the pallid light of dawn; Jesus has pardoned him, to be sure, but he has not forgotten, and he is grateful to Peter that he has not forgotten, either, and that he is downcast at the third question. Not that Jesus wishes to turn a knife in the wound, he is not a torturer, but it is necessary for the head of the Church, for him above all, to know without any possible doubt that he who is speaking to him and who has just shared a repast with him is indeed the Lord, the Lord himself, whom he denied, who has been killed and who has risen from the dead.

The fairness of Jesus Christ! It is necessary for these things to be perfectly clear. At the very moment when he alludes to Peter's triple and dreadful personal failure, Jesus confirms him in his universal pastoral charge. It must be made clear that the authority of the pope depends not upon his personal sanctity but only upon his investiture by Jesus Christ. Faithful to the teaching I have received and without wavering for an instant in the immense gratitude and veneration I feel for the person of John XXIII, I would have recognized with equal steadfastness in Alexander VI, the Borgia, the pastoral authority of the successor to Peter, if I had lived in his time. That too is Catholicism; its forms must not be confused.

Then Jesus rose and told Peter to follow him. John got up to accompany them.

Peter therefore, seeing him, said to Jesus, "Lord, and what of this man?" Jesus said to him, "If I wish him to remain until I come, what is it to thee? Do thou follow me." This saying therefore went abroad among the brethren, that that disciple was not to die. But Jesus had not said to him, "He is not to die"; but rather, "If I wish him to remain until I come, what is it to thee?"   John 21:21-23

The sojourn in Galilee had born its fruit. Jesus' corporeal reality and his self-identity after the Resurrection had triumphed over old habit, daily life, and the intensity of this luminous landscape. That is to say, this reality and this identity had been confirmed until they were, for these simple, reasonable men, who had never mistaken appearances for reality, the most unshakable of certainties.

One further appearance took place in Galilee, to a larger circle of disciples, the Eleven in the first rank, naturally. But this time there was no longer any question of Jesus' identifying himself—he had done that and done it well—but of defining his own dignity and the mission of his Church. Matthew gives the account and strikes once more the epic note, which, moreover, will be the style of the great apostolic conquests:

Matt. 28:16-20   But the eleven disciples went into Galilee, to the mountain where Jesus had directed them to go. And when they saw him they worshiped him; but some doubted. And Jesus drew near and spoke to them saying:

"All power in heaven and on earth has been given to me.

Go, therefore, and make disciples of all nations,

Baptizing them in the name of the Father, and of the Son, and of the Holy Spirit,

Teaching them to observe all that I have commanded you;

And behold, I am with you all days,

Even unto the consummation of the world."

CHAPTER XXV

The Ascension

AS ALWAYS, the Gospel of Mark is rapid and concise. "So then Mark 16:19 the Lord, after he had spoken to them, was taken up into heaven, and sits at the right hand of God." And I, out of these two lines, am to make a chapter!

Fortunately we have a more detailed account of the Ascension of the Lord. It is that of Luke in the Acts of the Apostles:

In the former book, O Theophilus, I spoke of all that Jesus did and taught Acts 1:1-11 from the beginning until the day on which he was taken up, after he had given commandments through the Holy Spirit to the apostles whom he had chosen. To them also he showed himself alive after his passion by many proofs, during forty days appearing to them and speaking of the kingdom of God.

And while eating with them, he charged them not to depart from Jerusalem, but to wait for the promise of the Father, "of which you have heard," said he, "by my mouth; for John indeed baptized with water, but you shall be baptized with the Holy Spirit not many days hence."

They therefore who had come together began to ask him, saying, "Lord, wilt thou at this time restore the kingdom to Israel?" But he said to them, "It is not for you to know *the times or dates* which the Father has fixed by his own authority; but you shall receive power when the Holy Spirit comes upon you, and *you shall be witnesses for me* in Jerusalem and in all Judea and Samaria and even to the very ends of the earth."

And when he had said this, he was lifted up before their eyes, and *a cloud* took him out of their sight. And while they were gazing up to heaven as he went, behold, two men stood by them in white garments, and said to them, "Men of Galilee, why do you stand looking up to heaven? This Jesus

449

who has been taken up from you into heaven, shall come in the same way as you have seen him going up to heaven."

And so we have now returned to Jerusalem, after the appearances in Galilee. There is a final meal together. Jesus must have had the same idea of friendship as Aristotle: to be friends one must have eaten a bushel of salt together—which means many dishes salted and many meals eaten in common. The number of meals mentioned in the Gospels is altogether amazing. Jesus truly wanted to be sure that no one could doubt his friendship for men.

Here, then, is Jesus' final repast with his Apostles. It is the brief meal of a morning before a battle. There is no longer time for effusions or long confidences, but only for brief orders and passwords. The last image Jesus will leave is that of a leader: he does not explain, he summarizes and commands.

And so he promises them the Holy Spirit. What Spirit? He has said on another occasion that they need only recall everything that has happened in the past three years and everything that has been said as well, and what John the Baptist himself said: "I indeed baptize you with water, for repentance. But he who is coming after me is mightier than I, whose sandals I am not worthy to bear. He will baptize you with the Holy Spirit and with fire."

Matt. 3:11

After the meal they gather around him and besiege him with questions: is he finally going to decide to claim and re-establish the kingdom in Israel? These blockheads have not yet abandoned all political ambition; they cling to their conception of the throne of David and of revenge upon the nations. Jesus no longer has the heart to rebuke them, but he cuts them short nevertheless, consistent as always in his conduct: from the beginning of his public life he has claimed for himself the title of "Son of Man" according to the prophecy of Daniel. Here he alludes once more to that prophecy when he speaks of the "times and seasons" reserved to the authority of his Father. Parenthetically, a text such as this gives little support to the theory of "consistent eschatology." Jesus is not willing to make pronouncements concerning dates. It is clear that he does not approve of our asking indiscreet questions about nonessentials. Here is the text from Daniel to which allusion is made:

Dan. 2:20-21

Blessed be the name of God
Forever and ever,
For wisdom and power are his.
He causes the changes of the times and seasons,
Makes kings and unmakes them. . . .

Jesus renews his promise of the Spirit, as a power that will put them in a position to accomplish the mission which he has left for them and with which he has invested them. What is this mission? Oh, very simple, the simplest possible, that they shall not forget him, that they shall never allow themselves to be distracted and that they shall live and die under the burden of this mission, a mission that is heavy, honorable, necessary, and redemptive. "You shall be my witnesses!" That is all, nothing more. But since it is necessary to be clear, let them remember carefully that the old and narrow nationalism is gone. Whether they like it or not, their mission of testimony has no frontiers: from Jerusalem they will have to pursue it into Judea, from Judea into the country of their brother enemies the Samarians, from Samaria to the confines of the world. Shame upon him who stops midway! They, however, will never stop, they will actually die on all the roads leading to the confines of the world, crushed by this burden. They will die as martyrs, and the whole of the then known world will resound with the rumor of their testimony.

But today when we, in our turn, are charged with this testimony, are we always on the roads of the world, what frontiers do we cross? What Samarians do we convert? Are we always at the borders of the known world, crying the testimony aloud? Yes, some of us . . . John XXIII. And so it is always possible, therefore it must always be undertaken and persevered in.

Still conversing, they arrived at the Mount of Olives, retracing the same road they had traveled on the sinister night of the betrayal. But this day was the day of definitive triumph. Then Jesus was gently lifted into the sky. And a cloud hid him from their eyes.

———————

Let us begin by asking certain foolish questions, questions of the sort children ask and grown people sometimes have trouble answering.

Christ has risen from the dead. It is a miraculous phenomenon, mystical and physical as well, but a phenomenon of the sort that we have no experience of, that is, therefore, impossible for us to judge on the physical plane. Those of us who believe in the physical fact of this Resurrection believe in it on the strength of the historically valid testimony of the Apostles, who were witnesses of it. These same witnesses have emphasized the strange phenomena that affected the risen body: it could change its appearance, it went through walls, it appeared and disappeared at will, and here we see that it was free of all weight and could of itself rise into the sky.

The apostolic testimony, and consequently our faith, does not rest so heavily on these diverse phenomena, which are secondary and consequent, as on the fact, which is indeed capital, of the bodily Resurrection of Jesus and his bodily entrance into eternal life. I have said—and I do not believe that it is absurd to maintain this—that the promotion of a human body to participation in eternity must be so formidable a shock for that body that it is not astonishing if, under the effect of such a transmutation, this body should become endowed with virtues that seem very strange to us on the basis of our sublunary experience. It is less strange for us today, however, habituated as we are to the marvelous exploits of physics, chemistry, and astronautics. Personally, what seems literally miraculous to me is the access of a body to immortality— miraculous but not incredible, granted the omnipotence of God. Once this last fact is admitted, it would seem suspect to me if such a prodigious change of state had not produced on this body the effect of endowing it with exceptional virtues.

Pursuing our investigation—our detective work, if you will, for there are alibis, too, to be verified—where was Jesus when he was not with his Apostles during those forty days that separated his Resurrection from his Ascension? Where is he now, I mean physically? Where is his body?

A first indication comes to us from Jesus' words to Mary Magdalene: "I have not yet ascended to my Father . . ." which seems to indicate that he ascended to his Father immediately after this meeting. The real Ascension of Christ in his risen body took place on Easter Day itself. It was "from his Father" that he came when he appeared to his disciples.

John 20:17

Then what is called his Ascension was only a visible and more solemn ascension, the decisive manifestation of his divine glory which drew his body into the heavens, with the accompaniment of a "cloud," in the tradition of the theophanies of Israel. This ascension was, so to speak, "the official Ascension," which publicly and cosmically confirmed the divine glorification of the body of the fairest of the children of men. Moreover, the Apostles, already witnesses of the Resurrection, needed also to be witnesses of the Ascension. This "official" Ascension nevertheless does not limit Jesus Christ's freedom of movement, for he will very soon appear bodily to Saul of Tarsus on the road to Damascus.

On the plane of our inquiry we have not advanced very far. Where is this "with his Father" of which Jesus speaks? Tradition designates this place "heaven," the "Paradise" of which henceforth Jesus is King. Alas! Here more than anywhere else the imagination can only lead us astray. For a body totally under the control of a glorified soul and participating in life eternal, the categories of space and time cannot be the same as for us. I do not believe that we can form an exact idea of the "location" of a glorious body any more than we can form an exact idea of what the hypothesis of a "curved universe" or an "expanding universe" means. But this borderland where the imagination loses its footing, this area that we so readily concede to science, why should we not leave it open to the statements of revelation?

In truth, however, the essential thing about this revelation does not lie in this: the essential thing remains that sins have been forgiven, that God has been reconciled with the universe and man within the universe, that purity has been recovered, and that Jesus Christ dominates the whole of creation even in his human nature, and that the access to eternal life is henceforth open to man, soul and body. The Apocalypse, last book of the Bible, says the same thing more fully: the general resurrection of all the dead, their judgment, the reward of the elect, the punishment of the damned; none of this is conceivable without a transmutation of the entire universe, of its laws and its categories, and without the establishment of a new physics in harmony with the new destiny of man.

And I saw a great white throne and the one who sat upon it; *from his face the earth and heaven fled away, and there was found no place for them.* And I saw the dead, the great and the small, standing before the throne, and scrolls were opened. And another scroll was opened, which is the book of life; and the dead were judged out of those things that were written in the scrolls, according to their works.

Apoc. 20:11-15; 21:1-7

And the sea gave up the dead that were in it, and death and hell gave up the dead that were in them; and they were judged each one, according to their works. And hell and death were cast into the pool of fire. This is the second death, the pool of fire. And if anyone was not found written in the book of life, he was cast into the pool of fire.

And I saw a new heaven and a new earth. For the first heaven and the first earth passed away, and the sea is no more. And I saw the holy city, New Jerusalem, coming down out of heaven from God, made ready as a bride adorned for her husband. And I heard a loud voice from the throne saying, "Behold the dwelling of God with men, and he will dwell with them. And they will be his people, and God himself will be with them as their God. And God will wipe away every tear from their eyes. And death shall be no more; neither shall there be mourning, nor crying, nor pain any more, *for the former things have passed away.*"

And he who was sitting on the throne said, "Behold, *I make all things new!*" And he said, "Write, for these words are trustworthy and true." And he said to me, "It is done! I am the Alpha and the Omega, the beginning and the end. To him who thirsts I will give of the fountain of the water of life freely. He who overcomes shall possess these things. . . ."

Once more, modern physics has so accustomed us to relativity and to views of the universe under aspects very different from those of classical physics that the idea of its total transmutation so that it may become the adequate dwelling place of God and his elect, glorified, even in body, contains nothing profoundly surprising. What we lack in order to judge it is the basic experience, the experience of glory reverberating on a risen body. I do not think that a reader who has meditated on these problems and who will reflect on what I am writing here can think that I am avoiding the difficulty. Within the limits of our present means of investigation it is a sign of unreasonable impatience, and is surely frivolous as well, to wish to judge a state of which we have absolutely no direct and basic experience.

Why would not God tell us more? Let us distrust our curiosity about secondary matters. What God wished in this terrestrial adventure of Christ, which has its first interval in the Ascension, was to become reconciled with the universe and, at the center of the universe, with man. This has been done: *the species is saved*. One could surely not dream of any such masterpiece of salvation for a created nature as we have here, henceforth to be associated personally with the very glory of God. In Christ the adventure has been superbly achieved, the human race is triumphant, it has been saved, and this salvation cannot again be compromised. By rising a single time to heaven, this man who is Jesus Christ has won the keys of the celestial dwelling, which is our definitive fatherland, and he opens to whom he will. He speaks our language, and we can speak his.

It is possible that the human species is not the only one composed of matter and spirit. Perhaps other planets than earth are inhabited. It is possible. Why not? As far as the Catholic faith is concerned, we can wait and see. Every discovery will be always welcome that upsets our intellectual complacency. Since science and technology have put on their seven-league boots, I can see at a glance what it is that will have trouble keeping up with them: it is our imagination, certainly not the Catholic faith. These two do not have the same geography nor do they pursue the same roads.

Today as yesterday man has need of reconciliation, not with himself alone, in the realm of nature, but with that source, above the world, of all purity and all holiness. It is here that Christianity has its place, a place that will never be taken away from it, not because it is the best place in the world's eyes but because it is the humblest in its patient, inflexible service to man in all his original misery.

Permit me to cite a novelist who, it seems to me, has gone farther than any other writer in his profound understanding of the modern world and its basic impoverishment: "One cannot deny that for a long time God has made Himself small, very small. Hence we conclude that He will make Himself as small tomorrow as today, smaller still, smaller and smaller. Nothing, however, obliges us to believe it. . . . The hour will come nevertheless when, in a world organized for despair, to preach hope will be exactly equivalent to throwing a burning torch into a powder barrel. Well then . . . We have left this unhappy world in your hands long enough. . . ." When Bernanos talks about "a world organized for despair," he means a world that allows no place for a single hope of a size appropriate to man and his profound nostalgia. Yes, that is exactly what it is all about: it is possible that economic expansion, luxury, high salaries, the conveniences of modern life, social and other kinds of insurance, even sensual pleasure and the daily news read, heard, or televised—it is indeed possible that all this is not sufficient to quench a spiritual thirst which, from one day to the next, can become more dreadful than the thirst of a traveler lost in the desert and writhing beside his empty water bottle.

That is why I have written this book, standing guard in my turn like the last of the soldiers over the redemptive testimony of Jesus Christ's Resurrection from the dead. I have borne in mind those who, consciously or not, are seeking beyond this world for a source of purity and reconciliation, precisely that source which our modern civilization has conclusively proved cannot be of this world. Those who seek beyond the world are on the right road: they "burn," as people say. Well and good, may they burn till they are consumed! A moment will surely come when man will grow aware of his true stature, and then he will seek further, always further. The hour of truth is bound to come. It is the hour when we feel we do not truly belong to this world. That hour comes for everyone at death. For some it comes long before. There are those who think the sooner it comes, the better.

I believe indeed that wisdom consists in trusting God concerning the manner of our resurrection. What is absolutely true and must be believed is that we shall arise, our souls regaining their bodies, to appear before the tribunal of Jesus Christ, where we shall be judged according to love. As for those who have preceded us and whom we long to see again, the manner in which Christ encountered his own after his Resurrection (especially his meeting with Mary Magdalene in the garden and his meeting with the Disciples on the shores of the Lake of Tiberias), this manner, so simple, frank, courteous, and full of tenderness, is a pledge to us of what our own meeting will be like with those whom we have loved and whom we shall find again, shorn of egotism and vanity, as we ourselves shall be, in the truth of the glory.

The sorrows of mourning confuse our powers of imagination, always inclined to credulity. Let us however be on our guard against easy answers: the Christian religion is not a soothsayer, a reader of cards, a fortune teller: ". . . a long voyage . . . joyful meeting . . . minor misfortune . . . delay . . . a friend from afar . . . there is someone close to you who wishes you ill, but there is another who wishes you much good . . . in the end all will be well . . ." Pooh!

The Catholic faith is that each will be raised in his own body to be judged with that body in the general confrontation of the Second Coming, at the trumpet sound. The most puerile conjectures have been made on this subject in less reputable theological quarters. They are of no interest whatever. Today we know that all the matter in our bodies is renewed every few months and that, despite this perpetual renewal of their substance, our bodies remain our bodies. There will be no lack of matter for that voracious principle of assimilation and of life that is the immortal soul, avid to regain a body to express itself.

I have said that we lack the necessary direct basic experience to judge the events of the Ascension. But we can find certain analogies to aid us in understanding it. The Ascension of the Lord is the supreme poetic event. The Word of God descended from God, he became flesh in order to reconcile God with the universe. Once this reconciliation was effected through his suffering, death, and Resurrection, he reascended to his natural dwelling place. Yes, but he bore with him the human nature he personally had assumed, and he bears it still, delivered forever from evil and from death. Moreover, Jesus himself sketched in advance the complete parable of his destiny in his saying to Nicodemus, "And no one has ascended into heaven except him who has descended from heaven: the Son of Man who is in heaven."

John 3:13

The Ascension is a gratuitous phenomen, finding its justification wholly in itself. An example will make my meaning clear. I am going to quote a poem by W. B. Yeats, a poem I like very much, but anyone can duplicate the experience with any poem at all, provided it is a true poem.

> Many ingenious lovely things are gone
> That seemed sheer miracle to the multitude,

Protected from the circle of the moon
That pitches common things about. There stood
Amid the ornamental bronze and stone
An ancient image made of olive wood—
And gone are Phidias' famous ivories
And all the golden grasshoppers and bees.

It is impossible to analyze or formulate the conquering charm of such a poem. One can take the words mounted in it and examine each one separately: they are all to be found in the dictionary; more than that, they are all of common usage: they are ordinary, banal, utilitarian, and possessed of down-to-earth meanings. But as soon as they are assembled by the poet, set by him in the poem, each one of them, without losing its own meaning, begins to shine with a new brilliance and a new glory. It is a question no longer of utility but of grace.

Jesus, arisen and glorious, has reconstituted the entire poem of creation. His body rises to heaven, as the word recovers its native innocence in the poem. For the word, any word at all, is more true, more significant, more itself, in the poem than in utilitarian discourse. The Ascension is the ascension of a human nature to the original level of its divine creation. Higher glory cannot be conceived of for that nature. Of all creatures, the Christ-man is henceforth the happiest who exists. I feel immense joy in knowing that at least he is happy, without shadows, without fear, without reproach, and that this happiness is due solely to a pure and generous victory without his having taken anything from anyone, but on the contrary after his having given all.

Thus the Word that is at the beginning of all is also at the end of all. The whole universe was created only in order to gain final expression through him, in him, in a long and gracious poem. The Ascension of the Lord is the first cry of joy in this long poem. The cry remains suspended in the sky, a summons that is addressed to us. It depends simply on us to enter into the poem, if only we would lose our utilitarian avarice and find again the mirror of our nativity.

The Word is at the beginning and at the end of all, as in a work of art the art of the artist is at the beginning of the work to conceive it, it is what then executes the work, and it is at the end of the work to judge it. This body that rises gracefully into heaven, under the sway of a restored and universal harmony, is the expression and the guaranty of the music of the world set free forever. I think I can divine the feelings of admiration, joy, respect, gratitude, and indeed inner liberation that animated the hearts of the Apostles at this perfection of accomplishment.

The seed of Abraham, which is also the seed of God, has arrived at its term. It has become a great tree, but a tree of inverse growth: its leafy branches fill the sky, but its roots too are in the sky:

> O chestnut tree, great rooted blossomer,
> Are you the leaf, the blossom or the bole?
> O body swayed to music, O brightening glance,
> How can we know the dancer from the dance?

The poem had its beginning in Jesus Christ. Thenceforth the history of Jesus Christ is mingled with the history of the world, its redemption, its salvation, and afterward its judgment. Jesus himself, having brushed for a moment against history, has passed to the farther side of history and of time. But he began the poem. And in this poem each of us has his predestined place. Our whole vocation is, while losing none of our immediate, natural significance and while accomplishing day by day our temporal tasks, to turn our ears toward the eternal harmony that summons us and so one day to find ourselves raised to the incorruptible glory of that divine poem wholly reconstituted.

Throughout this book I have been at pains to keep in contact on the one hand with the ancient prophecies of Israel and on the other with the preoccupations and the vocabulary of my time. It is with a prophecy made centuries before the birth of Jesus Christ but which he supremely fulfilled and which has lost nothing of the acuteness and sloemnity of its warning that I shall end this book, written as a testimony to the Catholic faith.

Isa. 55:3-11

> I will renew with you the everlasting covenant,
> The benefits assured to David.
>
> As I made him a witness to the peoples,
> A leader and commander of nations,
> So shall you summon a nation you knew not,
> And nations that knew you not shall run to you,
> Because of the Lord, your God, the Holy One of Israel,
> *Who has glorified you.*
>
> Seek the Lord while he may be found,
> Call him while he is near.
> Let the scoundrel forsake his way,
> And the wicked man his thoughts;
> Let him turn to the Lord for mercy;
> To our God, who is generous in forgiving.

For my thoughts are not your thoughts,
Nor are your ways my ways, says the Lord.

As high as the heavens are above the earth,
So high are my ways above your ways
And my thoughts above your thoughts.
For just as from the heavens the rain and snow come down
 And do not return there till they have watered the earth,
   making it fertile and fruitful,
     giving seed to him who sows and bread to him who eats,
So shall my word be that goes forth from my mouth;
It shall not return to me void,
But shall do my will,
Achieving the end for which I sent it.

That is Christianity. The Word of God came to share our lot, he rose again to God, drawing us upward in the wake of his glory. And, as Saint Paul said, death instead of wresting glory from us confirmed that glory. Christian honor consists in maintaining the sacred infancy of humanity, the hope of the glory due the sons of God:

1 Cor. 9:15

> *Gloriamur in spe gloriae*
> *filiorum Dei.*

Rom. 5:2

JUNE 1964

REFERENCE NOTES

Sources for Biblical quotations are given in the margins of the text. Following are the sources of the non-Biblical quotations, identified by page and line number.

Page 111, line 8—"The psychology of Satan . . ." Father Marie J. Lagrange, *L'Evangile de Jésus Christ.*

Page 134, line 16—"The fundamental constant . . ." Father Louis Bouyer, *La Bible et l'Evangile.*

Page 157, line 14—"And thus you see that Abraham . . ." *Mekilta* on Ex. 14: 31.

Page 182, Line 28—"Hail, true Body . . ." Denziger 355.

Page 196, line 3—"Of all the parties . . ." Isidore Epstein, *Judaism* (Penguin, 1959).

Page 209, line 16—"The caricaturist's art . . ." Henri Bergson, *Le Rire.*

Page 229, line 36—"There are two successive worlds . . ." Father Bouyer, *op. cit.*

Page 270, line 10—"How does this night . . ." Mishnah, Pesahim X: 5.

Page 275, line 30.—". . . was *fabricated* . . ." Saint Thomas Aquinas, *Summa Theologica,* III a, q. LXIV, art. 2, ad 3 m.

Page 340, line 31—"The first Christians . . ." Father Lagrange, *op. cit.*

Page 342, line 6—"And in this dream . . ." Victor Hugo.

Page 342, line 16—"It is a secret . . ." Cited in Leon Piliakov, *De Mahomet aux Marranes.*

Page 343, line 16—"O Tree . . ." Paul Claudel, *Tête d'Or,* second version.

Page 348, line 28—"An American magazine . . ." *Time*, May 17, 1963.

Page 401, line 11—"Better tacit concord . . ." Father Lagrange, *op. cit.*

Page 401, line 41—"The authenticity of this piece . . ." Father Braun, *Jésus.*

Page 419, line 23—"It is true that woman . . ." Aquinas, *op. cit.*, III a, q. LV, art. II, ad 3 m.

Page 456, line 40—"Many ingenious lovely things . . ." William Butler Yeats, "Nineteen Hundred and Nineteen," *Collected Poems of W. B. Yeats* (Macmillan, 1956).

Page 458, line 4—"O chestnut tree . . ." Yeats, "Among School Children," *op. cit.*